Excel® Data Analysis

Your visual blueprint™ for analyzing data, charts, and PivotTables, 4th Edition

Paul McFedries

Excel® Data Analysis: Your visual blueprint™ for analyzing data, charts, and PivotTables, 4th Edition

Published by
John Wiley & Sons, Inc.
10475 Crosspoint Boulevard
Indianapolis, IN 46256

www.wiley.com

Published simultaneously in Canada

Library of Congress Control Number: 2013938097

ISBN: 978-1-118-51714-7

Manufactured in the United States of America

10 9 8 7 6 5 4 3 2

Trademark Acknowledgments

Contact Us

For general information on our other products and services please contact our Customer Care Department within the U.S. at 877-762-2974, outside the U.S. at 317-572-3993 or fax 317-572-4002.

For technical support please visit www.wiley.com/techsupport.

Sales | Contact Wiley at (877) 762-2974 or fax (317) 572-4002.

Credits

Executive Editor
Jody Lefevere

Project Editor
Jade L. Williams

Technical Editor
Namir Shammas

Copy Editor
Marylouise Wiack

Editorial Director
Robyn Siesky

Business Manager
Amy Knies

Senior Marketing Manager
Sandy Smith

Vice President and Executive Group Publisher
Richard Swadley

Vice President and Executive Publisher
Barry Pruett

Project Coordinator
Katherine Crocker

Graphics and Production Specialists
Ronda David-Burroughs
Andrea Hornberger
Jennifer Mayberry

Quality Control Technician
Jessica Kramer

Proofreading
Joni Heredia Language Services

Indexing
Potomac Indexing, LLC

About the Author

Paul McFedries is a full-time technical writer. He has been authoring computer books since 1991 and has more than 80 books to his credit, including *Teach Yourself VISUALLY Excel 2013, Teach Yourself VISUALLY Windows 8, Windows 8 Visual Quick Tips, The Facebook Guide for People Over 50, iPhone 5 Portable Genius*, and *iPad 4th Generation and iPad mini Portable Genius, all available from Wiley*. Paul's books have sold more than 4 million copies worldwide. Paul is also the proprietor of Word Spy (`http://www.wordspy.com`), a website that tracks new words and phrases as they enter the English language. Paul invites you to drop by his personal website at `www.mcfedries.com`, or you can follow him on Twitter @paulmcf and @wordspy.

Author's Acknowledgments

It goes without saying that writers focus on text and I certainly enjoyed focusing on the text that you will read in this book. However, this book is more than just the usual collection of words and phrases designed to educate and stimulate the mind. A quick thumb through the pages will show you that this book is also chock full of treats for the eye, including copious screen shots, meticulous layouts, and sharp fonts. Those sure make for a beautiful book and that beauty comes from a lot of hard work by Wiley's immensely talented group of designers and layout artists.

They are all listed in the Credits section on the previous page, and I thank them for creating another gem. Of course, what you read in this book must also be accurate, logically presented, and free of errors. Ensuring all this was an excellent group of editors that I got to work with directly, including project editor Jade Williams, copy editor Marylouise Wiack, and technical editor Namir Shammas. Thanks to all of you for your exceptional competence and hard work. Thanks, as well, to Wiley Executive Editor Jody Lefevere for asking me to write this book.

How to Use This Visual Blueprint Book

Who This Book Is For

This book is for advanced computer users who want to take their knowledge of this particular technology or software application to the next level.

The Conventions in This Book

1 Steps

This book uses a step-by-step format to guide you easily through each task. Numbered steps are actions you must do; bulleted steps clarify a point, step, or optional feature; and indented steps give you the result.

2 Notes

Notes give additional information — special conditions that may occur during an operation, a situation that you want to avoid, or a cross reference to a related area of the book.

3 Icons and Buttons

Icons and buttons show you exactly what you need to click to perform a step.

4 Extra or Apply It

An Extra section provides additional information about the preceding task — insider information and tips for ease and efficiency. An Apply It section takes the code from the preceding task one step further and allows you to take full advantage of it.

5 Bold

Bold type shows text or numbers you must type.

6 Italics

Italic type introduces and defines a new term.

7 Courier Font

`Courier font` indicates the use of scripting language code such as statements, operators, or functions, and code such as objects, methods, or properties.

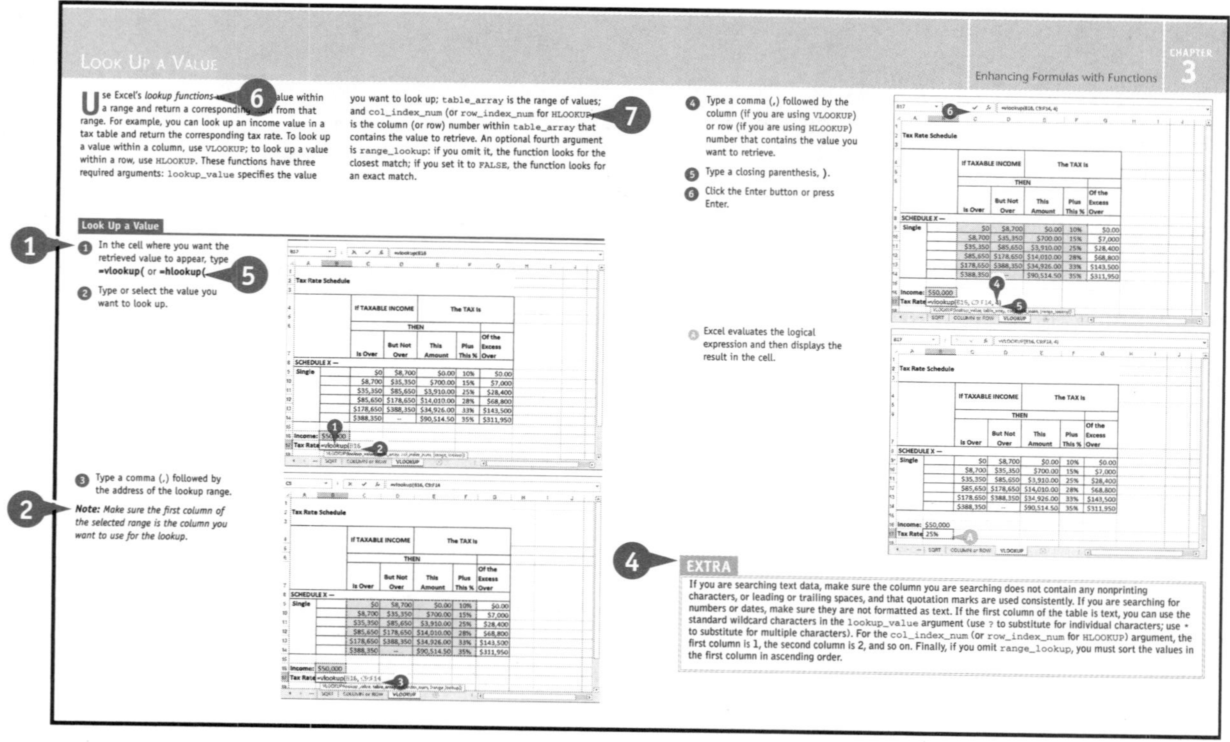

LOOK UP A VALUE

Enhancing Formulas with Functions

CHAPTER 3

Use Excel's *lookup functions* … alue within a range and return a correspondin… from that range. For example, you can look up an income value in a tax table and return the corresponding tax rate. To look up a value within a column, use `VLOOKUP`; to look up a value within a row, use `HLOOKUP`. These functions have three required arguments: `lookup_value` specifies the value you want to look up; `table_array` is the range of values; and `col_index_num` (or `row_index_num` for `HLOOKUP`) is the column (or row) number within `table_array` that contains the value to retrieve. An optional fourth argument is `range_lookup`: if you omit it, the function looks for the closest match; if you set it to `FALSE`, the function looks for an exact match.

Look Up a Value

1. In the cell where you want the retrieved value to appear, type **=vlookup(** or **=hlookup(**
2. Type or select the value you want to look up.
3. Type a comma (,) followed by the address of the lookup range.

Note: Make sure the first column of the selected range is the column you want to use for the lookup.

4. Type a comma (,) followed by the column (if you are using `VLOOKUP`) or row (if you are using `HLOOKUP`) number that contains the value you want to retrieve.
5. Type a closing parenthesis,).
6. Click the Enter button or press Enter.

- Excel evaluates the logical expression and then displays the result in the cell.

Is Over	But Not Over	This Amount	Plus This %	Of the Excess Over
$0	$8,700	$0.00	10%	$0.00
$8,700	$35,350	$700.00	15%	$7,000
$35,350	$85,650	$3,910.00	25%	$28,400
$85,650	$178,650	$14,010.00	28%	$68,800
$178,650	$388,350	$34,926.00	33%	$143,500
$388,350	--	$90,514.50	35%	$311,950

EXTRA

If you are searching text data, make sure the column you are searching does not contain any nonprinting characters, or leading or trailing spaces, and that quotation marks are used consistently. If you are searching for numbers or dates, make sure they are not formatted as text. If the first column of the table is text, you can use the standard wildcard characters in the `lookup_value` argument (use `?` to substitute for individual characters; use `*` to substitute for multiple characters). For the `col_index_num` (or `row_index_num` for `HLOOKUP`) argument, the first column is 1, the second column is 2, and so on. Finally, if you omit `range_lookup`, you must sort the values in the first column in ascending order.

Table of Contents

Chapter 1 Building Formulas for Data Analysis

Chapter 2 Troubleshooting Formulas

Chapter 3 Enhancing Formulas with Functions

Chapter 4 Analyzing Financial Data

Table of Contents

Chapter 5 Analyzing Statistical Data

Chapter 6 Building Tables for Data Analysis

Chapter 7 Sorting and Filtering Data

Chapter 8 Learning Data Analysis Techniques

Chapter 9 Working with Data Analysis Tools

Chapter 10 Tracking Trends and Making Forecasts

Chapter 11 Working with the Analysis ToolPak

Chapter 12 Analyzing Data with PivotTables

Chapter 13 Visualizing Data with Charts

Chapter 14 Importing Data into Excel

Chapter 15 Querying Data Sources

Chapter 16 Learning VBA for Data Analysis

Appendix A Using Excel Keyboard Shortcuts

Introducing Data Analysis

Data analysis is the application of tools and techniques to organize, study, reach conclusions, and sometimes make predictions about a specific collection of information. A sales manager might use data analysis to study the sales history of a product, determine the overall trend, and produce a forecast of future sales. A scientist might use data analysis to study experimental findings and determine the statistical significance of the results. A family might use data analysis to find the maximum mortgage that they can afford, or to determine how much they need to put aside each month to finance their retirement or their children's education.

Manipulate Raw Data

The point of data analysis is to understand information on some deeper, more meaningful level. By definition, *raw data* is a mere collection of facts that by themselves tell you little or nothing of any importance. To gain some understanding of the data, you must manipulate it in some meaningful way. This can be something as simple as finding the sum or average of a column of numbers or as complex as employing a full-scale regression analysis to determine the underlying trend of a range of values. Both are examples of data analysis, and Excel offers a number of tools, from the straightforward to the sophisticated, to meet even the most demanding needs.

Data

The "data" part of data analysis is a collection of numbers, dates, and text that represents the raw information you have to work with. In Excel, this data resides inside a worksheet and you get it there in one of two ways: you enter it by hand or you import it from an external source. You can then either leave the data as a regular range, or convert it into a table for easier data manipulation.

Data Entry

In many data analysis situations, you must enter the required data into the worksheet manually. For example, if you want to determine a potential monthly mortgage payment, you must first enter values such as the current interest rate, the principal, and the term. Manual data entry is suitable for small projects only, because entering hundreds or even thousands of values is time- consuming and can lead to errors.

Imported Data

Most data analysis projects involve large amounts of data, and the fastest and most accurate way to get that data onto a worksheet is to import it from a non-Excel data source. In the simplest scenario, you can copy the data from a text file, a Word table, or an Access datasheet and then paste it into a worksheet. However, most business and scientific data is stored in large databases, and Excel offers tools to import the data you need into your worksheet. See Chapter 14 for more about these tools.

Table

After you have your data in the worksheet, you can leave it as a regular range and still apply many data analysis techniques to the data. However, if you convert the range into a *table*, Excel treats the data as a simple flat-file database and enables you to apply a number of database-specific analysis techniques to the table. To learn how to do this, see Chapter 6.

Data Models

In many cases, you perform data analysis on worksheet values by organizing those values into a *data model*, a collection of cells designed as a worksheet version of some real-world concept or scenario. The model includes not only the raw data, but also one or more cells that represent some analysis of the data.

Formulas

A *formula* is a set of symbols and values that perform some kind of calculation and produce a result. All Excel formulas have the same general structure: an equal sign (=) followed by one or more operands separated by one or more operators. *Operands* can be a value, a cell reference, a range, a range name, or a function name. *Operators* are the symbols that combine the operands in some way, such as the plus sign (+) and the multiplication sign (*). For example, the formula `=A1+A2` adds the values in cells A1 and A2.

Functions

A *function* is a predefined formula that is built in to Excel. Each function takes one or more inputs called *arguments*, such as numbers or cell references, and then returns a result. Excel offers hundreds of functions and you can use them to compute averages, determine the future value of an investment, and much more.

What-If Analysis

One of the most common data analysis techniques is *what-if analysis*, where you set up worksheet models to analyze hypothetical situations. The what-if part comes from the fact that these situations usually come in the form of a question: “What happens to the monthly payment if the interest rate goes up by 2 percent?” Excel offers four what-if analysis tools: data tables, Goal Seek, Solver, and scenarios.

Data Tables

A *data table* is a range of cells where one column consists of a series of values, called *input cells*. You can then apply each of those inputs to a single formula, and Excel displays the results for each case. For example, you can use a data table to apply a series of interest rate values to a formula that calculates the monthly payment for a loan or mortgage.

Goal Seek

You use the Goal Seek tool in Excel when you want to manipulate one formula component, called the *changing cell*, in such a way that the formula produces a specific result. For example, in a *break-even analysis*, you can use Goal Seek to determine the number of units of a product that you must sell for the profit to be 0.

Solver

You use the Solver tool in Excel when you want to manipulate multiple formula components, called the *changing cells*, in such a way that the formula produces the optimal result. For example, you can use Solver to tackle the so-called *transportation problem*, where the goal is to minimize the cost of shipping goods from several product plants to various warehouses around the country.

Scenarios

A *scenario* is a collection of input values that you plug into formulas within a model to produce a result. The idea is that you make up scenarios for various situations — for example, best-case, worst-case, and so on — and the Excel Scenario Manager saves each one. Later you can apply any of the saved scenarios, and Excel automatically applies all the input values to the model.

Introducing Formulas

A *formula* is a set of symbols and values that perform some kind of calculation and produce a result. All Excel formulas have the same general structure: an equal sign (=) followed by one or more operands and operators. The equal sign tells Excel to interpret everything that follows in the cell as a formula. For example, if you type `=5+8` into a cell, Excel interprets the `5+8` text as a formula, and displays the result (`13`) in the cell.

To build accurate and useful formulas, you need to know the components of a formula, including operands and operators. You also need to understand the importance of precedence when building a formula.

Operands

Operands are the values that the formula uses as the raw material for the calculation. In a formula, the operands can be constants, cell or range references, range names, or worksheet functions.

Cell and Range References

The most common type of operand that you can use in a formula is a reference to a worksheet location. This makes intuitive sense because data analysis typically involves working with one or more values on a worksheet, so your formulas need some way to incorporate those worksheet values. In the simplest case, your formula can refer to the address of a single cell. For example, the following formula returns a result that adds 5 to the value in cell A1:

```
=A1 + 5
```

Your formulas can also work with ranges, in which case you include the range coordinates in your calculation. For example, the following formula uses the Excel `SUM` function to return the total of the values in the range B1:B5):

```
=SUM(B1:B5)
```

Range Names

Range names are labels applied to a single cell or to a range of cells. You can use a defined name in place of the range coordinates. In particular, to include the range in a formula, you use the name instead of selecting the range or typing its coordinates. Range names also make your formulas intuitive and easy to read. For example, assigning the name `BeverageSales` to a range such as F1:F10 immediately clarifies the purpose of a formula such as the following:

```
=SUM(BeverageSales)
```

Range names also increase the accuracy of your formulas because you do not have to specify range coordinates.

Constants

A *constant* is a fixed value that you insert into a formula and use as is. For example, suppose you want a calculated item to return a result that is 10 percent greater than the value of the `Beverage_Total` item. In that case, you create a formula that multiplies the `Beverage_Total` item by the constant 110 percent, as shown here:

```
=Beverage_Total * 110%
```

In Excel formulas, the constant values are usually numbers, although when using comparison formulas you may occasionally use a *string* (text surrounded by double quotation marks, such as `"January"`) as a constant.

Worksheet Functions

You can use any of the built-in worksheet functions in Excel as operands in a formula. For example, you can use the `AVERAGE` function to compute the average of two or more items, or you can use logic functions such as `IF` and `OR` to create complex formulas that make decisions. See Chapter 3 for more details.

Operators

It is possible to use only an operand in a formula. For example, if you reference just a cell address after the opening equal sign (=), then the value returned by the formula is identical to the value in the referenced cell.

A formula that is equal to an existing cell is not particularly useful in data analysis. To create formulas that perform more interesting calculations, you need to include one or more operators. The *operators* are the symbols that the formula uses to perform the calculation.

In an Excel formula that contains two or more operands, each operand is separated by an operator, which combines the operands in some way, usually mathematically. Example operators include the plus sign (+) and the multiplication sign (*). For example, the formula `=B1+B2` adds the values in cells B1 and B2. See the next section, "Understanding Formula Types," for a complete list of the available operators.

Operator Precedence

Most of your formulas include multiple operands and operators. In many cases, the order in which Excel performs the calculations is crucial. For example, consider the following formula:

```
=3 + 5 ^ 2
```

If you calculate from left to right, the answer you get is `64` (`3 + 5` equal `8`, and `8 ^ 2` equal `64`). However, if you perform the exponentiation first and then the addition, the result is `28` (`5 ^ 2` equal `25`, and `3 + 25` equal `28`). Therefore, a single formula can produce multiple answers, depending on the order in which you perform the calculations.

To control this problem, Excel evaluates a formula according to a predefined order of precedence. You can also control the order of precedence yourself using parentheses; see the Tip in the section, "Build a Formula," later in this chapter. This order of precedence enables Excel to calculate a formula unambiguously by determining which part of the formula it calculates first, which part second, and so on. The formula operators determine the order of precedence, as shown in the following table:

Symbol	Operator	Order of Precedence
( )	Parentheses	1st
: (space) ,	Reference	2nd
–	Negation	3rd
%	Percentage	4th
^	Exponentiation	5th
* and /	Multiplication and division	6th
+ and –	Addition and subtraction	7th
&	Concatenation	8th
= < <= > >= <>	Comparison	9th

Understanding Formula Types

Worksheet formulas fall into four distinct types: *arithmetic formulas* for computing numeric results; *comparison formulas* for comparing one value with another; *text formulas* for combining two or more text strings; and *reference formulas* that combine two cell references or ranges to create a single joint reference.

Because you usually deal with numeric values within a formula, the operators you use determine the type of formula. For example, arithmetic formulas use arithmetic operators and comparison formulas use comparison operators. This section shows you the operators that define all four formula types.

Arithmetic Formulas

An arithmetic formula combines numeric operands with mathematical operators to perform a calculation. Numeric operands are numeric constants, functions that return numeric results, and cells, ranges, or range names that contain numeric values. Because data analysis models primarily deal with numeric data, arithmetic formulas are by far the most common formulas used in analysis calculations.

The following table lists the seven arithmetic operators that you can use to construct arithmetic formulas. Most of these operators are straightforward, but the exponentiation operator might require further explanation. The formula =x ^ y means that the value x is raised to the power y. For example, the formula =3 ^ 2 produces the result 9 (that is, 3 * 3 = 9). Similarly, the formula =2 ^ 4 produces 16 (that is, 2 * 2 * 2 * 2 = 16).

Operator	Name	Example	Result
+	Addition	=10 + 5	15
–	Subtraction	=10 – 5	5
–	Negation	=–10	–10
•	Multiplication	=10 * 5	50
/	Division	=10 / 5	2
%	Percentage	=10%	0.1
^	Exponentiation	=10 ^ 5	100000

Comparison Formulas

A comparison formula, also called a relational formula, combines numeric operands with special operators to compare one operand with another. Numeric operands are numeric constants, functions that return numeric results, and cells, ranges, or range names that contain numeric values. A comparison formula always returns a logical result. This means that if the comparison is true, then the formula returns the value 1, which is equivalent to the logical value `TRUE`; if the comparison is false, then the formula returns the value 0, which is equivalent to the logical value `FALSE`.

The following table lists the six operators that you can use to construct comparison formulas:

Operator	Name	Example	Result
=	Equal to	=10 = 5	0
<	Less than	=10 < 5	0
<=	Less than or equal to	=10 <= 5	0
>	Greater than	=10 > 5	1
>=	Greater than or equal to	=10 >= 5	1
<>	Not equal to	=10 <> 5	1

Text Formulas

You use text formulas not to derive a result, but to combine two or more text strings, a process known as *concatenation*. There is only one text concatenation operator — the ampersand (&). You use the ampersand to join values together to produce one continuous text value. For example, if the text "John" is in cell A1 and the text "Smith" is in cell B1, the formula `= A1 & " " & B1` returns the concatenated string "John Smith" (in this formula, note that a space surrounded by double quotation marks returns a space). Your text formulas can also include text constants, which are text values surrounded by double quotation marks. For example, the formula `="John" & B1`, returns "John Smith", if "Smith" is in cell B1.

Reference Formulas

You use reference formulas to specify the range of cells you want to use in your formula. There are three reference operators: the colon (:), the comma (,), and the space. Excel refers to them as the range operator, the union operator, and the intersection operator, respectively. The colon references every cell included in and between the referenced cells. For example, A1:C3 includes cells A1, A2, A3, B1, B2, B3, C1, C2, and C3. The comma enables you to reference the union of two or more cells or ranges. For example, A1, B2:C3 references cells A1, B2, B3, C2, and C3. The intersection operator references all the cells that range operators have in common. For example, the reference B1:C3 C1:D3 references cells C1 to C3. You can use more than one reference operator in a single formula.

Operator	Name	Description
: (colon)	Range	Produces a range from two cell references (for example, A1:C5)
, (comma)	Union	Produces a range that is the union of two ranges (for example, A1:C5,B2:E8)
(space)	Intersection	Produces a range that is the intersection of two ranges (for example, A1:C5 B2:E8 references the intersecting range B2:C5)

Build a Formula

You can add a formula to a worksheet cell using a technique similar to adding data to a cell. To ensure that Excel treats the text as a formula, be sure to begin with an equal sign (=) and then type your operands and operators.

When you add a formula to a cell, Excel displays the formula result in the cell, not the actual formula. For example, if you add the formula `=C3+C4` to a cell, that cell displays the sum of the values in cells C3 and C4. To see the formula, you can click the cell and examine the Formula bar.

Build a Formula

1. Click in the cell in which you want to build the formula.
2. Type =.

   A. Your typing also appears in the Formula bar.

Note: You can also type the formula into the Formula bar.

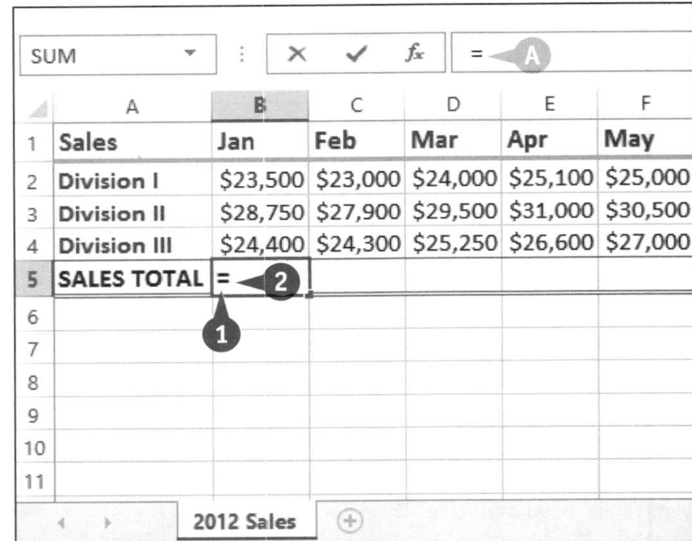

3. Type or click an operand. For example, to reference a cell in your formula, click in the cell.

   B. Excel inserts the address of the clicked cell into the formula.

FILE HOME INSERT PAGE LAYOUT FORMULAS DA

B2 =B2

	A	B	C	D	E	F
1	Sales	Jan	Feb	Mar	Apr	May
2	Division I	$23,500	$23,000	$24,000	$25,100	$25,000
3	Division II	$28,750	$27,900	$29,500	$31,000	$30,500
4	Division III	$24,400	$24,300	$25,250	$26,600	$27,000
5	SALES TOTAL	=B2				
6						
7						
8						
9						
10						
11						

4. Type an operator.
5. Repeat steps 3 and 4 to add other operands and operators to your formula.
6. Click the Enter button or press Enter.

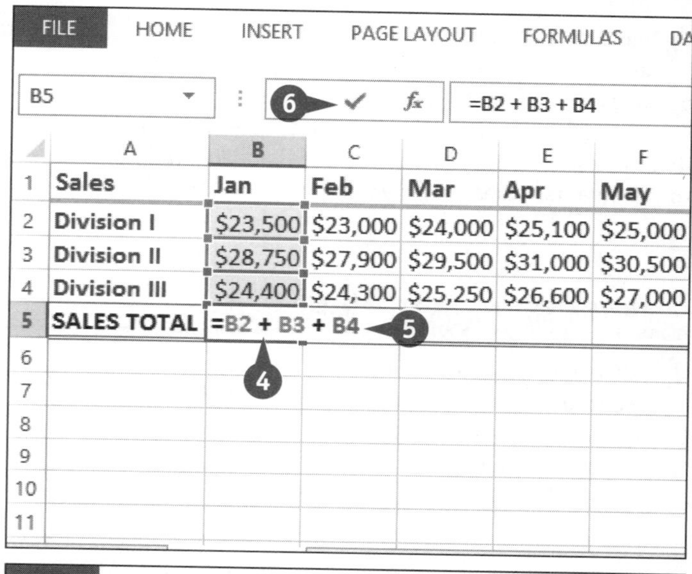

	A	B	C	D	E	F
1	Sales	Jan	Feb	Mar	Apr	May
2	Division I	$23,500	$23,000	$24,000	$25,100	$25,000
3	Division II	$28,750	$27,900	$29,500	$31,000	$30,500
4	Division III	$24,400	$24,300	$25,250	$26,600	$27,000
5	SALES TOTAL	=B2 + B3 + B4				

C. Excel displays the formula result in the cell.

	A	B	C	D	E	F
1	Sales	Jan	Feb	Mar	Apr	May
2	Division I	$23,500	$23,000	$24,000	$25,100	$25,000
3	Division II	$28,750	$27,900	$29,500	$31,000	$30,500
4	Division III	$24,400	$24,300	$25,250	$26,600	$27,000
5	SALES TOTAL	$76,650				

APPLY IT

Operator precedence seems straightforward, but it can lead to errors in your formula results. Consider a formula that calculates the gross margin for a business. Gross margin is profit — sales minus expenses — divided by expenses. Therefore, you might start with the following formula:

```
=Profit - Expenses / Expenses
```

However, when Excel processes this formula, operator precedence tells it to perform the division first, so the formula becomes `=Profit - 1`

This is clearly incorrect. To force Excel to perform a particular operation first, surround the expression with parentheses, as shown here:

```
=(Profit - Expenses) / Expenses
```

You can make your formulas easier to build, more accurate, and easier to read by using range names as operands instead of cell and range addresses. For example, the formula =SUM(B2:B10) is difficult to decipher on its own, particularly if you cannot see the range B2:B10 to examine its values. However, if you use the formula =SUM(Expenses) instead, it becomes immediately obvious what the formula is meant to do. The easiest way to define a range name is to select the range and then type the name in the Name box, which appears on the far-left side of the Excel Formula bar.

Add a Range Name to a Formula

1. Click in the cell in which you want to build the formula, type =, and then type any operands and operators you need before adding the range name.

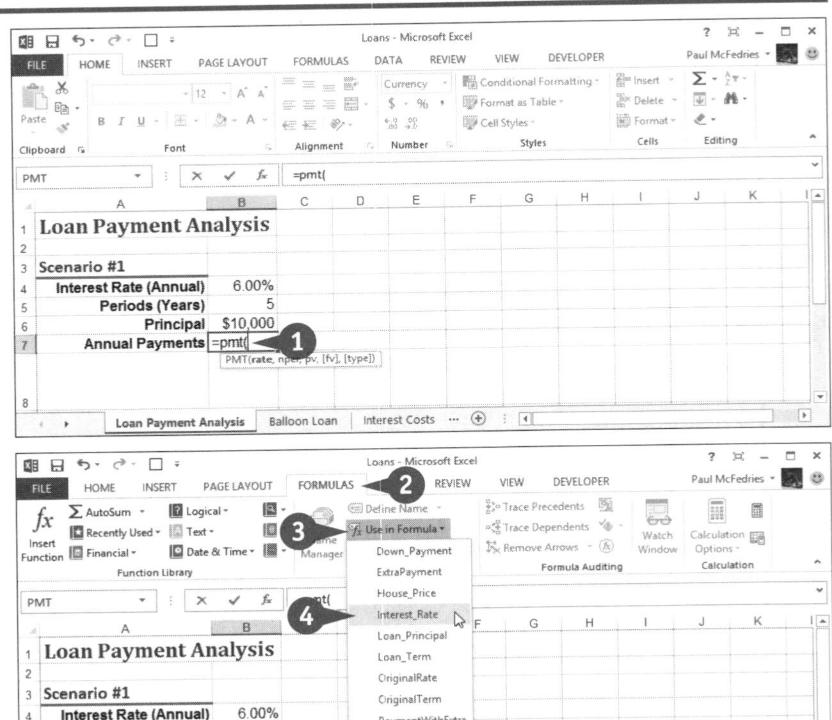

2. Click the Formulas tab.
3. Click Use in Formula.

   Ⓐ Excel displays a list of the range names in the current workbook.

4. Click the range name you want to use.

B Excel inserts the range name into the formula.

5 Type any operands and operators you need to complete your formula.

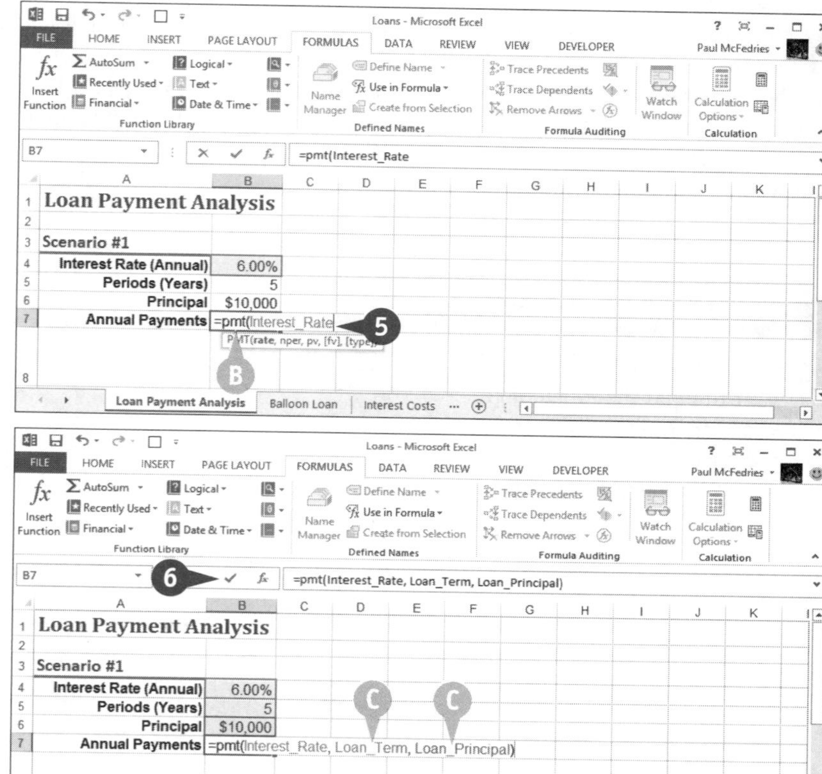

C If you need to insert other range names into your formula, repeat steps 2 to 5 for each name.

6 Click the Enter button or press Enter.

Excel calculates the formula result.

APPLY IT

Excel offers an Apply Names feature that replaces range references with their associated range names throughout a worksheet. Click the Formulas tab, click the Define Name list, and then click Apply Names to open the Apply Names dialog box. Click the range name you want to use, and then click OK.

As you build your formula, you can type the range name manually, if you know it. Alternatively, as you build your formula, click the cell, or select the range that has the defined name, and Excel adds the name to your formula instead of the range address.

Reference Another Worksheet Range in a Formula

You can enhance your data analysis and add flexibility to your formulas by adding references to ranges that reside in other worksheets. This enables you to take advantage of work that you or another person has done in other worksheets, so you do not have to waste time repeating that work in the current worksheet.

Referencing a range in another worksheet also gives you the advantage of having automatically updated information. For example, if the data in the other worksheet range changes, Excel automatically updates your formula to include the changed data. This saves you from constantly having to monitor the value in the other worksheet.

Reference Another Worksheet Range in a Formula

1. Click in the cell in which you want to build the formula, type =, and then type any operands and operators you need before adding the range reference.

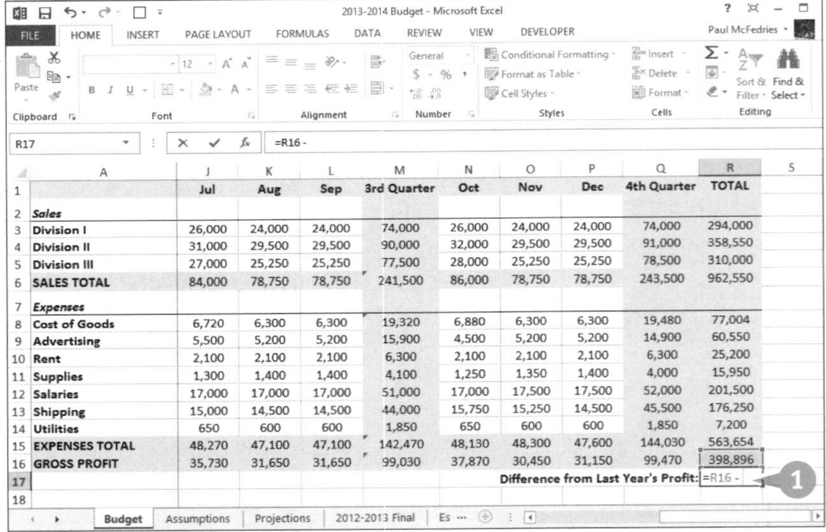

2. Press Ctrl+Page Down until the worksheet you want to use appears.

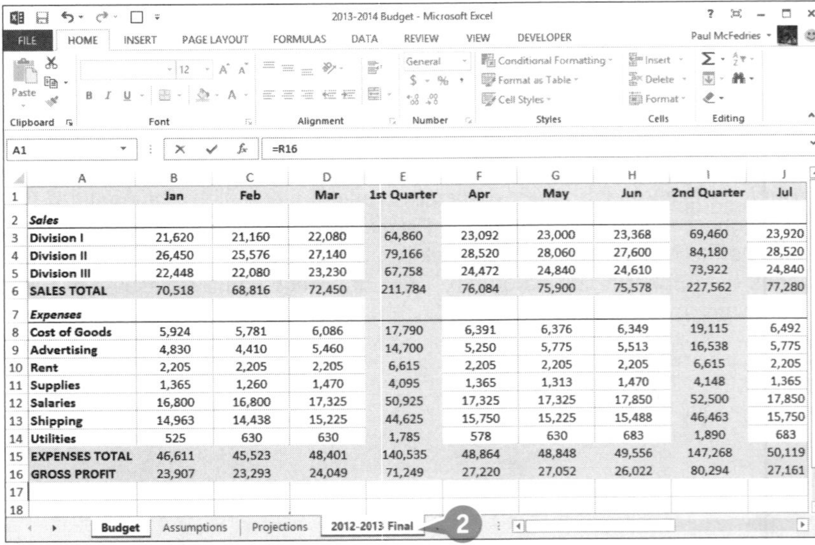

3 Select the range you want to use.

4 Press Ctrl+Page Up until you return to the original worksheet.

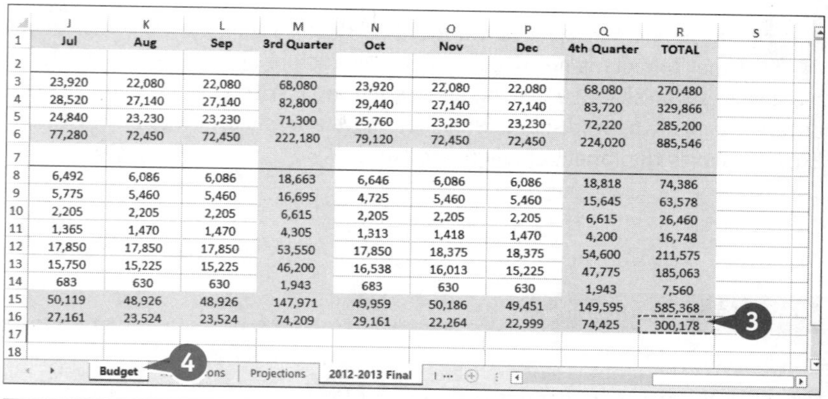

A A reference to the range on the other worksheet appears in your formula.

5 Type any operands and operators you need to complete your formula.

6 Click the Enter button or press Enter.

Excel calculates the formula result.

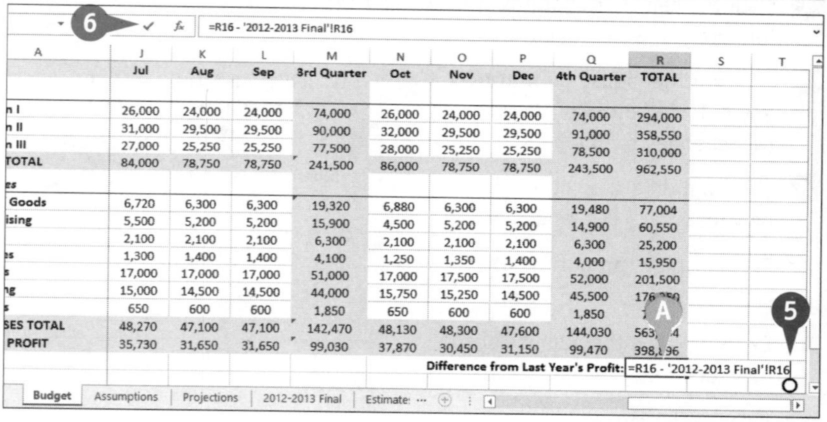

APPLY IT

Rather than selecting the other worksheet range with your mouse, you can type the range reference directly into your formula. Type the worksheet name, surrounded by single quotation marks (') if the name contains a space; type an exclamation mark (!); then type the cell or range address. Here is an example: 'Expenses 2013'!B2:B10.

To reference a range in another open workbook, click the Excel icon in the Windows taskbar, and then click the other workbook to switch to it. Click the worksheet that has the range you want to reference, and then select the range. Click the Excel taskbar icon and then click the original workbook to switch back to it. Excel adds the other workbook range reference to your formula.

When you add a formula to a worksheet, the location of that formula is not fixed. You can restructure or reorganize a worksheet by moving an existing formula to a different part of the worksheet. When you move a formula, Excel preserves the formula's range references.

Excel also enables you to make a copy of a formula, which is a useful technique if you require a duplicate of the formula elsewhere or if you require a formula that is similar to an existing formula. When you copy a formula, Excel adjusts the range references to the new location.

Move or Copy a Formula

Move a Formula

1. Click the cell that contains the formula you want to move.
2. Position the mouse pointer over any outside border of the cell (✥ changes to ✥).
3. Click and drag the cell to the new location (✥ changes to ↖).

- A Excel displays an outline of the cell.
- B Excel displays the address of the new location.

4. Release the mouse button.

- C Excel moves the formula to the new location.
- D Excel does not change the formula's range references.

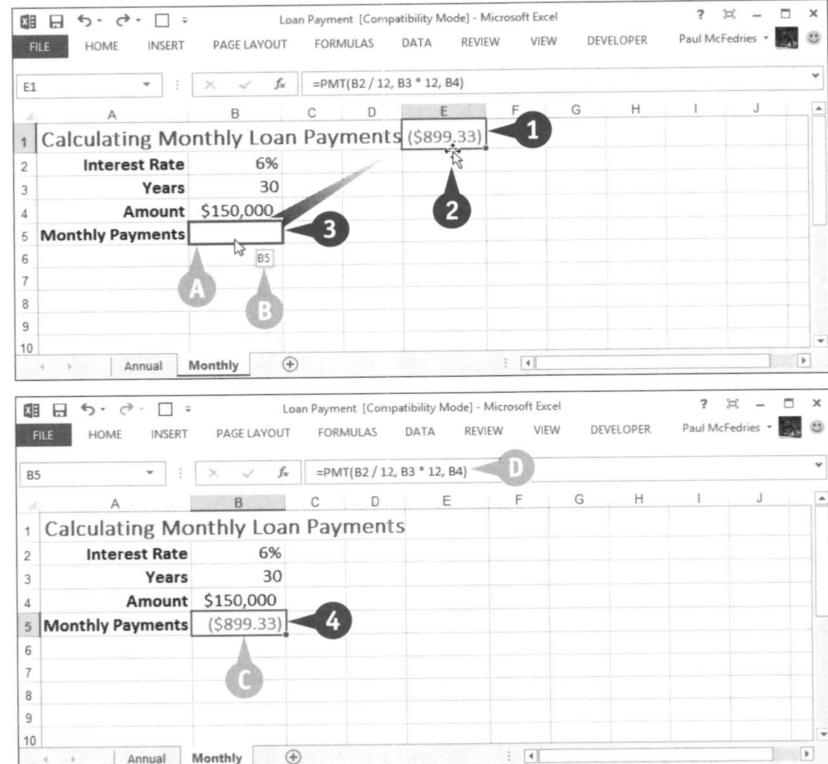

Copy a Formula

1. Click the cell that contains the formula you want to copy.
2. Press and hold the Ctrl key.
3. Position the mouse pointer over any outside border of the cell (✥ changes to ↖).
4. Click and drag the cell to the location where you want the copy to appear.

- E Excel displays an outline of the cell.
- F Excel displays the address of the new location.

5. Release the mouse button.
6. Release the Ctrl key.

- G Excel creates a copy of the formula in the new location.
- H Excel adjusts the range references.

Note: *You can make multiple copies by dragging the bottom-right corner of the cell. Excel fills the adjacent cells with copies of the formula. See the following section, "Switch to Absolute Cell References," for an example.*

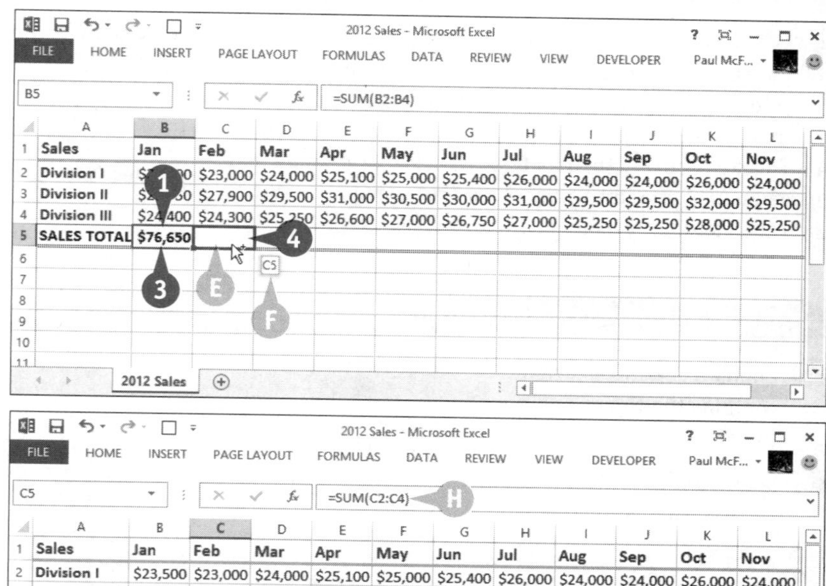

EXTRA

When you make a copy of a formula, Excel assumes that you want that copy to reference different ranges than in the original formula. In particular, Excel assumes that the ranges you want to use in the new formula are positioned relative to the ranges used in the original formula, and that the relative difference is equal to the number of rows and columns you dragged the cell to create the copy. For example, suppose your original formula references cell A1, and you make a copy of the formula in the cell one column to the right. In that case, Excel also adjusts the cell reference one column to the right, so it becomes B1 in the new formula.

Switch to Absolute Cell References

When you reference a cell in a formula, Excel treats it as a *relative cell reference*, which means it sees the reference as being relative to the formula's cell. For example, if the formula is in cell B5 and it references cell A1, Excel effectively treats A1 as the cell four rows up and one column to the left. If you copy the formula to cell D10, then the cell four rows up and one column to the left is now cell C6, so in the copied formula Excel changes A1 to C6.

To prevent that reference from changing, you must use the *absolute cell reference* format: $A$1. In this case, the copied formula in cell D10 also refers to $A$1.

Switch to Absolute Cell References

1. Double-click the cell that contains the formula you want to edit.
2. Select the cell reference you want to change.
3. Press F4.

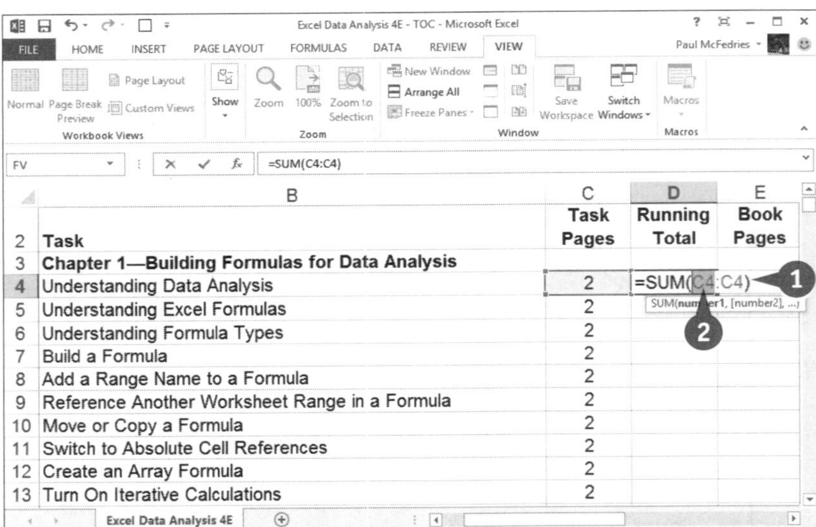

A. Excel switches the address to an absolute cell reference.

4. Repeat steps 2 and 3 to switch any other cell addresses that you require in the absolute reference format.
5. Click the Enter button or press Enter.

	B	C	D	E
2	**Task**	**Task Pages**	**Running Total**	**Book Pages**
3	**Chapter 1—Building Formulas for Data Analysis**			
4	Understanding Data Analysis	2	=SUM($C$4:C4)	
5	Understanding Excel Formulas	2		
6	Understanding Formula Types	2		
7	Build a Formula	2		
8	Add a Range Name to a Formula	2		
9	Reference Another Worksheet Range in a Formula	2		
10	Move or Copy a Formula	2		
11	Switch to Absolute Cell References	2		
12	Create an Array Formula	2		
13	Turn On Iterative Calculations	2		

Ⓑ Excel adjusts the formula.

❻ Copy the formula.

Note: *See the previous section, "Move or Copy a Formula," to learn how to copy a formula.*

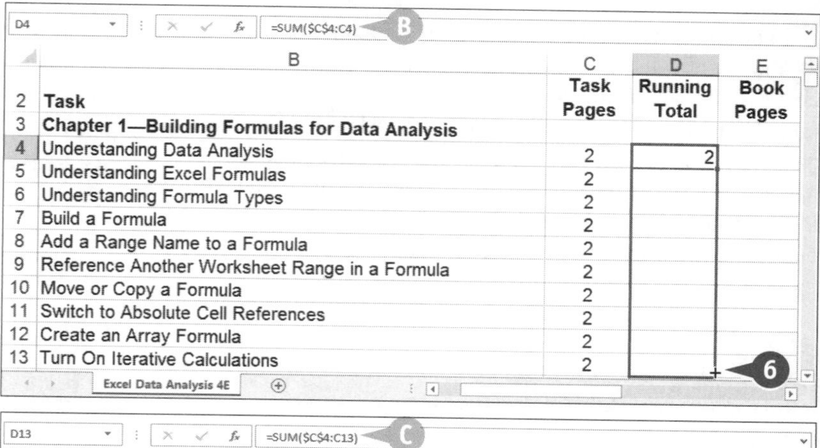

D4 =SUM($C$4:C4) Ⓑ

	B	C	D	E
2	**Task**	**Task Pages**	**Running Total**	**Book Pages**
3	**Chapter 1—Building Formulas for Data Analysis**			
4	Understanding Data Analysis	2	2	
5	Understanding Excel Formulas	2		
6	Understanding Formula Types	2		
7	Build a Formula	2		
8	Add a Range Name to a Formula	2		
9	Reference Another Worksheet Range in a Formula	2		
10	Move or Copy a Formula	2		
11	Switch to Absolute Cell References	2		
12	Create an Array Formula	2		
13	Turn On Iterative Calculations	2		

Excel Data Analysis 4E ❻

Ⓒ Excel preserves the absolute cell references in the copied formula.

D13 =SUM($C$4:C13) Ⓒ

	B	C	D	E
2	**Task**	**Task Pages**	**Running Total**	**Book Pages**
3	**Chapter 1—Building Formulas for Data Analysis**			
4	Understanding Data Analysis	2	2	
5	Understanding Excel Formulas	2	4	
6	Understanding Formula Types	2	6	
7	Build a Formula	2	8	
8	Add a Range Name to a Formula	2	10	
9	Reference Another Worksheet Range in a Formula	2	12	
10	Move or Copy a Formula	2	14	
11	Switch to Absolute Cell References	2	16	
12	Create an Array Formula	2	18	
13	Turn On Iterative Calculations	2	20	

Excel Data Analysis 4E

APPLY IT

To switch a cell reference from the absolute format back to the relative format, you can use the F4 keyboard technique, which actually runs the address through four different reference formats. Given a cell address in relative reference format, press F4 once to switch to the absolute cell reference format, such as $A$1. Press F4 again to switch to a mixed reference format that uses a relative column and absolute row (A$1). Press F4 a third time to switch to a mixed reference format that uses an absolute column and relative row ($A1). Finally, press F4 a fourth time to return to the relative cell reference (A1).

Create an Array Formula

If you find yourself repeating the same formula across a range of cells, you can make your formula-building chores easier and faster by taking advantage of the array formulas in Excel. An *array formula* is a special formula that generates multiple results. For example, if your worksheet has expense totals in cells C11, D11, and E11, and a budget increase value in cell C3, then you can calculate the new budget values with the following formulas:

```
=C11 * (1 + $C$3)
=D11 * (1 + $C$3)
=E11 * (1 + $C$3)
```

Rather than entering these formulas separately, you can enter just a single array formula:

```
{=C11:E11 * (1 + $C$3)}
```

The braces, { and }, mark this as an array formula, and Excel enters them automatically.

Create an Array Formula

Create a Multi-Cell Array Formula

1. Select the range where you want the formula results to appear.
2. Type the array formula.
3. Press Ctrl+Shift+Enter.

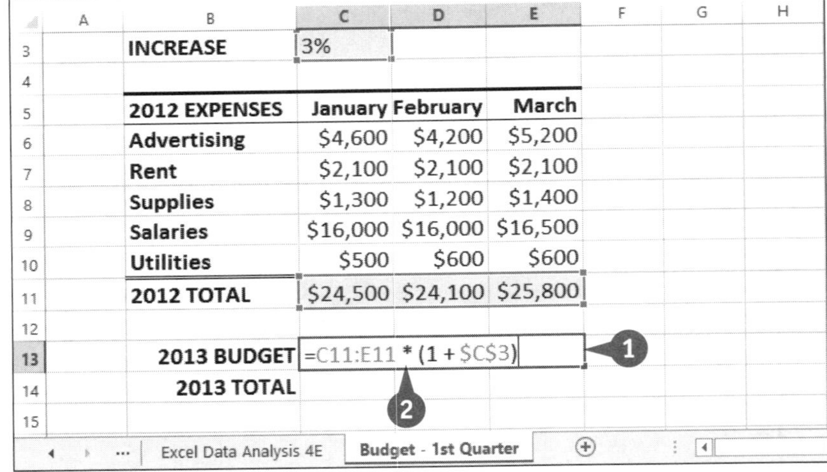

FV | =C11:E11 * (1 + $C$3)

	A	B	C	D	E	F	G	H
3		INCREASE	3%					
4								
5		2012 EXPENSES	January	February	March			
6		Advertising	$4,600	$4,200	$5,200			
7		Rent	$2,100	$2,100	$2,100			
8		Supplies	$1,300	$1,200	$1,400			
9		Salaries	$16,000	$16,000	$16,500			
10		Utilities	$500	$600	$600			
11		2012 TOTAL	$24,500	$24,100	$25,800			
12								
13		2013 BUDGET	=C11:E11 * (1 + $C$3)					
14		2013 TOTAL						
15								

A. Excel enters the formula as an array formula and automatically adds braces around it.

B. Excel enters the results in the range you selected.

C13 | {=C11:E11 * (1 + $C$3)} — A

	A	B	C	D	E	F	G	H
3		INCREASE	3%					
4								
5		2012 EXPENSES	January	February	March			
6		Advertising	$4,600	$4,200	$5,200			
7		Rent	$2,100	$2,100	$2,100			
8		Supplies	$1,300	$1,200	$1,400			
9		Salaries	$16,000	$16,000	$16,500			
10		Utilities	$500	$600	$600			
11		2012 TOTAL	$24,500	$24,100	$25,800			
12								
13		2013 BUDGET	$25,235	$24,823	$26,574	B		
14		2013 TOTAL						
15								

Excel Data Analysis 4E | Budget - 1st Quarter

Create a Single-Cell Array Formula

1. Select the cell where you want the formula result to appear.
2. Type the array formula.
3. Press Ctrl+Shift+Enter.

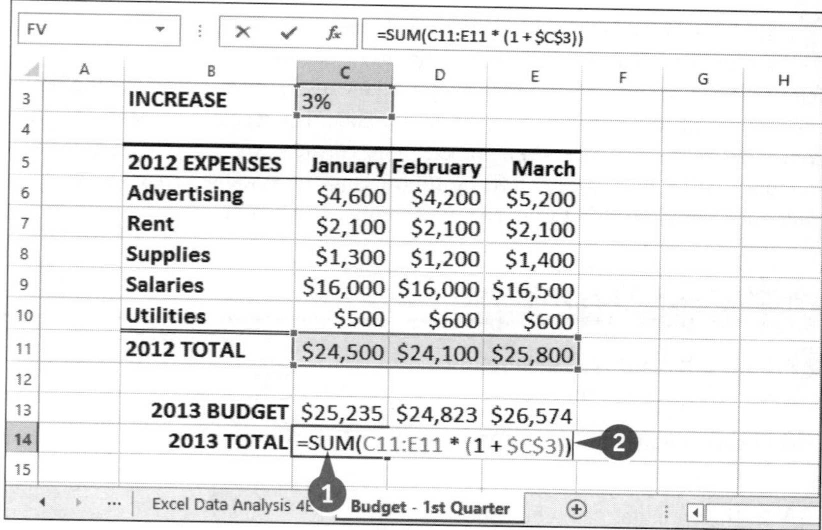
FV | =SUM(C11:E11 * (1 + $C$3))

	A	B	C	D	E	F	G	H
3		INCREASE	3%					
4								
5		2012 EXPENSES	January	February	March			
6		Advertising	$4,600	$4,200	$5,200			
7		Rent	$2,100	$2,100	$2,100			
8		Supplies	$1,300	$1,200	$1,400			
9		Salaries	$16,000	$16,000	$16,500			
10		Utilities	$500	$600	$600			
11		2012 TOTAL	$24,500	$24,100	$25,800			
12								
13		2013 BUDGET	$25,235	$24,823	$26,574			
14		2013 TOTAL	=SUM(C11:E11 * (1 + $C$3))					
15								

Excel Data Analysis 4E | Budget - 1st Quarter

C. Excel enters the formula as an array formula and automatically adds braces around it.

D. Excel enters the result in the cell you selected.

C14 | {=SUM(C11:E11 * (1 + $C$3))}

	A	B	C	D	E	F	G	H
3		INCREASE	3%					
4								
5		2012 EXPENSES	January	February	March			
6		Advertising	$4,600	$4,200	$5,200			
7		Rent	$2,100	$2,100	$2,100			
8		Supplies	$1,300	$1,200	$1,400			
9		Salaries	$16,000	$16,000	$16,500			
10		Utilities	$500	$600	$600			
11		2012 TOTAL	$24,500	$24,100	$25,800			
12								
13		2013 BUDGET	$25,235	$24,823	$26,574			
14		2013 TOTAL	$76,632					
15								

Excel Data Analysis 4E | Budget - 1st Quarter

EXTRA

It is important to remember that Excel treats multi-cell array formulas as a unit. This means that you cannot edit, move, or delete a single cell or any subset of cells within an array. If you need to work with an array, you must select the whole range. Note that you can select an array quickly by selecting one of its cells and pressing Ctrl+/.

If you want to reduce the size of an array, select it, select the Formula bar, and then press Ctrl+Enter to change the entry to a normal formula. You can then select the smaller range and reenter the array formula.

Turn On Iterative Calculations

In some Excel calculations, you cannot derive the answer directly. Instead, you perform a preliminary calculation, feed that answer into the formula to get a new result, feed the new result into the formula, and so on. Each new result *converges* on the actual answer. For example, consider a formula that calculates net profit by subtracting the amount paid out in profit sharing from the gross profit. This is not a simple subtraction because the profit sharing amount is calculated as a percentage of the net profit, so you must plug preliminary results back into the formula. This process is called *iteration*. To perform these types of Excel calculations, you must turn on the iterative calculation feature.

Turn On Iterative Calculations

1. Build a formula that requires an iterative calculation to solve.

   A. Circular reference arrows appear in the table.

   B. In the Formulas tab, you can click Remove Arrows to hide the circular reference arrows.

2. Click the File tab.

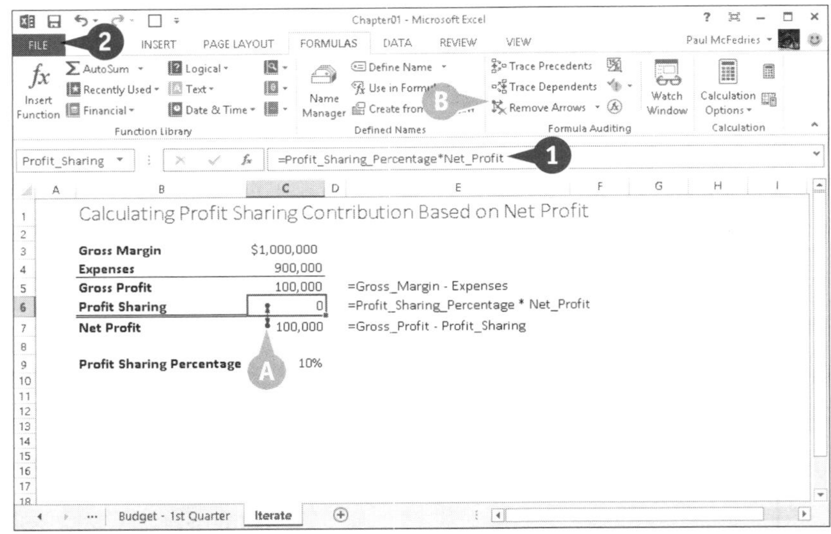

3. Click Options.

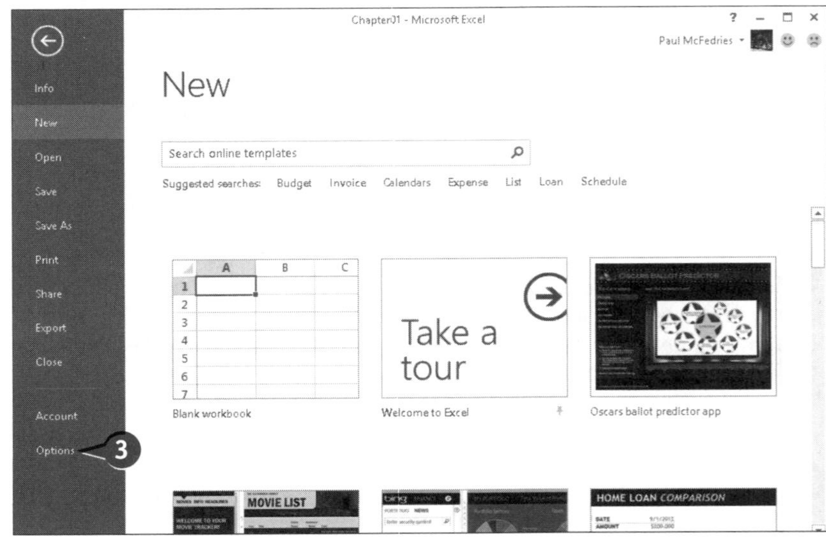

The Excel Options dialog box appears.

4 Click Formulas.

5 Click the Enable Iterative Calculation check box (☐ changes to ☑).

C If Excel fails to converge on the solution, you can try typing a higher value in the Maximum Iterations text box.

D If you want a more accurate solution, you can try typing a smaller value in the Maximum Change text box.

***Note:** The Maximum Change value tells Excel how accurate you want your results to be. The smaller the number, the more accurate the calculation, but the iteration takes longer.*

6 Click OK.

Excel performs the iteration.

E The iterated result appears in the formula cell.

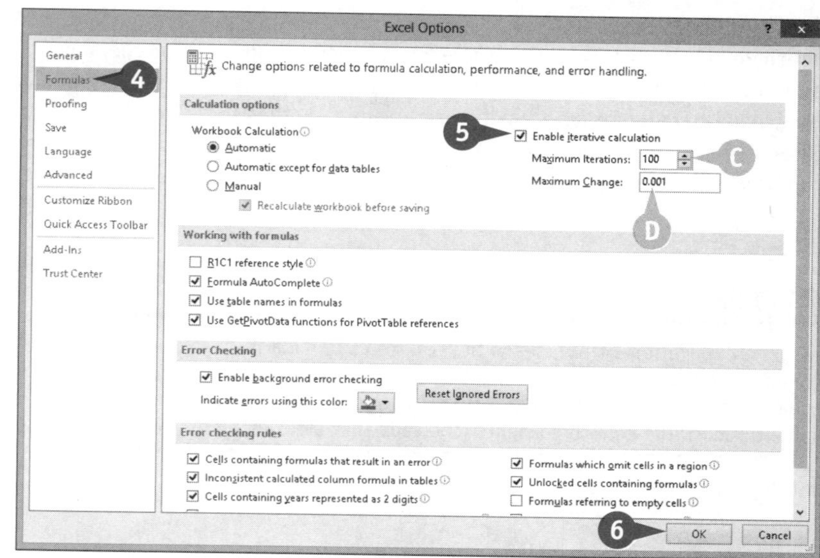

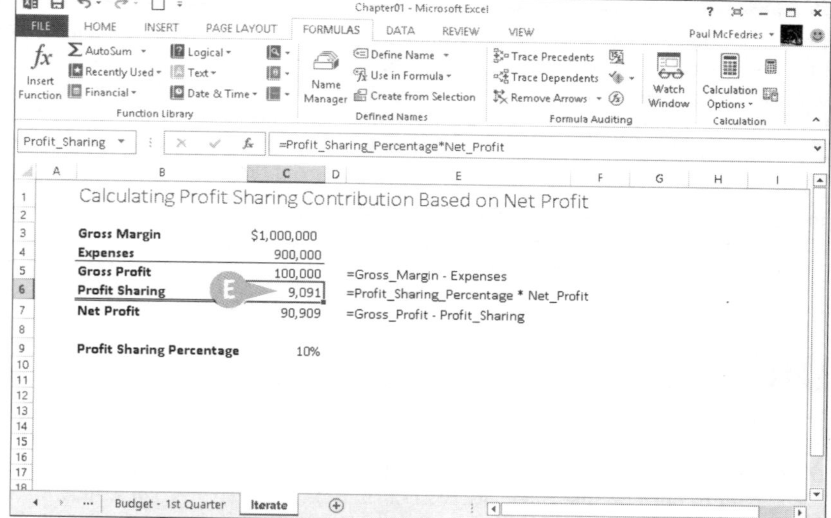

EXTRA

After you build a formula involving an iterative calculation, Excel displays circular reference arrows. These arrows usually indicate an error, but not in this case. When you set up an iterative calculation, you are by definition setting up a circular reference formula because there are terms on the left and right sides of the equal sign that depend on each other. In this example, the formula in C7 references the `Profit_Sharing` cell, which is C6. However, the `Profit_Sharing` cell references the `Net_Profit` cell, which is C7, so the references are circular.

Understanding Error Values in Excel

Excel formula errors fall into three main categories. First, there are the syntax errors, where Excel generates an error message when you press Enter to accept the formula. For example, if you forget a function's closing parenthesis, Excel displays an error letting you know that the parenthesis is missing. Next, there are the inaccuracy errors, where your worksheet data is wrong, one or more operators or operands in your formula are wrong, or both. Finally, there are the errors where Excel cannot compute a formula result and, instead, displays an error value. Excel has seven different error values — `#DIV/0!`, `#N/A`, `#NAME?`, `#NULL!`, `#NUM!`, `#REF!`, and `#VALUE!`.

#DIV/0!

The `#DIV/0!` error usually means that the cell's formula is trying to divide by zero, which is not allowed. The cause is usually a reference to a cell that either is blank or contains the value 0. Check the cell's precedents (the cells that are directly or indirectly referenced in the formula) to look for possible culprits. You also see `#DIV/0!` if you enter an inappropriate argument in some functions. The `MOD` function, for example, returns `#DIV/0!` if the second argument is 0.

#N/A

The `#N/A` error value is short for not available, and it means that the formula could not return a legitimate result. You usually see `#N/A` when you use an inappropriate argument (or if you omit a required argument) in a function. For example, the `HLOOKUP` and `VLOOKUP` functions return `#N/A` if the lookup value is smaller than the first value in the lookup range.

To solve the problem, first check the formula's input cells to see if any of them are displaying the `#N/A` error. If so, that is why your formula is returning the same error; the problem actually lies in the input cell. When you have found where the error originates, examine the formula's operands to look for inappropriate data types. In particular, check the arguments used in each function to ensure that they make sense for the function and that no required arguments are missing.

#NAME?

The `#NAME?` error appears when Excel does not recognize a name you used in a formula, or when it interprets text within the formula as an undefined name. This means that the `#NAME?` error pops up in a wide variety of circumstances, such as spelling a range name or function name incorrectly; using a range name that has not yet been defined; using a function that is part of an uninstalled add-in; using a string value without surrounding it with quotation marks; entering a range reference and accidentally omitting the colon; and entering a reference to a range on another worksheet and forgetting to enclose the sheet name in single quotation marks.

These are mostly syntax errors, so fixing them means double-checking your formula and correcting range name or function name misspellings, or inserting missing quotation marks or colons. Also, be sure to define any range names you use and to install the appropriate add-in modules for functions you use. When entering function names and defined names, use all lowercase letters. If Excel recognizes a name, it converts the function to all uppercase letters and the defined name to its original case. If a conversion does not occur, then you have misspelled the name, you have not defined it yet, or you are using a function from an add-in that is not loaded.

#NULL!

Excel displays the #NULL! error in a very specific case: when you use the intersection operator (a space) on two ranges that do not have cells in common. For example, the ranges A1:B2 and C3:D4 do not have common cells, so the following formula returns the #NULL! error:

```
=SUM(A1:B2 C3:D4)
```

Check your range coordinates to ensure that they are accurate. In addition, check to see if one of the ranges has been moved so that the two ranges in your formula no longer intersect.

#NUM!

The #NUM! error means there is a problem with a number in your formula. This usually means that you entered an invalid argument in a math or trig function. For example, you may have entered a negative number as the argument for the SQRT or LOG function. Check the formula's input cells — particularly those cells used as arguments for mathematical functions — to make sure the values are appropriate.

The #NUM! error also appears if you are using iteration (or a function that uses iteration) and Excel cannot calculate a result. There may not be a solution to the problem, or you may need to adjust the iteration parameters. For example, you could try increasing the maximum number of iterations or you could try reducing the maximum iteration change. To learn more about iteration, see Chapter 1.

#REF!

The #REF! error appears when your formula contains an invalid cell reference, which is usually caused by an action. Deleting a cell to which the formula refers will result in a #REF! error. In this case, you need to add the cell back in or adjust the formula reference.

Cutting a cell and then pasting it in a cell used by the formula will result in a #REF! error. In this case, you need to undo the cut and then paste the cell elsewhere (note that it is okay to copy a cell and paste it on a cell used by the formula).

Referencing a nonexistent cell address, such as B0, will result in a #REF! error. This can happen if you cut or copy a formula that uses relative references and paste it in such a way that the invalid cell address is created. For example, suppose that your formula references cell B1. If you cut or copy the cell containing the formula and paste it one row higher, the reference to B1 becomes invalid because Excel cannot move the cell reference up one row.

#VALUE!

When Excel generates a #VALUE! error, it means you have used an inappropriate argument in a function. This is most often caused by using the wrong data type. For example, you might have entered or referenced a string value instead of a numeric value. Similarly, you might have used a range reference in a function argument that requires a single cell or value. Excel also generates this error if you use a value that is larger or smaller than Excel can handle. (Excel can work with values between –1E–307 and 1E+307.) In all these cases, you solve the problem by double-checking your function arguments to find and edit the inappropriate arguments.

Show Formulas Instead of Results

You can more easily review and troubleshoot a worksheet by changing its display to show the formulas in each cell instead of those formulas' results. If you want to check a formula, you cannot do it by looking at the cell because Excel displays the formula result instead of the actual formula. You must click the cell to view the formula in the Formula bar. That works for a single cell, but what if you need to check all the formulas in a worksheet. You could click each cell that contains a formula, but that is impractical in a sheet with dozens of formulas. Instead, you can change the worksheet view to display the formulas in each cell rather than the formula results.

Show Formulas Instead of Results

1 Switch to the worksheet that contains the formulas you want to display.

2 Click the File tab.

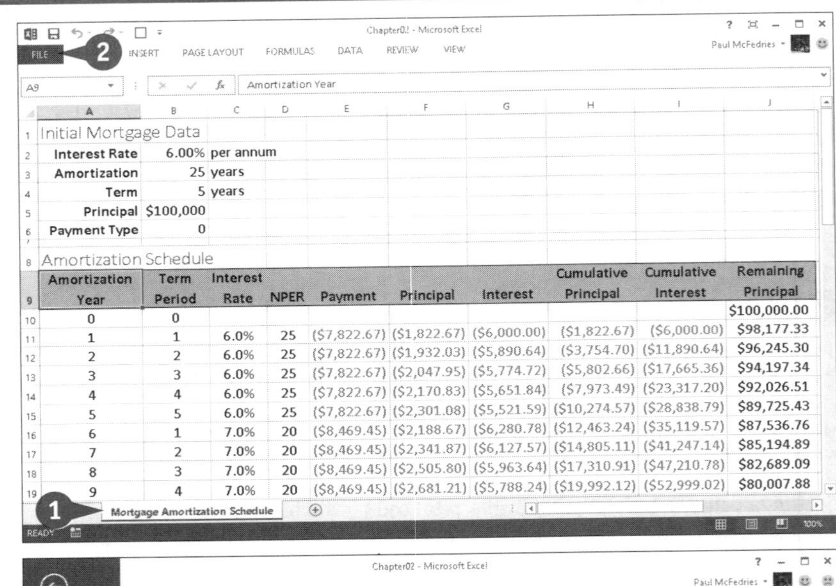

3 Click Options.

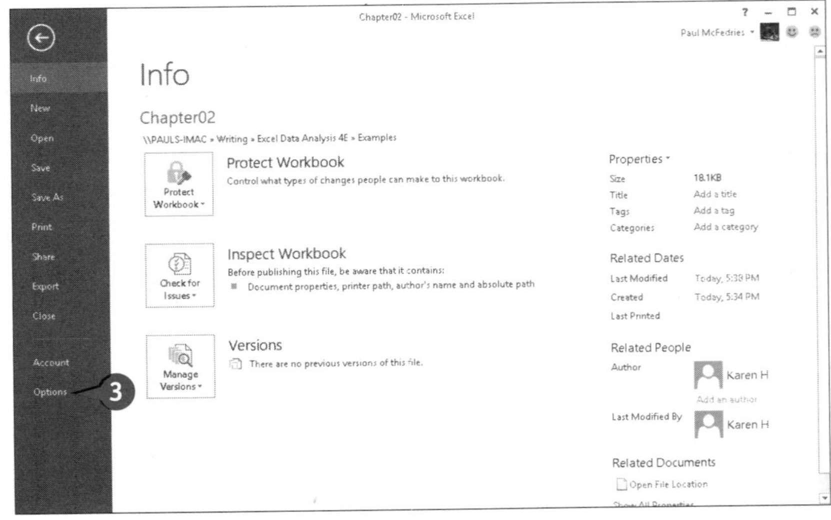

The Excel Options dialog box appears.

4. Click Advanced.
5. In the Display Options for This Worksheet section, click the Show Formulas in Cells Instead of Their Calculated Results check box (☐ changes to ☑).
6. Click OK.

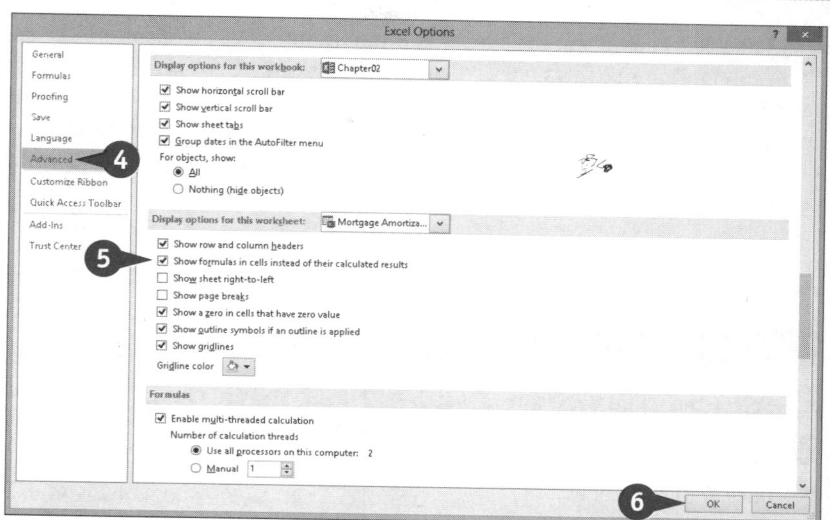

A. Excel displays the formulas instead of their results.

***Note:** You can also toggle the display between formulas and results by pressing Ctrl+`.*

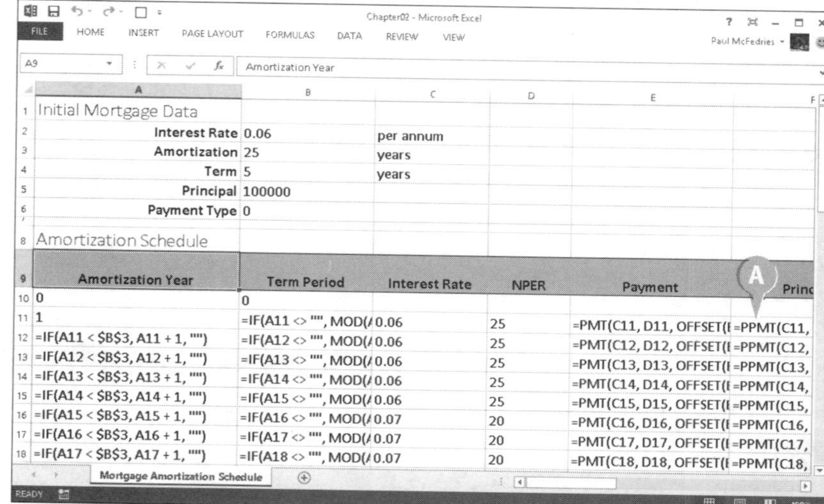

EXTRA

The technique of showing formulas instead of results applies only to the current worksheet. If you want to view the formulas in every sheet in a workbook, run the following VBA macro, which toggles formulas and results each time you run it. To learn how to add and run a VBA macro in Excel, see Chapter 16.

```
Sub ToggleFormulasAndResults()
    Dim win As Window
    Dim wv As WorksheetView
    For Each win In ActiveWorkbook.Windows
        For Each wv In win.SheetViews
            wv.DisplayFormulas = Not wv.DisplayFormulas
        Next 'wv
    Next 'win
End Sub
```

Use a Watch Window to Monitor a Cell Value

When you build a spreadsheet, it is often useful to monitor a cell's value, particularly if that cell contains a formula. For example, if a cell calculates the average of a range of values, you might want to monitor the average as the data changes to see if it reaches a particular value.

Monitoring a cell value is not easy if the cell's formula resides in a different worksheet or off-screen in the current worksheet. Rather than constantly navigating back and forth to check the cell value, you can use the Watch Window to monitor it. The Watch Window stays onscreen all the time, so no matter where you are within Excel, you can see the value of the cell.

Use a Watch Window to Monitor a Cell Value

1. Select the value you want to watch.
2. Click the Formulas tab.
3. Click Watch Window.

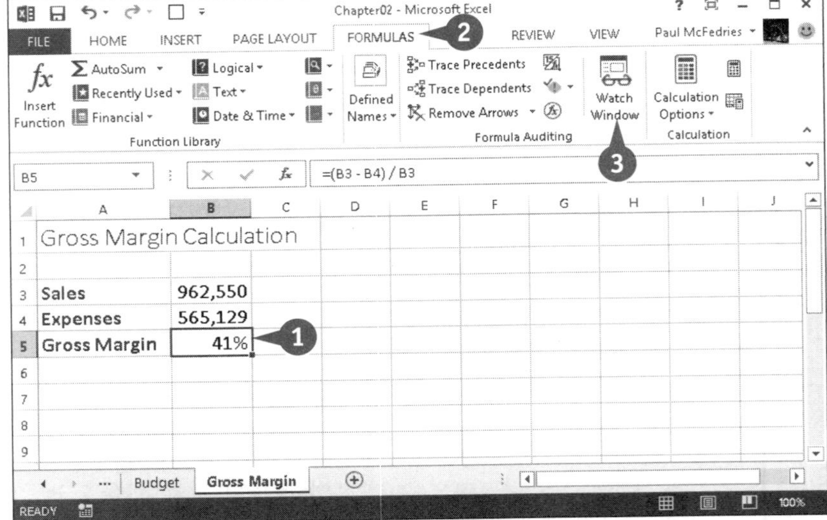

The Watch Window appears.

4. Click Add Watch.

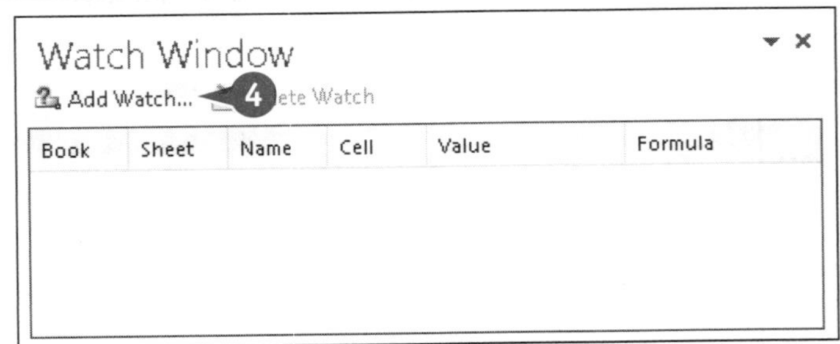

The Add Watch dialog box appears.

Ⓐ The selected cell appears in the reference box.

Ⓑ If the cell is incorrect, you can click the cell you want to monitor.

5 Click Add.

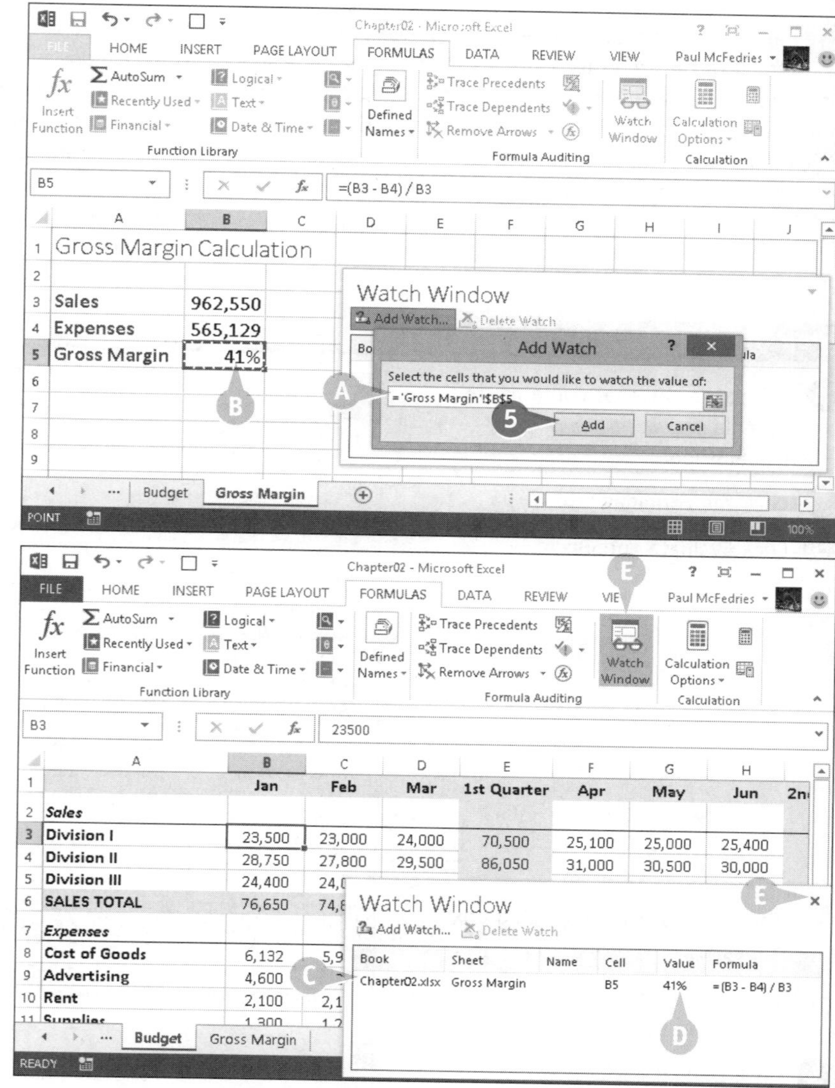

Ⓒ Excel adds the cell to the Watch Window.

Ⓓ The value of the cell appears here.

As you work with Excel, the Watch Window stays on top of the other windows so you can monitor the cell value.

Ⓔ If the Watch Window gets in the way, you can hide it by either clicking the Close button (X) or clicking Watch Window in the Formula tab.

EXTRA

You are not restricted to monitoring just a single cell in the Watch Window; you can add as many watch items, as you need. Note, too, that although you can use the Watch Window as a handy way to monitor a cell value, you can also use it to navigate. That is, if you double-click a watch item, Excel automatically selects the corresponding cell.

If you no longer need to monitor a particular cell value, you should delete the cell's watch item to reduce clutter in the Watch Window. Click the Formulas tab and then click Watch Window to open the Watch Window. Click the watch you no longer need, and then click Delete Watch. Excel removes the watch.

Many Excel formulas can be quite complex, with functions nested inside other functions, multiple sets of parentheses, several different operators, multiple range references, and so on. These more involved formulas are much harder to troubleshoot because it is often unclear what part of the formula is causing the trouble.

You can use the Evaluate Formula command to help troubleshoot such formulas. This command enables you to step through the various parts of the formula to see the preliminary results returned by each part. By examining these interim results, you can often see where your formula goes awry. If you still have trouble pinpointing the error, see the "Audit a Formula to Locate Errors" section in this chapter.

Step Through a Formula

1. Select the cell that contains the formula you want to troubleshoot.
2. Click the Formulas tab.
3. Click Evaluate Formula.

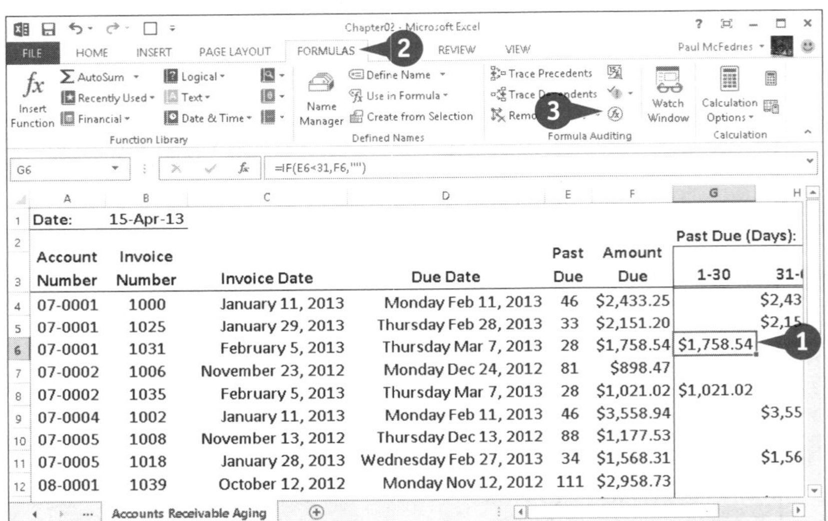

The Evaluate Formula dialog box appears.

A Excel underlines the first expression that it will evaluate.

4. Click Evaluate.

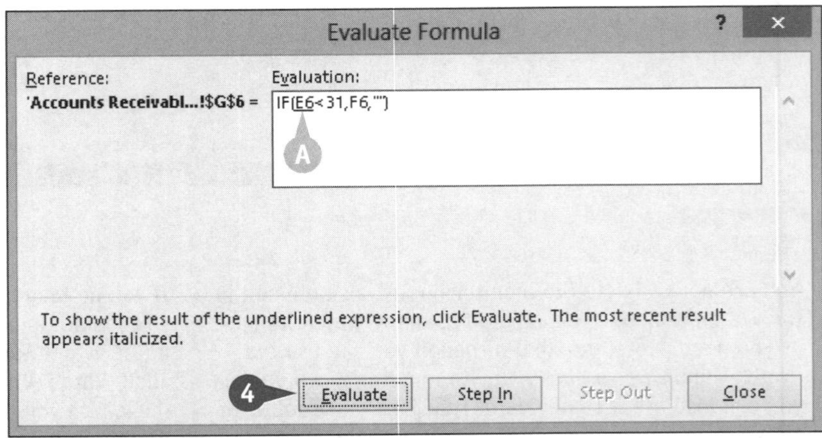

- B Excel evaluates the underlined term and then displays the result in italics.
- C Excel underlines the next expression that it will evaluate.

5 Click Evaluate.

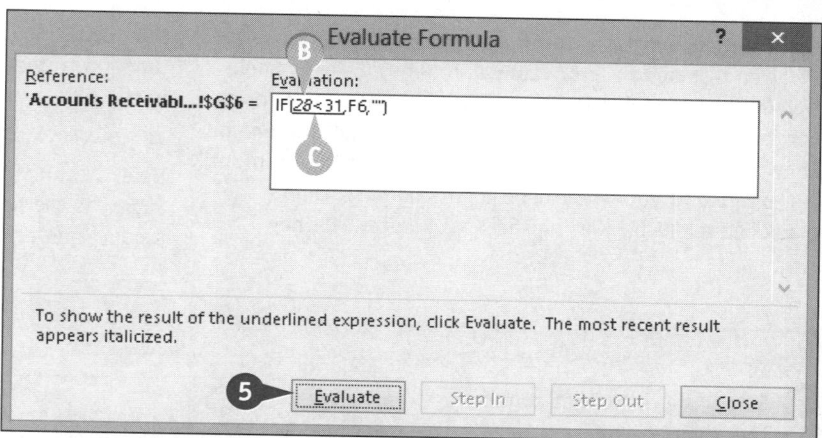

6 Repeat step 5 to continue evaluating the formula's expressions.

Note: *Continue evaluating the formula until you find the error or you want to stop the evaluation.*

- D If you evaluate all the terms in the formula, Excel displays the final result.

7 Click Close.

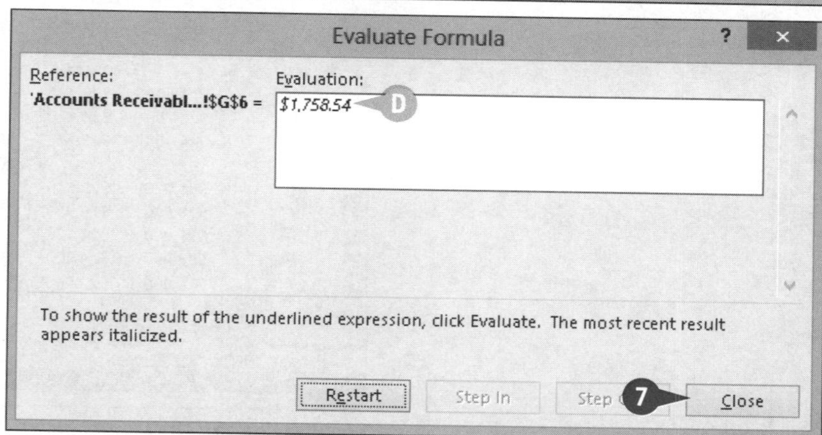

EXTRA

It is possible that the error exists in one of the cells referenced by the formula. To check this, when Excel underlines the cell reference, click Step In at the bottom of the Evaluate Formula dialog box. This tells Excel to display that cell's formula in the Evaluate Formula dialog box, so you can then evaluate this secondary formula to look for problems. To return to the main formula, click Step Out.

To evaluate just an expression within a formula, open the formula cell for editing, and then select the expression. Either click the Formulas tab and then click Calculate Now (▦) in the Calculation group, or press F9. Excel evaluates the selected expression. Press Esc when you are done.

If Excel encounters an error when calculating a formula, it often displays an error value as the result. For example, if your formula divides by zero, Excel indicates the error by displaying the value `#DIV/0`. There may be times when you know the error is temporary or is otherwise unimportant. For example, if your worksheet is missing data, then a blank cell might be causing the `#DIV/0` error. Rather than displaying an error value, you can use the `IFERROR` function to test for an error and display a more useful result in the cell:

`IFERROR(`*`value`*`, `*`value_if_error`*`)`

Here, *`value`* is the formula you are using, and *`value_if_error`* is the text you want Excel to display if the formula produces an error.

Display Text Instead of Error Values

1. Select the range that contains the formulas you want to edit.
2. Press F2.

- **A** Excel opens the first cell for editing.

3. After the formula's equals sign (=), type **iferror(**.

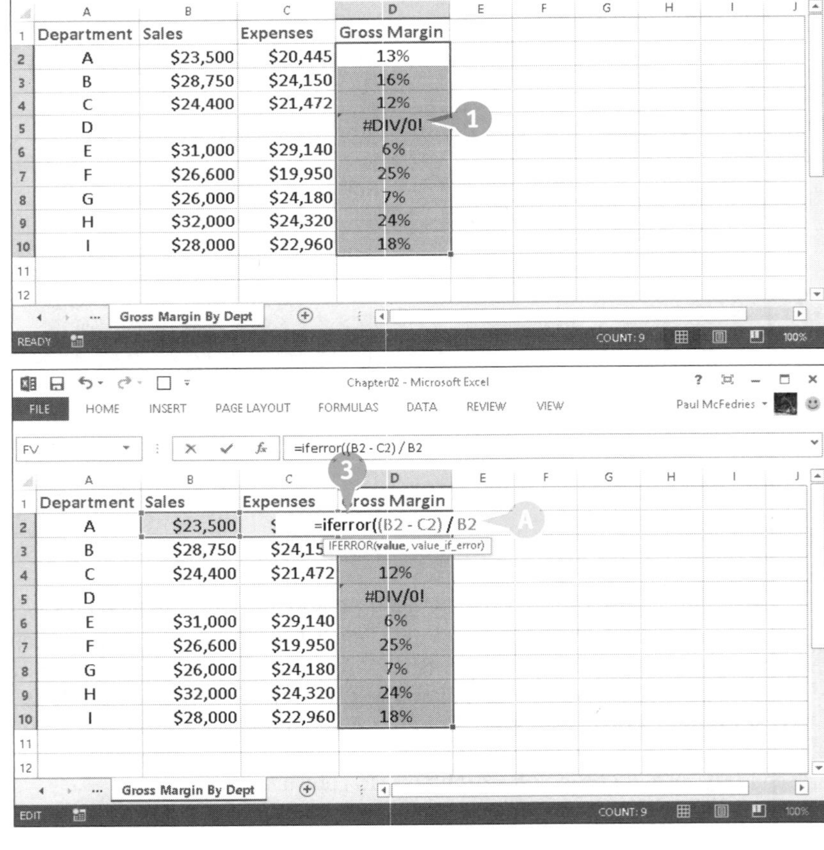

4 After the formula, type a comma followed by the text, in quotation marks, that you want Excel to display in place of any error, followed by a closing parenthesis.

5 Press Ctrl+Enter.

B Excel displays the formula result in cells where there is not an error.

C Excel displays the text message in cells that generate an error.

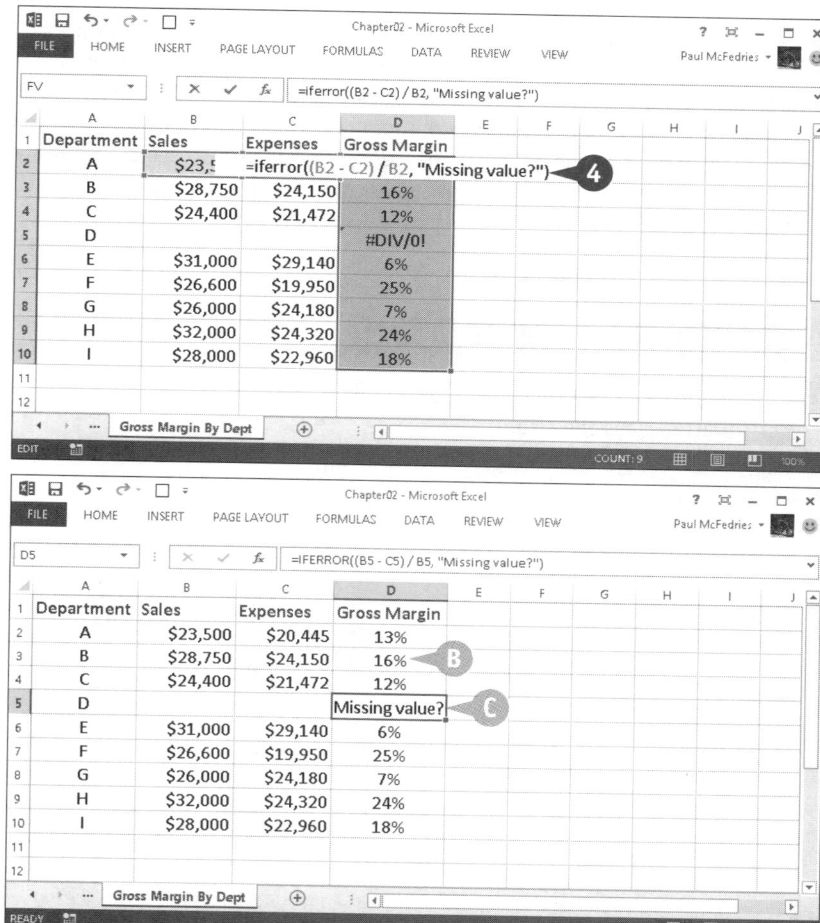

EXTRA

One of the main causes of worksheet errors is missing or mismatched parentheses. To help you avoid these types of errors, Excel provides two visual clues in the actual formula when you are editing it. The first clue occurs when you type a right parenthesis. Excel highlights both the right parenthesis and its corresponding left parenthesis. If you type what you think is the last right parenthesis and Excel does not highlight the first left parenthesis, your parentheses are unbalanced. The second clue occurs when you use the left and right arrow keys to navigate a formula. When you cross over a parenthesis, Excel highlights the other parenthesis in the pair and formats both parentheses with the same color.

Check for Formula Errors in a Worksheet

If you use Microsoft Word, you are probably familiar with the wavy green lines that appear under words and phrases that the grammar checker has flagged as being incorrect. Excel has a similar feature: the formula error checker. It is similar to the grammar checker, in that it uses a set of rules to determine correctness, and it operates in the background to monitor your formulas. If it detects that something is amiss, it displays an *error indicator* — a green triangle — in the upper-left corner of the cell containing the formula. You can then use the associated smart tag to see a description of the error and to either fix or ignore the error.

Check for Formula Errors in a Worksheet

1. Examine your worksheet for a cell that displays the error indicator.
2. Click the cell.

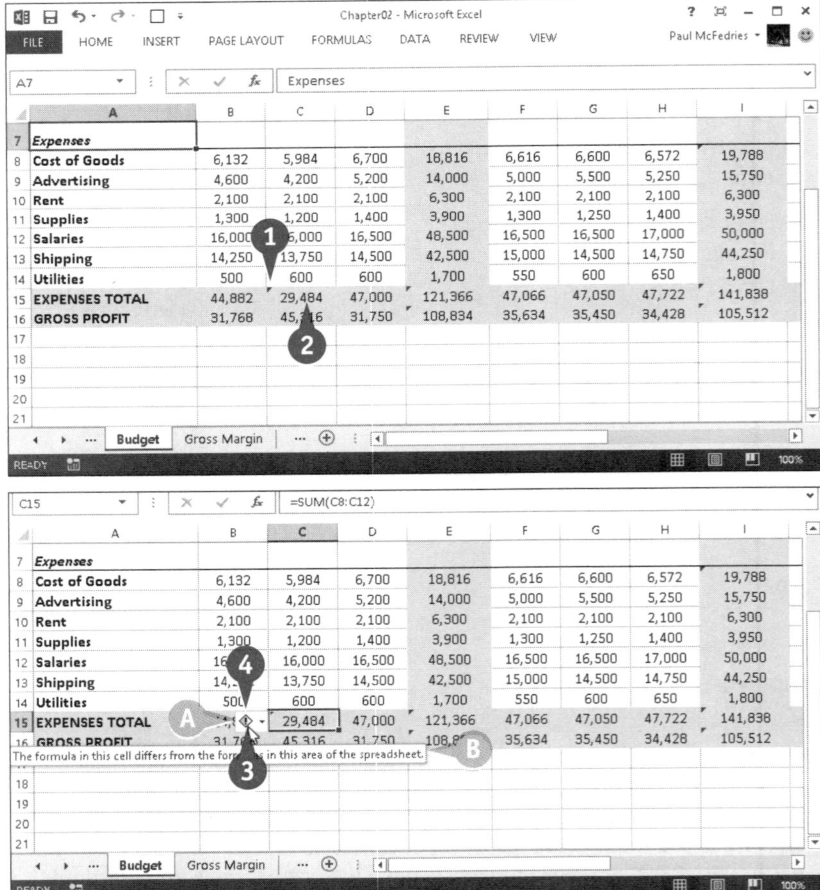

- A The error smart tag appears.

3. Position the mouse pointer over the smart tag.

- B Excel displays a description of the error.

4. Click the smart tag.

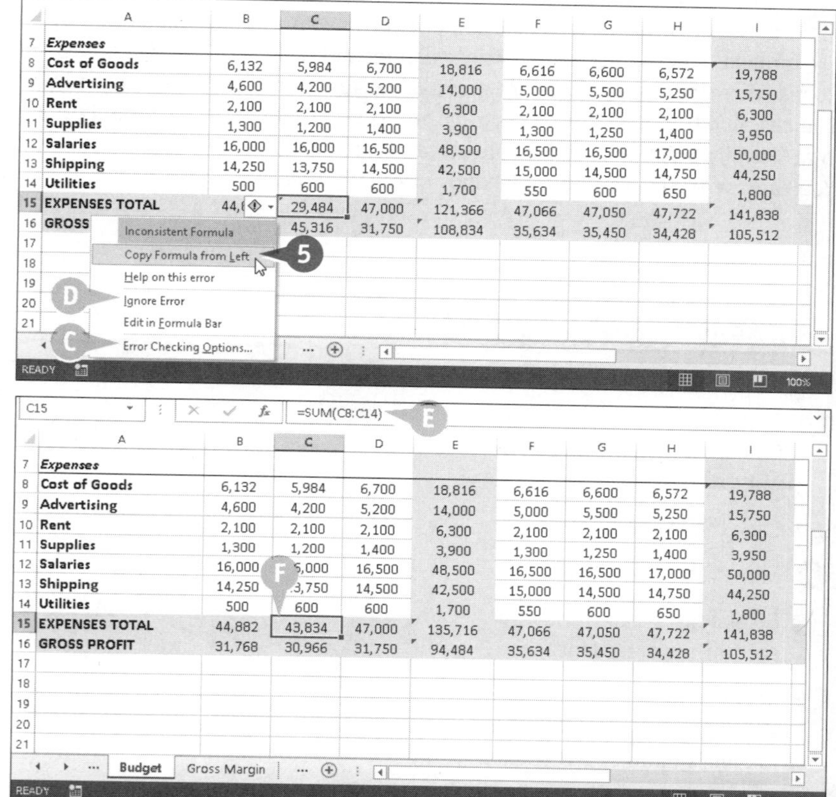

Ⓒ Excel displays the smart tag options.

5 Click the command that fixes the formula.

Note: *The name of the command depends on the error. You only see this command if Excel can fix the error.*

Ⓓ If the indicated error is not actually an error, you can just click Ignore Error.

Ⓔ Excel adjusts the formula.

Ⓕ Excel removes the error indicator from the cell.

6 Repeat steps 1 to 5 until you have checked all your worksheet formula errors.

EXTRA

To choose which error-checking rules you want Excel to enforce, click the File tab, click Options, and then click the Formulas tab. In the Error Checking Rules section, click to deselect the check box of any rule you do not want Excel to enforce. Click OK.

If your workbook uses green colors for text or cell backgrounds, or if you have graphics that use a great deal of green, you might not notice the error indicators. To use a different color, click the File tab, click Options, and then click the Formulas tab. In the Error Checking section, use the Indicate Errors Using This Color list to click the color you prefer, and then click OK.

Audit a Formula to Locate Errors

To determine which cell is causing an error in your formula, you can use the auditing features in Excel to visualize and trace a formula's input values and error sources. Auditing operates by creating *tracers* — arrows that literally point out the cells involved in a formula. You can use tracers to find three kinds of cells. *Precedents* are cells that are directly or indirectly referenced in a formula. *Dependents* are cells that are directly or indirectly referenced by a formula in another cell. *Errors* are cells that contain an error value and are directly or indirectly referenced in a formula.

Audit a Formula to Locate Errors

Trace Precedents

1. Click the cell containing the formula whose precedents you want to trace.
2. Click the Formulas tab.
3. Click Trace Precedents.

   A. Excel adds a tracer arrow to each direct precedent.

4. Repeat step 3 until you have added tracer arrows for all the formula's indirect precedents.

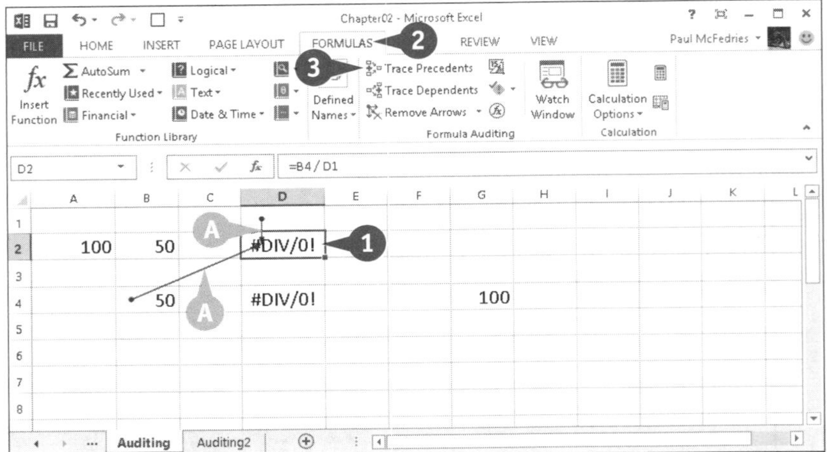

Trace Dependents

1. Click the cell containing the formula whose dependents you want to trace.
2. Click the Formulas tab.
3. Click Trace Dependents.

   B. Excel adds a tracer arrow to each direct dependent.

4. Repeat step 3 until you have added tracer arrows for all the formula's indirect dependents.

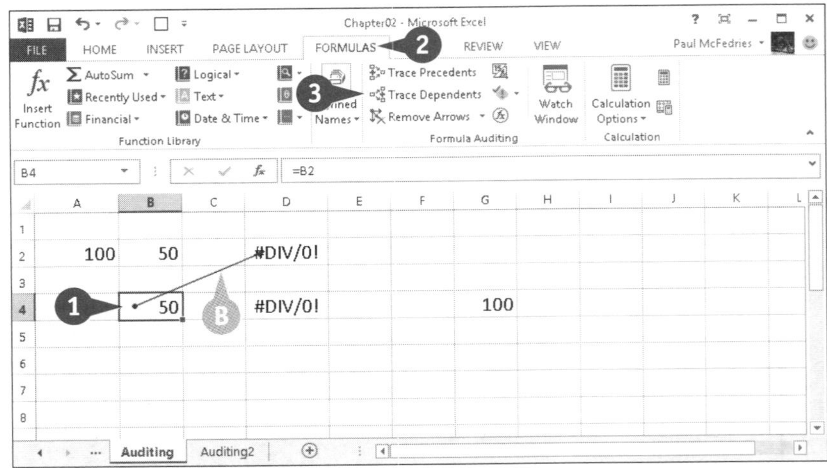

Trace Errors

1. Click the cell containing the error you want to trace.
2. Click the Formulas tab.
3. Click Remove Arrows.

Note: *You must first remove any existing arrows before you can trace an error.*

4. Click the Error Checking down arrow.
5. Click Trace Error.

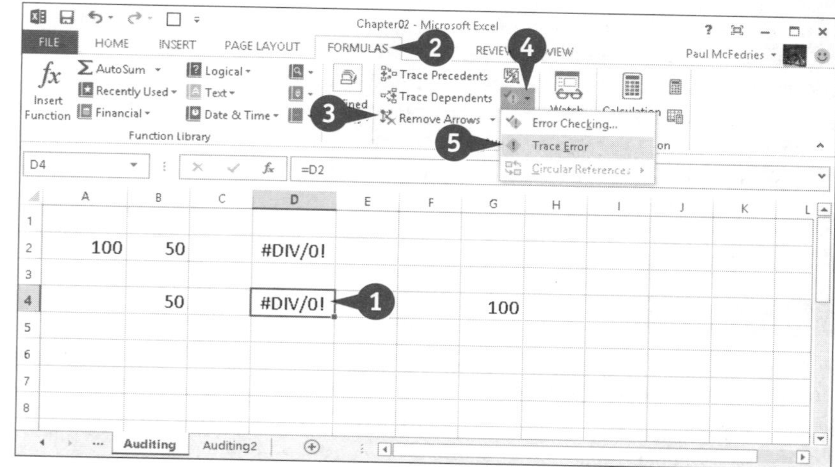

- **C** Excel selects the cells that contain the original error.
- **D** Excel displays tracer arrows showing the selected cells' precedents and dependents.
- **E** A red tracer arrow indicates an error.

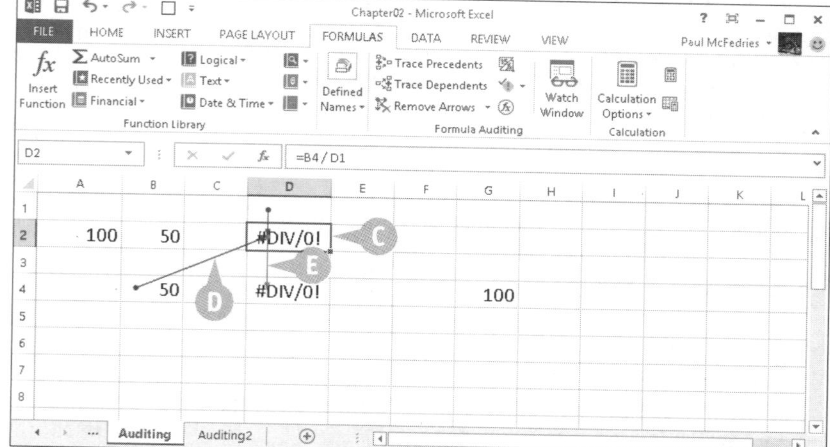

APPLY IT

You can use the Error Checking feature to look for and trace errors. To do so, click the Formulas tab and then click Error Checking (). The Error Checking dialog box displays the first error, if any. You choose to Trace Error, Show Calculation Steps, or Ignore Error. The Trace Error button appears if the error is caused by an error in another cell. You can click this button to display tracer arrows for the formula's precedents and dependents. The Show Calculation Steps button appears if the error is caused by the cell's formula. You can click this button to launch the Evaluate Formula feature. If you want to bypass the error, lick the Ignore Error button.

Understanding Excel Functions

A *function* is a predefined formula that accepts one or more inputs and then calculates a result. In Excel, a function is often called a *worksheet function* because you normally use it as part of a formula that you type in a worksheet cell. However, Excel enables you to use many of its worksheet functions in other parts of the program, such as VBA macros and the PivotTable formulas you create for calculated fields and items. This section introduces you to worksheet functions by showing you their advantages and structure and by examining a few other worksheet ideas that you should know.

Function Advantages

Functions are designed to take you beyond the basic arithmetic and comparison formulas. Functions do this in three ways:

- Functions make simple but cumbersome formulas easier to use. For example, suppose that you have a worksheet showing average house prices in various neighborhoods and you want to calculate the monthly mortgage payment for each price. Given a fixed monthly interest rate and a term in months, here is the general formula for calculating the monthly payment:

```
House Price * Interest Rate / (1 - (1 + Interest
Rate) ^ -Term)
```

  Fortunately, Excel offers an alternative to this intimidating formula — the `PMT` (payment) function:

```
PMT(Interest Rate, Term, House Price)
```

  Not only is this simpler than the equivalent worksheet formula, but Excel also helps you to enter a formula correctly by displaying a pop-up banner that shows you the exact syntax to use for each function.

- Functions enable you to include complex mathematical expressions in your worksheets that otherwise are difficult or impossible to construct using simple arithmetic operators. For example, you can calculate a range's average value using the `AVERAGE` function, but what if you prefer to know the *median* — the value that falls in the middle when all the values are sorted numerically — or the *mode*, which is the value that occurs most frequently? Either value can be time consuming to calculate by hand, but both are easy to calculate using the `MEDIAN` and `MODE` worksheet functions in Excel. Depending on your data analysis needs, you can also use functions to round formula results to a specified number of decimal places, calculate conditional sums and counts, and find square roots

- Functions enable you to include data in your applications that you could not access otherwise. For example, the powerful `IF` function enables you to test the value of a cell — for example, to see whether it contains a particular value — and then return one value or another, depending on the result. Similarly, the `INFO` function can tell you how much memory is available on your system, what operating system you are using, the version number of the operating system, the Excel version number, and more.

- Functions enable you to access other values in a worksheet depending on certain criteria, the result of another formula, and so on. These so-called *lookup* functions such as `VLOOKUP` and `HLOOKUP` can use a special range called a *lookup table* to seek a value in a specified *lookup column* that contains the values that you look up, and return a value from the *data column* that contains the data associated with each lookup value.

Function Structure

To use worksheet functions efficiently and to help you figure out how each function operates, you need to understand the structure of a typical function, particularly its name, and its arguments. Every worksheet function has the same basic structure of

```
NAME(Argument1, Argument2, ...)
```

Function Name

The NAME part identifies the function. In worksheet formulas, the function name always appears in uppercase letters: PMT, SUM, AVERAGE, and so on.

No matter how you type a function name, Excel always converts the name to all-uppercase letters. Therefore, when you type the name of a function that you want to use in a formula, you should always type the name using lowercase letters. This way, if you find that Excel does not convert the function name to uppercase characters, it means you misspelled the name, because Excel does not recognize it.

Arguments

The items that appear within the parentheses are the functions' *arguments*. The arguments are the inputs that functions use to perform calculations. For example, the SUM function adds its arguments and the PMT function calculates the loan payment based on arguments that include the interest rate, term, and present value of the loan. Some functions do not require any arguments at all, but most require at least one argument, and some as many as nine or ten. If a function uses two or more arguments, be sure to separate each argument with a comma, and be sure to enter the arguments in the order specified by the function.

Function arguments fall into two categories: required and optional. A *required argument* is one that you must specify when you use the function, and it must appear within the parentheses in the specified position; if you omit a required argument, Excel generates an error. An *optional argument* is one that you are free to use or omit, depending on your needs. If you omit an optional argument, Excel uses the argument's default value in the function. For example, the PMT function has an optional "future value" argument with which you can specify the value of the loan at the end of the term. The default future value is 0, so you need only specify this argument if your loan's future value is something other than 0.

Excel uses two methods for differentiating between required and optional arguments. When you enter a function in a cell, the optional arguments are shown surrounded by square brackets: [and]. When you build a function using the Insert Function dialog box, or look up a function in the Excel Help system, required arguments are shown in bold text and optional arguments are shown in regular text.

If a function has multiple optional arguments, you may need to skip one or more of these arguments. If you do this, be sure to include the comma that would normally follow each missing argument. For example, here is the full PMT function syntax (the required arguments are shown in bold text):

PMT(**rate**, **nper**, **pv**, *fv*, *type*)

Here is an example PMT function that uses the type argument but not the fv argument:

```
PMT(0.05, 25, 100000, ,1)
```

Understanding Function Types

Excel comes with hundreds of worksheet functions, and they are divided into various categories or types. These function types include Text, Information, Lookup and Reference, Date and Time, and Database. Although you will often use these categories for Excel data analysis, there are four function types that you will most likely use in most of your analytical formulas: Math, Statistical, Financial, and Logical. This section introduces you to these four function types and lists the most popular and useful functions in each category. Note that for each function, the required arguments appear in bold type.

Mathematical Functions

You use the mathematical worksheet functions in Excel to manipulate numbers. The following table lists a few of the most useful mathematical functions.

Function	Description
`CEILING`(***number***,***significance***)	Rounds *number* up to the nearest integer
`EVEN`(***number***)	Rounds *number* up to the nearest even integer
`FACT`(***number***)	Returns the factorial of *number*
`FLOOR`(***number***,***significance***)	Rounds *number* down to the nearest multiple of *significance*
`INT`(***number***)	Rounds *number* down to the nearest integer
`MOD`(***number***,***divisor***)	Returns the remainder of *number* after dividing by *divisor*
`ODD`(***number***)	Rounds *number* up to the nearest odd integer
`PI()`	Returns the value Pi
`PRODUCT`(***number1***,*number2*,...)	Multiplies the specified numbers
`RAND()`	Returns a random number between 0 and 1
`ROUND`(***number***,***digits***)	Rounds *number* to a specified number of *digits*
`ROUNDDOWN`(***number***,***digits***)	Rounds *number* down, toward 0
`ROUNDUP`(***number***,***digits***)	Rounds *number* up, away from 0
`SIGN`(***number***)	Returns the sign of *number* (1 = positive; 0 = zero; –1 = negative)
`SQRT`(***number***)	Returns the square root of *number*
`SUM`(***number1***,*number2*,...)	Adds the arguments
`TRUNC`(***number***,*digits*)	Truncates *number* to an integer

Statistical Functions

Excel offers statistical functions that calculate a wide variety of highly technical statistical measures. The following table lists the worksheet functions that perform these basic statistical operations. For more information, see Chapter 5.

Function	Description
`AVERAGE`(***number1***,*number2*,...)	Returns the average of the arguments
`COUNT`(***number1***,*number2*,...)	Counts the numbers in the argument list
`MAX`(***number1***,*number2*,...)	Returns the maximum value of the arguments
`MEDIAN`(***number1***,*number2*,...)	Returns the median value of the arguments
`MIN`(***number1***,*number2*,...)	Returns the minimum value of the arguments
`MODE`(***number1***,*number2*,...)	Returns the most common value of the arguments
`STDEV.P`(***number1***,*number2*,...)	Returns the standard deviation based on an entire population
`STDEV.S`(***number1***,*number2*,...)	Returns the standard deviation based on a sample

Statistical Functions (continued)

Function	Description
VAR.P(**number1**,*number2,...*)	Returns the variance based on an entire population
VAR.S(**number1**,*number2,...*)	Returns the variance based on a sample

Financial Functions

The financial functions in Excel offer you powerful tools for calculating such things as the future value of an annuity and the periodic payment for a loan. The financial functions that you can use within your worksheets use the following arguments.

Argument	Description
rate	The fixed rate of interest over the term of the loan or investment
nper	The number of payments or deposit periods over the term of the loan or investment
pmt	The periodic payment or deposit
pv	The present value of the loan (the principal) or the initial deposit in an investment
fv	The future value of the loan or investment
type	The type of payment or deposit: 0 (the default) for end-of-period payments or deposits; 1 for beginning-of-period payments or deposits

The following table lists some worksheet functions that perform basic financial analysis. For examples, see Chapter 4.

Function	Description
FV(***rate***,***nper***,***pmt***,*pv*,*type*)	Returns the future value of an investment or loan
IPMT(***rate***,***per***,***nper***,***pv***,*fv*,*type*)	Returns the interest payment for a specified period of a loan
NPER(***rate***,***pmt***,***pv***,*fv*,*type*)	Returns the number of periods for an investment or loan
PMT(***rate***,***nper***,***pv***,*fv*,*type*)	Returns the periodic payment for a loan or investment
PPMT(***rate***,***per***,***nper***,***pv***,*fv*,*type*)	Returns the principal payment for a specified period of a loan
PV(***rate***,***nper***,***pmt***,*fv*,*type*)	Returns the present value of an investment
RATE(***nper***,***pmt***,***pv***,*fv*,*type*,*guess*)	Returns the periodic interest rate for a loan or investment

Logical Functions

The logical functions operate with the logical values TRUE and FALSE, which in your worksheet calculations are interpreted as 1 and 0, respectively. In most cases, the logical values used as arguments are expressions that use comparison operators such as equal to (=) and greater than (>). The following table lists the logical functions that you can use in your formulas.

Function	Description
AND(***logical1***,*logical2,...*)	Returns 1 if all the arguments are true; returns 0, otherwise
IF(***logical_test***,***true_expr***,*false_expr*)	Performs a logical test; returns *true_expr* if the result is 1 (true); returns *false_expr* if the result is 0 (false)
NOT(***logical***)	Reverses the logical value of the argument
OR(***logical1***,*logical2,...*)	Returns 1 if any argument is true; returns 0, otherwise

Add a Function to a Formula

To get the benefit of an Excel function, you need to use it within a formula. You can use a function as the only operand in the formula, or you can include the function as part of a larger formula. To make it easy to choose the function you need and to add the appropriate arguments, Excel offers the Insert Function feature. This dialog box enables you to display functions by category and then choose the function you want from a list. You then see the Function Arguments dialog box that enables you to easily see and fill in the arguments used by the function.

Add a Function to a Formula

1. Click in the cell in which you want to build the formula.
2. Type =.
3. Type any operands and operators you need before adding the function.
4. Click the Insert Function button.

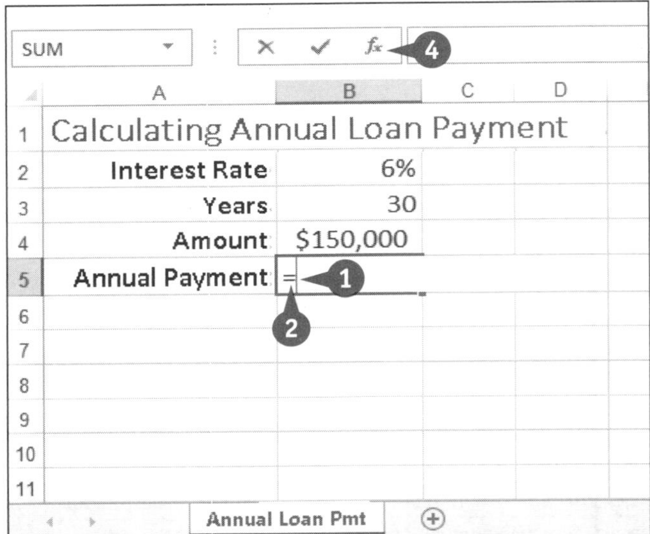

The Insert Function dialog box appears.

5. Click the down arrow and then select the category that contains the function you want to use from the drop-down list.
6. Click the function.
7. Click OK.

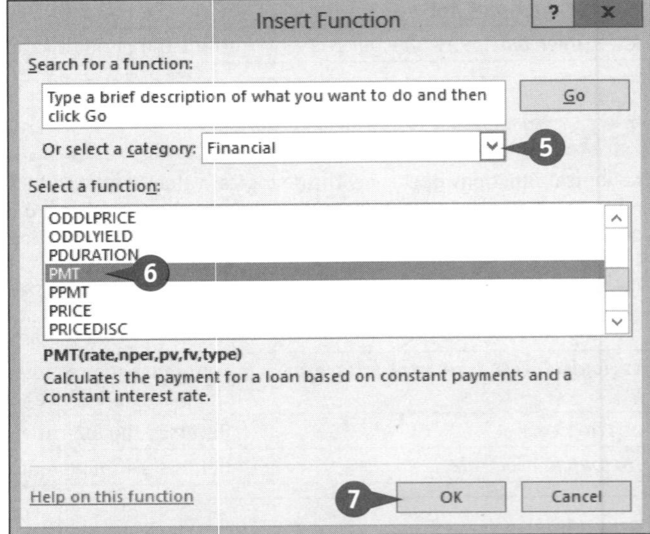

The Function Arguments dialog box appears.

8. Click inside an argument box.

9. Click the cell that contains the argument value.

   You can also type the argument value.

10. Repeat steps 8 and 9 to fill as many arguments as you need.

   A The function result appears below the edit boxes.

11. Click OK.

   B Excel adds the function to the formula.

   C Excel displays the formula result.

Note: *In this example, the result appears in the parentheses to indicate a negative value. In loan calculations, money that you pay out is always a negative amount.*

Note: *If your formula requires any other operands and operators, press F2 and then type what you need to complete your formula.*

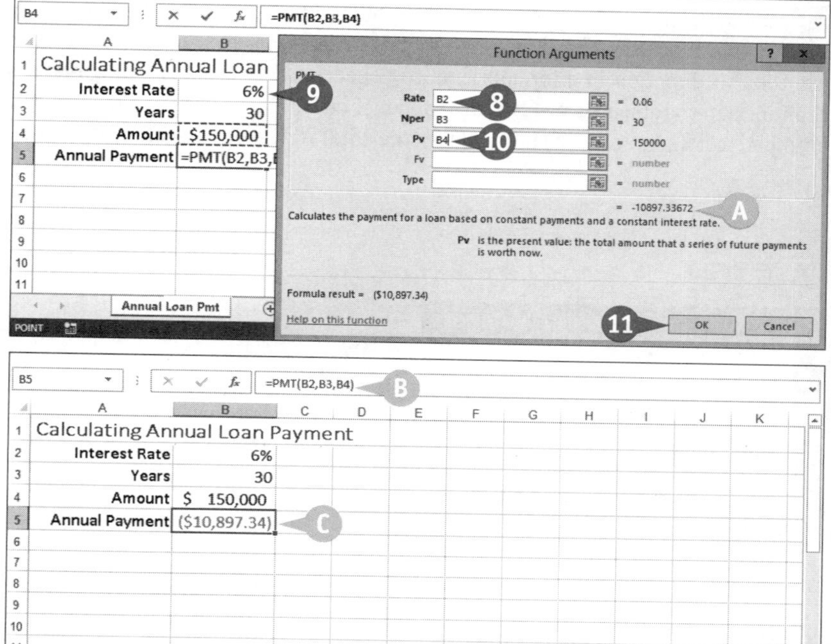

APPLY IT

How do you calculate a monthly financial result if you only have yearly values? For example, if your loan payment worksheet contains an annual interest rate and a loan term in years, how do you calculate the monthly payment using the `PMT` function? You need to convert the rate and term to monthly values. That is, you divide the annual interest rate by 12, and you multiply the term by 12. For example, if the annual rate is in cell B2, the term in years is in B3, and the loan amount is in B4, then the function `PMT(B2/12, B3*12, B4)` calculates the monthly payment.

Add a Row or Column of Numbers

You can quickly add worksheet numbers by building a formula that uses the Excel `SUM` function. When you use the `SUM` function in a formula, you can specify as the function's arguments a series of individual cells. For example, `SUM(A1, B2, C3)` calculates the total of the values in cells A1, B2, and C3. However, you can also use the `SUM` function to specify just a single argument, which is a range reference to either a row or a column of numbers. For example, `SUM(C3:C21)` calculates the total of the values in all the cells in the range C3 to C21.

Add a Row or Column of Numbers

1. Click in the cell where you want the sum to appear.
2. Type **=sum(**.

   A. When you begin a function, Excel displays a banner that shows you the function's arguments.

Note: *In the function banner, bold arguments are required, and arguments that appear in square brackets are optional.*

PMT | =sum(

	A	B	C	D
1				
2		Sales Rep	2011 Sales	2012 Sales
3		Nancy Freehafer	$996,336	$960,492
4		Andrew Cencini	$606,731	$577,983
5		Jan Kotas	$622,781	$967,580
6		Mariya Sergienko	$765,327	$771,399
7		Steven Thorpe	$863,589	$827,213
8		Michael Neipper	$795,518	$669,394
9		Robert Zare	$722,740	$626,945
10		Laura Giussani	$992,059	$574,472
11		Anne Hellung-Larsen	$659,380	$827,932
12		Kyra Harper	$509,623	$569,609
13		David Ferry	$987,777	$558,601
14		Paul Voyatzis	$685,091	$692,182
15		Andrea Aster	$540,484	$693,762
16		Charles Granek	$650,733	$823,034
17		Karen Aliston	$509,863	$511,569
18		Karen Hammond	[illegible]	$975,455
19		Vince Durbin	[illegible]	$599,514
20		Paul Sellars	[illegible]	$596,353
21		Gregg O'Donoghue	[illegible]	$652,171
22		TOTAL	=sum(	
23			SUM(**number1**, [number2], ...)	

Annual Loan Pmt | Sales Rep Sales

3. Click and drag the row or column of numbers that you want to add.

   B. Excel adds a reference for the range to the formula.

=sum(C3:C21

	A	B	C	D
1				
2		Sales Rep	2011 Sales	2012 Sales
3		Nancy Freehafer	$996,336	$960,492
4		Andrew Cencini	$606,731	$577,983
5		Jan Kotas	$622,781	$967,580
6		Mariya Sergienko	$765,327	$771,399
7		Steven Thorpe	$863,589	$827,213
8		Michael Neipper	$795,518	$669,394
9		Robert Zare	$722,740	$626,945
10		Laura Giussani	$992,059	$574,472
11		Anne Hellung-Larsen	$659,380	$827,932
12		Kyra Harper	$509,623	$569,609
13		David Ferry	$987,777	$558,601
14		Paul Voyatzis	$685,091	$692,182
15		Andrea Aster	$540,484	$693,762
16		Charles Granek	$650,733	$823,034
17		Karen Aliston	$509,863	$511,569
18		Karen Hammond	$503,699	$975,455
19		Vince Durbin	$630,263	[illegible]
20		Paul Sellars	$779,722	[illegible]
21		Gregg O'Donoghue	$592,802	[illegible]
22		TOTAL	=sum(C3:C21	
23			SUM(**number1**, [num... ...)	

Annual Loan Pmt | Sales Rep Sales

4 Type).

5 Click the Enter button or press Enter.

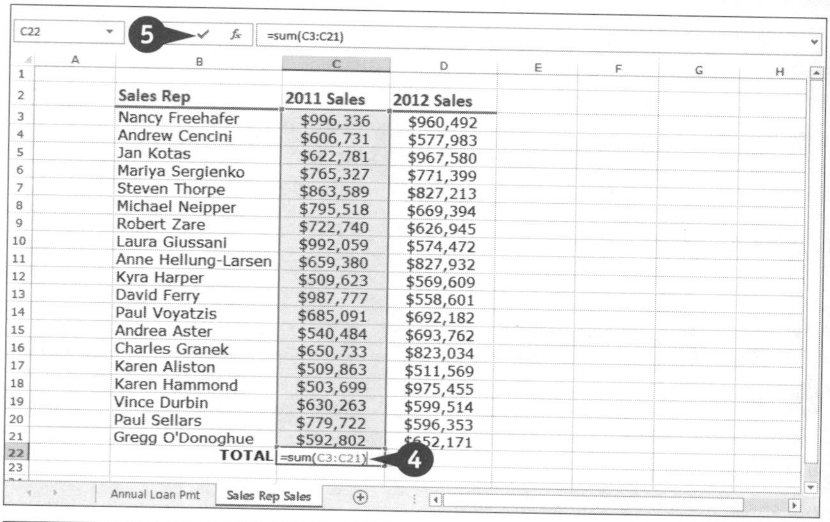

C22 | 5 | =sum(C3:C21)

	Sales Rep	2011 Sales	2012 Sales
3	Nancy Freehafer	$996,336	$960,492
4	Andrew Cencini	$606,731	$577,983
5	Jan Kotas	$622,781	$967,580
6	Mariya Sergienko	$765,327	$771,399
7	Steven Thorpe	$863,589	$827,213
8	Michael Neipper	$795,518	$669,394
9	Robert Zare	$722,740	$626,945
10	Laura Giussani	$992,059	$574,472
11	Anne Hellung-Larsen	$659,380	$827,932
12	Kyra Harper	$509,623	$569,609
13	David Ferry	$987,777	$558,601
14	Paul Voyatzis	$685,091	$692,182
15	Andrea Aster	$540,484	$693,762
16	Charles Granek	$650,733	$823,034
17	Karen Aliston	$509,863	$511,569
18	Karen Hammond	$503,699	$975,455
19	Vince Durbin	$630,263	$599,514
20	Paul Sellars	$779,722	$596,353
21	Gregg O'Donoghue	$592,802	$652,171
22	TOTAL	=sum(C3:C21) 4	

Annual Loan Pmt | Sales Rep Sales

C Excel displays the formula.

D Excel displays the sum in the cell.

C22 | =SUM(C3:C21) C

	Sales Rep	2011 Sales	2012 Sales
3	Nancy Freehafer	$996,336	$960,492
4	Andrew Cencini	$606,731	$577,983
5	Jan Kotas	$622,781	$967,580
6	Mariya Sergienko	$765,327	$771,399
7	Steven Thorpe	$863,589	$827,213
8	Michael Neipper	$795,518	$669,394
9	Robert Zare	$722,740	$626,945
10	Laura Giussani	$992,059	$574,472
11	Anne Hellung-Larsen	$659,380	$827,932
12	Kyra Harper	$509,623	$569,609
13	David Ferry	$987,777	$558,601
14	Paul Voyatzis	$685,091	$692,182
15	Andrea Aster	$540,484	$693,762
16	Charles Granek	$650,733	$823,034
17	Karen Aliston	$509,863	$511,569
18	Karen Hammond	$503,699	$975,455
19	Vince Durbin	$630,263	$599,514
20	Paul Sellars	$779,722	$596,353
21	Gregg O'Donoghue	$592,802	$652,171
22	TOTAL	$13,414,518 D	

Annual Loan Pmt | Sales Rep Sales

APPLY IT

You can use the SUM function to total rows and columns at the same time because the SUM function works not only with simple row and column ranges, but also with any rectangular range. After you type =sum(, click and drag the entire range that you want to sum.

You can also use the SUM function to total only certain values in a row or column. The SUM function can accept multiple arguments, so you can enter as many cells or ranges as you need. After you type =sum(, press and hold Ctrl and either click each cell that you want to include in the total, or use the mouse ✛ to click and drag each range that you want to sum.

Build an AutoSum Formula

Creating formulas that sum one or more ranges is one of the simplest and most common data analysis tasks. In many cases, you can reduce the time it takes to build a worksheet as well as reduce the possibility of errors by using the Excel AutoSum feature. This tool adds a SUM function formula to a cell and automatically adds the function arguments based on the structure of the worksheet data. For example, if there is a column of numbers above the cell where you want the SUM function to appear, AutoSum automatically includes that column of numbers as the SUM function argument.

Build an AutoSum Formula

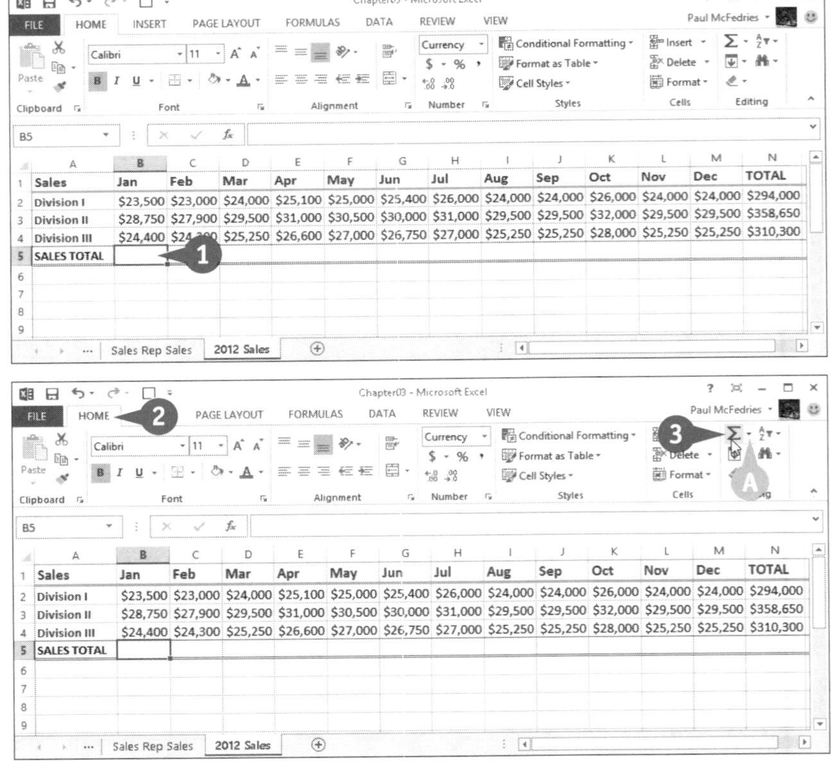

1. Click in the cell where you want the sum to appear.

***Note:** For AutoSum to work, the cell you select should be below or to the right of the range you want to sum.*

2. Click the Home tab.
3. Click the Sum button.

Ⓐ If you want to use a function other than SUM, click the Sum down arrow and then click the operation that you want to use from the drop-down list, for example: Average, Count Numbers, Max, or Min.

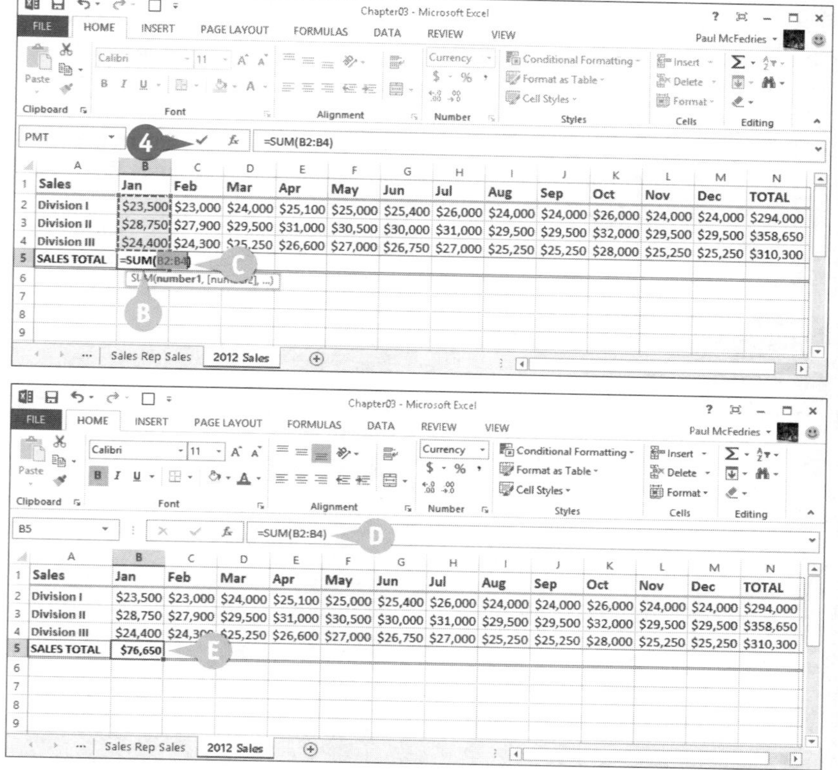

B Excel adds a SUM function formula to the cell.

***Note:** You can also press Alt+= instead of clicking the Sum button.*

C Excel guesses that the range above (or to the left of) the cell is the one you want to add.

If Excel guessed wrong, you can select the correct range manually.

4 Click the Enter button or press Enter.

D Excel displays the formula.

E Excel displays the sum in the cell.

EXTRA

You can use the Excel status bar to see the sum of a range without adding an AutoSum formula. When you select any range, Excel adds the range's numeric values and displays the result in the middle of the status bar — for example, `SUM: 76,650`.

There is a faster way to add an AutoSum formula if you know the range you want to sum, and that range is either a vertical column with a blank cell below it or a horizontal row with a blank cell to its right. Select the range (including the blank cell) and then click Sum (∑) or press Alt+=. Excel populates the blank cell with a `SUM` formula that totals the selected range.

Round a Number

When you need to round numbers, Excel offers the ROUND function, which rounds a value to the number of digits you specify. It takes two arguments: Number, the value you want to round, and Num_digits, the number of digits to which you want to round your number. If Num_digits is 1 or higher, Excel rounds to the number of decimal places that you specify. If Num_digits is 0, Excel rounds to the nearest integer. If Num_digits is –1 or lower, Excel rounds to the number of digits you specify that are to the left of the decimal point. For example, the function =ROUND(1234.5678,2) rounds to 1234.57, the function =ROUND(1234.5678,0) rounds to 1235, and the function =ROUND(1234.5678, -2) rounds to 1200.

Round a Number

1. Click the cell where you want the result to appear.
2. Click the Insert Function button.

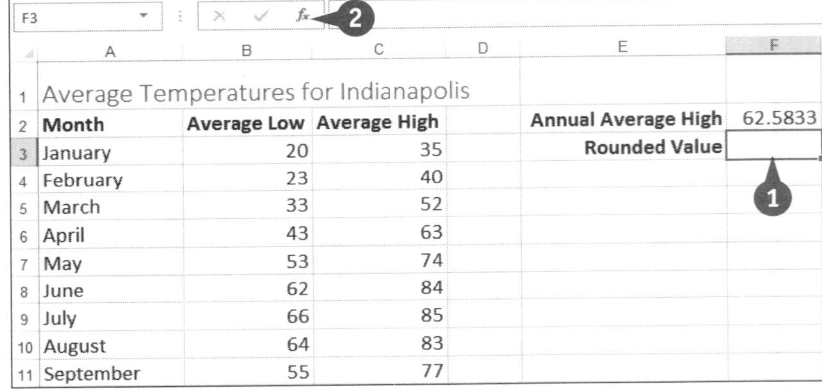

	A	B	C	D	E	F
1	Average Temperatures for Indianapolis					
2	**Month**	**Average Low**	**Average High**		**Annual Average High**	62.5833
3	January	20	35		**Rounded Value**	
4	February	23	40			
5	March	33	52			
6	April	43	63			
7	May	53	74			
8	June	62	84			
9	July	66	85			
10	August	64	83			
11	September	55	77			

The Insert Function dialog box appears.

3. Click the select a category down arrow and then select All from the drop-down list to list all the functions.
4. Double-click ROUND.

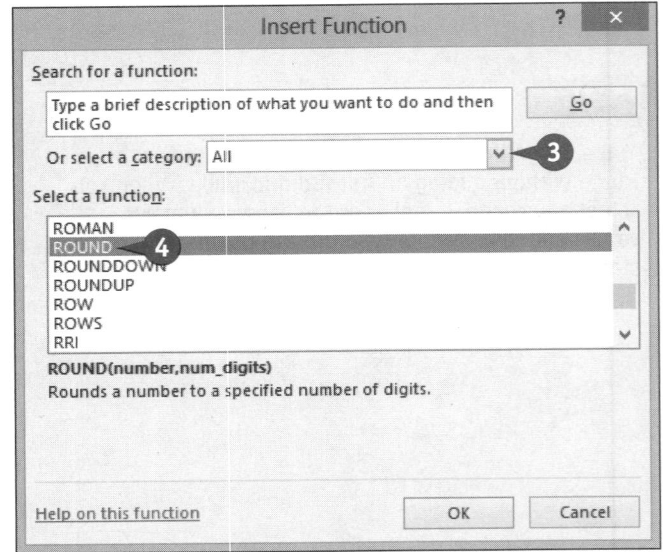

The Function Arguments dialog box appears.

5. Enter the cell address of the number you want to round.

   Alternatively, if the number is not in a cell, you can type the number into the Number field.

6. Type the number of decimal places to which you want to round.

7. Click OK.

A. Excel rounds the number.

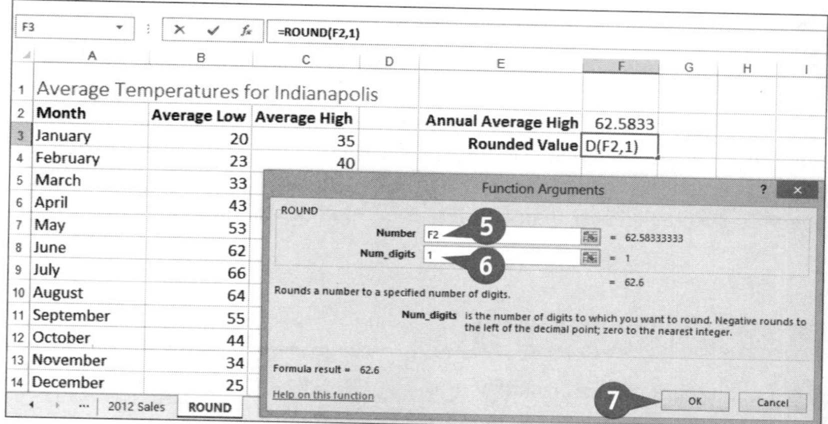

F3 =ROUND(F2,1)

	A	B	C	D	E	F
1	Average Temperatures for Indianapolis					
2	Month	Average Low	Average High		Annual Average High	62.5833
3	January	20	35		Rounded Value	62.6
4	February	23	40			
5	March	33	52			
6	April	43	63			
7	May	53	74			
8	June	62	84			
9	July	66	85			
10	August	64	83			
11	September	55	77			
12	October	44	65			
13	November	34	51			
14	December	25	42			

2012 Sales | ROUND

A

EXTRA

For even more sophisticated rounding operations, you can use the `INT` and `TRUNC` functions:

Function	Description
`INT`	Rounds down to the nearest integer. The `INT` function takes one argument: the number you want to round. The formula `=INT(7.9)` rounds the number 7.9 down to 7. The formula `=INT(–7.9)` rounds the number –7.9 down to –8, the next lowest integer.
`TRUNC`	Truncates to the number of digits you specify. The `TRUNC` function takes two arguments: `Number`, the number you want to truncate, and `Num_digits`, the number of digits to which you want to truncate your number. The formula `=TRUNC(7.9,0)` truncates the number 7.9 to 7. The formula `=TRUNC (–7.9,0)` truncates the number –7.9 to –7.

Create a Conditional Formula

A conditional formula uses the `IF` function to return a value based on whether a specified condition is true. The `IF` function takes three arguments: `logical_test`, `value_if_true`, and `value_if_false`. The `logical_test` argument is the condition being evaluated. It is a logical expression — that is, one that uses a comparison operator, such as greater than (>), less than or equal to (<=), or equal to (=) — that returns either the value `TRUE` or the value `FALSE`. The `value_if_true` argument is the result that the `IF` function returns if the `logical_test` argument is `TRUE`; the `value_if_false` argument is the result that the `IF` function returns if the `logical_test` argument is `FALSE`.

Create a Conditional Formula

1. Double-click the cell where you want your conditional formula to appear.
2. Type **=if(**.
3. Type the logical expression you want the `IF` function to evaluate.

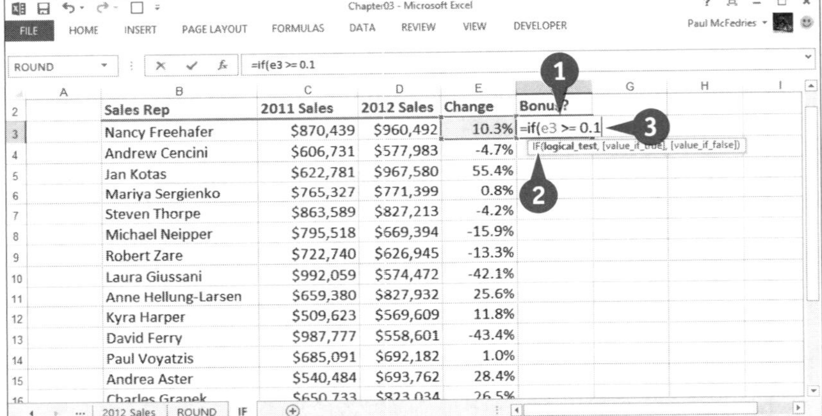

4. Type a comma (,) followed by the value you want the `IF` function to return if the logical expression evaluates to `TRUE`.

Note: *If the value is text, surround it with double quotation marks.*

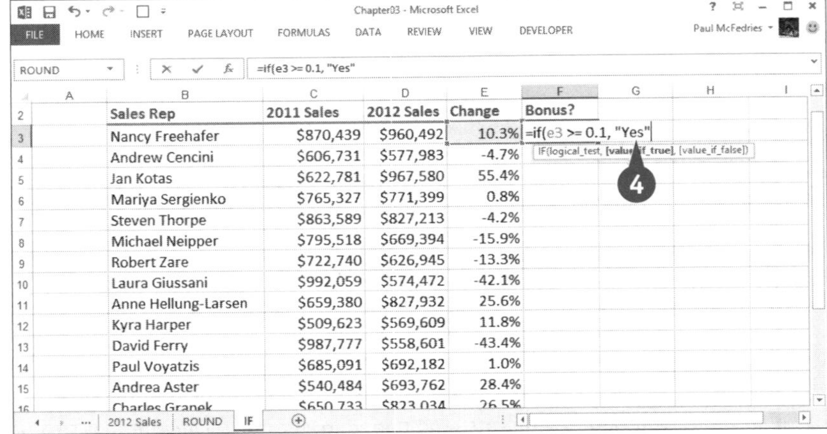

5. Type a comma (,) followed by the value you want the `IF` function to return if the logical expression evaluates to `FALSE`.

***Note:** If the value is text, surround it with double quotation marks.*

6. Type a closing parenthesis: **)**.

7. Click the Enter button or press Enter.

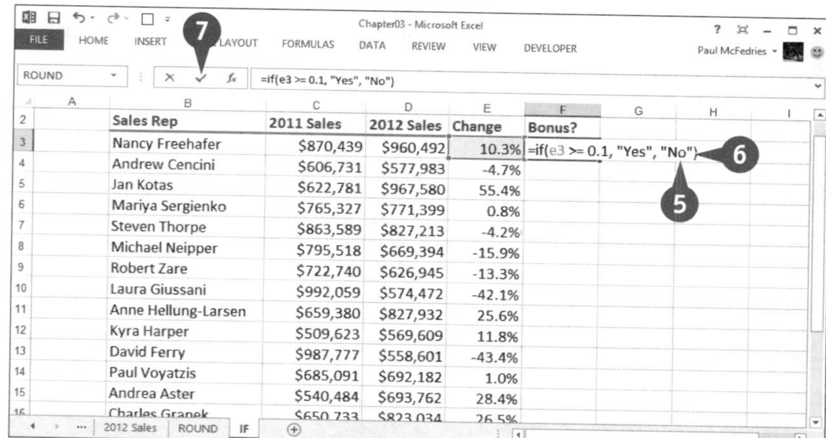

Ⓐ Excel evaluates the logical expression and then displays the result in the cell.

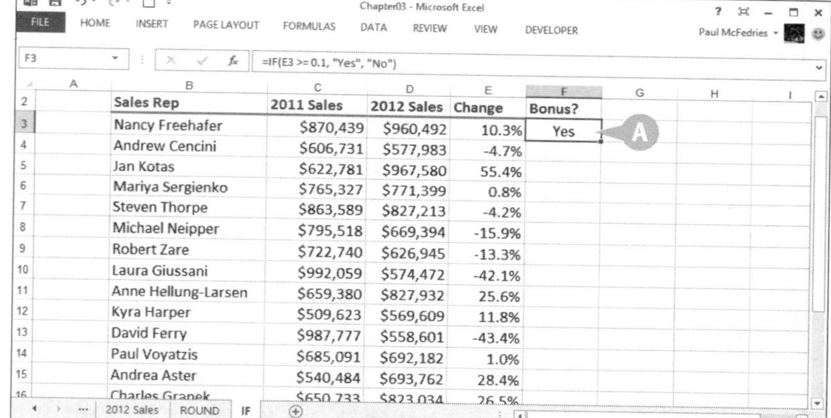

EXTRA

The `value_if_true` and `value_if_false` arguments are quite flexible since they can also be expressions that return a value. For example, you can use the `IF` function to avoid dividing by zero. To calculate the percentage change between some previous value and some new value, you would subtract the previous value from the new value and divide the result by the previous value:

```
=(New - Previous) / Previous
```

If `Previous` is 0, however, this formula returns the `#DIV/0!` error. To avoid that, use a conditional formula to check that `Previous` is not equal to 0:

```
=IF(Previous <> 0, (New - Previous) / Previous, "CAUTION: Previous value is zero!")
```

Calculate a Conditional Sum

In your data analysis, you might need to sum the values in a range, but only those values that satisfy some condition. You can do this by using the `SUMIF` function, an amalgam of `SUM` and `IF`, which sums only those cells in a range that meet the condition you specify. `SUMIF` takes up to three arguments: `range`, which is the range of cells you want to use to test the condition; `criteria`, which is a text string that determines which cells in `range` to sum; and the optional `sum_range`, which is the range from which you want the sum values to be taken. Excel sums only those cells in `sum_range` that correspond to the cells in `range` and meet the `criteria`.

Calculate a Conditional Sum

1. In the cell where you want the result to appear, type **=sumif(**.
2. Type the `range` argument.
3. Type a comma (,) and then the `criteria` argument.

Note: *Enclose the* `criteria` *argument in double quotation marks.*

4. If required, type a comma (,) and then the `sum_range` argument.

Note: *If you omit* `sum_range`*, Excel uses* `range` *for the sum.*

5. Type **)**.
6. Click the Enter button or press Enter.

Ⓐ Excel displays the conditional sum in the cell.

Note: *You can use the question mark (?) and asterisk (*) wildcards when creating your condition. A ? matches a single character, while an * matches multiple characters.*

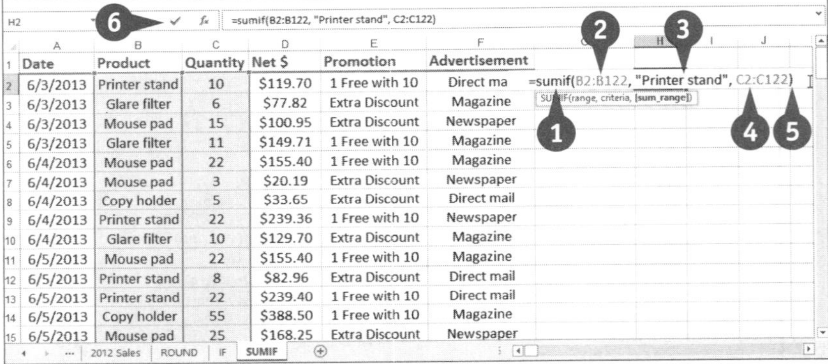

H2 | =sumif(B2:B122, "Printer stand", C2:C122)

	A	B	C	D	E	F	G
1	Date	Product	Quantity	Net $	Promotion	Advertisement	
2	6/3/2013	Printer stand	10	$119.70	1 Free with 10	Direct ma	=sumif(B2:B122, "Printer stand", C2:C122)
3	6/3/2013	Glare filter	6	$77.82	Extra Discount	Magazine	SUMIF(range, criteria, [sum_range])
4	6/3/2013	Mouse pad	15	$100.95	Extra Discount	Newspaper	
5	6/3/2013	Glare filter	11	$149.71	1 Free with 10	Magazine	
6	6/4/2013	Mouse pad	22	$155.40	1 Free with 10	Magazine	
7	6/4/2013	Mouse pad	3	$20.19	Extra Discount	Newspaper	
8	6/4/2013	Copy holder	5	$33.65	Extra Discount	Direct mail	
9	6/4/2013	Printer stand	22	$239.36	1 Free with 10	Newspaper	
10	6/4/2013	Glare filter	10	$129.70	Extra Discount	Magazine	
11	6/5/2013	Mouse pad	22	$155.40	1 Free with 10	Magazine	
12	6/5/2013	Printer stand	8	$82.96	Extra Discount	Direct mail	
13	6/5/2013	Printer stand	22	$239.40	1 Free with 10	Direct mail	
14	6/5/2013	Copy holder	55	$388.50	1 Free with 10	Magazine	
15	6/5/2013	Mouse pad	25	$168.25	Extra Discount	Newspaper	

2012 Sales | ROUND | IF | SUMIF

H2 | =SUMIF(B2:B122, "Printer stand", C2:C122)

	A	B	C	D	E	F	G	H
1	Date	Product	Quantity	Net $	Promotion	Advertisement		
2	6/3/2013	Printer stand	10	$119.70	1 Free with 10	Direct mail	Printer stands:	1343
3	6/3/2013	Glare filter	6	$77.82	Extra Discount	Magazine		
4	6/3/2013	Mouse pad	15	$100.95	Extra Discount	Newspaper		
5	6/3/2013	Glare filter	11	$149.71	1 Free with 10	Magazine		
6	6/4/2013	Mouse pad	22	$155.40	1 Free with 10	Magazine		
7	6/4/2013	Mouse pad	3	$20.19	Extra Discount	Newspaper		
8	6/4/2013	Copy holder	5	$33.65	Extra Discount	Direct mail		
9	6/4/2013	Printer stand	22	$239.36	1 Free with 10	Newspaper		
10	6/4/2013	Glare filter	10	$129.70	Extra Discount	Magazine		
11	6/5/2013	Mouse pad	22	$155.40	1 Free with 10	Magazine		
12	6/5/2013	Printer stand	8	$82.96	Extra Discount	Direct mail		
13	6/5/2013	Printer stand	22	$239.40	1 Free with 10	Direct mail		
14	6/5/2013	Copy holder	55	$388.50	1 Free with 10	Magazine		
15	6/5/2013	Mouse pad	25	$168.25	Extra Discount	Newspaper		

2012 Sales | ROUND | IF | SUMIF

When analyzing data, you might need to count the items in a range, a task normally handled by the `COUNT` function. However, in some cases you might need to count only those values that meet a condition. You can do this by using the `COUNTIF` function, which combines the `COUNT` and `IF` functions. `COUNTIF` counts only those cells in a range that meet the condition you specify. `COUNTIF` takes two arguments: `range`, which is the range of cells you want to use to test the condition; and `criteria`, which is a text string that determines which cells in `range` to count.

Calculate a Conditional Count

1. In the cell where you want the result to appear, type **=countif(**.
2. Type the `range` argument.
3. Type a comma (,) and then the `criteria` argument.

Note: *Enclose the `criteria` argument in double quotation marks.*

4. Type **)**.
5. Click the Enter button or press Enter.

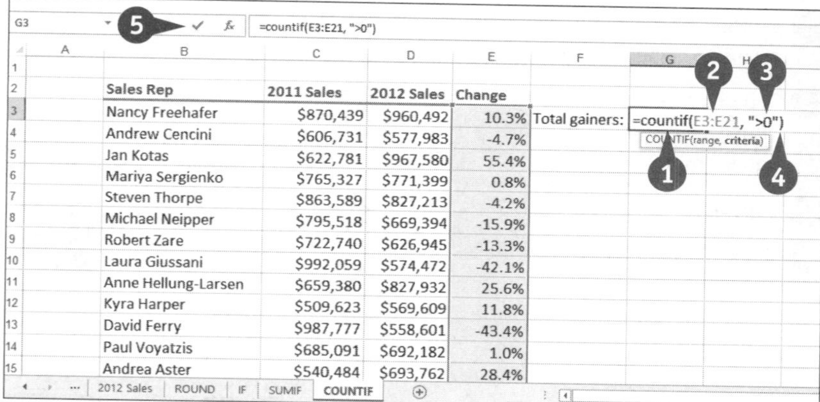

G3 | =countif(E3:E21, ">0")

	A	B	C	D	E	F	G
1							
2		Sales Rep	2011 Sales	2012 Sales	Change		
3		Nancy Freehafer	$870,439	$960,492	10.3%	Total gainers:	=countif(E3:E21, ">0")
4		Andrew Cencini	$606,731	$577,983	-4.7%		
5		Jan Kotas	$622,781	$967,580	55.4%		
6		Mariya Sergienko	$765,327	$771,399	0.8%		
7		Steven Thorpe	$863,589	$827,213	-4.2%		
8		Michael Neipper	$795,518	$669,394	-15.9%		
9		Robert Zare	$722,740	$626,945	-13.3%		
10		Laura Giussani	$992,059	$574,472	-42.1%		
11		Anne Hellung-Larsen	$659,380	$827,932	25.6%		
12		Kyra Harper	$509,623	$569,609	11.8%		
13		David Ferry	$987,777	$558,601	-43.4%		
14		Paul Voyatzis	$685,091	$692,182	1.0%		
15		Andrea Aster	$540,484	$693,762	28.4%		

Ⓐ Excel displays the conditional count in the cell.

Note: *You can use the question mark (?) and asterisk (*) wildcards when creating your condition. A ? matches a single character, while an * matches multiple characters.*

G3 | =COUNTIF(E3:E21, ">0")

	A	B	C	D	E	F	G
1							
2		Sales Rep	2011 Sales	2012 Sales	Change		
3		Nancy Freehafer	$870,439	$960,492	10.3%	Total gainers:	11
4		Andrew Cencini	$606,731	$577,983	-4.7%		
5		Jan Kotas	$622,781	$967,580	55.4%		
6		Mariya Sergienko	$765,327	$771,399	0.8%		
7		Steven Thorpe	$863,589	$827,213	-4.2%		
8		Michael Neipper	$795,518	$669,394	-15.9%		
9		Robert Zare	$722,740	$626,945	-13.3%		
10		Laura Giussani	$992,059	$574,472	-42.1%		
11		Anne Hellung-Larsen	$659,380	$827,932	25.6%		
12		Kyra Harper	$509,623	$569,609	11.8%		
13		David Ferry	$987,777	$558,601	-43.4%		
14		Paul Voyatzis	$685,091	$692,182	1.0%		
15		Andrea Aster	$540,484	$693,762	28.4%		

2012 Sales | ROUND | IF | SUMIF | COUNTIF

Find the Square Root

You can use the `SQRT` function to find a number's square root. However, Excel can only calculate the square roots of positive numbers. If a negative number is the argument, as in `SQRT(-9)`, Excel returns the error `#NUM`. To calculate the positive square root of a negative number, you can use `ABS` to first calculate the number's absolute value. The following formula returns 3: `=SQRT(ABS(-9))`. To find the power of any number, such as 2 to the fifth power, you can use the `POWER` function. This function takes two arguments: the number you want to raise to a power and the power to which you want to raise it. The formula `=POWER(2, 5)` raises the 2 to the fifth power, yielding 32.

Find the Square Root

1. In the cell where you want the result to appear, type **=sqrt(**.
2. Type or select the value of which you want to find the square root.
3. Type **)**.
4. Click the Enter button or press Enter.

Ⓐ Excel displays the square root in the cell.

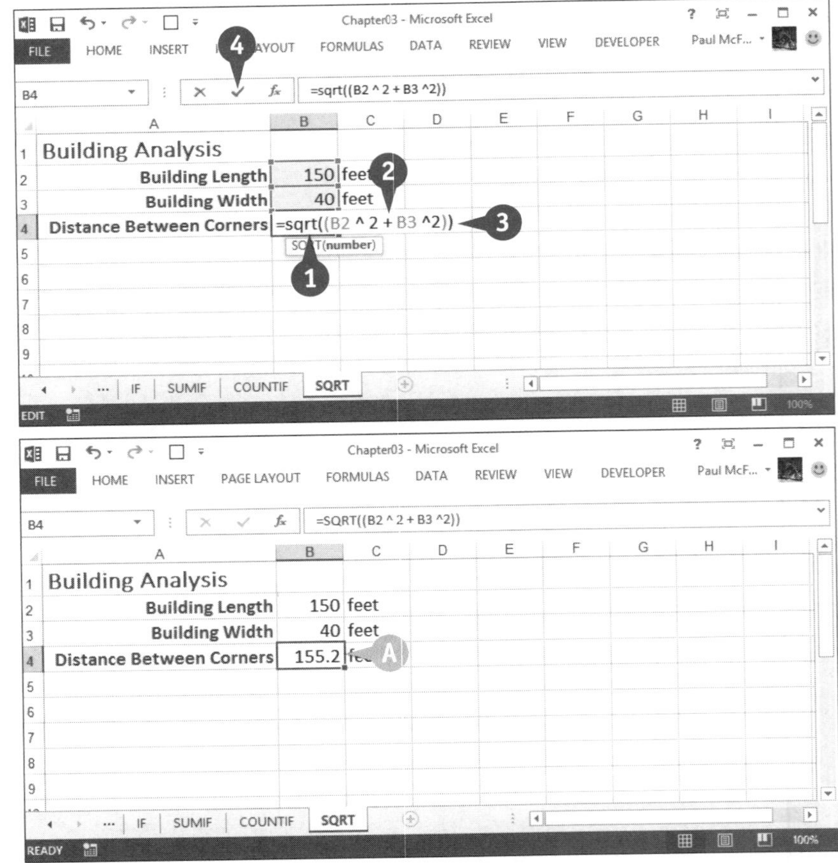

When you use functions such as VLOOKUP or INDEX, you enter a column number, a row number, or both. Entering an actual number means that number will not change when you copy the formula to another cell. If you want the number to change in the same way that relative cell addresses change, you can use the COLUMN function or the ROW function. These functions take one optional argument, reference, which is the cell or range for which you want to retrieve the row or column number. If you omit this argument, Excel returns the column or row number of the current cell. If you enter a range, Excel returns the column or row number of the range's upper-left corner cell.

Retrieve a Column or Row Number

1. In the cell where you want the result to appear, type **=column(** or **=row(**.
2. If needed, type or select the cell or range for which you want to retrieve the column or row number.
3. Type **)**.
4. Click the Enter button or press Enter.

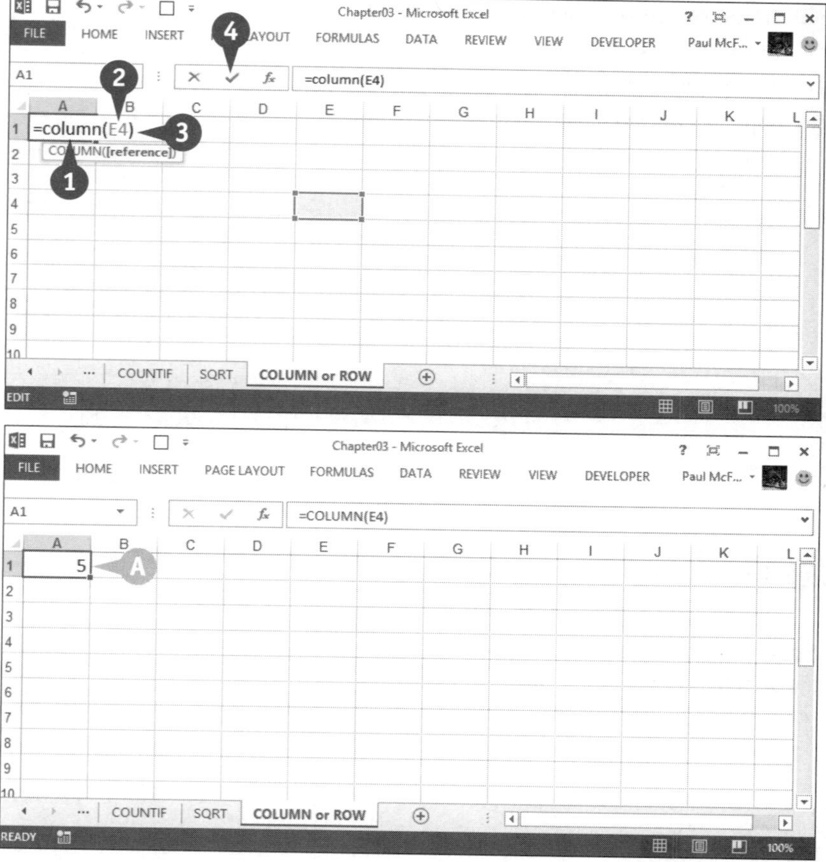

A. Excel displays the column or row number in the cell.

Use Excel's *lookup functions* to look up a value within a range and return a corresponding item from that range. For example, you can look up an income value in a tax table and return the corresponding tax rate. To look up a value within a column, use `VLOOKUP`; to look up a value within a row, use `HLOOKUP`. These functions have three required arguments: `lookup_value` specifies the value you want to look up; `table_array` is the range of values; and `col_index_num` (or `row_index_num` for `HLOOKUP`) is the column (or row) number within `table_array` that contains the value to retrieve. An optional fourth argument is `range_lookup`: if you omit it, the function looks for the closest match; if you set it to `FALSE`, the function looks for an exact match.

Look Up a Value

1. In the cell where you want the retrieved value to appear, type **=vlookup(** or **=hlookup(**.
2. Type or select the value you want to look up.

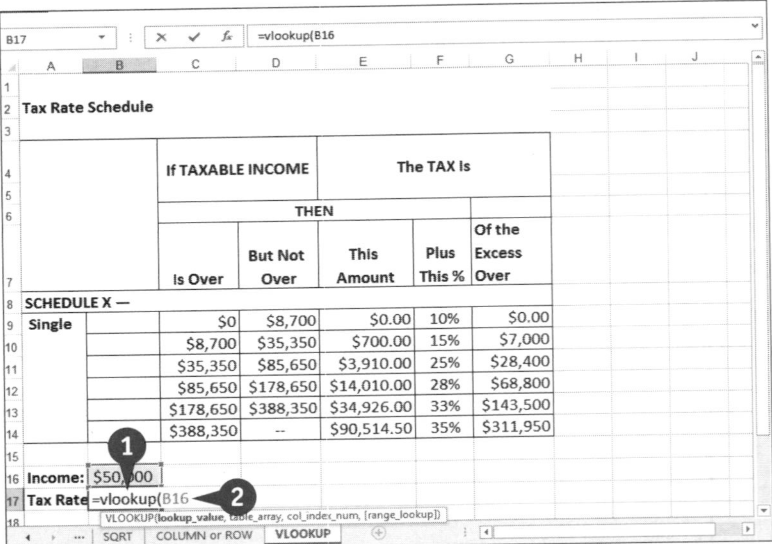

3. Type a comma (,) followed by the address of the lookup range.

Note: *Make sure the first column of the selected range is the column you want to use for the lookup.*

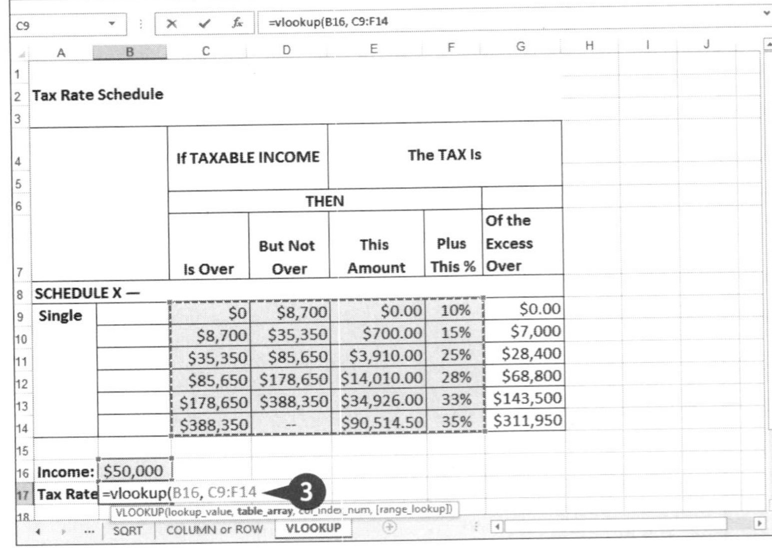

4 Type a comma (,) followed by the column (if you are using `VLOOKUP`) or row (if you are using `HLOOKUP`) number that contains the value you want to retrieve.

5 Type a closing parenthesis, **)**.

6 Click the Enter button or press Enter.

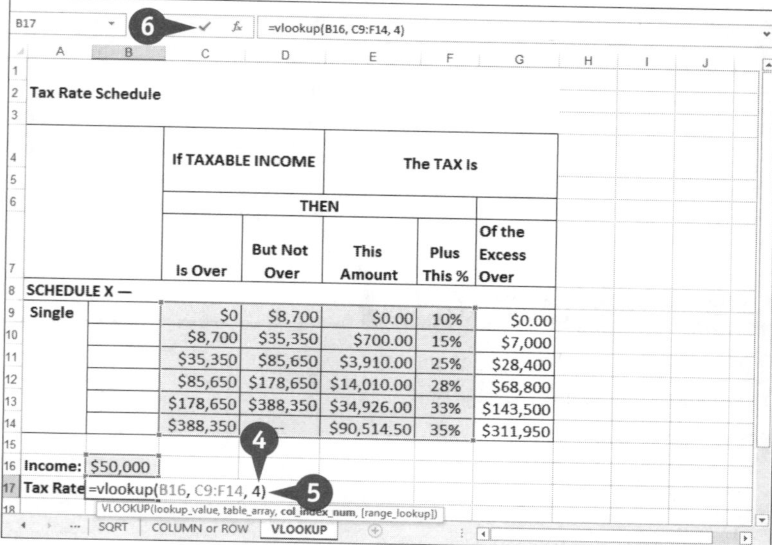

A Excel evaluates the logical expression and then displays the result in the cell.

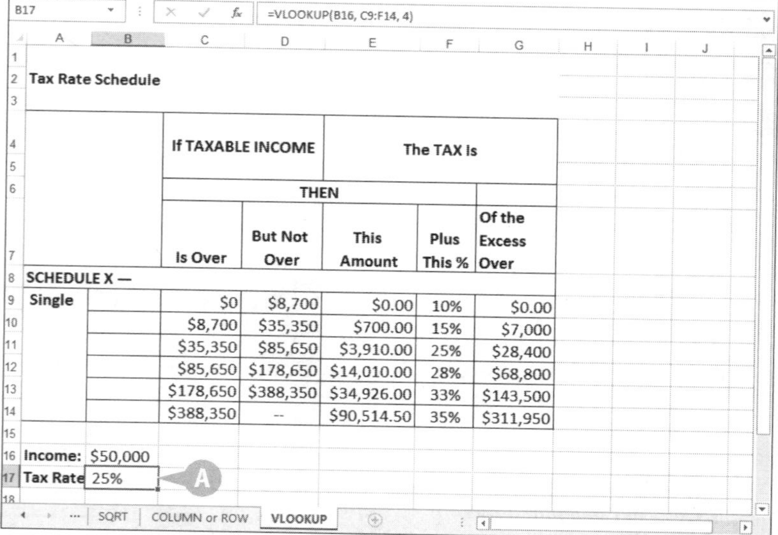

EXTRA

If you are searching text data, make sure the column you are searching does not contain any nonprinting characters, or leading or trailing spaces, and that quotation marks are used consistently. If you are searching for numbers or dates, make sure they are not formatted as text. If the first column of the table is text, you can use the standard wildcard characters in the `lookup_value` argument (use `?` to substitute for individual characters; use `*` to substitute for multiple characters). For the `col_index_num` (or `row_index_num` for `HLOOKUP`) argument, the first column is 1, the second column is 2, and so on. Finally, if you omit `range_lookup`, you must sort the values in the first column in ascending order.

Determine the Location of a Value

The `MATCH` function looks through a row or column for a value. If it finds a match, it returns the relative position of the match in the row or column. `MATCH` has three arguments: `lookup_value` is the value you want to find; `lookup_array` is the range you want to search; and the optional `match_type` specifies how to match values. If you omit `match_type` or enter 0, Excel finds the largest value less than or equal to `lookup_value`, and `lookup_array` must be in ascending order. If you enter –1, Excel returns the smallest value greater than or equal to `lookup_value`, and `lookup_array` must be in descending order. If you enter 0, Excel returns the first value that exactly matches `lookup_value`, and `lookup_array` can be in any order.

Determine the Location of a Value

1. In the cell where you want the result to appear, type **=match(**.
2. Type the value you want to locate or enter its address.
3. Type the address of the column or row you want to search.
4. Enter the `match_type` value.
5. Type **)**.
6. Click the Enter button or press Enter.

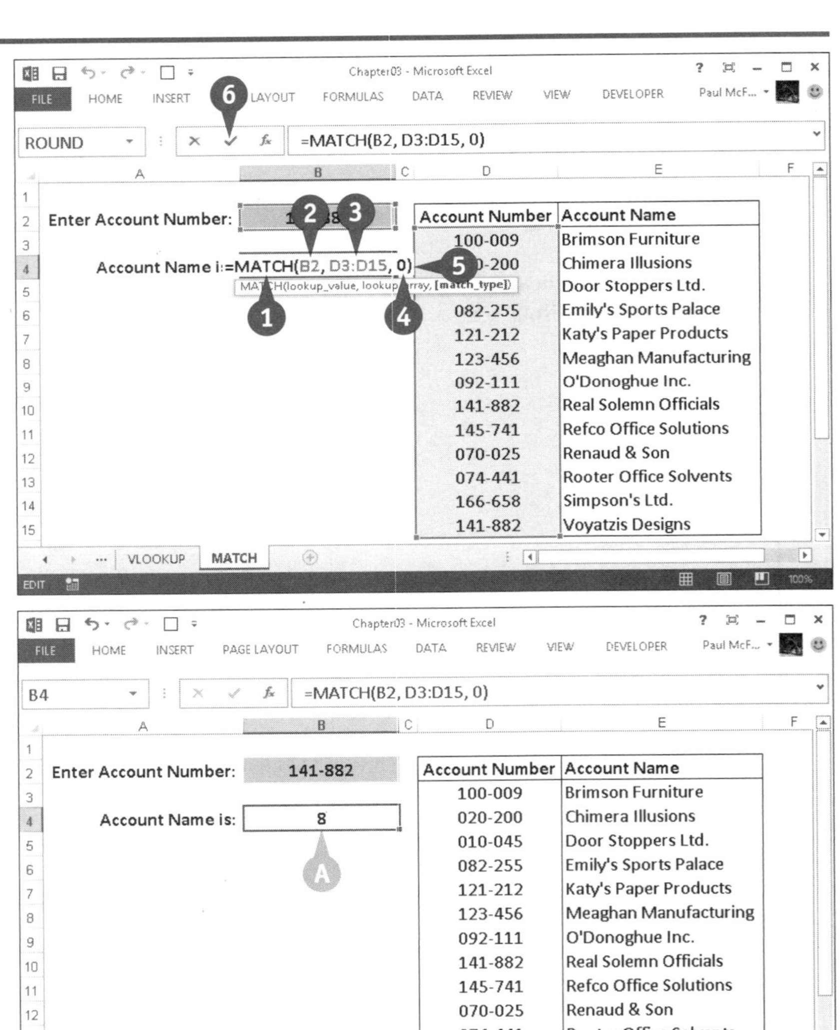

Ⓐ If Excel finds a match, it displays the relative position of the match within the row or column.

Note: *If you see the* #NA! *error, it means Excel did not find a match.*

If a particular value exists within a range, you can say that value resides at the intersection of a row and column number within the range. To retrieve that value, you can use the `INDEX` function. `INDEX` takes four arguments: `reference` specifies one or more ranges; `row_num` is the row number in `reference` from which to return a value; the optional `column_num` is the column number in `reference` from which to return a value; and `area_num` is the range you want to use if `reference` consists of multiple ranges, where the first range is 1, the second is 2, and so on. In most uses of `INDEX`, you use `MATCH`, described in the previous section, to return the `row_num` or `column_num` argument.

Return a Cell Value with INDEX

1. In the cell where you want the result to appear, type **=index(**.
2. Type the address of the range you want to search.
3. Type the row number of the value you want to return.
4. Type the column number of the value you want to return.

Note: *You can omit* `column_num` *if the range you are using is a single column.*

5. If you entered multiple ranges in step 2, type the range number you want to use (not shown).
6. Type **)**.
7. Click the Enter button or press Enter.

A. If Excel locates the cell, it displays the cell's value.

Note: *If you see the* `#NA!` *error, it means Excel did not locate the cell.*

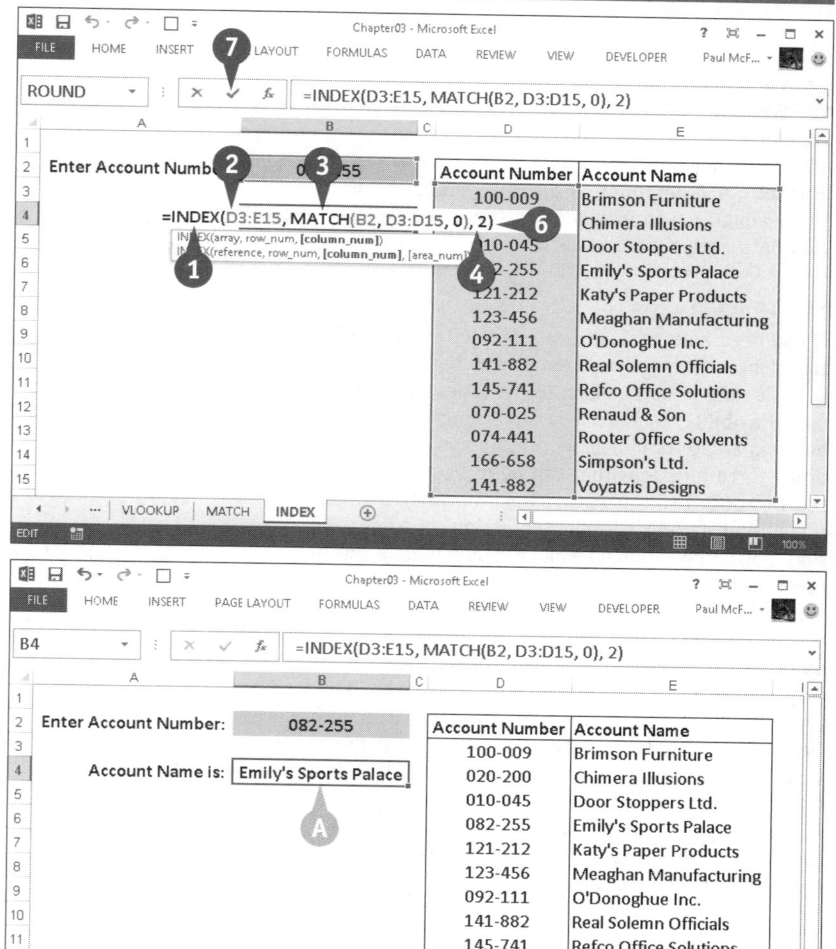

Perform Date and Time Calculations

In your Excel data analysis work, you will often have to perform date and time calculations. You can find, for example, the number of days that have elapsed between the start of a project and the end of a project or the number of hours worked from the start of the workday to the end of the workday.

Serial Numbers

Excel bases every date and time on a *serial number* that it can use to add and subtract. Excel calculates a date's serial number as the number of days after December 31, 1899, and represents each date with a whole number. Excel calculates a time's serial number as a value between 0 and 1, where midnight is 0, 6 a.m. is 0.25, noon is 0.5, and so on. A combined date and time serial number consists of the date to the left of the decimal and a time to the right. For example, August 23, 2013 6:00 p.m. has the serial number is 41509.75.

Date Calculations

Excel enables you to perform date calculations by returning a date serial number, returning parts of a date, such as the year or month, and determining the difference between two dates. This enables you to include sophisticated date calculations in your data analysis worksheets.

Return a Date

If you need a date for an expression operand or a function argument, you can always enter it by hand if you have a specific date in mind. Much of the time, however, you need more flexibility, such as always entering the current date or building a date from day, month, and year components. Excel offers three functions that can help: `TODAY`, `DATE`, and `DATEVALUE`. Use the `TODAY` function when you need to use the current date in a formula, function, or expression. Note that `TODAY` does not take any arguments. Use the `DATE` function to build a date from three separate values: the year, month, and day. `DATE` takes three arguments: `year`, which is the year component of the date (a number between 1900 and 9999); `month`, which is the month component of the date; and `day`, which is the day component of the date. For example, `DATE(2013, 12, 25)` returns the serial number of Christmas Day in 2013. Use `DATEVALUE` if you have a date value in string form and you want to convert it to a date serial number. `DATEVALUE` takes a single argument called `date_text` that is the string containing the date. For example, `DATEVALUE("August 23, 2013")` returns the date serial number for the string *August 23, 2013*.

Return Parts of a Date

The three components of a date — year, month, and day — can also be extracted individually from a given date. This might not seem very interesting at first, but many useful techniques actually arise out of working with a date's component parts. A date's components are extracted using the Excel `YEAR`, `MONTH`, and `DAY` functions, each of which takes a single argument called `serial_number`, which is the date you want to work with.

Calculate the Difference between Two Dates

Subtracting one date or time from another involves subtracting one serial number from another. For example, the serial number for August 14, 2013 is 41500 and the serial number for October 13, 2013 is 41560. To obtain the number of days between these two dates, subtract the later date from the earlier one. In this case, Excel performs the following calculation: `= 41560 - 41500`, which equal 60. However, when performing a date calculation, you do not need to display the serial number because Excel handles the conversion automatically.

Time Calculations

Excel enables you to perform time calculations by returning a time serial number; returning parts of a time, such as the hour or minute; and determining the difference between two times. These techniques enable you to include useful and sophisticated time calculations in your data analysis models.

Return a Time

The most straightforward way to work with times as operands or function arguments is to type the time values manually. Usually, however, your data analysis requires a more flexible approach, such as always using the current time or building a time using separate hour, minute, and second components. Excel offers three functions that can help: `NOW`, `TIME`, and `TIMEVALUE`. Use the `NOW` function when you need to use the current time in a formula, function, or expression. Note that `NOW` does not take any arguments. Use the `TIME` function to build a date from three separate values: the hour, minute, and second. `TIME` takes three arguments: `hour`, which is the hour component of the time (a number between 0 and 23); `minute`, which is the minute component of the time (between 0 and 59); and `second`, which is the second component of the time (between 0 and 59). For example, `TIME(13, 30, 15)` returns the serial number of the time 1:30:15 p.m. Use `TIMEVALUE` if you have a time value in string form and you want to convert it to a time serial number. `TIMEVALUE` takes a single argument called `time_text` that is the string containing the time. For example, `TIMEVALUE("4:45:00 PM")` returns the time serial number for the string *4:45:00 PM*.

Return Parts of a Time

If you require them for your formula, you can extract the three components of a time: hour, minute, and second. A time's components are extracted using the Excel `HOUR`, `MINUTE`, and `SECOND` functions, each of which takes a single argument called `serial_number`, which is the time you want to work with.

Calculate the Difference between Two Times

As with dates, you determine the difference between two time values by subtracting the later time from the earlier one. For example, if the later time is 6:00 p.m. and the earlier time is 9:00 a.m., Excel calculates the difference by using the serial numbers for the two times, which in this case is `=0.75 - 0.375`. The result is 0.375, which means the difference is 9 hours. When calculating the difference between two times, you want to know the hours and minutes that have elapsed, so you need to format your results as hours and minutes. Click the Home tab and then click the dialog box launcher in the Number group to open the Format Cells dialog box. Click the Number tab, click Time, click the format type 13:30, and then click OK. Also, when subtracting times that cross midnight, such as 11:00 p.m. to 2:00 a.m., you need to use the `MOD` function, which returns the remainder after dividing by a specified value. Here is the general formula to use:

```
=MOD (later time - earlier time, 1)
```

Calculate Future Value

If you have $1,000 and you plan to invest it at 5 percent interest, compounded annually for ten years, the amount you will receive at the end of ten years is called the future value of $1,000. You can use the Excel `FV` function to calculate the amount you will receive.

`FV` takes five arguments: `rate`, the interest rate; `nper`, the term of the investment; `pmt`, the amount of each deposit into the investment; the optional `pv`, your initial investment; and the optional `type`, a number indicating when deposits are due (0 or blank for end-of-period; 1 for beginning-of-period). When you are working with `FV`, cash outflows are considered negative amounts, so you need to enter the `pmt` and `pv` arguments as negative numbers.

Calculate Future Value

1. In the cell where you want the future value to appear, type **=fv(**.

2. Type the interest rate.

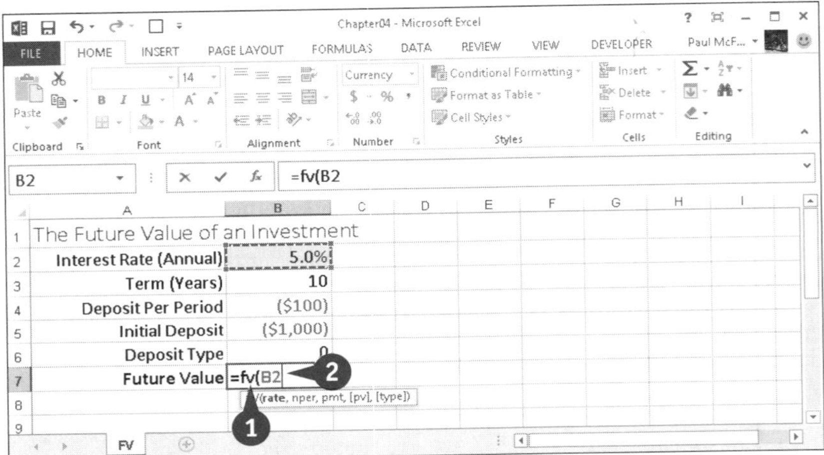

3. Type a comma and then the term.

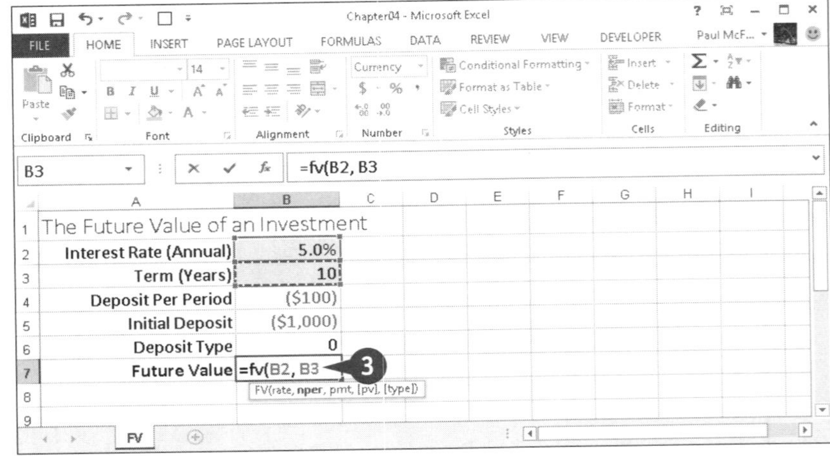

4. Type a comma and then the amount of each deposit.
5. If you had an initial investment, type a comma and then the amount.
6. If you need to specify the deposit type, type a comma and then **0** or **1**.
7. Type **)**.
8. Click the Enter button or press Enter.

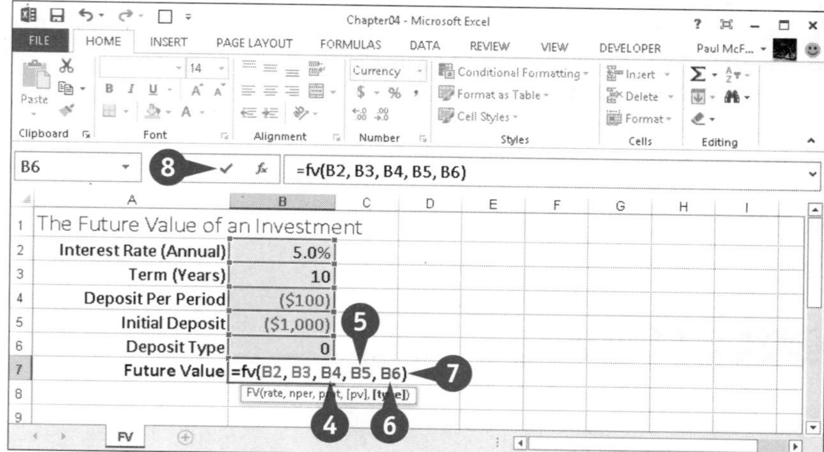

Ⓐ Excel calculates the future value.

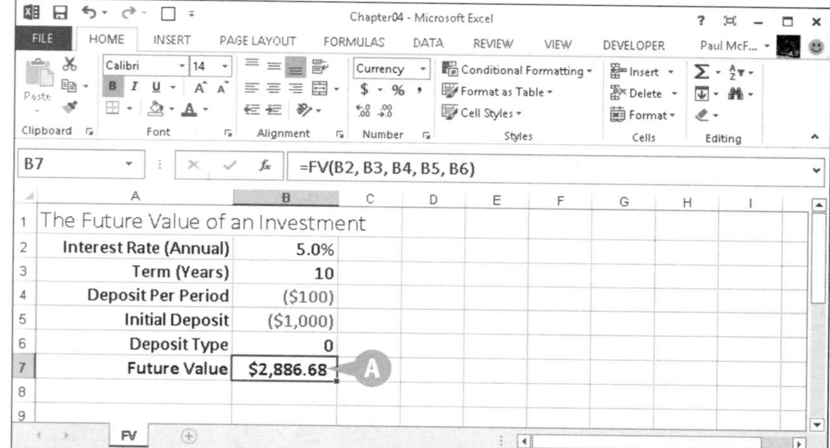

EXTRA

When calculating a future value, be careful of the values you use for the `rate` and `nper` arguments. If you are not making regular deposits or you are making a single deposit annually, you can use the annual interest rate for the `rate` argument and the number of years in the investment for the `nper` argument. For more frequent deposits, you need to adjust the `rate` and `nper` values accordingly. As a rule, divide the annual interest rate by the number of deposits per year, and multiply the term of the investment by the number of deposits per year. For example, with monthly deposits, divide the annual interest rate by 12 and multiply the term by 12.

Calculate Present Value

Investors use the concept of present value to recognize the time value of money. Because an investor can receive interest, $1,000 today is worth less than $1,000 ten years from today. For example, $1,000 invested today at 10 percent interest per year, compounded annually, would return $2,593.74. Therefore, the present value of $2,593.74 at 10 percent, compounded annually, for 10 years is $1,000, or worded differently, $1,000 today is worth $2,593.74 ten years from today.

To find the present value, you can use the Excel `PV` function, which takes five arguments: `rate`, the interest rate; `nper`, the number of periods in the term; `pmt`, the amount of each payment; `pv`, the amount you are trying to find the present value of; and `type`, a number indicating when payments are made.

Calculate Present Value

1. In the cell where you want the present value to appear, type **=pv(**.
2. Type the interest rate.
3. Type a comma and then the number of periods in the term.

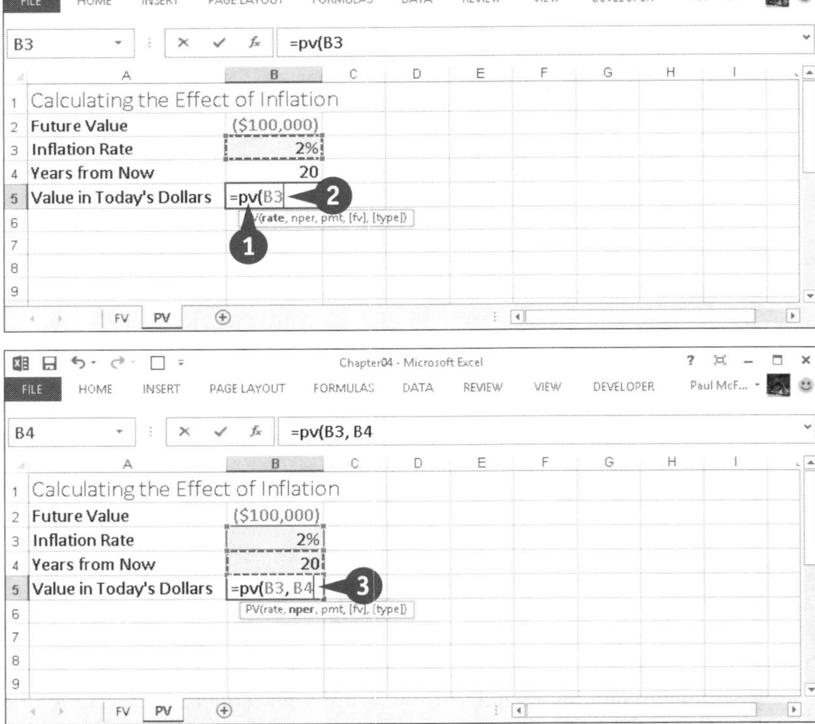

4. Type a comma and then the amount of each payment.

5. Type a comma and then the future value.

6. If you need to specify the deposit type, type a comma and then **0** or **1**.

7. Type **)**.

8. Click the Enter button or press Enter.

A. Excel calculates the present value.

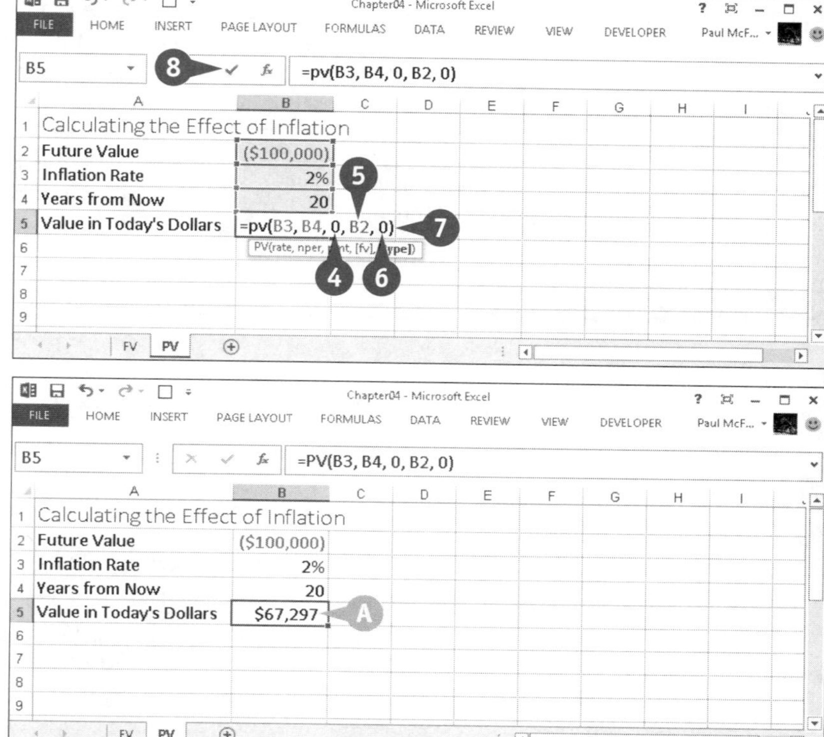

EXTRA

Present value also applies to loans and mortgages. The money you receive when you take out a loan is the present value of the loan. When calculating present value, be careful what you enter in the `rate` and `nper` arguments. You must divide the annual interest rate by the number of payments per year. For example, if payments are monthly, you should divide the annual interest rate by 12. You must also multiply the term by the number of payments. For example, if payments are monthly, multiply the term by 12. When you are working with the `PV` function, negative numbers are cash outflows and positive numbers are cash inflows. Enter a negative number when making a payment; enter a positive number when receiving cash.

Determine the Loan Payments

When borrowing money, whether it is for a mortgage, car financing, or a student loan, the most basic analysis is to calculate the regular payment you must make to repay the loan. You use the Excel `PMT` function to determine the payment.

The `PMT` function takes three required arguments and two optional ones. The required arguments are `rate`, the fixed rate of interest over the term of the loan; `nper`, the number of payments over the term of the loan; and `pv`, the loan principal. The two optional arguments are `fv`, the future value of the loan, which is usually an end-of-loan balloon payment; and `type`, the type of payment: 0 (the default) for end-of-period payments or 1 for beginning-of-period payments.

Determine the Loan Payments

1. In the cell where you want the payment amount to appear, type **=pmt(**.
2. Type the interest rate.

Note: *As shown here, if the interest rate is annual, you can divide it by 12 to get the monthly rate.*

3. Type a comma and then the number of periods in the term.

Note: *As shown here, if the term is expressed in years, you can multiply it by 12 to get the number of months in the term.*

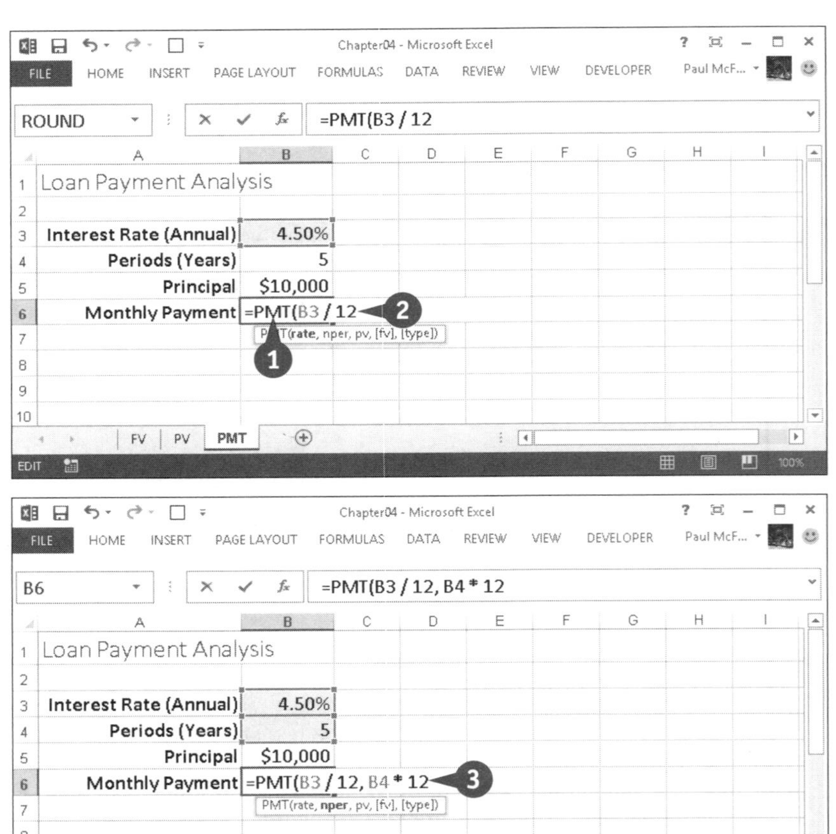

4 Type a comma and then the amount of the loan principal.

If the loan has a balloon payment, type a comma and then the amount of that payment.

Note: *A balloon payment covers any unpaid principal that remains at the end of a loan.*

If you need to specify the payment type, type a comma and then **0** or **1**.

5 Type **)**.

6 Click the Enter button or press Enter.

A Excel calculates the loan payment.

NOTE: The PMT *function returns a negative value because it is money that you pay out.*

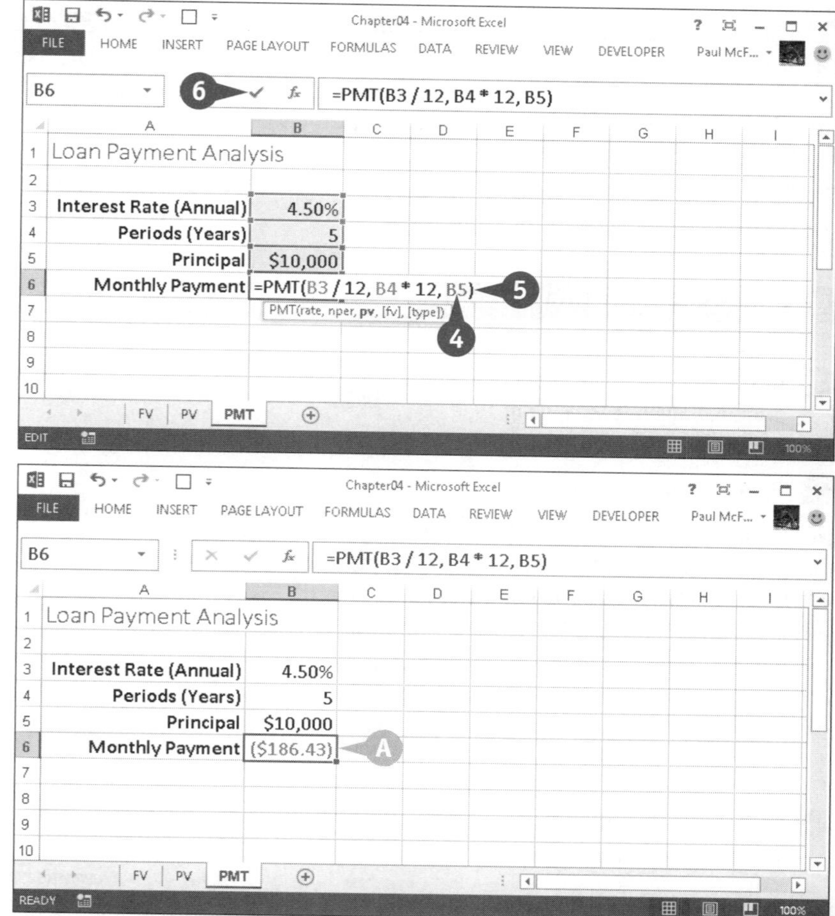

EXTRA

With many loans, the payments take care of only a portion of the principal, with the remainder due as an end-of-loan balloon payment. This payment is the future value of the loan, so you enter it into the PMT function as the fv argument. You might think that the pv argument should therefore be the partial principal — that is, the original loan principal minus the balloon amount — because the loan term is designed to pay off only the partial principal. That is not the case, however. In a balloon loan, you also pay interest on the balloon part of the principal. Therefore, the PMT function's pv argument must be the entire principal, with the balloon portion as the (negative) fv argument.

To break down a loan payment into principal and interest, you can use the PPMT and IPMT functions, respectively. As the loan progresses, the value of PPMT increases while the value of IPMT decreases, but the sum of the two is constant in each period and is equal to the loan payment.

Both functions take the same six arguments. The four required arguments are rate, the fixed rate of interest over the loan term; per, the number of the payment period; nper, the number of payments over the term of the loan; and pv, the loan principal. The two optional arguments are fv, the future value of the loan; and type, the type of payment: 0 for end-of-period or 1 for beginning-of-period.

Calculate the Principal or Interest

1. In the cell where you want the principal amount to appear, type **=ppmt(**.
2. Type the interest rate.

Note: *As shown here, if you will be filling the calculation into other cells, enter the interest rate address using the absolute reference format.*

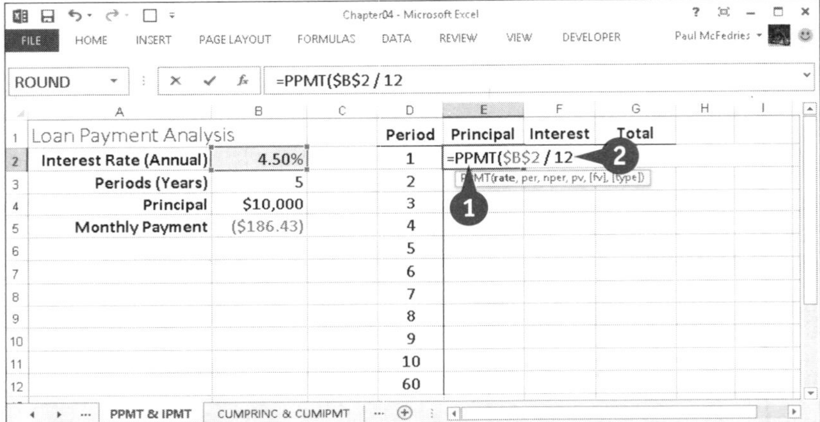

3. Type a comma and then the payment period.
4. Type a comma and then the number of periods in the term.

Note: *As shown here, if you will be filling the calculation into other cells, enter the term address using the absolute reference format.*

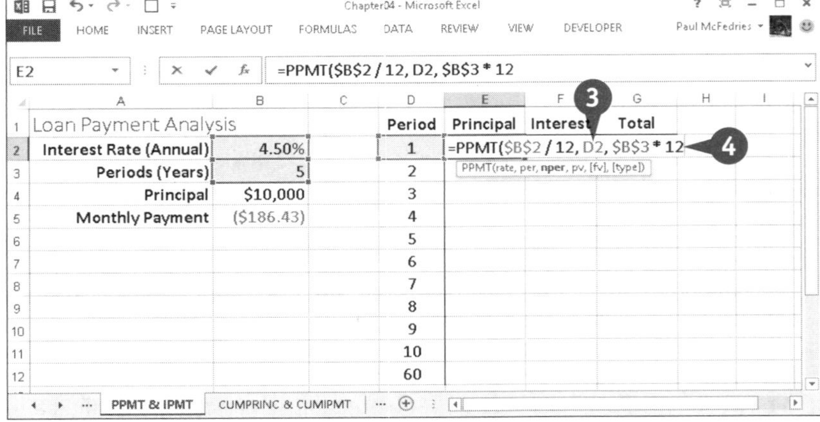

5 Type a comma and then the amount of the loan principal.

If the loan has a balloon payment, type a comma and then the amount of that payment.

If you need to specify the payment type, type a comma and then **0** or **1**.

6 Type **)**.

7 Click the Enter button or press Enter.

A Excel calculates the principal.

8 To calculate the interest, type **=ipmt(** in the cell and then follow steps 2 to 9.

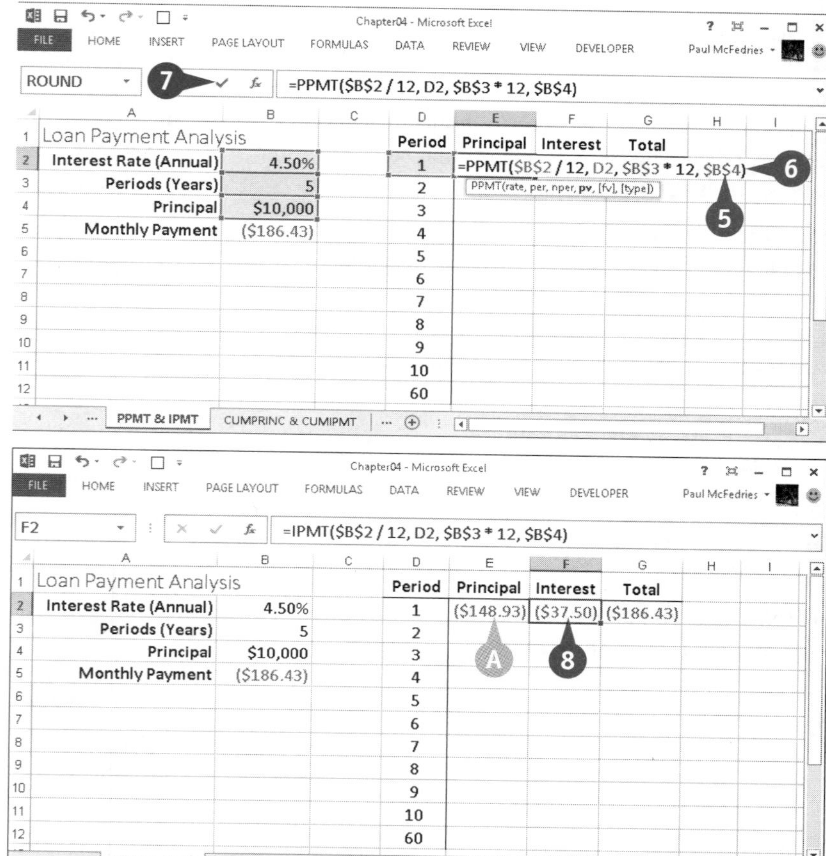

APPLY IT

To calculate how much principal or interest has accrued between two periods, use the `CUMPRINC` or the `CUMIPMT` function, respectively. Both functions require the same six arguments: `rate`, the fixed rate of interest over the term of the loan; `nper`, the number of payments over the term of the loan; `pv`, the loan principal; `start_period`, the first period to include in the calculation; `end_period`, the last period to include in the calculation; and `type`, the type of payment: 0 for end-of-period or 1 for beginning-of-period. For example, to find the cumulative principal or interest in the first year of a loan, set `start_period` to 1 and `end_period` to 12; for the second year, set `start_period` to 13 and `end_period` to 24.

If you know how much you want to borrow, how long a term you want, and what payments you can afford, you can calculate what interest rate will satisfy these parameters using the Excel `RATE` function. For example, you could use this calculation to put off borrowing money if current interest rates are higher than the value you calculate.

The `RATE` function takes three required arguments: `nper`, the number of payments over the term of the loan; `pmt`, the periodic payment; and `pv`, the loan principal. `RATE` can also take three optional arguments: `fv`, the future value of the loan; `type`, the type of payment (0 for end-of-period or 1 for beginning-of-period); and `guess`, a percentage value that Excel uses as a starting point for calculating the interest rate.

Find the Required Interest Rate

1. In the cell where you want the interest rate to appear, type **=rate(**.
2. Type the number of loan periods.

Note: *If you want an annual interest rate, you must divide the term by 12 if it is currently expressed in months.*

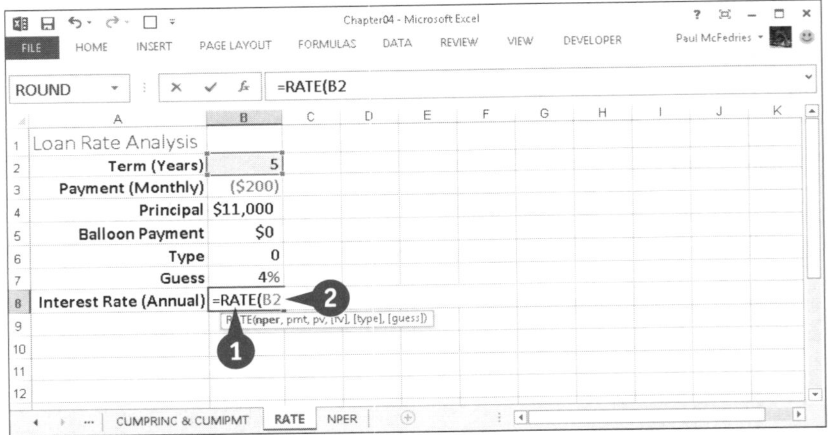

3. Type a comma and then the payment.

Note: *As shown here, if you have a monthly payment and you want an annual interest rate, you must multiply the payment by 12.*

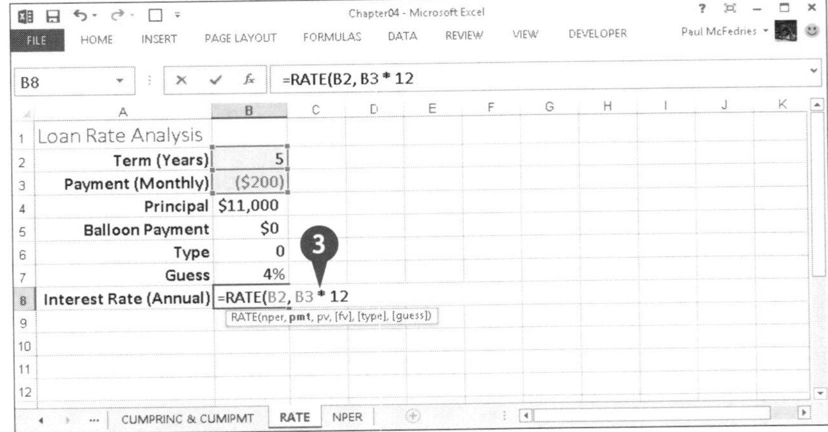

4 Type a comma and then the amount of the loan principal.

5 If the loan has a balloon payment, type a comma and then the amount of that payment.

6 If you need to specify the payment type, type a comma and then **0** or **1**.

7 If you want to supply an initial guess, type a comma and then specify the value.

8 Type **)**.

9 Click the Enter button or press Enter.

A Excel calculates the interest rate.

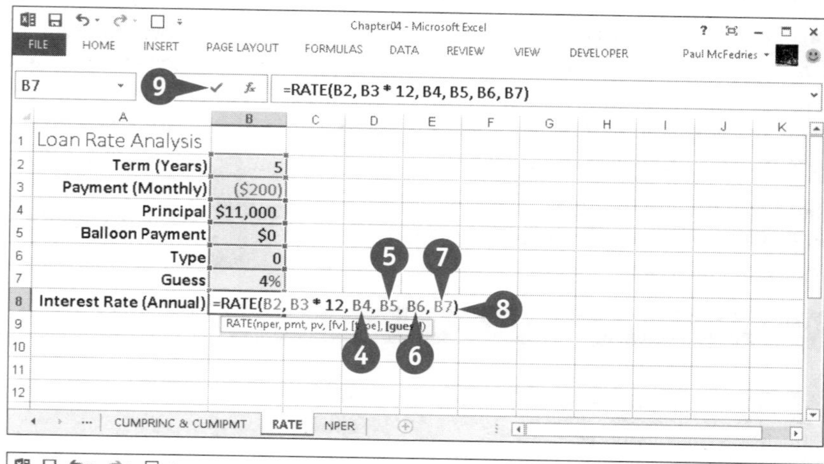

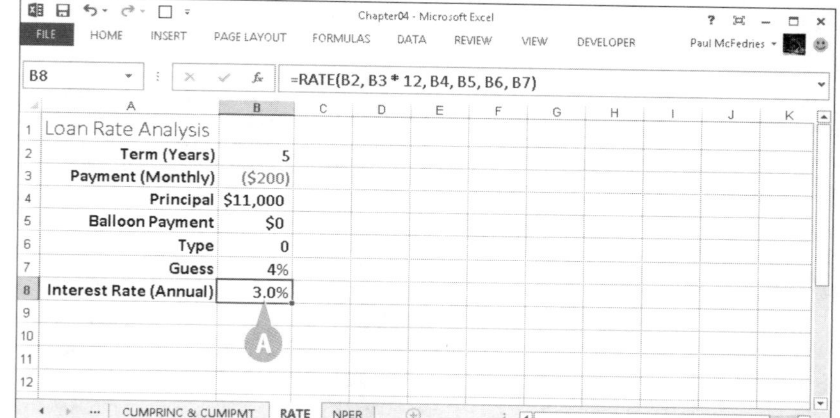

EXTRA

`RATE` uses an iterative process where Excel starts with an initial `guess` value and attempts to refine it to obtain the answer. If you omit `guess`, Excel uses a default value of 10 percent. If after 20 tries Excel cannot return a value, it returns a `#NUM!` error. You should enter a `guess` value and try again.

If you know the principal, the interest rate, and the payment, you can calculate the length of the loan by using the `NPER` function. The function's three required arguments are `rate`, the fixed rate of interest; `pmt`, the loan payment; and `pv`, the loan principal. The two optional arguments are `fv`, the future value of the loan, and `type`, the type of payment (0 or 1).

Determine the Internal Rate of Return

You can use the Excel `IRR` function to calculate the internal rate of return on an investment. The investment's cash flows do not have to be equal, but they must occur at regular intervals. `IRR` tells you the interest rate you receive on the investment.

IRR takes two arguments `values` and `guess`. The `values` argument is required. It represents the range of cash flows over the term of the investment. It must contain at least one positive and one negative value. The `guess` argument is optional. It specifies an initial estimate for the Excel iterative calculation of the internal rate of return (the default is 0.1). If after 20 tries Excel cannot return a value, it returns a `#NUM!` error. You should enter a `guess` value and try again.

Determine the Internal Rate of Return

1. Type the series of projected cash flows into a worksheet.

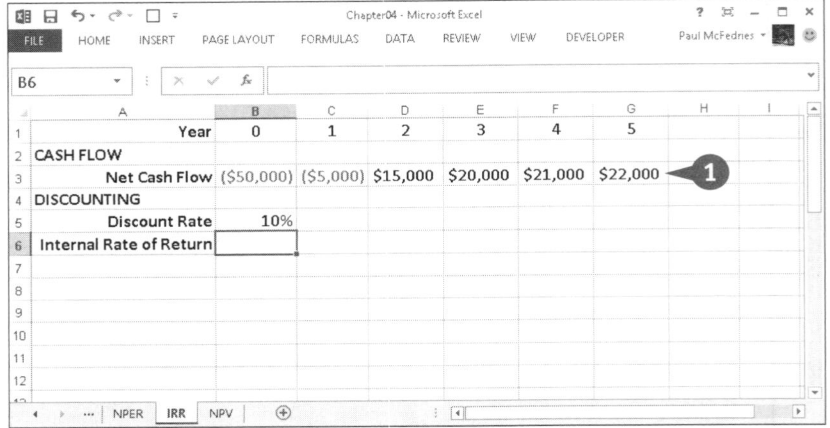

2. In the cell where you want the internal rate of return to appear, type **=irr(**.

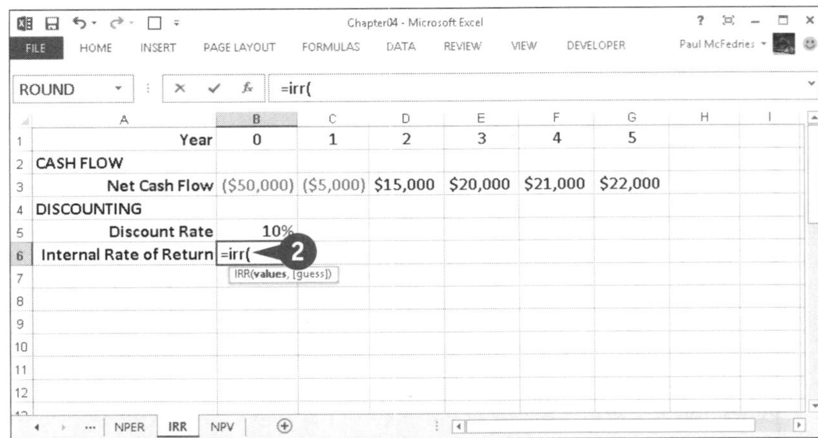

3. Type the address of the range of cash flows.
4. If you want to supply an initial guess, type a comma and then specify the value.
5. Type **)**.
6. Click the Enter button or press Enter.

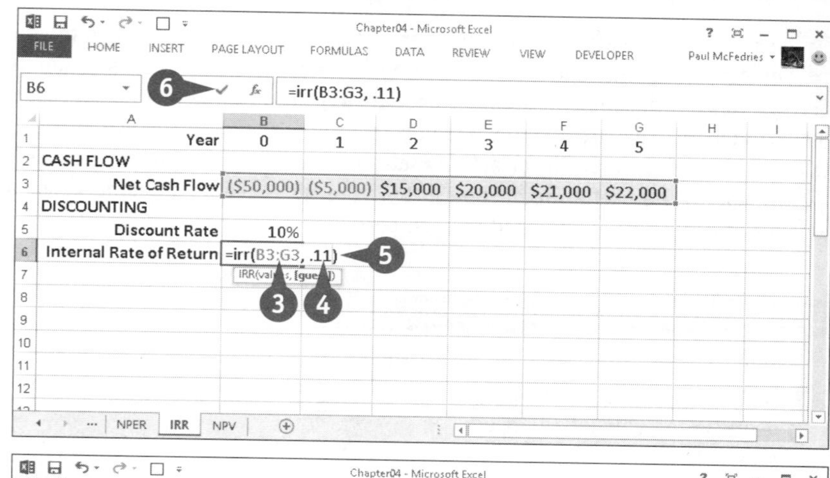

Ⓐ Excel calculates the internal rate of return.

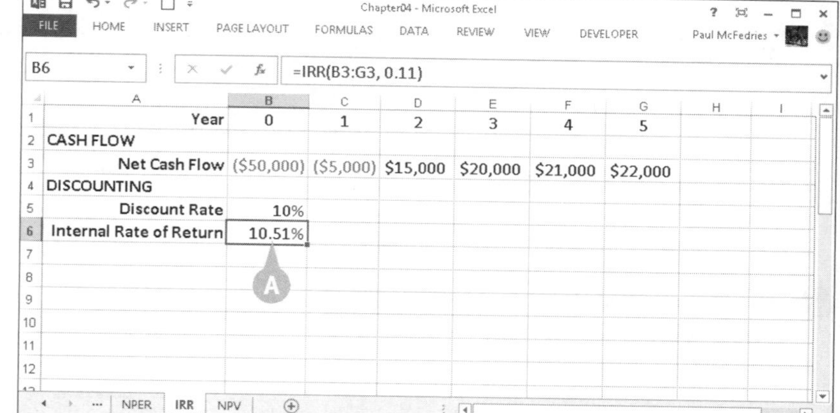

EXTRA

The internal rate of return is related to the net present value, which is the sum of a series of net cash flows, each of which has been discounted to the present using a fixed discount rate. The internal rate of return can be defined as the discount rate required to obtain a net present value of $0.

Use the `NPV` function to calculate the net present value of future cash flows. If all the cash flows are the same, you can use `PV` to calculate the present value. When you have a series of varying cash flows, use `NPV`, which requires two arguments: `rate`, the discount rate over the term of the asset or investment, and `values`, the range of cash flows.

Calculate Straight-Line Depreciation

The *straight-line* method of depreciation allocates depreciation evenly over the useful life of an asset. *Salvage value* is the value of an asset once its useful life has expired. To calculate straight-line depreciation, you take the cost of the asset, subtract any salvage value, and then divide by the useful life of the asset. The result is the amount of depreciation allocated to each period.

To calculate straight-line depreciation, you can use the Excel `SLN` function, which takes three arguments: `cost`, the initial cost of the asset; `salvage`, the salvage value of the asset; and `life`, the life of the asset in periods. If you purchase an asset mid-year, you can calculate depreciation in months instead of years.

Calculate Straight-Line Depreciation

1. In the cell where you want the depreciation amount to appear, type **=sln(**.
2. Type the cost of the asset.
3. Type a comma and then the salvage value of the asset.

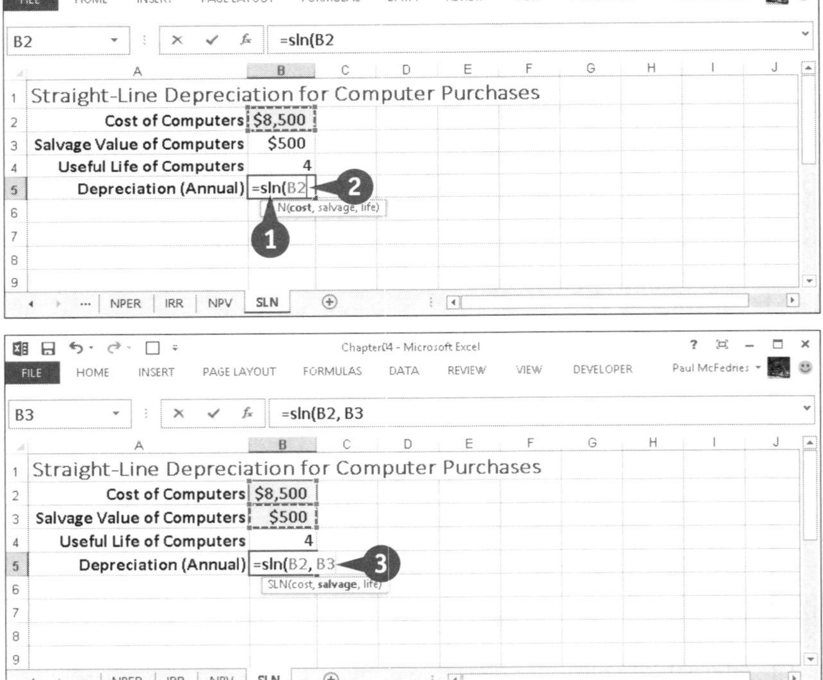

4 Type a comma and then the number of periods in the useful life of the asset.

5 Type).

6 Click the Enter button or press Enter.

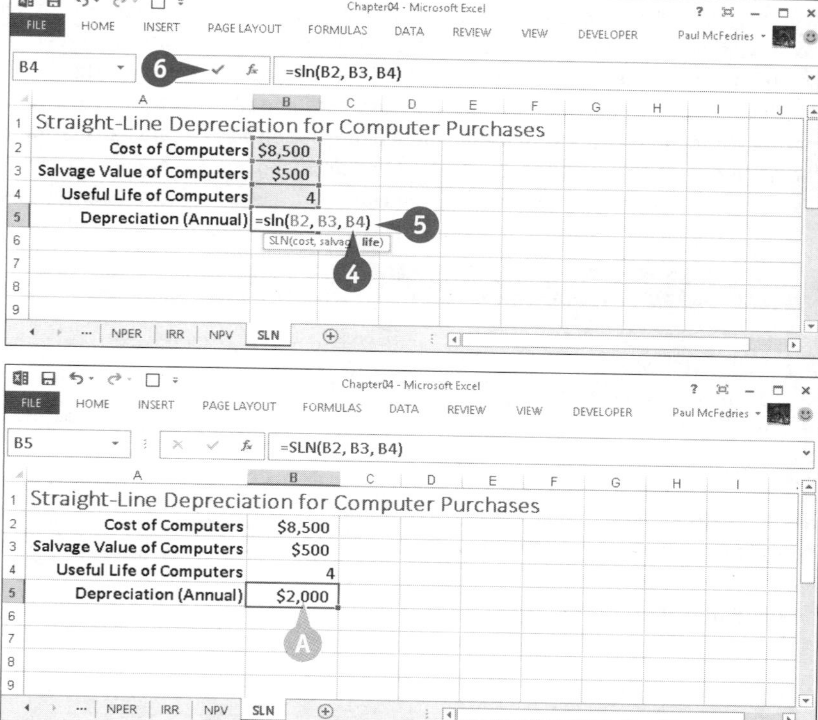

A Excel calculates the straight-line depreciation.

APPLY IT

The carrying value is the cost of an asset minus the total depreciation taken to date. The depreciation for an asset with a cost of $8,500, a salvage value of $500, and a useful life of four years would be allocated as follows:

Year	Annual Depreciation Expense	Accumulated Depreciation	Carrying Value
Beginning Year 1			$8,500
End Year 1	$2,000	$2,000	$6,500
End Year 2	$2,000	$4,000	$4,500
End Year 3	$2,000	$6,000	$2,500
End Year 4	$2,000	$8,000	$500

When calculating depreciation, accountants try to match the cost of an asset with the revenue it produces. Some assets produce more in earlier years than in later years. For those assets, accountants use accelerated methods of depreciation, which take more depreciation in the earlier years than in the later years. *Fixed-declining balance* is an accelerated method of depreciation.

To calculate fixed-declining balance depreciation, you can use the Excel `DB` function, which takes five arguments: `cost`, the cost of the asset; `salvage`, the salvage value; `life`, the useful life; `period`, the period for which you are calculating depreciation; and the optional `month`, the number of months in the first year. If you leave `month` blank, Excel uses a default value of 12.

Return the Fixed-Declining Balance Depreciation

1. In the cell where you want the depreciation amount to appear, type **=db(**.
2. Type the cost of the asset.

Note: *As shown here, if you will be filling the calculation into other cells, enter the cost address using the absolute reference format.*

3. Type a comma and then the salvage value of the asset.
4. Type a comma and then the number of periods in the useful life of the asset.

Note: *As shown here, if you will be filling the calculation into other cells, enter the salvage and life addresses using the absolute reference format.*

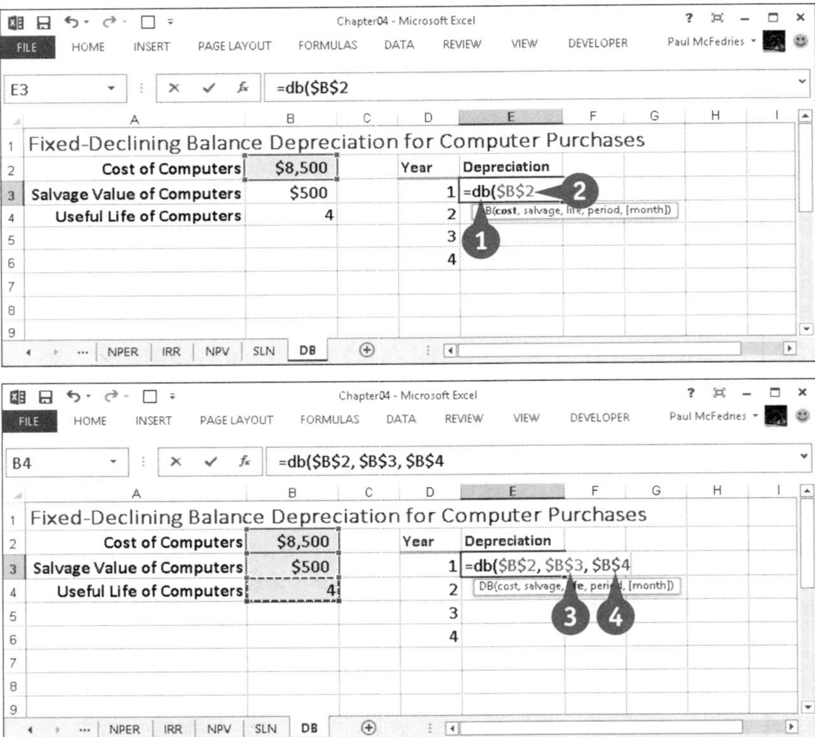

5. Type a comma and then the type of period for which you are calculating the depreciation.

   If the number of months in the first year is different than 12, type a comma and then type the number of months in the first year.

6. Type).

7. Click the Enter button or press Enter.

A. Excel calculates the fixed-declining balance depreciation.

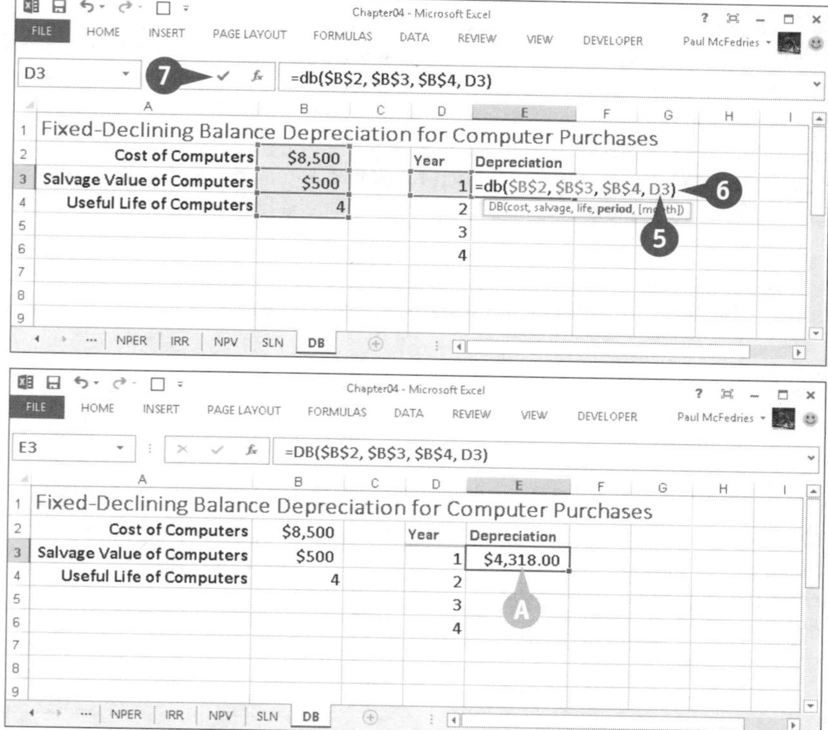

APPLY IT

The fixed-declining balance method of depreciation depreciates an asset with a cost of $8,500, a salvage value of $500, and a useful life of four years as follows:

Year	Annual Depreciation Expense	Accumulated Depreciation	Carrying Value
Beginning of Year 1			$8,500
End Year 1	$4,318	$4,318	$4,182
End Year 2	$2,124	$6,442	$2,058
End Year 3	$1,045	$7,488	$1,012
End Year 4	$512•	$8,000	$500

*Amount adjusted for rounding error.

Double-declining balance is an accelerated depreciation method that takes the rate you would apply by using straight-line depreciation, doubles it, and then applies the doubled rate to the carrying value of the asset. To determine the double-declining balance depreciation, you can use the Excel `DDB` function, which takes five arguments: `cost`, the cost of the asset; `salvage`, the salvage value; `life`, the useful life; `period`, the period for which you are calculating depreciation; and the optional `factor`, the rate at which the balance declines. The default value for `factor` is 2, but to use a value other than twice the straight-line rate, you can enter the factor you want to use, such as 1.5 for a rate of 150 percent.

Determine the Double-Declining Balance Depreciation

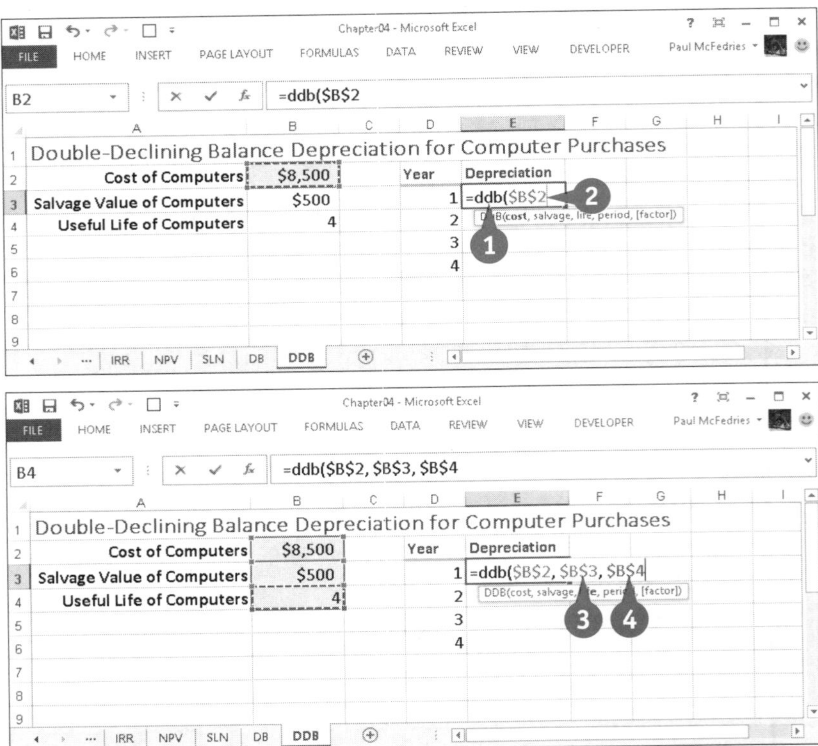

1. In the cell where you want the depreciation amount to appear, type **=ddb(**.

2. Type the cost of the asset.

Note: *As shown here, if you will be filling the calculation into other cells, enter the cost address using the absolute reference format.*

3. Type a comma and then the salvage value of the asset.

4. Type a comma and then the number of periods in the useful life of the asset.

Note: *As shown here, if you will be filling the calculation into other cells, enter the salvage and life addresses using the absolute reference format.*

5 Type a comma and then the type of period for which you are calculating the depreciation.

If you want to use a rate other than 2, type a comma and then type the factor value you want to use.

6 Type).

7 Click the Enter button or press Enter.

A Excel calculates the double-declining balance depreciation.

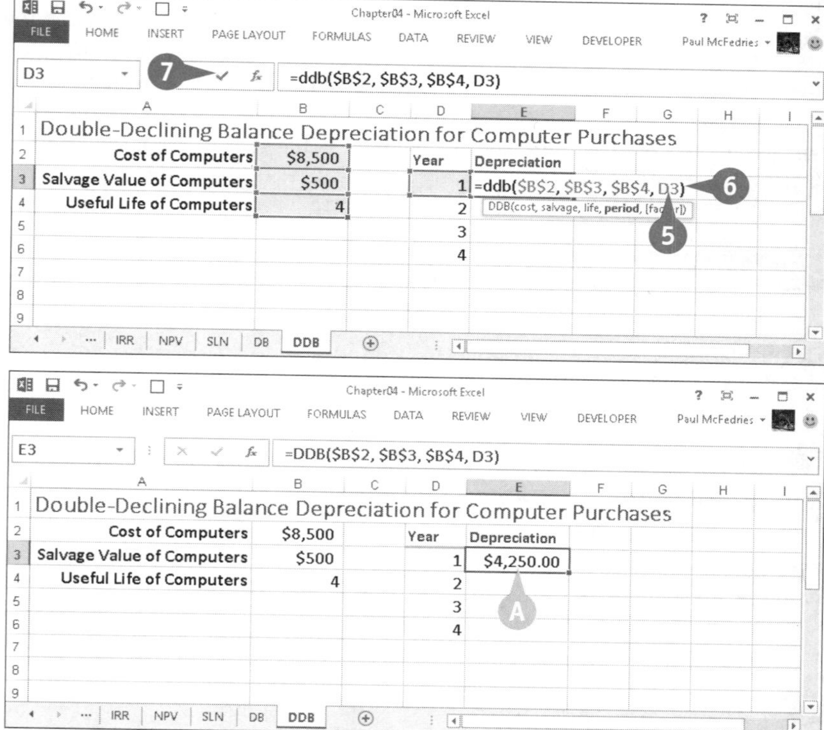

APPLY IT

The double-declining balance method of depreciation depreciates an asset with a cost of $8,500, a salvage value of $1,500, and a useful life of four years as follows:

Year	Annual Depreciation Expense	Accumulated Depreciation	Carrying Value
Beginning of Year			$8,500
End Year 1	$4,250	$4,250	$4,250
End Year 2	$2,125	$6,375	$2,125
End Year 3	$625•	$7,000	$1,500
End Year 4	$0•	$7,500	$1,500

*The DDB function does not depreciate the asset below the salvage value.

Sum-of-the-years-digits is an accelerated depreciation method. When you calculate sum-of-the-years-digits depreciation manually, you use a fraction to calculate annual depreciation. The numerator of the fraction is the remaining years of useful life. The denominator is the sum of the digits that make up the useful life.

To determine the sum-of-the-years-digits depreciation, you can use the Excel `SYD` function, which takes four arguments. The `cost` argument is the cost of the asset. The `salvage` argument is the salvage value. The `life` argument is the useful life. The `per` argument is the period for which you are calculating depreciation.

Figure the Sum-of-the-Years-Digits Depreciation

1. In the cell where you want the depreciation amount to appear, type **=syd(**.
2. Type the cost of the asset.

Note: *As shown here, if you will be filling the calculation into other cells, enter the cost address using the absolute reference format.*

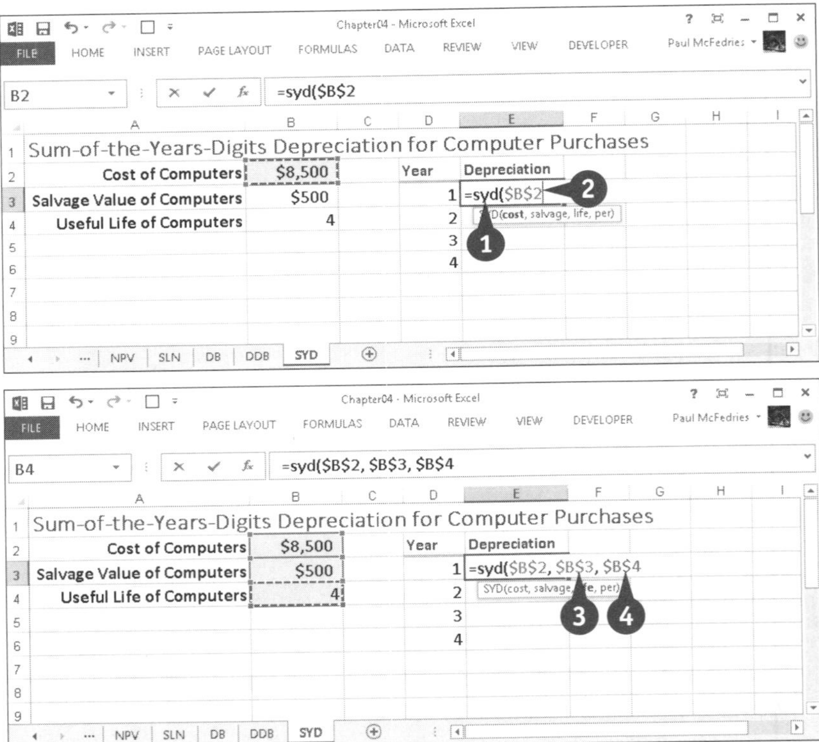

3. Type a comma and then the salvage value of the asset.
4. Type a comma and then the number of periods in the useful life of the asset.

Note: *As shown here, if you will be filling the calculation into other cells, enter the salvage and life addresses using the absolute reference format.*

5. Type a comma and then the type of period for which you are calculating the depreciation.

6. Type).

7. Click the Enter button or press Enter.

A. Excel calculates the sum-of-the-years-digits depreciation.

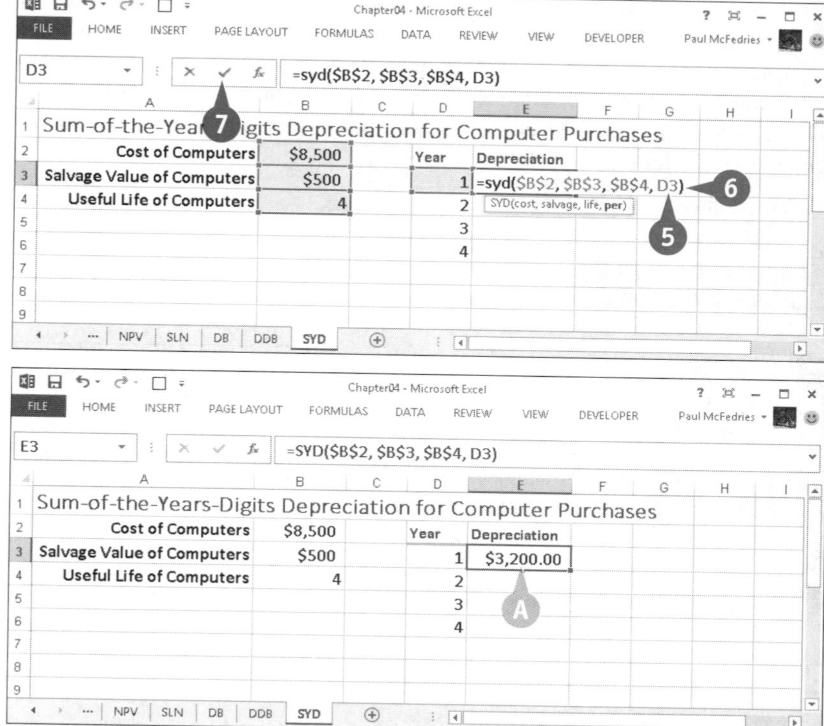

APPLY IT

The sum-of-the-years-digits method of depreciation depreciates an asset with a cost of $8,500, a salvage value of $500, and a useful life of four years as follows:

Year	Annual Depreciation Expense	Accumulated Depreciation	Carrying Value
Beginning of Year 1			$8,500
End Year 1	$3,200	$3,200	$5,300
End Year 2	$2,400	$5,600	$2,900
End Year 3	$1,600	$7,200	$1,300
End Year 4	$800	$8,000	$500

Calculate an Average

An average is the sum of two or more values divided by the number of values. You can calculate the average by creating a custom formula, but that is only practical for a small number of items. For larger collections, it is faster and more efficient to use the Excel cocktail `AVERAGE` function, which uses the following syntax:

```
AVERAGE(number1[, number2, ...])
```

You can enter up to 255 arguments, and each can be a number, a cell, a range, a range name, or an array (that is, a list of values enclosed in curly braces, such as {20, 25, 25, 30}). If a cell contains zero, Excel includes it in the calculation, but if a cell is blank, Excel does not include it.

Calculate an Average

1. In the cell where you want the average to appear, type **=average(**.
2. Type the values you want to average, separated by commas.
3. Type **)**.
4. Click the Enter button or press Enter.

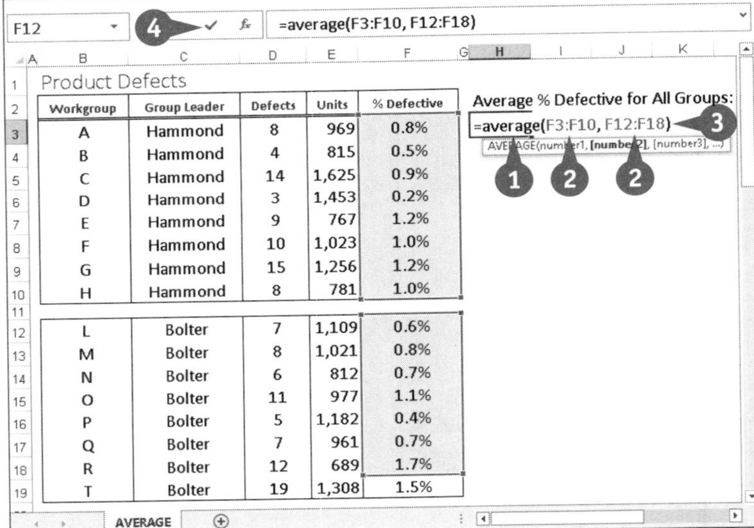

Product Defects

Workgroup	Group Leader	Defects	Units	% Defective
A	Hammond	8	969	0.8%
B	Hammond	4	815	0.5%
C	Hammond	14	1,625	0.9%
D	Hammond	3	1,453	0.2%
E	Hammond	9	767	1.2%
F	Hammond	10	1,023	1.0%
G	Hammond	15	1,256	1.2%
H	Hammond	8	781	1.0%
L	Bolter	7	1,109	0.6%
M	Bolter	8	1,021	0.8%
N	Bolter	6	812	0.7%
O	Bolter	11	977	1.1%
P	Bolter	5	1,182	0.4%
Q	Bolter	7	961	0.7%
R	Bolter	12	689	1.7%
T	Bolter	19	1,308	1.5%

Ⓐ Excel calculates the average.

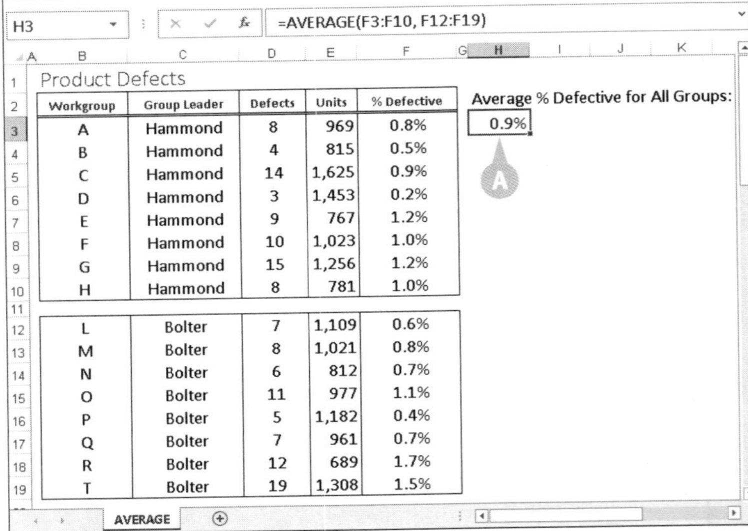

Product Defects

Workgroup	Group Leader	Defects	Units	% Defective
A	Hammond	8	969	0.8%
B	Hammond	4	815	0.5%
C	Hammond	14	1,625	0.9%
D	Hammond	3	1,453	0.2%
E	Hammond	9	767	1.2%
F	Hammond	10	1,023	1.0%
G	Hammond	15	1,256	1.2%
H	Hammond	8	781	1.0%
L	Bolter	7	1,109	0.6%
M	Bolter	8	1,021	0.8%
N	Bolter	6	812	0.7%
O	Bolter	11	977	1.1%
P	Bolter	5	1,182	0.4%
Q	Bolter	7	961	0.7%
R	Bolter	12	689	1.7%
T	Bolter	19	1,308	1.5%

In your data analysis, you might need to average the values in a range, but only those values that satisfy some condition. You can do this by using the AVERAGEIF function, an amalgam of AVERAGE and IF, which averages only those cells in a range that meet the condition you specify. AVERAGEIF takes up to three arguments: range, which is the range of cells you want to use to test the condition; criteria, which is a text string that determines which cells in range to sum; and the optional average_range, which is the range from which you want the average values to be taken. Excel sums only those cells in average_range that correspond to the cells in range and meet the criteria.

Calculate a Conditional Average

1. In the cell where you want the result to appear, type **=averageif(**.
2. Type the range argument.
3. Type a comma (,) and then the criteria argument.

Note: *Enclose the* criteria *argument in double quotation marks.*

4. If required, type a comma (,) and then the average_range argument.

Note: *If you omit* average_range, *Excel uses* range *for the average.*

5. Type **)**.
6. Click the Enter button or press Enter.

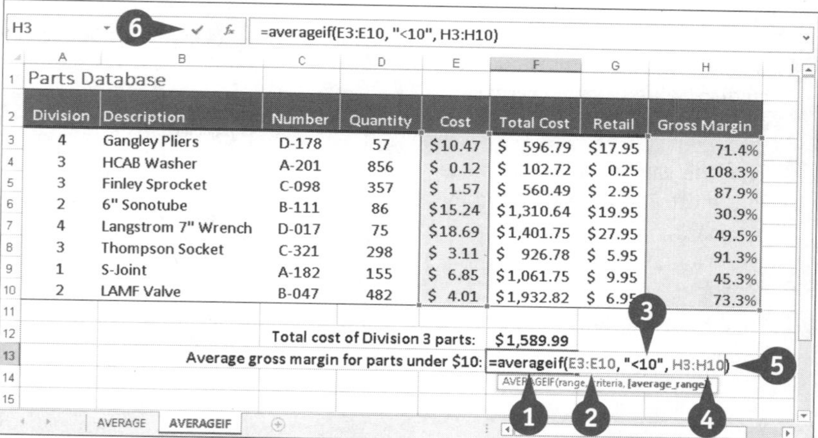

F13 =AVERAGEIF(E3:E10, "<10", H3:H10)

Parts Database

Division	Description	Number	Quantity	Cost	Total Cost	Retail	Gross Margin
4	Gangley Pliers	D-178	57	$10.47	$ 596.79	$17.95	71.4%
3	HCAB Washer	A-201	856	$ 0.12	$ 102.72	$ 0.25	108.3%
3	Finley Sprocket	C-098	357	$ 1.57	$ 560.49	$ 2.95	87.9%
2	6" Sonotube	B-111	86	$15.24	$1,310.64	$19.95	30.9%
4	Langstrom 7" Wrench	D-017	75	$18.69	$1,401.75	$27.95	49.5%
3	Thompson Socket	C-321	298	$ 3.11	$ 926.78	$ 5.95	91.3%
1	S-Joint	A-182	155	$ 6.85	$1,061.75	$ 9.95	45.3%
2	LAMF Valve	B-047	482	$ 4.01	$1,932.82	$ 6.95	73.3%

Total cost of Division 3 parts: $1,589.99

Average gross margin for parts under $10: 81.2% (A)

AVERAGE | AVERAGEIF

Ⓐ Excel displays the conditional average in the cell.

Note: *You can use the question mark (?) and asterisk (*) wildcards when creating your condition. A ? matches a single character; an * matches multiple characters.*

Determine the Median or the Mode

When analyzing data, you may need to find the median or the mode. The *median* is the midpoint in a series of numbers: the point at which half the values are greater and half the values are less when you arrange the values in numerical order. The *mode* is the most common value in a list of values. To calculate these values, you use the Excel `MEDIAN` and `MODE` functions, respectively:

`MEDIAN(`*`number1`*`[, `*`number2`*`, ...])`
`MODE(`*`number1`*`[, `*`number2`*`, ...])`

You can enter up to 255 arguments, and each can be a number, cell, range, range name, or array. Excel includes zeroes in the calculation, but not blanks.

Determine the Median or the Mode

Calculate the Median

1. In the cell where you want the median value to appear, type **=median(**.
2. Type the values you want to use in the calculation, separated by commas.
3. Type **)**.
4. Click the Enter button or press Enter.

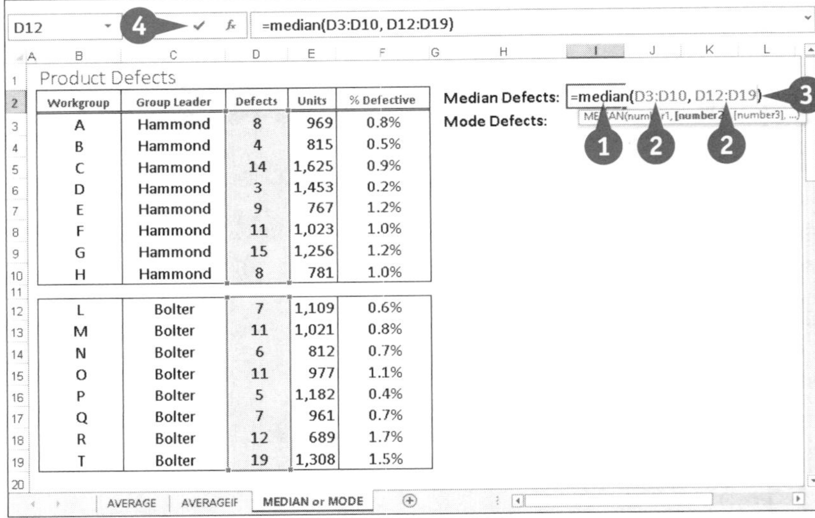

Workgroup	Group Leader	Defects	Units	% Defective
A	Hammond	8	969	0.8%
B	Hammond	4	815	0.5%
C	Hammond	14	1,625	0.9%
D	Hammond	3	1,453	0.2%
E	Hammond	9	767	1.2%
F	Hammond	11	1,023	1.0%
G	Hammond	15	1,256	1.2%
H	Hammond	8	781	1.0%
L	Bolter	7	1,109	0.6%
M	Bolter	11	1,021	0.8%
N	Bolter	6	812	0.7%
O	Bolter	11	977	1.1%
P	Bolter	5	1,182	0.4%
Q	Bolter	7	961	0.7%
R	Bolter	12	689	1.7%
T	Bolter	19	1,308	1.5%

Ⓐ Excel calculates the median value.

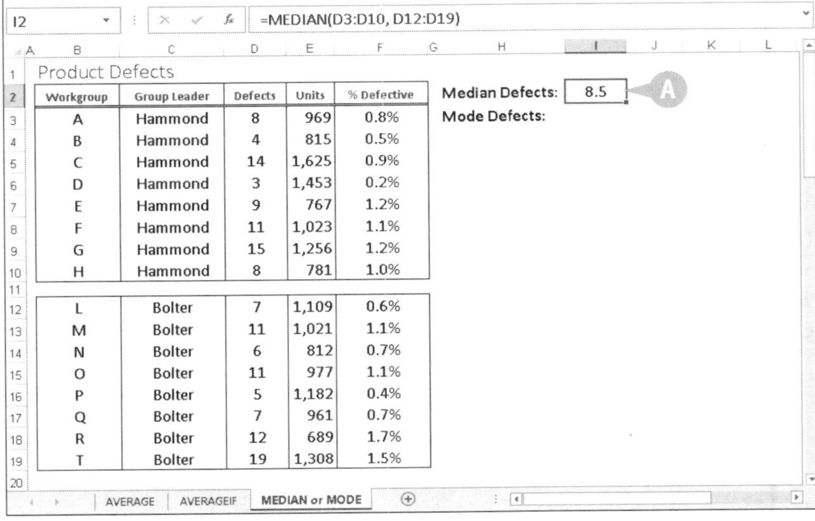

Workgroup	Group Leader	Defects	Units	% Defective
A	Hammond	8	969	0.8%
B	Hammond	4	815	0.5%
C	Hammond	14	1,625	0.9%
D	Hammond	3	1,453	0.2%
E	Hammond	9	767	1.2%
F	Hammond	11	1,023	1.1%
G	Hammond	15	1,256	1.2%
H	Hammond	8	781	1.0%
L	Bolter	7	1,109	0.6%
M	Bolter	11	1,021	1.1%
N	Bolter	6	812	0.7%
O	Bolter	11	977	1.1%
P	Bolter	5	1,182	0.4%
Q	Bolter	7	961	0.7%
R	Bolter	12	689	1.7%
T	Bolter	19	1,308	1.5%

Calculate the Mode

1. In the cell where you want the mode value to appear, type **=mode(**.
2. Type the values you want to include in the calculation, separated by commas.
3. Type **)**.
4. Click the Enter button or press Enter.

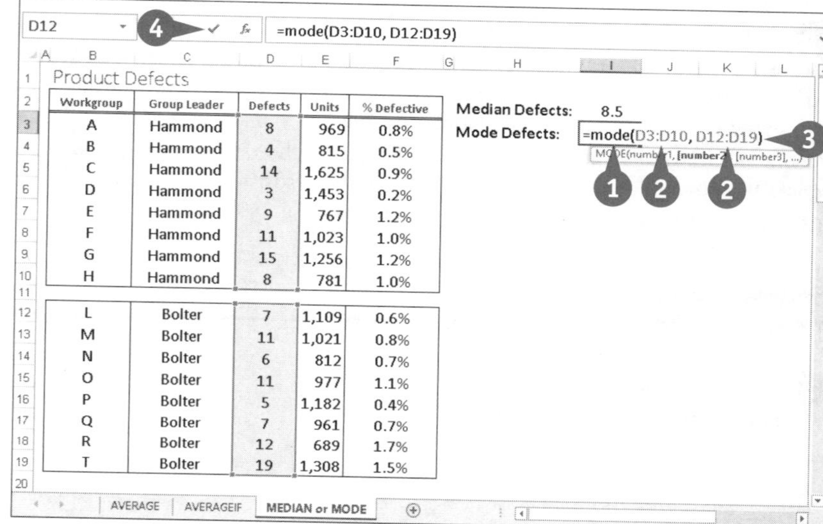

Product Defects

Workgroup	Group Leader	Defects	Units	% Defective
A	Hammond	8	969	0.8%
B	Hammond	4	815	0.5%
C	Hammond	14	1,625	0.9%
D	Hammond	3	1,453	0.2%
E	Hammond	9	767	1.2%
F	Hammond	11	1,023	1.0%
G	Hammond	15	1,256	1.2%
H	Hammond	8	781	1.0%
L	Bolter	7	1,109	0.6%
M	Bolter	11	1,021	0.8%
N	Bolter	6	812	0.7%
O	Bolter	11	977	1.1%
P	Bolter	5	1,182	0.4%
Q	Bolter	7	961	0.7%
R	Bolter	12	689	1.7%
T	Bolter	19	1,308	1.5%

B. Excel calculates the mode value.

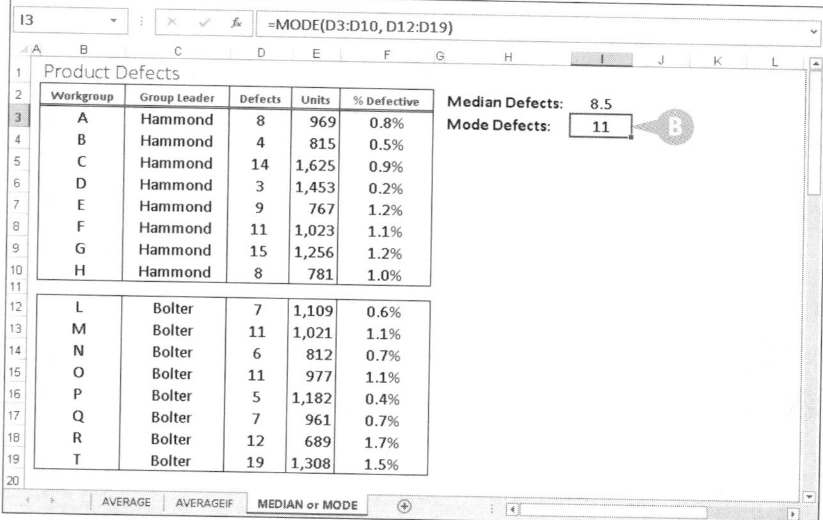

Product Defects

Workgroup	Group Leader	Defects	Units	% Defective
A	Hammond	8	969	0.8%
B	Hammond	4	815	0.5%
C	Hammond	14	1,625	0.9%
D	Hammond	3	1,453	0.2%
E	Hammond	9	767	1.2%
F	Hammond	11	1,023	1.1%
G	Hammond	15	1,256	1.2%
H	Hammond	8	781	1.0%
L	Bolter	7	1,109	0.6%
M	Bolter	11	1,021	1.1%
N	Bolter	6	812	0.7%
O	Bolter	11	977	1.1%
P	Bolter	5	1,182	0.4%
Q	Bolter	7	961	0.7%
R	Bolter	12	689	1.7%
T	Bolter	19	1,308	1.5%

EXTRA

Excel interprets the logical value `TRUE` as 1 and the logical value `FALSE` as 0, so you can use logical values as arguments when calculating the median or mode. However, if an array or a range of cells contains a logical value, `MEDIAN` and `MODE` do not include them in the calculation. Statisticians refer to an average as the mean. Central tendency is defined as a typical value in a distribution or a value that represents the majority of cases. The most commonly used measures of central tendency are mean, median, and mode. The Analysis Toolpak is an Excel add-in that you can use to calculate descriptive statistics such as the mean, median, and mode. To learn more, see Chapter 11.

Find the Rank

It is often useful to find how one item ranks relative to the other items in a list. For example, you might want to find out how a student's test score ranks in relation to the other students. You could do this by sorting the list, but in some situations, sorting is not advisable. For example, constantly changing data would require constant re-sorting. Instead, you can use the Excel `RANK.EQ` function to determine an item's rank relative to other items in a list. `RANK.EQ` takes three arguments: `number`, the item you want to rank; `ref`, the range that holds the list of items; and the optional `order`, the sort order you want Excel to use — the default is descending, but you can use any non-zero value for ascending.

Find the Rank

1. In the cell where you want the rank to appear, type **=rank(**.

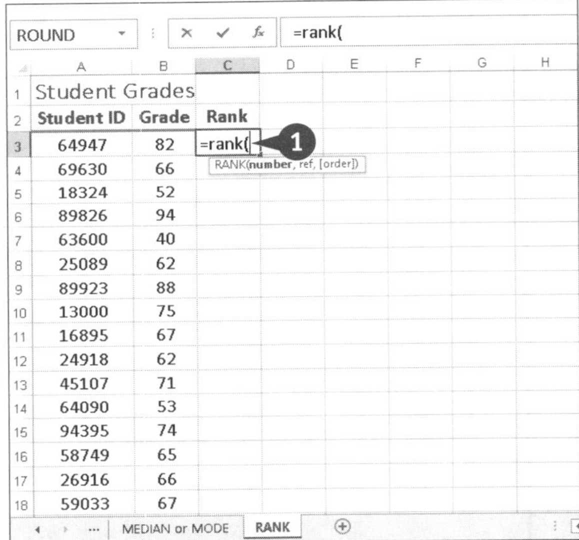

2. Type the item you want to rank.

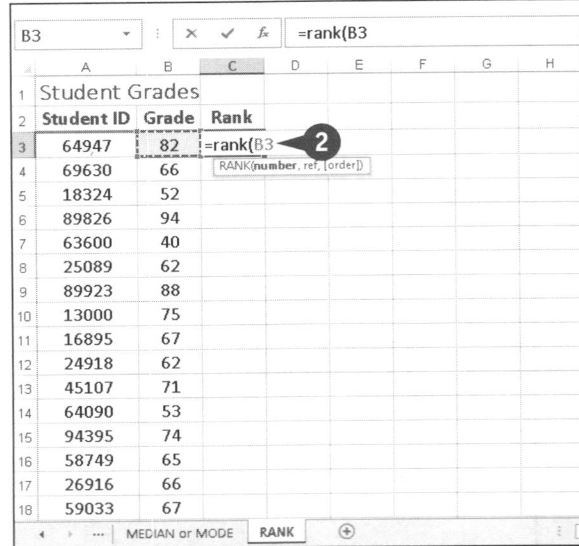

3. Type a comma and then enter the range that holds the list of items.

Note: *As shown here, if you will be filling the calculation into other cells, enter the range address using the absolute reference format.*

4. If you want to rank the item using a descending sort, type a comma and then a non-zero value such as 1 (not shown).

5. Type **)**.

6. Click the Enter button or press Enter.

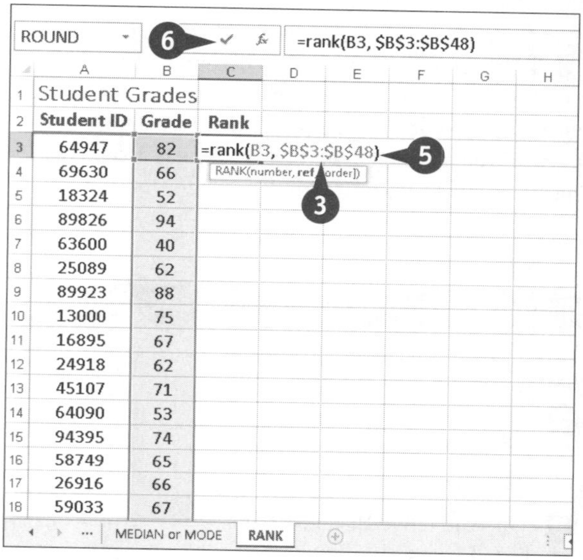

A. Excel calculates the rank.

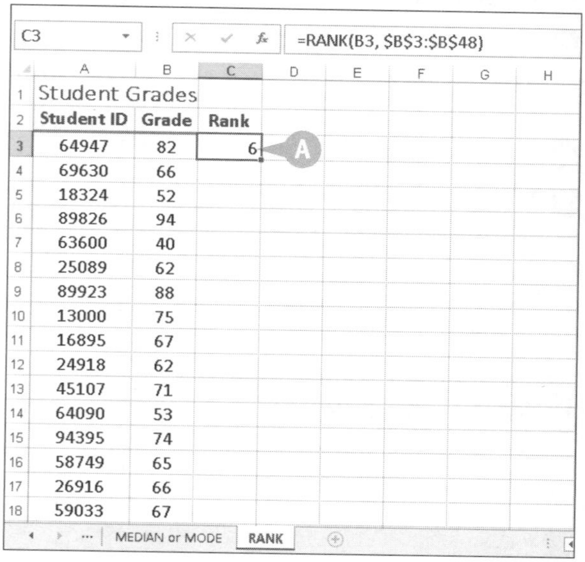

EXTRA

You can also use the RANK.AVG function to calculate the rank. With RANK.AVG, if two or more numbers have the same rank, Excel averages the rank. For example, in the list 100, 95, 90, 85, 85, 80, 70, the RANK.AVG function ranks the number 85 as 4.5, which is the average of 4 and 5. By contrast, RANK.EQ would give both instances of 85 the rank 4. With both RANK.EQ and RANK.AVG, if two or more numbers have the same rank, subsequent numbers are affected. In the preceding list, the number 80 ranks sixth. The RANK.AVG function takes the same three arguments as RANK.EQ: number, ref, and the optional order.

Determine the Nth Largest or Smallest Value

When given a list of values and an item from that list, you can use RANK to determine that item's rank (ascending or descending) within that list. A slightly different approach to this problem is to determine, given a list of values, what item in that list has a specified rank, such as first, third, or tenth.

You could solve this problem by sorting the list, but if the values change constantly, a better approach is to use the Excel LARGE or SMALL function, which returns the *n*th highest or smallest value in a list, respectively. Both functions take two arguments: `array`, the array or range you want to work with, and `k`, the rank order of the value you seek.

Determine the Nth Largest or Smallest Value

Calculate the Nth Highest Value

1. In the cell where you want the *n*th highest value to appear, type **=large(**.
2. Type the range that holds the list of items.
3. Type a comma and then the rank order of the value you want to return.
4. Type **)**.
5. Click the Enter button or press Enter.

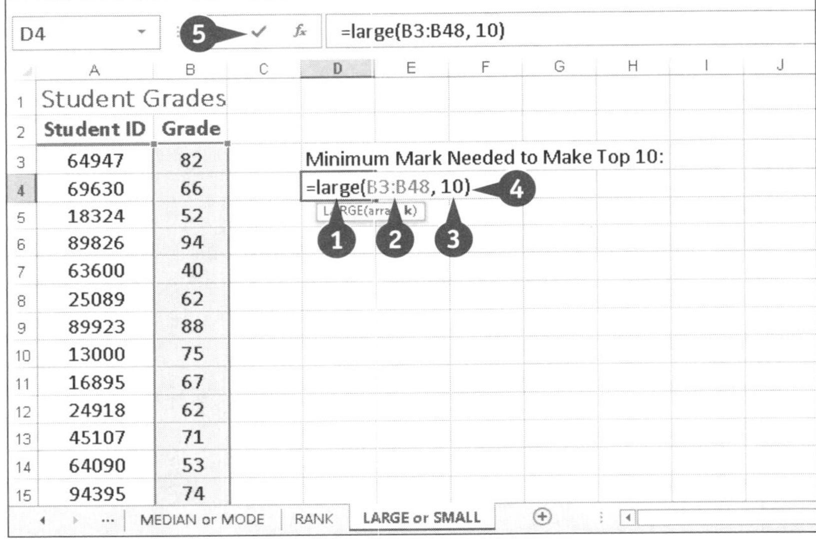

A. Excel returns the value in the list that matches the *n*th highest value.

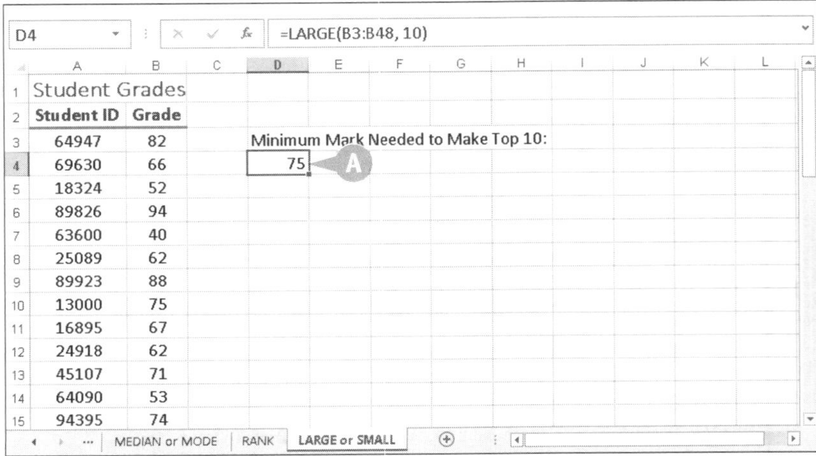

Calculate the Nth Smallest Value

1. In the cell where you want the *n*th smallest value to appear, type **=small(**.
2. Enter the range that holds the list of items.
3. Type a comma and then the rank order of the value you want to return.
4. Type **)**.
5. Click the Enter button or press Enter.

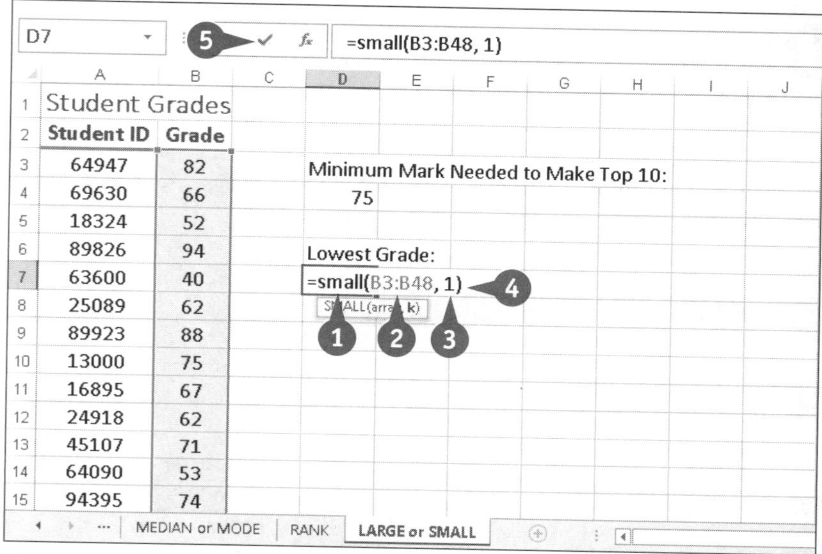

Ⓑ Excel returns the value in the list that matches the *n*th smallest value.

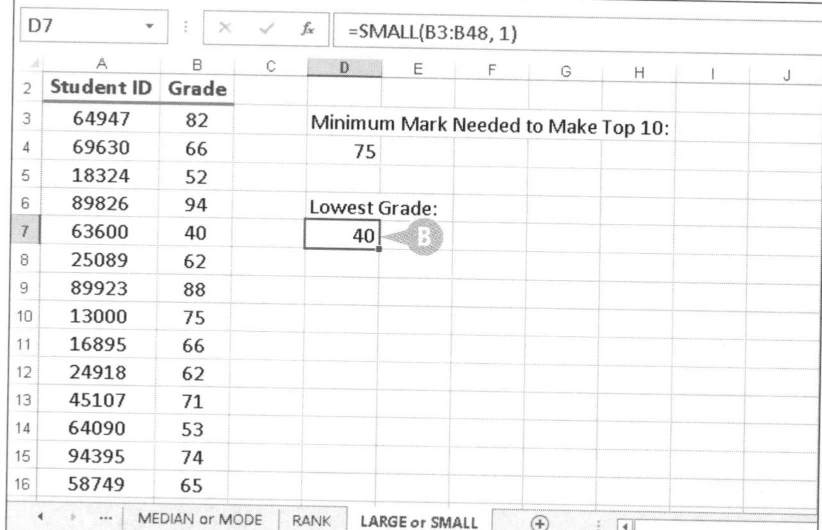

EXTRA

You can use the `PERCENTRANK.INC` function to determine the rank of a value as a percentage of all the values in your data set. `PERCENTRANK.INC` takes three arguments: `array`, the array or range you want to use; `x`, the value you want to rank; and the optional `significance`, the number of significant digits you want your results to return (the default is three). `PERCENTRANK.INC` gives equal values the same rank.

Excel also includes `PERCENTRANK.EXC` to comply with industry standards for calculating the rank of a value as a percentage of all the values in a data set. The `PERCENTRANK.EXC` function takes the same arguments as `PERCENTRANK.INC`, but it excludes the ranks of 0 and 100.

Create a Grouped Frequency Distribution

Organizing a large amount of data into a grouped frequency distribution can help you see patterns within the data. With student test scores, for example, the first group might be scores less than or equal to 50, the second group might be 51 to 60, and so on, up to scores between 91 and 100. You can use the Excel FREQUENCY function to return the number of occurrences in each group.

FREQUENCY takes two arguments: data_array is the list of values you want to group; bins_array is the list of groupings you want to use. You enter FREQUENCY as an array formula into the same number of cells as you have groups. For example, if you have six groups, you enter the formula into six cells.

Create a Grouped Frequency Distribution

1. Select the cells where you want the grouped frequency distribution to appear.
2. Type **=frequency(**.

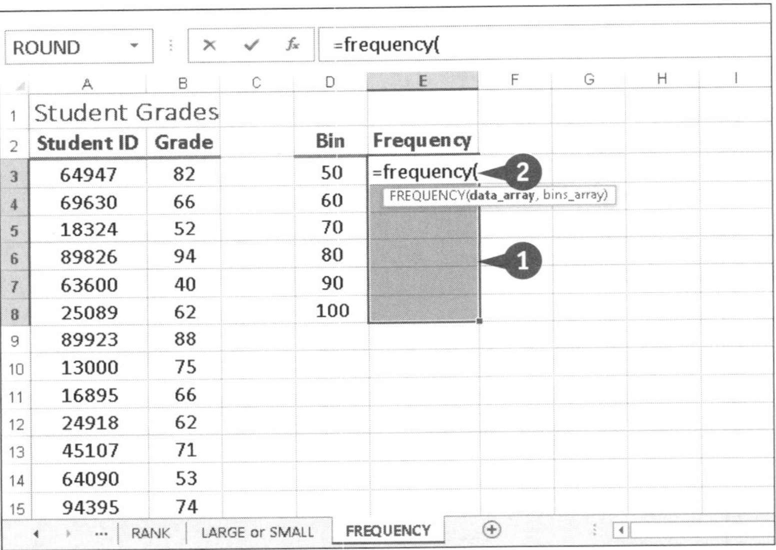

ROUND =frequency(

	A	B	C	D	E
1	Student Grades				
2	Student ID	Grade		Bin	Frequency
3	64947	82		50	=frequency(
4	69630	66		60	
5	18324	52		70	
6	89826	94		80	
7	63600	40		90	
8	25089	62		100	
9	89923	88			
10	13000	75			
11	16895	66			
12	24918	62			
13	45107	71			
14	64090	53			
15	94395	74			

3. Type or select the items you want to group.

ROUND =frequency(B3:B48

	A	B	C	D	E
1	Student Grades				
2	Student ID	Grade		Bin	Frequency
3	64947	82		50	=frequency(B3:B48
4	69630	66		60	
5	18324	52		70	
6	89826	94		80	
7	63600	40		90	
8	25089	62		100	
9	89923	88			
10	13000	75			
11	16895	66			
12	24918	62			
13	45107	71			
14	64090	53			
15	94395	74			

FREQUENCY(data_array, bins_array)

RANK | LARGE or SMALL | FREQUENCY

4. Type a comma and then enter or select the list of groupings.
5. Type).
6. Press and hold Ctrl+Shift and then press Enter or press Ctrl+Shift+Enter.

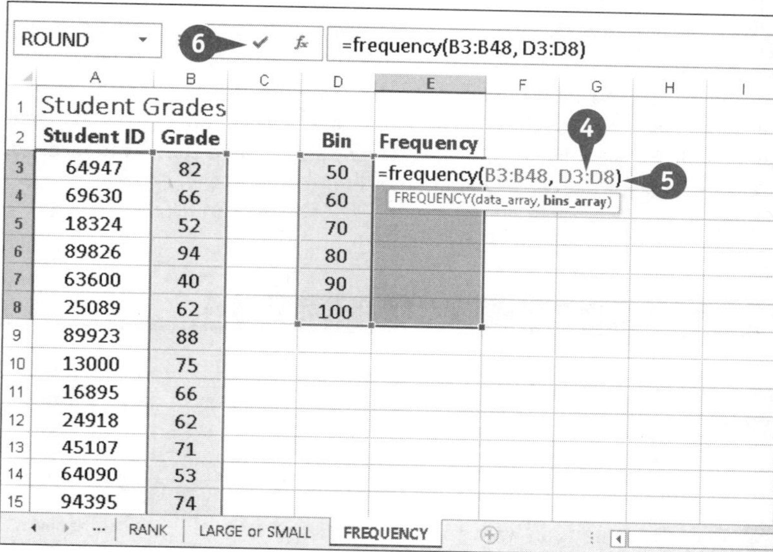

	A	B	C	D	E
1	Student Grades				
2	Student ID	Grade		Bin	Frequency
3	64947	82		50	=frequency(B3:B48, D3:D8)
4	69630	66		60	
5	18324	52		70	
6	89826	94		80	
7	63600	40		90	
8	25089	62		100	
9	89923	88			
10	13000	75			
11	16895	66			
12	24918	62			
13	45107	71			
14	64090	53			
15	94395	74			

A. Excel enters the array formula and returns the number of items in each grouping.

E3 {=FREQUENCY(B3:B48, D3:D8)}

	A	B	C	D	E
1	Student Grades				
2	Student ID	Grade		Bin	Frequency
3	64947	82		50	2
4	69630	66		60	4
5	18324	52		70	19
6	89826	94		80	15
7	63600	40		90	5
8	25089	62		100	1
9	89923	88			
10	13000	75			
11	16895	66			
12	24918	62			
13	45107	71			
14	64090	53			
15	94395	74			

A

RANK | LARGE or SMALL | FREQUENCY

EXTRA

When you create your frequency distribution, keep the number of groups reasonable: between five and ten is good. If you have too few or too many groups, you can lose your ability to convey information easily. Too few intervals can hide trends and too many intervals can mask details. You should also keep your intervals simple. Intervals of 5, 10, or 20 are good because they are easy to understand. Start your interval with a value that is divisible by the interval size, which will make your frequency distribution easy to read. Finally, all intervals should have the same number of values. Again, this makes your frequency distribution easy to understand.

Part of your analysis might involve determining how, on average, some values deviate from the mean. One method is to take the difference each number varies from the mean, square those differences, sum those squares, and then divide by the number of values. The result is called the *variance*, and in Excel, you calculate it using `VAR.P`:

```
VAR.P(number1[, number2, ...])
```

You can enter up to 255 arguments. However, because the variance is a squared value, it is difficult to interpret relative to the mean. Therefore, statisticians often calculate the *standard deviation*, which is the square root of the variance. You can use `STDEV.P`, which has the same syntax as `VAR.P`.

Calculate the Variance and Standard Deviation

Calculate the Variance

1. In the cell where you want the variance to appear, type **=var.p(**.
2. Type the values you want to use, separated by commas.
3. Type **)**.
4. Click the Enter button or press Enter.

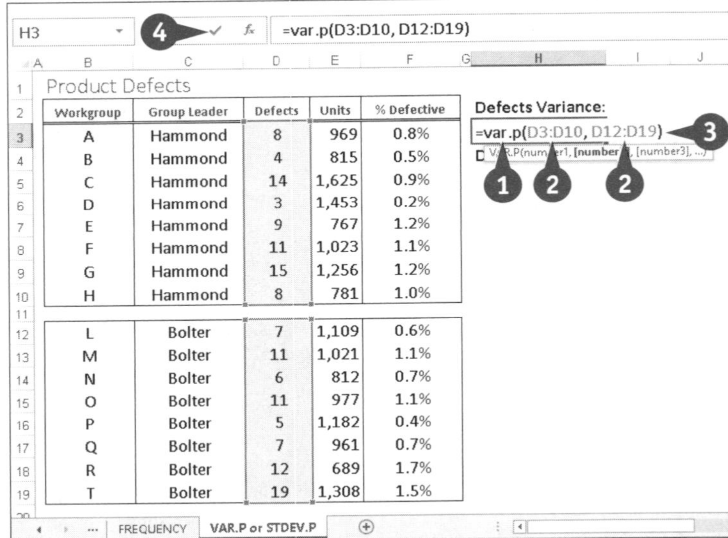

A Excel returns the variance of the data set.

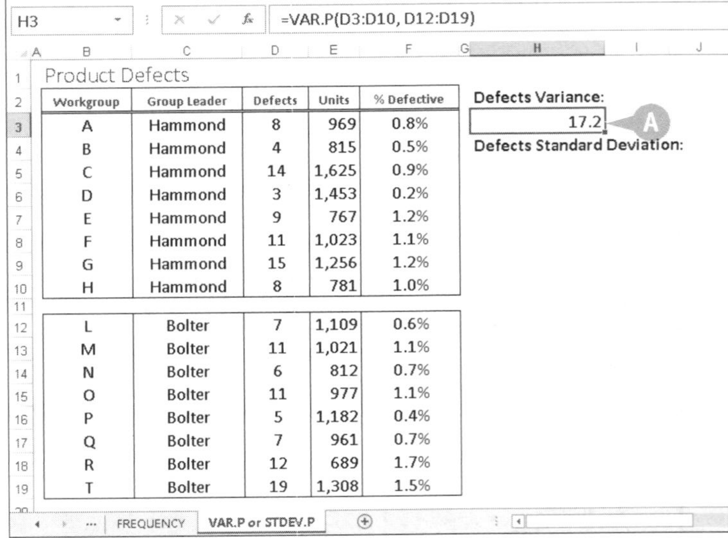

Calculate the Standard Deviation

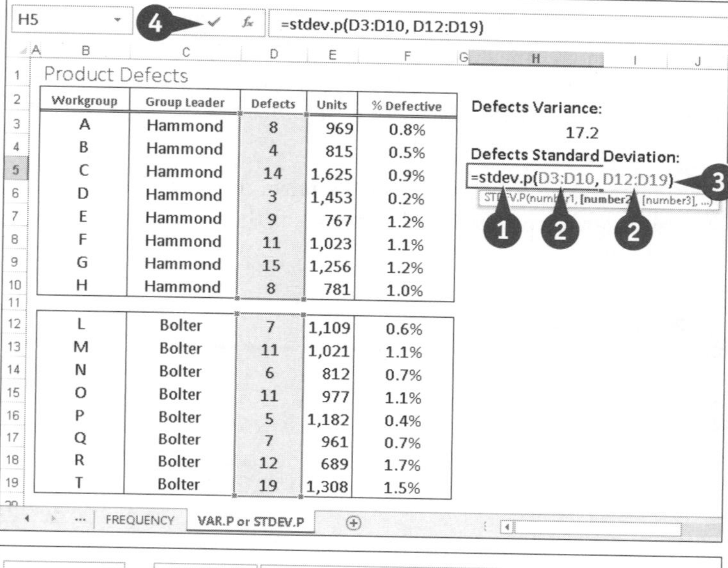

1. In the cell where you want the standard deviation to appear, type **=stdev.p(**.
2. Type the values you want to use, separated by commas.
3. Type **)**.
4. Click the Enter button or press Enter.

B. Excel returns the standard deviation of the data set.

H5 | =STDEV.P(D3:D10, D12:D19)

Product Defects

Workgroup	Group Leader	Defects	Units	% Defective
A	Hammond	8	969	0.8%
B	Hammond	4	815	0.5%
C	Hammond	14	1,625	0.9%
D	Hammond	3	1,453	0.2%
E	Hammond	9	767	1.2%
F	Hammond	11	1,023	1.1%
G	Hammond	15	1,256	1.2%
H	Hammond	8	781	1.0%
L	Bolter	7	1,109	0.6%
M	Bolter	11	1,021	1.1%
N	Bolter	6	812	0.7%
O	Bolter	11	977	1.1%
P	Bolter	5	1,182	0.4%
Q	Bolter	7	961	0.7%
R	Bolter	12	689	1.7%
T	Bolter	19	1,308	1.5%

Defects Variance: 17.2

Defects Standard Deviation: 4.2 (B)

FREQUENCY | VAR.P or STDEV.P

EXTRA

When finding standard deviation, use `STDEV.P` when your data set represents the entire population; use `STDEV.S` for a sample of the population. The relation of the values to each other in the data set affects the standard deviation. For example, a single outlier can distort the standard deviation, and a data set consisting of identical values gives you a standard deviation of zero. If two data sets have a similar mean, the set with a higher standard deviation has more data that are variable. If your data is distributed normally, about 68 percent of the data is found within one standard deviation of the mean; about 95 percent is within two standard deviations; and about 99 percent is within three standard deviations.

Find the Correlation

Correlation is a measure of the relationship between two sets of data. For example, if you have monthly figures for advertising expenses and sales, you might wonder whether higher advertising expenses lead to more sales, that is, whether they are related.

Keep in mind that a correlation does not prove that one thing causes another. The most you can say is that one number varies with the other.

To find a correlation in Excel, you use the `CORREL` function, which takes two arguments: `array1` and `array2`, which are two lists of numbers. `CORREL` returns the *correlation coefficient*, which is a number between −1 and 1 that has the properties outlined in the table at the end of this section.

Find the Correlation

1. In the cell where you want the correlation to appear, type **=correl(**.

ROUND | =correl(

Correlation Between Advertising and Sales

		Advertising	Sales		
Fiscal	1st Quarter	512,450	8,123,965	Correlation:	=correl(
2011	2nd Quarter	447,840	7,750,500		
	3rd Quarter	500,125	7,860,405		
	4th Quarter	515,600	8,005,800		
Fiscal	1st Quarter	482,754	8,136,444		
2012	2nd Quarter	485,750	7,950,426		
	3rd Quarter	460,890	7,875,500		
	4th Quarter	490,400	7,952,600		
Fiscal	1st Quarter	510,230	8,100,145		
2013	2nd Quarter	515,471	8,034,125		
	3rd Quarter	525,850	8,350,450		
	4th Quarter	520,365	8,100,520		

CORREL(array1, array2)

FREQUENCY | VAR.P or STDEV.P | CORREL

2. Type the range of the first list of values.

3. Type a comma and then enter the range of the second list of values.

Note: *You can select a list of subsets, but make sure the same subset is selected for each list.*

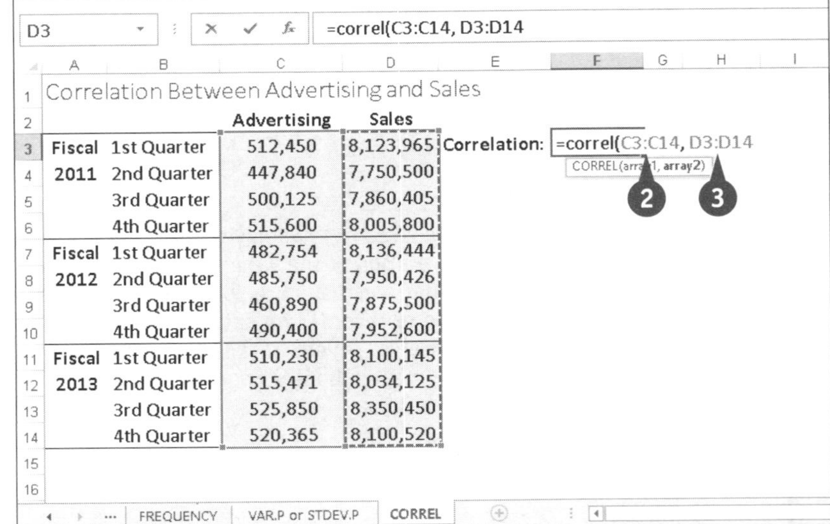

D3 | =correl(C3:C14, D3:D14

Correlation Between Advertising and Sales

		Advertising	Sales		
Fiscal	1st Quarter	512,450	8,123,965	Correlation:	=correl(C3:C14, D3:D14
2011	2nd Quarter	447,840	7,750,500		
	3rd Quarter	500,125	7,860,405		
	4th Quarter	515,600	8,005,800		
Fiscal	1st Quarter	482,754	8,136,444		
2012	2nd Quarter	485,750	7,950,426		
	3rd Quarter	460,890	7,875,500		
	4th Quarter	490,400	7,952,600		
Fiscal	1st Quarter	510,230	8,100,145		
2013	2nd Quarter	515,471	8,034,125		
	3rd Quarter	525,850	8,350,450		
	4th Quarter	520,365	8,100,520		

CORREL(array1, array2)

FREQUENCY | VAR.P or STDEV.P | CORREL

4. Type **)**.
5. Click the Enter button or press Enter.

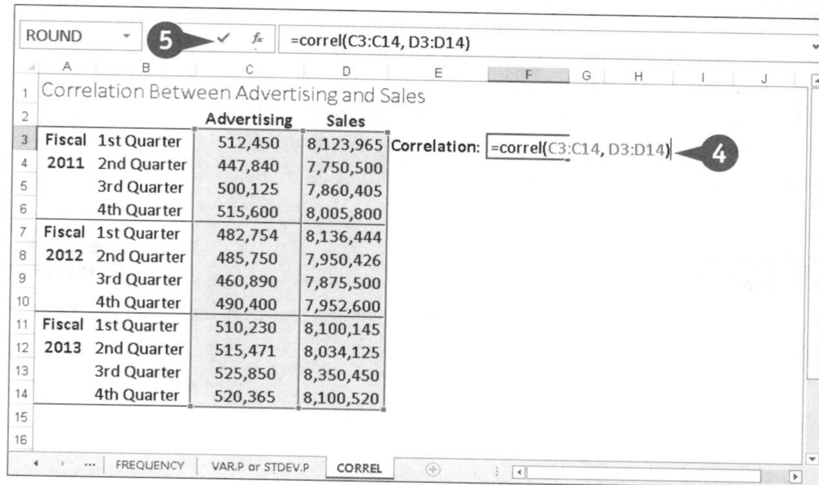

Ⓐ Excel calculates the correlation.

Note: *The sign suggests whether the relationship is positive (+) or negative (–). See the following table to help interpret the result.*

F3 =CORREL(C3:C14, D3:D14)

Correlation Between Advertising and Sales

		Advertising	Sales		
Fiscal	1st Quarter	512,450	8,123,965	Correlation:	0.74
2011	2nd Quarter	447,840	7,750,500		
	3rd Quarter	500,125	7,860,405		
	4th Quarter	515,600	8,005,800		
Fiscal	1st Quarter	482,754	8,136,444		
2012	2nd Quarter	485,750	7,950,426		
	3rd Quarter	460,890	7,875,500		
	4th Quarter	490,400	7,952,600		
Fiscal	1st Quarter	510,230	8,100,145		
2013	2nd Quarter	515,471	8,034,125		
	3rd Quarter	525,850	8,350,450		
	4th Quarter	520,365	8,100,520		

APPLY IT

You can use the following table to help you interpret the correlation result:

Correlation Coefficient	Interpretation
1	The data sets are perfectly and positively correlated. For example, a 10-percent increase in advertising produces a 10-percent increase in sales.
Between 0 and 1	The data sets are positively correlated. The higher the number is, the higher the correlation is between the data.
0	There is no correlation between the data.
Between 0 and –1	The data sets are negatively correlated. The lower the number is, the more negatively correlated the data is.
–1	The data sets have a perfect negative correlation. For example, a 10-percent increase in advertising leads to a 10-percent decrease in sales.

Understanding Tables

In Excel, a *table* is a rectangular range of cells used to store data; it includes special tools for entering, editing, and analyzing that data. A table is designed to store collections of related information. For example, one table might store business data such as customers, invoices, and inventory, whereas another might store personal data such as contacts, movies, and household items. You can use Excel tables to create, retrieve, and manage large or small collections of information. To get the most out of Excel tables, you need to understand a few basic concepts, such as how a table is like a database, the advantages of tables, and how tables help with data analysis.

A Table Is a Database

Microsoft Access is a powerful database management tool that lets you work with large, complex databases. If your needs are simpler, you can use a table as a database where the data is organized into columns and rows. In this case, each column is the equivalent of a database field, which is a single type of information, such as a name, address, or phone number, and each row is the equivalent of a database record, which is a collection of associated field values, such as the information for a specific contact.

Data Analysis

Tables are also useful tools for analyzing your data. For example, you can easily use a table as the basis of a PivotTable, which is a powerful tool for summarizing and analyzing data. Tables also offer a number of useful data analysis techniques. For example, you can to sort the table data, both on a single field and on multiple fields. You can also make the table data easier to manage by filtering the data to show only the subset of records you want to work with.

Advantages of a Table

Because a table is a collection of rows and columns on a worksheet, it looks very much like a regular Excel range. However, a table is actually a special type of range because Excel makes available with the table a set of tools that makes it easier to work with the data in the table. These tools allow you to convert existing worksheet data into a table, select the rows and fields you want to work with, add new records and fields to the table, delete existing records and fields, and insert rows to show totals.

Table Considerations

Before creating your tables, you should spend some time thinking about what type of data each table should contain. This involves thinking about what purpose your tables will serve, which fields you will need in each table, and how you will differentiate between each record in the table. Each table should have a single, well-defined purpose. For example, a table may store customer contact information, product inventory, or personnel records. Combining multiple purposes in a single table results in needless duplication and increases the chance of data-entry error. If you think that you may need to sort or filter by a certain type of information, make it a separate field. Finally, it is usually a good idea to have at least one field that is unique to each record to differentiate between them.

Although a table looks much like a regular Excel range, it offers a number of features that differentiate it from a range and enable you to manipulate and analyze the table data. To understand these differences and make it as easy as possible to learn how to build and use tables for your data analysis needs, you need to know the various features that are available in a typical table, such as the table tools, the table rows and columns, the table cells, the table headers, and the filter buttons.

Explore Table Features

A Table Column

A single type of information, such as names, addresses, or phone numbers. In an Excel table, each column is the equivalent of a database field.

B Table Tools

A contextual tab that appears when you select any cell within a table. The Design tab contains most of the table-related commands, options, and features in Excel.

C Column Headers

The unique names you assign to every table column that serve to label the type of data in each column. These names are always found in the first row of the table.

D Table Cell

An item in a table column that represents a single instance of that column's data, such as a name, address, or phone number. In an Excel table, each cell is equivalent to a database field value.

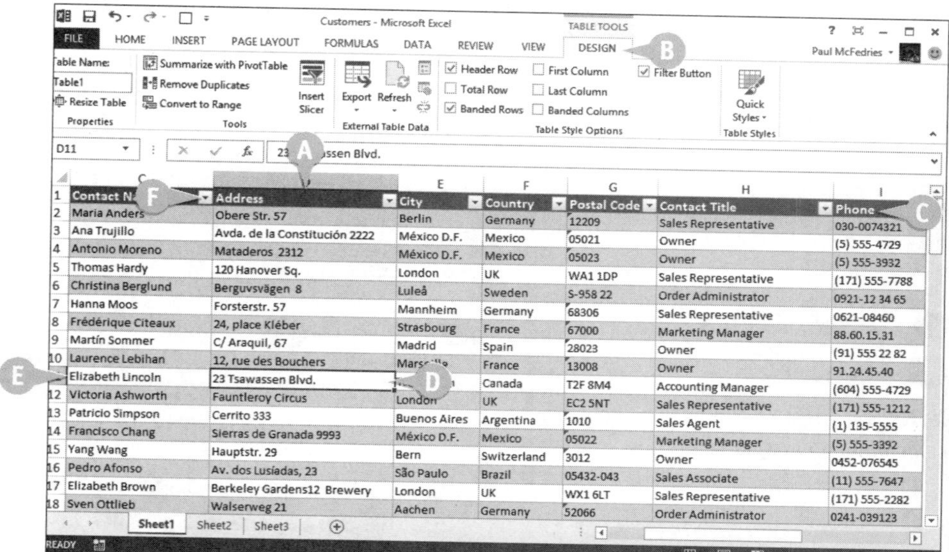

E Table Row

A collection of associated table cells, such as the data for a single contact. In Excel tables, each row is the equivalent of a database record.

F Column Filter Button

A feature that gives you access to a set of commands that perform various actions on a column, such as sorting or filtering the column data.

Convert a Range to a Table

In Excel 2013, you cannot create a table from scratch and then fill that table with data. Instead, you must first create a range that includes at least some of the data you want in your table and then convert that range to a table.

Note that you do not need to enter all of your data before converting the range to a table. Once you have the table, you can add new rows and columns as needed. However, it is best to decide first whether you want your table to have column headers and, if so, to add those headers before converting the range to a table.

Convert a Range to a Table

1. Click a cell within the range that you want to convert to a table.

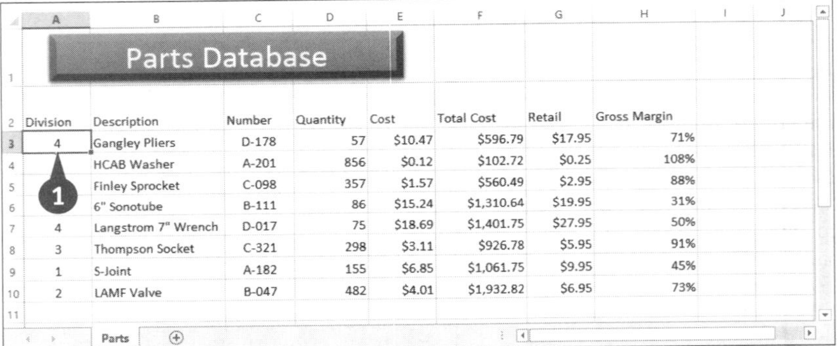

Division	Description	Number	Quantity	Cost	Total Cost	Retail	Gross Margin
4	Gangley Pliers	D-178	57	$10.47	$596.79	$17.95	71%
	HCAB Washer	A-201	856	$0.12	$102.72	$0.25	108%
	Finley Sprocket	C-098	357	$1.57	$560.49	$2.95	88%
	6" Sonotube	B-111	86	$15.24	$1,310.64	$19.95	31%
4	Langstrom 7" Wrench	D-017	75	$18.69	$1,401.75	$27.95	50%
3	Thompson Socket	C-321	298	$3.11	$926.78	$5.95	91%
1	S-Joint	A-182	155	$6.85	$1,061.75	$9.95	45%
2	LAMF Valve	B-047	482	$4.01	$1,932.82	$6.95	73%

2. Click the Insert tab.
3. Click Table.

Note: *You can also choose the Table command by pressing Ctrl+T.*

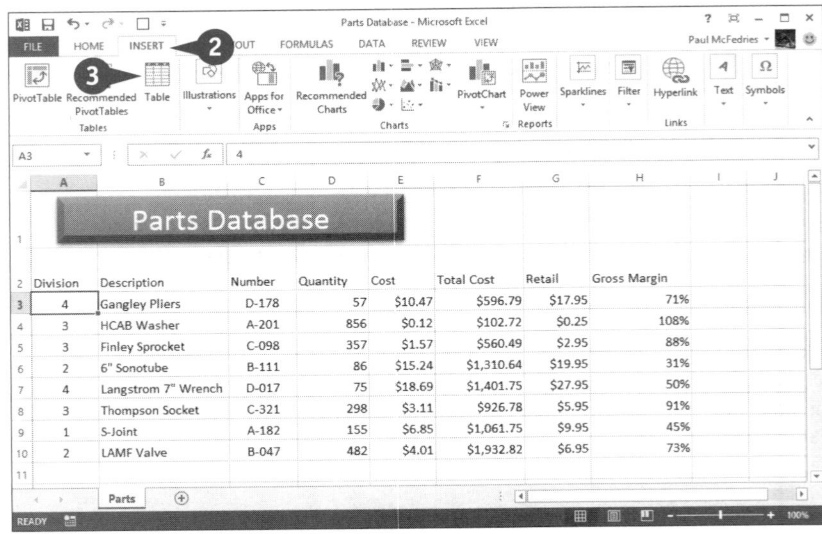

Division	Description	Number	Quantity	Cost	Total Cost	Retail	Gross Margin
4	Gangley Pliers	D-178	57	$10.47	$596.79	$17.95	71%
3	HCAB Washer	A-201	856	$0.12	$102.72	$0.25	108%
3	Finley Sprocket	C-098	357	$1.57	$560.49	$2.95	88%
2	6" Sonotube	B-111	86	$15.24	$1,310.64	$19.95	31%
4	Langstrom 7" Wrench	D-017	75	$18.69	$1,401.75	$27.95	50%
3	Thompson Socket	C-321	298	$3.11	$926.78	$5.95	91%
1	S-Joint	A-182	155	$6.85	$1,061.75	$9.95	45%
2	LAMF Valve	B-047	482	$4.01	$1,932.82	$6.95	73%

The Create Table dialog box appears.

A Excel selects the range that it will convert to a table.

B If you want to change the range, click inside the range box and then drag the mouse over the new range.

4 If your range has labels that you want to use as column headers, click to select the My Table Has Headers check box.

5 Click OK.

Excel converts the range to a table.

C Excel applies a table format to the range.

D The Table Tools contextual tab appears.

E Filter buttons appear in each column heading.

6 Click the Design tab to see the Excel table design tools.

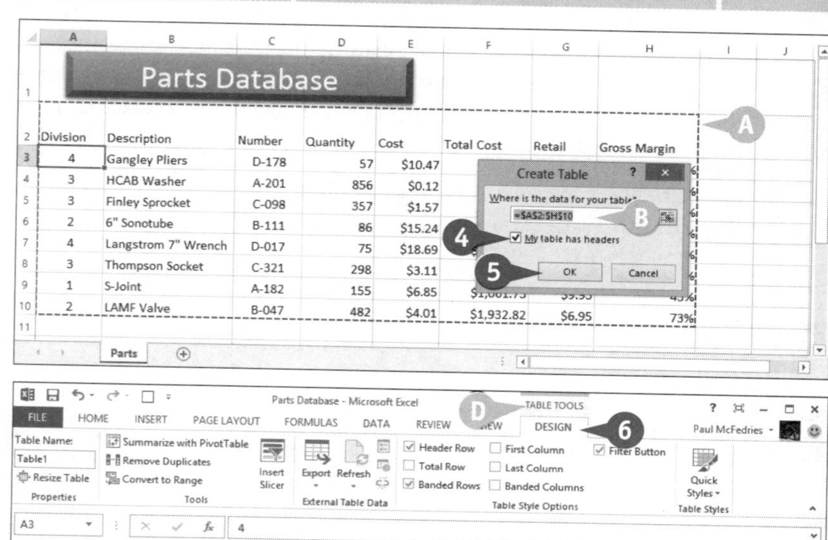

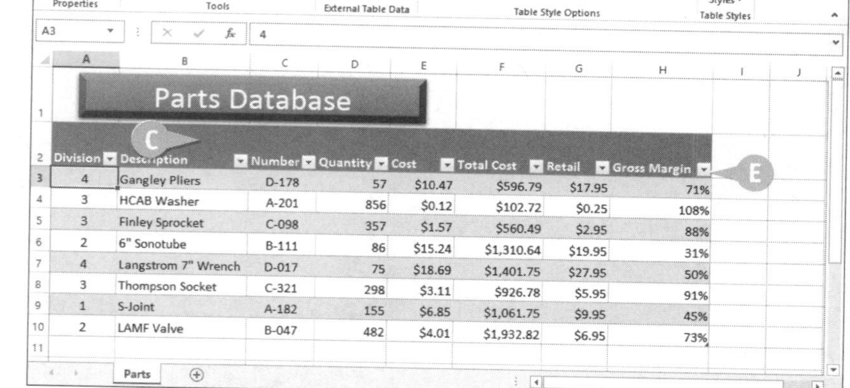

APPLY IT

If your range does not have column headers, follow steps 1 to 3 to display the Create Table dialog box, and then click to deselect the My Table Has Headers check box (☑ changes to ☐). After you click OK, Excel converts the range to a table and automatically adds headers to each column. These headers use the generic names Column1, Column2, and so on.

To redefine the range used in the table, first select any cell in the table. Under the Table Tools contextual tab, click the Design tab and then click Resize Table (⊞) to open the Resize Table dialog box. Drag the mouse ✚ over the new range and then click OK.

If you want to work with part of a table, you first need to select that part of the table. For example, if you want to apply a format to an entire column or copy an entire row, you first need to select that column or row.

The normal range-selection techniques in Excel often do not work well with a table. For example, selecting an entire worksheet column or row does not work because a table does not use up an entire worksheet column or row. Instead, Excel provides several tools for selecting a table column (just the data or the data and the header), a table row, or the entire table.

Select Table Data

Select a Table Column

1. Click any cell in the column you want to select.
2. Right-click the selected cell.
3. Click Select.
4. Click Table Column Data.

Excel selects all the column's data cells.

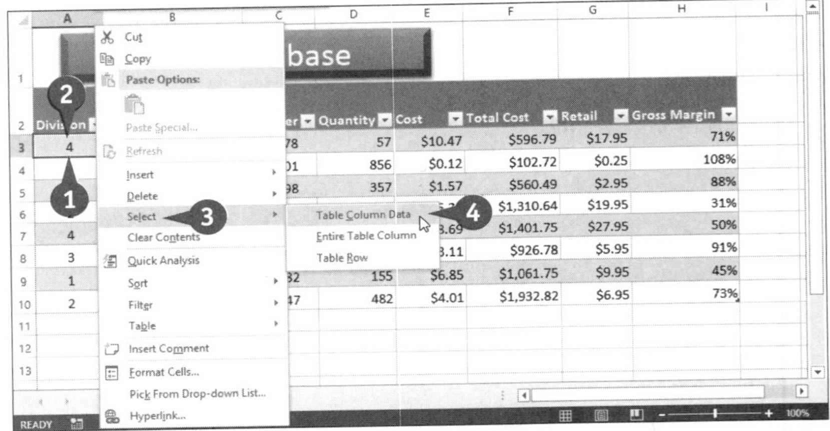

Select a Table Column and Header

1. Click any cell in the column you want to select.
2. Right-click the selected cell.
3. Click Select.
4. Click Entire Table Column.

Excel selects the column's data and header.

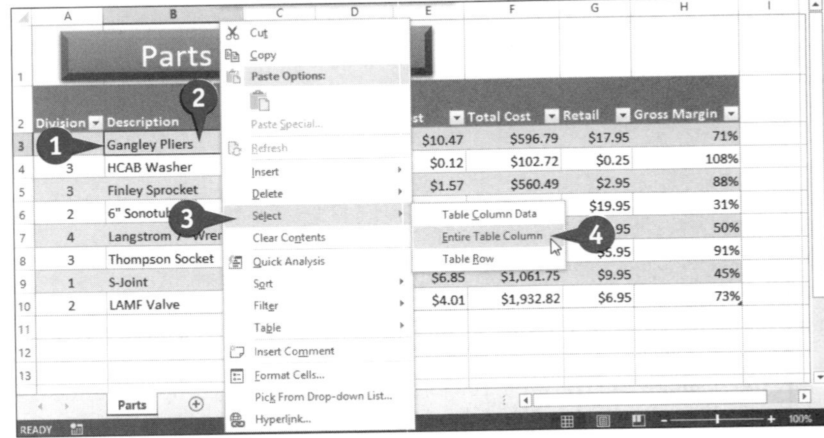

Select a Table Row

1. Click any cell in the row you want to select.
2. Right-click the selected cell.
3. Click Select.
4. Click Table Row.

Excel selects all the data within the row.

Select the Entire Table

1. Click any cell within the table.
2. Press Ctrl+A.

Excel selects the entire table.

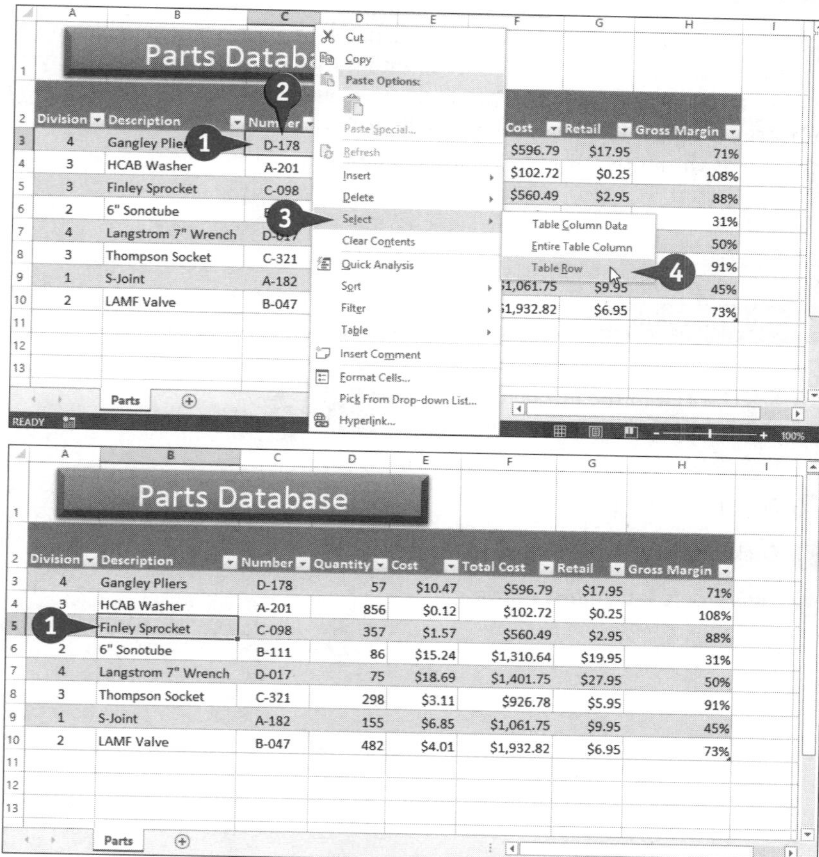

APPLY IT

To select multiple table columns, first select one cell in each of the columns you want to select. If the columns are not adjacent, click the first cell, press and hold Ctrl, and then click each of the other cells. Right-click any selected cell, click Select, and then click Table Column Data (or Entire Table Column if you also want to include the column headers in the selection).

To select multiple table rows, first select one cell in each of the rows you want to select. Again, if the rows are not adjacent, click the first cell and then press and hold Ctrl as you click each of the other cells. Right-click any selected cell, click Select, and then click Table Row.

Insert a Table Row

You can add a new record to an Excel table by inserting it as a new row. You can insert a row either within the table or at the end of the table. After you have entered the initial set of data into your table, you will likely add most new records within the table by inserting a new row above a current row. However, when you are in the initial data entry phase, you will most likely prefer to add new records by adding a row to the end of the table.

Insert a Table Row

1. Select a cell in the row below which you want to insert the new row.
2. Click the Home tab.
3. Click Insert.
4. Click Insert Table Rows Above.

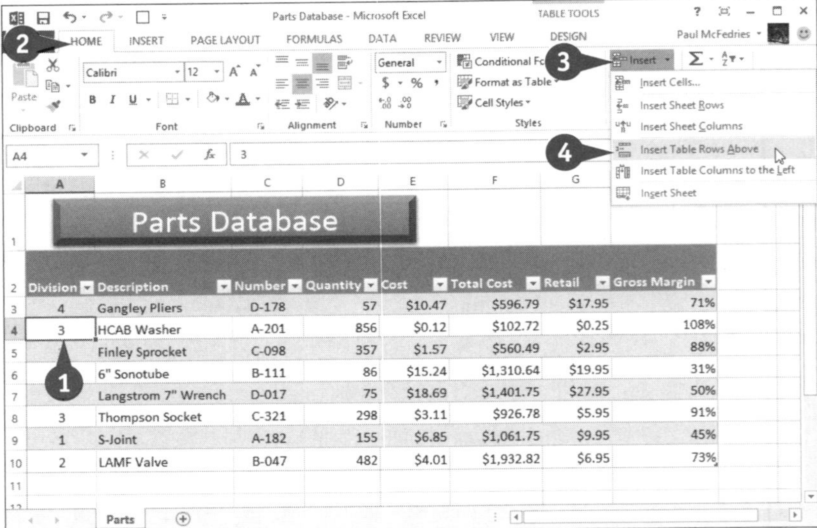

- A Excel inserts the new row.
- B To insert a new row at the end of the table, select the lower-right table cell and then press Tab.

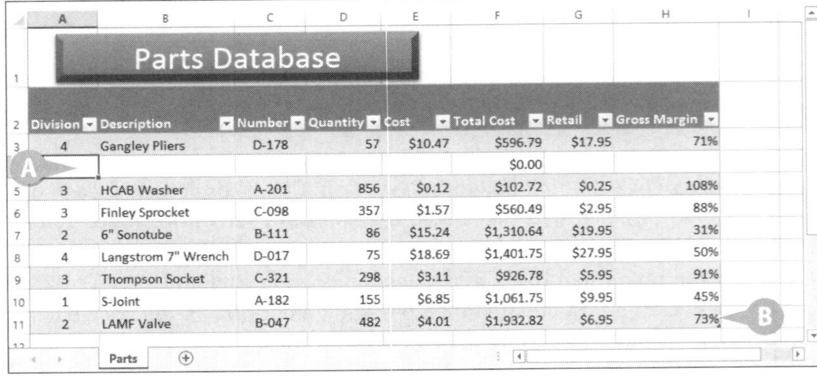

You can add a new field to your Excel table by inserting a new column. You can insert a column either within the table or at the end of the table. To make data entry easier and more efficient, you should decide in advance all the fields you want to include in the table. However, if you later realize you forgot a particular field, you can still add it to the table. Inserting a table column is also useful if you imported or inherited the data from elsewhere and you see that the data is missing a field that you require.

Insert a Table Column

1. Select a cell in the column to the left of which you want to insert the new column.

   A. If you want to insert the new column at end of the table, select a cell in the last table column.

2. Click the Home tab.
3. Click Insert.
4. Click Insert Table Columns to the Left.

   To insert a column at the end of the table instead, click Insert Table Columns to the Right (not shown).

   B. Excel inserts the new column.

5. Name the new field by editing the column header.

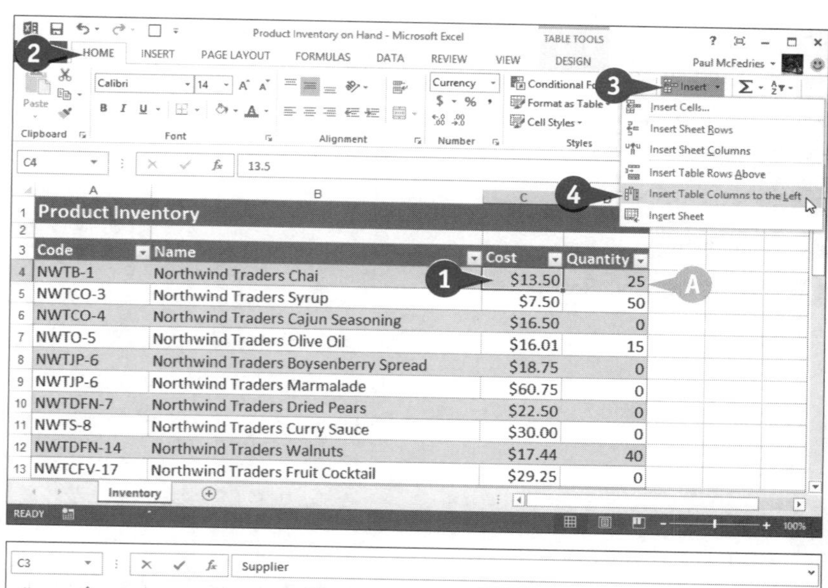

C3 Supplier

Product Inventory

Code	Name	Supplier		Quan
NWTB-1	Northwind Traders Chai		$13.50	25
NWTCO-3	Northwind Traders Syrup		$7.50	50
NWTCO-4	Northwind Traders Cajun Seasoning		$16.50	0
NWTO-5	Northwind Traders Olive Oil		$16.01	15
NWTJP-6	Northwind Traders Boysenberry Spread		$18.75	0
NWTJP-6	Northwind Traders Marmalade		$60.75	0
NWTDFN-7	Northwind Traders Dried Pears		$22.50	0
NWTS-8	Northwind Traders Curry Sauce		$30.00	0
NWTDFN-14	Northwind Traders Walnuts		$17.44	40
NWTCFV-17	Northwind Traders Fruit Cocktail		$29.25	0

Inventory

5

B

Delete a Table Row

If your table contains a record that includes inaccurate, outdated, or unnecessary data, you should delete that row to preserve your table's data integrity. An Excel table is a repository of data that you can use as a reference source or to analyze or summarize the data. However, when you use the table, it is only as beneficial as its data is accurate. You should take extra care to ensure the data you enter is correct. If you find that an entire record is inaccurate, out of date, or no longer needed, Excel enables you to delete that row quickly.

Delete a Table Row

1. Select a cell in the row you want to delete.

Note: *To delete multiple rows, select a cell in each row you want to delete.*

2. Click the Home tab.
3. Click Delete.
4. Click Delete Table Rows.

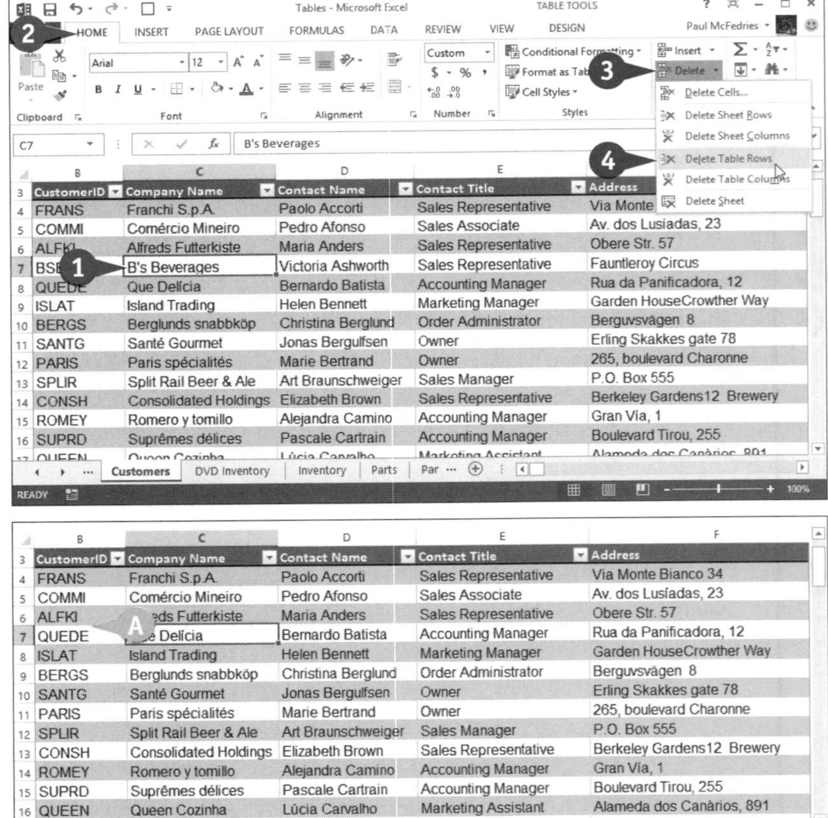

Ⓐ Excel deletes the row.

If your table contains a field that you do not require, you should delete that column to make your table easier to work with, navigate, and analyze. You analyze and summarize your table information based on the data in one or more fields. For example, you use the items in one or more table fields to sort and filter the table data. If your table contains a field that you never look at and that you never use for analysis or summaries, consider deleting that column to reduce table clutter and make your table easier to navigate.

Delete a Table Column

1. Select a cell in the column you want to delete.

Note: *To delete multiple columns, select a cell in each column you want to delete.*

2. Click the Home tab.
3. Click Delete.
4. Click Delete Table Columns.

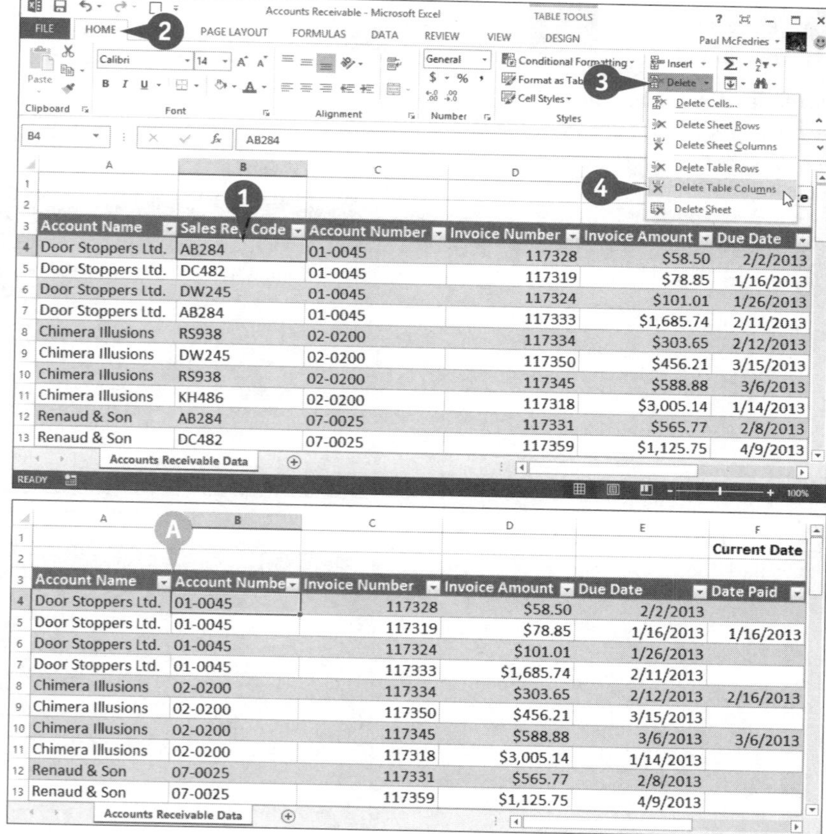

Ⓐ Excel deletes the column.

Add a Column Subtotal

To get your table analysis tasks started, note that you can get more out of your table data by summarizing a field with a subtotal that appears at the bottom of the column.

Although the word *subtotal* implies that you are summing the numeric values in a column, Excel uses the term more broadly. That is, a subtotal can be not only a numeric sum, but also an average, a maximum or minimum, or a count of the values in the field. You can also choose more advanced subtotals, such as the standard deviation or the variance.

Add a Column Subtotal

1. Select all the data in the column you want to total.

Note: *See the "Select Table Data" section earlier in the chapter to learn how to select column data.*

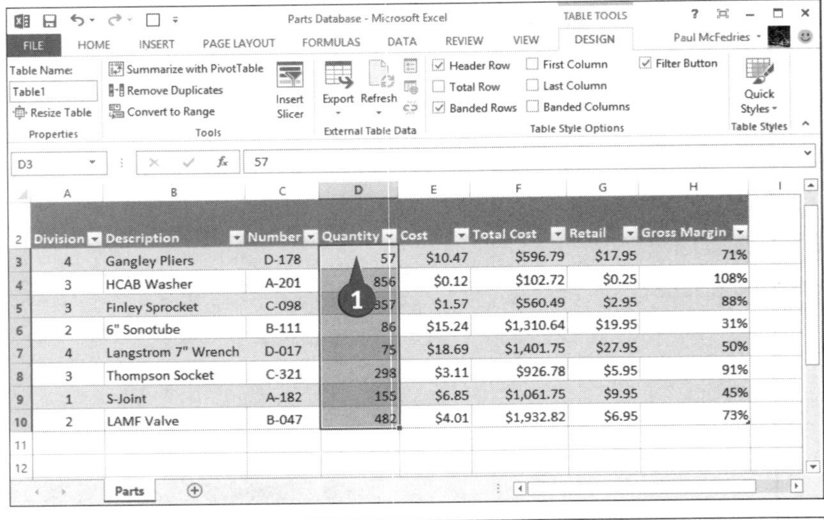

2. Click the Quick Analysis smart tag.

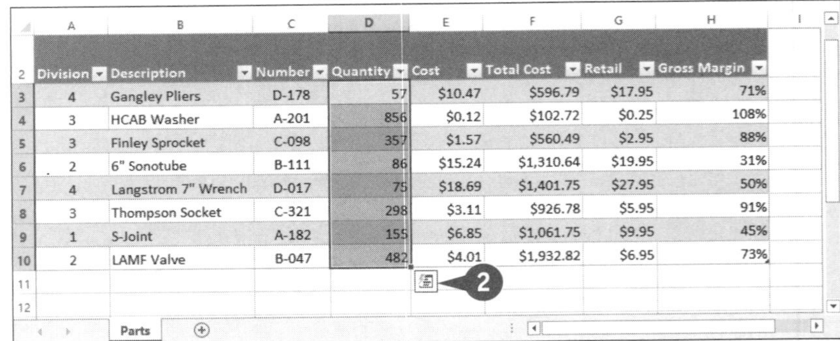

The Quick Analysis options appear.

3. Click Totals.

4. Click the type of calculation you want to use.

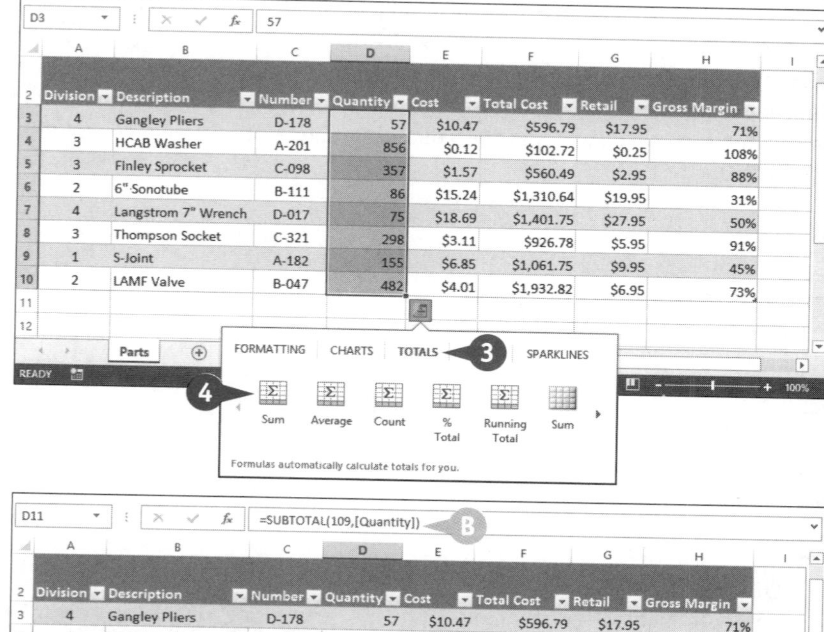

Division	Description	Number	Quantity	Cost	Total Cost	Retail	Gross Margin
4	Gangley Pliers	D-178	57	$10.47	$596.79	$17.95	71%
3	HCAB Washer	A-201	856	$0.12	$102.72	$0.25	108%
3	Finley Sprocket	C-098	357	$1.57	$560.49	$2.95	88%
2	6" Sonotube	B-111	86	$15.24	$1,310.64	$19.95	31%
4	Langstrom 7" Wrench	D-017	75	$18.69	$1,401.75	$27.95	50%
3	Thompson Socket	C-321	298	$3.11	$926.78	$5.95	91%
1	S-Joint	A-182	155	$6.85	$1,061.75	$9.95	45%
2	LAMF Valve	B-047	482	$4.01	$1,932.82	$6.95	73%

A. Excel adds a Total row to the bottom of the table.

B. Excel inserts a SUBTOTAL function to perform the calculation you chose in step 4.

C. Click the cell's down arrow and select a different type of subtotal from the drop-down list.

D11 =SUBTOTAL(109,[Quantity]) (B)

Division	Description	Number	Quantity	Cost	Total Cost	Retail	Gross Margin
4	Gangley Pliers	D-178	57	$10.47	$596.79	$17.95	71%
3	HCAB Washer	A-201	856	$0.12	$102.72	$0.25	108%
3	Finley Sprocket	C-098	357	$1.57	$560.49	$2.95	88%
2	6" Sonotube	B-111	86	$15.24	$1,310.64	$19.95	31%
4	Langstrom 7" Wrench	D-017	75	$18.69	$1,401.75	$27.95	50%
3	Thompson Socket	C-321	298	$3.11	$926.78	$5.95	91%
1	S-Joint	A-182	155	$6.85	$1,061.75	$9.95	45%
2	LAMF Valve	B-047	482	$4.01	$1,932.82	$6.95	73%
		(A)	2366 (C)				

Parts

EXTRA

If the column you want to total is the last column in the table, you can add the total row and include a SUBTOTAL function for that column with just a few mouse clicks. Click any cell within the table. Click the Design tab and then click to select the Total Row check box (☐ changes to ☑). Excel automatically inserts a row named Total at the bottom of the table. Excel also adds a SUBTOTAL function below the last column. Click the cell's down arrow and then click the type of subtotal you want to use from the drop-down list.

Perform a Simple Sort or Filter

You can make a range easier to analyze by *sorting* it based on a column's values. You can sort the data using either an ascending sort, which arranges the values alphabetically from A to Z or numerically from 0 to 9, or a descending sort, which arranges the values from Z to A or from 9 to 0.

You can also analyze data by *filtering* it to show only the items you want to work with. The easiest way to filter a range is to use the Filter buttons, each of which presents you with a list of check boxes for each unique value in a column. You filter the data by activating the check boxes for the items you want to see.

Perform a Simple Sort or Filter

Sort a List

1. Click a cell in the column you want to sort.
2. Click the Data tab.
3. Click a sort direction.

A. Click Sort A to Z to sort from lowest to highest — ascending order.

B. Click Sort Z to A to sort from highest to lowest — descending order.

C. Excel sorts your list by the column you selected.

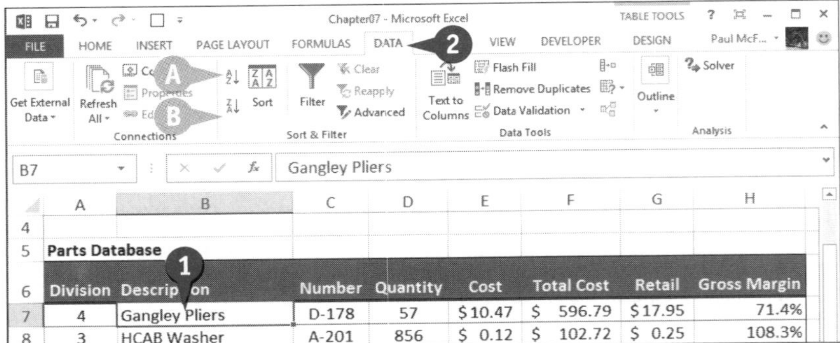

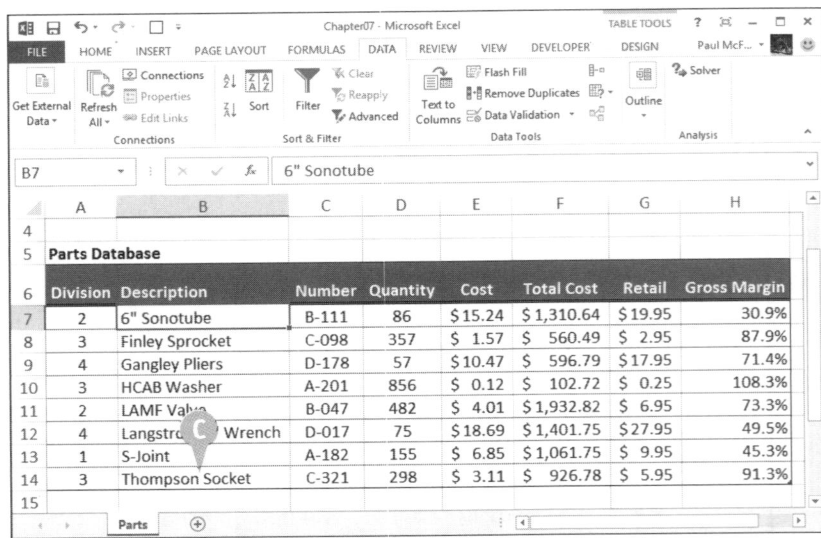

Filter a List

1. Click a cell in the range you want to filter.
2. Click the Data tab.
3. Click Filter.

   D AutoFilter buttons appear next to your field headers.
4. Click an AutoFilter button.

   The Sort & Filter menu appears.
5. Click items to deselect the ones you do not want (☑ changes to ☐).
6. Click OK.

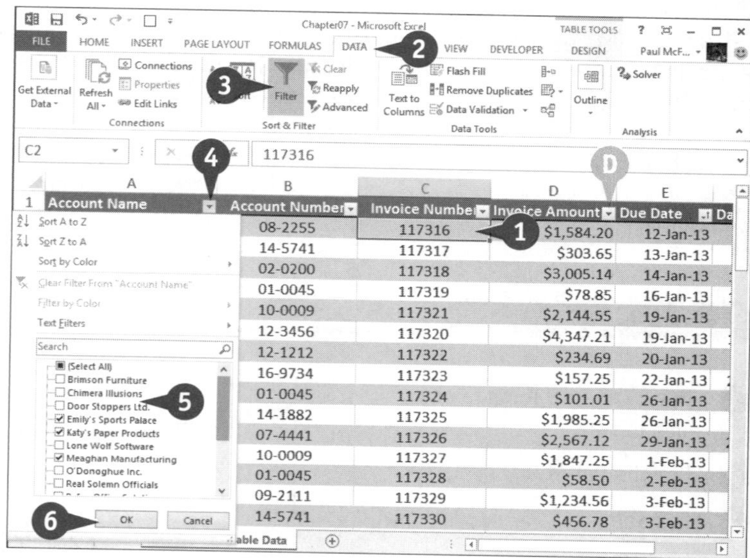

E Excel filters your list.

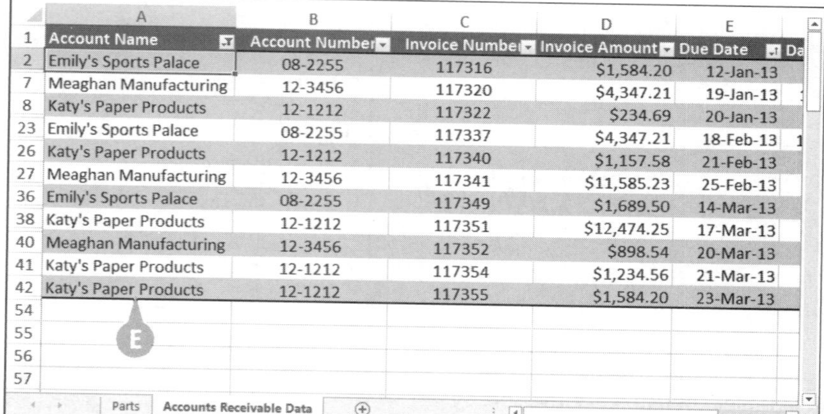

	Account Name	Account Number	Invoice Number	Invoice Amount	Due Date
2	Emily's Sports Palace	08-2255	117316	$1,584.20	12-Jan-13
7	Meaghan Manufacturing	12-3456	117320	$4,347.21	19-Jan-13
8	Katy's Paper Products	12-1212	117322	$234.69	20-Jan-13
23	Emily's Sports Palace	08-2255	117337	$4,347.21	18-Feb-13
26	Katy's Paper Products	12-1212	117340	$1,157.58	21-Feb-13
27	Meaghan Manufacturing	12-3456	117341	$11,585.23	25-Feb-13
36	Emily's Sports Palace	08-2255	117349	$1,689.50	14-Mar-13
38	Katy's Paper Products	12-1212	117351	$12,474.25	17-Mar-13
40	Meaghan Manufacturing	12-3456	117352	$898.54	20-Mar-13
41	Katy's Paper Products	12-1212	117354	$1,234.56	21-Mar-13
42	Katy's Paper Products	12-1212	117355	$1,584.20	23-Mar-13

EXTRA

When you activate the Data tab's Filter button (▼), Excel places an AutoFilter button (▾) next to each column header. When you filter the data using a particular field, Excel modifies that field's AutoFilter button to include a Field Filter icon (▾). Similarly, when you sort a column in ascending order, Excel modifies that field's AutoFilter to include a Field Sort Ascending button (▾). When you sort a column in descending order, Excel modifies that field's AutoFilter to include a Field Sort Descending button (▾). To clear all filters, click the Data tab and then click Clear Filter (▼). To remove the AutoFilter buttons next to your field names, click the Data tab and then click Filter (▼).

Perform a Multilevel Sort

A simple sort is one that arranges data based on the contents of a single column. Simple sorts are fine for many data analysis applications, but Excel enables you to take sorting to a higher level. Specifically, you can sort your data on two or more fields, creating a *multilevel* sort.

For example, with a database of customer information, a simple sort might organize that data in ascending order by country name. However, within each country, you might also want the customers sorted by region (such as the state or province). You do that by creating a multilevel sort where the country is the first level and the region is the second level.

Perform a Multilevel Sort

1. Click a cell in the range you want to sort.
2. Click the Data tab.
3. Click Sort.

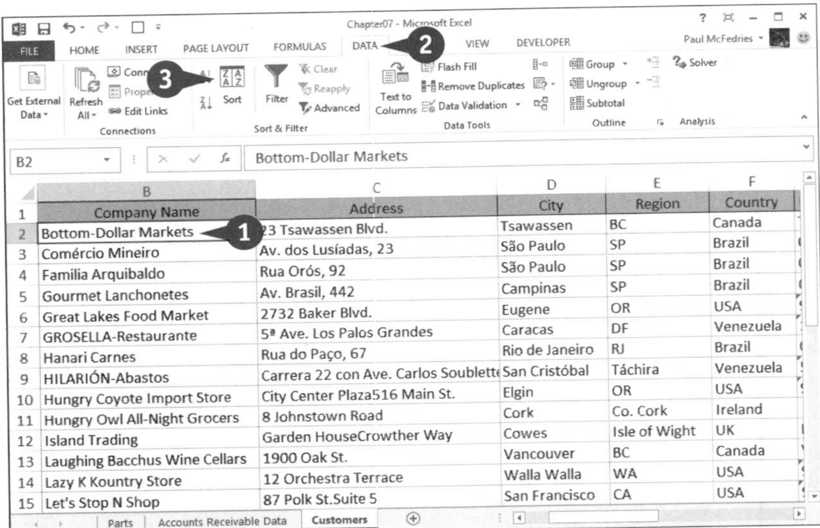

The Sort dialog box appears.

4. Under Column, click the Sort by down arrow and then click the column you want to use as the first sort level.
5. Under Sort On, click the Sort by down arrow and then click Values.
6. Under Order, click the Sort by down-arrow and then click a sort order.
7. Click Add Level.

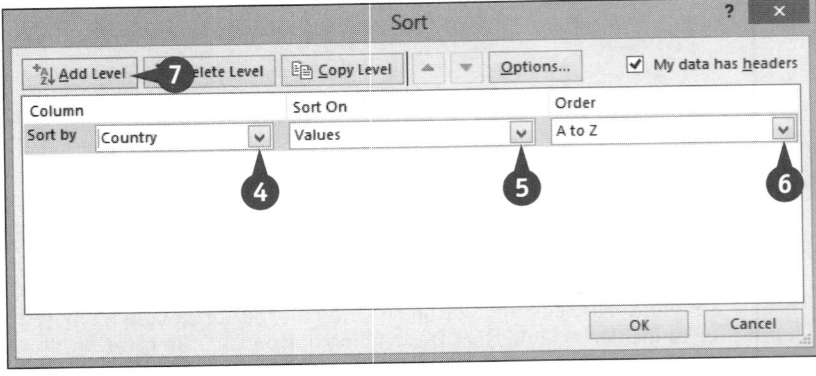

8. Under Column, click the Then by down arrow and then click the column you want to use for this sort level.
9. Under Sort On, click the Then by down arrow and then click Values.
10. Under Order, click the Then by down arrow and then click a sort order.
11. Repeat steps 7 to 10 to add additional sort levels.
12. Click OK.

A. Excel sorts the list.

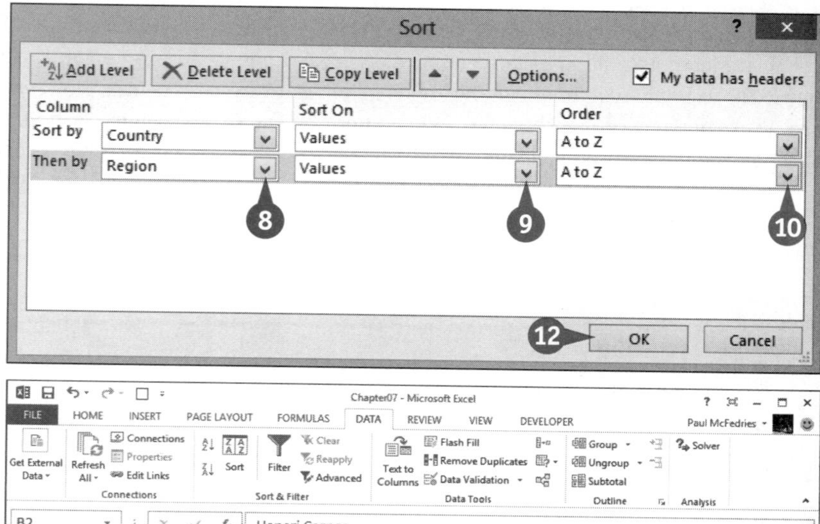

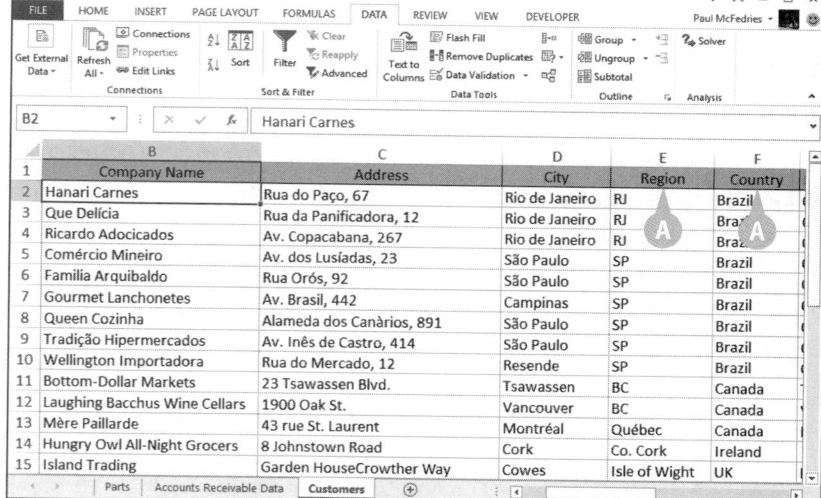

EXTRA

If you are sorting a table, click any cell in the table and Excel selects the entire table when you open the Sort dialog box. If you are sorting a range of cells that are not a table, select the cells and then open the Sort dialog box. If your data does not have column headers, deselect the My Data Has Headers check box (☑ changes to ☐).

To rearrange the sort levels, follow steps 1 to 3 to open the Sort dialog box, click a level, and then click either Move Up (▲) or Move Down (▼). To remove a sort level, open the Sort dialog box, click the level you want to remove, and then click Delete Level.

Create a Custom Sort

When you are analyzing data, you might find that a standard ascending or descending sort is what you need. For example, you might prefer to sort your dates by the weekday name or month name. You can perform such sorts by basing them on a *custom list* of values.

Excel comes with several predefined custom lists that enable you to sort dates by weekday names or month names. However, if your range data includes a unique set of values, or if you have a data series that you use often, you can create a custom list based on the values, and then use that list for sorting the range.

Create a Custom Sort

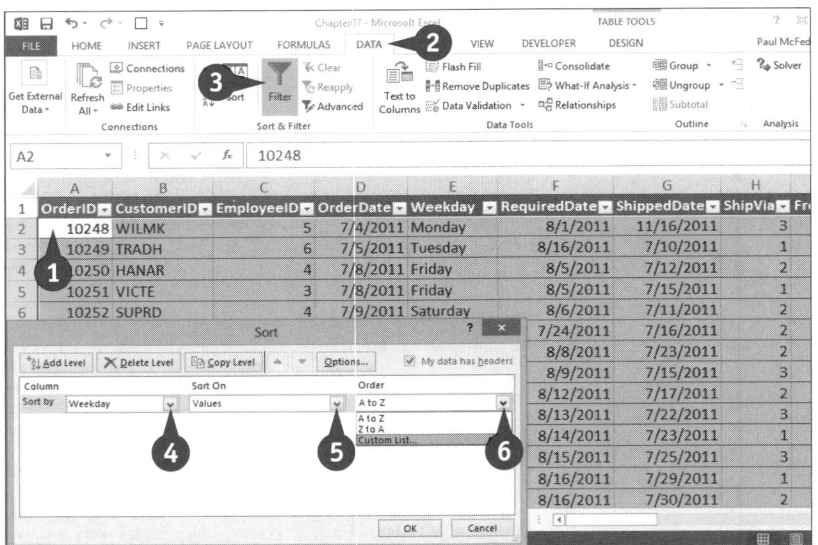

1. Click a cell in the range you want to sort.
2. Click the Data tab.
3. Click the Sort button.

   The Sort dialog box appears.
4. Click here and then click the column you want to use as the first sort level.
5. Click here and then click Values.
6. Click here and then click Custom List.

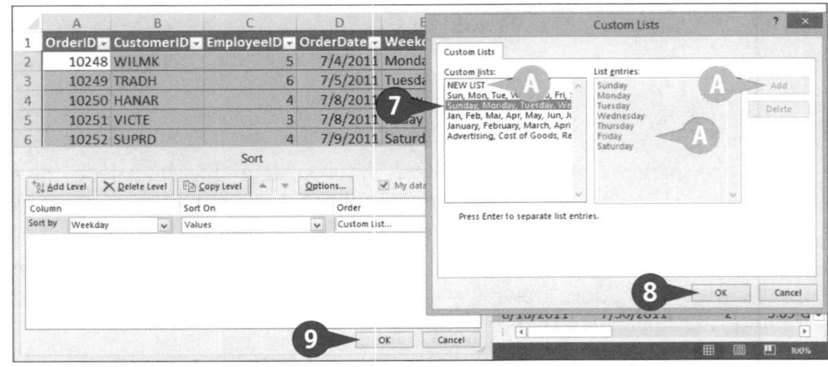

The Custom Lists dialog box appears.

7. Click the list you want to use as the sort order.

   A. To create your own custom list, click NEW LIST, type your entries, and then click Add.
8. Click OK.
9. Click OK.

   Excel sorts the data using the custom list.

You can use conditional formatting to format your data with cell colors, font colors, or cell icons. You can then use the Sort dialog box to sort data based on one or more of these formats. When you choose Cell Color, Font Color, or Cell Icon in the Sort On drop-down list of the Sort dialog box, Excel places a list of cell colors, font colors, or cell icons in the Order field. You can then choose On Top to place the selection on the next highest level or On Bottom to place the selection on the next lowest level.

Sort by Cell Color, Font Color, or Cell Icon

1. Click a cell in the range you want to sort.
2. Click the Data tab.
3. Click Sort.

   The Sort dialog box appears.
4. Click here and then select a sort column.
5. Click here and then select Cell Color, Font Color, or Cell Icon.
6. Click here and then select a cell color, font color, or cell icon.
7. Click here and then select On Top or On Bottom.
8. Click Add Level.
9. Repeat steps 4 to 8 until you are finished.
10. Click OK.

- A. Excel sorts the column by cell color, font color, or cell Icon.

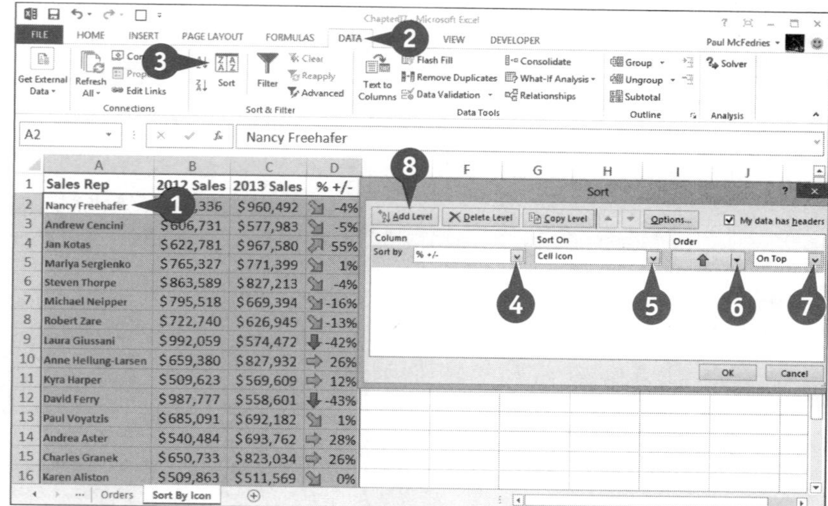

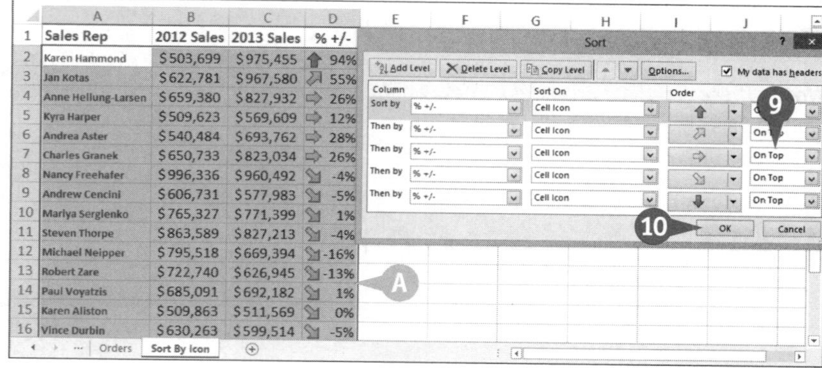

When you filter a range using a *filter list*, you filter the data by selecting the check boxes for the records you want to see. A more complex technique uses *quick filters*, which enable you to specify criteria for a field, such as only showing those records where the field value is greater than a specified amount.

Excel offers three types of quick filters: *date filters* for date fields; *text filters* for text fields; and *number filters* for numeric fields. When you select one of these options, a menu appears. From this menu, you can select the criteria you want to apply. You can also apply multiple filters.

Using Quick Filters for Complex Sorting

1. Click a cell in the range you want to filter.
2. Click the Data tab.
3. Click Filter.

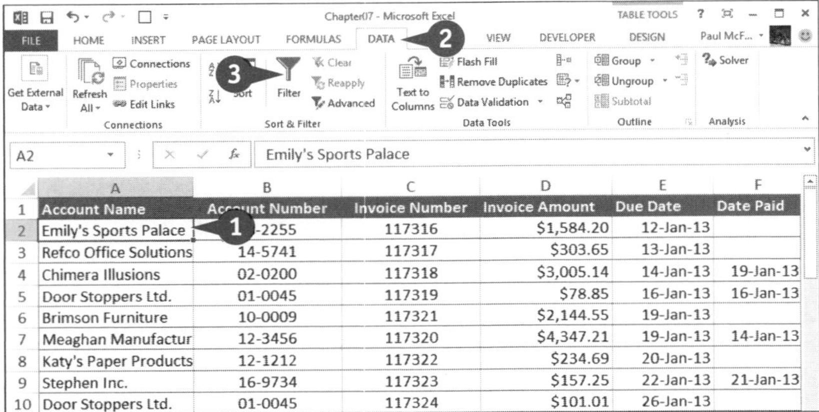

Ⓐ AutoFilter buttons appear next to your field headers.

4. Click an AutoFilter button.
5. Click Number Filters.

Note: *If the field is a date field, click Date Filters; if the field is a text field, click Text Filters.*

6. Click the filter you want to use.

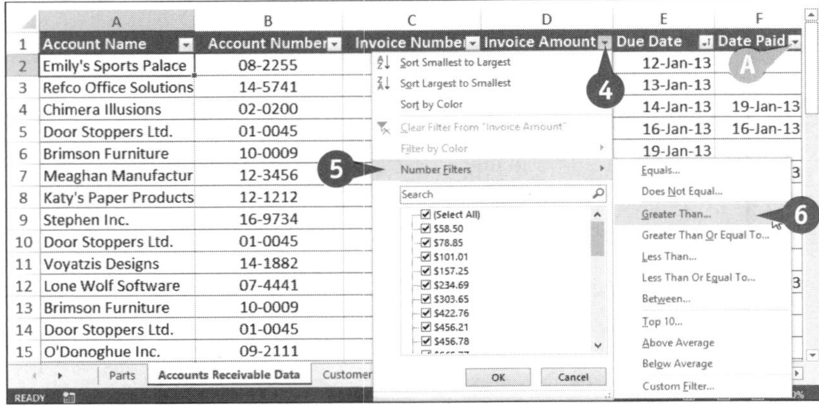

The Custom AutoFilter dialog box appears.

Note: *Some quick filters do not require extra input, so you can skip the next two steps.*

7 Type the value you want to use, or click the down arrow and select a unique value from the drop-down list.

8 Click OK.

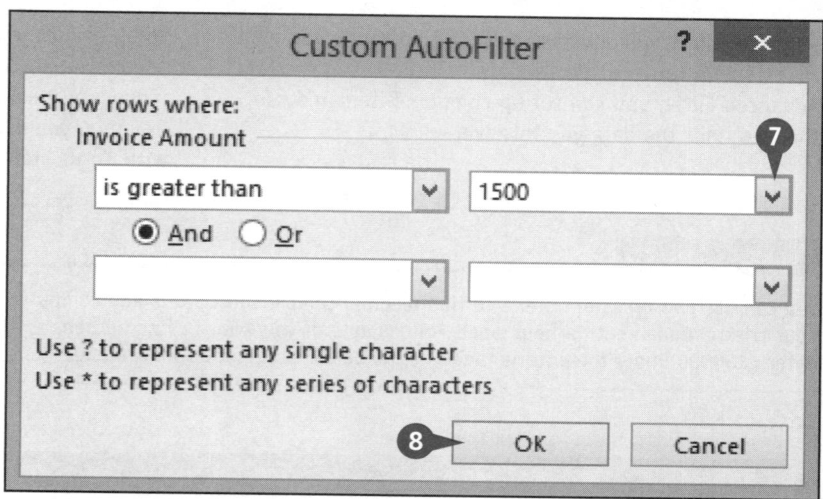

B Excel filters the table to show only those records that have the field values you selected.

C Excel displays the number of records found.

D If you have AutoFilter buttons displayed, the field's button displays a filter icon.

E To remove the filter, click Clear.

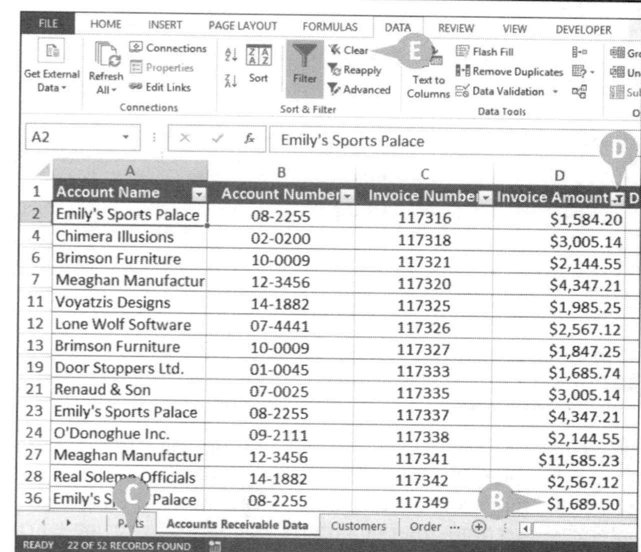

APPLY IT

You can create custom quick filters that use two different criteria, and you can tell Excel to filter records that match both or at least one of the two criteria. Follow steps 1 to 5 and then click Custom Filter. The Custom AutoFilter dialog box offers two sets of list boxes. Use the lists on the left to choose operators, such as Equal and Is Greater Than; use the lists on the right to specify field values.

If you want Excel to match both criteria, click the And option (○ changes to ◉); if you want Excel to match at least one of the criteria, click the Or option (○ changes to ◉). Click OK.

Enter Criteria to Find Records

Once you have converted a range to a table, you may want to retrieve specific information. Using the Excel Advanced Filter, you can set up complex filters and use them to limit the data you retrieve.

When using the Advanced Filter feature, you must set up a worksheet area called the *criteria range*. In the criteria range, you tell Excel exactly what you are looking for. For example, you can tell Excel you want to retrieve all people with an income of $100,000 or more.

Types of Criteria

You can use two types of criteria to find records: comparison criteria and computed criteria. With *comparison criteria*, you enter your criteria underneath a field label. For example, if you want to find all people with an income greater than $100,000, you enter >100000 under the criteria range field labeled `Income`, as shown here.

Criteria Range

Last Name	First Name	Property Tax	Income Tax	Income
				>100000

Table

Last Name	First Name	Property Tax	Income Tax	Income
Jones	Serena	4,143	23,487	75,436
Jacobs	Tom	4,230	14,537	146,621
Cohen	James	3,875	12,844	64,220
Jones	Libby	3,933	25,174	125,871

With *computed criteria*, you use a formula to find records. You use computed criteria when your table does not have a field that specifies the data you want to use as the filter. For example, if you want to extract all records from the table where the property tax plus the income tax is greater than $20,000, you can use the formula `=Property Tax+Income Tax>20000` as your criteria.

When you use computed criteria, at least one variable in the formula must be a field in your table. However, the criteria range label cannot be one of the field labels used by your table. For example, you can create a new criteria range label called `Total Tax` and place your formula under that label. Excel interprets all criteria that use field labels from your table as comparison criteria. Excel interprets all criteria that do not use field labels as computed criteria. The following is an example of computed criteria.

Criteria Range

Last Name	First Name	Property Tax	Income Tax	Income	Total Tax
					=Property Tax+Income Tax>20000

Set Up Your Criteria Range

You can place your criteria range anywhere in your workbook, but the best places are above your table or on a separate worksheet. You should create one row that lists your field labels. You do not have to include all your labels, but you must include every label for which you are going to enter comparison criteria. You should also place the labels that you are going to use for computed criteria on this row. You also need at least one additional row to use for the criteria.

Enter Comparison Criteria

You can use comparison criteria to find text, numbers, dates, and logical values. If you want to match a series of characters, you can place the characters under the field label. For example, if you want to find all records for people with the last name Jones, you type Jones under the field label `Last Name` in the criteria range.

For more flexibility with text criteria, you can use wildcard characters. You use a question mark (?) to match any single character. For example, J?ne finds Jane and June. You use an asterisk (*) to match any series of characters. For example, *son finds Jackson and Johnson. If you need to find a question mark or an asterisk, you can place a tilde (~) in front of the question mark or asterisk. Excel assumes that there is an asterisk after every search entry. Therefore, if you type John under the `Last Name` field label, Excel finds everyone whose last name begins with John. If you want to find an exact match for a text value, you can enter your criteria in the format ="=text". For example, if you want to find John, but not Johnson, you type ="=John".

You can also use comparison operators. To do this, you type the comparison operator followed by the value you are trying to find. For example, to find all records where the income is equal to or greater than $100,000, you type >=100000 under the `Income` field label. To find all last names that are alphabetically greater than Cohen, you type >Cohen under the `Last Name` field label. Comparison criteria are not case-sensitive. To find all blank fields, you type an equal sign with nothing after it. To find all nonblank fields, you type the unequal operator (<>) with nothing after it. To learn more about comparison operators, see Chapter 1.

Enter Computed Criteria

When you enter computed criteria, you must use a formula that evaluates to the logical value `TRUE` or the logical value `FALSE`, based on whether your criteria match records in your table, and your formula must include a reference to at least one field label from your table. If you use computed criteria, your field labels must conform to the rules for naming a range. To learn more about naming ranges, see Chapter 1.

You create your formula by using a relative cell reference to the first data row in your table. For example, `=C8+D8>20000` is a valid formula if the first data row in your formula is row 8. If you name the data fields in the first row of your table, you can use range names in your formula. For example, if C8 is named `Property Tax` and D8 is named `Income Tax`, you can use the formula `=Property Tax + Income Tax > 20000`.

You create a new label and place your formula under that label in the criteria range. The cell displays either the value `TRUE` or the value `FALSE`.

Apply Multiple Criteria

You can use a criteria range to specify multiple criteria. For example, you can find all people with the last name Jones whose incomes are more than $50,000. You can also find all people whose property tax is more than $4,000 or whose income tax is more than $20,000. To meet both criteria, you can place your criteria on the same row. To meet either criterion, you can place your criteria on separate rows.

Meet both criteria:

Last Name	First Name	Property Tax	Income Tax	Income
Jones				>50000

Meet either criterion:

Last Name	First Name	Property Tax	Income Tax	Income
		>4000		
			>20000	

Create an Advanced Filter

You can go beyond the limitations of the AutoFilter command by creating an advanced filter that uses criteria to specify the records you want to see. You have two options when creating an advanced filter: you can have the filtered items appear in place, under the column headings of your table; or, you can have your filtered items appear in another location, thereby, enabling you to also view your original table data. If you choose the latter, you should select a worksheet location beside or below the original table and make sure the location has enough room below it to include all the values that Excel returns in the filter results. For more information on using criteria, see the section, "Enter Criteria to Find Records,"

Create an Advanced Filter

1. Set up your criteria range by typing the headings for the columns you want to filter.

Note: *In most cases, it is easiest just to copy the column headings from the original table.*

2. Type the criteria you want to use for your filter.
3. Click a cell inside the original table.

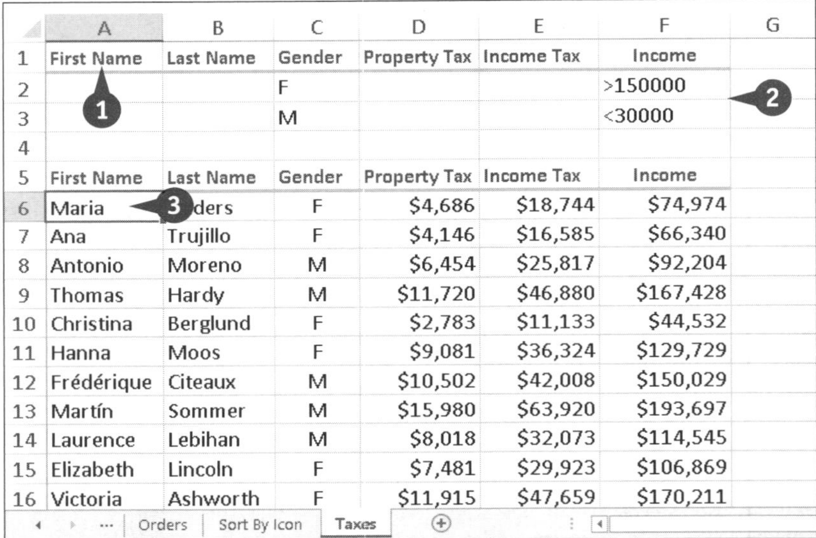

	A	B	C	D	E	F
1	First Name	Last Name	Gender	Property Tax	Income Tax	Income
2			F			>150000
3			M			<30000
4						
5	First Name	Last Name	Gender	Property Tax	Income Tax	Income
6	Maria	Anders	F	$4,686	$18,744	$74,974
7	Ana	Trujillo	F	$4,146	$16,585	$66,340
8	Antonio	Moreno	M	$6,454	$25,817	$92,204
9	Thomas	Hardy	M	$11,720	$46,880	$167,428
10	Christina	Berglund	F	$2,783	$11,133	$44,532
11	Hanna	Moos	F	$9,081	$36,324	$129,729
12	Frédérique	Citeaux	M	$10,502	$42,008	$150,029
13	Martín	Sommer	M	$15,980	$63,920	$193,697
14	Laurence	Lebihan	M	$8,018	$32,073	$114,545
15	Elizabeth	Lincoln	F	$7,481	$29,923	$106,869
16	Victoria	Ashworth	F	$11,915	$47,659	$170,211

4. Click the Data tab.
5. Click Advanced.

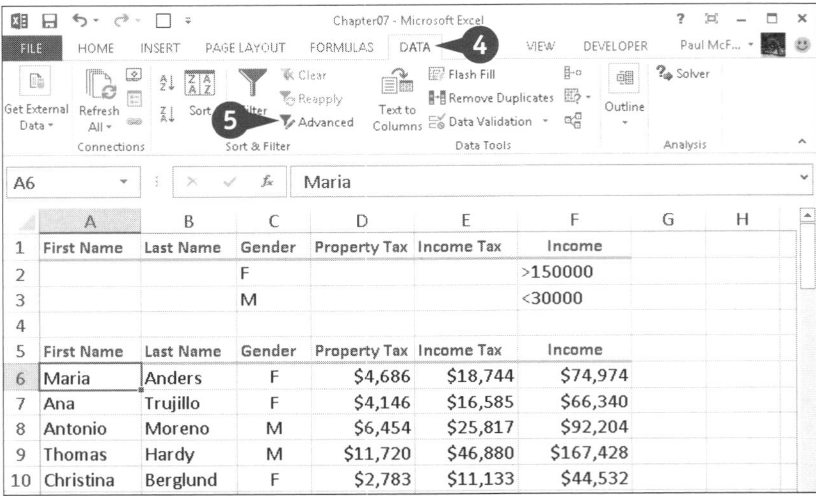

	A	B	C	D	E	F
1	First Name	Last Name	Gender	Property Tax	Income Tax	Income
2			F			>150000
3			M			<30000
4						
5	First Name	Last Name	Gender	Property Tax	Income Tax	Income
6	Maria	Anders	F	$4,686	$18,744	$74,974
7	Ana	Trujillo	F	$4,146	$16,585	$66,340
8	Antonio	Moreno	M	$6,454	$25,817	$92,204
9	Thomas	Hardy	M	$11,720	$46,880	$167,428
10	Christina	Berglund	F	$2,783	$11,133	$44,532

The Advanced Filter dialog box appears.

6 Select where to place the filter results (◯ changes to ◉).

7 Enter the criteria range address, including the column headings.

A If you chose Copy to Another Location in step 6, enter the first cell of the copy location.

8 Click OK.

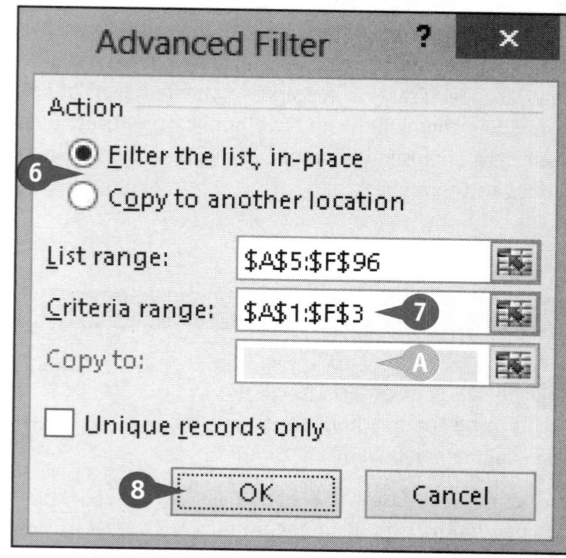

B Excel filters the table to show only those records that have the field values you selected.

C Excel displays the number of records found.

	A	B	C	D	E	F	G	H
1	First Name	Last Name	Gender	Property Tax	Income Tax	Income		
2			F			>150000		
3			M			<30000		
4								
5	First Name	Last Name	Gender	Property Tax	Income Tax	Income		
16	Victoria	Ashworth	F	$11,915	$47,659	$170,211		
17	Patricio	Simpson	M	$960	$3,839	$25,594		
24	Ann	Devon	F	$11,206	$44,824	$160,087		
28	Martine	Rancé	F	$10,643	$42,573	$152,048		
30	Peter	Franken	M	$789	$3,156	$21,042		
38	Manuel	Pereira	M	$1,068	$4,272	$28,483		
49	Renate	Messner	F	$11,698	$46,791	$167,110		
55	Catherine	Dewey	F	$10,997	$43,988	$157,100		
62	Marie	Bertrand	F	$11,152	$44,607	$159,309		
73	Michael	Holz	M	$769	$3,078	$20,517		
80	Art	Braunschw	M	$845	$3,380	$22,531		
83	Liu	Wong	F	$10,613	$42,452	$151,616		
89	Mary	Saveley	F	$12,311	$49,245	$175,874		
93	Paula	Parente	F	$10,572	$42,287	$151,024		

Orders | Sort By Icon | Taxes

READY 14 OF 91 RECORDS FOUND 100%

APPLY IT

Criteria are not case-sensitive, meaning that if you enter bill, Excel matches bill and Bill. For a case-sensitive filter, include the `EXACT` function. In your criteria range, create a column label named, say, `Exact Match`. In the field below the `Exact Match` column label, type the `EXACT` function as follows:

```
EXACT(column, value)
```

Replace `column` with a reference to the first cell in the column you want to filter, and `value` with the text string you want to match. For example, `=EXACT(A6, "Bill")` sets up a case-sensitive filter for the items in column A (assuming the first item in that column is in cell A6) to match the text Bill.

Display Unique Records in the Filter Results

It is not uncommon to have a range or table with duplicate items, meaning the values in two or more rows are identical. For example, a simple list of books sold over some time will likely have duplicate entries. As part of your data analysis, you might prefer to see only the unique values in the range.

You can use the advanced filtering tool in Excel to identify and filter the duplicates. You must specify a criteria range by which you want to filter your data. Your criteria consist of at least two rows, one with one or more headings and the other with the criteria. See the section, "Enter Criteria to Find Records," for information on how to set up your criteria range.

Display Unique Records in the Filter Results

1. Set up your criteria range by typing the headings for the columns you want to filter.

Note: *In most cases, it is easiest just to copy the column headings from the original table.*

2. Type the criteria you want to use for your filter.

3. Click a cell inside the original table.

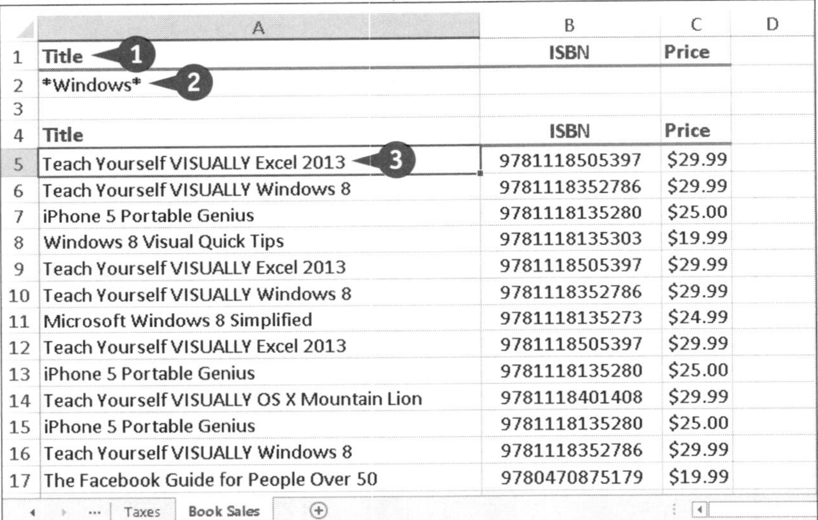

	A	B	C
1	Title	ISBN	Price
2	*Windows*		
3			
4	Title	ISBN	Price
5	Teach Yourself VISUALLY Excel 2013	9781118505397	$29.99
6	Teach Yourself VISUALLY Windows 8	9781118352786	$29.99
7	iPhone 5 Portable Genius	9781118135280	$25.00
8	Windows 8 Visual Quick Tips	9781118135303	$19.99
9	Teach Yourself VISUALLY Excel 2013	9781118505397	$29.99
10	Teach Yourself VISUALLY Windows 8	9781118352786	$29.99
11	Microsoft Windows 8 Simplified	9781118135273	$24.99
12	Teach Yourself VISUALLY Excel 2013	9781118505397	$29.99
13	iPhone 5 Portable Genius	9781118135280	$25.00
14	Teach Yourself VISUALLY OS X Mountain Lion	9781118401408	$29.99
15	iPhone 5 Portable Genius	9781118135280	$25.00
16	Teach Yourself VISUALLY Windows 8	9781118352786	$29.99
17	The Facebook Guide for People Over 50	9780470875179	$19.99

4. Click the Data tab.

5. Click Advanced.

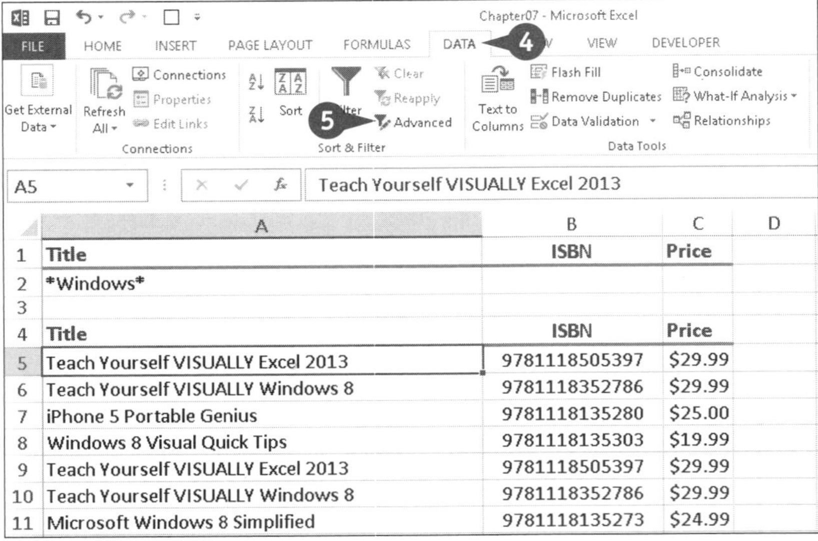

	A	B	C
1	Title	ISBN	Price
2	*Windows*		
3			
4	Title	ISBN	Price
5	Teach Yourself VISUALLY Excel 2013	9781118505397	$29.99
6	Teach Yourself VISUALLY Windows 8	9781118352786	$29.99
7	iPhone 5 Portable Genius	9781118135280	$25.00
8	Windows 8 Visual Quick Tips	9781118135303	$19.99
9	Teach Yourself VISUALLY Excel 2013	9781118505397	$29.99
10	Teach Yourself VISUALLY Windows 8	9781118352786	$29.99
11	Microsoft Windows 8 Simplified	9781118135273	$24.99

The Advanced Filter dialog box appears.

6 Select where to place the filter results (○ changes to ◉).

7 Enter the criteria range address, including the column headings.

A If you chose Copy to Another Location in step 6, enter the first cell of the copy location.

8 Click the Unique Records Only check box (☐ changes to ☑).

9 Click OK.

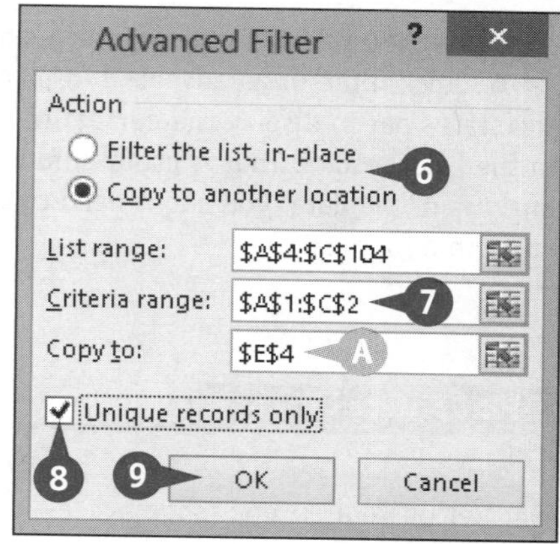

B In this example, Excel copies the unique records from the filter results to the specified location.

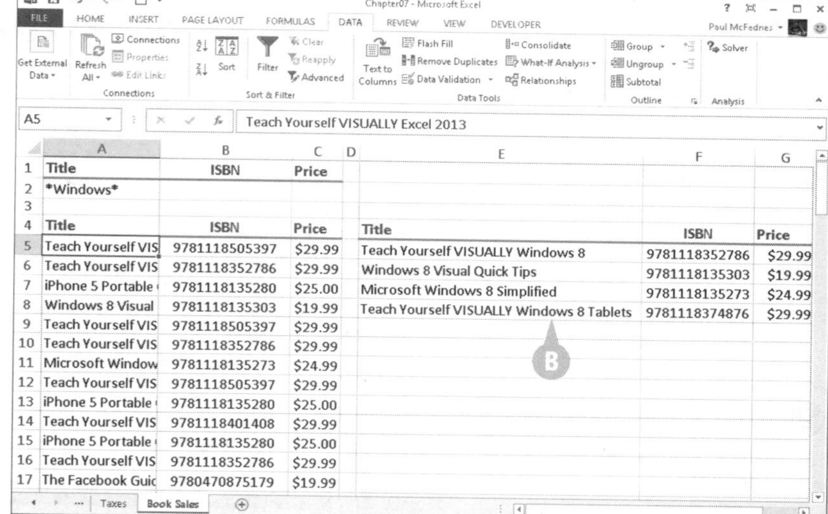

EXTRA

Using an advanced filter temporarily removes the duplicate records from view. This is usually the behavior you want, but in some cases, having duplicate records is an error (for example, having two identical invoices or customers). In such cases, it is better to delete the duplicate records permanently. See Chapter 8 to learn about an Excel feature that makes it easy to remove duplicate records.

You can make working with advanced filters faster and easier by applying special names to your ranges. Specifically, name your original range Database, your criteria range Criteria, and your copy range Extract. If you do this, Excel fills in the addresses for these ranges automatically when you display the Advanced Filter dialog box.

Count Filtered Records

When you filter a range or table using an AutoFilter, a quick filter, or an advanced in-place filter, Excel uses the status bar to display the number of records returned in the filter results. That is useful information, but in your analysis of the data, you might need to use that count value in a formula.

You can do this by using `DCOUNT`, one of the database functions in Excel, which returns the number of items in a range that satisfy your criteria. `DCOUNT` takes three arguments: `database` specifies the range that contains the data; `field` specifies the column you want to count; and `criteria` specifies the address of the criteria range.

Count Filtered Records

1. Set up your criteria range by typing the headings for the columns you want to filter.

Note: *In most cases, it is easiest just to copy the column headings from the original table.*

2. Type the criteria you want to use for your filter.

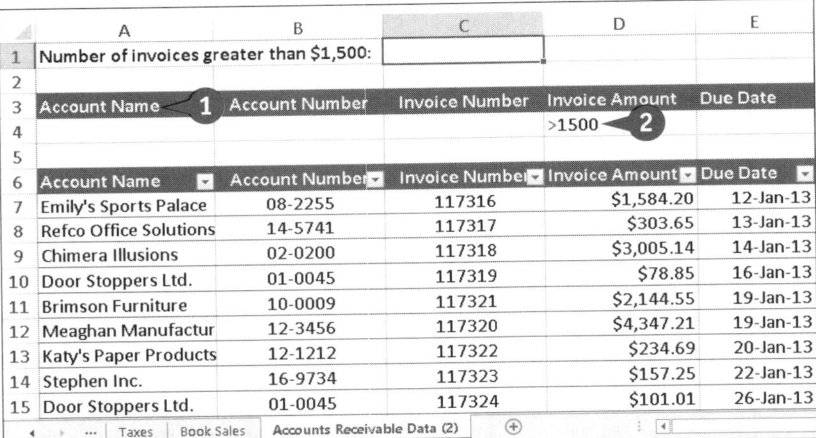

	A	B	C	D	E
1	Number of invoices greater than $1,500:				
2					
3	Account Name	Account Number	Invoice Number	Invoice Amount	Due Date
4				>1500	
5					
6	Account Name	Account Number	Invoice Number	Invoice Amount	Due Date
7	Emily's Sports Palace	08-2255	117316	$1,584.20	12-Jan-13
8	Refco Office Solutions	14-5741	117317	$303.65	13-Jan-13
9	Chimera Illusions	02-0200	117318	$3,005.14	14-Jan-13
10	Door Stoppers Ltd.	01-0045	117319	$78.85	16-Jan-13
11	Brimson Furniture	10-0009	117321	$2,144.55	19-Jan-13
12	Meaghan Manufactur	12-3456	117320	$4,347.21	19-Jan-13
13	Katy's Paper Products	12-1212	117322	$234.69	20-Jan-13
14	Stephen Inc.	16-9734	117323	$157.25	22-Jan-13
15	Door Stoppers Ltd.	01-0045	117324	$101.01	26-Jan-13

3. In the cell where you want the count result to appear, type **=dcount(**.

Note: *The* `DCOUNT` *function counts only cells containing numbers. For non-numeric data, use the* `DCOUNTA` *function.*

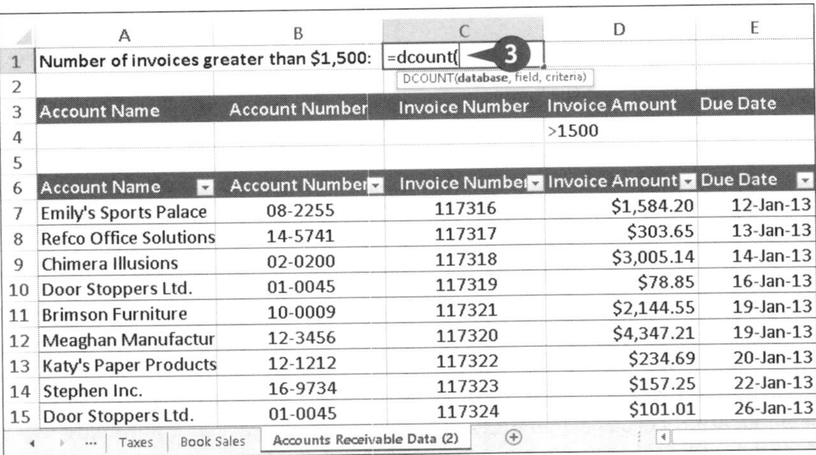

	A	B	C	D	E
1	Number of invoices greater than $1,500:		=dcount(		
2					
3	Account Name	Account Number	Invoice Number	Invoice Amount	Due Date
4				>1500	
5					
6	Account Name	Account Number	Invoice Number	Invoice Amount	Due Date
7	Emily's Sports Palace	08-2255	117316	$1,584.20	12-Jan-13
8	Refco Office Solutions	14-5741	117317	$303.65	13-Jan-13
9	Chimera Illusions	02-0200	117318	$3,005.14	14-Jan-13
10	Door Stoppers Ltd.	01-0045	117319	$78.85	16-Jan-13
11	Brimson Furniture	10-0009	117321	$2,144.55	19-Jan-13
12	Meaghan Manufactur	12-3456	117320	$4,347.21	19-Jan-13
13	Katy's Paper Products	12-1212	117322	$234.69	20-Jan-13
14	Stephen Inc.	16-9734	117323	$157.25	22-Jan-13
15	Door Stoppers Ltd.	01-0045	117324	$101.01	26-Jan-13

4 Enter the address or name of the data range.

Note: *As shown here, if the data is in a table, type the table name followed by* ***[#All]****.*

5 Type the column name in quotation marks.

Alternatively, type the column number.

6 Type the address of the criteria range.

7 Type **)**.

8 Click the Enter button or press Enter.

A Excel displays the count of the records that match the criteria.

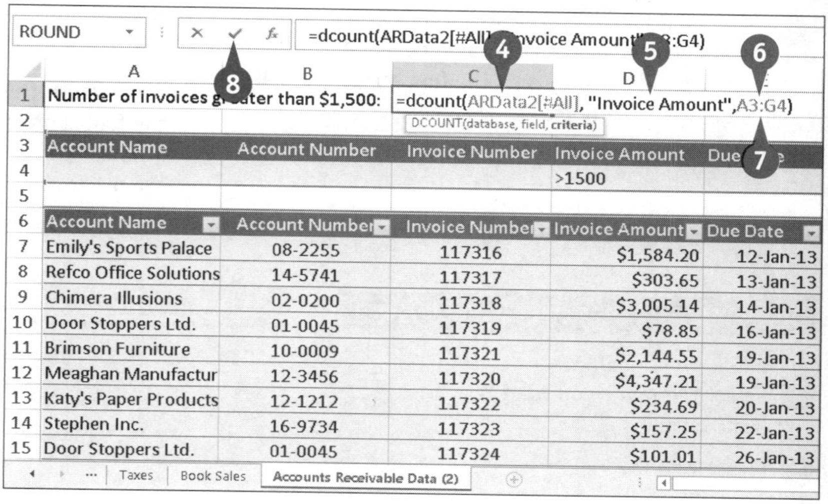

ROUND | =dcount(ARData2[#All], "Invoice Amount",A3:G4)

	A	B	C	D	E
1	Number of invoices greater than $1,500:		=dcount(ARData2[#All], "Invoice Amount",A3:G4) DCOUNT(database, field, criteria)		
2					
3	Account Name	Account Number	Invoice Number	Invoice Amount	Due Date
4				>1500	
5					
6	Account Name	Account Number	Invoice Number	Invoice Amount	Due Date
7	Emily's Sports Palace	08-2255	117316	$1,584.20	12-Jan-13
8	Refco Office Solutions	14-5741	117317	$303.65	13-Jan-13
9	Chimera Illusions	02-0200	117318	$3,005.14	14-Jan-13
10	Door Stoppers Ltd.	01-0045	117319	$78.85	16-Jan-13
11	Brimson Furniture	10-0009	117321	$2,144.55	19-Jan-13
12	Meaghan Manufactur	12-3456	117320	$4,347.21	19-Jan-13
13	Katy's Paper Products	12-1212	117322	$234.69	20-Jan-13
14	Stephen Inc.	16-9734	117323	$157.25	22-Jan-13
15	Door Stoppers Ltd.	01-0045	117324	$101.01	26-Jan-13

Taxes | Book Sales | Accounts Receivable Data (2)

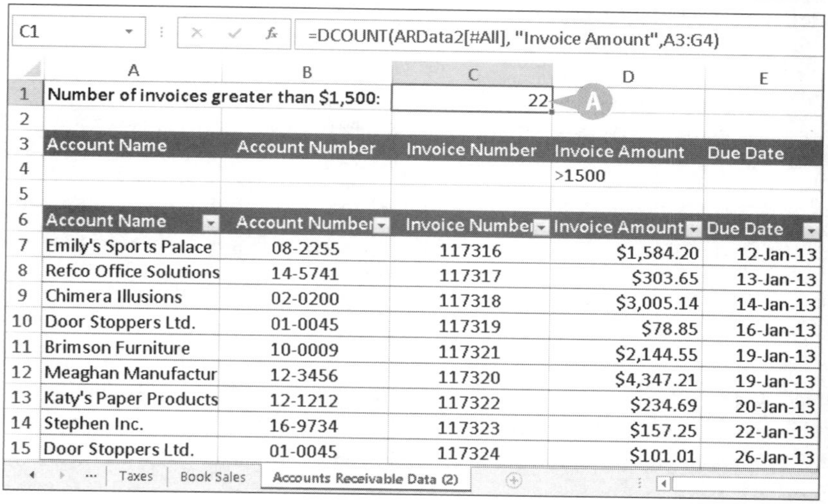

C1 | =DCOUNT(ARData2[#All], "Invoice Amount",A3:G4)

	A	B	C	D	E
1	Number of invoices greater than $1,500:		22		
2					
3	Account Name	Account Number	Invoice Number	Invoice Amount	Due Date
4				>1500	
5					
6	Account Name	Account Number	Invoice Number	Invoice Amount	Due Date
7	Emily's Sports Palace	08-2255	117316	$1,584.20	12-Jan-13
8	Refco Office Solutions	14-5741	117317	$303.65	13-Jan-13
9	Chimera Illusions	02-0200	117318	$3,005.14	14-Jan-13
10	Door Stoppers Ltd.	01-0045	117319	$78.85	16-Jan-13
11	Brimson Furniture	10-0009	117321	$2,144.55	19-Jan-13
12	Meaghan Manufactur	12-3456	117320	$4,347.21	19-Jan-13
13	Katy's Paper Products	12-1212	117322	$234.69	20-Jan-13
14	Stephen Inc.	16-9734	117323	$157.25	22-Jan-13
15	Door Stoppers Ltd.	01-0045	117324	$101.01	26-Jan-13

Taxes | Book Sales | Accounts Receivable Data (2)

EXTRA

Excel's other database functions take the same arguments as `DCOUNT`. The `DAVERAGE` function returns the average of the matching records. `DGET` returns a single matching record. `DMAX` returns the maximum of the matching records, while `DMIN` returns the minimum. `DPRODUCT` returns the product of the matching records. `DSTDEV` returns the standard deviation if the matching records are a sample of the population, while `DSTDEVP` returns the standard deviation if the matching records are the entire population. `DSUM` returns the sum of the matching records. `DVAR` returns the variance if the matching records are a sample of the population, while `DVARP` returns the variance if the matching records are the entire population.

Highlight Cells That Meet Some Criteria

A *conditional format* is formatting that Excel applies only to cells that meet the criteria you specify. For example, you can tell Excel to apply only the formatting if a cell's value is greater than or less than some specified amount, between two specified values, or equal to some value. You can also look for cells that contain specified text, dates that occur during a specified timeframe, and more.

When you set up your conditional format, you can specify the font, border, and background pattern. This helps to ensure that the cells that meet your criteria stand out from the other cells in the range.

Highlight Cells That Meet Some Criteria

1. Select the range you want to work with.
2. Click the Home tab.
3. Click Conditional Formatting.
4. Click Highlight Cells Rules.
5. Click the operator you want to use for the condition.

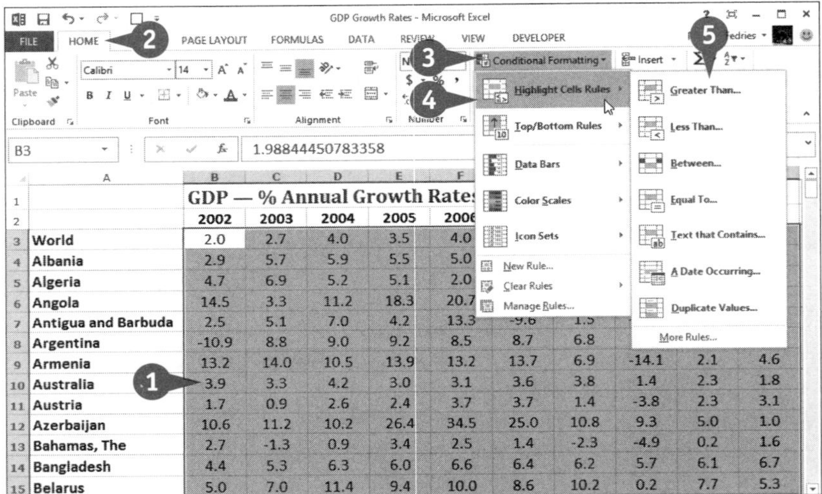

A dialog box appears with a name corresponding to the operator you clicked in step 5.

6. Type the value to use for the condition.

Ⓐ You can also click here and then click a worksheet cell.

Depending on the operator, you may need to specify two values.

7. Click the down arrow and then click the formatting to use.

Ⓑ To create your own format, click Custom Format.

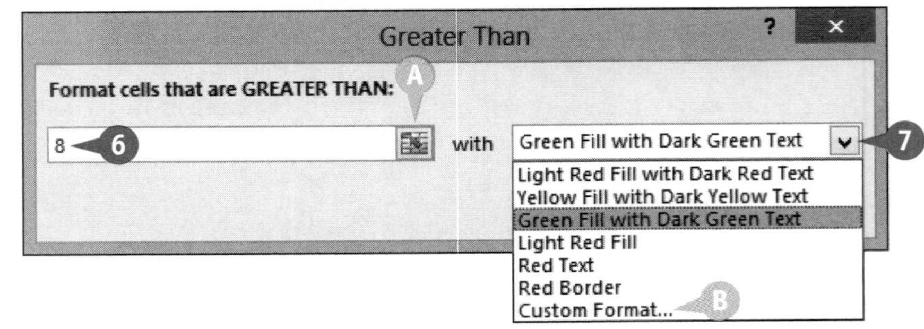

8 Click OK.

Ⓒ Excel applies the formatting to cells that meet the condition you specified.

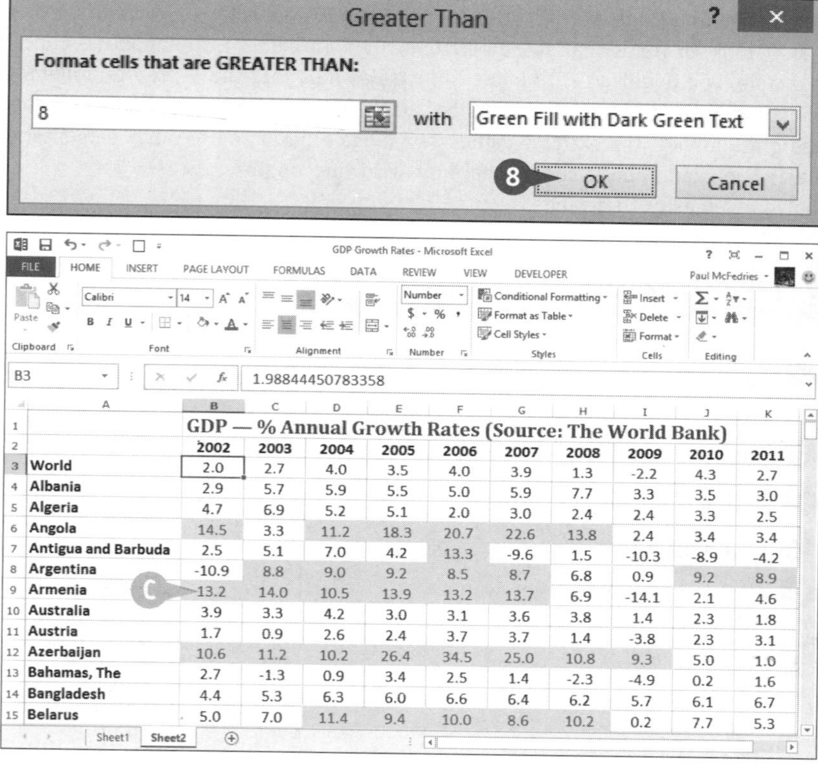

	2002	2003	2004	2005	2006	2007	2008	2009	2010	2011
World	2.0	2.7	4.0	3.5	4.0	3.9	1.3	-2.2	4.3	2.7
Albania	2.9	5.7	5.9	5.5	5.0	5.9	7.7	3.3	3.5	3.0
Algeria	4.7	6.9	5.2	5.1	2.0	3.0	2.4	2.4	3.3	2.5
Angola	14.5	3.3	11.2	18.3	20.7	22.6	13.8	2.4	3.4	3.4
Antigua and Barbuda	2.5	5.1	7.0	4.2	13.3	-9.6	1.5	-10.3	-8.9	-4.2
Argentina	-10.9	8.8	9.0	9.2	8.5	8.7	6.8	0.9	9.2	8.9
Armenia	13.2	14.0	10.5	13.9	13.2	13.7	6.9	-14.1	2.1	4.6
Australia	3.9	3.3	4.2	3.0	3.1	3.6	3.8	1.4	2.3	1.8
Austria	1.7	0.9	2.6	2.4	3.7	3.7	1.4	-3.8	2.3	3.1
Azerbaijan	10.6	11.2	10.2	26.4	34.5	25.0	10.8	9.3	5.0	1.0
Bahamas, The	2.7	-1.3	0.9	3.4	2.5	1.4	-2.3	-4.9	0.2	1.6
Bangladesh	4.4	5.3	6.3	6.0	6.6	6.4	6.2	5.7	6.1	6.7
Belarus	5.0	7.0	11.4	9.4	10.0	8.6	10.2	0.2	7.7	5.3

EXTRA

Excel enables you to specify multiple conditional formats. For example, you could set up one condition for cells that are greater than some value, and a separate condition for cells that are less than some other value. You can apply unique formats to each condition. Follow steps 1 to 8 to configure the new condition.

If you no longer require a conditional format, you can delete it. Follow steps 1 to 3 to select the range and display the Conditional Formatting drop-down list and then click Manage Rules. Excel displays the Conditional Formatting Rules Manager dialog box. Click the conditional format you want to remove and then click Delete Rule.

Highlight the Top or Bottom Values in a Range

When analyzing worksheet data, it is often useful to look for items that stand out from the norm. For example, you might want to know which sales reps sold the most last year, or which departments had the lowest gross margins. To view the extreme values in a range quickly and easily, you can apply a conditional format to the top or bottom values of that range.

You can do this by setting up *top/bottom rules*, where Excel applies a conditional format to those items that are at the top or bottom of a range of values. For the top or bottom values, you can specify a number, such as the top 5 or 10, or a percentage, such as the bottom 20 percent.

Highlight the Top or Bottom Values in a Range

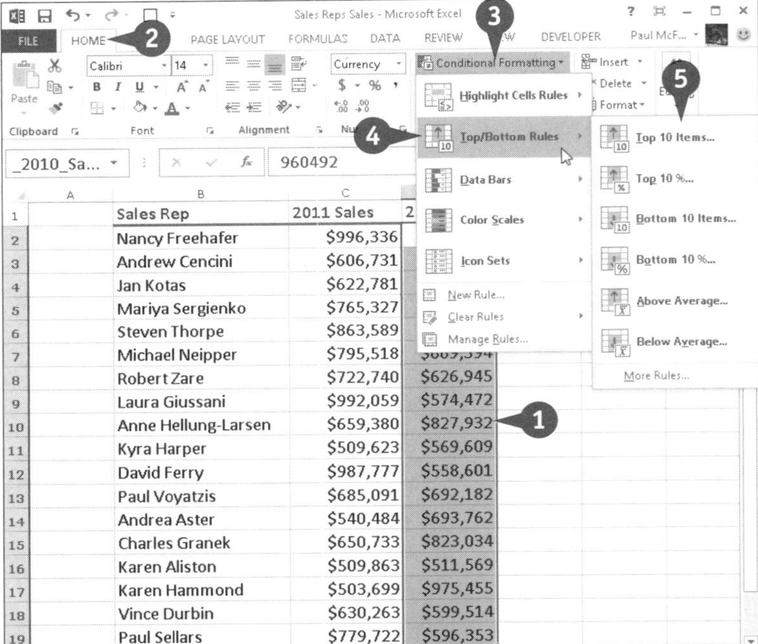

1. Select the range you want to work with.
2. Click the Home tab.
3. Click Conditional Formatting.
4. Click Top/Bottom Rules.
5. Click the type of rule you want to create.

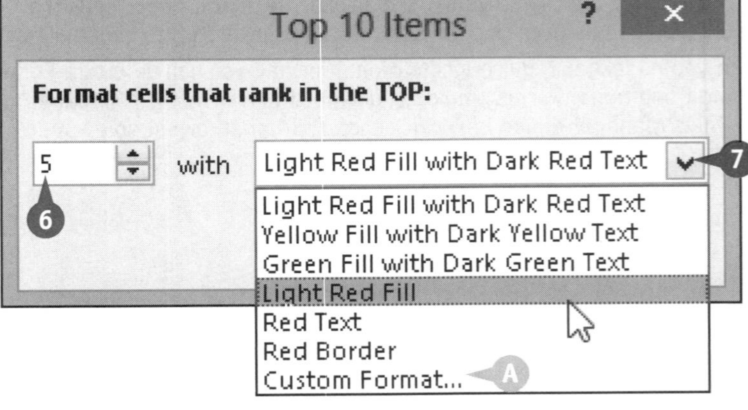

A dialog box appears with a name corresponding to the type of rule you clicked in step 5.

6. Type the value you want to use for the condition.
7. Click the down arrow and then click the formatting you want to use.

(A) To create your own format, click Custom Format.

8 Click OK.

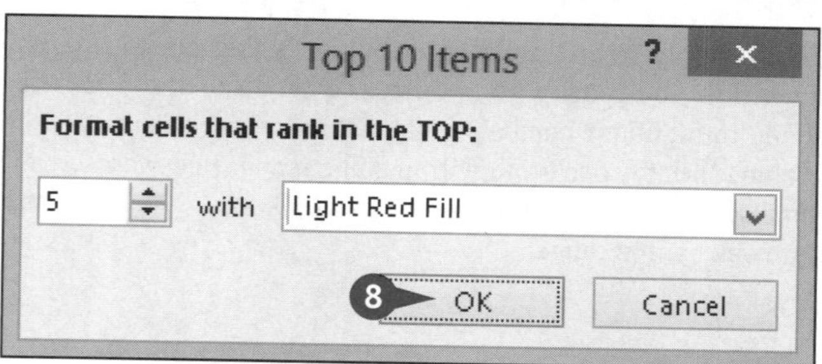

B Excel applies the formatting to cells that meet the condition you specified.

Sales Rep	2011 Sales	2012 Sales
Nancy Freehafer	$996,336	$960,492
Andrew Cencini	$606,731	$577,983
Jan Kotas	$622,781	$967,580
Mariya Sergienko	$765,327	$771,399
Steven Thorpe	$863,589	$827,213
Michael Neipper	$795,518	$669,394
Robert Zare	$722,740	$626,945
Laura Giussani	$992,059	$574,472
Anne Hellung-Larsen	$659,380	$827,932
Kyra Harper	$509,623	$569,609
David Ferry	$987,777	$558,601
Paul Voyatzis	$685,091	$692,182
Andrea Aster	$540,484	$693,762
Charles Granek	$650,733	$823,034
Karen Aliston	$509,863	$511,569
Karen Hammond	$503,699	$975,455
Vince Durbin	$630,263	$599,514
Paul Sellars	$779,722	$596,353

EXTRA

When you set up your top/bottom rule, select a format that ensures the cells that meet your criteria stand out from the other cells in the range. If none of the predefined formats suits your needs, you can always click Custom Format and then use the Format Cells dialog box to create a suitable formatting combination. Use the Font, Border, and Fill tabs to specify the formatting you want to apply, and then click OK.

If you no longer require a top/bottom rule, you can delete it. Follow steps 1 to 3 to select the range and display the Conditional Formatting drop-list. Click Clear Rules, and then click Clear Rules from Selected Cells. Excel removes the rule from the range.

Show Duplicate Values

Excel can apply a conditional format to cells that meet the criteria you specify. You mostly use conditional formatting to highlight numbers greater than or less than some value, or dates occurring within some range. However, you can also use conditional formatting to look for duplicate values in a range.

Many range or table columns require unique values. For example, a column of student IDs or part numbers should not have duplicate values. With conditional formatting, you can specify a font, border, and background pattern that helps to ensure that any duplicate cells in a range or table stand out from the other cells.

Show Duplicate Values

1. Select the range you want to work with.
2. Click the Home tab.
3. Click Conditional Formatting.
4. Click Highlight Cells Rules.
5. Click Duplicate Values.

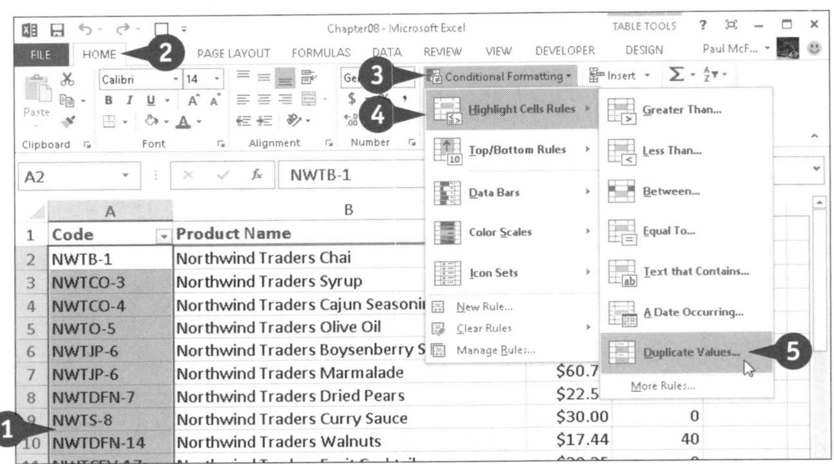

A dialog box appears with a name corresponding to the operator you clicked in step 5.

A. To highlight the unique values in the range, click the down arrow, and then click Unique.

6. Click the down arrow and then click the formatting to use.

   To create your own format, click Custom Format.

7. Click OK.

B. Excel applies the formatting to any cells that have duplicate values in the range.

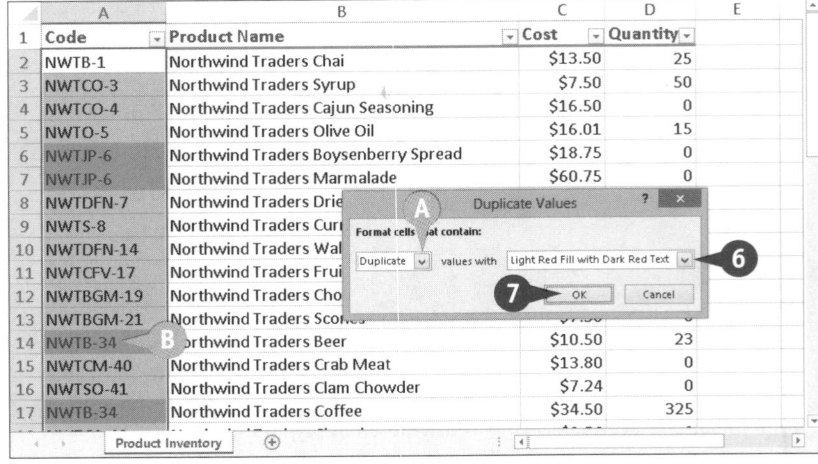

When you create top/bottom rules that apply a conditional format to cells at the top or bottom of a range of values, you mostly use these rules on either raw values or percentages. However, Excel also enables you to create top/bottom rules based on the average value in the range.

Specifically, you can highlight values that are either above or below the average of all the values in the range. You can specify a font, border, and background pattern that helps to ensure that these values stand out from the other cells.

Show Cells That Are Above or Below Average

1. Select the range you want to work with.
2. Click the Home tab.
3. Click Conditional Formatting.
4. Click Top/Bottom Rules.
5. Click either Above Average or Below Average.

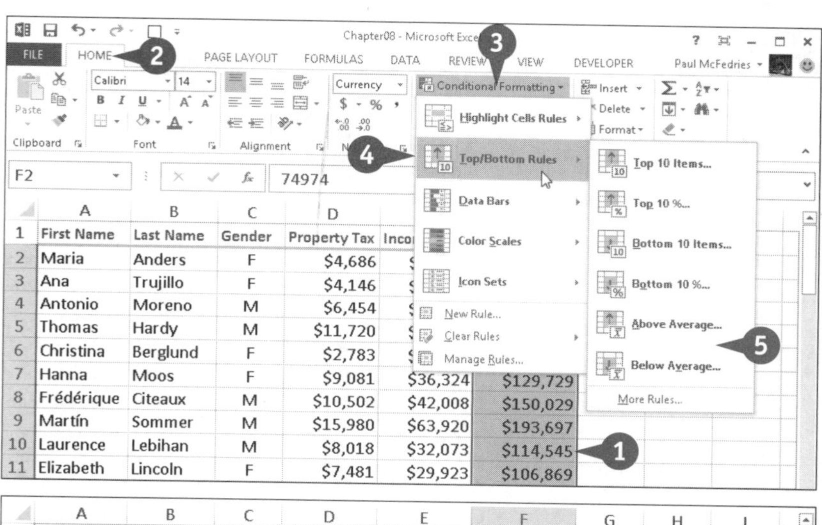

A dialog box appears with a name corresponding to the type of rule you clicked in step 5.

6. Click the down arrow and then click the formatting you want to use.

To create your own format, click Custom Format.

7. Click OK.

A. Excel applies the formatting to cells that are either above or below average.

Above Average

Format cells that are ABOVE AVERAGE:

for the selected range with Green Fill with Dark Green Text

OK Cancel

Analyze Cell Values with Data Bars

In some data analysis scenarios, you might be interested more in the relative values within a range than the absolute values. For example, if you have a table of products that includes a column showing unit sales, you may want to compare the relative sales of all the products.

This sort of analysis is often easiest if you visualize the relative values. You can do that by using *data bars*, a data visualization feature that applies colored, and horizontal bars to each cell in a range of values — these bars appear behind the values in the range. The length of the data bar that appears in each cell depends on the value in that cell: the larger the value, the longer the data bar.

Analyze Cell Values with Data Bars

1. Select the range you want to work with.

	A	B	C	D
1	Product Name	Units	$ Total	
2	Northwind Traders Almonds	20	$ 200	
3	Northwind Traders Beer	487	$ 6,818	
4	Northwind Traders Boysenberry Spread	100	$ 2,500	
5	Northwind Traders Cajun Seasoning	40	$ 880	
6	Northwind Traders Chai	40	$ 720	
7	Northwind Traders Chocolate	200	$ 2,550	
8	Northwind Traders Chocolate Biscuits Mix	85	$ 782	
9	Northwind Traders Clam Chowder	290	$ 2,799	
10	Northwind Traders Coffee	650	$ 29,900	
11	Northwind Traders Crab Meat	120	$ 2,208	
12	Northwind Traders Curry Sauce	65	$ 2,600	
13	Northwind Traders Dried Apples	40	$ 2,120	
14	Northwind Traders Dried Pears	40	$ 1,200	
15	Northwind Traders Dried Plums	75	$ 263	
16	Northwind Traders Fruit Cocktail	40	$ 1,560	
17	Northwind Traders Gnocchi	10	$ 380	
18	Northwind Traders Green Tea	275	$ 822	

2. Click the Home tab.
3. Click Conditional Formatting.
4. Click Data Bars.

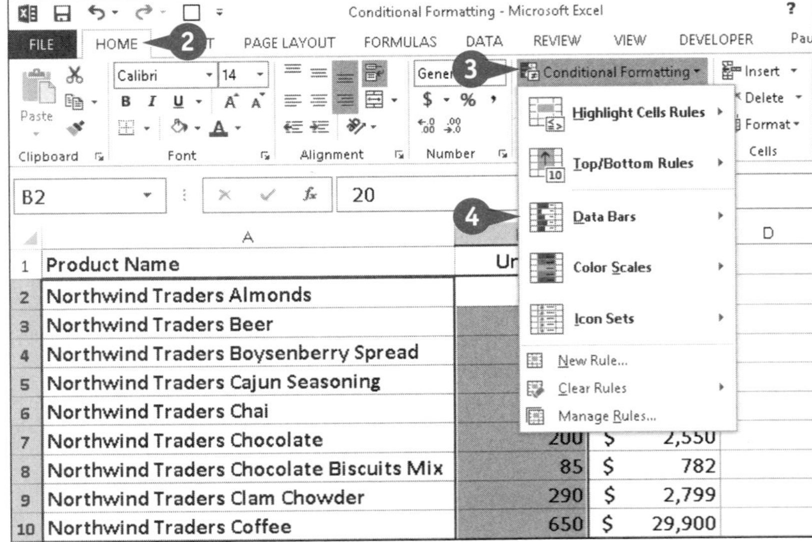

5 Click the fill type of data bars you want to create.

A Gradient fill data bars begin with a solid color and then gradually fade to a lighter color.

B Solid fill data bars are a solid color.

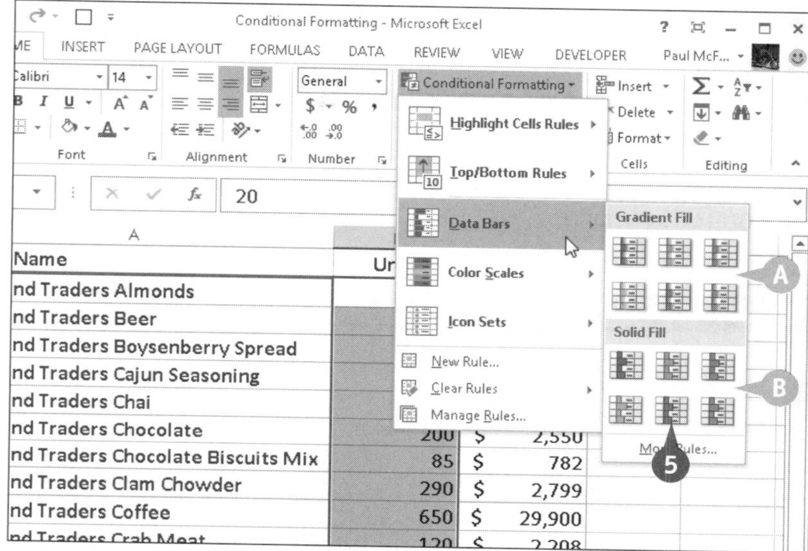

C Excel applies the data bars to each cell in the range.

	A	B	C
1	Product Name	Units	$ Total
2	Northwind Traders Almonds	20	$ 200
3	Northwind Traders Beer	487	$ 6,818
4	Northwind Traders Boysenberry Spread	100	$ 2,500
5	Northwind Traders Cajun Seasoning	40	$ 880
6	Northwind Traders Chai	40	$ 720
7	Northwind Traders Chocolate	200	$ 2,550
8	Northwind Traders Chocolate Biscuits Mix	85	$ 782
9	Northwind Traders Clam Chowder	290	$ 2,799
10	Northwind Traders Coffee	650	$ 29,900
11	Northwind Traders Crab Meat	120	$ 2,208
12	Northwind Traders Curry Sauce	65	$ 2,600
13	Northwind Traders Dried Apples	40	$ 2,120
14	Northwind Traders Dried Pears	40	$ 1,200
15	Northwind Traders Dried Plums	75	$ 263
16	Northwind Traders Fruit Cocktail	40	$ 1,560
17	Northwind Traders Gnocchi	10	$ 380
18	Northwind Traders Green Tea	275	$ 822

EXTRA

If your range includes right-aligned values, the gradient fill data bars are a better choice than the solid fill data bars. This is because even the longest gradient fill bars fade to white towards the right edge of the cell, so your range values should mostly appear on a white background, making them easier to read.

If you no longer require the data bars, you can remove them. Follow steps 1 to 3 to select the range and display the Conditional Formatting drop-down list, and then click Manage Rules. Excel displays the Conditional Formatting Rules Manager dialog box. Click the data bar rule you want to remove, click Delete Rule, and then click OK.

Analyze Cell Values with Color Scales

It is often useful to get some idea about the overall distribution of values in a range. For example, you might want to know whether a range has many low values and just a few high values. *Color scales* can help you analyze your data in this way. A color scale compares the relative values in a range by applying shading to each cell, where the color reflects each cell's value.

Color scales can also tell you whether your data includes *outliers*, values that are much higher or lower than the others are. Similarly, color scales can help you make value judgments about your data. For example, high sales and low numbers of product defects are good, whereas low margins and high employee turnover rates are bad.

Analyze Cell Values with Color Scales

1. Select the range you want to work with.

GDP — % Annual Growth Rates (Source: The World Bank)

	2002	2003	2004	2005	2006	2007	2008	2009	2010	2011
World	2.0	2.7	4.0	3.5	4.0	3.9	1.3	-2.2	4.3	2.7
Albania	2.9	5.7	5.9	5.5	5.0	5.9	7.7	3.3	3.5	3.0
Algeria	4.7	6.9	5.2	5.1	2.0	3.0	2.4	2.4	3.3	2.5
Angola	14.5	3.3	11.2	18.3	20.7	22.6	13.8	2.4	3.4	3.4
Antigua and Barbuda	2.5	5.1	7.0	4.2	13.3	-9.6	1.5	-10.3	-8.9	-4.2
Argentina	-10.9	8.8	9.0	9.2	8.5	8.7	6.8	0.9	9.2	8.9
Armenia	13.2	14.0	10.5	13.9	13.2	13.7	6.9	-14.1	2.1	4.6
Australia	3.9	3.3	4.2	3.0	3.1	3.6	3.8	1.4	2.3	1.8
Austria	1.7	0.9	2.6	2.4	3.7	3.7	1.4	-3.8	2.3	3.1
Azerbaijan	10.6	11.2	10.2	26.4	34.5	25.0	10.8	9.3	5.0	1.0
Bahamas, The	2.7	-1.3	0.9	3.4	2.5	1.4	-2.3	-4.9	0.2	1.6
Bangladesh	4.4	5.3	6.3	6.0	6.6	6.4	6.2	5.7	6.1	6.7
Belarus	5.0	7.0	11.4	9.4	10.0	8.6	10.2	0.2	7.7	5.3
Belgium	1.4	0.8	3.3	1.8	2.7	2.9	1.0	-2.8	2.2	1.9

2. Click the Home tab.
3. Click Conditional Formatting.
4. Click Color Scales.

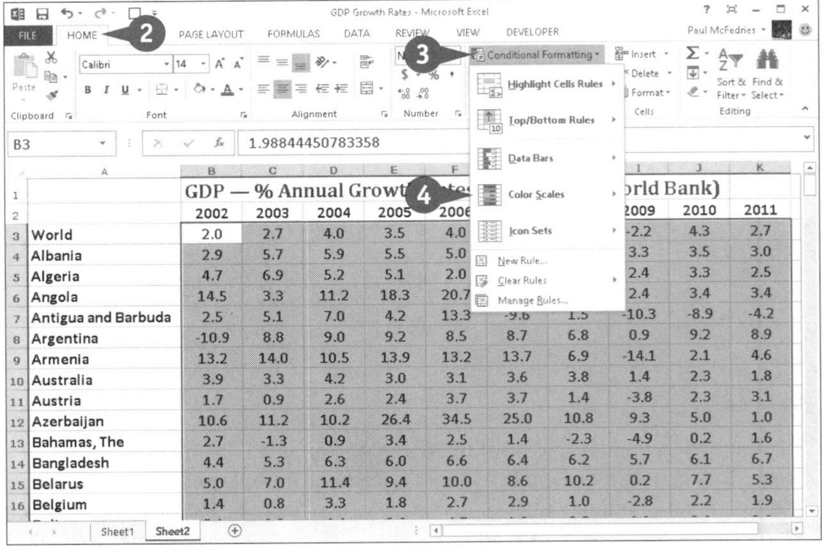

5 Click the color scale that has the color scheme you want to apply.

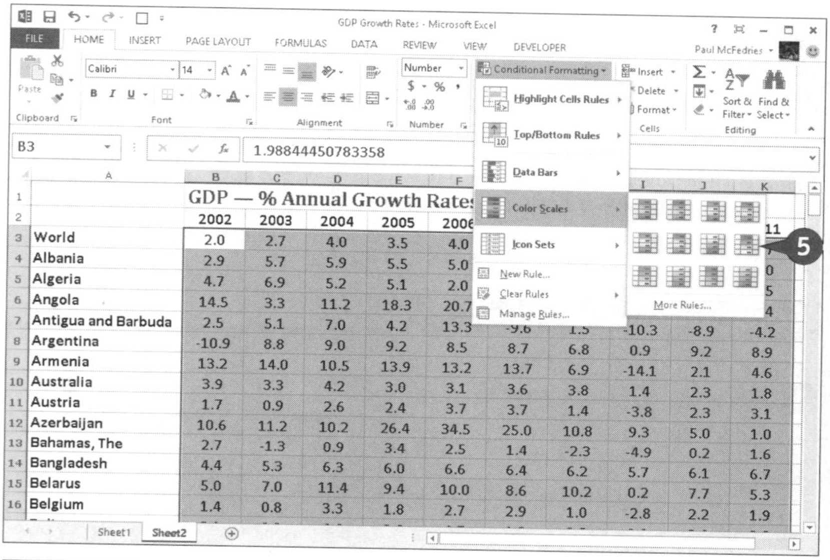

A Excel applies the color scales to each cell in the range.

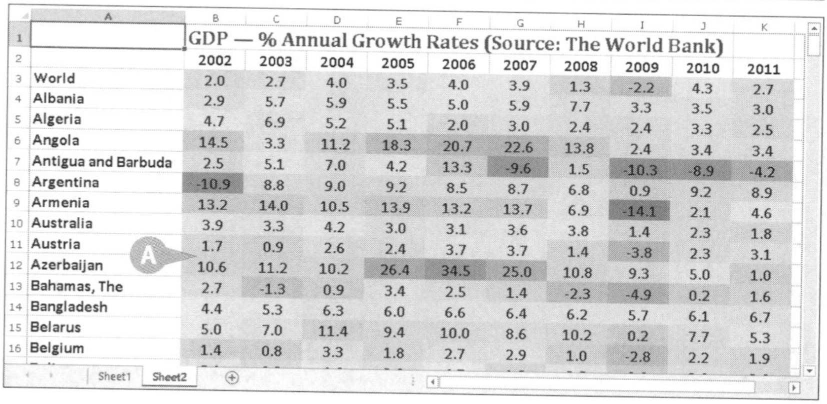

EXTRA

Excel color scales come in two varieties: 3-color scales and 2-color scales. If your goal is to look for outliers or to make value judgments about your data, go with a 3-color scale because outliers stand out more, and you can assign your own values to the colors (such as positive, neutral, and negative). Use a 2-color scale when you want to look for patterns in the data, as 2-color scale offers less contrast.

To delete a color scale, follow steps 1 to 3 to select the range and display the Conditional Formatting drop-down list, and then click Manage Rules. In the Conditional Formatting Rules Manager dialog box, click the rule you want to remove and then click Delete Rule.

Analyze Cell Values with Icon Sets

You can help analyze large sets of data by applying to each cell an icon that has a symbolic association. This gives you a visual clue about the cell's relative value compared with the overall distribution of values in the range.

Symbols that have common or well-known associations are often useful for analyzing large amounts of data. For example, a check mark usually means something is good, finished, or acceptable, whereas an X means something is bad, unfinished, or unacceptable. Similarly, a green circle is positive, whereas a red circle is negative (think traffic lights). Excel puts these and other symbolic associations to good use with the *icon sets* feature. You use icon sets to visualize the relative values of cells in a range.

Analyze Cell Values with Icon Sets

1. Select the range you want to work with.

	A	B
1	Student ID	Grade
2	64947	82
3	69630	66
4	18324	52
5	89826	94
6	63600	40
7	25089	62
8	89923	88
9	13000	75
10	16895	66
11	24918	62
12	45107	71
13	64090	53
14	94395	74
15	58749	65
16	26916	66
17	59033	67
18	15450	68

GDP Growth Rates | Student Grades

2. Click the Home tab.
3. Click Conditional Formatting.
4. Click Icon Sets.

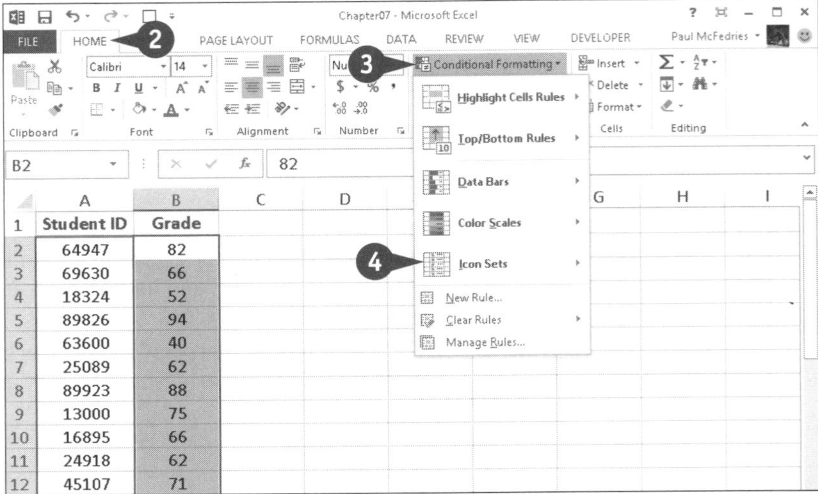

5. Click the type of icon set you want to apply.

   The categories include Directional, Shapes, Indicators, and Ratings.

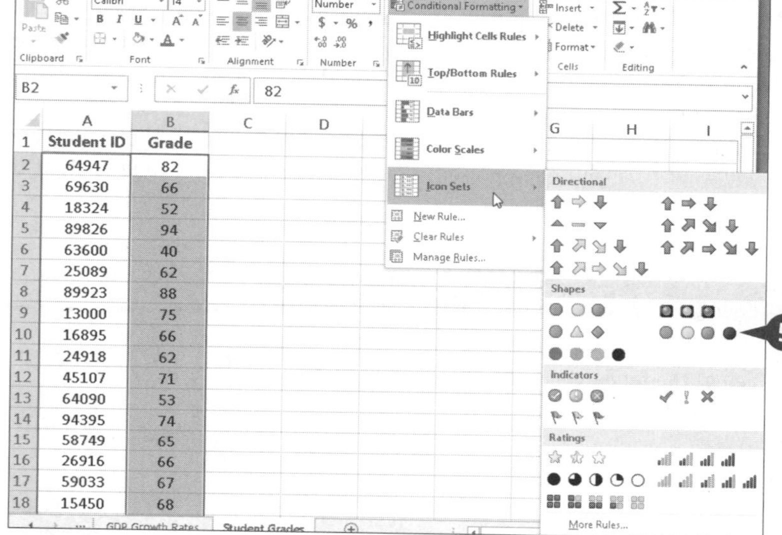

Ⓐ Excel applies the icons to each cell in the range.

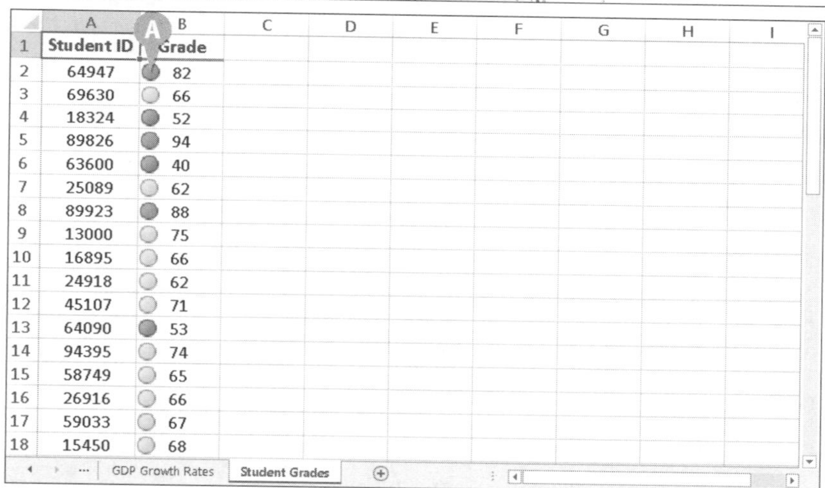

APPLY IT

With icon sets, Excel adds a particular icon to each cell in the range, and that icon tells you something about the cell's value relative to the rest of the range. For example, the highest values might be assigned an upward-pointing arrow, the lowest values a downward-pointing arrow, and the values in between a horizontal arrow.

The Excel icon sets come in four categories: use Directional icon sets for indicating trends and data movement; use Shapes icon sets for pointing out the high (green) and low (red) values; use Indicators to add value judgments; and use Ratings to show where each cell resides in the overall range of data values.

Create a Custom Conditional Formatting Rule

The conditional formatting rules in Excel — highlight cells rules, top/bottom rules, data bars, color scales, and icon sets — offer an easy way to analyze data through visualization. You can tailor your format-based data analysis by creating a custom conditional formatting rule that suits how you want to analyze and present the data.

These predefined rules do not suit particular types of data or data analysis. For example, the icon sets assume that higher values are more positive than lower values, but that is not always true. To get the type of data analysis you prefer, you can create a custom conditional formatting rule and apply it to your range.

Create a Custom Conditional Formatting Rule

1. Select the range you want to work with.

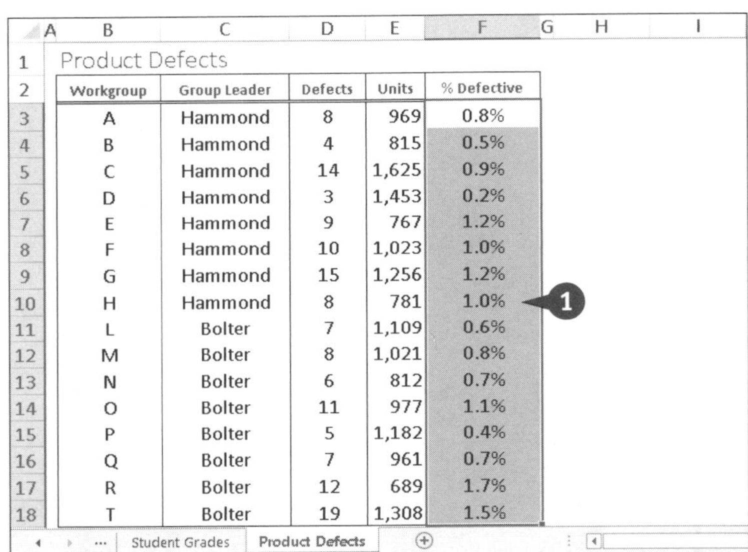

Product Defects

Workgroup	Group Leader	Defects	Units	% Defective
A	Hammond	8	969	0.8%
B	Hammond	4	815	0.5%
C	Hammond	14	1,625	0.9%
D	Hammond	3	1,453	0.2%
E	Hammond	9	767	1.2%
F	Hammond	10	1,023	1.0%
G	Hammond	15	1,256	1.2%
H	Hammond	8	781	1.0%
L	Bolter	7	1,109	0.6%
M	Bolter	8	1,021	0.8%
N	Bolter	6	812	0.7%
O	Bolter	11	977	1.1%
P	Bolter	5	1,182	0.4%
Q	Bolter	7	961	0.7%
R	Bolter	12	689	1.7%
T	Bolter	19	1,308	1.5%

2. Click the Home tab.
3. Click Conditional Formatting.
4. Click New Rule.

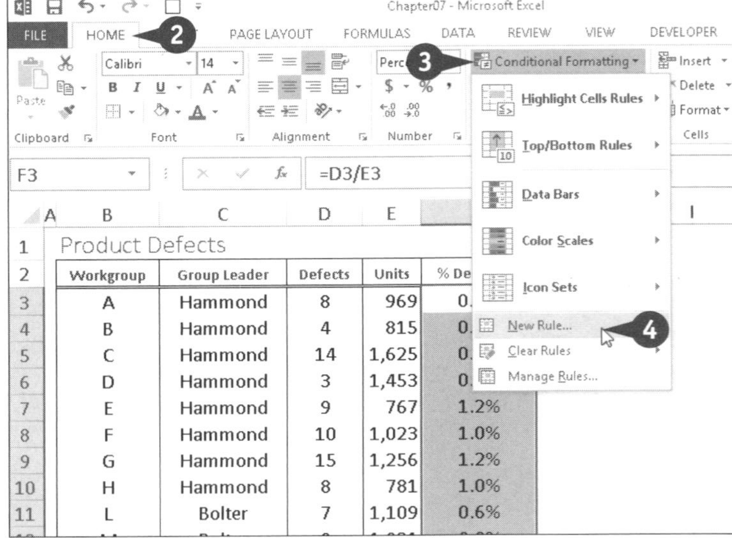

The New Formatting Rule dialog box appears.

5 Click the type of rule you want to create.

6 Edit the rule's style and formatting.

The controls you see depend on the rule type you selected.

A With Icon Sets, click Reverse Icon Order if you want to reverse the normal icon assignments, as shown here.

7 Click OK.

B Excel applies the conditional formatting to each cell in the range.

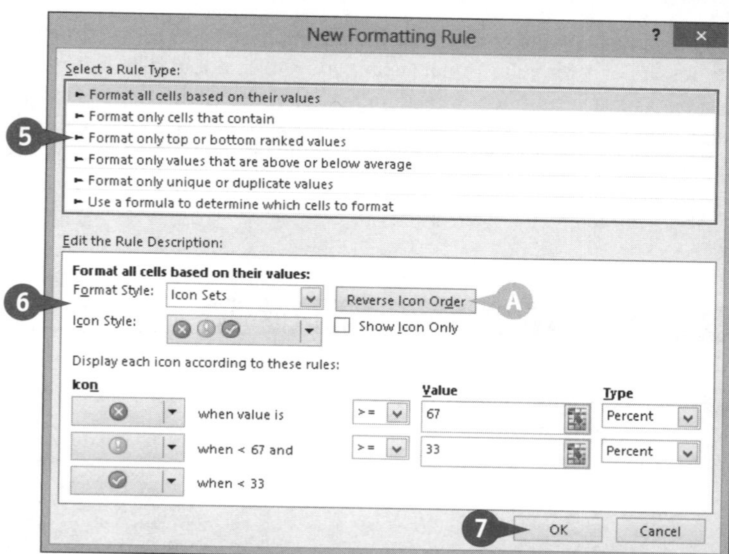

2	Workgroup	Group Leader	Defects	Units	Defective
3	A	Hammond	8	969	0.8%
4	B	Hammond	4	815	0.5%
5	C	Hammond	14	1,625	0.9%
6	D	Hammond	3	1,453	0.2%
7	E	Hammond	9	767	1.2%
8	F	Hammond	10	1,023	1.0%
9	G	Hammond	15	1,256	1.2%
10	H	Hammond	8	781	1.0%
11	L	Bolter	7	1,109	0.6%
12	M	Bolter	8	1,021	0.8%
13	N	Bolter	6	812	0.7%
14	O	Bolter	11	977	1.1%
15	P	Bolter	5	1,182	0.4%
16	Q	Bolter	7	961	0.7%
17	R	Bolter	12	689	1.7%
18	T	Bolter	19	1,308	1.5%

Student Grades | Product Defects

B

APPLY IT

Custom conditional formatting rules are ideal for situations where the normal value judgments — that is, that higher values are good and lower values are bad — do not apply. For example, although the icon sets assume higher values are more positive than lower values, this assumption is not always true. In a database of product defects, lower values are better than higher ones. Similarly, data bars are based on the relative numeric values in a range, but you might prefer to base them on the relative percentages or on percentile rankings.

Highlight Cells Based On a Formula

You can also apply conditional formatting based on the results of a formula. In particular, you set up a logical formula as the conditional formatting criteria. For each cell where that formula returns `TRUE`, Excel applies the formatting you specify; for all the other cells, Excel does not apply the formatting.

In most cases, you use a comparison formula, or you use an `IF` function, often combined with another logical function such as `AND` or `OR`. In each case, your formula's comparison value must reference only the first value in the range. For example, if the range you are working with is a set of dates in A2:A100, the comparison formula =WEEKDAY(A2)=6 would apply conditional formatting to every cell in the range that occurs on a Friday.

Create a Custom Conditional Formatting Rule

1 Select the range you want to work with.

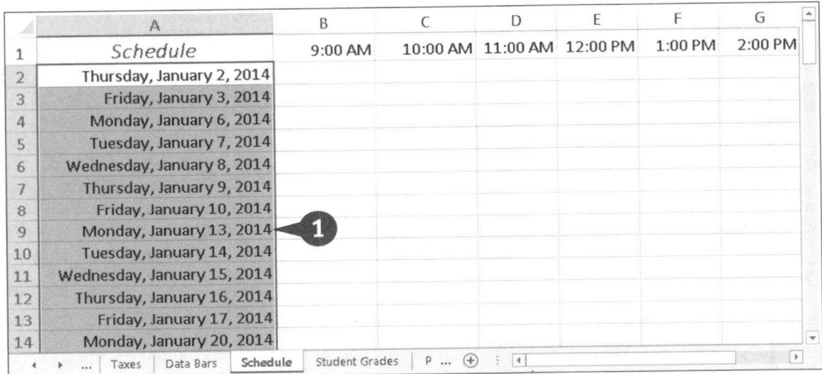

2 Click the Home tab.

3 Click Conditional Formatting.

4 Click New Rule.

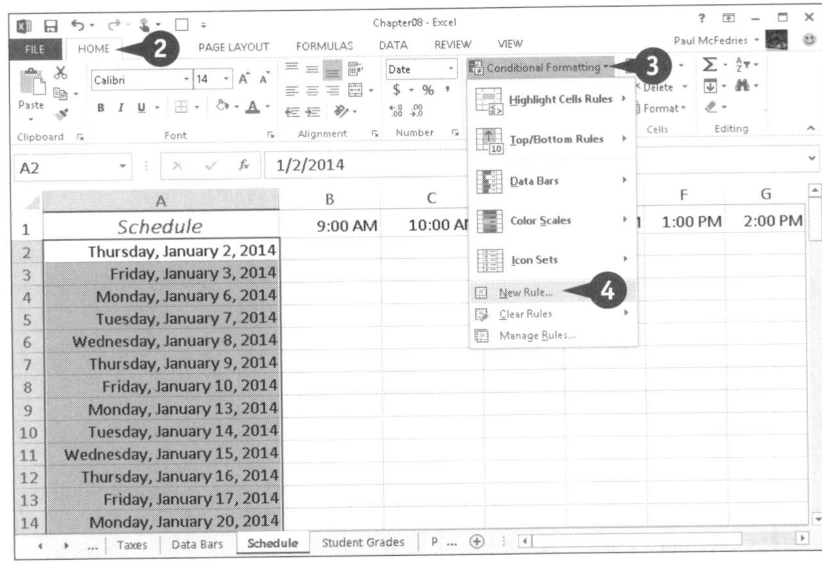

The New Formatting Rule dialog box appears.

5 Click Use a Formula to Determine Which Cells to Format.

6 Type the logical formula.

7 Edit the rule's style and formatting.

8 Click OK.

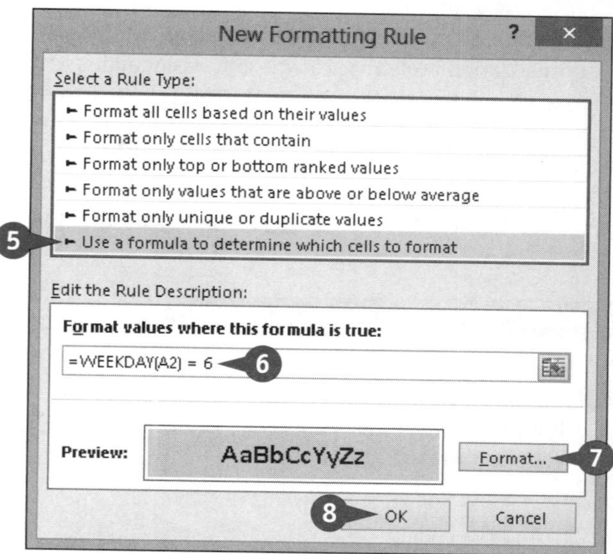

A Excel applies the conditional formatting to each cell in the range where the logical formula returns `TRUE`.

	A	B
1	Schedule	9:00 AM
2	Thursday, January 2, 2014	
3	Friday, January 3, 2014	
4	Monday, January 6, 2014	
5	Tuesday, January 7, 2014	
6	Wednesday, January 8, 2014	
7	Thursday, January 9, 2014	
8	Friday, January 10, 2014	
9	Monday, January 13, 2014	
10	Tuesday, January 14, 2014	
11	Wednesday, January 15, 2014	
12	Thursday, January 16, 2014	
13	Friday, January 17, 2014	
14	Monday, January 20, 2014	

... Taxes | Data Bars | Schedule | Student Gra

APPLY IT

It is often advantageous to apply a conditional format based on a formula that compares all the cells in a range to one value in that range. The simplest case is a formula that applies conditional formatting to those range cells that are equal to a cell value in the range. The logical formula to use for such a comparison is `=range=cell`.

Here, `range` is an absolute reference to the range of cells you want to work with, and `cell` is a relative reference to the comparison cell. For example, to apply a conditional format to those cells in the range A1:A50 that are equal to the value in cell A1, you would use the logical formula `=$A$1:$A$50=A1`.

Modify a Conditional Formatting Rule

Conditional formatting rules are excellent data visualization tools that can make it easier and faster to analyze your data. Whether it is highlighting cells based on criteria, showing cells that are in the top or bottom of the range, or using features such as data bars, color scales, and icon sets, conditional formatting enables you to interpret your data quickly. Based on this, you might find that the conditional formatting you used was not correct because it does not enable you to visualize your data the way you had hoped. Similarly, a change in data might require a change in criteria. Whatever the reason, you can modify your conditional formatting rules to ensure you get the best visualization for your data.

Modify a Conditional Formatting Rule

1 Select the range that includes the conditional formatting rule you want to modify.

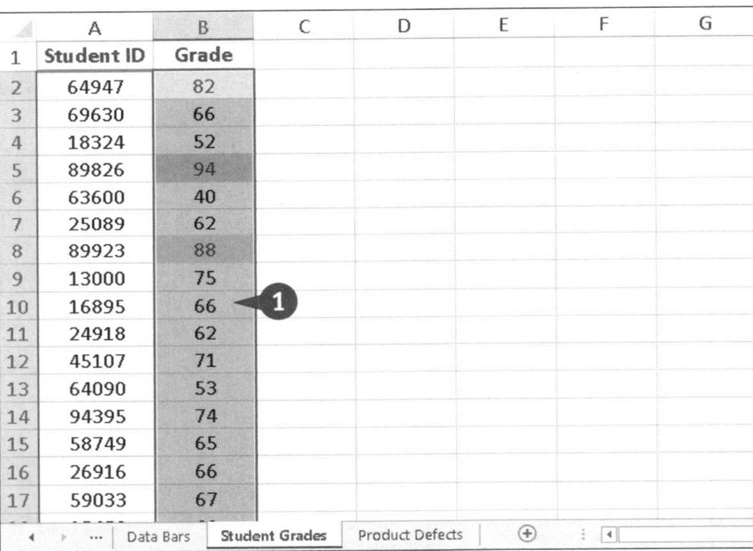

2 Click the Home tab.

3 Click Conditional Formatting.

4 Click Manage Rules.

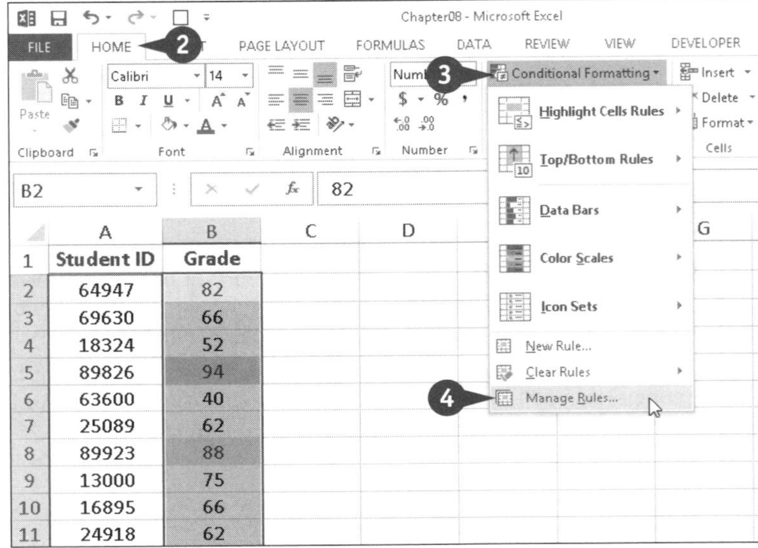

The Conditional Formatting Rules Manager dialog box appears.

5 Click the rule you want to modify.

6 Click Edit Rule.

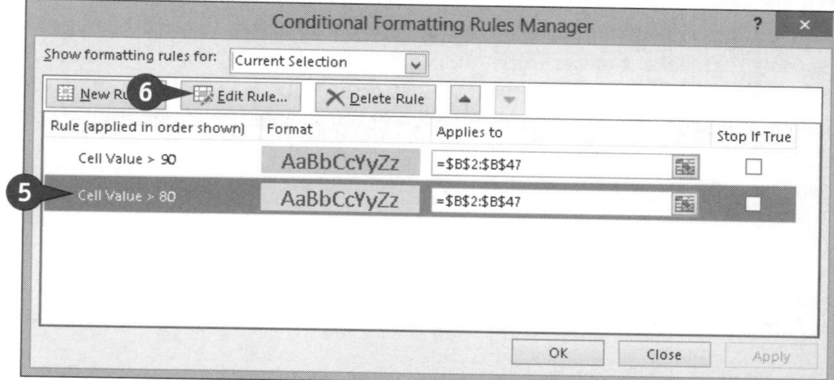

The Edit Formatting Rule dialog box appears.

7 Make your changes to the rule.

8 Click OK.

Excel returns you to the Conditional Formatting Rules Manager dialog box.

9 Click OK (not shown).

Excel updates the conditional formatting.

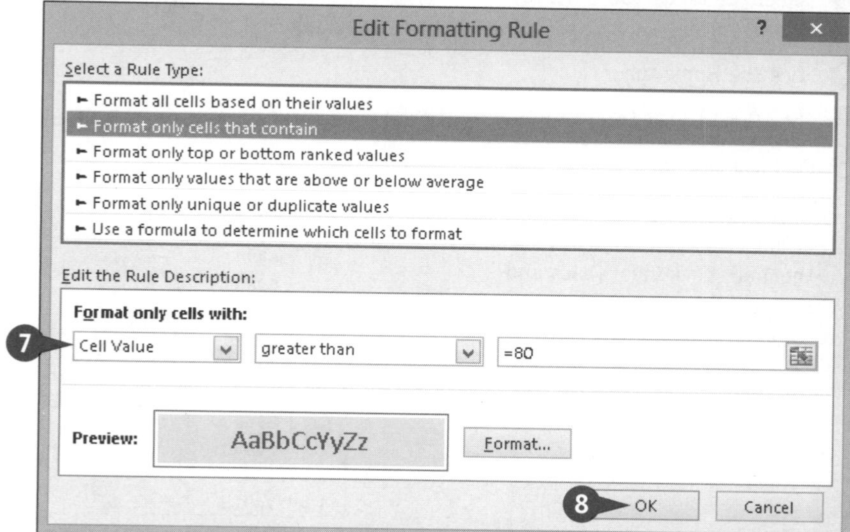

EXTRA

If you have multiple conditional formatting rules applied to a range, the visualization is affected by the order in which Excel applies the rules. Specifically, if a cell already has a conditional format applied, Excel does not overwrite that format with a new one. For example, suppose you have two conditional formatting rules applied to a list of student grades: one for grades over 90 and one for grades over 80. If you apply the over-80 conditional format first, Excel will never apply the over-90 format because those values are already covered by the over-80 format. To fix this, in the Conditional Formatting Rules Manager dialog box, click the rule you want to modify, and then click the Move down (▾) or Move Up (▴) sort button to set the order.

Remove Conditional Formatting from a Range

Conditional formatting rules are useful data visualization tools that make it easier to perform certain types of data analysis. For example, if your data is essentially random, then conditional formatting rules will not enable you to see patterns in that data. You might also find that conditional formatting is not helpful for certain collections of data or certain types of data. On the other hand, you might find conditional formatting useful for getting a handle on your data set, but then prefer to remove the formatting. If, for whatever reason, you find that a range's conditional formatting is not helpful or no longer required, you can remove the conditional formatting from that range.

Remove Conditional Formatting from a Range

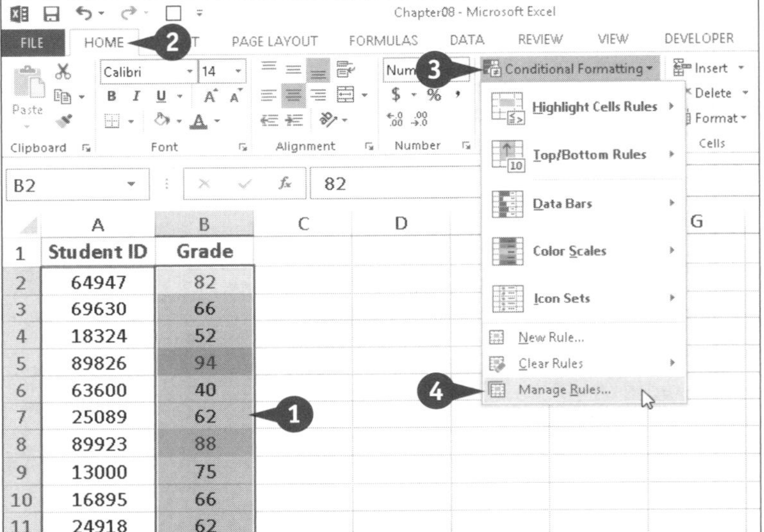

1. Select the range you want to work with.
2. Click the Home tab.
3. Click Conditional Formatting.
4. Click Manage Rules.

   If you have multiple rules defined and you want to remove them all, click Clear Rules and then click Clear Rules from Selected Cells.

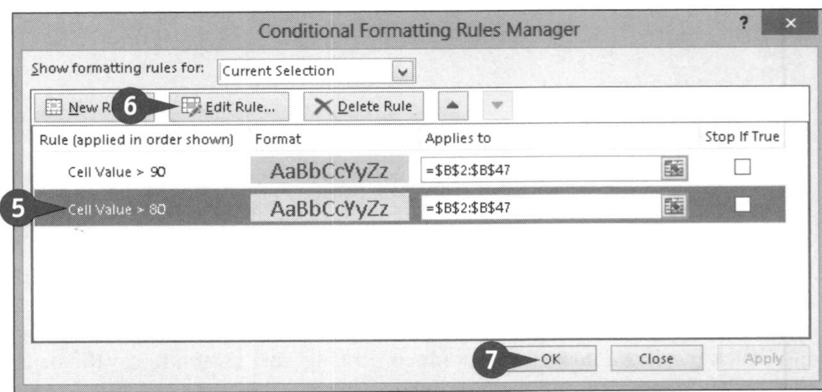

The Conditional Formatting Rules Manager dialog box appears.

5. Click the rule you want to remove.
6. Click Delete Rule.

   Excel removes the rule from the range.

7. Click OK.

Remove Conditional Formatting from a Worksheet

Although the data visualization aspect of conditional formatting rules is part of the appeal of this Excel feature, as with all things visual it is possible to overdo it. That is, you might end up with a worksheet that has multiple conditional formatting rules and therefore some unattractive and confusing combinations of highlighted cells, data bars, color scales, and icon sets.

If you find that a worksheet's conditional formatting is hindering your data analysis efforts rather than helping them, you can remove conditional formatting from that worksheet. You can either remove individual conditional formatting rules or clear the worksheet of all its conditional formatting.

Remove Conditional Formatting from a Worksheet

1. Select the worksheet.
2. Click the Home tab.
3. Click Conditional Formatting.
4. Click Manage Rules.

   If you have multiple rules defined and you want to remove them all, click Clear Rules and then click Clear Rules from Entire Sheet.

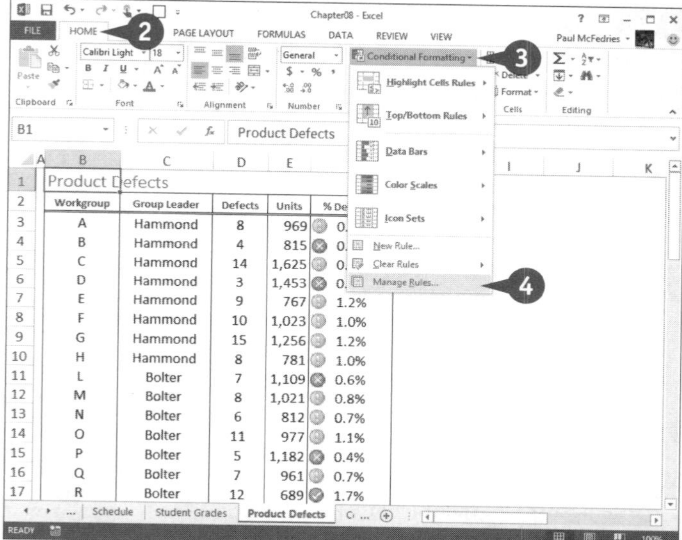

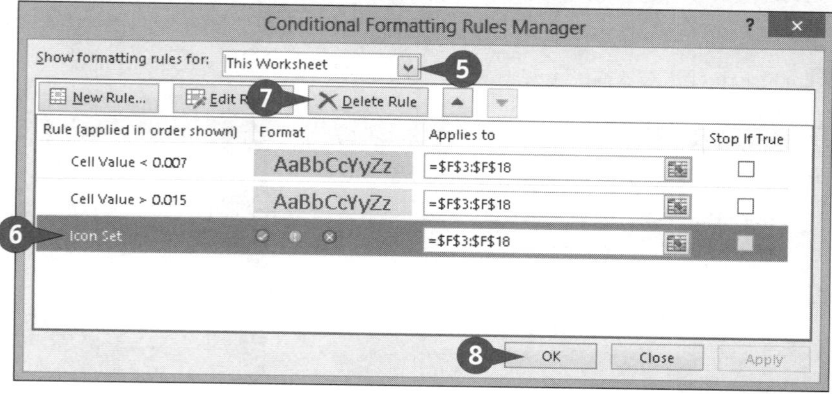

The Conditional Formatting Rules Manager dialog box appears.

5. Click the Show Formatting Rules For down arrow and select This Worksheet.
6. Click the rule you want to remove.
7. Click Delete Rule.

   Excel removes the rule from the worksheet.

8. Click OK.

Set Data Validation Rules

You can make Excel data entry more efficient by setting up data entry cells to accept only certain values. To do this, you can set up a cell with data validation criteria that specify the allowed value or values. This is called a *data validation rule*. You can work with numbers, dates, times, or even text length, and you can set up criteria that are between two values, equal to a specific value, greater than a value, and so on.

Excel also lets you tell the user what to enter by defining an input message that appears when the user selects the cell. You can also configure the data validation rule to display a message when the user tries to enter an invalid value.

Set Data Validation Rules

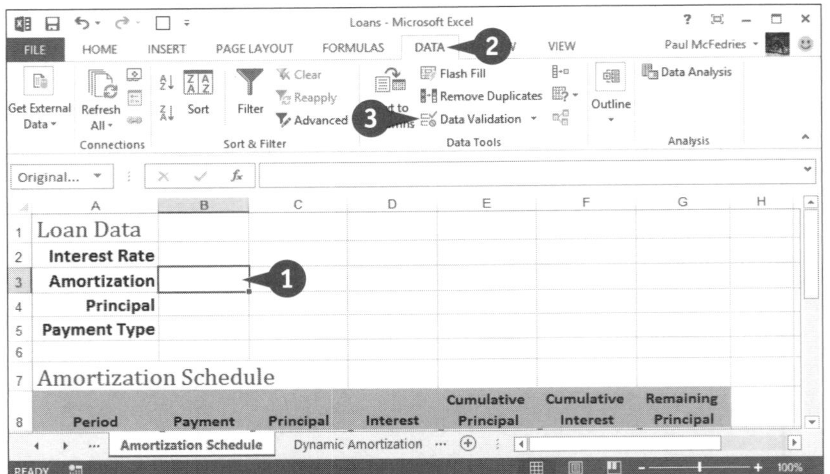

1. Click the cell you want to restrict.
2. Click the Data tab.
3. Click Data Validation.

The Data Validation dialog box appears.

4. Click the Settings tab.
5. Click the Allow down arrow and select the type of data to allow in the cell.
6. Click the Data down arrow and select the operator to use to define the allowable data.
7. Specify the validation criteria, such as the Minimum and Maximum allowable values shown here.

Note: *The criteria boxes you see depend on the operator you chose in step 6.*

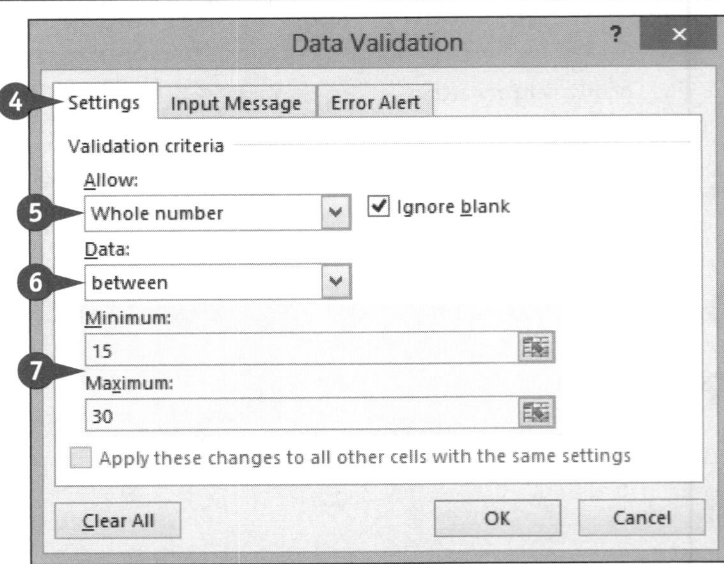

8 Click the Input Message tab.

9 Click the Show Input Message When Cell Is Selected check box if it is not selected (☐ changes to ☑).

10 Type a message title in the Title text box.

11 Type the message you want to display in the Input Message text box.

12 Click OK.

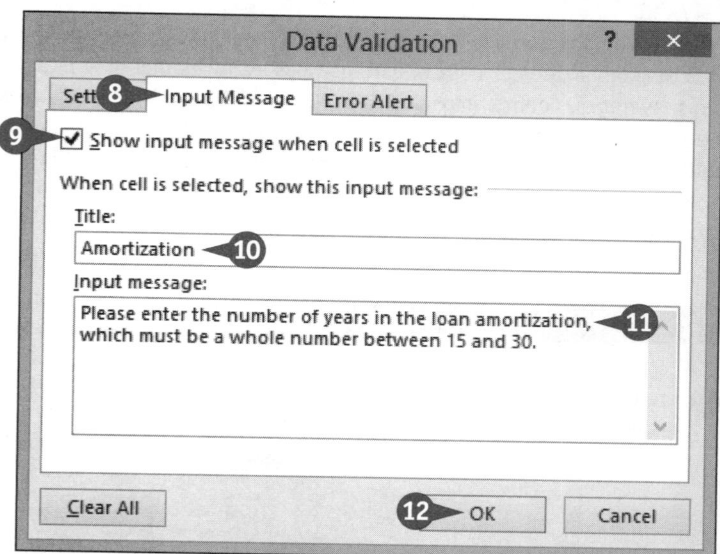

Excel configures the cell to accept only values that meet your criteria.

A When the user selects the cell, the input message appears.

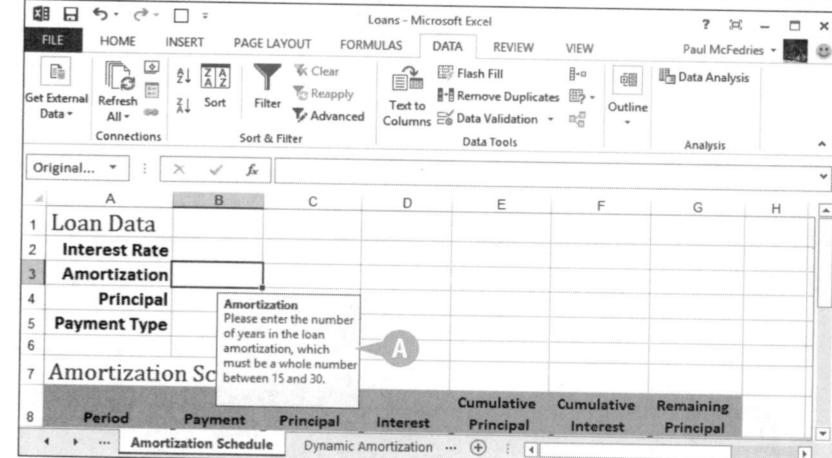

APPLY IT

You can configure the cell to display a message if the user tries to enter an invalid value. Follow steps 1 to 3 to open the Data Validation dialog box, and then click the Error Alert tab. Make sure the Show Error Alert After Invalid Data Is Entered check box is selected (☑), and then specify the Style, Title, and Error Message. Click OK.

If you no longer need to use data validation on a cell, you should clear the settings. Follow steps 1 to 3 to display the Data Validation dialog box and then click Clear All. Excel removes all the validation criteria, as well as the input message and the error alert. Click OK.

Summarize Data with Subtotals

Although you can use formulas and worksheet functions to summarize your data in various ways — including sums, averages, counts, maximums, and minimums — if you are in a hurry, or if you just need a quick summary of your data, you can get Excel to do the work for you. The secret here is a feature called *automatic subtotals*, formulas that Excel adds to a worksheet automatically.

Excel sets up automatic subtotals based on data groupings in a selected field. For example, if you ask for subtotals based on the Customer field, Excel runs down the Customer column and creates a new subtotal each time the name changes. To get useful summaries, you can sort the range on the field containing the data groupings in which you are interested.

Summarize Data with Subtotals

1. Click a cell within the range you want to subtotal.

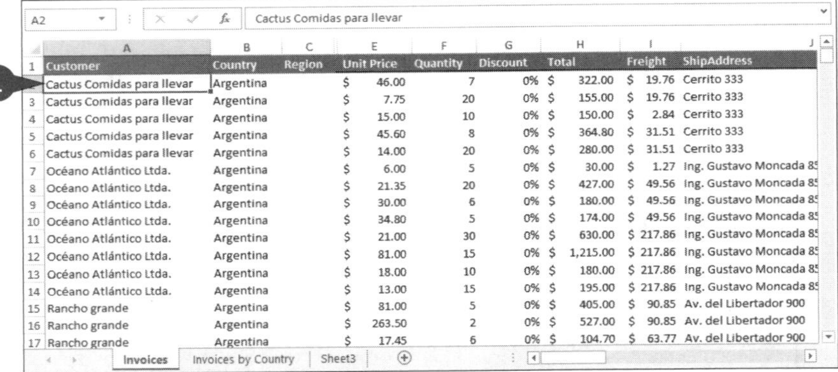

2. Click the Data tab.
3. Click Subtotal.

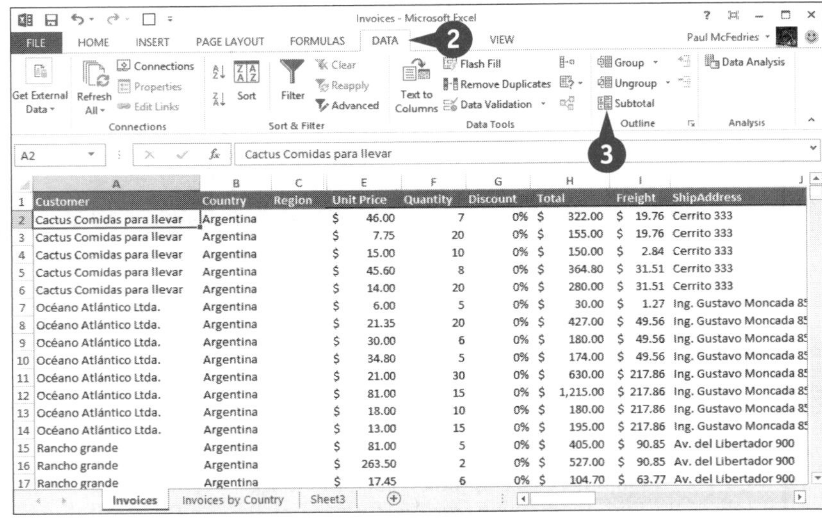

The Subtotal dialog box appears.

4. Click the down arrow and then click the column you want to use to group the subtotals.
5. In the Add Subtotal To list, click the check box for the column you want to summarize (☐ changes to ☑).
6. Click OK.

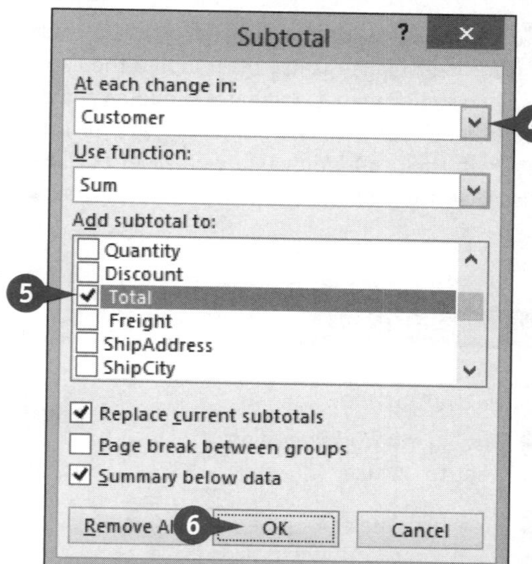

Ⓐ Excel calculates the subtotals and adds them into the range.

Ⓑ Excel adds outline symbols to the range.

Note: *See the next section, "Group Related Data," to learn more about outlining in Excel.*

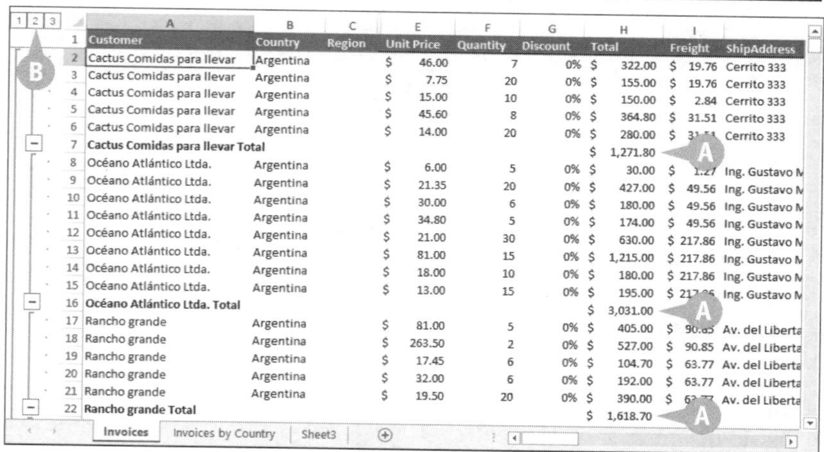

EXTRA

Note that in the phrase, automatic subtotals, the word subtotals is misleading because it implies that you can only summarize your data with totals. That is not the case, however. Using this feature, you can also count the values (all the values or just the numeric values), calculate the average of the values, determine the maximum or minimum value, and calculate the product of the values. For statistical analysis, you can also calculate the standard deviation and variance, both of a sample and of a population. To change the summary calculation, follow steps 1 to 4, click the Use Function drop-down list, and then click the function you want to use for the summary.

Group Related Data

To help you analyze a worksheet, you can control a worksheet range display by grouping the data based on the worksheet formulas and data. Grouping the data creates a worksheet outline, which works similarly to the outline feature in Microsoft Word. In a worksheet outline, you can *collapse* sections of the sheet to display only summary cells (such as quarterly or regional totals), or *expand* hidden sections to show the underlying detail. Note that when you add subtotals to a range, Excel automatically groups the data and displays the outline tools. For more information, see the section, "Summarize Data with Subtotals."

Group Related Data

Create the Outline

1. Display the worksheet you want to outline.
2. Click the Data tab.
3. Click the Group down arrow.
4. Click Auto Outline.

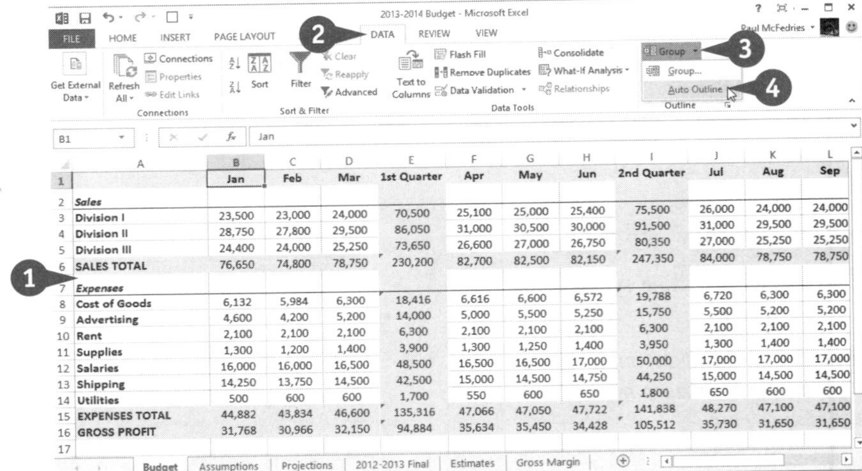

A. Excel outlines the worksheet data.

B. Excel uses level bars to indicate the grouped ranges.

C. Excel displays level symbols to indicate the various levels of the detail that are available in the outline.

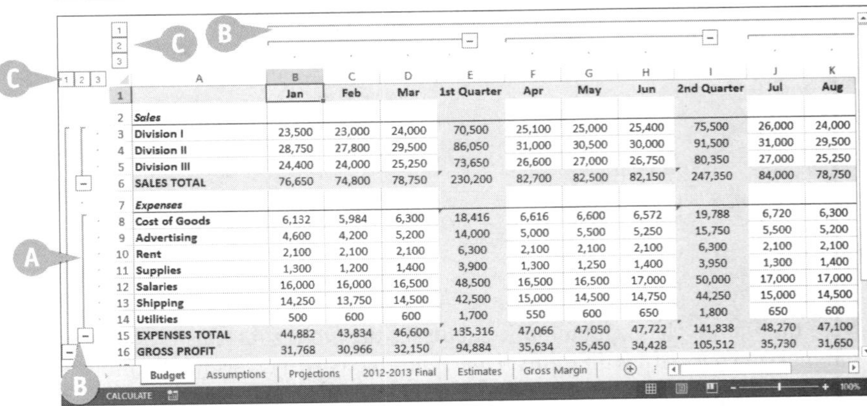

Use the Outline to Control the Range Display

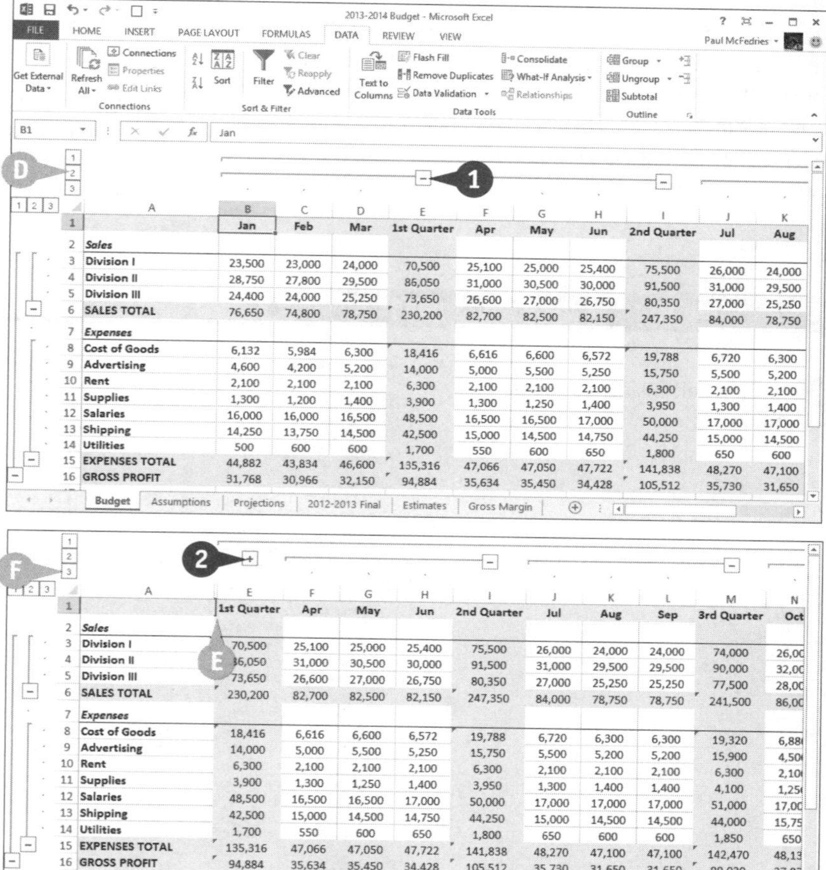

1 Click a Collapse symbol to hide the range indicated by the level bar.

D You can also collapse multiple ranges that are on the same outline level by clicking the appropriate level symbol.

E Excel collapses the range.

2 Click the Expand symbol to view the range again.

F You can also show multiple ranges that are on the same outline level by clicking the appropriate level symbol.

EXTRA

Not all worksheets can be grouped, so you need to make sure your worksheet is a candidate for outlining. First, the worksheet must contain formulas that reference cells or ranges directly adjacent to the formula cell. Worksheets with `SUM` functions that subtotal cells above or to the left are particularly good candidates for outlining.

Second, there must be a consistent pattern to the direction of the formula references. For example, a worksheet with formulas that always reference cells above or to the left can be outlined. Excel will not outline a worksheet with, say, `SUM` functions that reference ranges above and below a formula cell.

Remove Duplicate Values from a Range or Table

You can make your Excel data more accurate for analysis by removing any duplicate records. Duplicate records throw off your calculations by including the same data two or more times. To prevent this, you should delete duplicate records. Rather than looking for duplicates manually, you can use the Remove Duplicates command, which can quickly find and remove duplicates in even the largest ranges or tables.

Before you use the Remove Duplicates command, you must decide what defines a duplicate record in your data. That is, you must specify whether every field has to be identical or whether it is enough that only certain fields are identical.

Remove Duplicate Values from a Range or Table

1. Click a cell inside the range or table.

2. Click the Data tab.

3. Click Remove Duplicates.

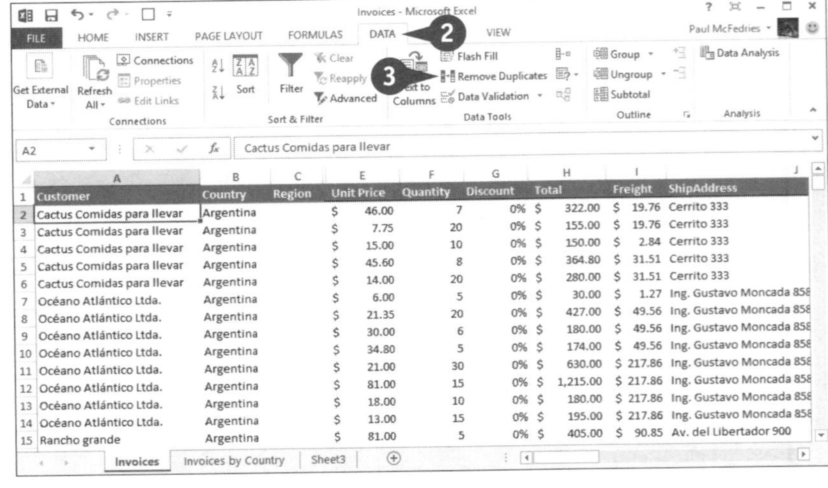

The Remove Duplicates dialog box appears.

4 Click the check box beside each field that you want Excel to check for duplication values (☐ changes to ☑).

Note: *Excel does not give you a chance to confirm the deletion of the duplicate records, so be sure you want to do this before proceeding.*

5 Click OK.

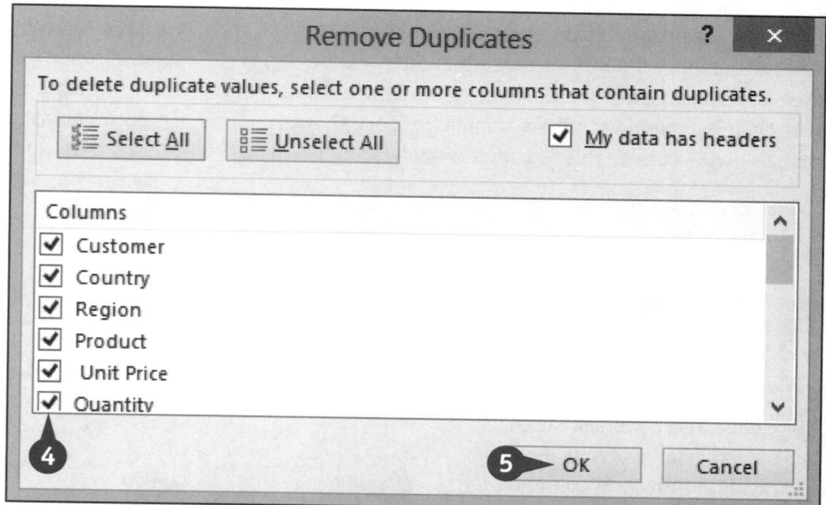

Excel deletes any duplicate records that it finds.

A Excel tells you the number of duplicate records that it deleted.

6 Click OK.

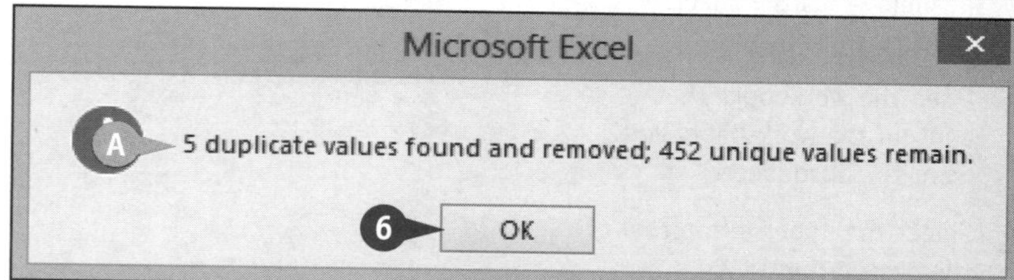

APPLY IT

If your data has many columns, you may want Excel to use only one or two of those fields to look for duplicates. To make this easier, first click Unselect All in the Remove Duplicates dialog box to clear all the check boxes; then select just the check boxes you want Excel to use.

To remove duplicates when your range does not have column headers, open the Remove Duplicates dialog box and deselect the My Data Has Headers check box (☑ changes to ☐). Use the check boxes labeled Column A, Column B, and so on to choose the columns that you want Excel to check for duplicate values.

Consolidate Data from Multiple Worksheets

Companies often distribute similar worksheets to multiple departments to capture budget numbers, inventory values, survey data, and so on. Those worksheets must then be combined into a summary report showing company-wide totals. This is called *consolidating* the data.

Rather than doing this manually, Excel can consolidate your data automatically. You can use the Consolidate feature to consolidate the data either by position or by category. In both cases, you specify one or more source ranges (the ranges that contain the data you want to consolidate) and a destination range (the range where the consolidated data will appear).

Consolidate Data from Multiple Worksheets

Consolidate by Position

1 Create a new worksheet that uses the same layout — including row and column headers — as the sheets you want to consolidate.

2 Open the workbooks that contain the worksheets you want to consolidate.

3 Select the upper-left corner of the destination range.

4 Click the Data tab.

5 Click Consolidate.

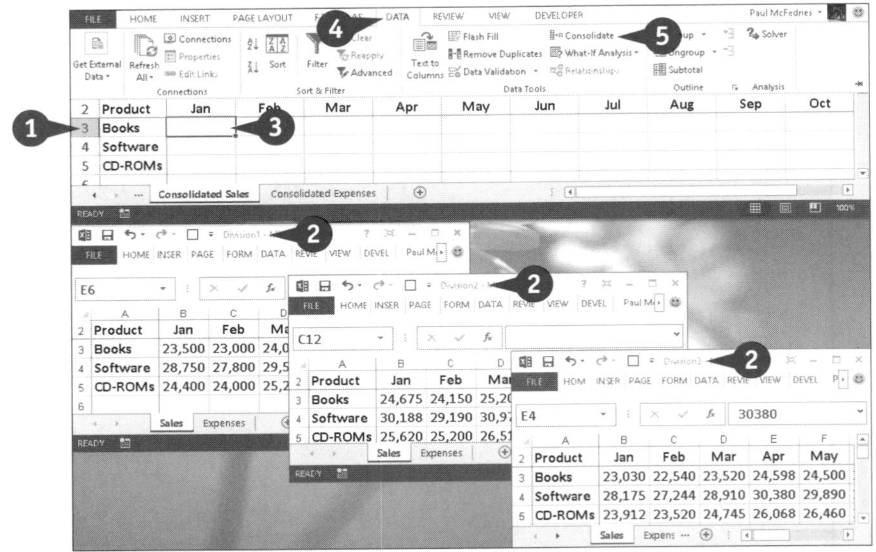

The Consolidate dialog box appears.

6 Click the Function down arrow and then click the summary function you want to use.

7 Click inside the Reference text box.

8 Select one of the ranges you want to consolidate.

9 Click Add.

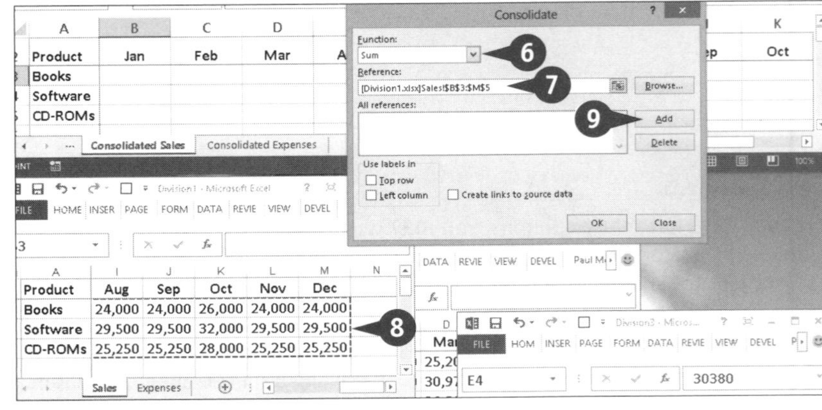

Ⓐ Excel adds the range to the All References list.

10 Repeat steps 7 to 9 to add all of the consolidation ranges.

11 Click OK.

Ⓑ Excel consolidates the data from the source ranges and displays the summary in the destination range.

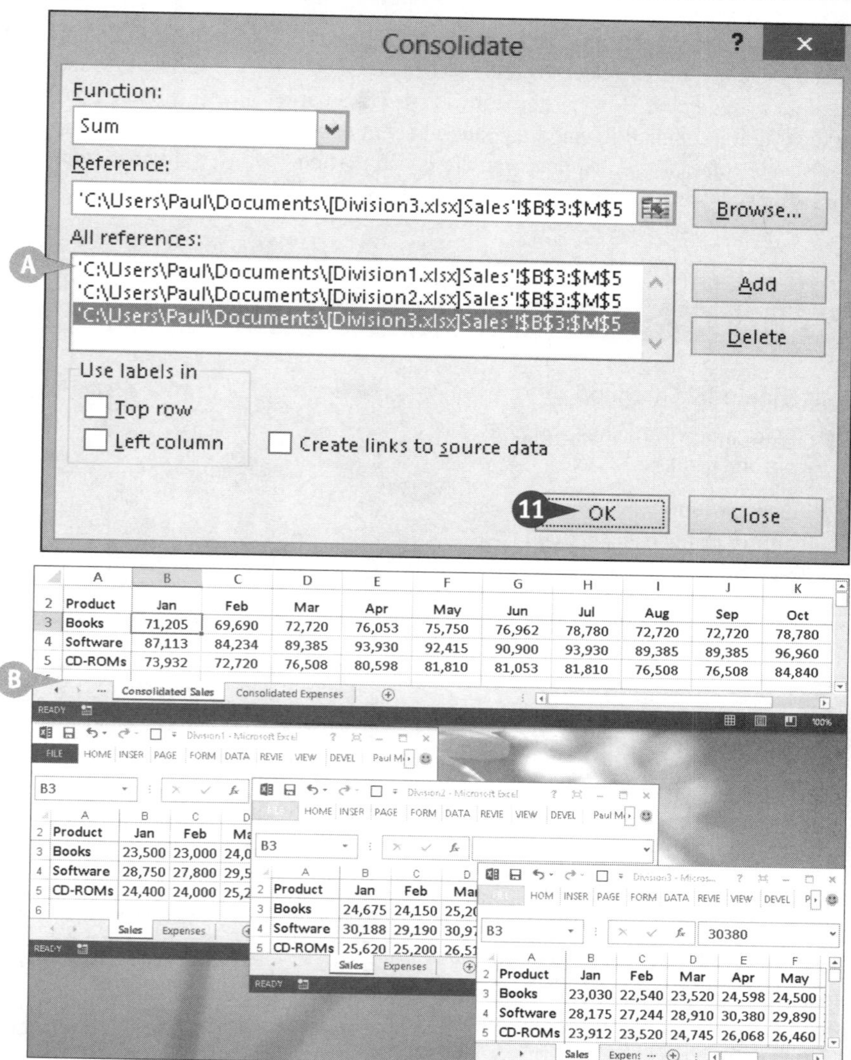

	A	B	C	D	E	F	G	H	I	J	K
2	Product	Jan	Feb	Mar	Apr	May	Jun	Jul	Aug	Sep	Oct
3	Books	71,205	69,690	72,720	76,053	75,750	76,962	78,780	72,720	72,720	78,780
4	Software	87,113	84,234	89,385	93,930	92,415	90,900	93,930	89,385	89,385	96,960
5	CD-ROMs	73,932	72,720	76,508	80,598	81,810	81,053	81,810	76,508	76,508	84,840

APPLY IT

If the source data changes, then you probably want to reflect those changes in the consolidation worksheet. Rather than running the entire consolidation over again, a much easier solution is to click the Create Links to Source Data check box (☐ changes to ☑) in the Consolidate dialog box. This enables you to update the consolidation worksheet by clicking the Data tab and then clicking Refresh All.

This also means that Excel creates an outline in the consolidation sheet, and you can use that outline to see the detail from each of the source ranges. See the section, "Group Related Data," to learn more about outlines in Excel.

continued ➤

If the worksheets you want to summarize do not use the same layout, you need to tell Excel to consolidate the data *by category*. This method consolidates the data by looking for common row and column labels in each worksheet. For example, suppose you are consolidating sales. Division A sells software, books, and videos. Division B sells books and CD-ROMs. Division C sells books, software, videos, and CD-ROMs. When you consolidate this data, Excel summarizes the software and videos from Divisions A and C, the CD-ROMs from Divisions B and C, and the books from all three.

Consolidate Data from Multiple Worksheets (continued)

Consolidate by Category

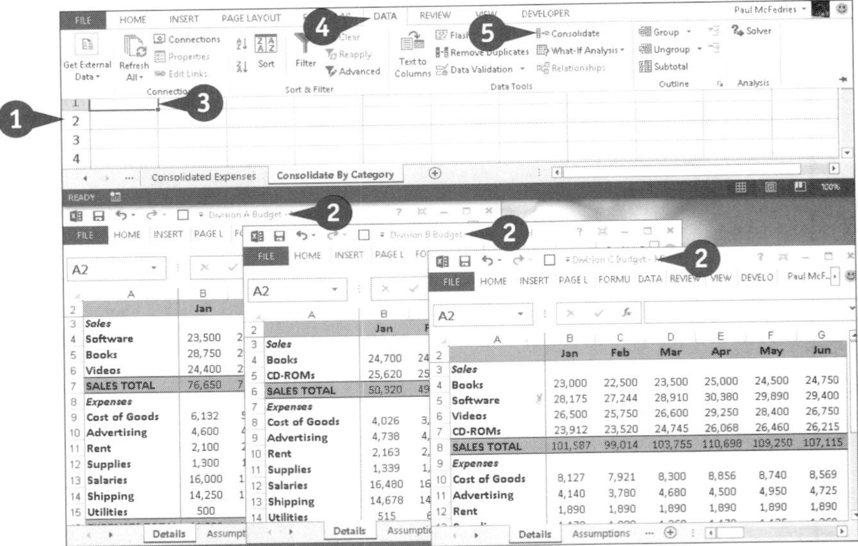

1. Create a new worksheet for the consolidation.
2. Open the workbooks that contain the worksheets you want to consolidate.
3. Select the upper-left corner of the destination range.
4. Click the Data tab.
5. Click Consolidate.

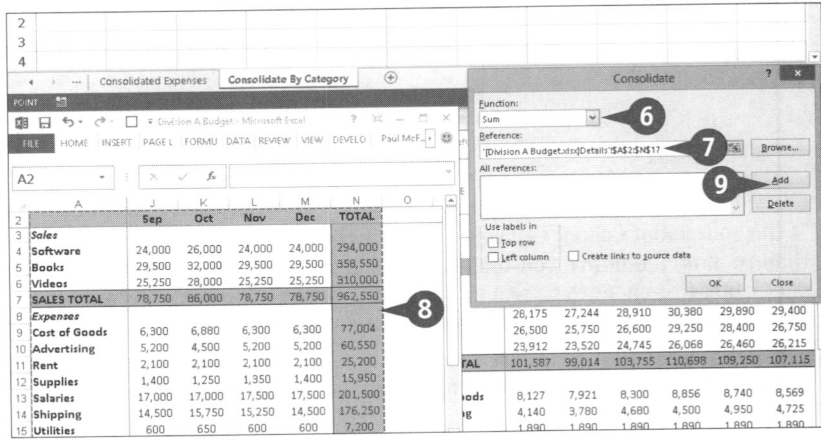

The Consolidate dialog box appears.

6. Click the Function down arrow and then click the summary function you want to use.
7. Click inside the Reference text box.
8. Select one of the ranges you want to consolidate.

Note: *Be sure to include the row and column labels in the range.*

9. Click Add.

Ⓐ Excel adds the range to the All References list.

10. Repeat steps 7 to 9 to add all of the consolidation ranges.

11. If you have labels in the top row of each range, click the Top Row check box to select it (☐ changes to ☑).

12. If you have labels in the left-column row of each range, click the Left Column check box to select it (☐ changes to ☑).

13. Click OK.

Ⓑ Excel consolidates the data from the source ranges and displays the summary in the destination range.

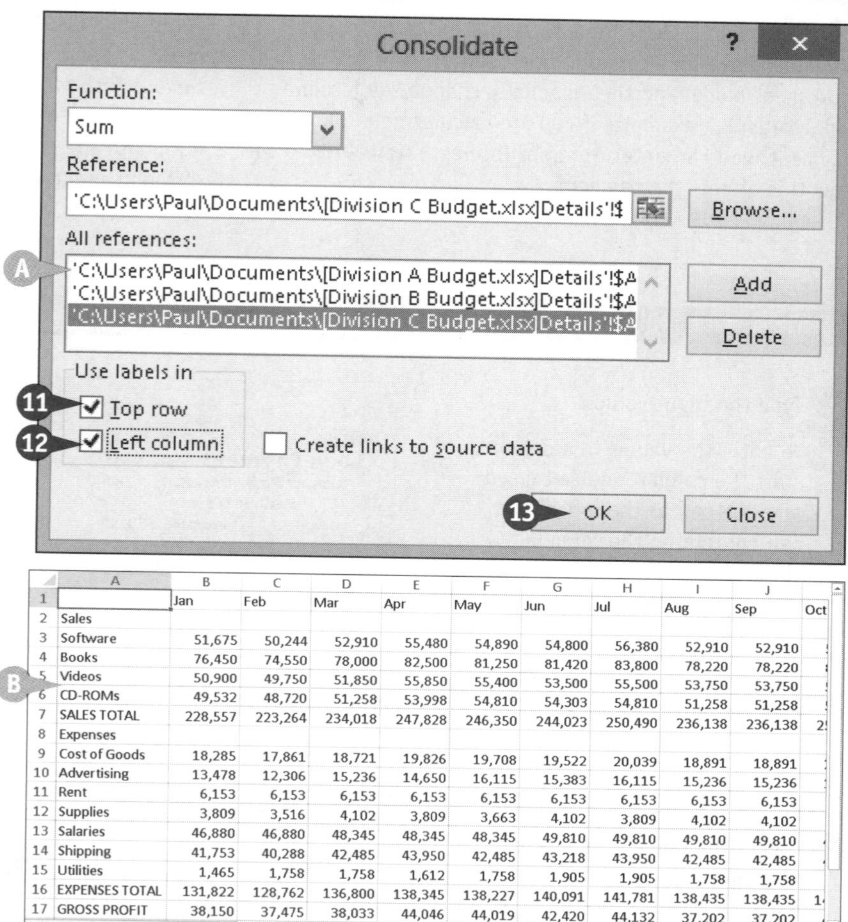

	A	B	C	D	E	F	G	H	I	J
1		Jan	Feb	Mar	Apr	May	Jun	Jul	Aug	Sep
2	Sales									
3	Software	51,675	50,244	52,910	55,480	54,890	54,800	56,380	52,910	52,910
4	Books	76,450	74,550	78,000	82,500	81,250	81,420	83,800	78,220	78,220
5	Videos	50,900	49,750	51,850	55,850	55,400	53,500	55,500	53,750	53,750
6	CD-ROMs	49,532	48,720	51,258	53,998	54,810	54,303	54,810	51,258	51,258
7	SALES TOTAL	228,557	223,264	234,018	247,828	246,350	244,023	250,490	236,138	236,138
8	Expenses									
9	Cost of Goods	18,285	17,861	18,721	19,826	19,708	19,522	20,039	18,891	18,891
10	Advertising	13,478	12,306	15,236	14,650	16,115	15,383	16,115	15,236	15,236
11	Rent	6,153	6,153	6,153	6,153	6,153	6,153	6,153	6,153	6,153
12	Supplies	3,809	3,516	4,102	3,809	3,663	4,102	3,809	4,102	4,102
13	Salaries	46,880	46,880	48,345	48,345	48,345	49,810	49,810	49,810	49,810
14	Shipping	41,753	40,288	42,485	43,950	42,485	43,218	43,950	42,485	42,485
15	Utilities	1,465	1,758	1,758	1,612	1,758	1,905	1,905	1,758	1,758
16	EXPENSES TOTAL	131,822	128,762	136,800	138,345	138,227	140,091	141,781	138,435	138,435
17	GROSS PROFIT	38,150	37,475	38,033	44,046	44,019	42,420	44,132	37,202	37,202

APPLY IT

If the layout of the source data changes, then you need to run the consolidation again. If you consolidated by position, then before you can re-run the consolidation, you must first adjust the layout of the consolidation worksheet to match the changes to the source data. (You do not need to do this if you consolidated by category.)

Regardless of the consolidation method you used, before you run the consolidation again, you must delete the existing source ranges. Click the Data tab and then click Consolidate to display the Consolidate dialog box. For each source range, click the range in the All References list and then click Delete.

If you want to study the effect that different input values have on a formula, one solution is to set up the worksheet model and then manually change the formula's input cells. For example, if you are calculating a loan payment, you can enter different interest rate values to see how this affects the payment.

The problem with this method is that you see only a single result at one time. A better solution is to set up a *data table*, which is a range that consists of the formula you are using and multiple input values for that formula. Excel automatically creates a solution to the formula for each different input value.

Create a Data Table

1 Type the input values:

To enter the values in a column, start the column one cell down and one cell to the left of the cell containing the formula, as shown here.

To enter the values in a row, start the row one cell up and one cell to the right of the cell containing the formula.

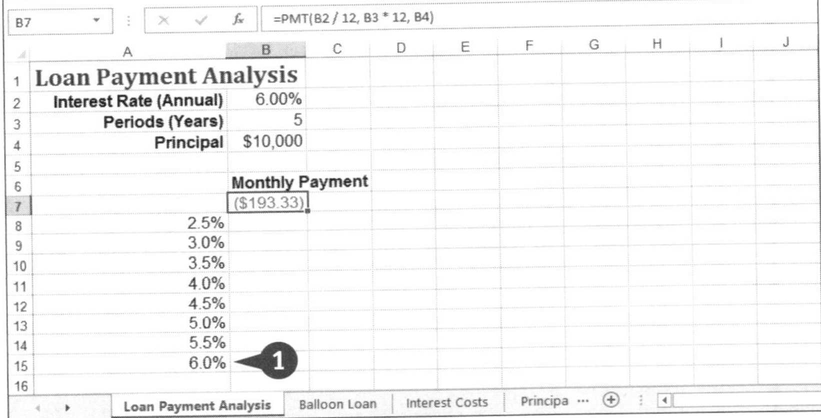

2 Select the range that includes the input values and the formula.

3 Click the Data tab.

4 Click What-If Analysis.

5 Click Data Table.

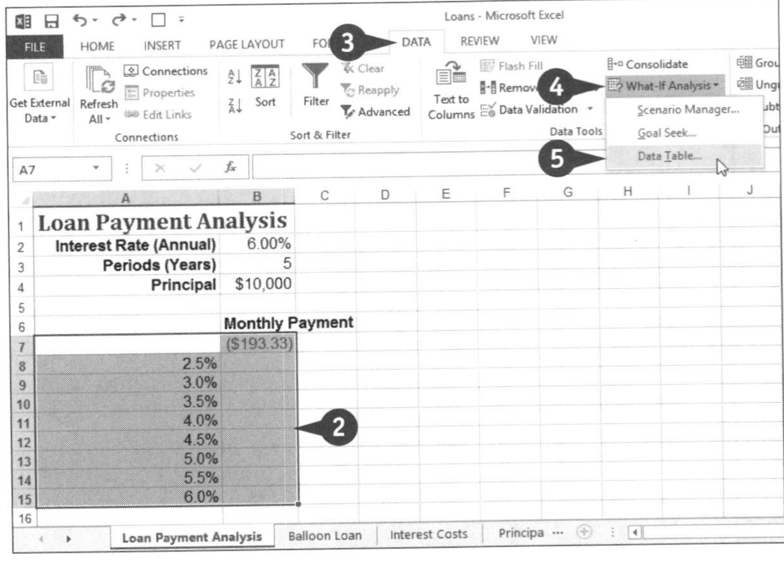

The Data Table dialog box appears.

6 Specify the formula cell you want to use as the data table's input cell:

If the input values are in a column, type the input cell's address in the Column Input Cell text box.

If you entered the input values in a row, type the input cell's address in the Row Input Cell text box.

7 Click OK.

A Excel displays the results.

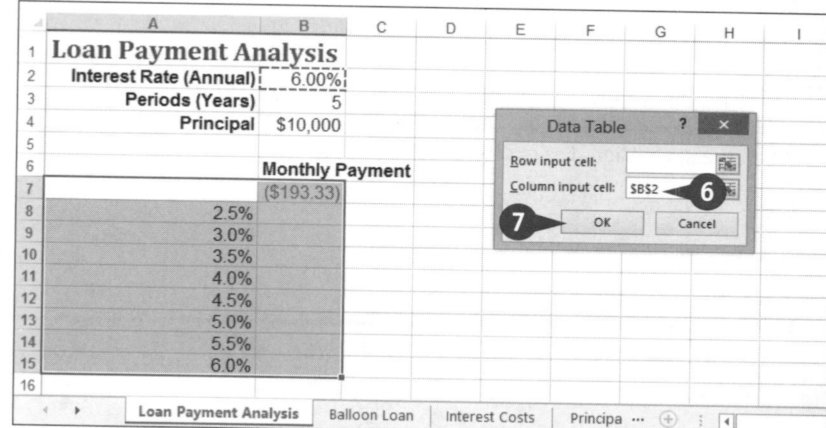

B8 {=TABLE(,B2)}

	A	B
1	Loan Payment Analysis	
2	Interest Rate (Annual)	6.00%
3	Periods (Years)	5
4	Principal	$10,000
5		
6		Monthly Payment
7		($193.33)
8	2.5%	($177.47)
9	3.0%	($179.69)
10	3.5%	($181.92)
11	4.0%	($184.17)
12	4.5%	($186.43)
13	5.0%	($188.71)
14	5.5%	($191.01)
15	6.0%	($193.33)
16		

A

Loan Payment Analysis | Balloon Loan | Interest Costs | Principa ...

EXTRA

Data tables are an example of what-if analysis, which is perhaps the most basic method for analyzing worksheet data. With what-if analysis, you first calculate a formula D, based on the input from variables A, B, and C. You then say, "What happens to the result if I change the value of variable A?" "What happens if I change B or C?," and so on.

Do not confuse data tables with the Excel tables in Chapter 6. A data table is a special range that Excel uses to calculate multiple solutions to a formula.

Create a Two-Input Data Table

If your worksheet model is a data table that varies only one of the formula's input cells, then this is an example of a *one-input* data table. However, Excel also enables you to set up a *two-input* data table that varies two formula inputs at the same time. For example, in a loan payment worksheet, you could set up a two-input data table that varies the interest rate and the term.

To set up a two-input data table, you must set up two ranges of input cells. One range must appear in a column directly below the formula, and the other range must appear in a row directly to the right of the formula.

Create a Two-Input Data Table

1 Type the input values:

A To enter the column values, start the column one cell down and one cell to the left of the cell containing the formula.

B To enter the row values, start the row one cell up and one cell to the right of the cell containing the formula.

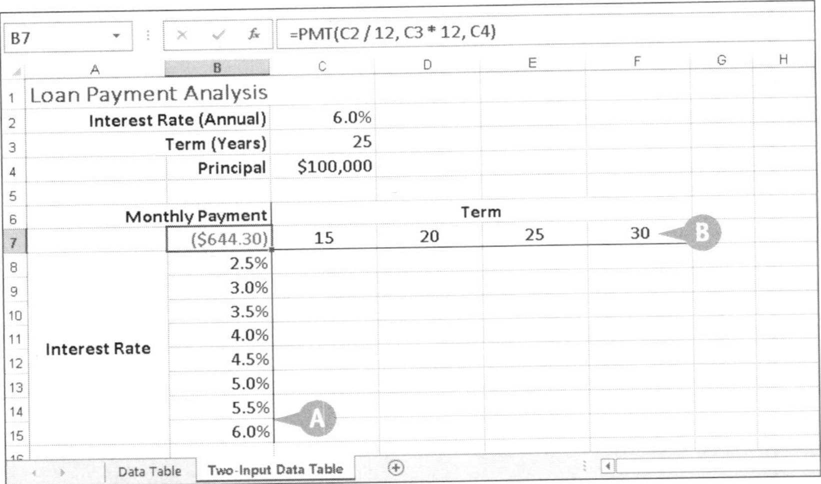

2 Select the range that includes the input values and the formula.

3 Click the Data tab.

4 Click What-If Analysis.

5 Click Data Table.

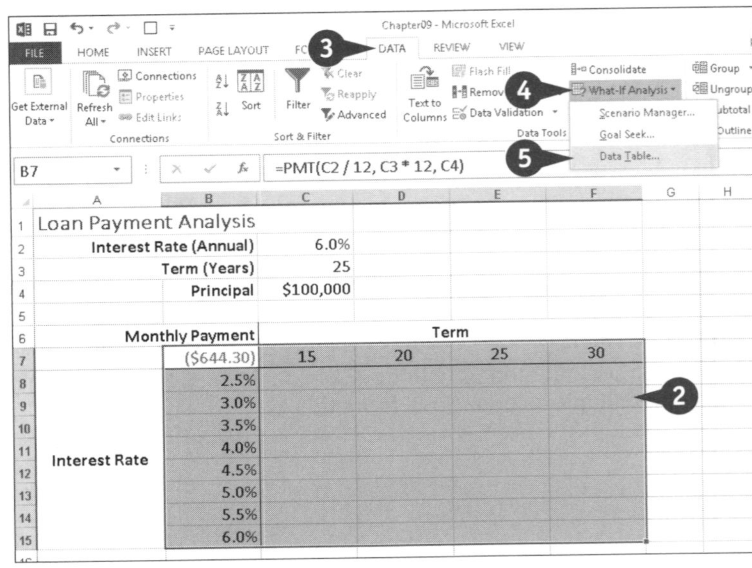

The Data Table dialog box appears.

6 In the Row Input Cell text box, type the cell address of the input cell that corresponds to the row values you entered.

7 In the Column Input Cell text box, type the cell address of the input cell you want to use for the column values.

8 Click OK.

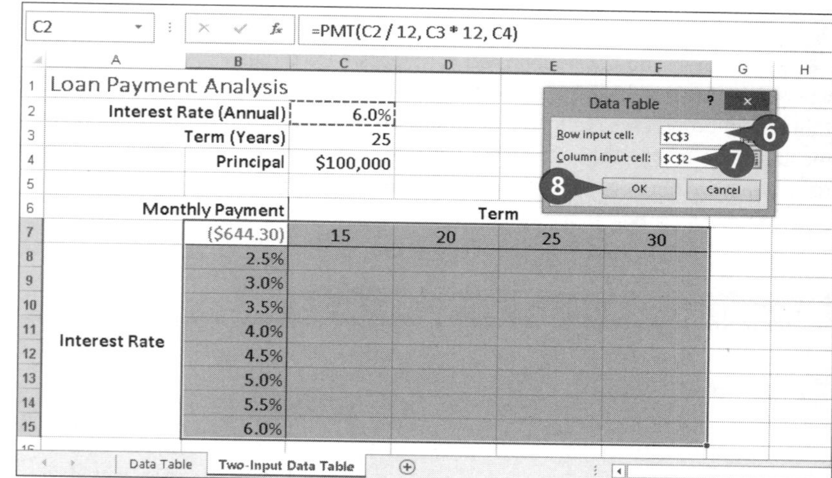

C Excel displays the results.

C8 {=TABLE(C3,C2)}

	A	B	C	D	E	F
1	Loan Payment Analysis					
2		Interest Rate (Annual)	6.0%			
3		Term (Years)	25			
4		Principal	$100,000			
5						
6		Monthly Payment		Term		
7		($644.30)	15	20	25	30
8		2.5%	($666.79)	($529.90)	($448.62)	($395.12)
9		3.0%	($690.58)	($554.60)	($474.21)	($421.60)
10		3.5%	($714.88)	($579.96)	($500.62)	($449.04)
11	Interest Rate	4.0%	($739.69)	($605.98)	($527.84)	($477.42)
12		4.5%	($764.99)	($632.65)	($555.83)	($506.69)
13		5.0%	($790.79)	($659.96)	($584.59)	($536.82)
14		5.5%	($817.08)	($687.89)	($614.09)	($567.79)
15		6.0%	($843.86)	($716.43)	($644.30)	($599.55)

Data Table | Two-Input Data Table

EXTRA

When you run the Data Table command, Excel enters an array formula in the interior of the data table. This formula is a `TABLE` function (a special function available only by using the Data Table command) with the following syntax:

```
{=TABLE(row_input_ref, column_input_ref)}
```

Here, `row_input_ref` and `column_input_ref` are the cell references you entered in the Data Table dialog box. The braces ({ }) indicate an array, which means that you cannot change or delete individual elements within the results. If you want to change the results, you need to select the entire data table and then run the Data Table command again. If you want to delete the results, you must select the entire array and then delete it.

Skip Data Tables When Calculating Workbooks

You can reduce the time it takes for Excel to calculate a workbook if you configure Excel to bypass data tables when it is recalculating the workbook. Because a data table is an array, Excel treats it as a unit, so a worksheet recalculation means that the entire data table is always recalculated. This is not a big problem for a small data table with a few dozen formulas. However, it is not uncommon to have data tables with hundreds or even thousands of formulas, and these larger data tables can really slow down worksheet recalculation. To avoid this problem, you can configure Excel to skip data tables when it calculates worksheets.

Skip Data Tables When Calculating Workbooks

1 Click the File tab.

Chapter09 - Microsoft Excel

B7 =PMT(C2 / 12, C3 * 12, C4)

	A	B	C	D	E	F	G	H
1	Loan Payment Analysis							
2		Interest Rate (Annual)	6.0%					
3		Term (Years)	25					
4		Principal	$100,000					
5								
6		Monthly Payment			Term			
7		($644.30)	15	20	25	30		
8		2.5%						
9		3.0%						
10		3.5%						
11	Interest Rate	4.0%						
12		4.5%						
13		5.0%						
14		5.5%						

2 Click Options.

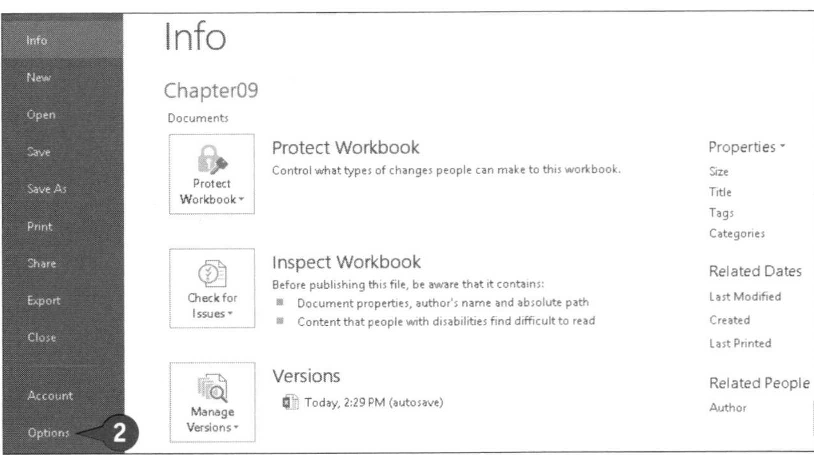

The Excel Options dialog box appears.

3 Click Formulas.

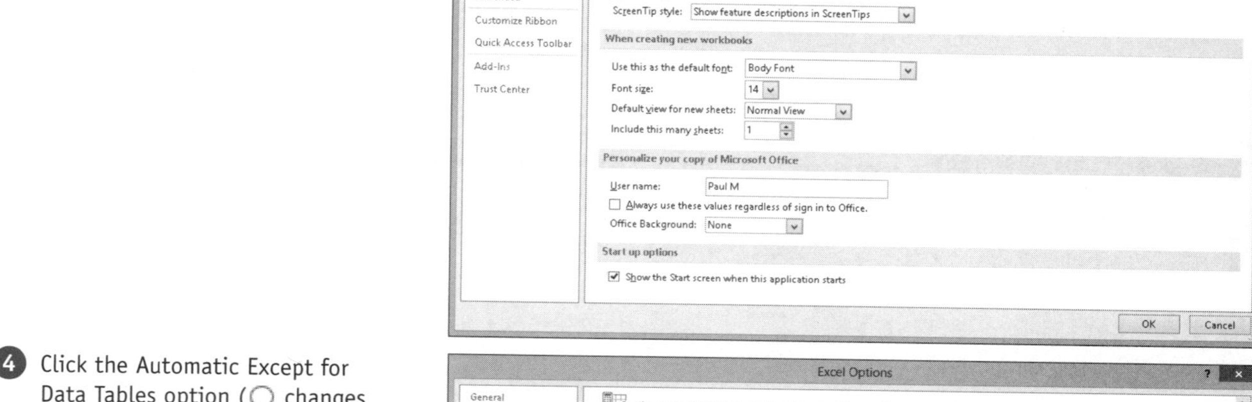

4 Click the Automatic Except for Data Tables option (○ changes to ◉).

5 Click OK.

The next time you calculate a workbook, Excel bypasses the data tables.

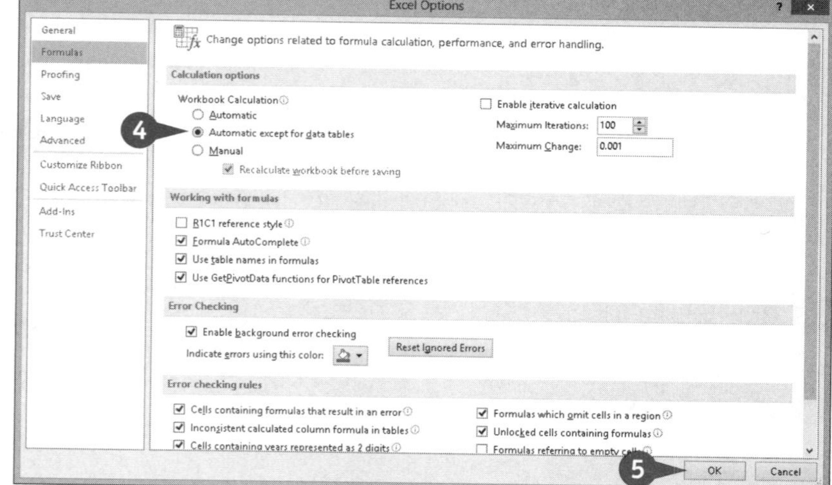

APPLY IT

When you want to recalculate a data table, you can follow steps 1 to 3, click to deselect the Automatic Except for Data Tables option, click OK, and then recalculate the workbook. On the other hand, you might prefer to leave the Automatic Except for Data Tables option selected. In that case, to recalculate the data table, select any cell inside the data table and press F9. If you often turn the Automatic Except for Data Tables option on and off, Excel offers a faster method for toggling this setting. Click the Formulas tab, click Calculation Options, and then select the Automatic Except for Data Tables option. Alternatively, from the keyboard, press Alt+M, then press X, and then press E.

Analyze Data with Goal Seek

If you already know the formula result you want, but you must find an input value that produces that result, you can use Goal Seek to solve the problem. For example, you might know that you want to have $50,000 saved to purchase new equipment five years from now, so you need to calculate how much to invest each year.

You must do three things to set up your worksheet for Goal Seek. First, you need to set up one cell as the *changing cell*, which is the value that Goal Seek will manipulate to reach the goal. Second, you must set up the other input values for the formula and give them proper initial values. Third, you need to create a formula for Goal Seek to use to reach the goal.

Analyze Data with Goal Seek

1 Set up your worksheet model.

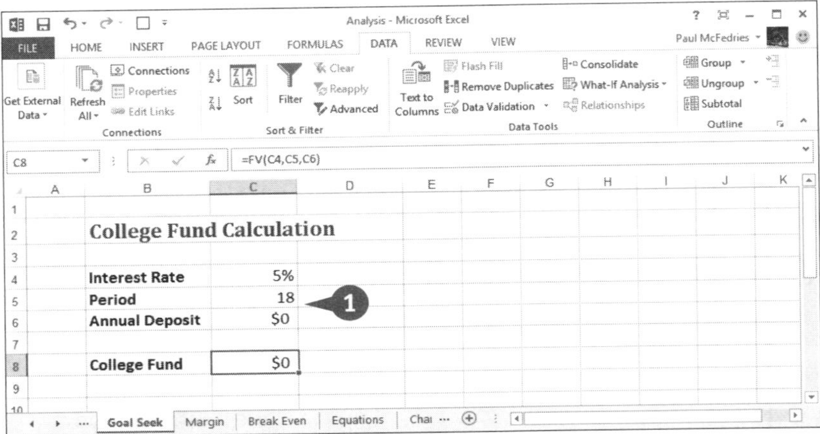

2 Click the Data tab.

3 Click What-If Analysis.

4 Click Goal Seek.

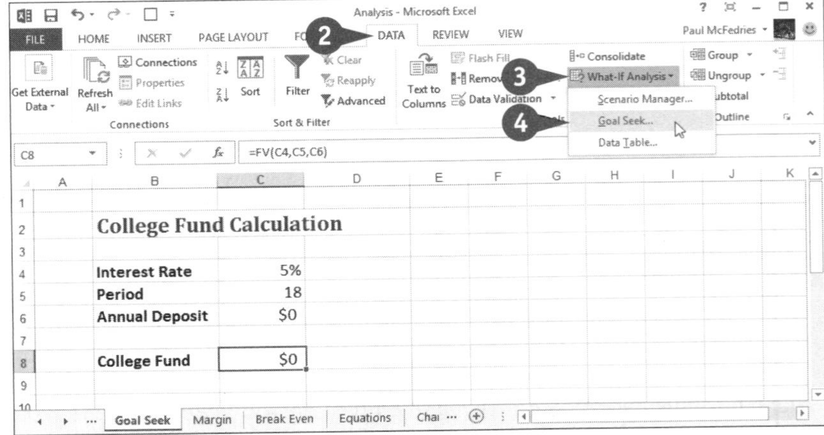

The Goal Seek dialog box appears.

5. Click in the Set Cell box.
6. Click the cell that contains the formula you want Goal Seek to work with.
7. In the To Value text box, type the value that you want Goal Seek to find.
8. Click in the By Changing Cell box.
9. Click the cell that you want Goal Seek to modify.
10. Click OK.

A. Goal Seek adjusts the changing cell value until it reaches a solution.

B. The formula now shows the value you entered in step 7.

11. Click OK.

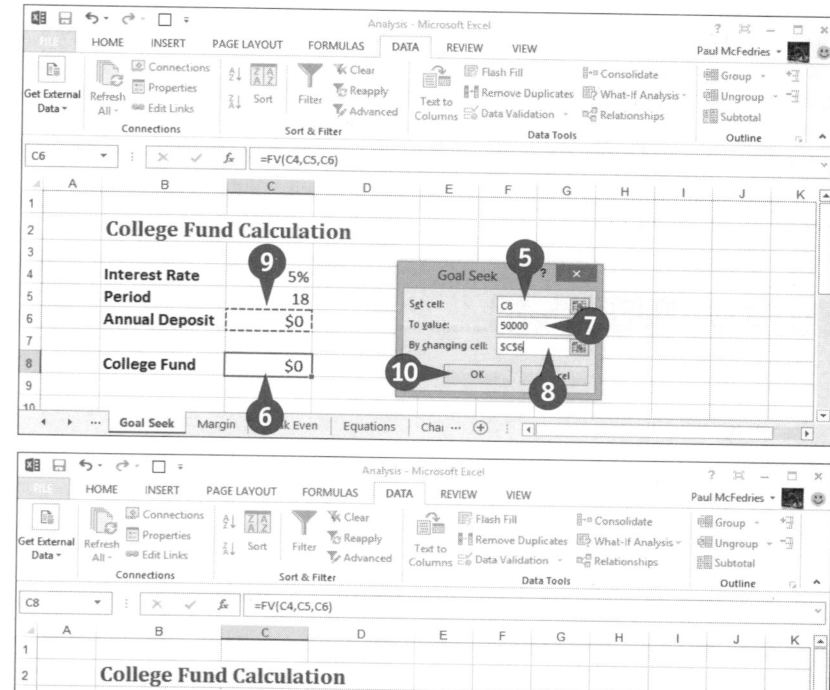

EXTRA

In some cases, Goal Seek may not find an exact solution to your model. That can happen if it takes Goal Seek a relatively long time to find a solution, because Goal Seek stops after 100 iterations or if the current result is within 0.001 of the desired result. You can get a more accurate solution by increasing the number of iterations that Goal Seek can use, by reducing the value that Goal Seek uses to mark a solution as "close enough," or both. Click the File tab, click Options, and then click Formulas. Increase the value of the Maximum Iterations spin box, decrease the value in the Maximum Change text box, or both, and then click OK.

You can analyze the result of a formula by creating sets of values that enable you to use those values quickly as the inputs for the formula. Many formulas take a number of input values to produce a result. When you are analyzing the formula's results, it helps to manipulate the input values in some systematic way. For example, one set of values might represent a best-case approach, while another might represent a worst-case approach. In Excel, each of these coherent sets of input values — known as *changing cells* — is called a *scenario*. By creating multiple scenarios, you can easily apply these different value sets to analyze how the result of a formula changes under different conditions.

Analyze Data with Scenarios

Create a Scenario

1. Set up your worksheet model.

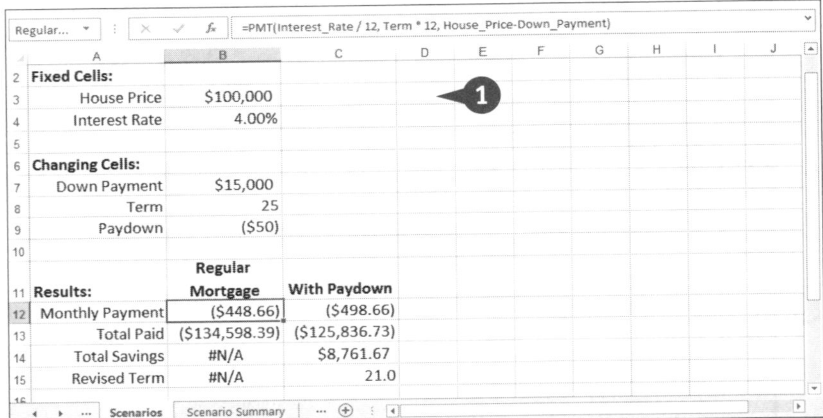

2. Click the Data tab.
3. Click What-If Analysis.
4. Click Scenario Manager.

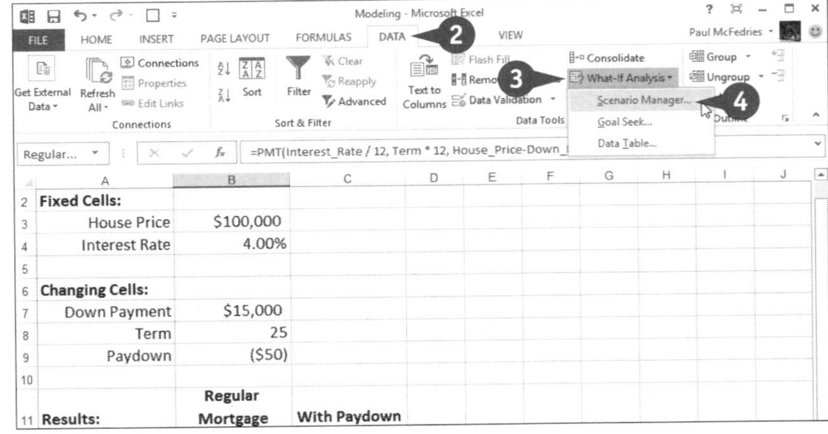

The Scenario Manager dialog box appears.

5 Click Add.

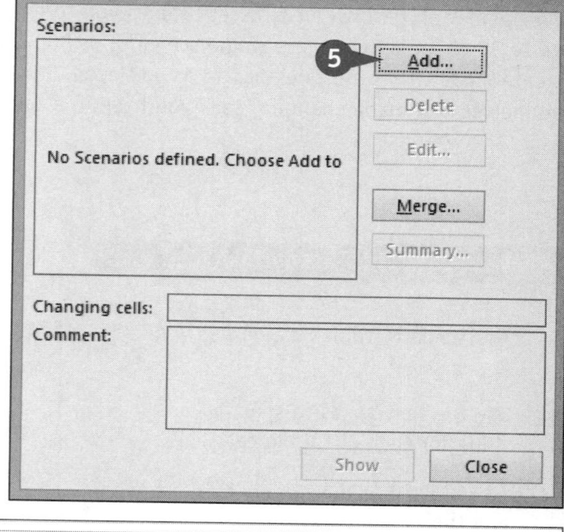

The Add Scenario dialog box appears.

6 Type a name for the scenario.

7 Click in the Changing Cells box.

8 Select the cells you want to change in the scenario.

9 Type a description for the scenario.

10 Click OK.

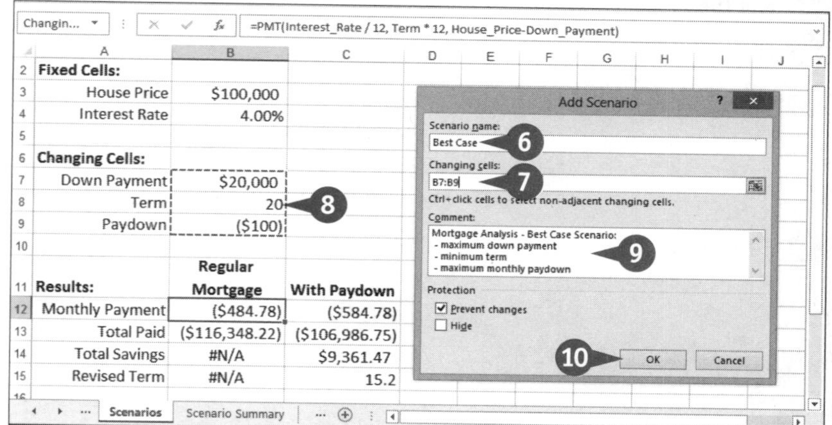

APPLY IT

When building a worksheet model, you can use a couple techniques to make the model more suited to scenarios. First, group all your changing cells in one place and label them. Second, make sure that each changing cell is a constant value. If you use a formula for a changing cell, another cell could change the formula result and throw off your scenarios.

Your scenarios appear in the Scenario Manager, and for each scenario, you see its changing cells and its description. The description is often very useful, particularly if you have several scenarios defined, so be sure to write a detailed description in step 9 to help you differentiate your scenarios later on.

continued

Excel scenarios are a powerful data analysis tool for a number of reasons. First, Excel enables you to enter up to 32 changing cells in a single scenario, so you can create models that are as elaborate as you need. Second, no matter how many changing cells you have in a scenario, Excel enables you to show the scenario's result with just a few mouse clicks. Third, because the number of scenarios you can define is limited only by the available memory on your computer, you can effectively use as many scenarios as you need to analyze your data model.

Analyze Data with Scenarios (continued)

The Scenario Values dialog box appears.

11 Use the text boxes to specify a value for each changing cell.

A To add more scenarios, click Add and then repeat steps 6 to 11.

12 Click OK.

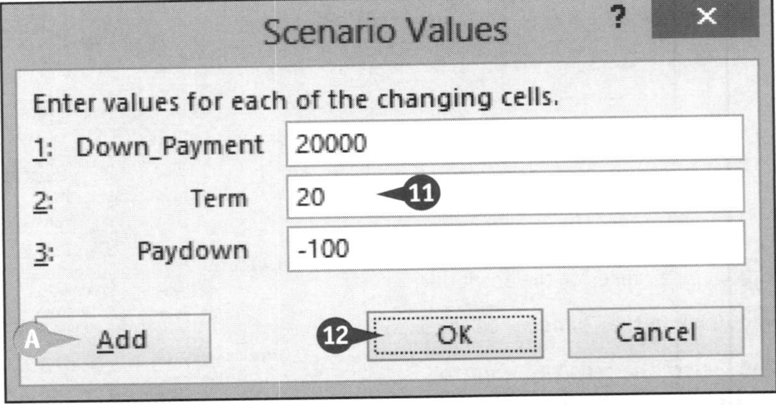

13 Click Close.

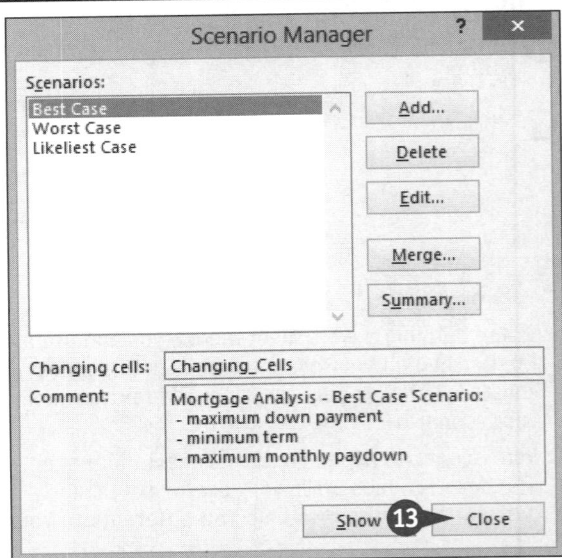

Display Scenarios

1 Click the Data tab.

2 Click What-If Analysis.

3 Click Scenario Manager.

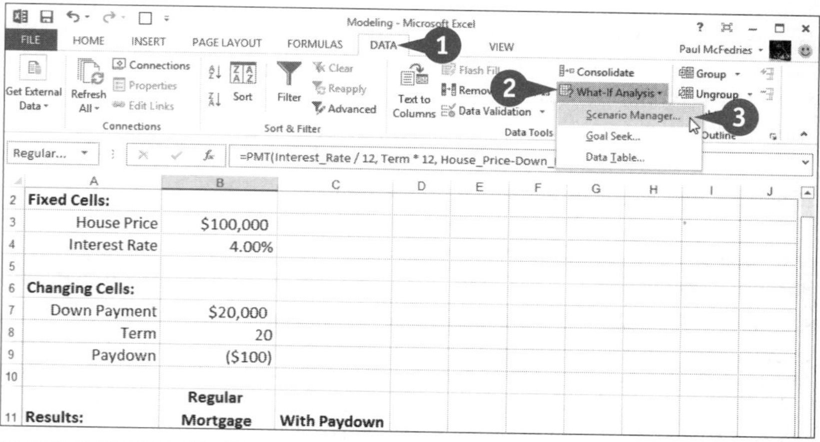

The Scenario Manager dialog box appears.

4 Click the scenario you want to display.

5 Click Show.

B Excel enters the scenario values into the changing cells and displays the formula result.

6 Repeat steps 4 and 5 to display other scenarios.

7 Click Close.

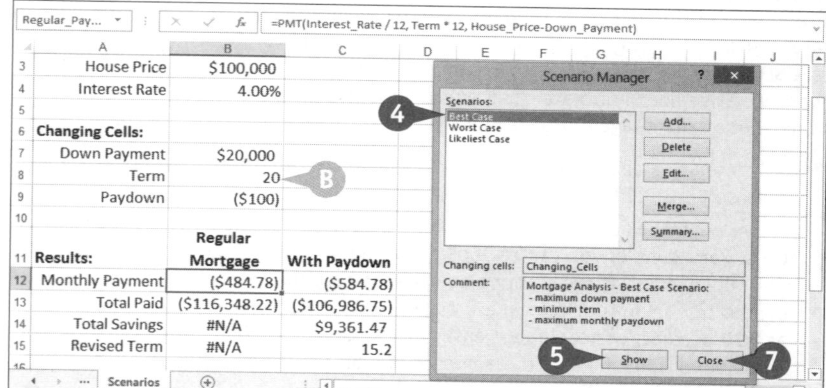

APPLY IT

If you need to make changes to a scenario, you can edit the name, the changing cells, the description, and the scenario's input values. Click the Data tab, click What-If Analysis, and then click Scenario Manager. In the Scenario Manager dialog box, click the scenario you want to modify, and then click Edit.

If you have a scenario that you no longer need, you should delete it to reduce clutter in the Scenario Manager. Click the Data tab, click What-If Analysis, and then click Scenario Manager. Click the scenario you want to delete. Note that Excel does not ask you to confirm the deletion, so double-check that you have selected the correct scenario. Click Delete and then click Close.

Spreadsheet tools such as Goal Seek that change a single variable are useful, but unfortunately, most problems in business are not so easy. You will usually face formulas with at least two and sometimes dozens of variables. Often, a problem will have more than one solution, and your challenge will be to find the *optimal* solution (that is, the one that maximizes profit, or minimizes costs, or matches other criteria). For these bigger challenges, you need a more muscular tool. Excel has just the answer: Solver. Solver is a sophisticated optimization program that enables you to find the solutions to complex problems that would otherwise require high-level mathematical analysis.

Solver Advantages

Solver, like Goal Seek, uses an iterative method to perform its calculations. This means that Solver tries a solution, analyzes the results, and tries another solution, and so on. However, this cyclic iteration is not just guesswork on Solver's part. The program looks at how the results change with each new iteration and through some sophisticated mathematical processes, can usually tell in what direction it should head for the solution. However, the fact that Goal Seek and Solver are both iterative does not make them equal. In fact, Solver brings a number of advantages to the table:

- Solver enables you to specify multiple adjustable cells. You can use up to 200 adjustable cells in all.
- Solver enables you to set up constraints on the adjustable cells. For example, you can tell Solver to find a solution that not only maximizes profit, but also satisfies certain conditions, such as achieving a gross margin between 20 and 30 percent, or keeping expenses at less than $100,000. These conditions are said to be constraints on the solution.
- Solver seeks not only a desired result (the goal in Goal Seek), but also the optimal one. This means you can find a solution that is the maximum or minimum possible.
- For complex problems, Solver can generate multiple solutions. You can then save these different solutions under different scenarios.

Using Solver

Solver is a powerful tool that most Excel users do not need. It would be overkill, for example, to use Solver to compute net profit given fixed revenue and cost figures. Many problems, however, require nothing less than the Solver approach. These problems cover many different fields and situations, but they all have the following characteristics in common:

- They have a single *objective cell* (also called the *target cell*) that contains a formula you want to maximize, minimize, or set to a specific value. This formula could be a calculation, such as total transportation expenses or net profit.
- The objective cell formula contains references to one or more *variable cells* (also called *unknowns* or *changing cells*). Solver adjusts these cells to find the optimal solution for the objective cell formula. These variable cells might include items such as units sold, shipping costs, or advertising expenses.
- Optionally, one or more *constraint cells* must satisfy certain criteria. For example, you might require that advertising be less than 10 percent of total expenses, or that the discount to customers be an amount between 40 and 60 percent.

Understanding Solver's Messages

When Solver finishes its calculations, it displays the Solver dialog box and a message that tells you what happened. Some of these messages are straightforward, but others are more cryptic. This section looks at the most common messages and gives their translations.

Solver Finds a Solution

If Solver finds a solution successfully, you see one of the messages shown in the following table.

Message	Description
Solver found a solution. All constraints and optimality conditions are satisfied.	This is the message you hope to see. It means that the value you wanted for the objective cell has been found, and Solver was able to find the solution while meeting your constraints within the precision and integer tolerance levels you set.
Solver has converged to the current solution. All constraints are satisfied.	Solver normally assumes that it has a solution if the value of the objective cell formula remains virtually unchanged during a few iterations. This is called *converging to a solution*. Such is the case with this message, but it does not necessarily mean that Solver has found a solution. The iterative process might just be taking a long time, or the initial values in the variable cells might have been set too far from the solution. You should try rerunning Solver with different values. You can also try using a higher precision setting (that is, entering a smaller number in the Constraint Precision text box).
Solver cannot improve the current solution. All constraints are satisfied.	This message tells you that Solver has found a solution, but it might not be the optimal one. Try setting the precision to a smaller number or, if you are using the GRG Nonlinear engine, try using the central differencing method for partial derivatives.

Solver Does Not Find a Solution

If Solver does not find a solution, you see one of the messages in the following table.

Message	Description
The Set Cell values do not converge.	This means that the value of the objective cell formula has no finite limit. For example, if you are trying to maximize profit based on product price and unit costs, Solver will not find a solution; The reason is that continually higher prices and lower costs lead to higher profit. You need to add (or change) constraints in your model, such as setting a maximum price or minimum cost level (for example, the amount of fixed costs).
Solver could not find a feasible solution.	Solver could not find a solution that satisfied all your constraints. Check your constraints to make sure they are realistic and consistent.
Stop chosen when the maximum x limit was reached.	This message appears when Solver reaches either the maximum time limit or the maximum iteration limit. If it appears that Solver is heading toward a solution, click Keep Solver Solution and try again.
The conditions for Assume Linear Model are not satisfied.	Solver based its iterative process on a linear model, but when the results are put into the worksheet, they do not conform to the linear model. You need to select the GRG Nonlinear engine and try again.

Load the Solver Add-In

An *add-in* is software that adds one or more features to Excel. Installing add-ins gives you additional Excel features that are not available in the Ribbon by default. Bundled add-in software is included with Excel but is not automatically installed when you install Excel. Excel comes with several standard add-ins, including Solver, which enables you to solve optimization problems.

You install the bundled add-ins by using the Excel Options dialog box; you can find them in the Add-Ins section. Once installed, add-ins are available right away. They usually appear on a tab related to their function. For example, Solver appears on the Data tab.

Load the Solver Add-In

1 Click the File tab.

2 Click Options.

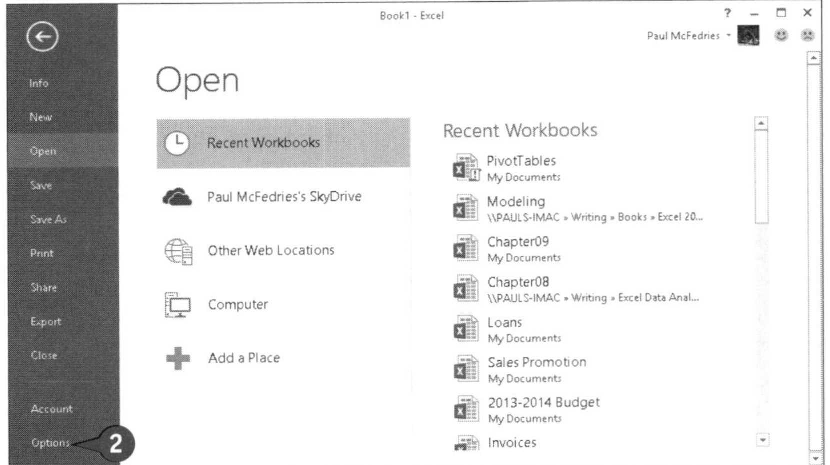

The Excel Options dialog box appears.

3 Click Add-Ins.

4 Click the Manage down arrow and select Excel Add-Ins from the drop-down list.

5 Click Go.

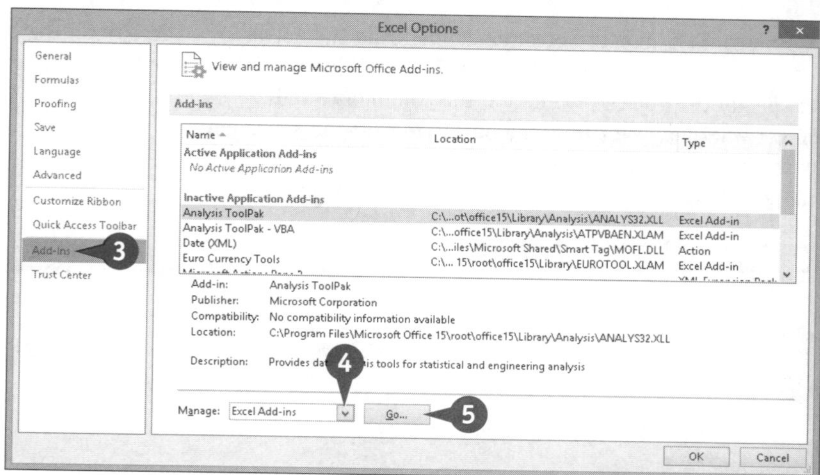

Excel displays the Add-Ins dialog box.

6 In the Add-Ins Available list, click the Solver Add-In check box (☐ changes to ☑).

7 Click OK.

Excel adds a Solver button to the Data tab's Analysis group.

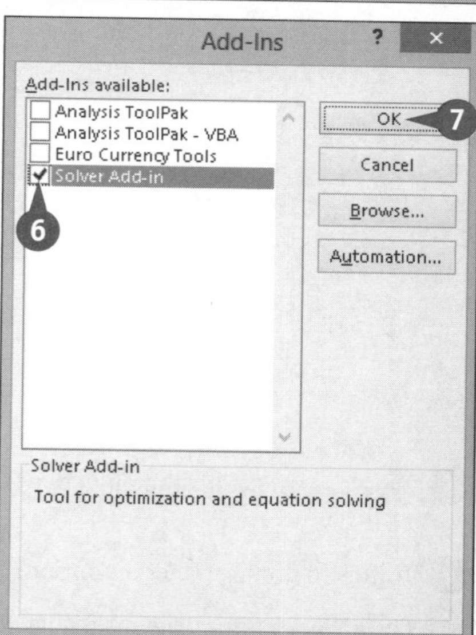

EXTRA

When you click OK in the Add-Ins dialog box, Excel first checks to see if Solver is installed on your computer. This is usually the case, but if Excel finds that Solver is not installed, it displays a dialog box to let you know. In this case, click Yes to have Excel install the add-in. If you find that you no longer use Solver, you should remove it to save memory and reduce clutter in the Ribbon's Data tab. Follow steps 1 to 5 to display the Add-Ins dialog box. In the Add-Ins Available list, deselect the Solver Add-In check box (☑ changes to ☐), and then click OK.

Optimize a Result with Solver

You can set up your Solver model by using the Solver Parameters dialog box. You use the Set Objective field to specify the objective cell, and the To group to tell Solver what you want from the objective cell: the maximum possible value, the minimum possible value, or a specific value. Finally, you use the By Changing Variable Cells box to specify the cells that Solver can use to plug in values to optimize the result.

When Solver finds a solution, you can choose either Keep Solver Solution or Restore Original Values. If you choose Keep Solver Solution, Excel permanently changes the worksheet. You cannot undo the changes.

Optimize a Result with Solver

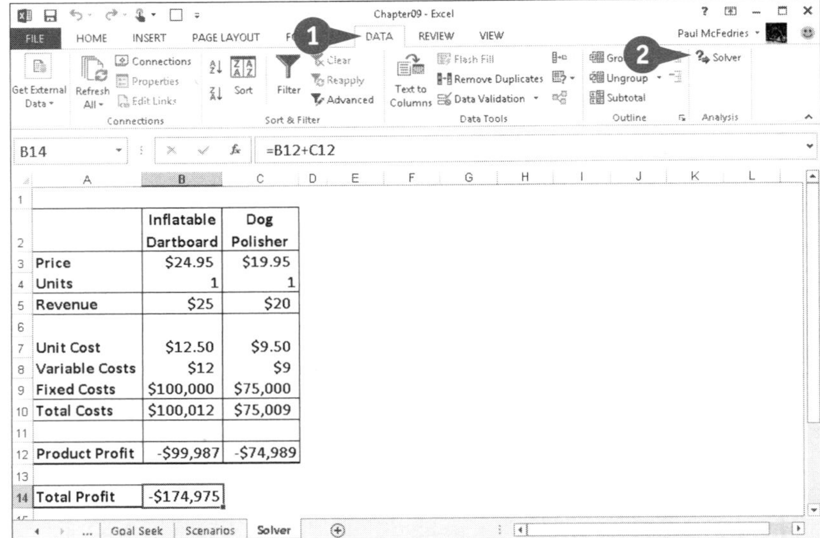

1. Click the Data tab.
2. Click Solver.

   The Solver Parameters dialog box appears.

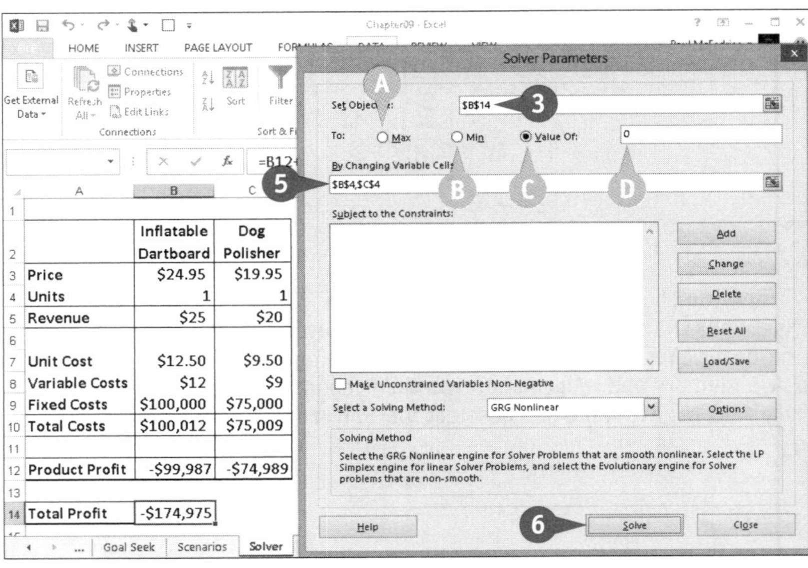

3. Type a reference to the objective cell.
4. In the To group, select an option:
   - A Click Max to return the maximum possible value.
   - B Click Min to return the minimum possible value.
   - C Click Value Of and type a number to set the objective cell to that number.
5. In the By Changing Variable Cells box, type the cells you want Solver to change while it looks for a solution.
6. Click Solve.

As Solver works on the problem, you might see one or more Show Trial Solution dialog boxes.

7 Click Continue.

8 Repeat step 7 as often as necessary.

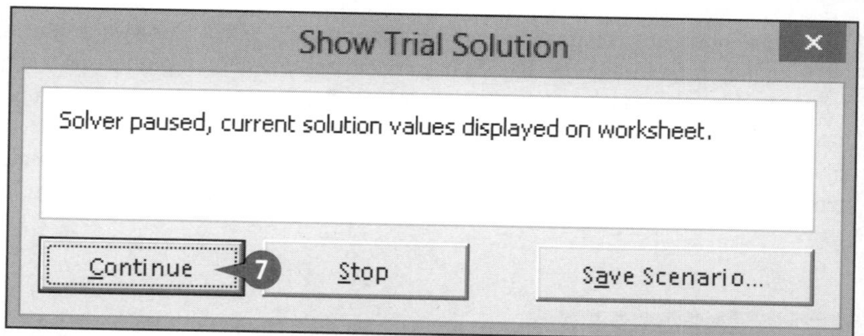

When the optimization is complete, Excel displays the Solver Results dialog box.

D The Solver result message appears here.

9 Click the Keep Solver Solution option (○ changes to ◉).

E If you do not want to accept the result, click the Restore Original Values option instead (○ changes to ◉).

10 Click OK.

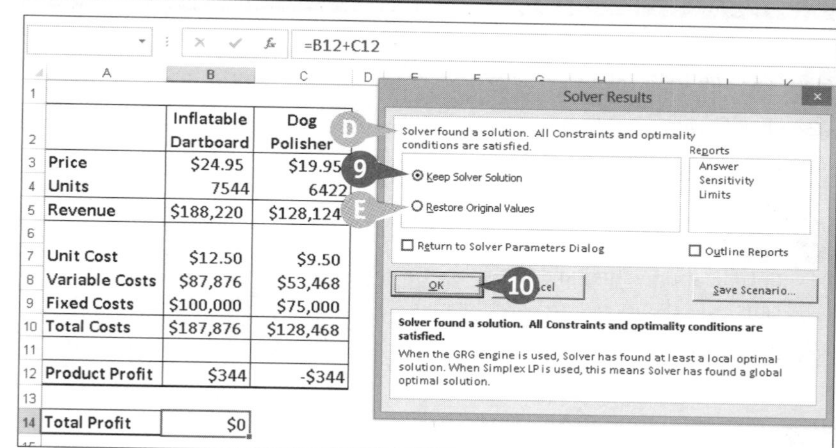

EXTRA

You can ask Solver to display one or more reports that give you extra information about the results. In the Solver Results dialog box, use the Reports list to click each report you want to view. The Answer report displays information about the model's objective cell, variable cells, and constraints. For the objective cell and variable cells, Solver shows the original and final values. The Sensitivity report attempts to show how sensitive a solution is to changes in the model's formulas. The layout of the Sensitivity report depends on the type of model you are using. The Limits report displays the objective cell and its value, as well as the variable cells and their addresses, names, and values.

Add Constraints to Solver

The real world puts restrictions and conditions on formulas. A factory might have a maximum capacity of 10,000 units a day, the number of employees in a company has to be a number greater than or equal to zero, and your advertising costs might be restricted to 10 percent of total expenses. Similarly, if you are running a break-even analysis on two products, without restrictions Solver might set one product at a slight loss and the other at a slight profit, whereas in your analysis you might prefer to set both products at the break-even point. These are all examples of what Solver calls *constraints*. Adding constraints tells Solver to find a solution so that these conditions are not violated.

Add Constraints to Solver

1. Click the Data tab.
2. Click Solver.

   The Solver Parameters dialog box appears.

3. Specify the objective cell, optimization value, and variable cells.
4. Click Add.

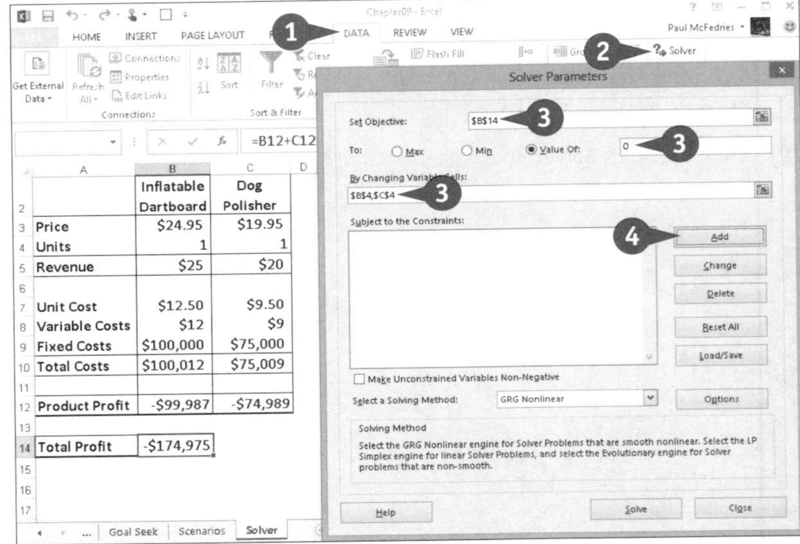

Excel displays the Add Constraint dialog box.

5. In the Cell Reference box, type the cell you want to constrain.
6. Click here and then click the operator you want to use.
7. If you chose a comparison operator in step 6, use the Constraint box to enter the value by which you want to restrict the cell.
8. To specify more constraints, click Add and repeat steps 5 to 7.
9. Click OK.

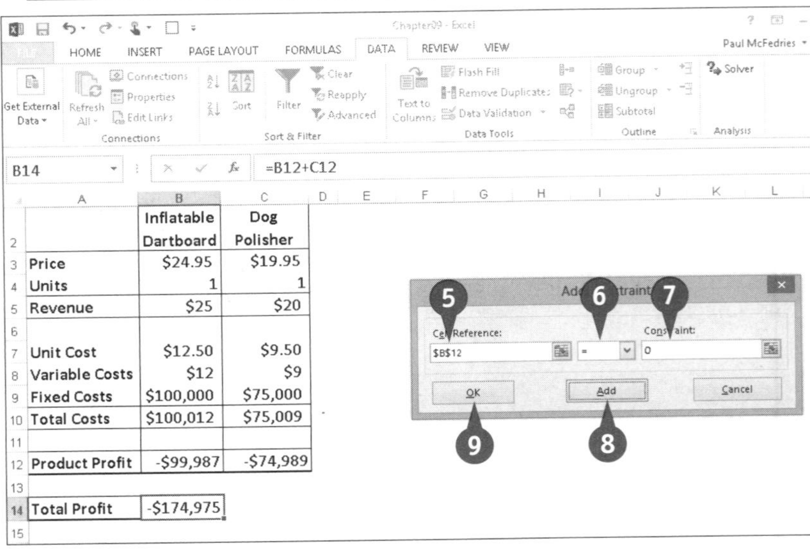

Excel returns to the Solver Parameters dialog box.

A Excel displays your constraints in the Subject to the Constraints list box.

10 Click Solve.

11 If you see one or more Show Trial Solution dialog boxes (not shown), click Continue in each.

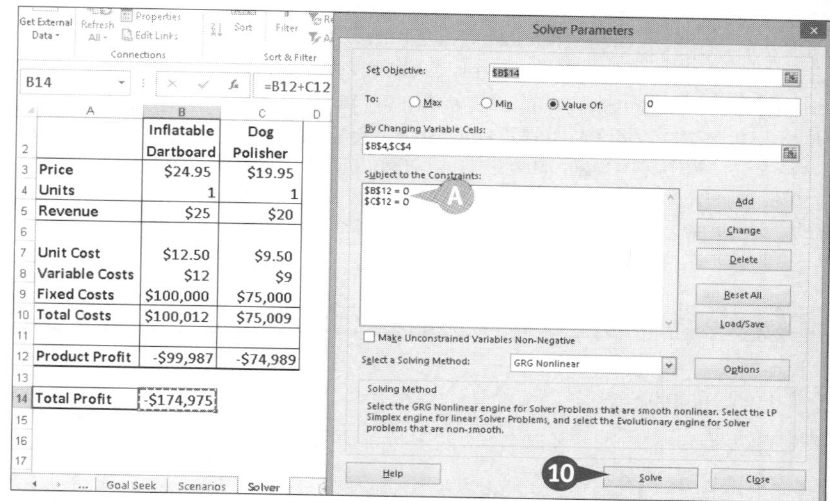

When the optimization is complete, Excel displays the Solver Results dialog box.

B The Solver result message appears here.

12 Click the Keep Solver Solution option (○ changes to ◉).

C If you do not want to accept the result, click the Restore Original Values option instead (○ changes to ◉).

13 Click OK.

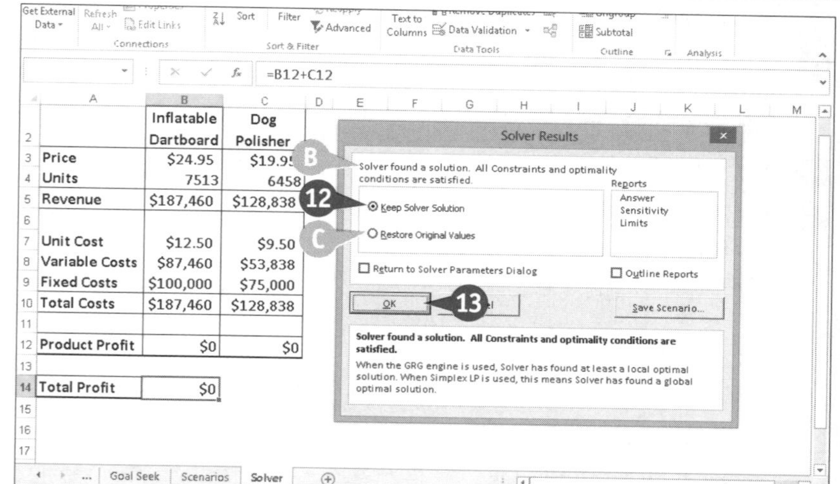

EXTRA

Use the `int` (integer) operator when you need a constraint, such as total employees, to be an integer value instead of a real number. Use the `bin` (binary) operator when you have a constraint that must be either `TRUE` or `FALSE` (or 1 or 0). You can add a maximum of 100 constraints. Also, if you need to make a change to a constraint before you begin solving, click the constraint in the Subject to the Constraints list box, click Change, and then make your adjustments in the Change Constraint dialog box that appears. If you want to delete a constraint that you no longer need, click it and then click Delete.

Save a Solver Solution as a Scenario

If you use Solver frequently to try out different types of analyses on the same set of data, you can make your analysis faster and more efficient by saving your solutions as scenarios that you can recall quickly. Whenever you have a spreadsheet model that uses a coherent set of input values — known as *changing cells* — you have what Excel calls a *scenario*. With Solver, these changing cells are its variable cells, so a Solver solution amounts to a kind of scenario.

However, Solver does not give you an easy way to save and rerun a particular solution. To work around this problem, you can save a solution as a scenario that you can later recall using the Excel Scenario Manager feature.

Save a Solver Solution as a Scenario

1. Click the Data tab.
2. Click Solver.

   The Solver Parameters dialog box appears.
3. Specify the objective cell, optimization value, variable cells, and constraints.
4. Click Solve.
5. If you see one or more Show Trial Solution dialog boxes (not shown), click Continue in each.

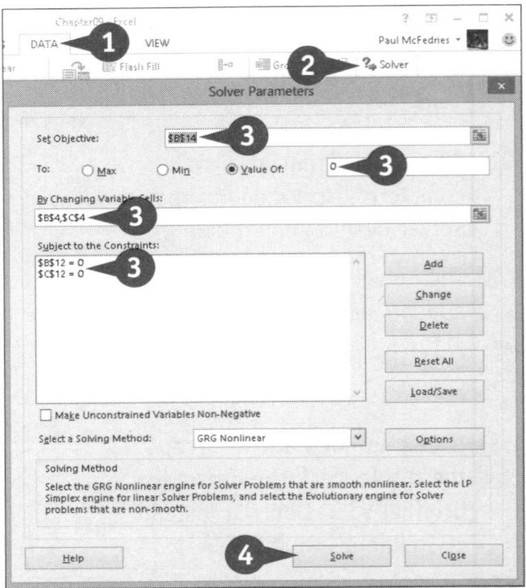

When the optimization is complete, Excel displays the Solver Results dialog box.

6. Click Save Scenario.

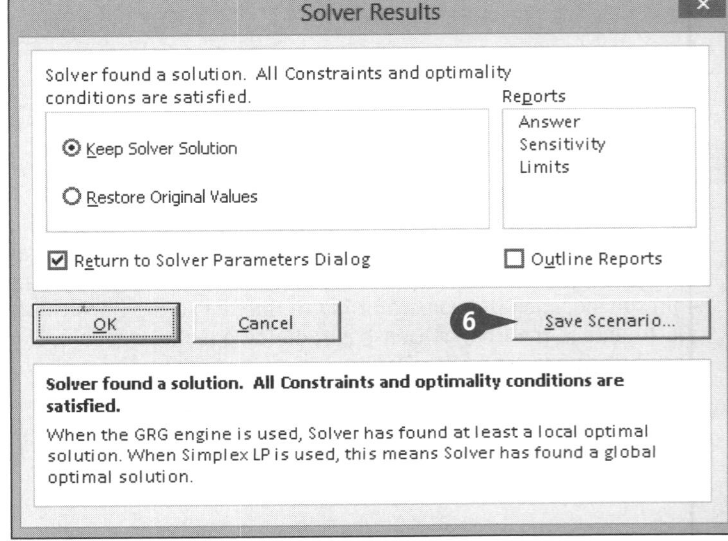

Excel displays the Save Scenario dialog box.

7 Type a name for the scenario.

8 Click OK.

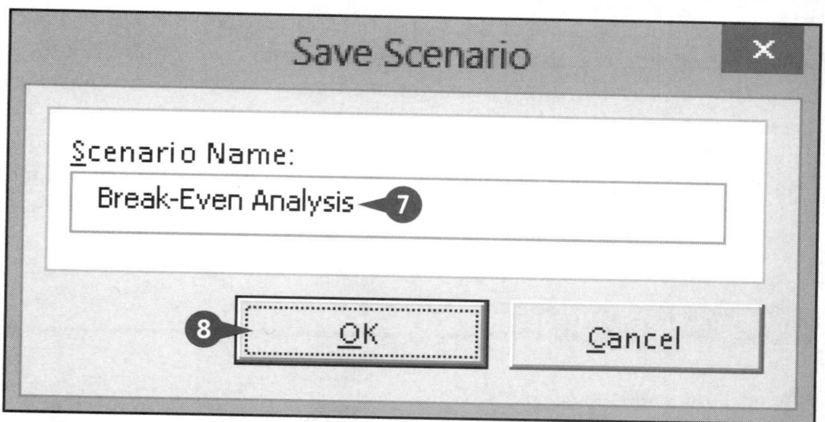

Excel returns you to the Solver Results dialog box.

9 Click the Keep Solver Solution option (○ changes to ◉).

A If you do not want to accept the result, click the Restore Original Values option instead (○ changes to ◉).

10 Click OK.

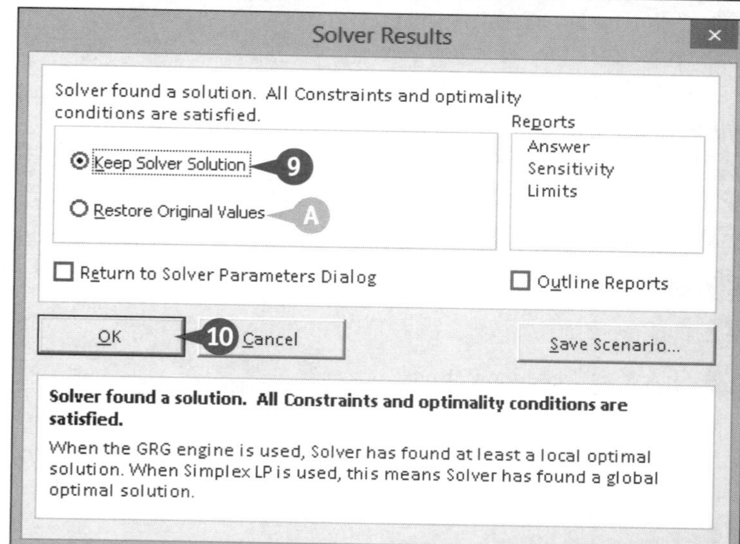

EXTRA

Solver can use one of several solving methods. In the Solver Parameters dialog box, click the Select a Solving Method down arrow and select Simplex LP, GRG Nonlinear, or Evolutionary. Select the Simplex LP method if your worksheet model is linear. In the simplest possible terms, a linear model is one in which the variables are not raised to any powers and none of the so-called transcendent functions, such as `SIN` and `COS`, are used. Select the GRG Nonlinear method if your worksheet model is nonlinear and smooth. In general terms, a smooth model is one in which a graph of the equation used does not show sharp edges or breaks. Select the Evolutionary method if your worksheet model is nonlinear and nonsmooth.

Plotting a Best-Fit Trendline

If you want to get a sense of the overall trend displayed by a set of data, the easiest way is to use a chart to plot a *best-fit trendline*. This is a straight line through the chart's data points where the differences between the chart points that reside above the line and those that reside below the line cancel each other out.

A best-fit trendline is an example of *regression analysis*, which is a statistical tool for analyzing the relationship between two phenomena, where one depends upon the other. For example, housing sales depend upon interest rates. In this case, you would say that housing sales are the *dependent variable* and interest rates are the *independent variable*.

Plotting a Best-Fit Trendline

1. Click the chart to select it.
2. If your chart has multiple data series, click the series you want to analyze.

Note: *To add a best-fit trendline, you must plot your data series as an XY (Scatter) chart.*

3. Click the Design tab.
4. Click Add Chart Element.
5. Click Trendline.
6. Click More Trendline Options.

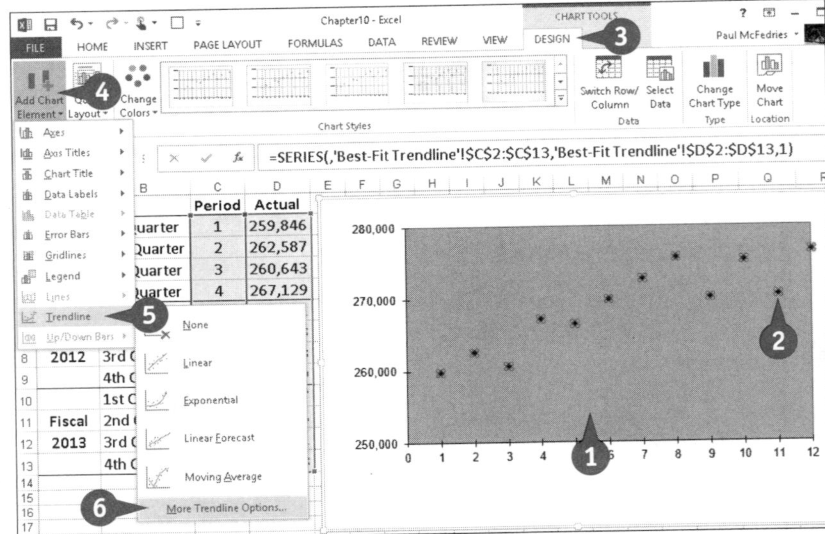

The Format Trendline pane appears.

7. Click the Trendline Options tab.
8. Click the Linear option (○ changes to ◉).

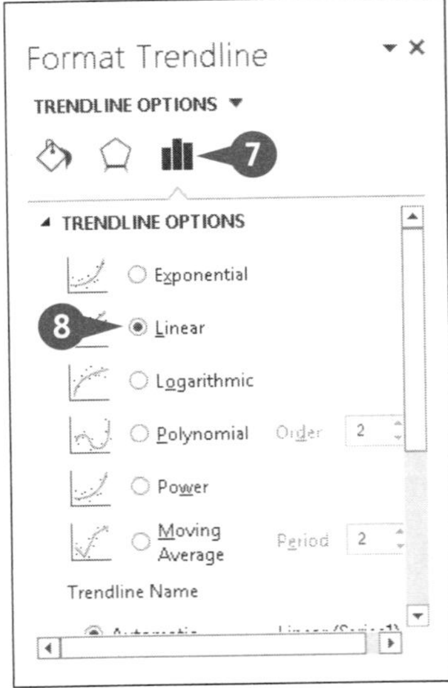

9. Scroll down and click the Display Equation on Chart check box (☐ changes to ☑).
10. Click the Display R-Squared Value on Chart check box (☐ changes to ☑).
11. Click Close.

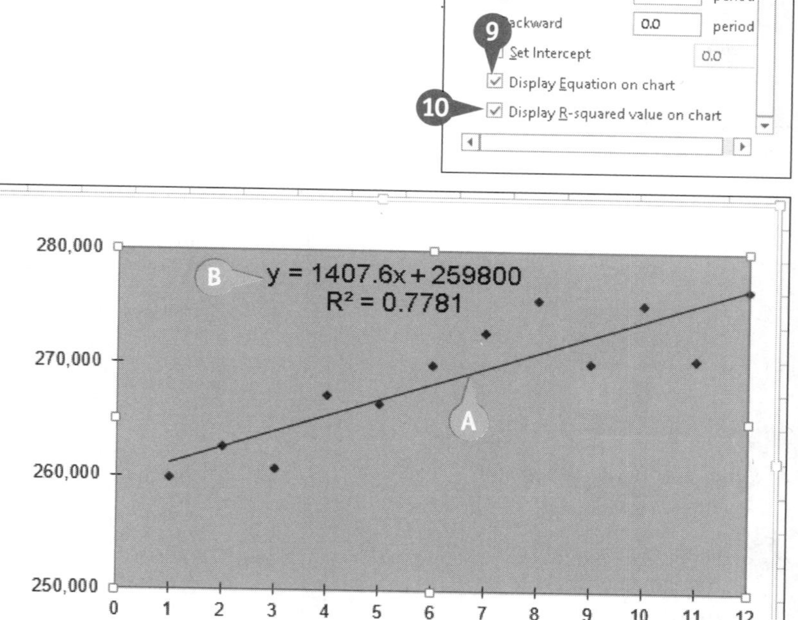

A. Excel plots the best-fit trendline.

B. Excel displays the regression equation and the R^2 value.

EXTRA

The regression equation tells you the exact relationship between the dependent variable and the independent variable. With linear regression, where the best-fit trendline is a straight line, the regression equation looks like this:

```
y = mx + b
```

`y` is the dependent variable; `x` is the independent variable; `m` is the slope of the trendline; and `b` is the starting value for the trend. R^2 is the coefficient of determination, which is the square of the correlation, and it tells you how well the trendline fits the data. In general, the closer R^2 is to 1, the better the fit. Values of R^2 below 0.7 mean that the trendline is not a very good fit for the data.

Calculating Best-Fit Values

If your analysis requires exact trend values, you could plot the best-fit trendline and then use the regression equation to calculate the values. However, if the data values change, you need to recalculate the values. A better solution is to use the `TREND` function.

`TREND` takes up to four arguments. The only required argument is `known_y's`, which is a range reference or array of the dependent values. The `known_x's` argument is a range reference or array of the independent values (the default is the array `{1,2,3,...],n}`, where `n` is the number of `known_y's`). The `new_x's` argument is for forecasting, so it is not required here. The `const` argument determines the y-intercept: `FALSE` places it at 0, and `TRUE` (the default) calculates the y-intercept based on the `known_y's`.

Calculating Best-Fit Values

1. Select the cells in which you want the best-fit values to appear.
2. Type **=trend(**.

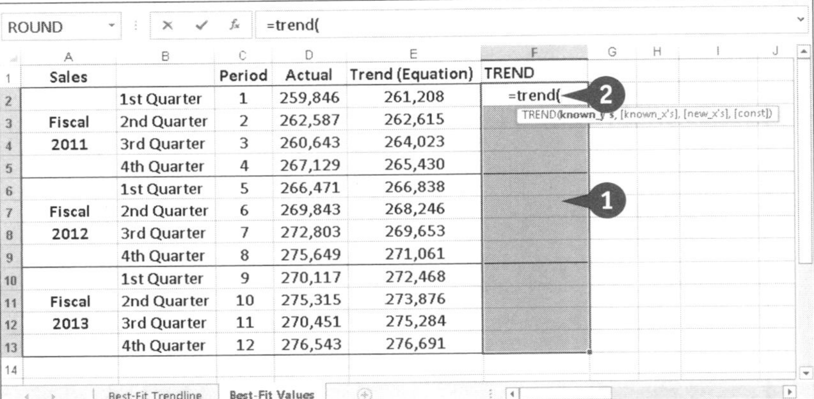

	A	B	C	D	E	F
1	Sales		Period	Actual	Trend (Equation)	TREND
2		1st Quarter	1	259,846	261,208	=trend(
3	Fiscal	2nd Quarter	2	262,587	262,615	
4	2011	3rd Quarter	3	260,643	264,023	
5		4th Quarter	4	267,129	265,430	
6		1st Quarter	5	266,471	266,838	
7	Fiscal	2nd Quarter	6	269,843	268,246	
8	2012	3rd Quarter	7	272,803	269,653	
9		4th Quarter	8	275,649	271,061	
10		1st Quarter	9	270,117	272,468	
11	Fiscal	2nd Quarter	10	275,315	273,876	
12	2013	3rd Quarter	11	270,451	275,284	
13		4th Quarter	12	276,543	276,691	

3. Type a reference or array that represents the dependent values.
4. Type a comma and then type a reference or array that represents the independent values.

Note: *In the example shown here, the independent values are the period numbers 1, 2, 3, and so on. However, these are the default values for the* `known_x's` *argument, so technically you could omit this argument in this example.*

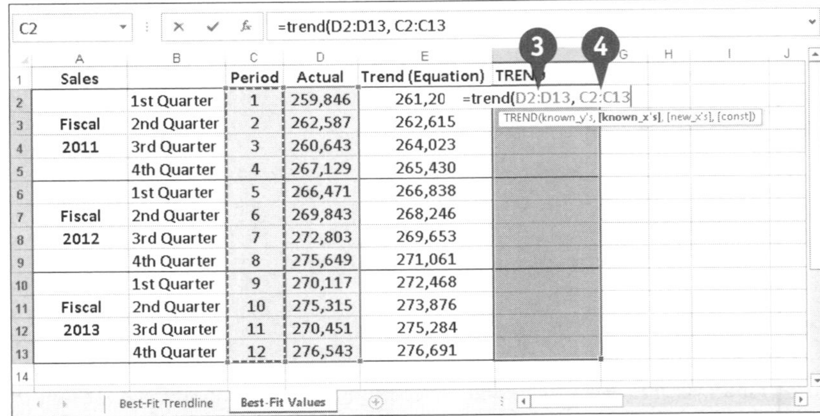

	A	B	C	D	E	F
1	Sales		Period	Actual	Trend (Equation)	TREN
2		1st Quarter	1	259,846	261,20	=trend(D2:D13, C2:C13
3	Fiscal	2nd Quarter	2	262,587	262,615	
4	2011	3rd Quarter	3	260,643	264,023	
5		4th Quarter	4	267,129	265,430	
6		1st Quarter	5	266,471	266,838	
7	Fiscal	2nd Quarter	6	269,843	268,246	
8	2012	3rd Quarter	7	272,803	269,653	
9		4th Quarter	8	275,649	271,061	
10		1st Quarter	9	270,117	272,468	
11	Fiscal	2nd Quarter	10	275,315	273,876	
12	2013	3rd Quarter	11	270,451	275,284	
13		4th Quarter	12	276,543	276,691	

5 If you prefer to use a trend starting point of 0, type two commas and then type **FALSE** (not shown).

6 Type **)**.

7 Press and hold Ctrl + Shift and then click the Enter button or press Enter.

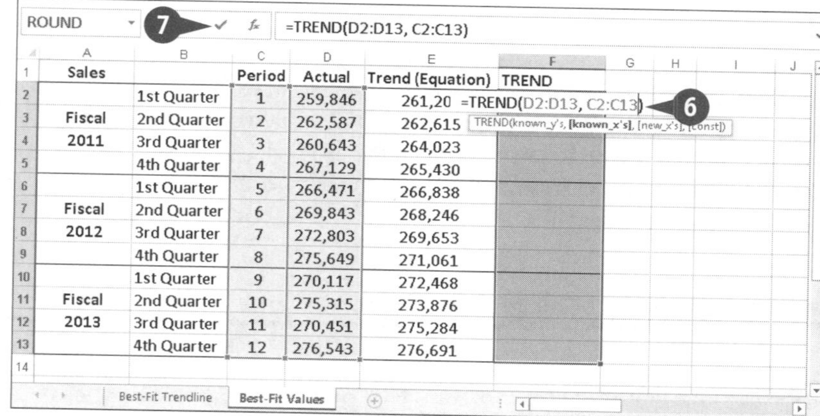

ROUND =TREND(D2:D13, C2:C13)

	A	B	C	D	E	F
1	Sales		Period	Actual	Trend (Equation)	TREND
2		1st Quarter	1	259,846	261,20	=TREND(D2:D13, C2:C13)
3	Fiscal	2nd Quarter	2	262,587	262,615	
4	2011	3rd Quarter	3	260,643	264,023	
5		4th Quarter	4	267,129	265,430	
6		1st Quarter	5	266,471	266,838	
7	Fiscal	2nd Quarter	6	269,843	268,246	
8	2012	3rd Quarter	7	272,803	269,653	
9		4th Quarter	8	275,649	271,061	
10		1st Quarter	9	270,117	272,468	
11	Fiscal	2nd Quarter	10	275,315	273,876	
12	2013	3rd Quarter	11	270,451	275,284	
13		4th Quarter	12	276,543	276,691	

A Excel calculates the best-fit trend values and enters them as an array.

F2 {=TREND(D2:D13, C2:C13)}

	A	B	C	D	E	F
1	Sales		Period	Actual	Trend (Equation)	TREND
2		1st Quarter	1	259,846	261,208	261,208
3	Fiscal	2nd Quarter	2	262,587	262,615	262,615
4	2011	3rd Quarter	3	260,643	264,023	264,023
5		4th Quarter	4	267,129	265,430	265,431
6		1st Quarter	5	266,471	266,838	266,838
7	Fiscal	2nd Quarter	6	269,843	268,246	268,246
8	2012	3rd Quarter	7	272,803	269,653	269,654
9		4th Quarter	8	275,649	271,061	271,061
10		1st Quarter	9	270,117	272,468	272,469
11	Fiscal	2nd Quarter	10	275,315	273,876	273,876
12	2013	3rd Quarter	11	270,451	275,284	275,284
13		4th Quarter	12	276,543	276,691	276,692

Best-Fit Trendline | Best-Fit Values

EXTRA

You can use the `LINEST` function to calculate the trendline's slope (`m`) and y-intercept (`b`), which you can then plug into the general regression equation (`y = mx + b`) to calculate individual trend values. `LINEST` takes three of the same arguments as `TREND`: `known_y's`, `known_x's`, and `const`. A fourth argument named `stats` is an optional logical value that determines whether `LINEST` returns additional regression statistics besides the slope and intercept. The default is `FALSE`. When you use `LINEST` without the `stats` argument, enter the function as a `1x2` array, where the value in the first column is the slope of the trendline and the value in the second column is the intercept. With `stats`, enter the function as a 5x2 array.

Plotting Forecasted Values

If you find that the best-fit trendline or the best-fit values indicate that the dependent and independent variables are well correlated, then you can take advantage of that correlation to forecast future values. This analysis assumes that the major factors underlying the existing data will remain more or less constant over the number of periods in your forecast.

The easiest way to calculate forecasted values is to use a chart to extend the best-fit trendline into one or more future periods. However, note that to work with a best-fit trendline and use it to plot forecasted values, you must plot your data series as an XY (Scatter) chart.

Plotting Forecasted Values

1. Click the chart to select it.
2. If your chart has multiple data series, click the series you want to analyze.
3. Click the Design tab.
4. Click Add Chart Element.
5. Click Trendline.
6. Click More Trendline Options.

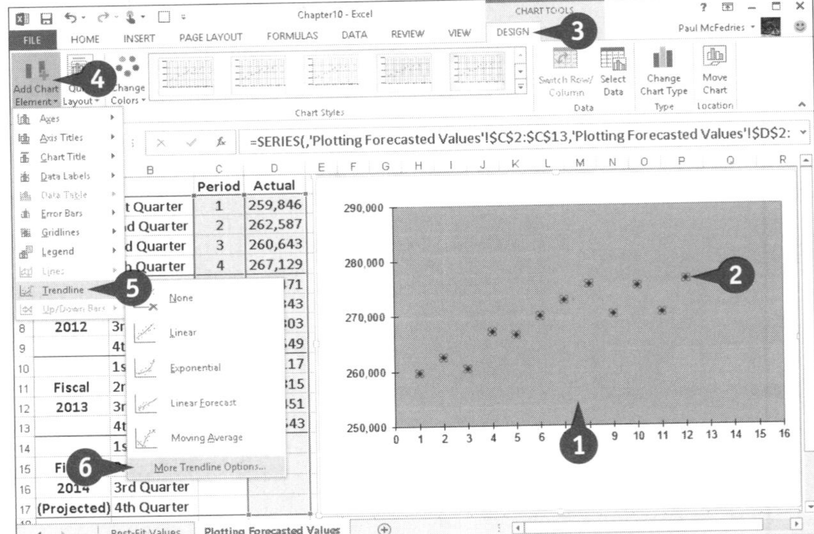

The Format Trendline pane appears.

7. Click the Trendline Options tab.
8. Click the Linear option (○ changes to ◉).

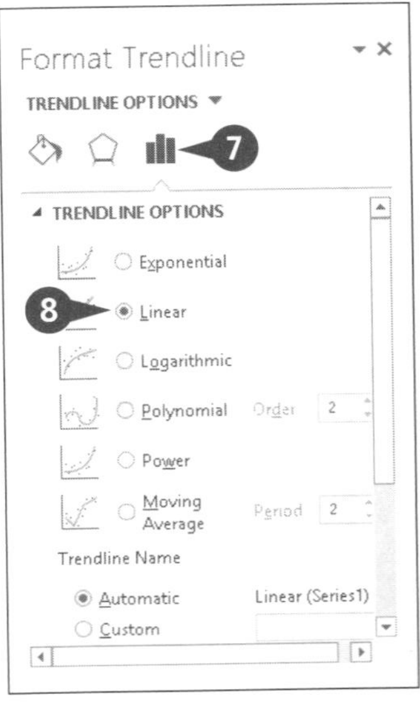

9 Scroll down and type the number of units you want to project the trendline into in the future the Forward text box.

10 Click the Display Equation on Chart check box (☐ changes to ☑).

11 Click the Display R-Squared Value on Chart check box (☐ changes to ☑).

12 Click Close.

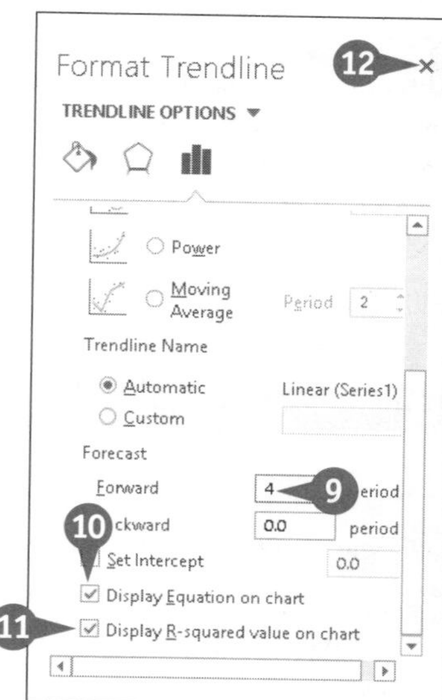

A Excel plots the forecasted values.

B Excel displays the regression equation and the R^2 value.

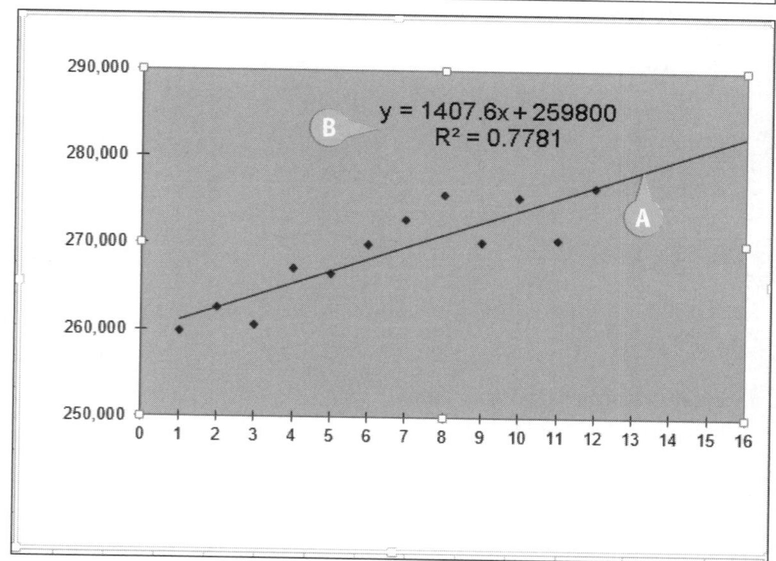

EXTRA

Another way to come up with forecasted dependent variable values is to calculate them directly using the regression equation that Excel generates when you click the Display Equation on Chart check box in the Format Trendline pane. The general regression equation for a linear model is as follows:

```
y = mx + b
```

`y` is the dependent variable; `x` is the independent variable; `m` is the slope of the trendline; and `b` is the starting value for the trend. Both `m` and `b` are constants, so to calculate the dependent variable value for the next period in your forecast, substitute that period's independent variable value for `x`.

Extending a Linear Trend

If forecasting is part of your data analysis, you can use the Excel fill handle and Series command to extend a linear trend into one or more future periods. With a *linear trend*, the dependent variable is related to the independent variable by some constant amount. For example, you might find that housing sales (the dependent variable) increase by 100,000 units whenever interest rates (the independent variable) decrease by 1 percent. Similarly, you might find that company revenue (the dependent variable) increases by $250,000 for every $50,000 you spend on advertising (the independent variable). With this linear relationship, you can forecast future periods by using Excel's fill handle and Series command to extend your existing data.

Extending a Linear Trend

Using the Fill Handle

1. Select the existing data.
2. Click and drag the fill handle to extend the selection over the number of future periods you want to forecast.

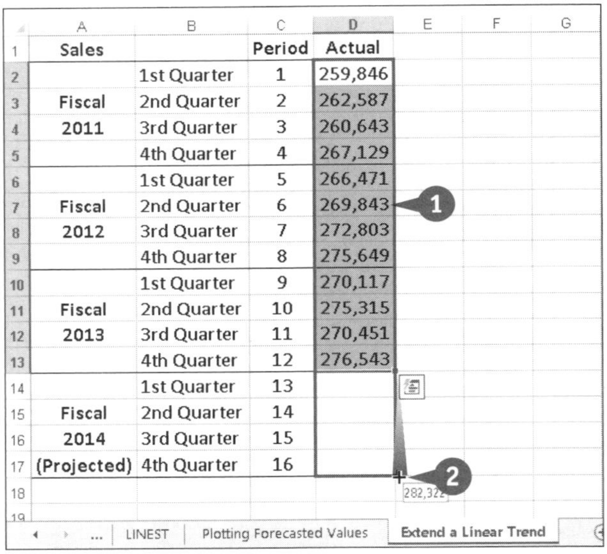

	A	B	C	D	E	F	G
1	Sales		Period	Actual			
2		1st Quarter	1	259,846			
3	Fiscal	2nd Quarter	2	262,587			
4	2011	3rd Quarter	3	260,643			
5		4th Quarter	4	267,129			
6		1st Quarter	5	266,471			
7	Fiscal	2nd Quarter	6	269,843			
8	2012	3rd Quarter	7	272,803			
9		4th Quarter	8	275,649			
10		1st Quarter	9	270,117			
11	Fiscal	2nd Quarter	10	275,315			
12	2013	3rd Quarter	11	270,451			
13		4th Quarter	12	276,543			
14		1st Quarter	13				
15	Fiscal	2nd Quarter	14				
16	2014	3rd Quarter	15				
17	(Projected)	4th Quarter	16				
18					282,322		

LINEST | Plotting Forecasted Values | Extend a Linear Trend

Ⓐ Excel extends the existing data with the forecasted values.

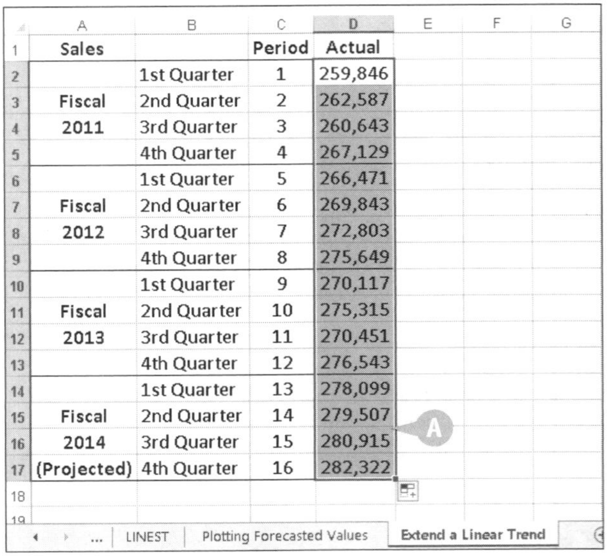

	A	B	C	D	E	F	G
1	Sales		Period	Actual			
2		1st Quarter	1	259,846			
3	Fiscal	2nd Quarter	2	262,587			
4	2011	3rd Quarter	3	260,643			
5		4th Quarter	4	267,129			
6		1st Quarter	5	266,471			
7	Fiscal	2nd Quarter	6	269,843			
8	2012	3rd Quarter	7	272,803			
9		4th Quarter	8	275,649			
10		1st Quarter	9	270,117			
11	Fiscal	2nd Quarter	10	275,315			
12	2013	3rd Quarter	11	270,451			
13		4th Quarter	12	276,543			
14		1st Quarter	13	278,099			
15	Fiscal	2nd Quarter	14	279,507			
16	2014	3rd Quarter	15	280,915			
17	(Projected)	4th Quarter	16	282,322			
18							

LINEST | Plotting Forecasted Values | Extend a Linear Trend

Using the Series Command

1. Select the existing data and the cells where you want the forecasted data to appear.
2. Click the Home tab.
3. Click Fill.
4. Click Series.

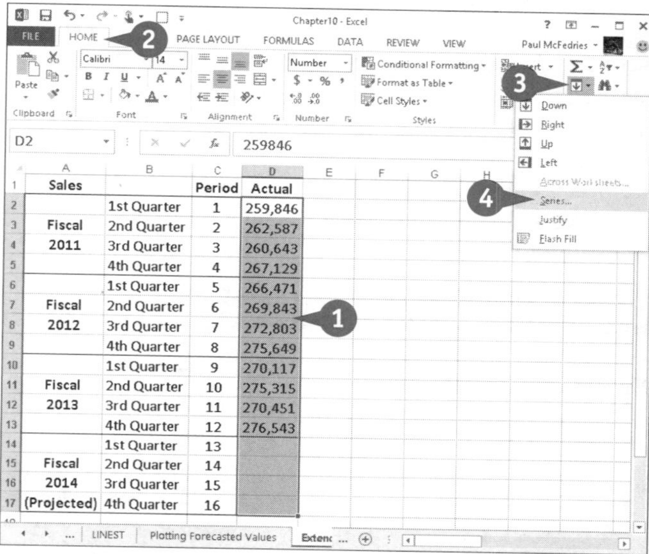

Excel displays the Series dialog box.

5. Click the AutoFill option (○ change to ◉).
6. Click OK.

B Excel extends the existing linear trend with the forecasted values.

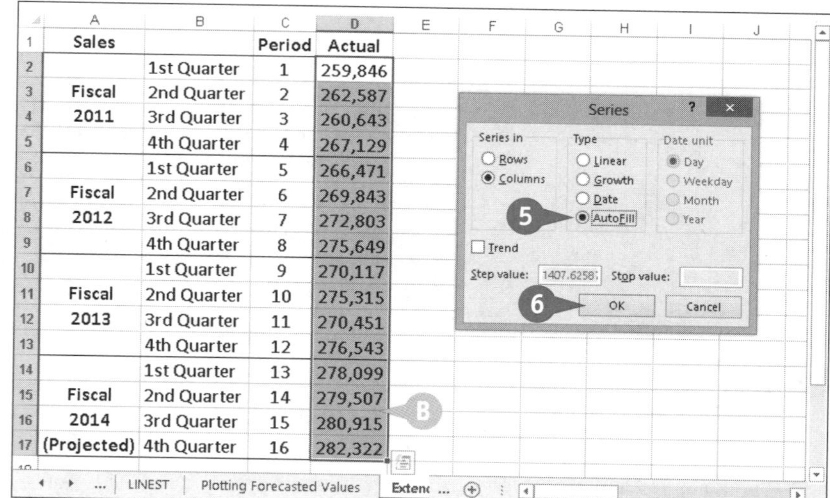

APPLY IT

If your data analysis requires that you see the actual values that make up a linear trend, the Series command can help. To begin, copy the historical data into an adjacent row or column, and then select the range that includes both the copied historical data and the blank cells that will contain the projections. Click the Home tab, click Fill, and then click Series to open the Series dialog box. Click the Trend check box (☐ changes to ☑), click the Linear option (○ changes to ◉), and then click OK. Excel replaces the copied historical data with the best-fit trend numbers and projects the trend onto the blank cells.

Calculating Forecasted Linear Values

If your analysis requires exact forecast values, you could extend the best-fit trendline and then use the regression equation to calculate the values, or you could use the fill handle or Series command to extend the linear trend. These are easy methods, but if the historical values change, then you need to repeat these procedures to recalculate the forecasted values. A more efficient solution is to use the `TREND` function.

In this situation, you need to use `TREND` not only with the `known_y's` argument (a reference to the dependent values) and optionally the `known_x's` argument (a reference to the independent values), but also the `new_x's` argument. The `new_x's` argument is a range reference or array that represents the new independent values for which you want forecasted dependent values.

Calculating Forecasted Linear Values

1. Select the cells in which you want the forecasted values to appear.
2. Type **=trend(**.

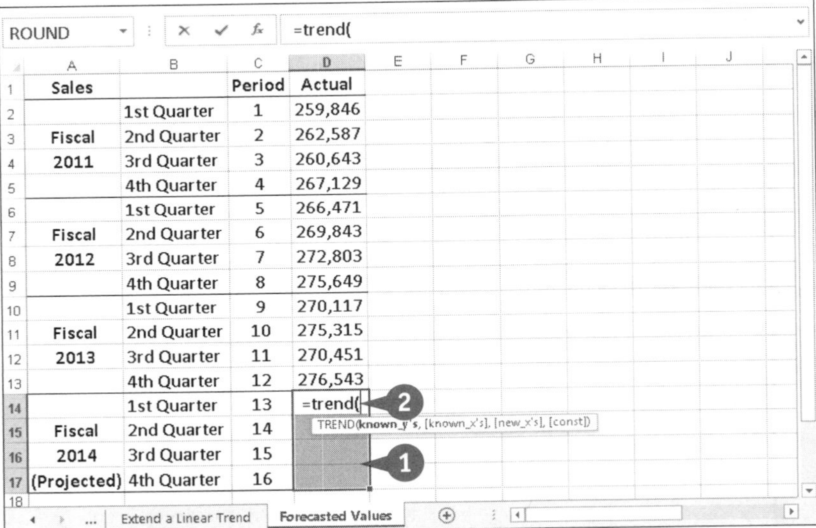

ROUND | =trend(

	A	B	C	D
1	Sales		Period	Actual
2		1st Quarter	1	259,846
3	Fiscal	2nd Quarter	2	262,587
4	2011	3rd Quarter	3	260,643
5		4th Quarter	4	267,129
6		1st Quarter	5	266,471
7	Fiscal	2nd Quarter	6	269,843
8	2012	3rd Quarter	7	272,803
9		4th Quarter	8	275,649
10		1st Quarter	9	270,117
11	Fiscal	2nd Quarter	10	275,315
12	2013	3rd Quarter	11	270,451
13		4th Quarter	12	276,543
14		1st Quarter	13	=trend(
15	Fiscal	2nd Quarter	14	
16	2014	3rd Quarter	15	
17	(Projected)	4th Quarter	16	

3. Type a reference or array that represents the dependent values.
4. Type a comma and then type a reference or array that represents the independent values.

Note: *In the example shown here, the independent values are the period numbers 1, 2, 3, and so on. However, these are the default values for the* `known_x's` *argument, so technically you could omit this argument in this example.*

D14 | =trend(D2:D13, C2:C13

	A	B	C	D
1	Sales		Period	Actual
2		1st Quarter	1	259,846
3	Fiscal	2nd Quarter	2	262,587
4	2011	3rd Quarter	3	260,643
5		4th Quarter	4	267,129
6		1st Quarter	5	266,471
7	Fiscal	2nd Quarter	6	269,843
8	2012	3rd Quarter	7	272,803
9		4th Quarter	8	275,649
10		1st Quarter	9	270,117
11	Fiscal	2nd Quarter	10	275,315
12	2013	3rd Quarter	11	270,451
13		4th Quarter	12	276,543
14		1st Quarter	13	=trend(D2:D13, C2:C13
15	Fiscal	2nd Quarter	14	
16	2014	3rd Quarter	15	
17	(Projected)	4th Quarter	16	

TREND(known_y's, [known_x's], [new_x's], [const])

Extend a Linear Trend | Forecasted Values

5 Type a comma and then a reference or array that represents the new independent values.

6 If you prefer to use a trend starting point of 0, type a comma and then type **FALSE** (not shown).

7 Type **)**.

8 Press and hold Ctrl + Shift and then click the Enter button or press Enter.

D14 | 8 | =trend(D2:D13, C2:C13, C14:C17)

	A	B	C	D
1	Sales		Period	Actual
2		1st Quarter	1	259,846
3	Fiscal	2nd Quarter	2	262,587
4	2011	3rd Quarter	3	260,643
5		4th Quarter	4	267,129
6		1st Quarter	5	266,471
7	Fiscal	2nd Quarter	6	269,843
8	2012	3rd Quarter	7	272,803
9		4th Quarter	8	275,649
10		1st Quarter	9	270,117
11	Fiscal	2nd Quarter	10	275,315
12	2013	3rd Quarter	11	270,451
13		4th Quarter	12	276,543
14		1st Quarter	13	=trend(D2:D13, C2:C13, C14:C17)
15	Fiscal	2nd Quarter	14	
16	2014	3rd Quarter	15	
17	(Projected)	4th Quarter	16	

5 7 TREND(known_y's, [known_x's], [new_x's], [const])

Extend a Linear Trend | Forecasted Values

A Excel calculates the forecasted values.

D14 | {=TREND(D2:D13, C2:C13, C14:C17)} A

	A	B	C	D
1	Sales		Period	Actual
2		1st Quarter	1	259,846
3	Fiscal	2nd Quarter	2	262,587
4	2011	3rd Quarter	3	260,643
5		4th Quarter	4	267,129
6		1st Quarter	5	266,471
7	Fiscal	2nd Quarter	6	269,843
8	2012	3rd Quarter	7	272,803
9		4th Quarter	8	275,649
10		1st Quarter	9	270,117
11	Fiscal	2nd Quarter	10	275,315
12	2013	3rd Quarter	11	270,451
13		4th Quarter	12	276,543
14		1st Quarter	13	278,099
15	Fiscal	2nd Quarter	14	279,507
16	2014	3rd Quarter	15	280,915
17	(Projected)	4th Quarter	16	282,322

A

Extend a Linear Trend | Forecasted Values

EXTRA

When you use the `LINEST` function to calculate the linear trend's slope (`m`) and y-intercept (`b`), you can use these results to forecast new values. That is, given a new independent value `x`, the forecasted dependent value is given by the regression equation:

```
y = mx + b
```

You can also calculate a forecasted value by using the `FORECAST` function, which takes three arguments: `x` is the new independent value for which you want to forecast a new dependent value; `known_y's` and `known_x's` are the same as with the `TREND` function, except that with `FORECAST`, the `known_x's` argument is required.

You can apply regression analysis to nonlinear data, such as an *exponential* trend, which rises or falls at an increasing rate. It is called exponential because the trendline resembles the graph of a number being raised to successively higher values of an exponent. For example, the series 2^1, 2^2, 2^3 starts slowly (2, 4, 8, and so on), but by the time you get to 2^{20}, the series value is up to 1,048,576, and 2^{100} is a number that is 31 digits long.

To visualize such a trend, you can plot an *exponential trendline*. This is a curved line through the data points where the differences between the points on one side of the line and the points on the other side of the line cancel each other out.

Plotting an Exponential Trendline

1. Click the chart to select it.
2. If your chart has multiple data series, click the series you want to analyze.
3. Click the Design tab.
4. Click Add Chart Element.
5. Click Trendline.
6. Click More Trendline Options.

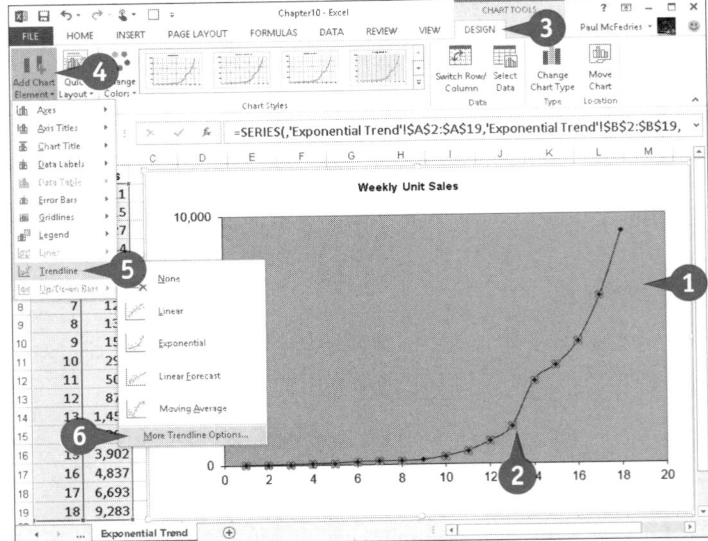

The Format Trendline pane appears.

7. Click the Trendline Options tab.
8. Click the Exponential option (○ changes to ◉).

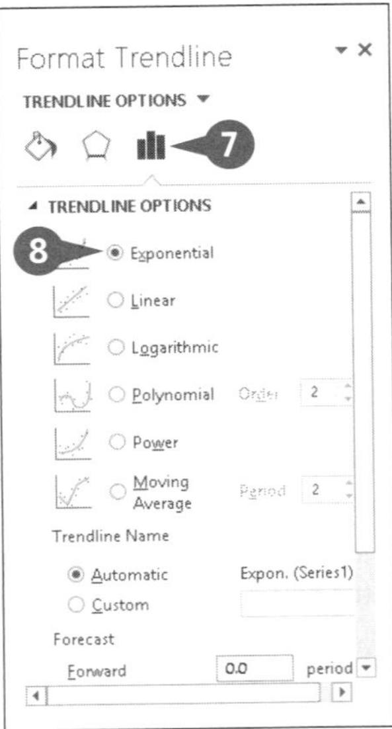

9 Scroll down and click the Display Equation on Chart check box (☐ changes to ☑).

10 Click the Display R-Squared Value on Chart check box (☐ changes to ☑).

11 Click Close.

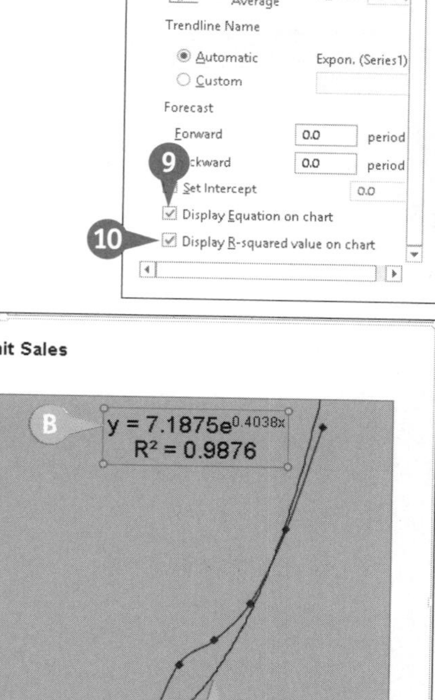

A Excel plots the exponential trendline.

B Excel displays the regression equation and the R^2 value, as described in the Extra section.

Weekly Unit Sales

$y = 7.1875e^{0.4038x}$

$R^2 = 0.9876$

EXTRA

The regression equation tells you the specific relationship between the dependent variable and the independent variable. With nonlinear regression, when the best-fit trendline is an exponential curve, the regression equation takes the following general form:

```
y = be^mx
```

`y` is the dependent variable; `x` is the independent variable; `b` and `m` are constants; and `e` is a constant (approximately 2.71828) that represents the base of the natural logarithm.

R^2 is the coefficient of determination, which is the square of the correlation, and it tells you how well the trendline fits the data. In general, the closer R^2 is to 1, the better the fit. Values of R^2 below 0.7 mean that the trendline is not a very good fit for the data.

Calculating Exponential Trend Values

If you require exact exponential trend values, you could plot the trendline and then use the regression equation to calculate them. However, if the data values change, you need to recalculate the trend values. A better solution is to use the `GROWTH` function.

`GROWTH` takes up to four arguments. The `known_y's` argument is required and is a reference to the dependent values. The `known_x's` argument is a reference to the independent values (the default is the array `{1,2,3,...],n}`, where `n` is the number of `known_y's`). The `new_x's` argument is a reference to the new independent values for which you want forecasted dependent values. The `const` argument determines the value of `b` in the regression equation: `FALSE` places it at 1, while `TRUE` (the default) calculates `b` based on the `known_y's`.

Calculating Exponential Trend Values

1. Select the cells in which you want the trend values to appear.
2. Type **=growth(**.

	A	B	C	D	E	F
1	Historical Data				Future Data	
2	Week	Units	Trend		Week	Forecast
3	1	11	11		19	=growth(
4	2	15	16		20	GROWTH(known_y's, [known_x's], [new_x's], [const])
5	3	27	24		21	
6	4	44	36		22	
7	5	59	54			
8	6	112	81			
9	7	125	121			
10	8	136	182			
11	9	157	272			
12	10	298	408			
13	11	503	610			
14	12	875	914			
15	13	1,452	1,369			
16	14	3,293	2,049			
17	15	3,902	3,069			
18	16	4,837	4,596			
19	17	6,693	6,882			
20	18	9,283	10,306			

Calculating Exponential Trend

3. Type a reference or array that represents the dependent values.
4. Type a comma and then type a reference or array that represents the independent values.

Note: *In the example shown here, the independent values are the period numbers 1, 2, 3, and so on. However, these are the default values for the* `known_x's` *argument, so technically you could omit this argument in this example.*

	A	B	C	D	E	F
1	Historical Data				Future Data	
2	Week	Units	Trend		Week	Forecast
3	1	11	11		19	=growth(B3:B20, A3:A20
4	2	15	16		20	GROWTH(known_y's, [known_x's], [new_x's], [const])
5	3	27	24		21	
6	4	44	36		22	
7	5	59	54			
8	6	112	81			
9	7	125	121			
10	8	136	182			
11	9	157	272			
12	10	298	408			
13	11	503	610			
14	12	875	914			
15	13	1,452	1,369			
16	14	3,293	2,049			
17	15	3,902	3,069			
18	16	4,837	4,596			
19	17	6,693	6,882			
20	18	9,283	10,306			

Calculating Exponential Trend

5 Type a comma and then a reference or array that represents the new independent values.

6 If you prefer to use a trend starting point of 0, type a comma and then type **FALSE** (not shown).

7 Type).

8 Press Ctrl + Shift and then click the Enter button or press Enter.

F3 | =growth(B3:B20, A3:A20, E3:E6)

	A	B	C	D	E	F
1	Historical Data				Future Data	
2	Week	Units	Trend		Week	Forecast
3	1	11	11		19	=growth(B3:B20, A3:A20, E3:E6)
4	2	15	16		20	GROWTH(known_y's, [known_x's], [new_x's], [const])
5	3	27	24		21	
6	4	44	36		22	
7	5	59	54			
8	6	112	81			
9	7	125	121			
10	8	136	182			
11	9	157	272			
12	10	298	408			
13	11	503	610			
14	12	875	914			
15	13	1,452	1,369			
16	14	3,293	2,049			
17	15	3,902	3,069			
18	16	4,837	4,596			
19	17	6,693	6,882			
20	18	9,283	10,306			

A Excel calculates the exponential trend values.

F3 | {=GROWTH(B3:B20, A3:A20, E3:E6)}

	A	B	C	D	E	F
1	Historical Data				Future Data	
2	Week	Units	Trend		Week	Forecast
3	1	11	11		19	15,433
4	2	15	16		20	23,111
5	3	27	24		21	34,608
6	4	44	36		22	51,825
7	5	59	54			
8	6	112	81			
9	7	125	121			
10	8	136	182			
11	9	157	272			
12	10	298	408			
13	11	503	610			
14	12	875	914			
15	13	1,452	1,369			
16	14	3,293	2,049			
17	15	3,902	3,069			
18	16	4,837	4,596			
19	17	6,693	6,882			
20	18	9,283	10,306			

EXTRA

You can use the `LOGEST` function to calculate the exponential trend equation's `m` and `b` constants, which you can then plug into the equation, $y = be^{mx}$, to calculate individual trend values. `LOGEST` takes three of the same arguments as `GROWTH`: `known_y's`, `known_x's`, and `const`. A fourth argument named `stats` is an optional logical value that determines whether `LOGEST` returns additional regression statistics. The default is `FALSE`. When you use `LOGEST` without the `stats` argument, enter the function as a 1x2 array, where the value in the second column is `b`; to derive `m`, you must use the `LN` function to take the natural logarithm of the value in the first column of the array. With `stats`, enter the function as a 5x2 array.

Plotting a Logarithmic Trendline

You can apply regression analysis to nonlinear data, such as data that exhibits logarithmic behavior. A *logarithmic trend* is one in which the data rises or falls very quickly at the beginning, but then slows down and levels off over time. An example of a logarithmic trend is the sales pattern of a highly anticipated new product, which typically sells in large quantities for a short time and then levels off.

To visualize such a trend, you can plot a *logarithmic trendline*. This is a curved line through the data points where the differences between the points on one side of the line and those on the other side of the line cancel each other out.

Plotting a Logarithmic Trendline

1. Click the chart to select it.
2. If your chart has multiple data series, click the series you want to analyze.
3. Click the Design tab.
4. Click Add Chart Element.
5. Click Trendline.
6. Click More Trendline Options.

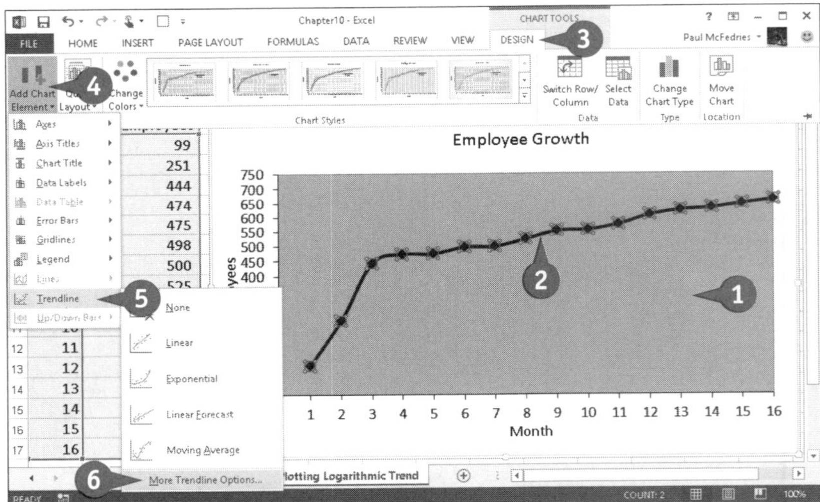

The Format Trendline pane appears.

7. Click the Trendline Options tab.
8. Click the Logarithmic option (○ changes to ◉).

9. Scroll down and click the Display Equation on Chart check box (☐ changes to ☑).
10. Click the Display R-Squared Value on Chart check box (☐ changes to ☑).
11. Click Close.

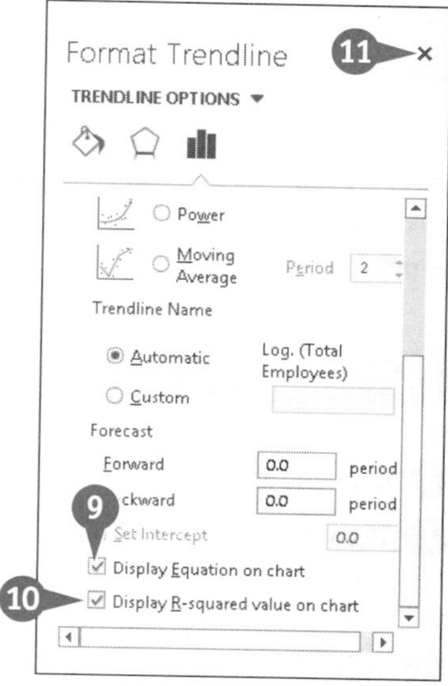

A. Excel plots the logarithmic trendline.

B. Excel displays the regression equation and the R^2 value.

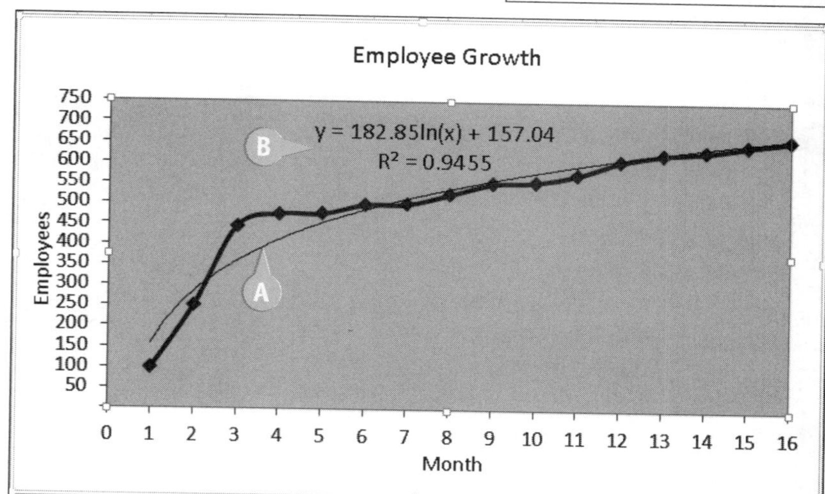

EXTRA

The regression equation tells you the exact relationship between the dependent and independent variables. With nonlinear regression, when the best-fit trendline is a logarithmic curve, the regression equation takes the following general form:

```
y = m * ln(x) + b
```

`y` is the dependent variable; `x` is the independent variable; `b` and `m` are constants; and `ln` is the natural logarithm, for which you can use the Excel function `LN`.

Excel does not have a function that calculates the values of `b` and `m` directly. However, you can use the `LINEST` function if you "straighten out" the logarithmic curve by using a logarithmic scale for the independent values:

```
{=LINEST(known_y's, LN(known_x's), const, stats)}
```

Plotting a Power Trendline

In many cases of regression analysis, the best fit is provided by a *power trend*, where the data increases or decreases steadily. Such a trend is clearly not exponential or logarithmic, both of which imply extreme behavior, either at the end (in the case of exponential) of the trend or at the beginning (in the case of logarithmic). Examples of power trends include revenues, profits, and margins in successful companies, all of which show steady increases in the rate of growth year after year.

A power trend sounds linear, but plotting the *power trendline* shows a curved best-fit line through the data points. In your analysis of such data, it is usually best to try a linear trendline first. If that does not give a good fit, switch to a power trendline.

Plotting a Power Trendline

1. Click the chart to select it.
2. If your chart has multiple data series, click the series you want to analyze.
3. Click the Design tab.
4. Click Add Chart Element.
5. Click Trendline.
6. Click More Trendline Options.

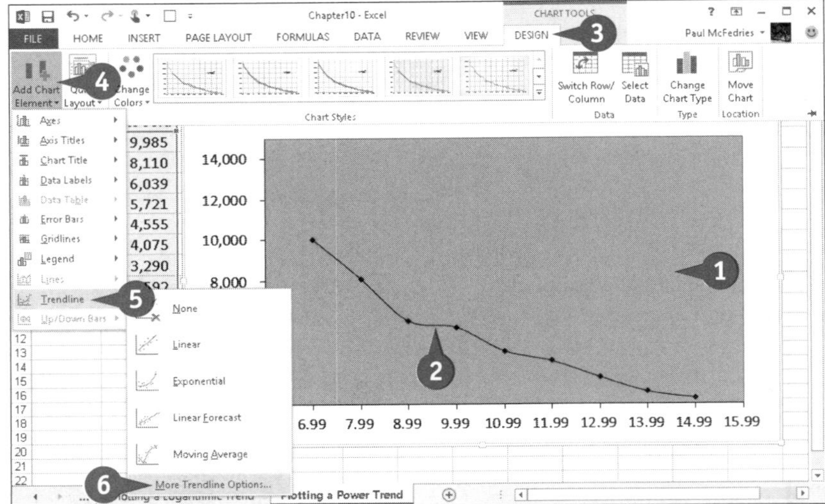

The Format Trendline pane appears.

7. Click the Trendline Options tab.
8. Click the Power option (○ changes to ◉).

9. Click the Display Equation on Chart check box (☐ changes to ☑).
10. Click the Display R-Squared Value on Chart check box (☐ changes to ☑).
11. Click Close.

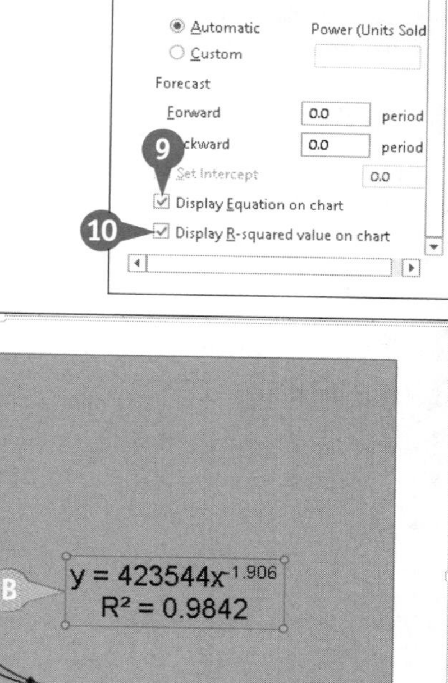

A. Excel plots the power trendline.

B. Excel displays the regression equation and the R^2 value.

EXTRA

The relationship between the dependent and independent variables is given by the regression equation. With nonlinear regression, when the best-fit trendline is a power curve, the regression equation takes the following general form:

```
y = m * x^b
```

`y` is the dependent variable; `x` is the independent variable; and `b` and `m` are constants.

There is no worksheet function available to calculate the values of `b` and `m` directly. However, you can use the `LINEST` function if you "straighten out" the power curve by applying a logarithmic scale to the dependent and independent values:

```
{=LINEST(LN(known_y's), LN(known_x's), const, stats)}
```

Plotting a Polynomial Trendline

For data that fluctuates, your analysis must take into account nonlinear polynomial behavior. In many real-world scenarios, the relationship between the dependent and independent variables is not unidirectional. For example, rather than constantly rising — uniformly, as in a linear trend, sharply as in an exponential or logarithmic trend, or steadily as in a power trend — data such as unit sales, profits, and costs might move up and down.

To visualize such a trend, you can plot a *polynomial trendline*. This is a best-fit line of multiple curves derived using an equation that uses multiple powers of x. The number of powers of x is the *order* of the polynomial equation. Generally, the higher the order, the tighter the curve fits your existing data, but the more unpredictable your forecasted values are.

Plotting a Polynomial Trendline

1. Click the chart to select it.
2. If your chart has multiple data series, click the series you want to analyze.
3. Click the Design tab.
4. Click Add Chart Element.
5. Click Trendline.
6. Click More Trendline Options.

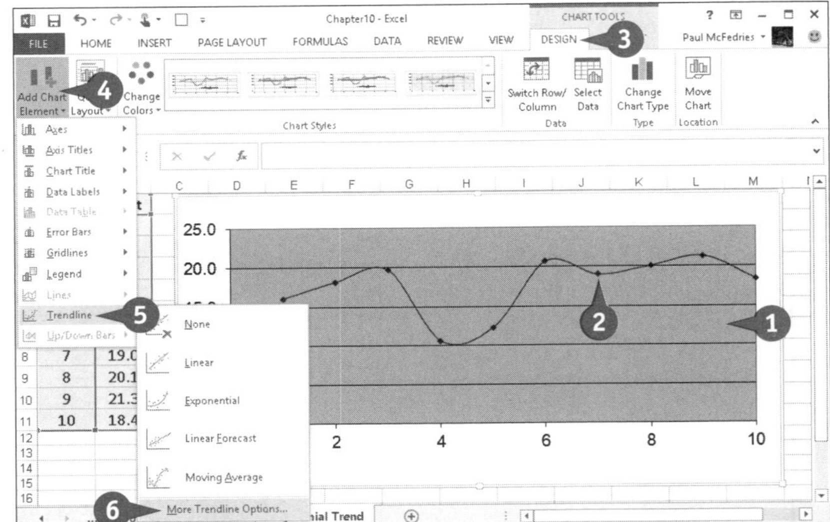

The Format Trendline pane appears.

7. Click the Trendline Options tab.
8. Click the Polynomial options (○ changes to ◉).
9. Click the Order spin box arrows and select the order of the polynomial equation you want.

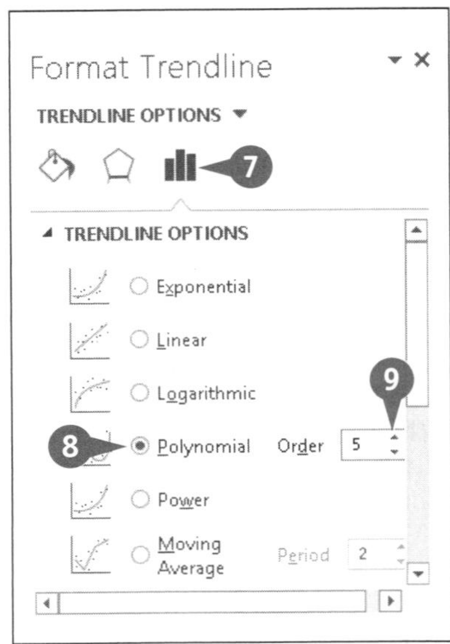

10 Click the Display Equation on Chart check box (☐ changes to ☑).

11 Click the Display R-Squared Value on Chart check box (☐ changes to ☑).

12 Click Close.

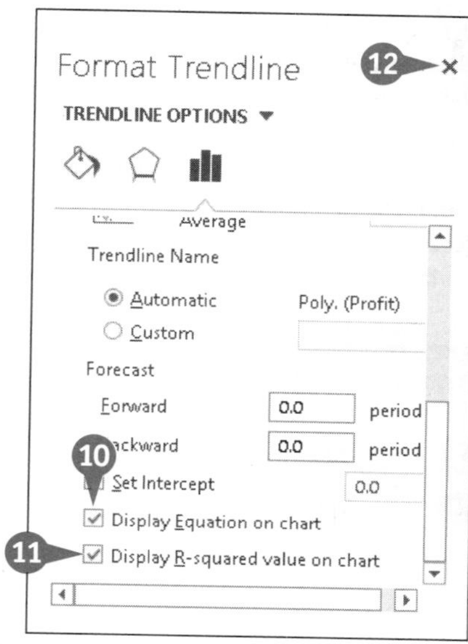

A Excel plots the polynomial trendline.

B Excel displays the regression equation and the R^2 value.

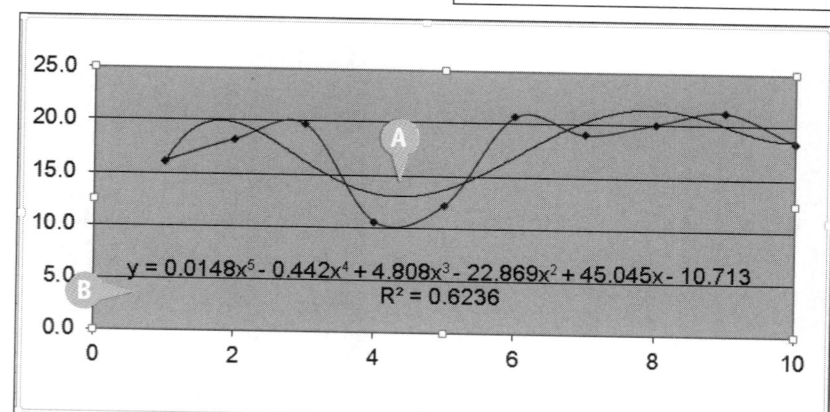

EXTRA

When the best-fit trendline is a polynomial curve, the regression equation takes the following form:

```
y = mnxn + ... + m2x2 + m1x + b
```

y is the dependent variable; x is the independent variable; and b and mn through m1 are constants. To calculate the latter, you can use LINEST if you raise the known_x's values to the powers from 1 to n for an nth-order polynomial:

```
{=LINEST(known_y's, known_x's ^ {1,2,...,n}, const, stats)}
```

Alternatively, you can use the TREND function:

```
{=TREND(known_y's, known_x's ^ {1,2,...,n}, new_x's, const)}
```

Load the Analysis ToolPak

You can get access to a number of powerful statistical analysis tools by loading the Analysis ToolPak add-in. The Analysis ToolPak consists of 19 statistical tools that calculate statistical measures such as correlation, regression, rank and percentile, covariance, and moving averages. You can also use the analysis tools to generate descriptive statistics (such as median, mode, and standard deviation), random numbers, and histograms.

Many of these tools have equivalent worksheet functions. For example, you can calculate correlation using the `CORREL` function, rank and percentile using the `RANK` and `PERCENTILE` functions, and so on. Each Analysis ToolPak tool also displays a dialog box that makes it easier for you to configure the tool and select the options you need for your analysis, although the tool results are static values, not formulas.

Load the Analysis ToolPak

1. Click the File tab (not shown).
2. Click Options.

The Excel Options dialog box appears.

3. Click Add-Ins.
4. Click the Manage down arrow and then select Excel Add-ins from the drop-down list.
5. Click Go.

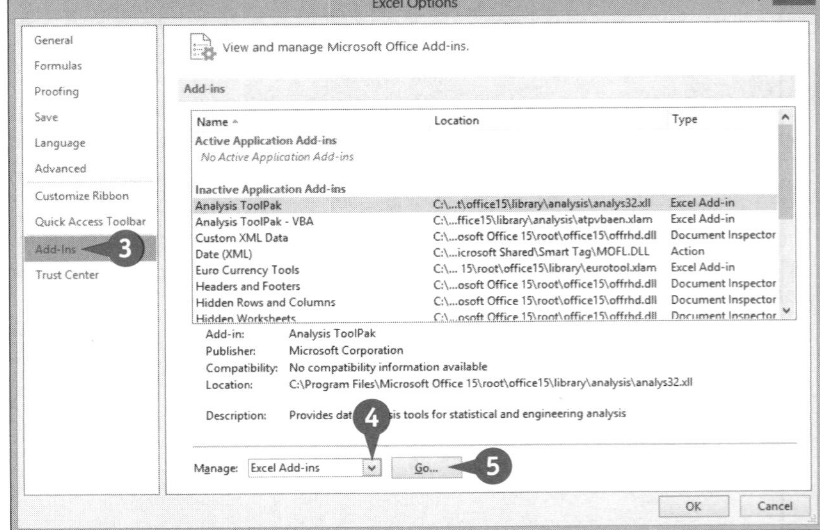

The Add-Ins dialog box appears.

6 Click the Analysis ToolPak check box (☐ changes to ☑).

7 Click OK.

Excel loads the Analysis ToolPak add-in.

8 Click the Data tab.

9 Click Data Analysis.

The Data Analysis dialog box appears where you can access the Analysis ToolPak tools.

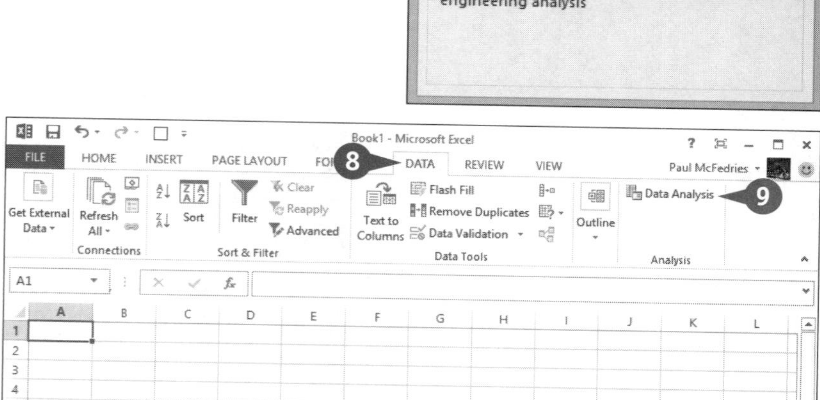

APPLY IT

To use one of the Analysis ToolPak's statistical tools, click the Data tab and then click Data Analysis. In the Data Analysis dialog box that appears, click the tool you want to use, and then click OK. Excel displays a dialog box for the tool. Use the dialog box to specify the tool settings you want to use (the controls vary from tool to tool), and then click OK. If you no longer need the Analysis ToolPak, you can disable the add-in to reduce clutter on the Ribbon's Data tab and to save space on your computer's hard drive. Follow steps 1 to 5 to display the Add-Ins dialog box. Click to deselect the Analysis ToolPak check box, and then click OK.

Calculate a Moving Average

A *moving average* smoothes a data series by averaging the series values over a specified number of preceding periods. For example, a 7-day moving average takes the average of the first 7 days, and then for each subsequent day to the end of the series, calculates a new average based on the previous 7 days. In this example, 7 is called the *interval* of the moving average.

Using a moving average can reveal trends that are masked when you use a simple average because a simple average gives equal weight to each value. A moving average weighs recent values equally and ignores older values, thereby enabling you to spot trends. You can use a moving average to forecast sales, stock prices, or other trends.

Calculate a Moving Average

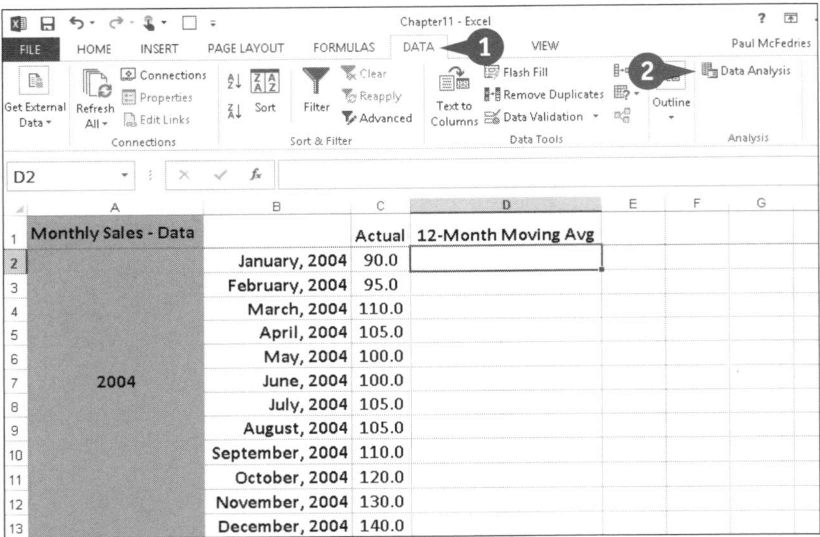

	A	B	C	D
1	Monthly Sales - Data		Actual	12-Month Moving Avg
2		January, 2004	90.0	
3		February, 2004	95.0	
4		March, 2004	110.0	
5		April, 2004	105.0	
6		May, 2004	100.0	
7	2004	June, 2004	100.0	
8		July, 2004	105.0	
9		August, 2004	105.0	
10		September, 2004	110.0	
11		October, 2004	120.0	
12		November, 2004	130.0	
13		December, 2004	140.0	

1. Click the Data tab.
2. Click Data Analysis.

The Data Analysis dialog box appears.

3. Click Moving Average.
4. Click OK.

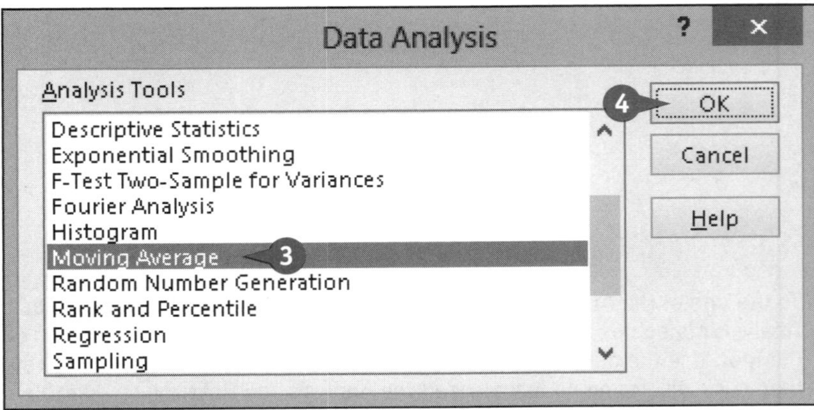

The Moving Average dialog box appears.

5 Type or select the range of values you want to analyze.

A If the first row contains labels, click the Labels in First Row check box (☐ changes to ☑).

6 Type the interval you want to use for the moving average.

7 Type or select the range where you want the moving average values to appear.

8 Click OK.

B Excel calculates the moving average. In this example, cell D13 shows the moving average for cells C2 to C13.

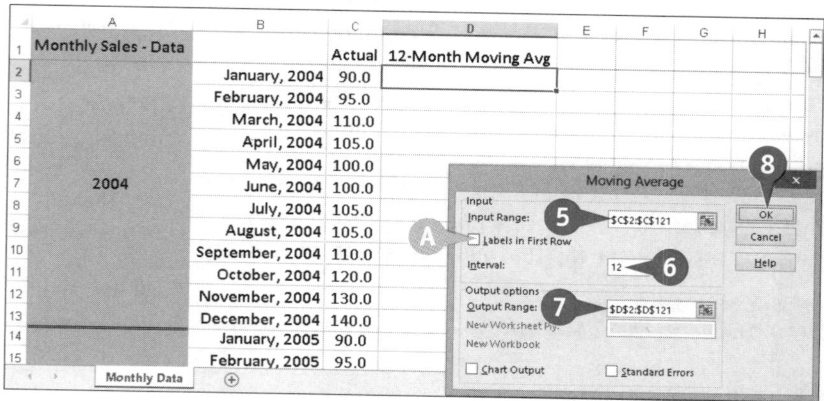

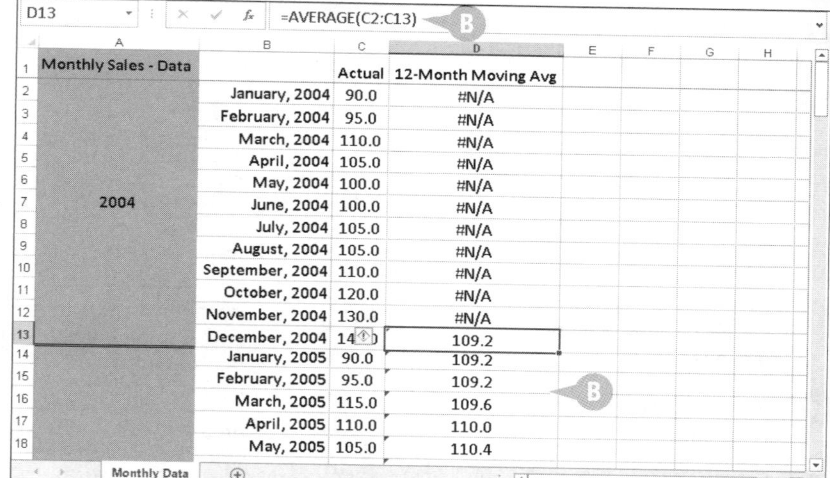

EXTRA

When you use the Moving Average tool, the first few values in the column contain the value #N/A. The number of cells that contain #N/A is one less than the number specified for the Interval value because for those initial cells, Excel does not yet have enough values to calculate the moving average. To create a moving average of interval n using the `AVERAGE` function, enter the initial formula `=AVERAGE(range)`, where `range` is a reference to the first n values in the series. Be sure to use relative references in the range coordinates. That way, when you fill the formula down to the subsequent cells to the end of the series, Excel updates the formula to create a moving average.

Compare Variances

Variance is a measure of how much a group of values varies from the group's mean. You can use an F-test to compare two variances. In particular, a *one-tailed* F-test determines whether the variance of the first group is greater than or less than the variance of the second group. The result of the F-test is an F statistic (F), and the more that F deviates from 1, the more likely it is that the two variances are different and that you must reject the *null hypothesis* that the variances of the two groups are the same.

You must also specify an *alpha level*, or the statistical confidence level you expect. This value between 0 and 1 represents the probability of the null hypothesis being true. The default level of .05 is equivalent to a 95-percent confidence level.

Compare Variances

1 Click the Data tab.

2 Click Data Analysis.

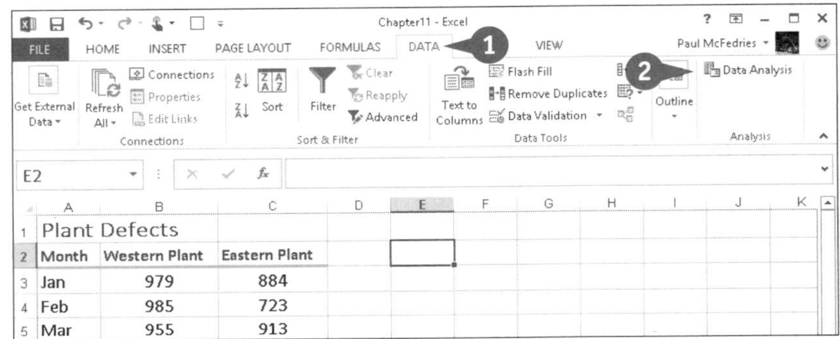

The Data Analysis dialog box appears.

3 Click F-Test Two-Sample for Variances.

4 Click OK.

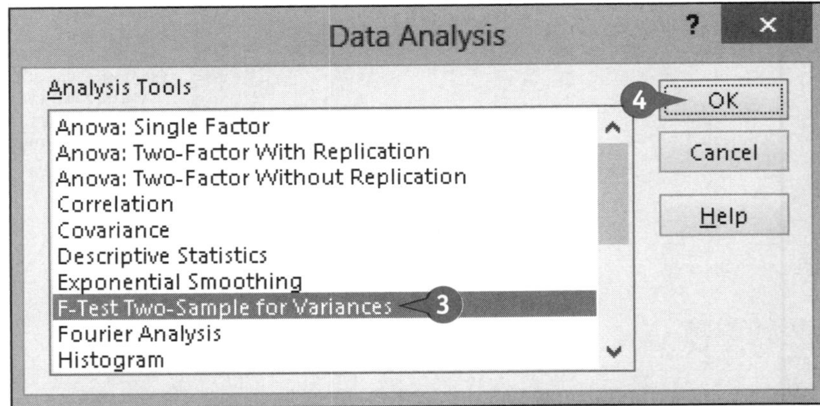

The F-Test Two-Sample for Variances dialog box appears.

5 Type the first range of cells to analyze.

6 Type the second range of cells to analyze.

A If your data range has labels, click the Labels check box (☐ changes to ☑).

7 Type an alpha value between 0 and 1.

8 Click the Output Range option (○ changes to ◉).

9 Type the upper-left corner of the output range.

10 Click OK.

B Excel compares the variances between the two groups.

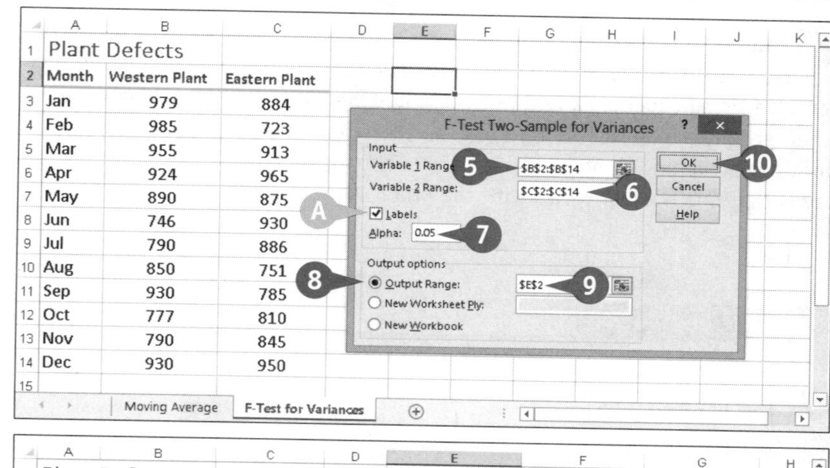

Month	Western Plant	Eastern Plant
Jan	979	884
Feb	985	723
Mar	955	913
Apr	924	965
May	890	875
Jun	746	930
Jul	790	886
Aug	850	751
Sep	930	785
Oct	777	810
Nov	790	845
Dec	930	950

F-Test Two-Sample for Variances

	Western Plant	Eastern Plant
Mean	878.8	859.8
Variance	7194.2	6119.1
Observations	12	12
df	11	11
F	1.1757	
P(F<=f) one-tail	0.3966	
F Critical one-tail	2.8179	

EXTRA

The F-test analysis tool calculates several values, including means, variances, and observations. `F` is the ratio of the first group variance to the second group variance. For the value `P(F<=f) one-tail`, if `F` is less than 1, this is the probability that the actual F statistic (designated as `f`) is less than `F`. If `F` is greater than 1, this is the probability that `f` is greater than `F`. `F Critical one-tail` is the value at which you must reject the null hypothesis. If `F` is less than 1, you reject the null hypothesis if `F` is less than `F Critical`. If `F` is greater than 1, you reject the null hypothesis if `F` is greater than `F Critical`.

Correlation is a measure of the relationship between two sets of data. For example, if you have quarterly figures for advertising expenses and sales, you might wonder whether they are related. Note, however, that a correlation does not prove one thing causes another. The most you can say is that one number varies with the other.

You can use the `CORREL` function to calculate the correlation, but it is often easier and faster to use the Analysis ToolPak's Correlation tool. This tool takes two ranges as inputs and then returns a 2x2 array where the value in the lower-left corner is the correlation, which is a number between –1 and 1.

Calculate Correlation

1. Click the Data tab.
2. Click Data Analysis.

Correlation Between Advertising and Sales

		Advertising	Sales
Fiscal 2011	1st Quarter	512,450	8,123,965
	2nd Quarter	447,840	7,750,500
	3rd Quarter	500,125	7,860,405
	4th Quarter	515,600	8,005,800
Fiscal 2012	1st Quarter	482,754	8,136,444
	2nd Quarter	485,750	7,950,426
	3rd Quarter	460,890	7,875,500
	4th Quarter	490,400	7,952,600
Fiscal 2013	1st Quarter	510,230	8,100,145
	2nd Quarter	515,471	8,034,125
	3rd Quarter	525,850	8,350,450
	4th Quarter	520,365	8,100,520

Correlation:

The Data Analysis dialog box appears.

3. Click Correlation.
4. Click OK.

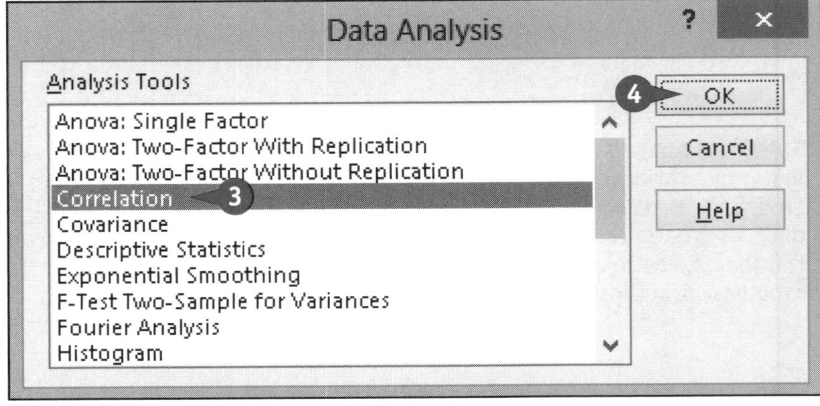

The Correlation dialog box appears.

5 Type the range of cells to analyze.

6 Click the Columns or Rows option to specify whether your data is grouped in columns or rows (○ changes to ◉).

A If your data range has labels, click the Labels in first row check box (☐ changes to ☑).

7 Click the Output Range option (○ changes to ◉).

8 Type the upper-left corner of the output range.

9 Click OK.

B Excel calculates the correlation.

Note: *The sign indicates whether the relationship is positive (+) or negative (–).*

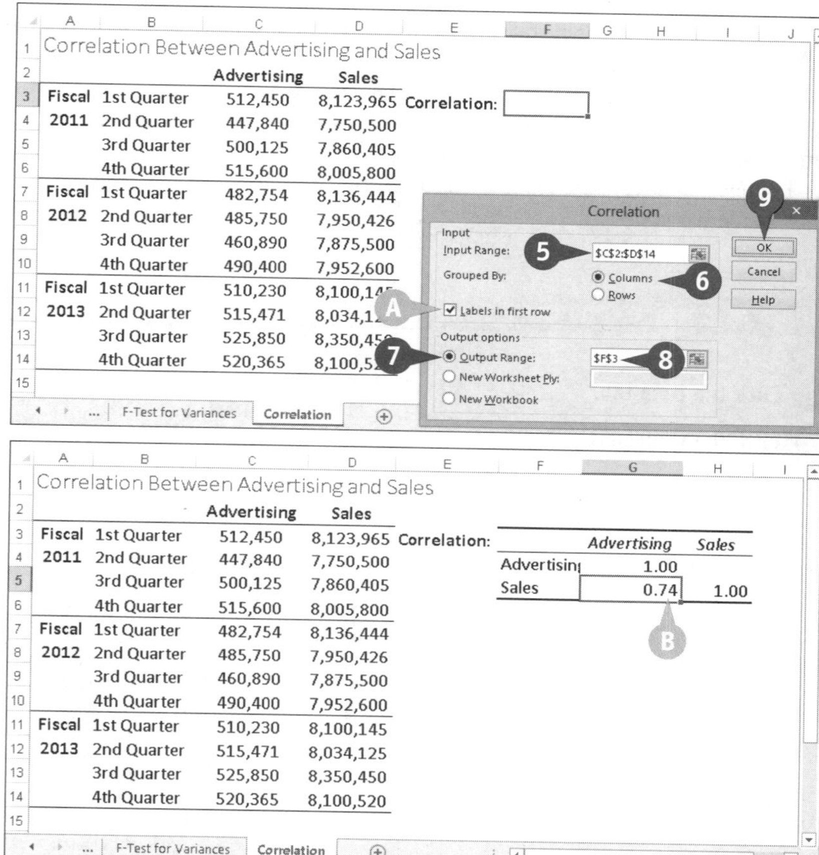

APPLY IT

You interpret the correlation result as follows: a result of 1 means the data sets are perfectly and positively correlated; for example, a 10-percent increase in advertising correlates to a 10-percent increase in sales. Between 0 and 1 means the data sets are positively correlated and the higher the number, the higher the correlation is between the data. Zero means there is no correlation between the data. Between 0 and –1 means the data sets are negatively correlated (an increase in advertising correlates to a decrease in sales); the lower the number, the more negatively correlated the data. Negative 1 means the data sets have a perfect negative correlation; for example, a 10-percent increase in advertising correlates to a 10-percent decrease in sales.

Run a Regression Analysis

A *regression analysis* is a statistical tool for interrogating the relationship between two phenomena, where one depends upon the other. For example, housing sales generally rise when interest rates fall, and fall when interest rates rise. In this case, you can say that housing sales are the *dependent variable* (Y) and interest rates are the *independent variable* (X).

You can run a regression analysis in various ways, including plotting best-fit trendlines and using functions such as `TREND` and `LINEST`. However, it is usually easier to use the Analysis ToolPak's Regression tool, which returns multiple linear regression statistics.

Run a Regression Analysis

1. Click the Data tab.
2. Click Data Analysis.

Sales		Period	Actual
	1st Quarter	1	259,846
Fiscal	2nd Quarter	2	262,587
2011	3rd Quarter	3	260,643
	4th Quarter	4	267,129
	1st Quarter	5	266,471
Fiscal	2nd Quarter	6	269,843
2012	3rd Quarter	7	272,803
	4th Quarter	8	275,649
	1st Quarter	9	270,117
Fiscal	2nd Quarter	10	275,315
2013	3rd Quarter	11	270,451
	4th Quarter	12	276,543

The Data Analysis dialog box appears.

3. Click Regression.
4. Click OK.

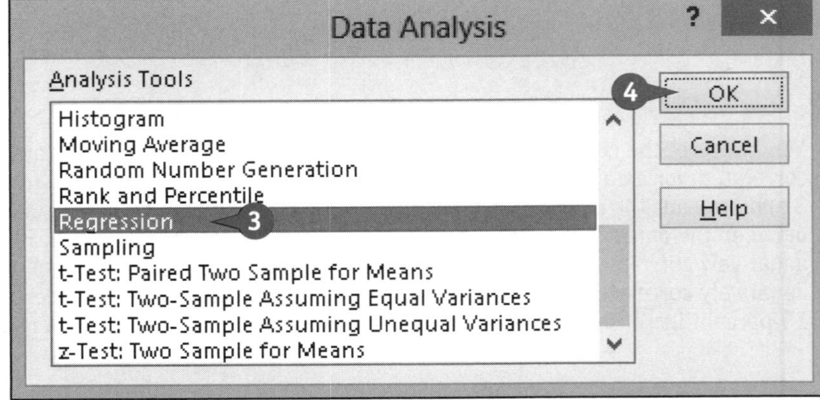

The Regression dialog box appears.

5 Type the range of dependent data.

6 Type the range of independent data.

A If your data range has labels, click the Labels check box (☐ changes to ☑).

7 Click the Output Range option (○ changes to ◉).

8 Type the upper-left corner of the output range.

9 Click OK.

B Excel calculates the regression statistics.

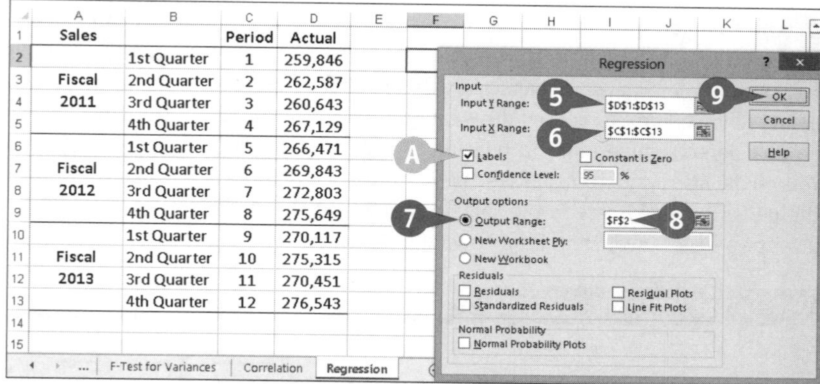

	F	G	H	I	J	K	L
2	SUMMARY OUTPUT						
3							
4	*Regression Statistics*						
5	Multiple R	0.88					
6	R Square	0.78					
7	Adjusted R Square	0.76					
8	Standard Error	2842.50					
9	Observations	12.00					
10							
11	ANOVA						
12		*df*	*SS*	*MS*	*F*	*Significance F*	
13	Regression	1.00	283341716.02	283341716.02	35.07	0.0001	
14	Residual	10.00	80798022.23	8079802.22			
15	Total	11.00	364139738.25				
16							
17		*Coefficients*	*Standard Error*	*t Stat*	*P-value*	*Lower 95%*	*Upper 95%*
18	Intercept	259800.18	1749.44	148.50	0.00	255902.19	263698.17
19	Period	1407.63	237.70	5.92	0.00015	877.99	1937.26

F-Test for Variances | Correlation | Regression

APPLY IT

The Regression tool returns several results. `Multiple R` is the correlation. `R Square` is the proportion of the variance in the dependent variable that can be explained by the independent variable. If `Significance F` is less than 0.05, the overall regression result is statistically significant. In the linear regression equation `y = mx + b`, the `Coefficients` are `b` (the intercept), and `m`, (the period). The larger the `t Stat` value, the less likely that the coefficients are 0. The `P-value` is the probability that the coefficients are actually 0. `Lower 95%` and `Upper 95%` mean that there is a 95-percent chance that the actual values for the coefficients fall within the displayed lower and upper bounds.

Determine Rank and Percentile

One common form of data analysis is calculating where an item ranks relative to the other items in a group. For example, in a dataset that shows the number of product defects by workgroup, you might want to find out how one group's defects value ranks in relation to the other groups. You might also want to calculate the *percentile*, which is the percentage of items in the sample that are at the same level or a lower level than a given value.

You can calculate the rank using the Excel `RANK.EQ` and `RANK.AVG` functions, and you can calculate the percentile using the `PERCENTILE.EXC` and `PERCENTILE.INC` functions. However, if you do not mind using static results, you can calculate these values more easily by using the Analysis ToolPak's Rank and Percentile tool.

Determine Rank and Percentile

1. Click the Data tab.
2. Click Data Analysis.

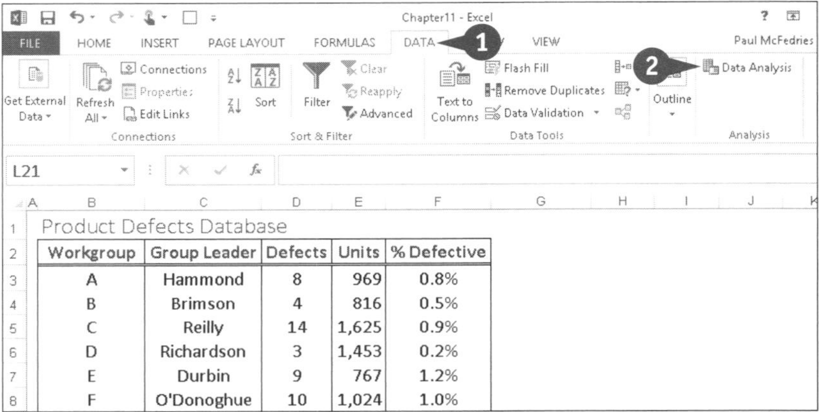

Workgroup	Group Leader	Defects	Units	% Defective
A	Hammond	8	969	0.8%
B	Brimson	4	816	0.5%
C	Reilly	14	1,625	0.9%
D	Richardson	3	1,453	0.2%
E	Durbin	9	767	1.2%
F	O'Donoghue	10	1,024	1.0%

The Data Analysis dialog box appears.

3. Click Rank and Percentile.
4. Click OK.

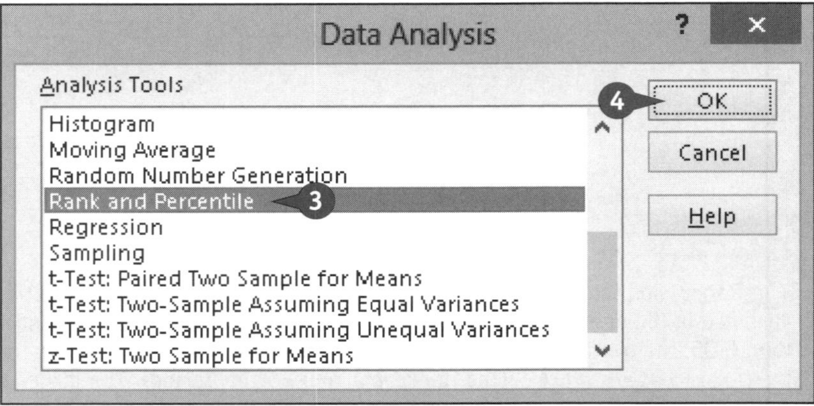

The Rank and Percentile dialog box appears.

5. Type the range of cells to analyze.
6. Click the Columns or Rows option to specify whether your data is grouped in columns or rows (○ changes to ◉).

A. If your data range has labels, click the Labels in First Row check box (☐ changes to ☑).

7. Click the Output Range option (○ changes to ◉).
8. Type the upper-left corner of the output range.
9. Click OK.

B. Excel calculates the rank and percentile.

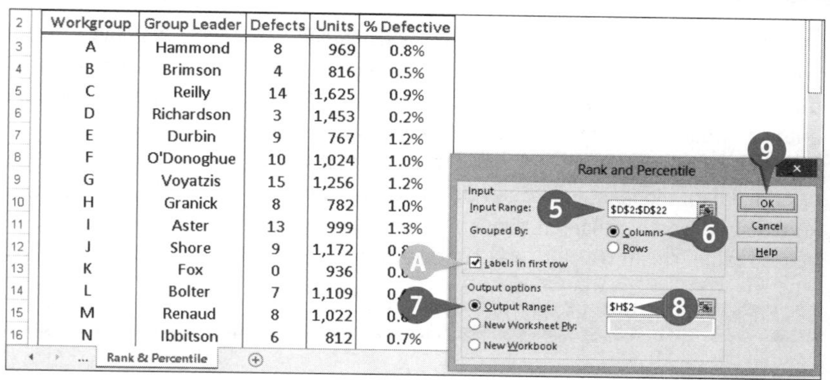

Workgroup	Group Leader	Defects	Units	% Defective		Point	Defects	Rank	Percent
A	Hammond	8	969	0.8%		20	19	1	100.00%
B	Brimson	4	816	0.5%		7	15	2	94.70%
C	Reilly	14	1,625	0.9%		3	14	3	89.40%
D	Richardson	3	1,453	0.2%		9	13	4	84.20%
E	Durbin	9	767	1.2%		18	12	5	78.90%
F	O'Donoghue	10	1,024	1.0%		15	11	6	73.60%
G	Voyatzis	15	1,256	1.2%		6	10	7	63.10%
H	Granick	8	782	1.0%		19	10	7	63.10%
I	Aster	13	999	1.3%		5	9	9	52.60%
J	Shore	9	1,172	0.8%		10	9	9	52.60%
K	Fox	0	936	0.0%		1	8	11	36.80%
L	Bolter	7	1,109	0.6%		8	8	11	36.80%
M	Renaud	8	1,022	0.8%		13	8	11	36.80%
N	Ibbitson	6	812	0.7%		12	7	14	26.30%
O	Harper	11	978	1.1%		17	7	14	26.30%
P	Ferry	5	1,183	0.4%		14	6	16	21.00%
Q	Richens	7	961	0.7%		16	5	17	15.70%
R	Munson	12	690	1.7%		2	4	18	10.50%
S	Little	10	1,105	0.9%		4	3	19	5.20%
T	Jones	19	1,309	1.5%		11	0	20	0.00%

Rank & Percentile

EXTRA

Excel creates a four-column table containing the rank and percentile data:

COLUMN	DESCRIPTION
Point	The location of the data value within the specified input range. For example, if the value was originally the third numeric value in the input data, the point value is 3.
Column	The input values, sorted based upon their ranking. *Column* refers to the name of the original input data column.
Rank	The rank for each input value, with 1 being the highest-ranking value in the list.
Percent	The percentile result for each input value.

Calculate Descriptive Statistics

You can speed up your data analysis by using the Descriptive Statistics tool to quickly generate up to 16 different statistical measurements. When you use this tool on a range of data, Excel produces a table containing statistical calculations for that range, including the mean, standard error, median, mode, standard deviation, sample variance, kurtosis, skewness, range, minimum, maximum, sum, count, largest value, smallest value, and confidence level.

You can use the four check boxes in the Descriptive Statistics dialog box to specify which descriptive statistic values Excel returns. The Summary Statistics option calculates all the common statistic values. The Confidence Level for Mean option calculates the confidence level. Both the Kth Largest and the Kth Smallest options enable you to find specific values in the group, such as the second-largest or third-smallest number.

Calculate Descriptive Statistics

1. Click the Data tab.
2. Click Data Analysis.

   The Data Analysis dialog box appears.

3. Click Descriptive Statistics.
4. Click OK.

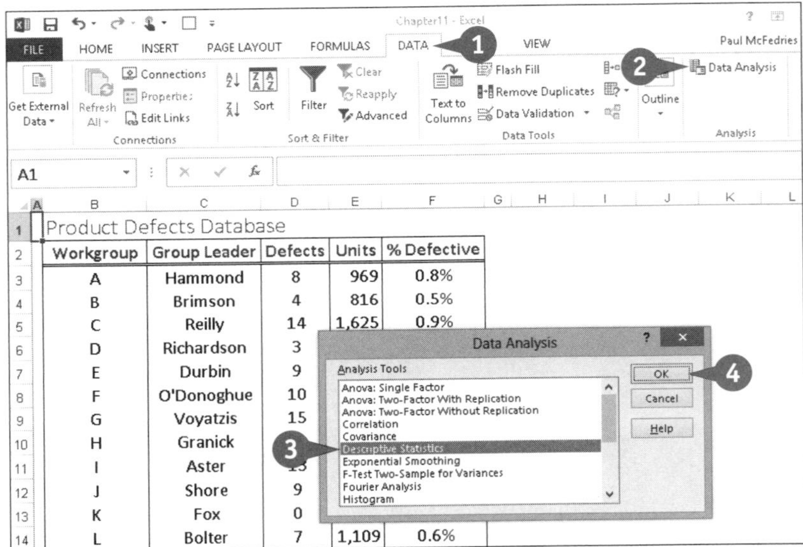

The Descriptive Statistics dialog box appears.

5. Type the range of cells to analyze.
6. Click the Columns or Rows option to specify whether your data is grouped in columns or rows (◯ changes to ◉).

Ⓐ If your data range has labels, click the Labels in First Row check box (☐ changes to ☑).

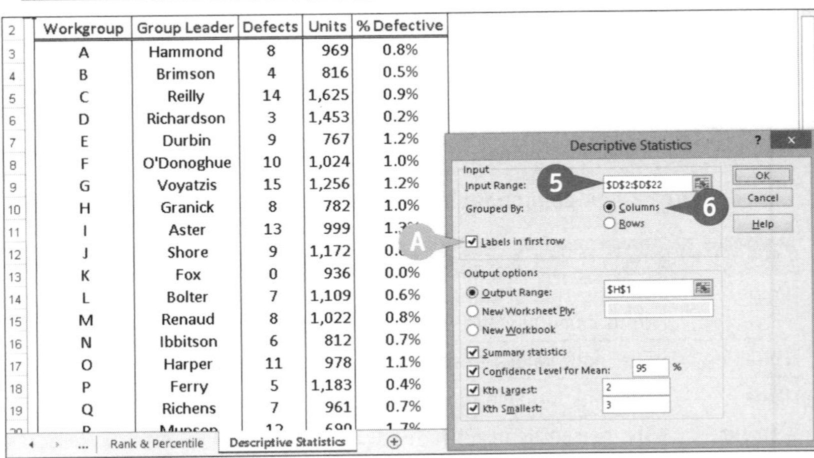

7. Click the Output Range option (○ changes to ◉).
8. Type the upper-left corner of the output range.
9. Click the check box for each type of measure you want returned (☐ changes to ☑).
10. Click OK.

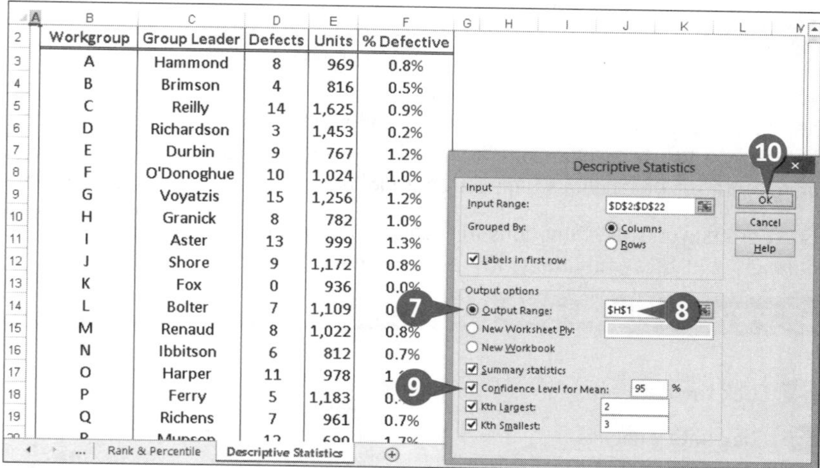

B. Excel calculates the descriptive statistics.

Workgroup	Group Leader	Defects	Units	% Defective
A	Hammond	8	969	0.8%
B	Brimson	4	816	0.5%
C	Reilly	14	1,625	0.9%
D	Richardson	3	1,453	0.2%
E	Durbin	9	767	1.2%
F	O'Donoghue	10	1,024	1.0%
G	Voyatzis	15	1,256	1.2%
H	Granick	8	782	1.0%
I	Aster	13	999	1.3%
J	Shore	9	1,172	0.8%
K	Fox	0	936	0.0%
L	Bolter	7	1,109	0.6%
M	Renaud	8	1,022	0.8%
N	Ibbitson	6	812	0.7%
O	Harper	11	978	1.1%
P	Ferry	5	1,183	0.4%
Q	Richens	7	961	0.7%
R	Munson	12	690	1.7%
S	Little	10	1,105	0.9%
T	Jones	19	1,309	1.5%

Mean	8.9
Standard Error	1.0
Median	8.5
Mode	8.0
Standard Deviation	4.41
Sample Variance	19.46
Kurtosis	0.51
Skewness	0.25
Range	19
Minimum	0
Maximum	19
Sum	178
Count	20
Largest(2)	15
Smallest(3)	4
Confidence Level(95.0%)	2.06

Rank & Percentile | Descriptive Statistics

EXTRA

Most of the statistical measures returned by the Descriptive Statistics tool are straightforward, but there are a few less known measures. The standard error is the square root of the sample size divided into the standard deviation over the square root of the sample size (n). The kurtosis is a measure of the flatness of the data distribution, where a negative value implies a flat distribution and a positive value implies a peaked distribution. The closer the skewness value is to 0, the closer the data distribution is to the normal curve. The confidence level for mean calculates, when using sample data, the chance that the true mean falls within the confidence interval.

Generate Random Numbers

When you are building a data analysis model, you need data for testing. If you do not have available data, you can enter temporary test values, but that process can be tedious and time-consuming. A faster and more efficient approach is to use the Random Number Generation tool to generate a set of random values for your model.

Excel offers worksheet functions for generating random numbers, but these functions, while useful, have limited capabilities. For example, `RAND` generates random numbers between 0 and 1, and `RANDBETWEEN` generates random numbers between two specified values. However, the Random Number Generation tool allows you to generate random values using various *distributions* that specify the pattern of the values. For example, the Normal distribution produces numbers in a bell curve pattern.

Generate Random Numbers

1. Click the Data tab.
2. Click Data Analysis.

   The Data Analysis dialog box appears.
3. Click Random Number Generation.
4. Click OK.

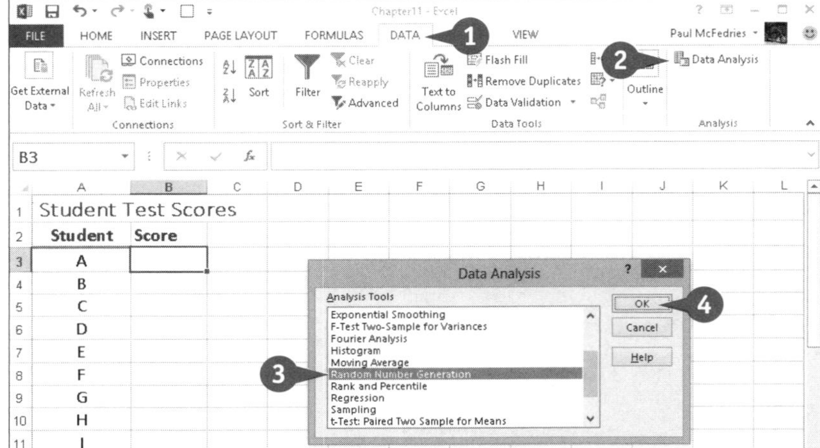

The Random Number Generation dialog box appears.

5. Type how many random number sets you want.
6. Type how many random numbers you want.
7. Select the type of distribution.

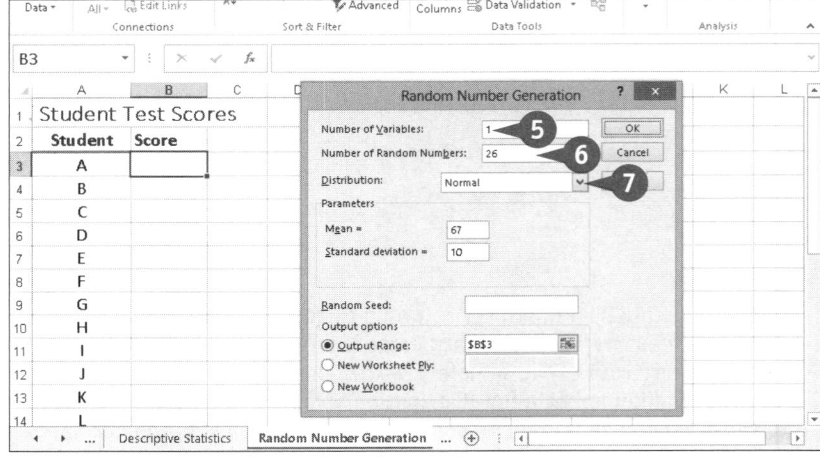

8. Type the distribution parameters.

Note: ***Note:*** *The options you see depend on the distribution you selected in step 7.*

9. Click the Output Range option (○ changes to ◉).

10. Type the upper-left corner of the output range.

11. Click OK.

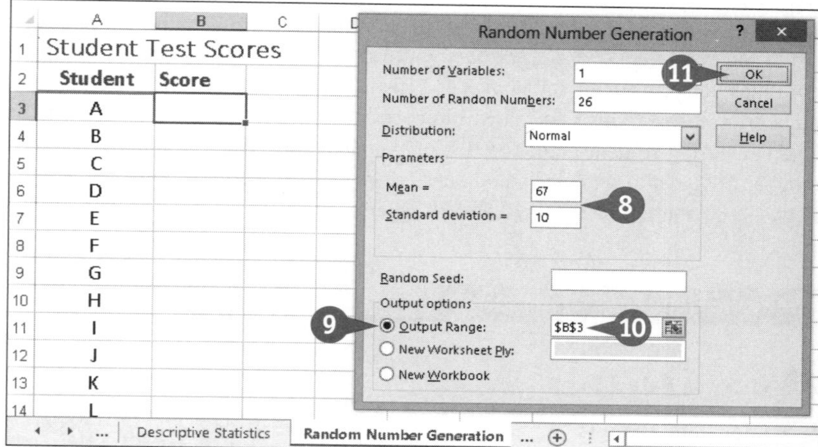

A. Excel generates the random numbers.

	A	B
1	Student Test Scores	
2	Student	Score
3	A	51
4	B	80
5	C	72
6	D	80
7	E	58
8	F	52
9	G	61
10	H	68
11	I	57
12	J	63
13	K	65
14	L	79

EXTRA

The Random Number Generation tool offers several distribution types. The Uniform distribution generates numbers with equal probability from the range of values you provide. Normal produces numbers in a bell curve distribution based on a mean and standard deviation. Bernoulli generates a random series of 1s and 0s based on the probability of success on a single trial. Binomial generates random numbers characterized by the probability of success over a number of trials. Poisson generates random numbers based on the probability of a designated number of events occurring in a time frame. Patterned generates random numbers according to a pattern given by a lower and upper bound, step value, and repetition rate. Discrete generates random numbers from a series of values and probabilities for these values.

Create a Frequency Distribution

When analyzing a large amount of data, you might require a *frequency distribution*, which organizes the data into numeric ranges called *bins* and then tells you the number of observations that fall within each bin. For example, when analyzing student grades, you might want to know the number of students who received grades between 90 and 100, between 80 and 89, between 70 and 79, and so on.

Although you could calculate the frequency distribution using multiple formulas that use the `COUNTIFS` function, Excel offers an easier and faster method: the Analysis ToolPak's Histogram tool. This tool requires two worksheet ranges: the *input range* of observations and the *bin range*, which is a range of numbers, where each number defines a boundary of the bin.

Create a Frequency Distribution

1. Click the Data tab.
2. Click Data Analysis.

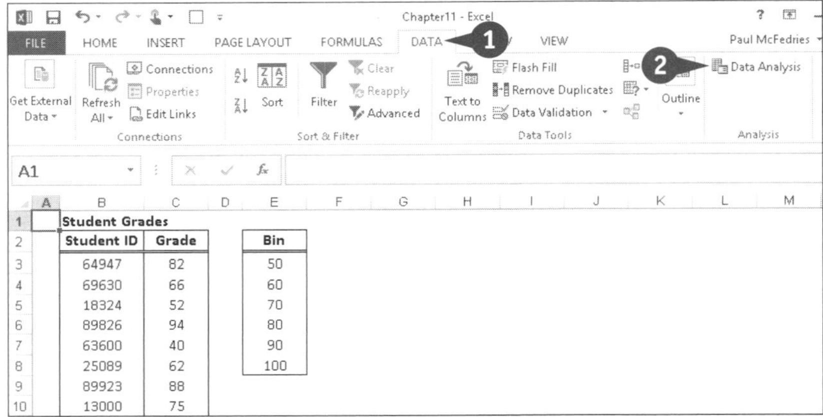

The Data Analysis dialog box appears.

3. Click Histogram.
4. Click OK.

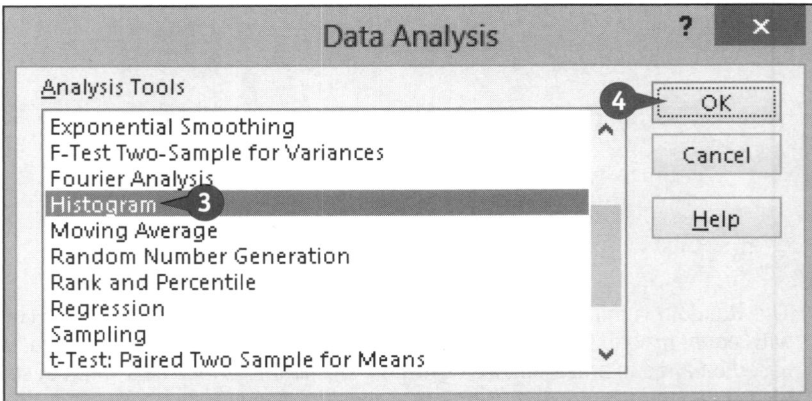

The Histogram dialog box appears.

5. Type the input range.
6. Type the bin range.
   - A If the ranges have labels, click the Labels check box (☐ changes to ☑).
7. Click the Output Range option (○ changes to ◉).
8. Type the upper-left corner of the output range.
9. Click OK.
   - B Excel generates the frequency distribution.

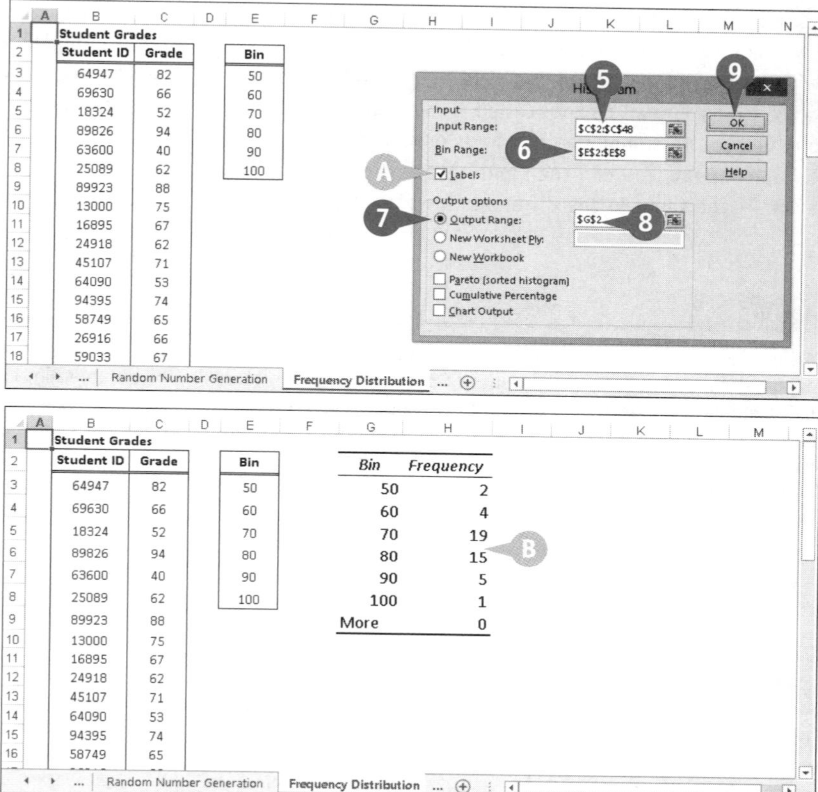

EXTRA

Here is the general formula for determining the frequency for a single bin using the `COUNTIFS` function:

```
=COUNTIFS(range, lower_criteria, range, upper_criteria)
```

Here, both instances of `range` refer to the range of observations: `lower_criteria` are the criteria that define the lower end of the bin, and `upper_criteria` define the upper end of the bin. Using the example data shown in this section, the following formula returns the number of student grades that are greater than or equal to 80 and less than 90:

```
=COUNTIFS(C3:C48, ">=80", C3:C48, "<90")
```

UNDERSTANDING PIVOTTABLES

Tables and external databases can contain thousands of records. Analyzing that much data can be a nightmare without the right kinds of tools. To help, Excel offers a powerful data analysis tool called a *PivotTable*, which enables you to summarize hundreds of records in a concise tabular format. You can then manipulate the layout of — or *pivot* — the table to see different views of your data.

PivotTables help you analyze large amounts of data by performing three operations: grouping the data into categories, summarizing the data using calculations, and filtering the data to show just the records you want to work with.

Grouping

A PivotTable is a powerful data-analysis tool in part because it automatically groups large amounts of data into smaller, more manageable categories. For example, suppose you have a data source with a Region field where each cell contains one of four values: East, West, North, and South. The original data may contain thousands of records, but if you build your PivotTable using the Region field, the resulting table has just four rows — one each for the four unique Region values in your data.

You can also create your own grouping after you build your PivotTable. For example, if your data has a Country field, you can build the PivotTable to group together all the records that have the same Country value. When you have done that, you can further group the unique Country values into continents: North America, South America, Europe, and so on.

Summarizing

In conjunction with grouping data according to the unique values in one or more fields, Excel also displays summary calculations for each group. The default calculation is Sum, which means for each group, Excel totals all the values in some specified field. For example, if your data has a Region field and a Sales field, a PivotTable can group the unique Region values and display the total of the Sales values for each one. Excel has other summary calculations, including Count, Average, Maximum, Minimum, and Standard Deviation.

Even more powerful, a PivotTable can display summaries for one grouping broken down by another. For example, suppose your sales data also has a Product field. You can set up a PivotTable to show the total Sales for each Product, broken down by Region.

Filtering

A PivotTable also enables you to view just a subset of the data. For example, by default the PivotTable's groupings show all the unique values in the field. However, you can manipulate each grouping to hide those that you do not want to view. Each PivotTable also comes with a report filter that enables you to apply a filter to the entire PivotTable. For example, suppose your sales data also includes a Customer field. By placing this field in the PivotTable's report filter, you can filter the PivotTable report to show just the results for a single Customer.

PivotTables are worth learning about because they come with a long list of benefits. For example, PivotTables are easy to build and maintain, and they perform large and complex calculations amazingly fast. You can update PivotTables quickly and easily to account for new data. Because they are dynamic, you can easily move, filter, and add components. PivotTables are fully customizable so you can build each report the way you want, and they can use most of the formatting options that you can apply to regular Excel ranges.

You can get up to speed with PivotTables very quickly after you learn a few key concepts. You need to understand the features that make up a typical PivotTable, particularly the four areas — row, column, data, and filter — to which you add fields from your data.

Get Familiar with PivotTable Features

A Filter

Displays a drop-down list that contains the unique values from a field. When you select a value from the list, Excel filters the PivotTable results to include only the records that match the selected value.

B Column Area

Displays horizontally the unique values from a field in your data.

C Row Area

Displays vertically the unique values from a field in your data.

D Data Area

Displays the results of the calculation that Excel applied to a numeric field in your data.

E Row Field Header

Identifies the field contained in the row area. You also use the row field header to filter the field values that appear in the row area.

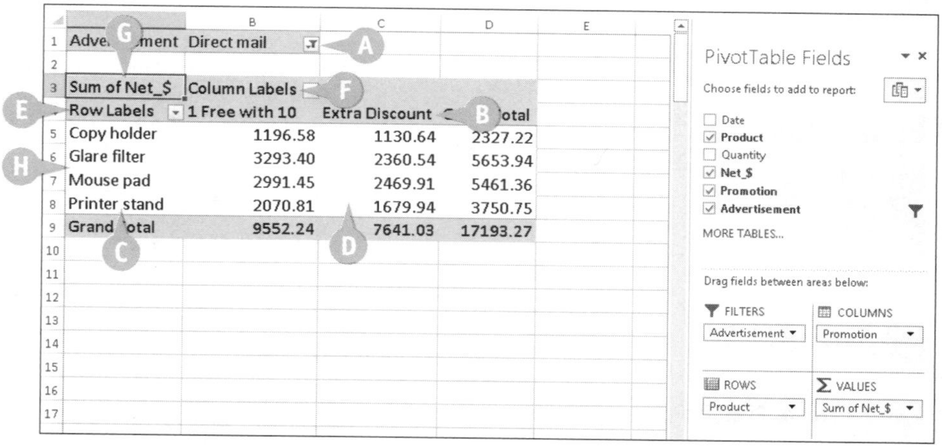

Advertisement	Direct mail		
Sum of Net_$	Column Labels		
Row Labels	1 Free with 10	Extra Discount	Grand Total
Copy holder	1196.58	1130.64	2327.22
Glare filter	3293.40	2360.54	5653.94
Mouse pad	2991.45	2469.91	5461.36
Printer stand	2070.81	1679.94	3750.75
Grand Total	9552.24	7641.03	17193.27

PivotTable Fields

Choose fields to add to report:

- Date
- Product
- Quantity
- Net_$
- Promotion
- Advertisement

MORE TABLES...

Drag fields between areas below:

FILTERS: Advertisement | COLUMNS: Promotion | ROWS: Product | VALUES: Sum of Net_$

F Column Field Header

Identifies the field contained in the column area. You also use the column field header to filter the field values that appear in the column area.

G Data Field Header

Specifies both the calculation (such as Sum) and the field (such as Invoice Total) used in the data area.

H Field Items

Consists of the unique values for the field added to the particular area.

If the data you want to analyze exists as an Excel range or table, you can use the PivotTable command to easily build a PivotTable report based on your data. You need only specify the location of your source data and then choose the location of the resulting PivotTable.

Excel creates an empty PivotTable in a new worksheet or in the location you specified. Excel also displays the PivotTable Fields pane, which contains four areas: FILTERS, COLUMNS, ROWS, and VALUES. To complete the PivotTable, you must populate some or all of these areas with one or more fields from your data.

Build a PivotTable from an Excel Range or Table

1 Click a cell within the range or table that you want to use as the source data.

2 Click the Insert tab.

3 Click PivotTable.

ID	Date	Product	Quantity	Net_$	Promotion	Advertisement
1	6/3/2013	Printer stand	10	$119.70	1 Free with 10	Direct mail
2	6/3/2013	Glare filter	6	$77.82	Extra Discount	Magazine
3	6/3/2013	Mouse pad	15	$100.95	Extra Discount	Newspaper
4	6/3/2013	Glare filter	11	$149.71	1 Free with 10	Magazine
5	6/4/2013	Mouse pad	22	$155.40	1 Free with 10	Magazine
6	6/4/2013	Mouse pad	3	$20.19	Extra Discount	Newspaper
7	6/4/2013	Copy holder	5	$33.65	Extra Discount	Direct mail
8	6/4/2013	Printer stand	22	$239.36	1 Free with 10	Newspaper
9	6/4/2013	Glare filter	10	$129.70	Extra Discount	Magazine
10	6/5/2013	Mouse pad	22	$155.40	1 Free with 10	Magazine
11	6/5/2013	Printer stand	8	$82.96	Extra Discount	Direct mail
12	6/5/2013	Printer stand	22	$239.40	1 Free with 10	Direct mail

The Create PivotTable dialog box appears.

4 Click the New Worksheet option (○ changes to ◉).

A If you want to place the PivotTable in an existing location, click the Existing Worksheet option (○ changes to ◉) and then use the Location range box to select the worksheet and cell where you want the PivotTable to appear.

5 Click OK.

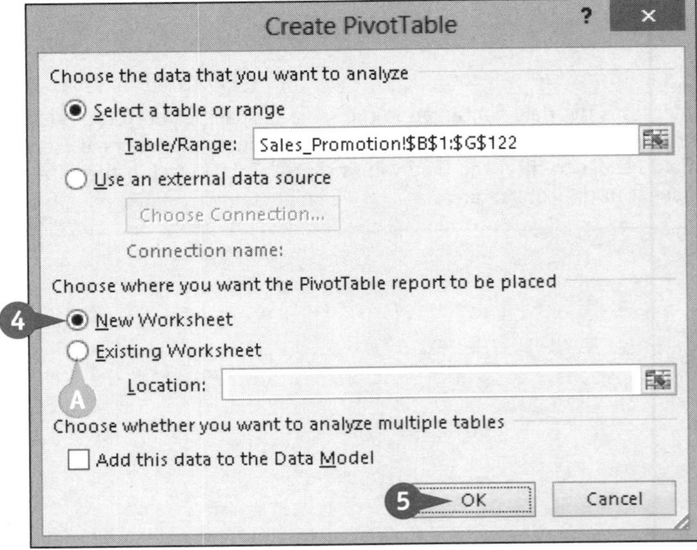

B Excel creates a blank PivotTable.

C Excel displays the PivotTable Fields pane.

6 Click and drag a field and drop it inside the ROWS area.

D Excel adds the field's unique values to the PivotTable's row area.

7 Click and drag a numeric field and drop it inside the VALUES area.

E Excel sums the numeric values based on the row values.

8 If desired, click and drag fields and drop them in the COLUMNS area and the FILTERS area.

Each time you drop a field in an area, Excel updates the PivotTable to include the new data.

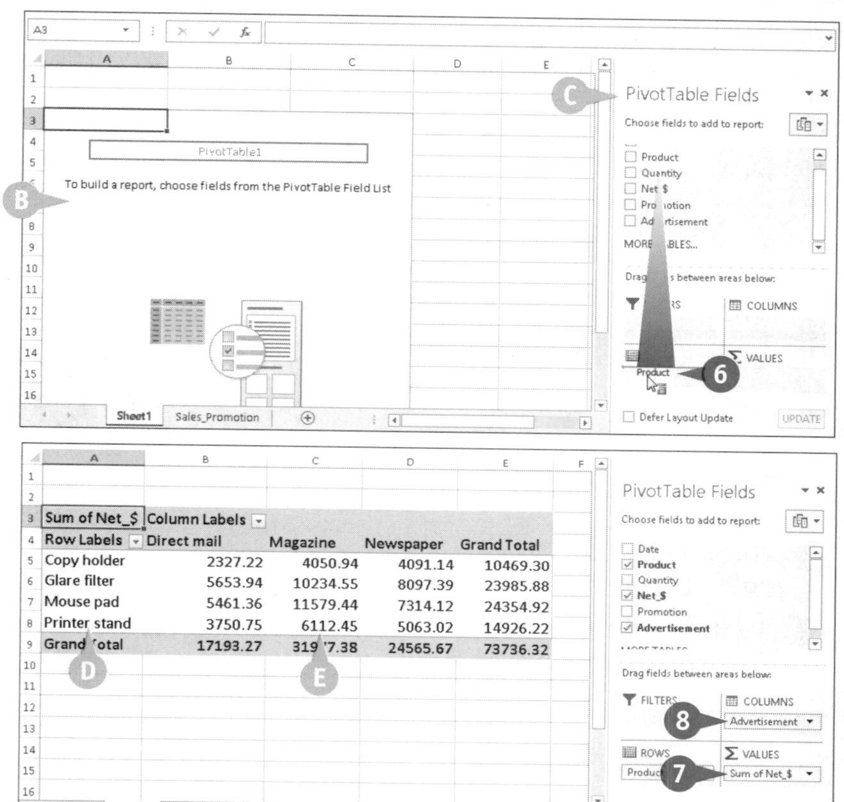

EXTRA

Excel offers a few shortcut techniques for building PivotTables. In the PivotTable Fields pane, click a check box for a text or date field (☐ changes to ☑) to add it to the ROWS area; click a check box for a numeric field (☐ changes to ☑) to add it to the VALUES area. You can also right-click a field and then click the area that you want to use. You use the FILTERS box to add a filter field to the PivotTable, which enables you to display a subset of the data based on an item from that field. Click the down arrow in the filter field, select the item that you want to use as a filter from the drop-down list, and then click OK.

Create a PivotTable from External Data

Rather than creating a PivotTable from data within an Excel worksheet, you may want to create a PivotTable using an external data source. This enables you to build reports from extremely large datasets and from relational database systems.

The data you are analyzing might not exist in an Excel range or table, but outside of Excel in a relational database management system (RDBMS) such as Microsoft Access or SQL Server. With these programs, you can set up a table, query, or other object that defines the data you want to work with. You can then build your PivotTable based on this external data source.

Create a PivotTable from External Data

1. Press Alt+D and then press P.

   The PivotTable and PivotChart Wizard - Step 1 of 3 dialog box appears.

2. Click the External Data Source option (○ changes to ◉).
3. Click the PivotTable option (○ changes to ◉).
4. Click Next.

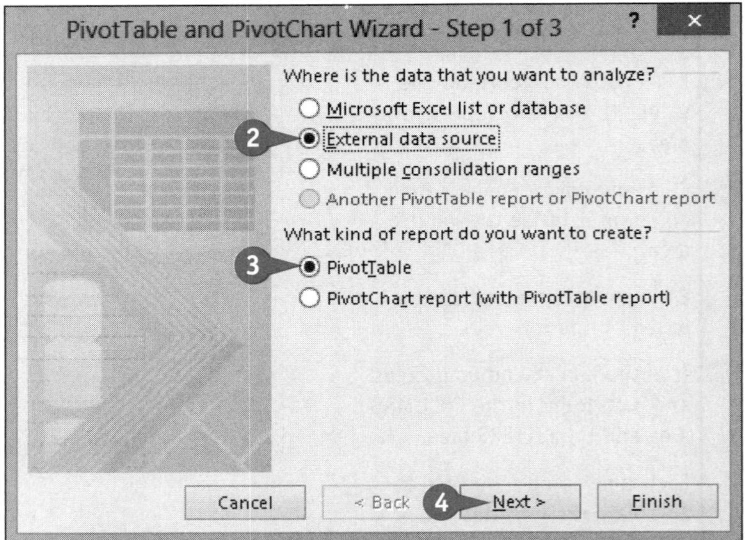

   The PivotTable and PivotChart Wizard - Step 2 of 3 dialog box appears.

5. Click Get Data.

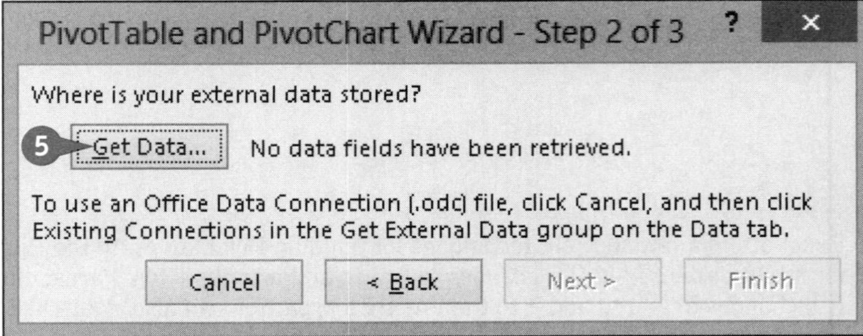

The Choose Data Source dialog box appears.

6 Click the type of data source you want to use.

7 Click OK.

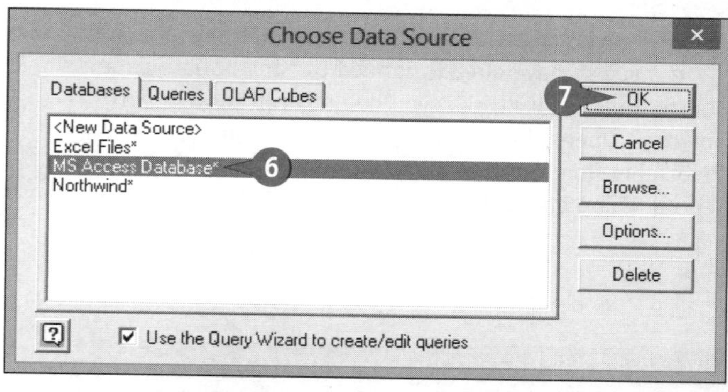

The Select Database dialog box appears.

8 Click the folder that contains the database.

9 Click the database.

10 Click OK.

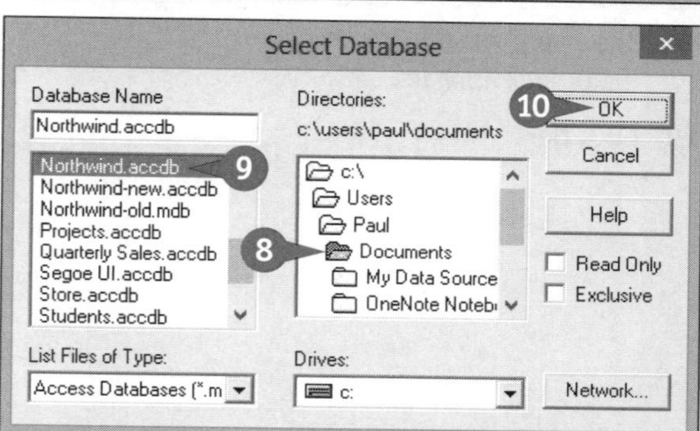

The Query Wizard - Choose Columns dialog box appears.

11 Click the table or column you want to use as the source data for your PivotTable.

12 Click Add.

A The table's fields appear in this list.

13 Click Next.

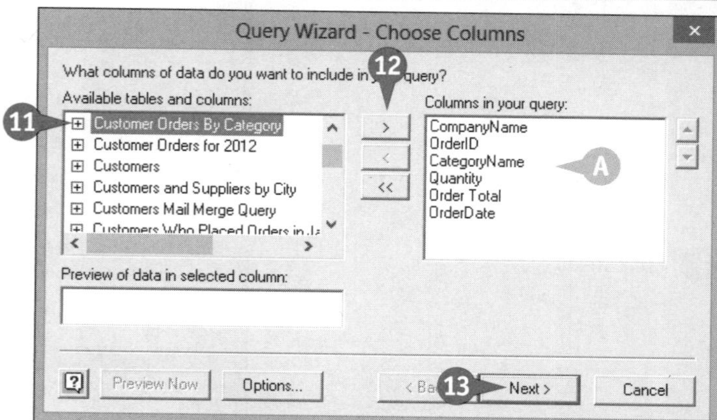

EXTRA

To create a data source, click the Excel Data tab, click Get External Data, click From Other Sources, and then click From Microsoft Query. In the Choose Data Source dialog box, click New Data Source. Click to deselect the Use the Query Wizard to Create/Edit Queries check box (☑ changes to ☐), and then click OK. In the Create New Data Source dialog box, type a name for your data source, select the database driver that your data source requires, and then click OK.

continued

When you create a PivotTable from external data, you need to have already defined the appropriate data source. Note, as well, that you do not need to work with Microsoft Query directly. Note, too, that when you create a PivotTable from external data, you can skip over the Query Wizard dialog boxes that enable you to filter and sort the external data, because this is not usually pertinent for a PivotTable.

When you create a PivotTable from external data, you do not need the external data to be imported to Excel. Rather, the external data resides only in the new PivotTable; you do not see the actual data in your workbook.

Create a PivotTable from External Data (continued)

The Query Wizard - Filter Data dialog box appears.

14 Click Next.

Query Wizard - Filter Data

Filter the data to specify which rows to include in your query.
If you don't want to filter the data, click Next.

Column to filter:
CompanyName
OrderID
CategoryName
Quantity
Order Total
OrderDate

Only include rows where:
And Or
And Or
And Or

< Back 14 Next > Cancel

The Query Wizard - Sort Order dialog box appears.

15 Click Next.

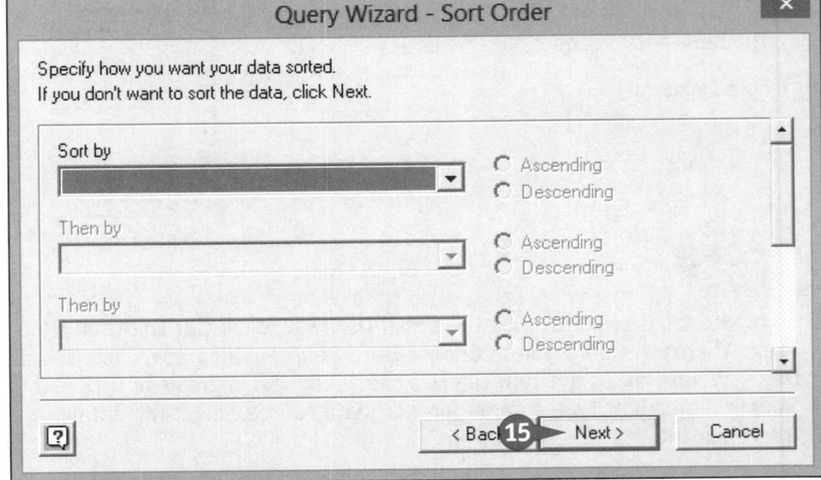

The Query Wizard - Finish dialog box appears.

16 Click the Return Data to Microsoft Excel options (○ changes to ◉).

17 Click Finish.

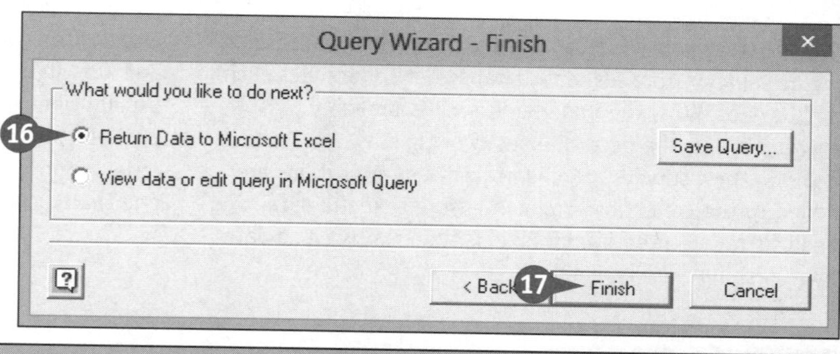

Excel returns you to the PivotTable and PivotChart Wizard - Step 2 of 3 dialog box.

18 Click Finish.

Excel creates an empty PivotTable.

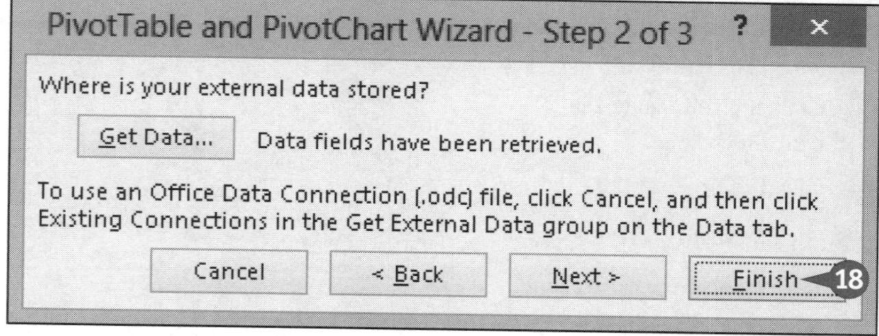

A The fields available in the table or query that you chose in step 11 appear in the PivotTable Fields pane.

19 Click and drag fields from the PivotTable Fields pane and drop them in the PivotTable areas.

B Excel summarizes the external data in the PivotTable.

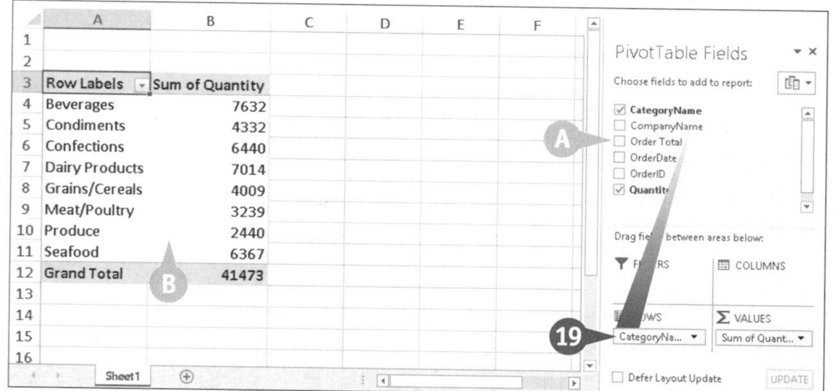

EXTRA

The most common drawback to using an external data source is that you often have no control over the actual external file. For example, if you attempt to refresh the PivotTable, Excel may display an error message. If you suspect the problem is a change to the database login data, click OK to display the Login dialog box and find out the new login name and password from the database administrator.

The problem might also be that the database file has been moved or renamed. Click OK in the error message, and then click Database in the Login dialog box. You can then use the Select Database dialog box to find and select the database file.

Whether your PivotTable is based on financial results, survey responses, or a database of collectibles such as books or DVDs, the underlying data is probably not static. That is, the data changes over time as new results come in, new surveys are undertaken, and new items are added to the collection. You can ensure that the data analysis represented by the PivotTable remains up to date by refreshing the PivotTable.

Excel offers two methods for refreshing a PivotTable: manual and automatic. A manual refresh is one that you perform, usually when you know that the source data has changed, or if you simply want to be sure that the latest data is reflected in your PivotTable report. An automatic refresh is one that Excel handles for you.

Refresh PivotTable Data

Refresh Data Manually

1. Click any cell inside the PivotTable.
2. Click the Analyze tab.
3. Click Refresh.

   You can also press Alt+F5.

   Ⓐ To update every PivotTable in the workbook, click the Refresh down arrow and then click Refresh All.

   You can also update all PivotTables by pressing Ctrl+Alt+F5.

   Excel updates the PivotTable data.

Refresh Data Automatically

1. Click any cell inside the PivotTable.
2. Click the Analyze tab.
3. Click PivotTable.
4. Click Options.

Note: *You can also right-click any cell in the PivotTable and then click PivotTable Options.*

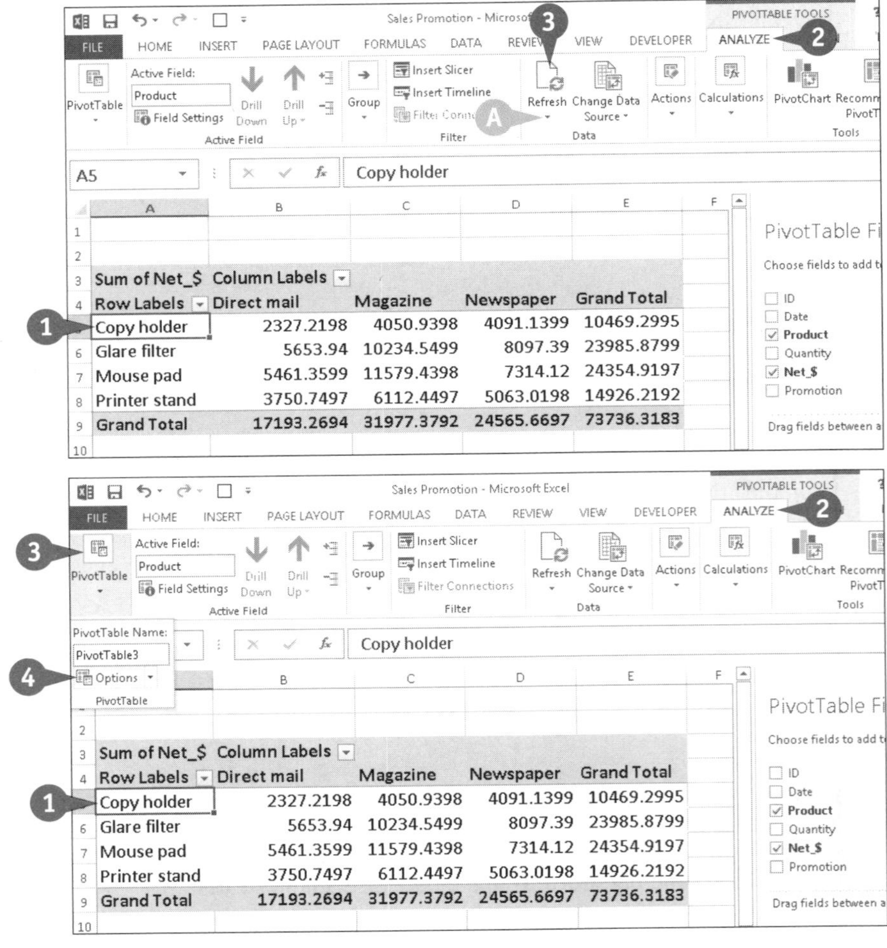

The PivotTable Options dialog box appears.

5 Click the Data tab.

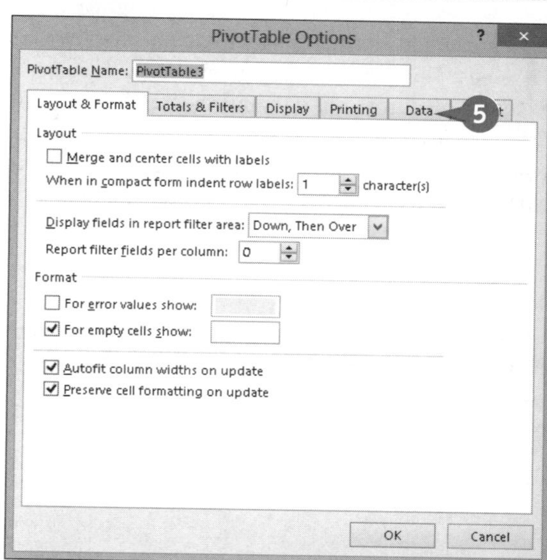

6 Click the Refresh Data When Opening the File check box (☐ changes to ☑).

7 Click OK.

Excel applies the refresh options.

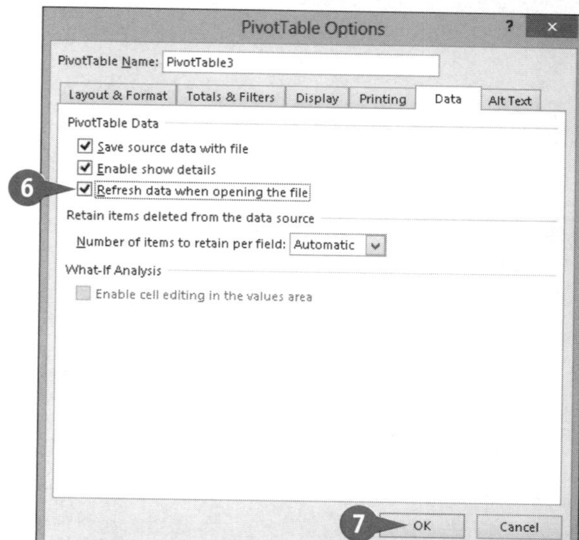

APPLY IT

If your PivotTable is based on external data, you can set up a schedule that automatically refreshes the PivotTable at a specified interval. Click any cell inside the PivotTable, click the Analyze tab, click the Refresh down arrow, and then select Connection Properties from the drop-down list. Click the Refresh Every check box (☐ changes to ☑), and then use the spin box to specify the refresh interval, in minutes.

Note, however, that when you set up an automatic refresh, you might prefer not to have the source data updated too frequently. Depending on where the data resides and how much data you are working with, the refresh could take some time, which may slow down the rest of your work.

Add Multiple Fields to the Row or Column Area

You can add multiple fields to any of the PivotTable areas. This powerful feature enables you to perform further analysis of your data by viewing the data differently. For example, suppose that you are analyzing the results of a sales campaign that ran different promotions in several types of advertisements. A basic PivotTable might show you the sales for each Product (the row field) according to the Advertisement used (the column field). You might also be interested in seeing, for each product, the breakdown in sales for each promotion. You can do that by adding the Promotion field to the row area.

Add Multiple Fields to the Row or Column Area

Add a Field to the ROWS Area

1 Click a cell within the PivotTable.

2 Click the check box of the text or date field that you want to add (☐ changes to ☑).

A Excel adds the field to the ROWS box.

B Excel adds the field's unique values to the PivotTable's row area.

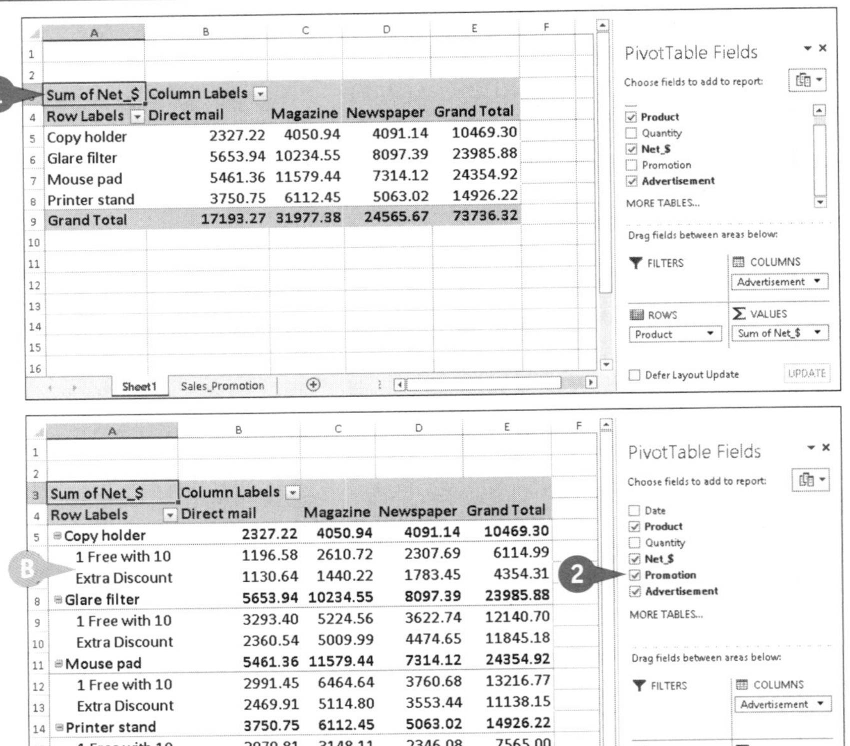

Add a Field to the ROWS or COLUMNS Area

1. Click a cell within the PivotTable.
2. From the list in the PivotTable Fields pane, click and drag the field that you want to add and drop the field in either the ROWS box or the COLUMNS box.

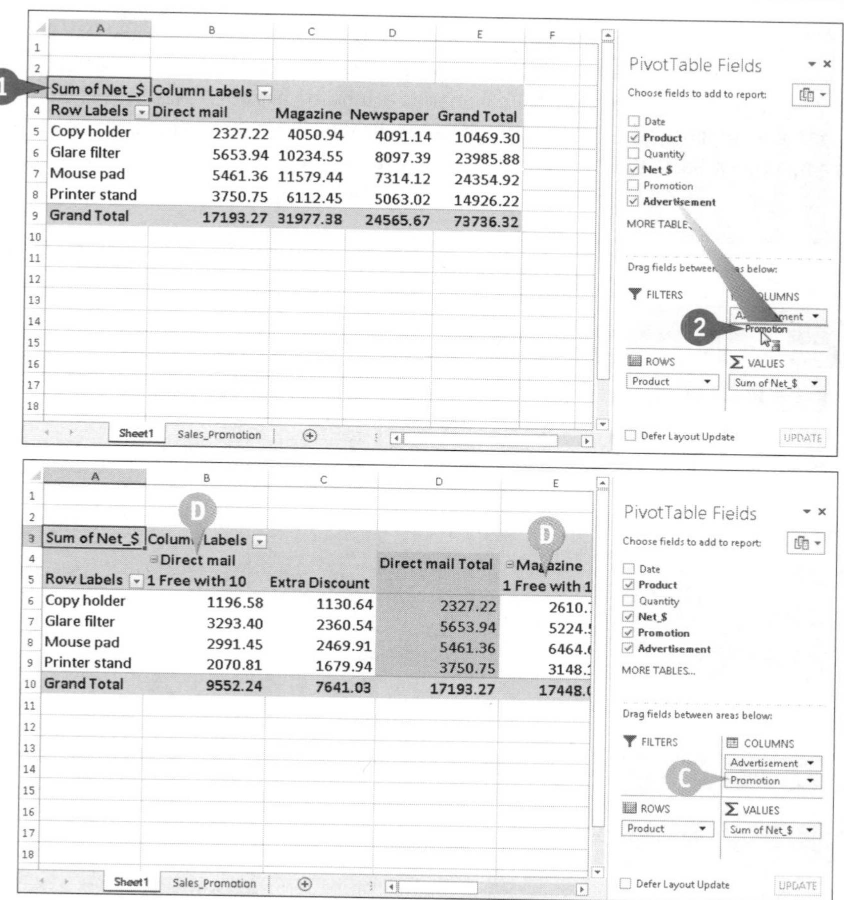

- C Excel adds the field to the ROWS or COLUMNS box.
- D Excel adds the field's unique values to the PivotTable's row or column area.

APPLY IT

After you add a second field to the row or column area, you can change the field positions to change the PivotTable view. In the PivotTable Field List, use the ROWS box or the COLUMNS box to click and drag the button of the field you want to move and then drop the field above or below an existing field button.

Excel does not restrict you to just two fields in the row or column area. Depending on your data analysis requirements, you are free to add three, four, or more fields to the row area or to the column area.

Add Multiple Fields to the Data Area

Excel enables you to add multiple fields to the PivotTable's data area, which enhances your analysis by enabling you to see multiple summaries at one time. For example, suppose you are analyzing the results of a sales campaign. A basic PivotTable might show you the sum of the quantity sold. You might also be interested in seeing the net dollar amount sold. You can do that by adding the Net $ field to the data area. You can add multiple fields to the data area either by using the PivotTable Fields pane or by dragging a field to the data area.

Add Multiple Fields to the Data Area

Add a Field to the Data Area with a Check Box

1. Click a cell within the PivotTable.

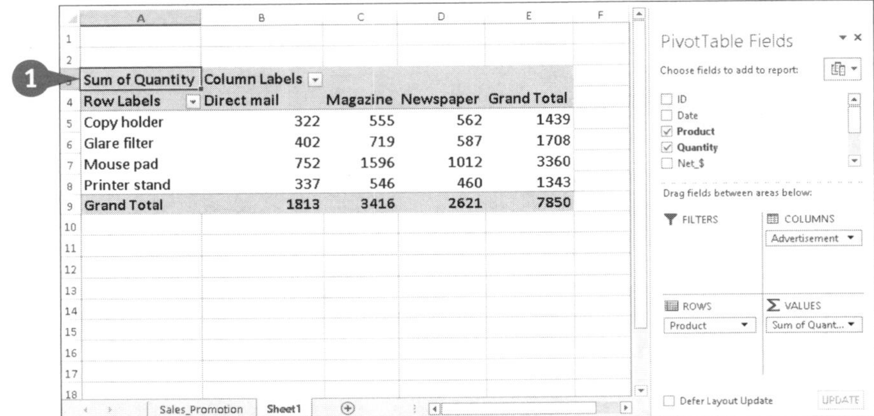

2. Select the check box of the field you want to add to the data area.

- A Excel adds a button for the field to the VALUES box.
- B Excel adds the field to the PivotTable's data area.

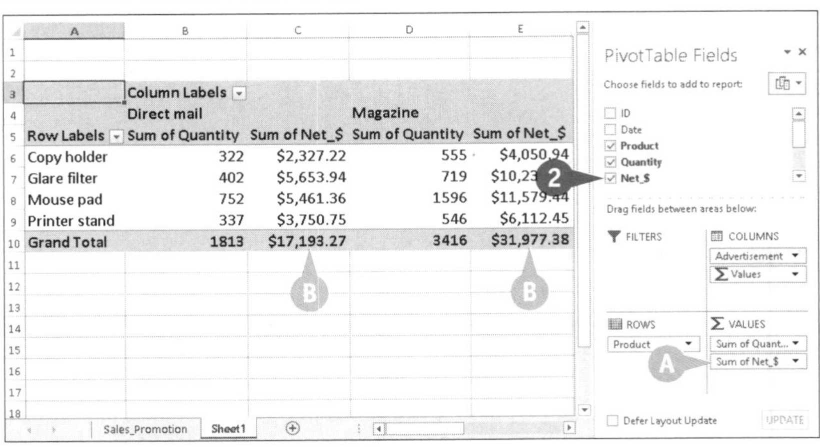

Add a Field to the Data Area by Dragging

1. Click a cell within the PivotTable.

2. In the PivotTable Fields pane, click and drag the field you want to add and drop the field in the VALUES box.

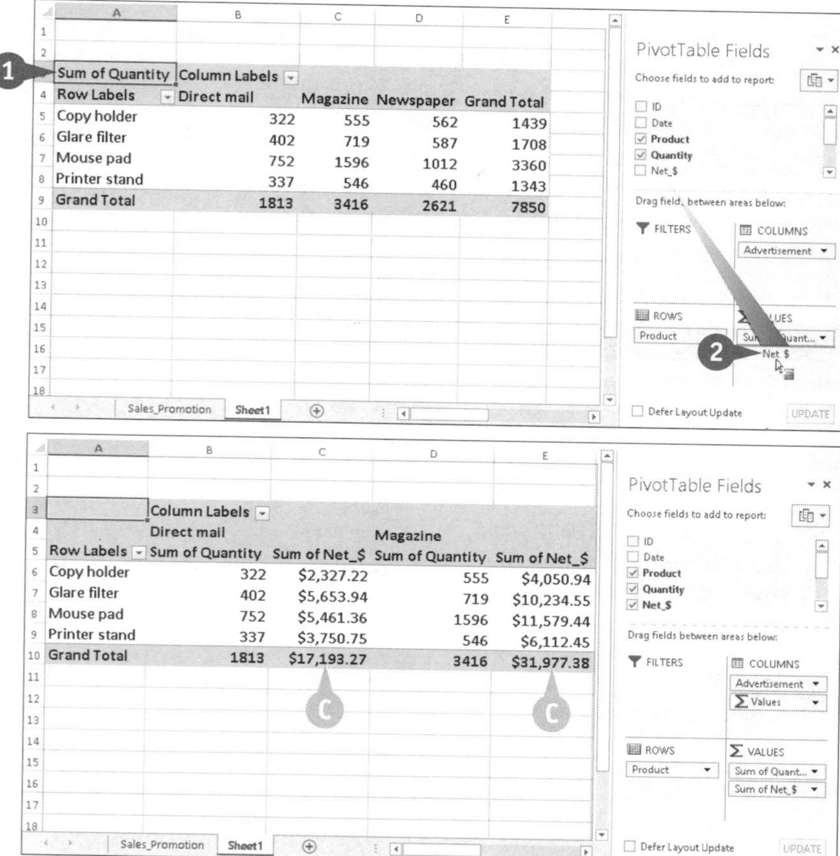

C Excel adds the field to the PivotTable's data area.

EXTRA

When you add a second field to the data area, Excel moves the labels, such as Sum of Quantity and Sum of Net $, into the column area for easier reference. This is also reflected in the addition of a Values button in the COLUMNS box section of the PivotTable Fields pane. This enables you to pivot the values within the report. Excel does not restrict you to just two fields in the data area. You are free to add three, four, or more data fields to enhance your analysis of the data.

Move a Field to a Different Area

A PivotTable is a powerful data analysis tool because it can take hundreds or even thousands of records and summarize them into a compact, comprehensible report. However, unlike most of the other data-analysis features in Excel, a PivotTable is not a static collection of worksheet cells. Instead, you can move a PivotTable's fields from one area of the PivotTable to another. This enables you to view your data from different perspectives, which can greatly enhance the analysis of the data. Moving a field within a PivotTable is called *pivoting* the data.

The most common way to pivot the data is to move fields between the row and column areas. However, you can also pivot data by moving a row or column field to the filter area.

Move a Field to a Different Area

Move a Field between the Row and Column Areas

1. Click a cell within the PivotTable.
2. Click and drag a COLUMNS field button and drop it within the ROWS box.

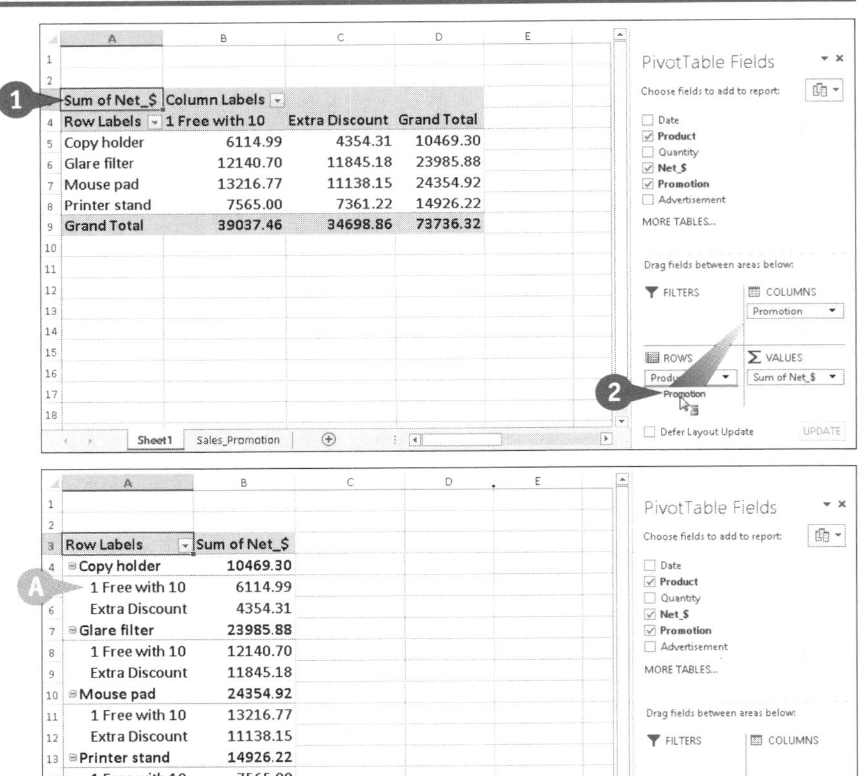

A. Excel displays the field's values within the row area.

You can also drag a field button from the ROWS box area and drop it within the COLUMNS box.

Move a Row or Column Field to the Filters Area

1. Click a cell within the PivotTable.
2. Click and drag a field from the ROWS box and drop it within the FILTERS box.

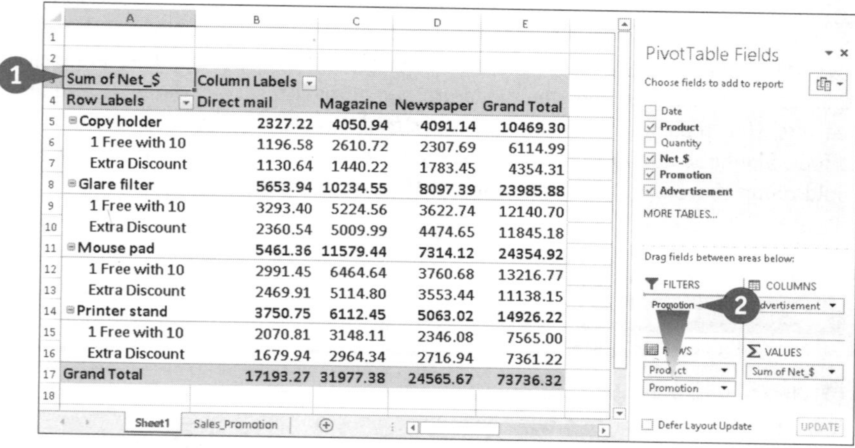

Sum of Net_$	Column Labels			
Row Labels	Direct mail	Magazine	Newspaper	Grand Total
Copy holder	2327.22	4050.94	4091.14	10469.30
1 Free with 10	1196.58	2610.72	2307.69	6114.99
Extra Discount	1130.64	1440.22	1783.45	4354.31
Glare filter	5653.94	10234.55	8097.39	23985.88
1 Free with 10	3293.40	5224.56	3622.74	12140.70
Extra Discount	2360.54	5009.99	4474.65	11845.18
Mouse pad	5461.36	11579.44	7314.12	24354.92
1 Free with 10	2991.45	6464.64	3760.68	13216.77
Extra Discount	2469.91	5114.80	3553.44	11138.15
Printer stand	3750.75	6112.45	5063.02	14926.22
1 Free with 10	2070.81	3148.11	2346.08	7565.00
Extra Discount	1679.94	2964.34	2716.94	7361.22
Grand Total	17193.27	31977.38	24565.67	73736.32

Ⓑ Excel moves the field button to the report filter.

You can also drag a field button from the COLUMNS box and drop it within the FILTERS box.

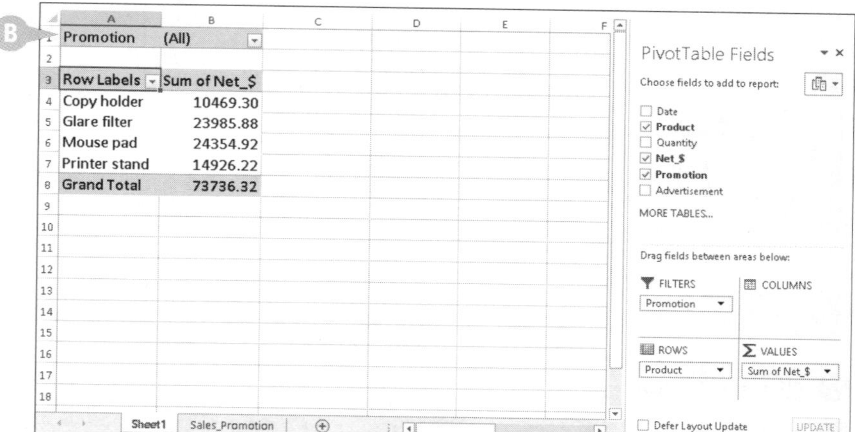

Promotion	(All)
Row Labels	Sum of Net_$
Copy holder	10469.30
Glare filter	23985.88
Mouse pad	24354.92
Printer stand	14926.22
Grand Total	73736.32

APPLY IT

You can move any row, column, or filter field to the PivotTable's data area. This may seem strange because row, column, and page fields are almost always text values, and the default data area calculation is Sum. How can you sum text values? You cannot, of course. Instead, the default Excel PivotTable summary calculation for text values is Count. Therefore, for example, if you drag the Promotion field and drop it inside the data area, Excel creates a second data field named Count of Promotion.

Group PivotTable Values

To make a PivotTable with a large number of row or column items easier to work with, you can group the items together. For example, you could group months into quarters, thus reducing the number of items from twelve to four. Similarly, a report that lists dozens of countries could group those countries by continent, thus reducing the number of items to four or five, depending on where the countries are located. Finally, if you use a numeric field in the row or column area, you may have hundreds of items, one for each numeric value. You can improve the report by creating just a few numeric ranges.

Group PivotTable Values

1. Click any item in the numeric field that you want to group.

2. Click the Analyze tab.
3. Click Group.
4. Click Group Field.

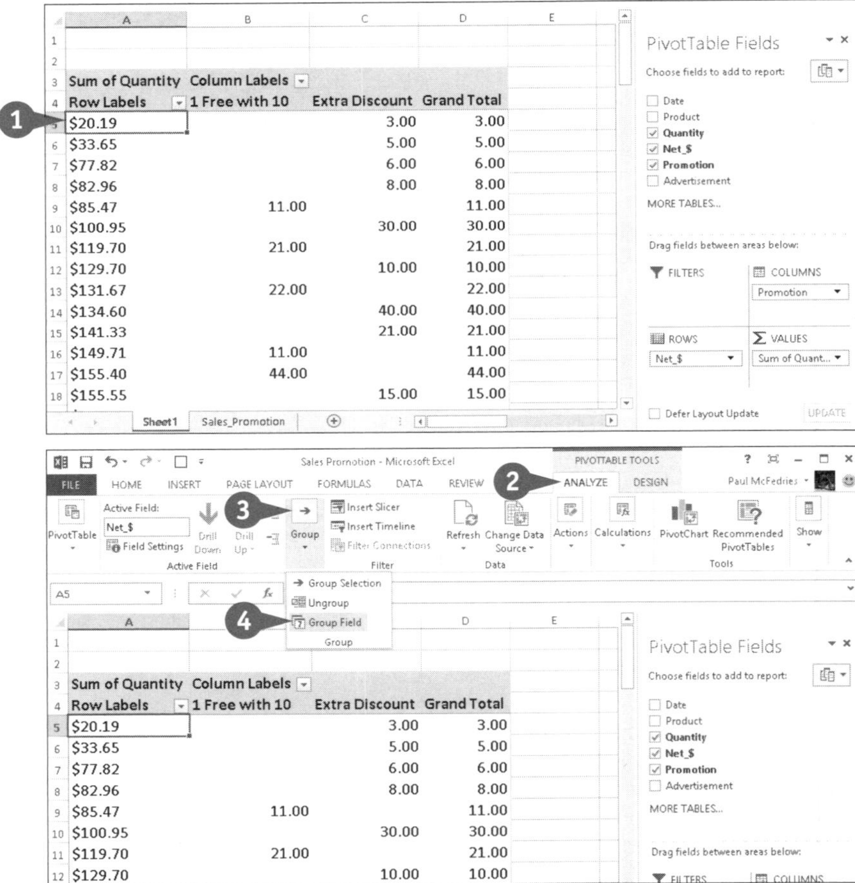

The Grouping dialog box appears.

5 Type the starting numeric value.

A Click these check boxes (☐ changes to ☑) to have Excel extract the minimum and maximum values of the numeric items and place those values in the text boxes.

6 Type the ending numeric value.

7 Type the size that you want to use for each grouping.

8 Click OK.

B Excel groups the numeric values.

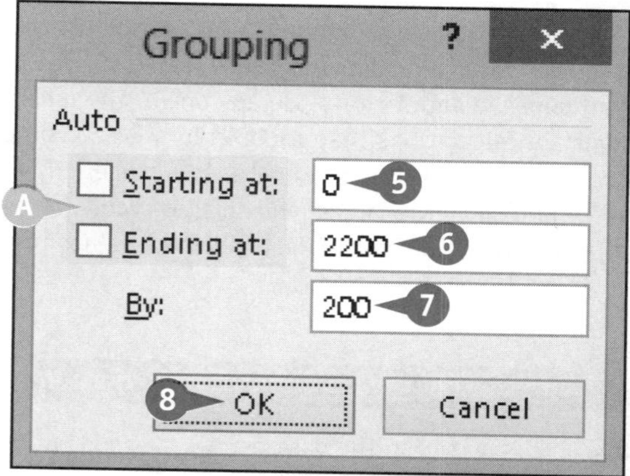

3	Sum of Quantity	Column Labels		
4	Row Labels	1 Free with 10	Extra Discount	Grand Total
5	0-200	186.00	203.00	389.00
6	200-400	429.00	430.00	859.00
7	400-600	638.00	619.00	1257.00
8	600-800	363.00	286.00	649.00
9	800-1000	440.00	791.00	1231.00
10	1000-1200	473.00	632.00	1105.00
11	1200-1400	429.00	293.00	722.00
12	1400-1600	473.00	120.00	593.00
13	1600-1800	110.00	254.00	364.00
14	1800-2000	132.00	274.00	406.00
15	2000-2200	275.00		275.00
16	Grand Total	3948.00	3902.00	7850.00

APPLY IT

To group dates and times, first click any item in the field. Click the Analyze tab, click Group, and then click Group Field. In the Grouping dialog box, type the starting date or time and the ending date or time. In the By list, click the type of grouping that you want, such as Months or Quarters. Click OK. To group text values, you must create custom groups. For example, to group by country, you could create custom groups named North America, Europe, and so on. Select the items that you want to include in a group, click the Analyze tab, click Group, and then click Group Selection. Click the group label, type a new name for the group, press Enter, and repeat for each custom group.

Change the PivotTable Summary Calculation

If your data analysis requires a calculation other than Sum (for numeric data) or Count (for text), you can configure the data field to use any one of the nine other summary calculations that are built into Excel. For example, Average calculates the mean value in a numeric field. Max and Min display the largest and smallest value, respectively, in a numeric field. Product multiplies the values in a numeric field, while Count Nums displays the total number of numeric values in the source field. StdDev and StdDevp calculate the standard deviation of a population sample and entire population, respectively. Var and Varp calculate the variance of a population sample and entire population, respectively.

Change the PivotTable Summary Calculation

1. Click any cell in the data field.
2. Click the Analyze tab.
3. Click Active Field.
4. Click Field Settings.

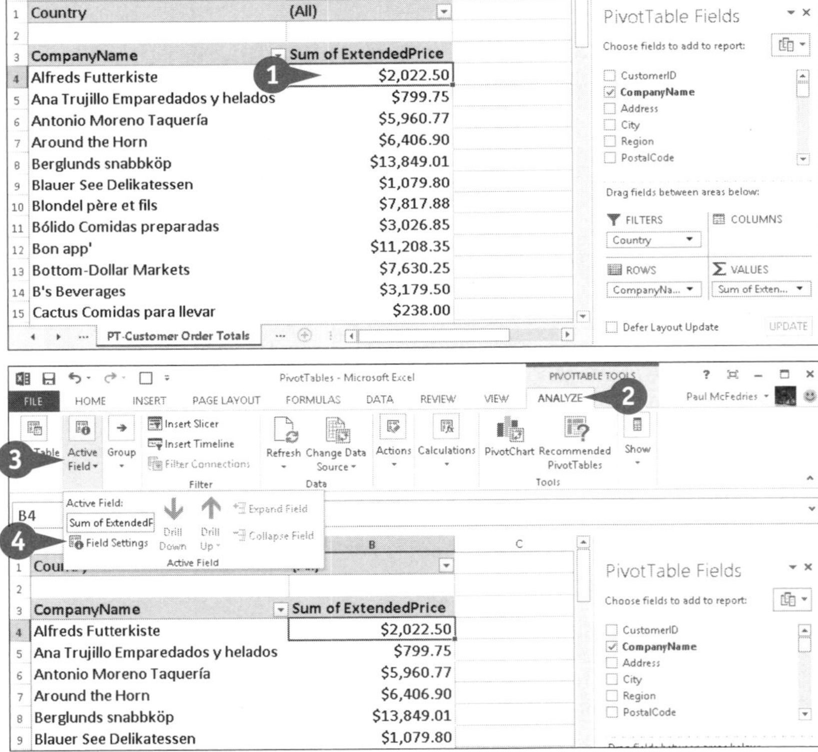

The Value Field Settings dialog box appears with the Summarize Values By tab displayed.

5 Click the summary calculation you want to use.

6 Click OK.

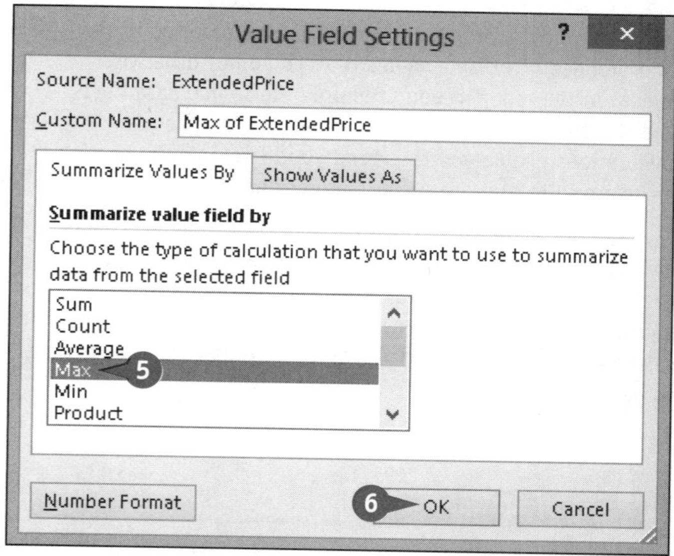

A Excel recalculates the PivotTable results.

B Excel renames the data field label to reflect the new summary calculation.

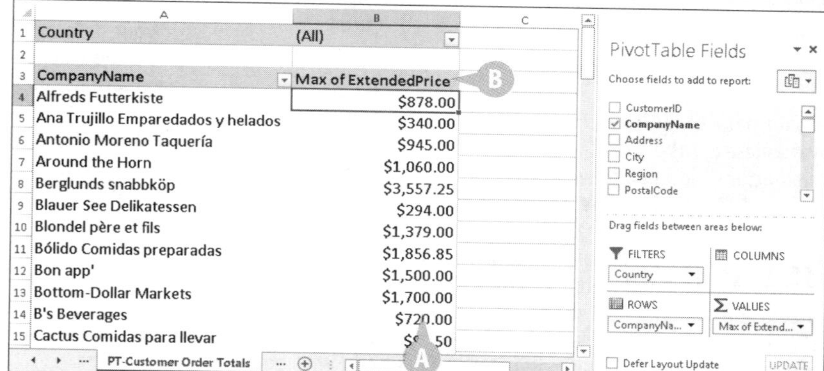

EXTRA

If your PivotTable results do not look correct, check the summary calculation that Excel has applied to the field to see if it is using Count instead of Sum. If the data field includes one or more text cells or one or more blank cells, Excel defaults to the Count summary function instead of Sum. When you add a second field to the row or column area, Excel displays a subtotal for each item in the outer field. To change the subtotal summary calculation, click any cell in the outer field, click the Analyze tab, click Active Field, and then click Field Settings. Select the Custom option (○ changes to ◉), and then click the summary calculation you want to use for the subtotals. Click OK.

Introducing Custom Calculations

A *custom calculation* is a formula that you define to produce PivotTable values that would not otherwise appear in the report if you used only the source data fields and the built-in summary calculations in Excel. Custom calculations enable you to extend your data analysis to include results that are specific to your needs.

For example, suppose your PivotTable shows employee sales by quarter and you want to award a 10-percent bonus to each employee with sales of more than $25,000 in any quarter. You can create a custom calculation that checks for sales greater than $25,000 and then multiplies them by 0.1 to get the bonus number.

Excel applies a custom calculation to your source data to produce a summary result. In most cases, the custom calculation is just like the PivotTable summary calculations that are built into Excel, except that you define the specifics of the calculation. Because you are creating a formula, you can use most of the formula power available in Excel, which gives you tremendous flexibility to create custom calculations that suit your data-analysis needs. By placing these calculations within the actual PivotTable, as opposed to adding them to your source data, you can easily update the calculations as needed and refresh the report results.

Custom Calculation Types

When building a custom calculation for a PivotTable, Excel offers two types: a calculated field and a calculated item.

Calculated Field

If your data analysis requires a PivotTable field that is not available from the data source or via Excel's built-in summary calculations, you can insert a custom formula to derive the field you need. A *calculated field* is a new data field in which the values are the result of a custom calculation formula. You can display the calculated field along with another data field or on its own. A calculated field is really a custom summary calculation, so in almost all cases, the calculated field references one or more fields in the source data. For more information, see the "Insert a Custom Calculated Field" section later in this chapter.

Calculated Item

If your data analysis requires a PivotTable item that is not available from the data source or via Excel's built-in summary calculations, you can insert a custom formula to derive the item you need. A *calculated item* is a new item in a row or column field in which the values are the result of a custom calculation. In this case, the calculated item's formula references one or more items in the same field.

Understanding Custom Calculation Limitations

Whether they are calculated fields or calculated items, custom calculations are powerful additions to your PivotTable analysis toolbox. However, although custom calculation formulas look like regular worksheet formulas, you cannot assume that you can do everything with a custom PivotTable formula that you can do with a worksheet formula. In fact, there are a number of limitations that Excel imposes on custom formulas, such as not being able to reference data outside the pivot cache, and not being able to use custom items in conjunction with grouping.

General Limitations

The major limitation inherent in custom calculations is that, with the exception of constant values such as numbers, you cannot reference anything outside the PivotTable's source data:

- You cannot use a cell reference, range address, or range name as an operand in a custom calculation formula.
- You cannot use any worksheet function that requires a cell reference, range, or defined name. However, you can still use many of the Excel worksheet functions by substituting either a field or an item in place of a cell reference or range name. For example, if you want a calculated item that returns the average of items named Jan, Feb, and Mar, you could use the following formula:

```
=AVERAGE(Jan, Feb, Mar)
```

- You cannot use the PivotTable's subtotals, row totals, column totals, or Grand Total as an operand in a custom calculation formula.

Calculated Field Limitations

When you are working with calculated fields, it is important to understand how references to other PivotTable fields work within your calculations and what limitations you face when using field references.

Field References

When you reference a field in your formula, Excel interprets this reference as the *sum* of that field's values. For example, the formula `=Sales + 1` does not add 1 to each Sales value and return the sum of these results; that is, Excel does not interpret the formula as `=Sum of (Sales + 1)`. Instead, the formula adds 1 to the sum of the Sales values; Excel interprets the formula as `=(Sum of Sales) + 1`.

Field Reference Problems

The fact that Excel defaults to a Sum calculation when you reference another field in your custom calculation can lead to problems. The trouble is that it does not make sense to sum certain types of data. For example, suppose you have inventory source data with `UnitsInStock` and `UnitPrice` fields. You want to calculate the total value of the inventory, so you create a custom field based on the following formula:

```
=UnitsInStock * UnitPrice
```

Unfortunately, this formula does not work because Excel treats the `UnitPrice` operand as Sum of `UnitPrice`. Of course, it does not make sense to "add" the prices together, so your formula produces an incorrect result.

Calculated Item Limitations

Excel imposes the following limitations on the use of calculated items:

- A formula for a calculated item cannot reference items from any field except the one in which the calculated item resides.
- You cannot insert a calculated item into a PivotTable that has at least one grouped field. You must ungroup all the PivotTable fields before you can insert a calculated item.
- You cannot group a field in a PivotTable that has at least one calculated item.
- You cannot insert a calculated item into a page field. Also, you cannot move a row or column field that has a calculated item into the page area.
- You cannot insert a calculated item into a PivotTable in which a field has been used more than once.
- You cannot insert a calculated item into a PivotTable that uses the Average, StdDev, StdDevp, Var, or Varp summary calculations.

Insert a Custom Calculated Field

If your data analysis requires a PivotTable field that is not available using just the data source fields and the summary calculations that are built into Excel, you can insert a calculated field that uses a custom formula to derive the results you need. A custom calculated field is based on a formula that looks much like an Excel worksheet formula. However, you do not enter the formula for a calculated field into a worksheet cell. Instead, Excel offers the Calculated Field feature, which provides a dialog box for you to name the field and construct the formula. Excel then stores the formula along with the rest of the PivotTable data in the pivot cache.

Insert a Custom Calculated Field

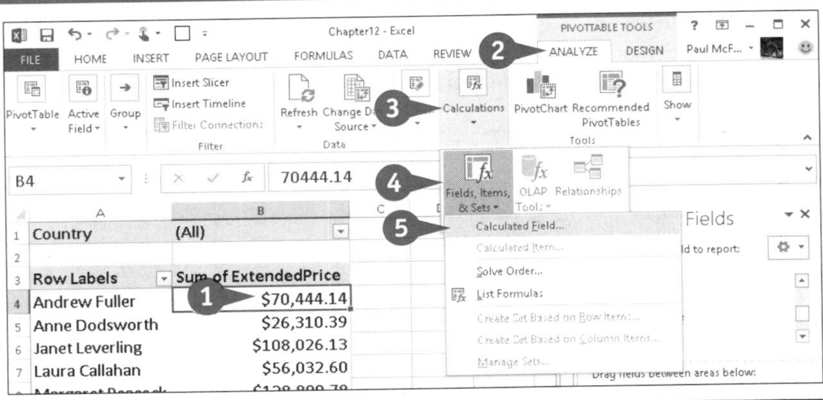

1. Click any cell inside the PivotTable's data area.
2. Click Analyze.
3. Click Calculations.
4. Click Fields, Items, & Sets.
5. Click Calculated Field.

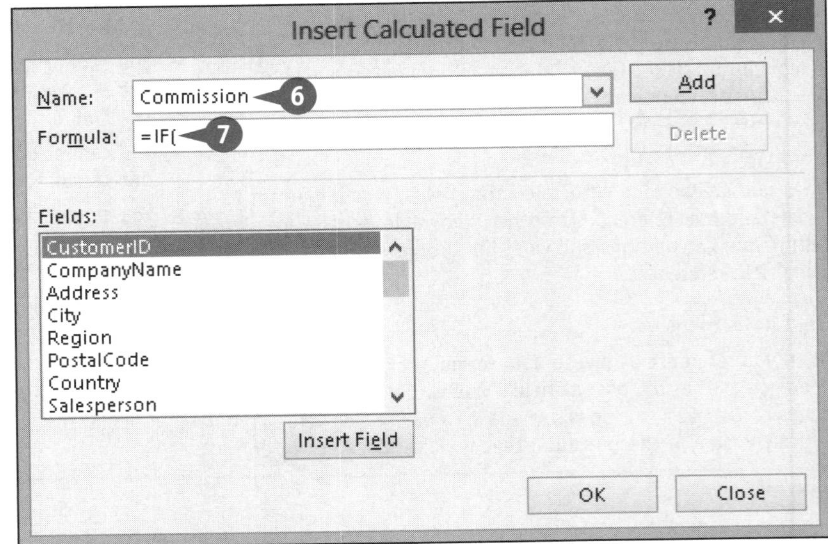

The Insert Calculated Field dialog box appears.

6. Type a name for the calculated field.
7. Start the formula for the calculated field.

8. To insert a field into the formula at the current cursor position, click the field.
9. Click Insert Field.
10. When the formula is complete, click Add.
11. Click OK.

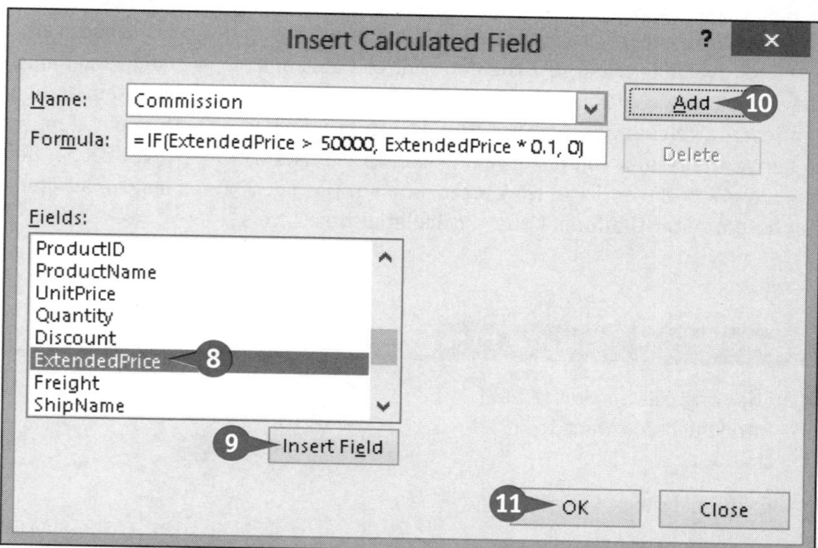

A. Excel adds the calculated field to the PivotTable's data area.

B. Excel adds the calculated field to the PivotTable Fields pane.

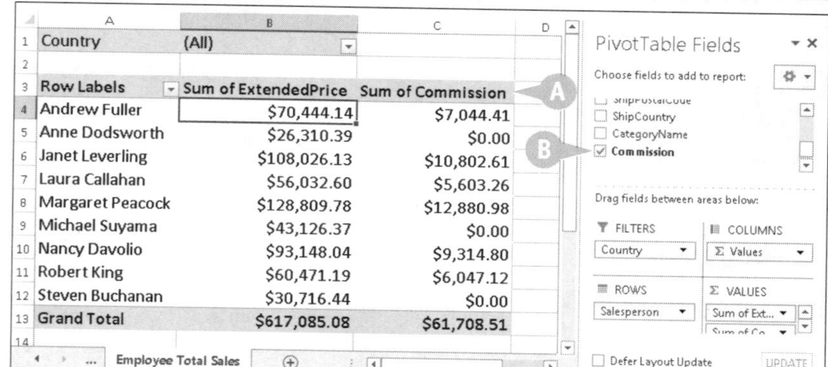

Country	(All)	
Row Labels	Sum of ExtendedPrice	Sum of Commission
Andrew Fuller	$70,444.14	$7,044.41
Anne Dodsworth	$26,310.39	$0.00
Janet Leverling	$108,026.13	$10,802.61
Laura Callahan	$56,032.60	$5,603.26
Margaret Peacock	$128,809.78	$12,880.98
Michael Suyama	$43,126.37	$0.00
Nancy Davolio	$93,148.04	$9,314.80
Robert King	$60,471.19	$6,047.12
Steven Buchanan	$30,716.44	$0.00
Grand Total	$617,085.08	$61,708.51

EXTRA

When you add a calculated field to the PivotTable, Excel also applies the custom calculation to the Grand Total value. Unfortunately, this total is often inaccurate and you should be careful not to assume that it is correct. The problem is that it is not a sum of the values in the calculated field. Instead, Excel applies the calculated field's formula to the sum of whatever field or fields you referenced in the formula. When inserting a custom calculated field example, Excel applies the formula to the Sum of Extended Price field's Grand Total value, which is not the correct way to calculate the total commission. To work around this problem, you need to set up a formula outside the PivotTable that sums the commission values.

Insert a Custom Calculated Item

If your data analysis requires a PivotTable item that is not available using just the data source fields and the summary calculations that are built into Excel, you can insert a calculated item that uses a custom formula to derive the results you need. A calculated item uses a formula much like an Excel worksheet formula. However, you do not enter the formula for a calculated item into a worksheet cell. Instead, Excel offers the Calculated Item command, which displays a dialog box where you name the item and construct the formula. Excel then stores the formula along with the rest of the PivotTable data in the pivot cache. Before you create a calculated item, be sure to remove all groupings from your PivotTable.

Insert a Custom Calculated Item

1. Click any cell inside the field into which you want to insert the item.
2. Click Analyze.
3. Click Calculations.
4. Click Fields, Items, & Sets.
5. Click Calculated Item.

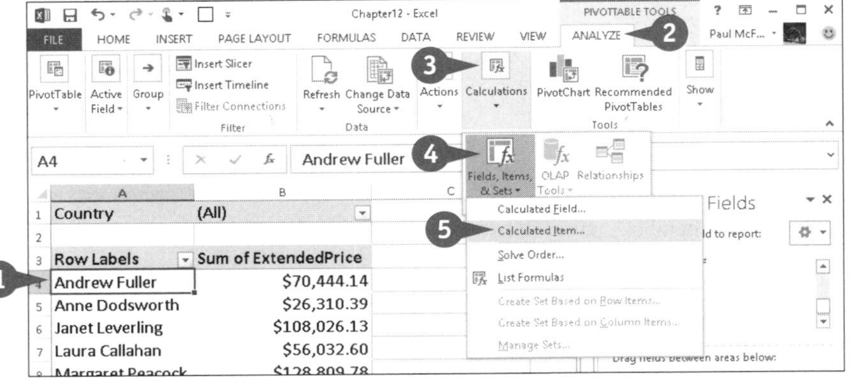

The Insert Calculated Item dialog box appears.

6. Type a name for the calculated item.
7. Start the formula for the calculated item.
8. To insert a field into the formula at the current cursor position, click the field.
9. Click Insert Field.

You can also double-click the field.

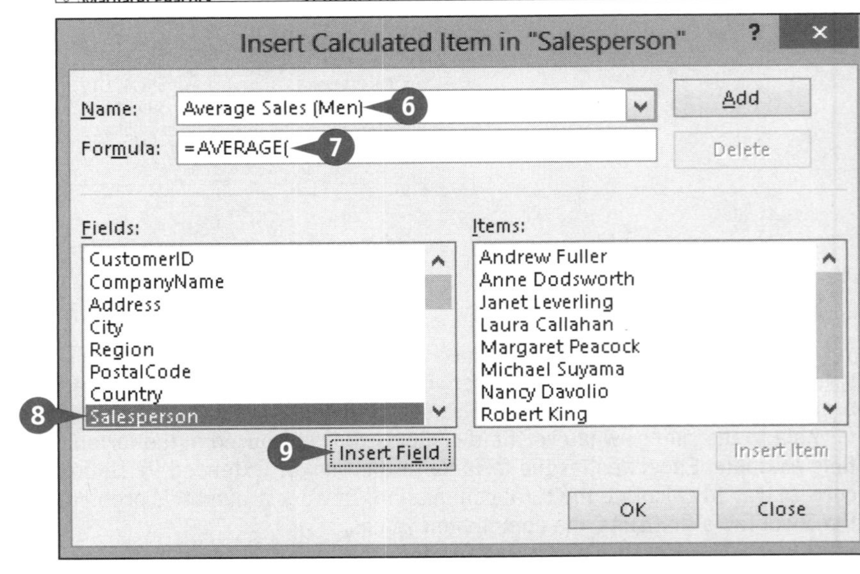

10 To insert an item into the formula at the current cursor position, click the field containing the item.

11 Click the item.

12 Click Insert Item.

You can also double-click the item.

13 When the formula is complete, click Add.

14 Repeat steps 6 to 13 to add other calculated items.

15 Click OK.

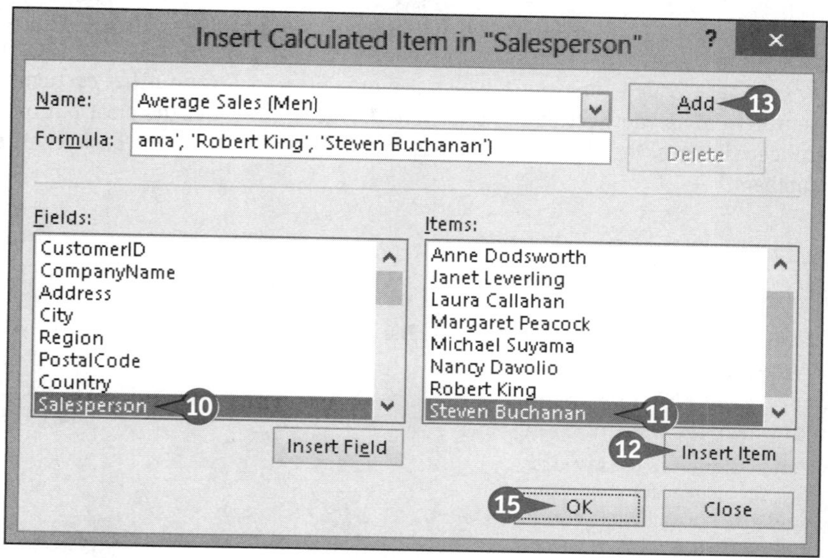

A Excel adds the calculated item to the field.

B The calculated item's formula appears in the Formula bar when you click the result.

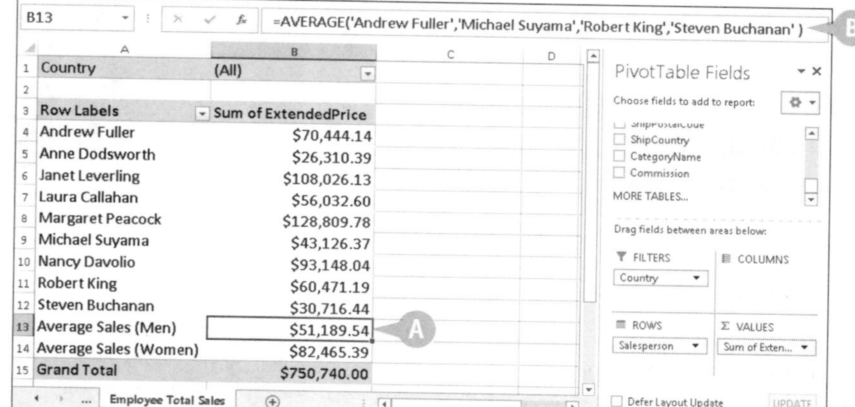

EXTRA

When you insert an item into a field, that item becomes part of the field within the pivot cache. For example, when you select the field in the Insert Calculated Item dialog box, the calculated item appears in the Items list along with the regular field items. This is handy because it enables you to use the calculated item's result in other formulas.

The downside to having the calculated item become part of the field is that Excel includes the calculated item's result in the PivotTable subtotals, row or column totals, and Grand Total. This almost always causes the totals for the affected field to be inaccurate, so double-check field totals when you use a calculated item.

Examine Chart Elements

One of the best ways to analyze your worksheet data, or get your point across to other people, is to display your data visually in a *chart*, which is a graphic representation of spreadsheet data. As the data in the spreadsheet changes, the chart also changes to reflect the new numbers.

You have dozens of different chart formats to choose from, and if none of the built-in Excel formats is just right, you can further customize these charts to suit your needs. To get the most out of charts, you need to become familiar with the basic chart elements.

A Category Axis

The axis (usually the X axis) that contains the category groupings.

B Chart Title

The title of the chart.

C Data Marker

A symbol that represents a specific data value. The symbol used depends on the chart type.

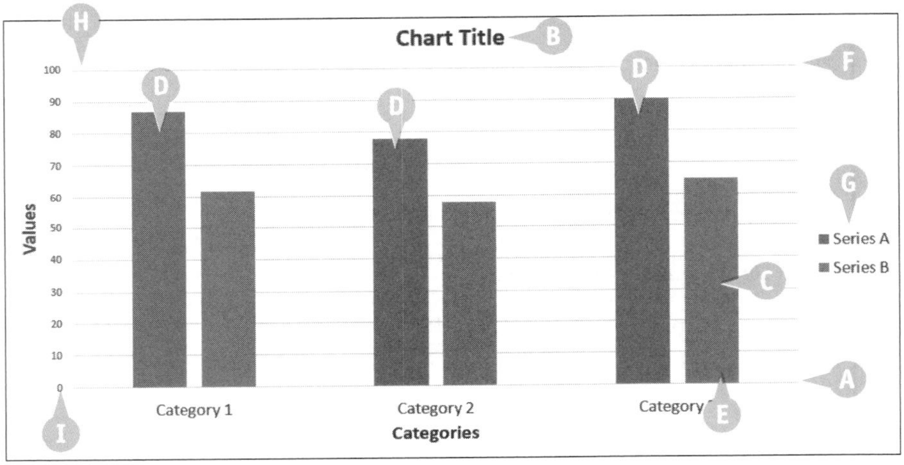

D Data Series

A collection of related data values. Normally, the marker for each value in a series has the same pattern.

E Data Value

A single piece of data, also called a *data point*.

F Gridlines

Optional horizontal and vertical extensions of the axis tick marks. These lines make data values easier to read.

G Legend

A guide that shows the colors, patterns, and symbols used by the markers for each data series.

H Plot Area

The area bounded by the category and value axes. The plot area contains the data points and gridlines.

I Value Axis

The axis (usually the Y axis) that contains the data values.

Understanding Chart Types

Excel offers 11 different types of charts, including column charts, bar charts, line charts, and pie charts. The chart type you use depends on the type of data and how you want to present that data visually.

Chart Types and Their Descriptions

Chart Type	Description
Area chart	A chart that shows the relative contributions over time that each data series makes to the whole picture.
Bar chart	A chart that compares distinct items or shows single items at distinct intervals. A bar chart is laid out with categories along the vertical axis and values along the horizontal axis.
Bubble chart	A chart that is similar to an XY chart, except that there are three data series, and in the third series the individual plot points appear as bubbles (the larger the value, the larger the bubble).
Column chart	A chart that, like a bar chart, compares distinct items or shows single items at distinct intervals. However, a column chart is laid out with categories along the horizontal axis and values along the vertical axis.
Doughnut chart	A chart that, like a pie chart, shows the proportion of the whole that is contributed by each value in a data series. The advantage of a doughnut chart is that you can plot multiple data series.
Line chart	A chart that shows how a data series changes over time. The category (X) axis usually represents a progression of even increments (such as days or months), and the value (Y) axis shows the series points.
Pie chart	A chart that shows the proportion of the whole that is contributed by each value in a single data series. The whole is represented as a circle (the "pie"), and each value is displayed as a proportional "slice" of the circle.
Radar chart	A chart that makes comparisons within a data series and between data series relative to a center point. Each category is shown with a value axis extending from the center point.
Stock chart	A chart that is designed to plot stock-market prices, such as a stock's daily high, low, and closing values.
Surface chart	A chart that analyzes two sets of data and determines the optimum combination of the two.
XY chart	A chart that shows the relationship between numeric values in two different data series. It can also plot a series of data pairs in XY coordinates. (This is also called a *scatter* chart.)

Create a Chart

To help analyze your data, you can create a chart with just a few mouse clicks. When Excel creates a chart, it examines both the shape and the contents of the range you select. From this, Excel makes various assumptions to determine what should be on the category axis, what should be on the value axis, how to label the categories, and so on. For example, Excel assumes that there are more categories than data series. This assumption makes sense, because most charts plot a small number of series over many different intervals.

Excel offers nearly 100 default chart configurations, so there should always be a type that best visualizes your data. Regardless of the chart type you choose originally, you can change to a different chart type at any time.

Create a Chart

1. Select the data that you want to visualize in a chart.

   A. If your data includes headings, be sure to include those headings in the selection.

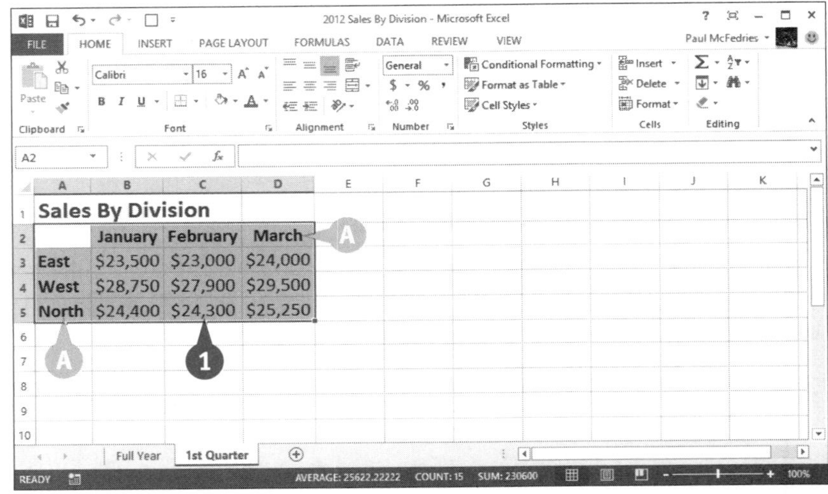

2. Click the Insert tab.
3. Click a chart type.

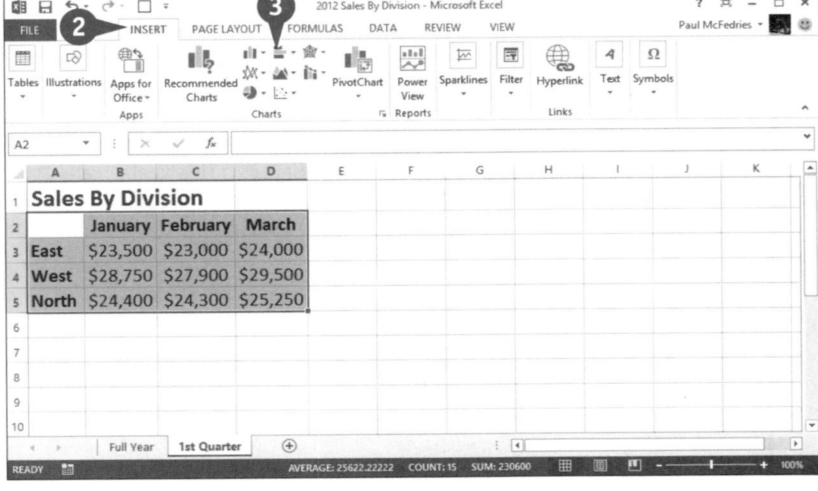

B Excel displays a gallery of configurations for the chart type.

4 Click the chart configuration you want to use.

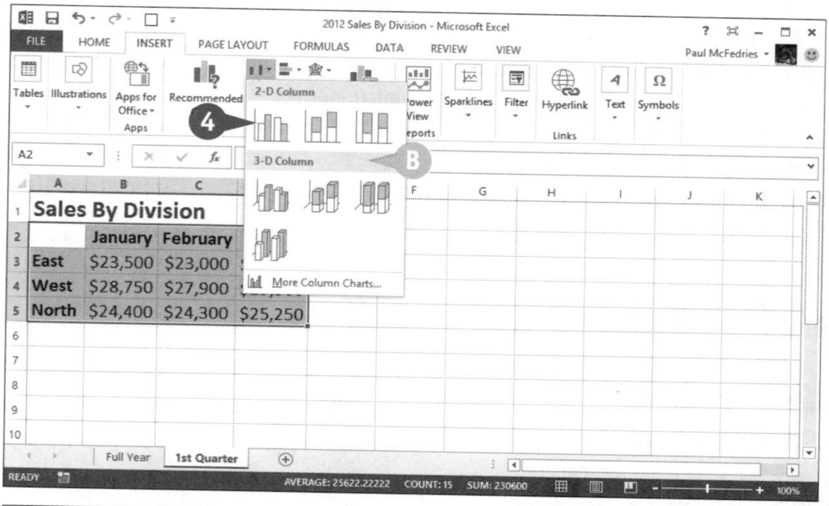

C Excel inserts the chart.

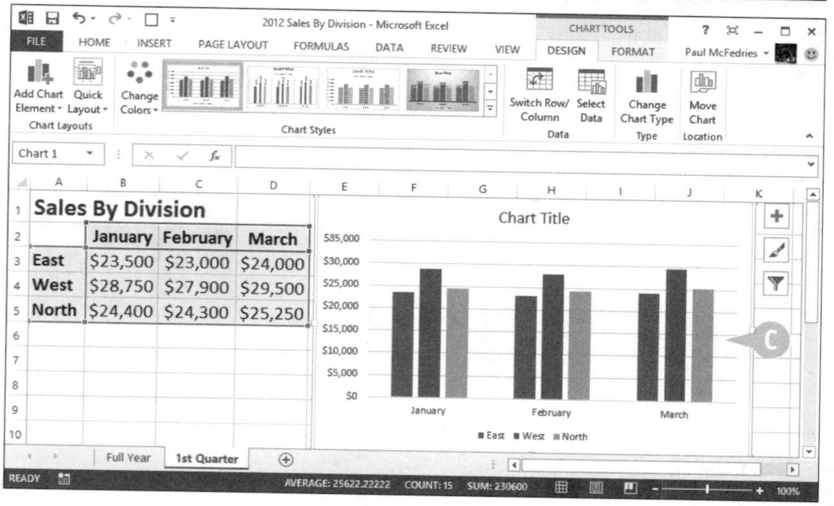

APPLY IT

You can also create a chart on a separate chart sheet. If you have not yet created your chart, select the worksheet data, right-click any worksheet tab, and then click Insert to display the Insert dialog box. Click the General tab, click Chart, and then click OK. Excel creates a new chart sheet and inserts the chart.

If you have already created your chart, you can move it to a separate chart sheet. Click the chart, click the Design tab, and then click Move Chart to open the Move Chart dialog box. Select the New Sheet option (○ changes to ◉). In the New Sheet text box, type a name for the new sheet, and then click OK.

Display a Data Table

When using a chart for data analysis, it is often useful just to see the overall shape of the data, but more often you will want to analyze the data that underlies the chart. You can usually do this from the chart by, for example, comparing column chart data markers to the value axis numbers. However, you can make it easier for yourself and others to interpret your chart by adding a data table. A *data table* is a tabular grid where each row is a data series from the chart, each column is a chart category, and each cell is a chart data point. Excel gives you the option of displaying the data table with or without *legend keys*, which are markers that identify each series.

Display a Data Table

1. Click the chart.
2. Click the Design tab.
3. Click Add Chart Element.
4. Click Data Table.
5. Click With Legend Keys.

A. If you prefer not to display the legend keys, click No Legend Keys.

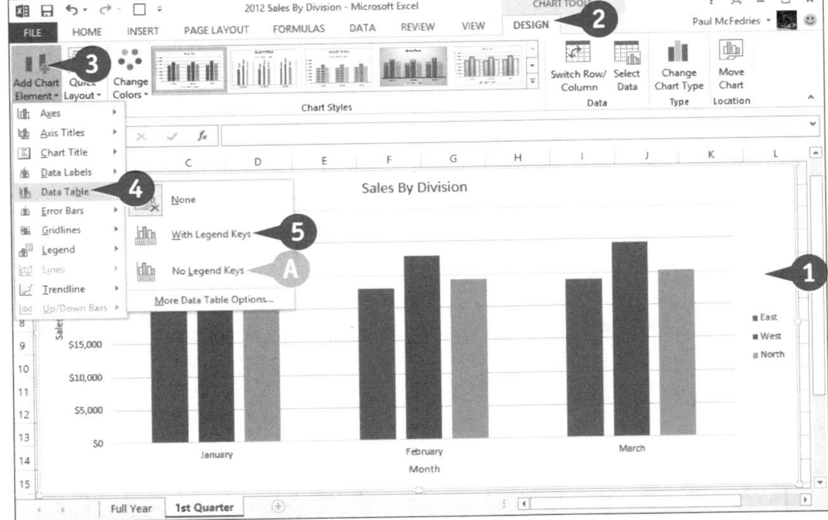

B. Excel adds the data table below the chart.

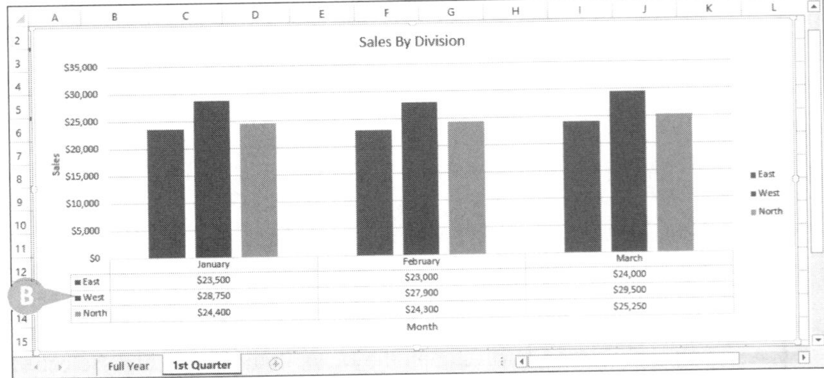

You can enhance your chart-related data analysis by adding chart elements such as data labels, a legend, and gridlines. However, adding and positioning these elements can be time-consuming. You can avoid this problem by taking advantage of tools in Excel for quickly formatting your chart by applying a different chart layout and chart style.

The chart layout includes elements such as the titles, data labels, legend, gridlines, and data table. The Quick Layouts feature in Excel enables you to apply these elements in different combinations with just a few mouse clicks. The chart style represents the colors used by the chart data markers and background.

Change the Chart Layout and Style

1. Click the chart.
2. Click the Design tab.
3. Click Quick Layout.
4. Click the layout you want to use.

A. Excel applies the layout.

5. Click the Chart Styles.

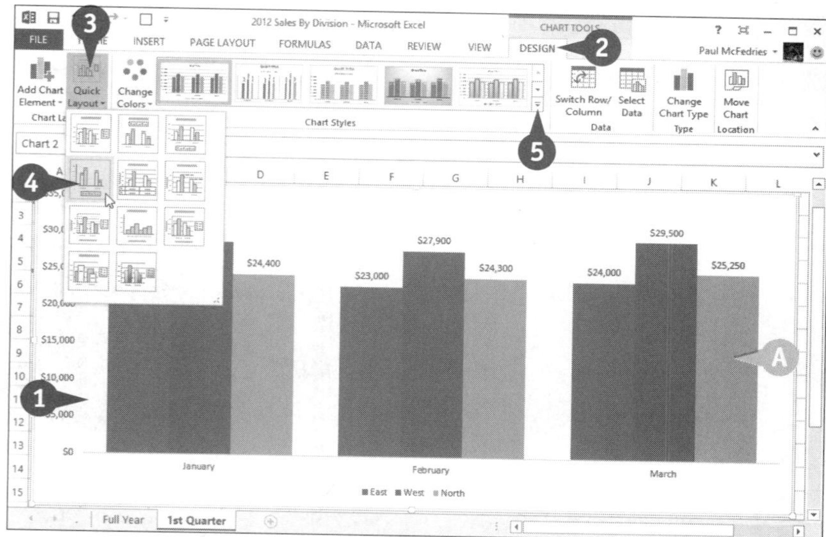

6. Click the chart style you want to use.

B. Excel applies the style to the chart.

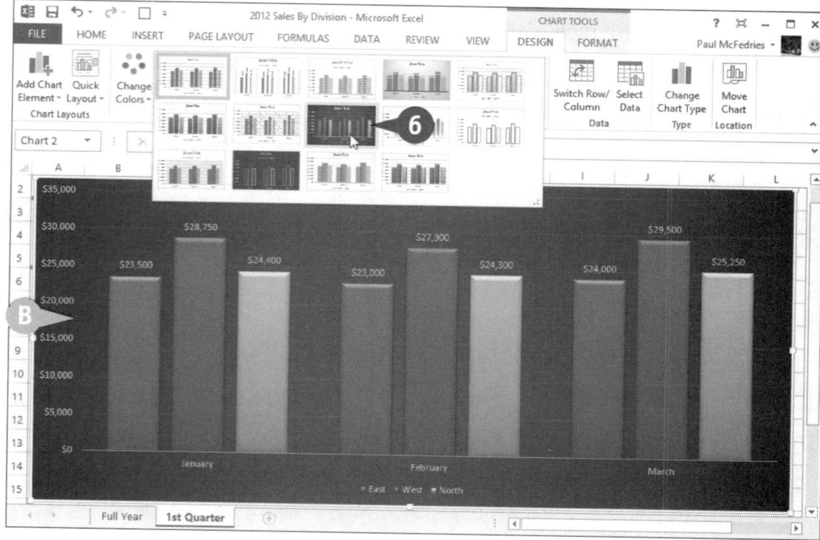

Select a Different Chart Type

If you feel that the current chart type is not showing your data in the best way, you can change the chart type. This enables you to experiment not only with the ten different chart types that Excel offers, but also with its nearly 100 chart type configurations.

For example, if you are graphing a stock's high, low, and closing prices, a line chart shows you each value, but a stock chart gives you a better sense of the daily price movements. Similarly, if you are using a bar chart to show percentages of some whole, you can more readily visualize the data by switching to a pie chart.

Select a Different Chart Type

1. Click the chart.
2. Click the Design tab.
3. Click Change Chart Type.

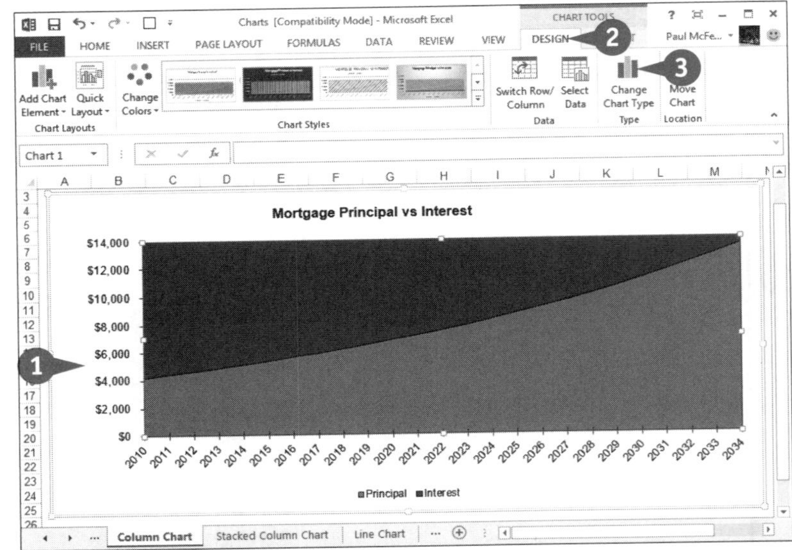

The Change Chart Type dialog box appears.

4. Click the chart type you want to use.

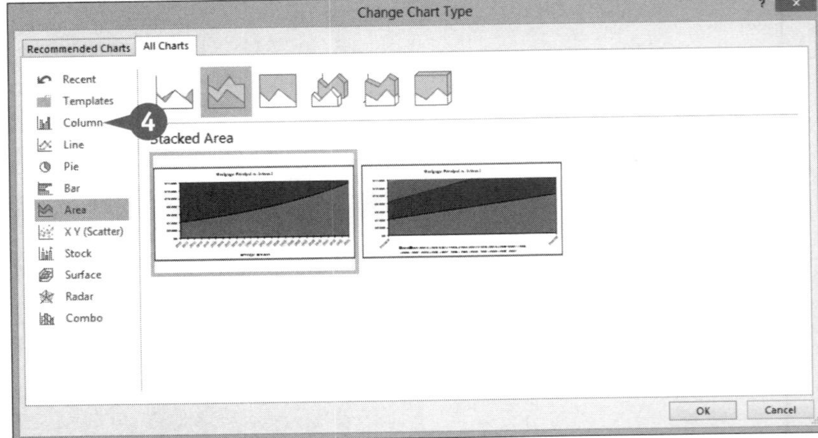

Excel displays the chart type configurations.

5 Click the configuration you want to use.

6 Click OK.

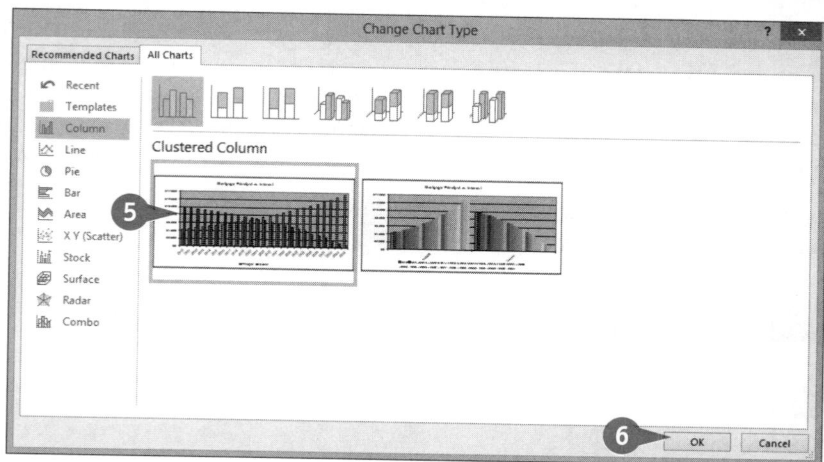

A Excel applies the new chart type.

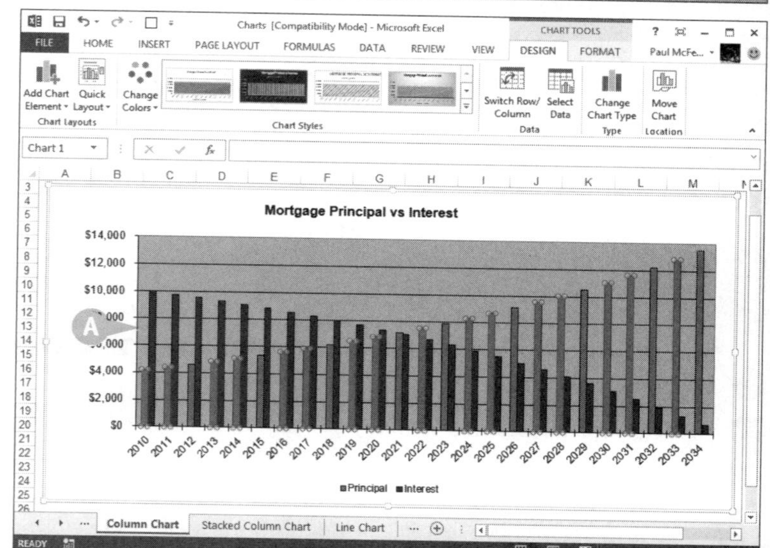

APPLY IT

You can save the chart type and formatting so that you can reuse it later on a different chart. You do this by saving your work as a chart template. Follow the steps in this section and use the tools in the Design tab's Add Chart Element list to set the chart type, titles, labels, legend position, gridlines, layout, and style. Right-click the chart's plot area or background, click Save as Template, type a name for the template, and then click Save. To reuse the template, follow steps 1 to 3 in this section, click Templates, click your template, and then click OK.

If you want a quick visualization of your data without having a chart take up a large amount of worksheet space, you can add a sparkline to a single cell. A *sparkline* is a small chart that visualizes a row or column of data and fits inside a single cell.

Excel offers three types of sparklines. The Line type is similar to a line chart and it shows you how the data fluctuates. The Column type is similar to a column chart, in that the size of each data marker corresponds to the relative size of its underlying value: negative values appear below the zero line, and positive values appear above the zero line. The Win/Loss type is similar to the Column type, except the size of each column is the same.

Add a Sparkline to a Cell

1. Select the row or column of data you want to visualize.
2. Click the Insert tab.
3. Click the type of sparkline you want to create.

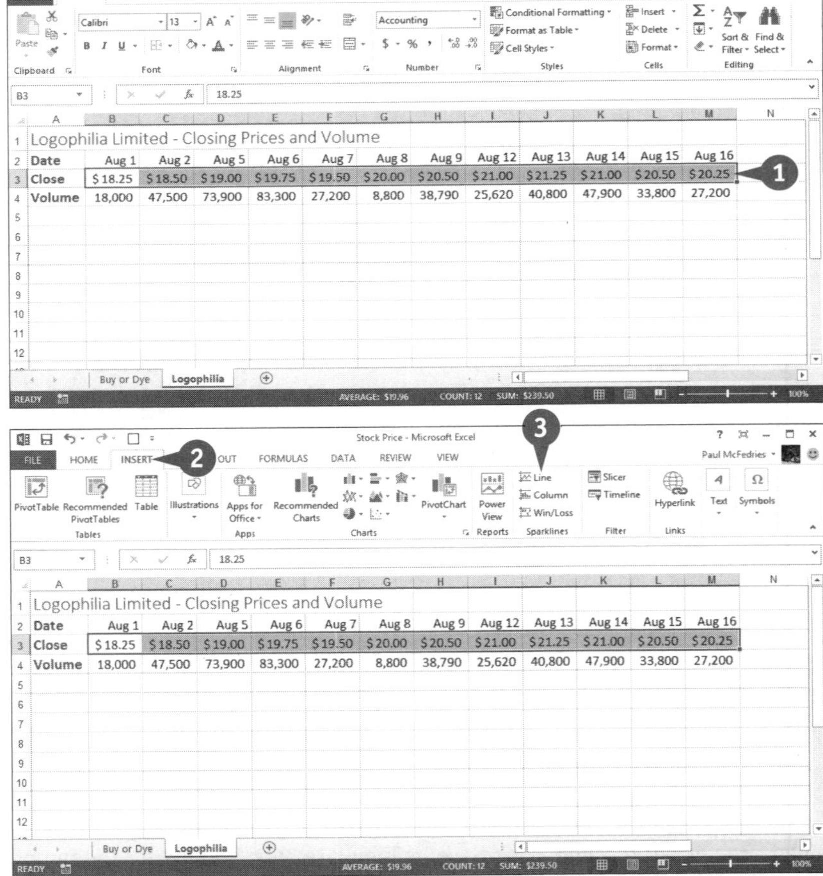

The Create Sparklines dialog box appears.

4 Click inside the Location Range box.

5 Click the cell where you want the sparkline to appear.

6 Click OK.

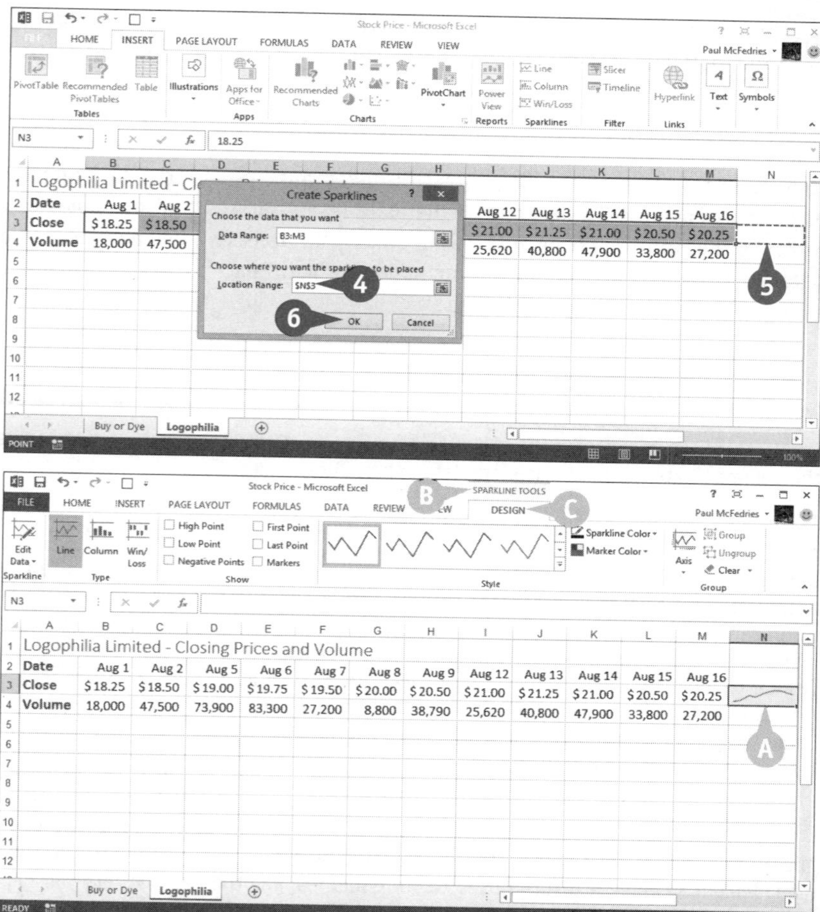

A Excel adds the sparkline to the cell.

B Excel displays the Sparkline Tools tab.

C You can use the tools in the Design tab to format your sparkline.

EXTRA

To add sparklines to multiple rows or columns of data, first select the rows or columns you want to visualize. Follow steps 2 and 3 to open the Create Sparklines dialog box and click inside the Location Range box. Select a single cell for each row or column that you have selected. For example, if you have selected five rows, select five cells. Click OK. Excel adds a sparkline for each selected row or column.

When you click a field that contains a sparkline, the Sparkline Tools appear. If you activate the Design tab, you can use the Style gallery to apply a style to your sparklines. To change the sparkline type, use the Type group to click the type you want.

Understanding External Data

External data is data that resides outside of Excel in a file, database, server, or website. You can import external data into an Excel worksheet for additional types of data analysis. A vast amount of data exists in the world, and most of it resides in some kind of non-workbook format. Some data exists in simple text files, perhaps as comma-separated lists of items. Other data resides in tables, either in Word documents or, more likely, in Access databases. There is also an increasing amount of data that resides in web pages and in XML files.

By definition, all this data is not directly available to you via Excel. However, Excel offers a number of tools that enable you to import external data into the program. Depending on your needs and on the type of data, you can either import the data into a worksheet or you can import the data directly into a PivotTable. In most cases, Excel also enables you to refresh the data so that you are always working with the most up-to-date version of the data.

External Data Types

Excel can access a wide variety of external data types. Some of the common external data types are data source files, Access tables, Word tables, text files, web pages, and XML files.

Data Source File

Open Database Connectivity (ODBC) data sources give you access to data residing in databases such as Access and dBase or on servers such as SQL Server and Oracle. However, there are many other data-source types, including data connection files (which connect to specific objects in a data source, such as an Access table), web queries, OLAP (Online Analytical Processing) cubes, query files (saved via Microsoft Query), web-based data retrieval services, and XML files.

Access Table

Microsoft Access is the Office suite's relational database management system. It is often used to store and manage the bulk of the data used by a person, team, department, or company. You can connect to Access tables either via Microsoft Query or by importing table data directly into Excel.

Word Table

Simple collections of nonrelational data are often stored in a table embedded in a Word document. You can only perform so much analysis on that data within Word, and so it is often useful to import the data from the Word table into an Excel worksheet.

Text File

Text files often contain useful data. If that data is formatted properly — for example, where each line has the same number of items, all separated by spaces, commas, or tabs — then it is possible to import that data into Excel for further analysis.

Web Page

People and companies often store useful data on web pages that reside either on the Internet or on company intranets. This data is often a combination of text and tables, but you cannot analyze web-based data in any meaningful way in your web browser. Fortunately, Excel enables you to create a web query that lets you import text and tables from a web page.

XML

XML (Extensible Markup Language) is redefining how data is stored. This is reflected in the large number of tools that Excel now has for dealing with XML data, particularly tools for importing XML data into Excel.

Access to External Data

To use external data, you must have access to it. This usually means knowing at least one of the following: the location of the data or the login information required to authorize your use of the data.

Location

By definition, external data resides somewhere other than in an Excel worksheet on your system. Therefore, to access this external data, you must at least know where it is located. Here are some of the possibilities:

- **On your computer.** The data may reside in a file on your hard drive, on a CD or DVD, or on a memory card or other removable storage medium.
- **On your network.** The data may reside in a folder on a computer that is part of your local or wide area network. If that folder has been shared with the network, and if you have the appropriate permissions to view files in that folder, then you can access the data within the files.
- **On a server.** The data may be part of a large, server-based database management system, such as SQL Server or Oracle. In this case, you need to know the name or network address of the server.
- **On a web page.** The data may reside on a web page, either as text or as a table, in which case you need to know the address of the web page.
- **On a web server.** The data may reside on a special web server that runs data retrieval services such as Windows SharePoint Services. In this case, you need to know the address of the server and the location of the data on that server.

Login

Knowing where the data is located is probably all that you require if you are dealing with a local file or database or, usually, a web page. However, after you start accessing data remotely — on a network, database server, or web server — you also require authorization to secure that access. You need to see the administrator of the resource to obtain a username or login ID as well as a password.

Import Data

After you have access to the data, your next step is to import it into Excel for analysis and manipulation. You have two choices: importing to a worksheet or to a PivotTable.

Import to Worksheet

In all cases, you can import the data directly into an Excel worksheet. Depending on the amount of data, this can make your worksheet quite large. However, having direct access to the data gives you maximum flexibility when it comes to analyzing the data. Not only can you create a PivotTable from the worksheet data, but you can also use Excel with other data-analysis tools: lists, database functions, scenarios, and what-if analysis.

Import to PivotTable

If you are building a PivotTable using the external data as the source, then in most cases Excel enables you to import the data directly into the PivotTable. The advantage here is that Excel does not have to store two copies of the data, one on a worksheet and another in the pivot cache. The disadvantage is that you can only analyze the data using the PivotTable report. Other types of data analysis that require direct access to worksheet data are not possible.

Import Data from a Data Source

You can quickly import data into just about any format by importing the data from a defined data source file. A *data connection file* is a data source that connects you to a wide variety of data, including ODBC, SQL Server, SQL Server OLAP Services, Oracle, and web-based data retrieval services.

You can also create data connection files that point to specific objects in a database, such as an Access table. Excel also considers file types such as Access databases and projects, web pages, and text files to be data sources.

Import Data from a Data Source

1. Click the Data tab.
2. Click Get External Data.
3. Click Existing Connections.

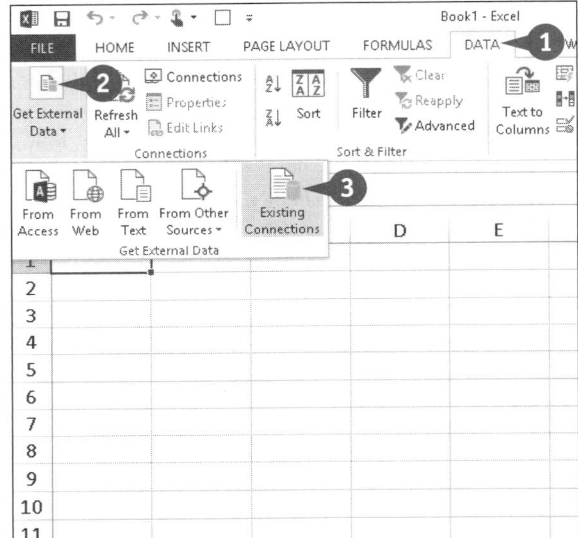

The Existing Connections dialog box appears.

4. Click the data source you want to import.
5. Click Open.

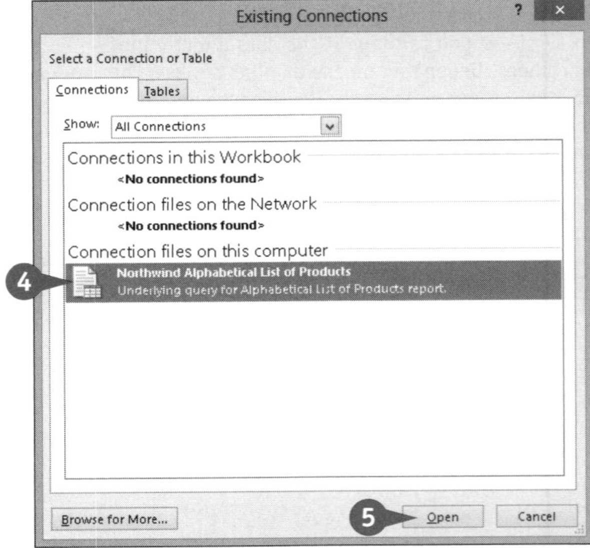

The Import Data dialog box appears.

6 Click the Table option (○ changes to ◉).

A To import the data directly into a PivotTable, click the PivotTable Report option (○ changes to ◉).

7 Click the Existing Worksheet option (○ changes to ◉).

8 Click the cell where you want the imported data to appear.

B To import the data into a new sheet, click the New Worksheet option (○ changes to ◉).

9 Click OK.

Excel imports the data into the worksheet.

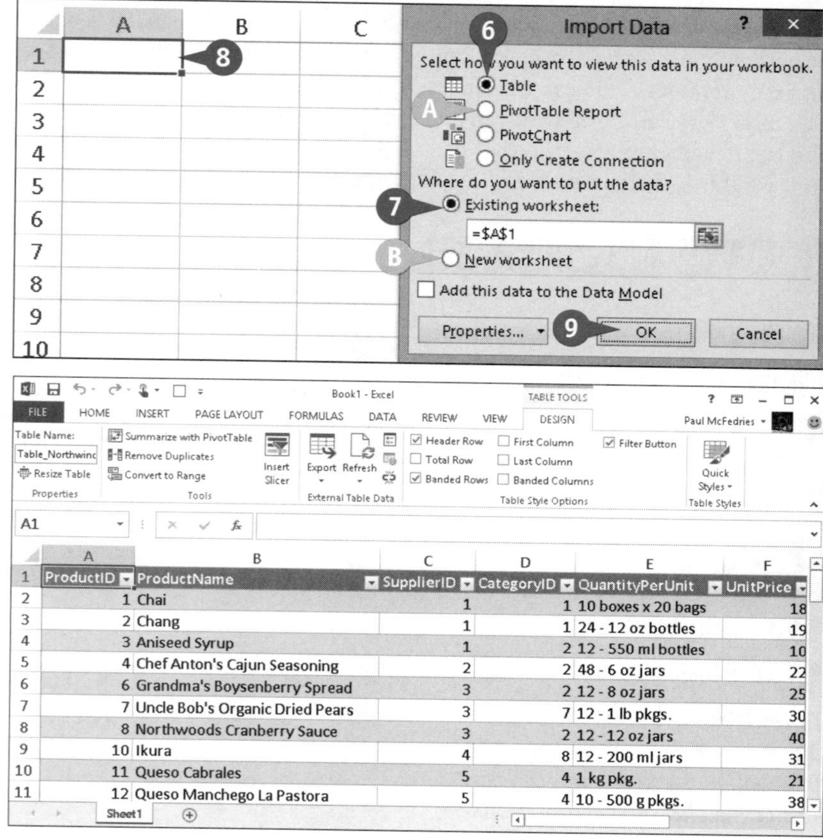

EXTRA

To create a data connection (.odc) file, click the Data tab, click Get External Data, click From Other Sources, and then click From Data Connection Wizard. Click the data source you want and then click Next. The next steps depend on the data source. For example, for Microsoft SQL Server or Oracle, you specify the server name or address and your server login data; similarly, for ODBC DSN (Database Source Name), you choose the ODBC data source, specify the location of the file, and select the table or query you want to connect to. When you get to the Import Data dialog box, click OK to import the data or click Cancel if you just want to create the data source file.

Import Data from an Access Table

If you want to use Excel to analyze data from a table within an Access database, you can import the table into an Excel worksheet. You can use Microsoft Query to perform this task. However, Excel gives you an easier way to do this: You can import the table directly from the Access database. To make this technique even easier, Excel automatically creates a data connection file for the database and table that you import. Therefore, you can import the same table in the future simply by opening the data connection file. Note, too, that you can also use the steps in this section to import data from any query that is already defined in the Access database.

Import Data from an Access Table

1. Click the Data tab.
2. Click Get External Data.
3. Click From Access.

   The Select Data Source dialog box appears.

4. Open the folder that contains the database.
5. Click the file.
6. Click Open.

Note: *If the Data Link Properties dialog box appears, make sure the login information is correct and then click Test Connection until you can connect; then click OK.*

   The Select Table dialog box appears.

7. Click the table or query you want to import.
8. Click OK.

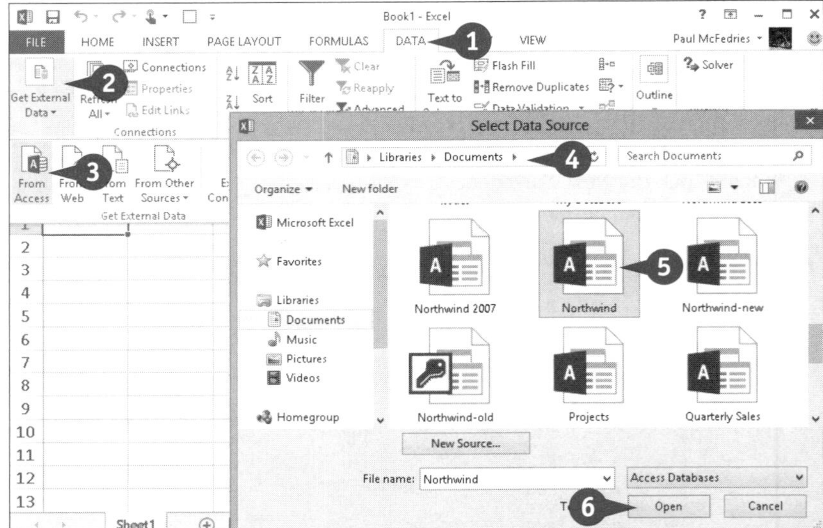

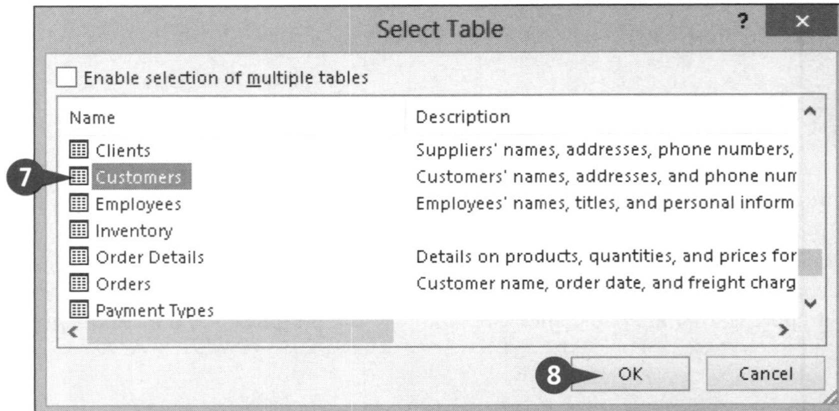

The Import Data dialog box appears.

9. Click the Table option (○ changes to ◉).

A. To import the data directly into a PivotTable, click the PivotTable Report option (○ changes to ◉).

10. Click the Existing Worksheet option (○ changes to ◉).

11. Click the cell where you want the imported data to appear.

B. To import the data into a new sheet, click the New Worksheet option (○ changes to ◉).

12. Click OK.

Excel imports the data into the worksheet.

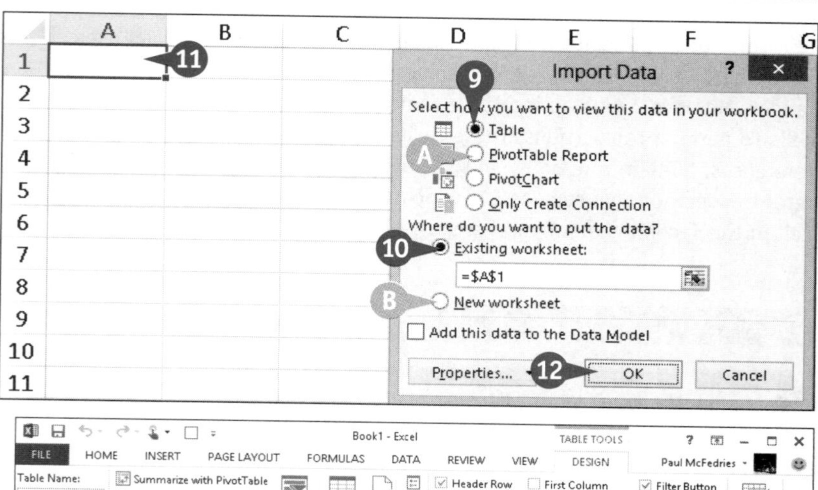

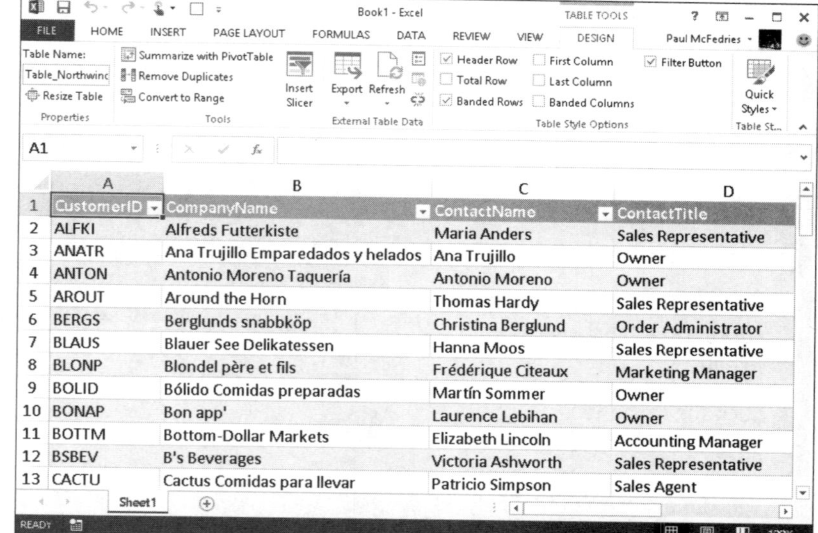

EXTRA

If the Access database requires a login password, you may need to type the password again when you refresh the imported data. To avoid this extra step, tell Excel to save the database password along with the external data. If you have the Import Data dialog box onscreen, click the Properties button; if you have already imported the data, click the Data tab, click the Refresh All down arrow, and then select Connection Properties from the drop-down list. In the Connection Properties dialog box, click the Definition tab, click the Save Password check box (☐ changes to ☑), click Yes, and then click OK.

Import Data from a Word Table

Word tables are collections of rows, columns, and cells, which means they look something like Excel ranges. Moreover, you can insert fields into Word table cells to perform calculations. These fields support cell references, built-in functions, and operators. Cell references refer to specific cells, such as B1, which refers to the cell in the second column and first row of a table. You can use cell references with built-in functions such as SUM and AVERAGE, and operators such as addition (+), multiplication (*), and greater than (>), to build formulas that calculate results based on the table data. However, Excel still offers far more sophisticated data-analysis tools. Therefore, to analyze your Word table data properly, you should import the table into an Excel worksheet.

Import Data from a Word Table

1. Launch Microsoft Word and open the document that contains the table.
2. Click a cell inside the table you want to import.
3. Click the Layout tab.
4. Click Select.
5. Click Select Table.

   A. You can also select the table by clicking the table selection handle.

6. Click the Home tab.
7. Click Copy.

   You can also press Ctrl+C.

   Word copies the table to the Clipboard.

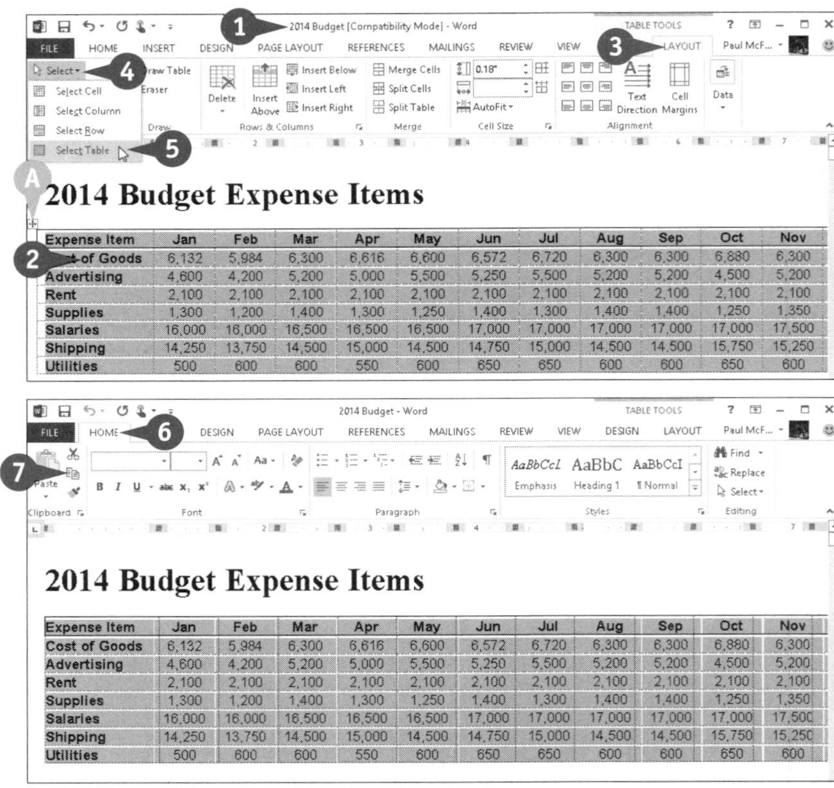

8. Switch to the Excel workbook into which you want to import the table.
9. Click the cell where you want the table to appear.
10. Click the Home tab.
11. Click Paste.

    You can also press Ctrl+V.

    Excel pastes the Word table data.

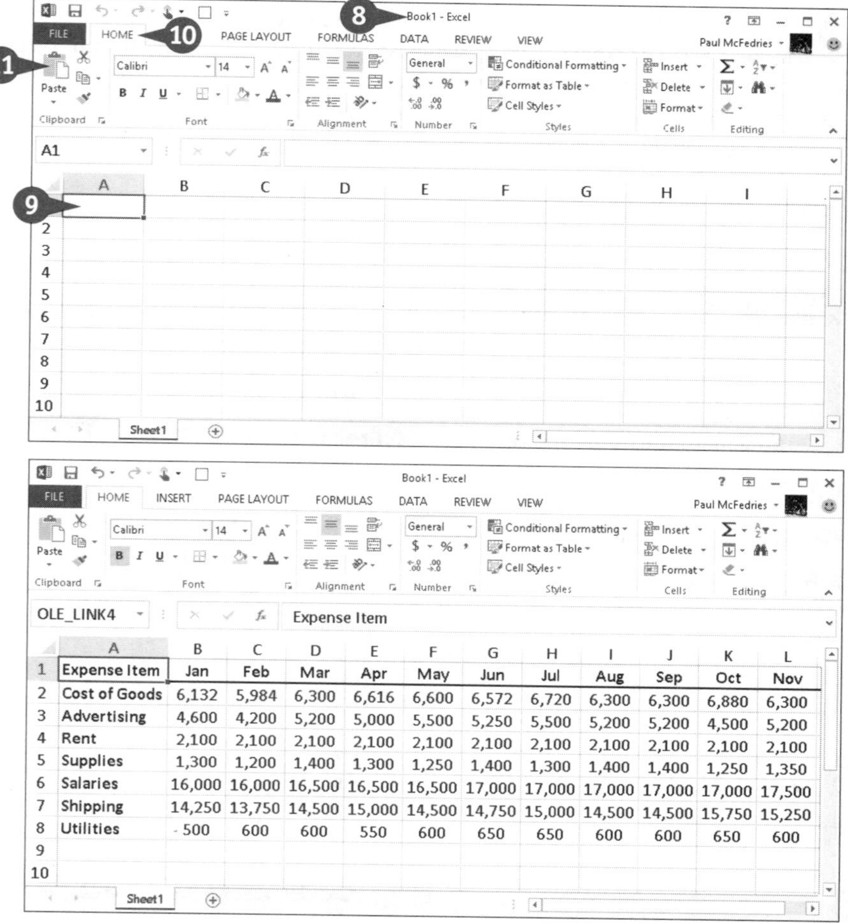

Expense Item	Jan	Feb	Mar	Apr	May	Jun	Jul	Aug	Sep	Oct	Nov
Cost of Goods	6,132	5,984	6,300	6,616	6,600	6,572	6,720	6,300	6,300	6,880	6,300
Advertising	4,600	4,200	5,200	5,000	5,500	5,250	5,500	5,200	5,200	4,500	5,200
Rent	2,100	2,100	2,100	2,100	2,100	2,100	2,100	2,100	2,100	2,100	2,100
Supplies	1,300	1,200	1,400	1,300	1,250	1,400	1,300	1,400	1,400	1,250	1,350
Salaries	16,000	16,000	16,500	16,500	16,500	17,000	17,000	17,000	17,000	17,000	17,500
Shipping	14,250	13,750	14,500	15,000	14,500	14,750	15,000	14,500	14,500	15,750	15,250
Utilities	500	600	600	550	600	650	650	600	600	650	600

EXTRA

If you make changes to the Word data, those changes are not automatically reflected in the Excel data. If this is a concern, shift the data's container application from Word to Excel. After you paste the table data into Excel, copy the Excel range, switch to Word, click the Home tab, click the Paste down arrow, and then click Paste Special. In the Paste Special dialog box, click HTML Format in the As list, click the Paste Link option (○ changes to ◉), and then click OK. The resulting table is linked to the Excel data, which means that any changes you make to the data in Excel automatically appear in the Word table. However, if you change the data in Word, you cannot update the data in Excel.

Nowadays, most data resides in some kind of special format: Excel workbook, Access database, web page, and so on. However, it is still relatively common to find data stored in simple text files because text is a universal format that users can work with on any system and in a wide variety of programs. You can analyze the data contained in certain text files by importing the data into an Excel worksheet. Note, however, that you cannot import just any text file into Excel; it needs to be in the form of *delimited* or *fixed-width* text files.

Import Data from a Text File

Start the Text Import Wizard

1. Click the cell where you want the imported data to appear.
2. Click the Data tab.
3. Click Get External Data.
4. Click From Text.

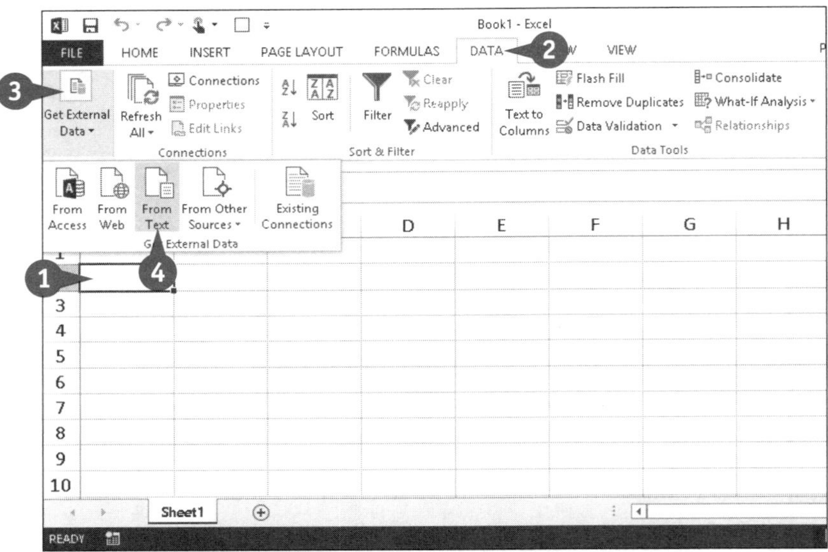

The Import Text File dialog box appears.

5. Open the folder that contains the text file.
6. Click the text file.
7. Click Import.

The Text Import Wizard – Step 1 of 3 dialog box appears.

***Note:** For delimited text, continue to the steps under "Import Delimited Data"; for fixed-width text, skip to "Import Fixed-Width Data."*

Import Delimited Data

1. Click the Delimited option (◯ changes to ◉).
2. Click the Start Import at Row spin box arrows to set the first row you want to import.
3. If the first import row consists of column headers, click the My Data Has Headers check box (☐ changes to ☑).
4. Click Next.

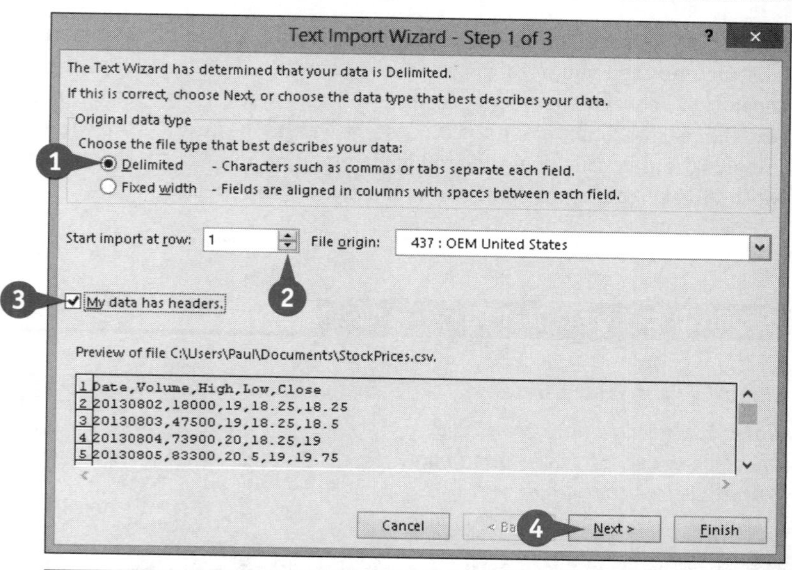

The Text Import Wizard – Step 2 of 3 dialog box appears.

5. Click the check box beside the delimiter character that your text data uses (☐ changes to ☑).

A If you choose the correct delimiter, the data appears in separate columns.

6. Click Next.

The Text Import Wizard – Step 3 of 3 dialog box appears.

***Note:** To complete this section, follow the steps under the subsection, "Finish the Text Import Wizard."*

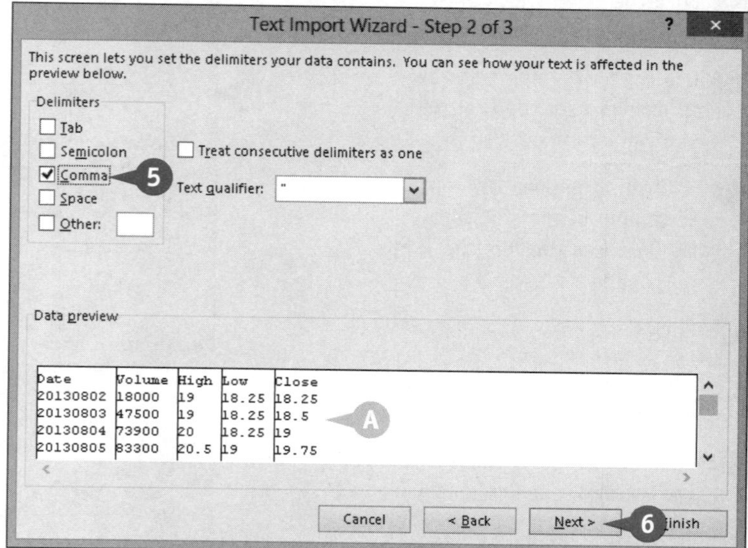

EXTRA

A delimited text file uses a structure in which each item on a line of text is separated by a character called a delimiter. The most common text delimiter is the comma (,). When Excel imports a delimited text file, it treats each line of text as a record and each item between the delimiter as a field.

A fixed-width text file uses a structure in which all the items on a line of text use a set amount of space — for example, 10 characters or 20 characters — and these fixed widths are the same on every line of text. Excel imports a fixed-width text file by treating each line of text as a record and each fixed-width item as a field.

continued

If you are importing data that uses the fixed-width structure, then you need to tell Excel where the separation between each field occurs. In a fixed-width text file, each column of data is a constant width. The Text Import Wizard is usually quite good at determining the width of each column of data, and in most cases the wizard automatically sets up *column break lines*, which are vertical lines that separate one field from the next. However, titles or introductory text at the beginning of the file can impair the wizard's calculations, so you should check carefully that the proposed break lines are accurate.

Import Data from a Text File (continued)

Import Fixed-Width Data

Note: *You need to have completed the steps under "Start the Text Import Wizard" before continuing with this section.*

1. Click the Fixed Width option (○ changes to ◉).
2. Use the Start Import at Row spin box to set the first row you want to import.
3. If the first import row consists of column headers, click the My Data Has Headers check box (☐ changes to ☑).
4. Click Next.

   The Text Import Wizard – Step 2 of 3 dialog box appears.
5. Click and drag a break line to set the width of each column.

   To create a break line, you can click the ruler at the point where you want the break to appear.

   To delete a break line, you can double-click it.
6. Click Next.

   The Text Import Wizard – Step 3 of 3 dialog box appears.

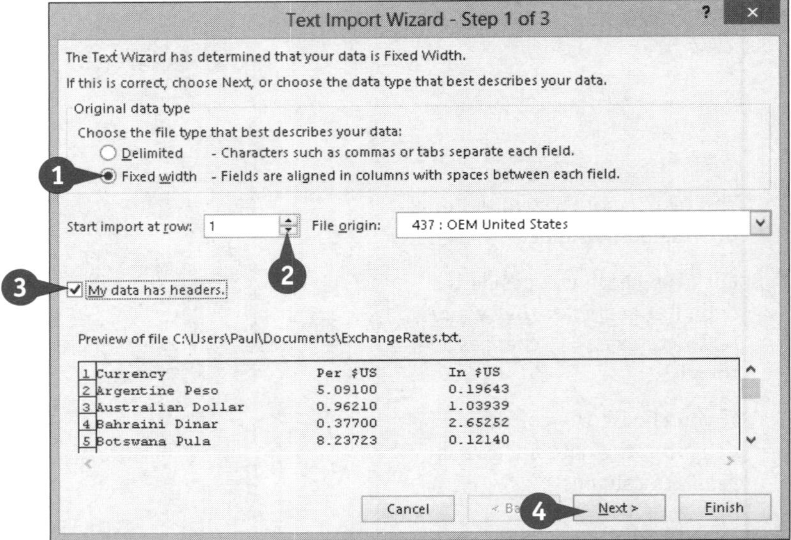

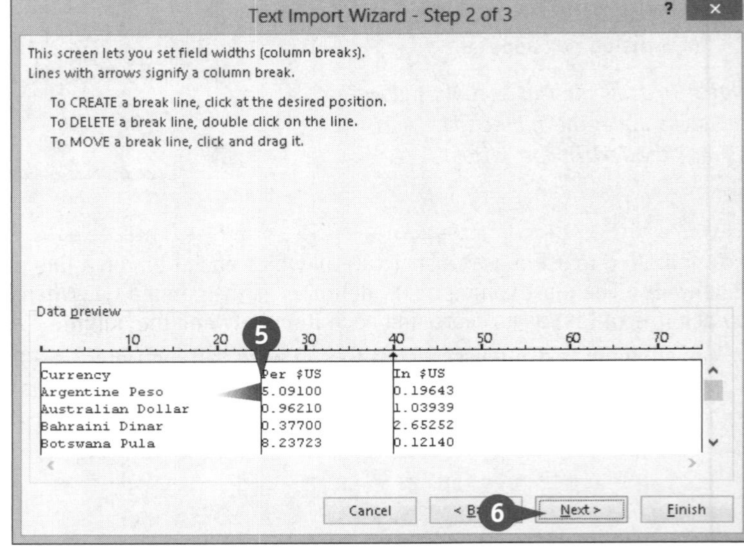

Finish the Text Import Wizard

1. Click a column.
2. Click the Column data format option that you want Excel to apply to the column (○ changes to ◉).

   A If you select the Date option, click the down arrow and select the date format your data uses from the drop-down list.

3. Repeat steps 1 and 2 to set the data format for all of the columns.
4. Click Finish.

   The Import Data dialog box appears.

5. Click the Existing Worksheet option (○ changes to ◉).

   B If you want the data to appear in a new sheet, you can click the New Worksheet option instead (○ changes to ◉).

6. Click OK.

   Excel imports the data to the worksheet.

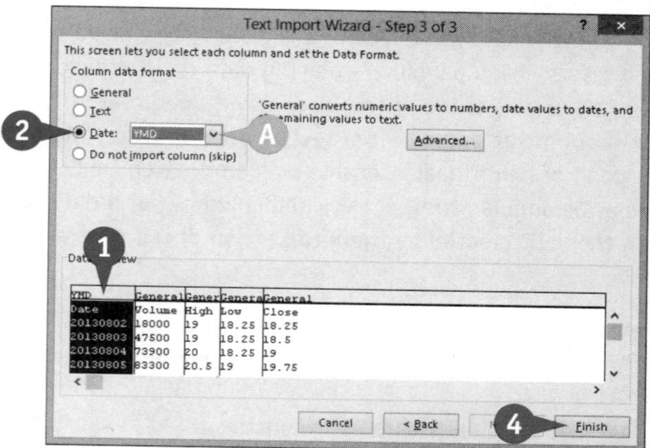

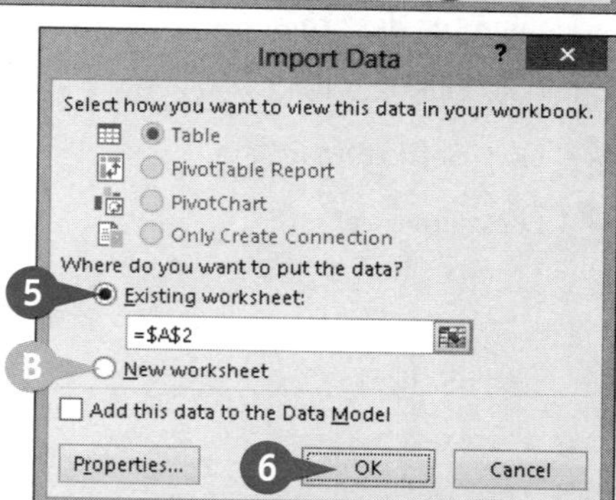

	A	B	C	D	E
1					
2	Date	Volume	High	Low	Close
3	8/2/2013	18000	19	18.25	18.25
4	8/3/2013	47500	19	18.25	18.5
5	8/4/2013	73900	20	18.25	19
6	8/5/2013	83300	20.5	19	19.75
7	8/6/2013	27200	20.25	19.5	19.5
8	8/9/2013	8800	20.25	19.5	20
9	8/10/2013	387900	20.5	19.5	20.5
10	8/11/2013	256200	21.75	20.25	21.5

EXTRA

Some text files use a comma instead of a dot as the decimal separator. To import such data, click the Advanced button in the Text Import Wizard – Step 3 of 3 dialog box to display the Advanced Text Import Settings dialog box. Click the Decimal separator down arrow and then click the text's decimal separator. If you make a mistake when importing a text file, you do not need to start the import from the beginning. Click any cell in the imported data, click the Data tab, click the Refresh All down arrow, and then select Connection Properties from the drop-down list. Click the Definition tab and then click Edit Query. Click the file you want to import and then click Import. Excel launches the Import Text Wizard again.

Import Data from a Web Page

To make data more readily available to a wide variety of users, many people are placing data on web pages that are accessible through the Internet or a corporate network. Although this data is often text, most web page data comes in one of two formats: a table or preformatted text. A *table* is a rectangular array of rows and columns, with data values in the cells created by the intersection of the rows and columns. *Preformatted text* is text that has been structured with predefined spacing. In many cases, you can use this spacing to organize data into columns with fixed widths. Both types of data are suitable for import into Excel, which enables you to perform more extensive data analysis using the Excel tools.

Import Data from a Web Page

1. Click the cell where you want the imported data to appear.
2. Click the Data tab.
3. Click Get External Data.
4. Click From Web.

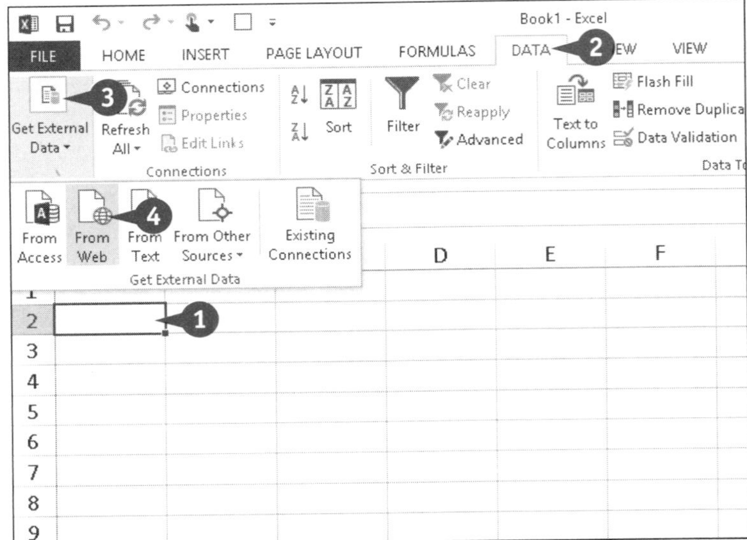

The New Web Query dialog box appears.

5. Type the address of the web page.
6. Click Go.

A. Excel loads the page into the dialog box.

7. Click the Select Table icon beside the table that you want to import.

B. Excel selects the table.

8. Click Import.

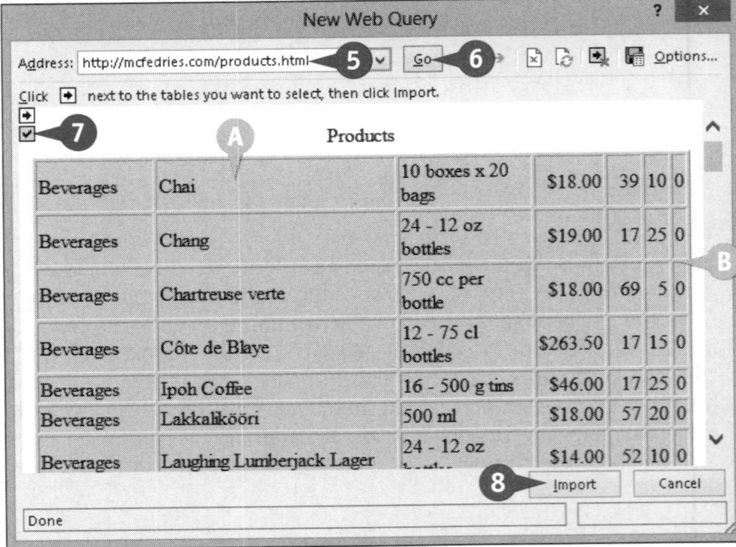

The Import Data dialog box appears.

9 Click the Existing Worksheet option (○ changes to ◉).

C If you want the data to appear in a new sheet, you can click the New Worksheet option instead (○ changes to ◉).

10 Click OK.

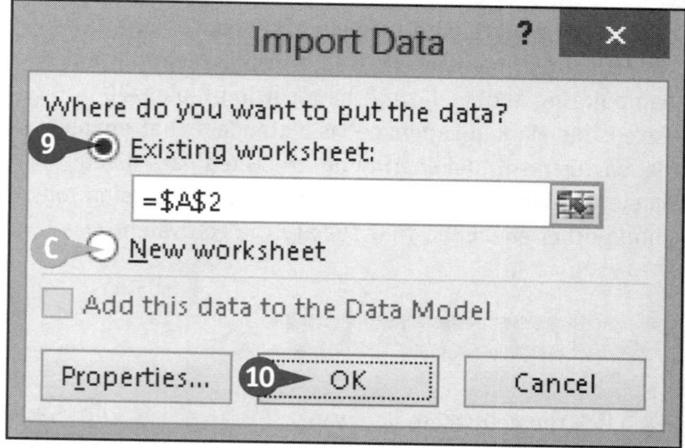

Excel imports the data to the worksheet.

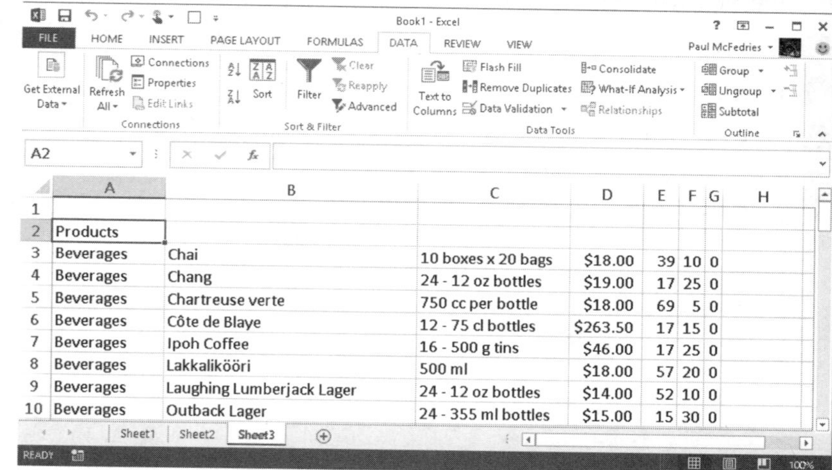

APPLY IT

Excel gives you two other methods for creating web queries:

- Right-click the page and then click Export to Microsoft Excel.
- Copy the web page text, switch to Excel, and then paste the text. When the Paste Options smart tag appears, click the smart tag down arrow and then click Refreshable Web Query.

Each of these methods opens the New Web Query dialog box and automatically loads the web page. If you want to save the web query for future use in other workbooks, click Save Query (💾) in the New Web Query dialog box and then use the Save Workspace dialog box to save the query file.

Import Data from an XML File

You can analyze data that currently resides in XML format by importing that data into Excel and then manipulating and analyzing the resulting table. *XML* (Extensible Markup Language) is a standard that enables the management and sharing of structured data using simple text files. These XML files organize data using *tags,* among other elements, that specify the equivalent of a table name and field names. Because XML is just text, if you want to perform data analysis on the XML file, you must import the file into an Excel worksheet. Excel usually stores imported XML data in an *XML table,* a range that looks and operates much like a regular Excel table, except that it has a few XML-specific features.

Import Data from an XML File

1. Click the cell where you want the imported data to appear.
2. Click the Data tab.
3. Click Get External Data.
4. Click From Other Sources.
5. Click From XML Data Import.

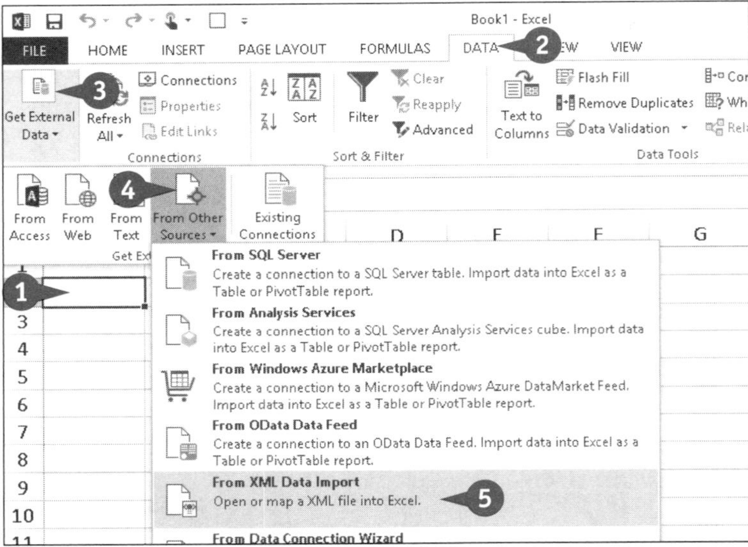

The Select Data Source dialog box appears.

6. Select the folder that contains the XML file you want to import.
7. Click the XML file.
8. Click Open.

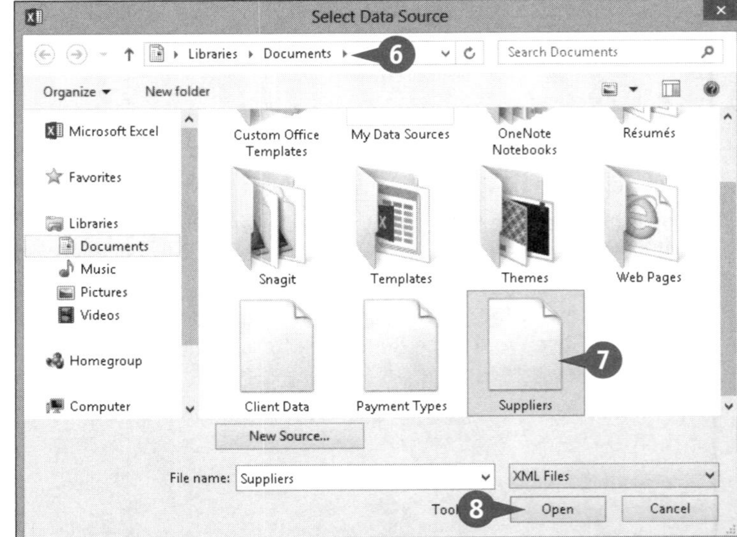

Note: *If you see a dialog box telling you there is a problem with the data, click OK.*

The Import Data dialog box appears.

9 Click the XML Table in Existing Worksheet option (○ changes to ◉).

10 Click OK.

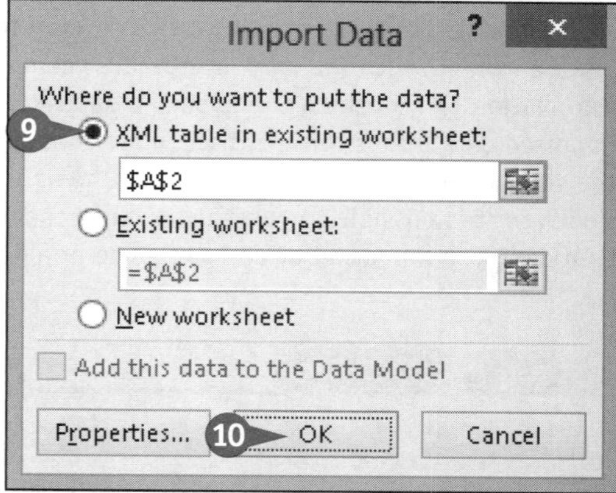

Excel imports the data into the worksheet as an XML table.

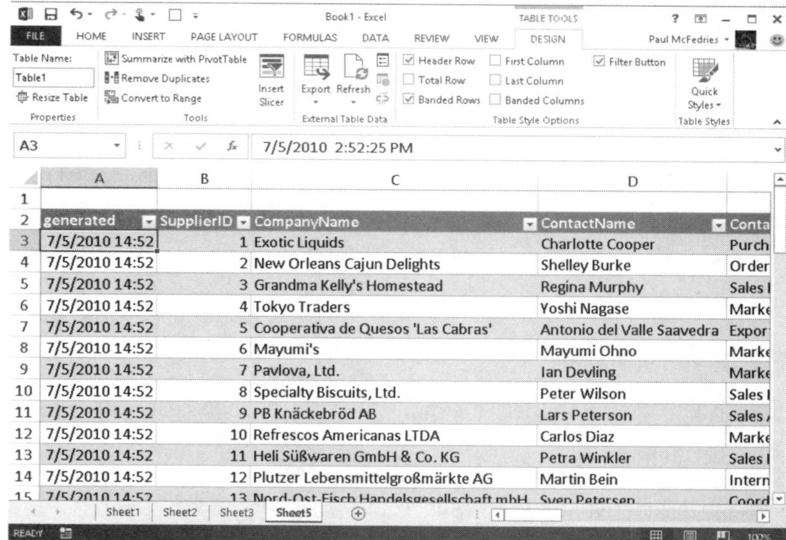

EXTRA

An XML file is a text file that uses a specific structure. Here is a simple XML example that constitutes a single record in a table named Product:

```
<Products>
<ProductName>Chai</ProductName>
<CompanyName>Exotic Liquids</CompanyName>
<ContactName>Charlotte Cooper</ContactName>
</Products>
```

To remove a field from the XML table, right-click the table, click XML, and then click XML Source to display the XML Source pane. To remove an element, right-click it and then click Remove Element.

Refresh Imported Data

External data often changes; you can ensure that you are working with the most up-to-date version of the information by refreshing the imported data. Refreshing the imported data means retrieving the most current version of the source data. This is usually a straightforward operation. However, it is possible to construct a query that accesses confidential information or destroys some or all of the external data. Therefore, when you refresh imported data, Excel always lets you know the potential risks and asks if you are sure the query is safe. Remember that most external data resides on servers or in remote network locations. Therefore, the refresh may take some time, depending on the amount of data, the load on the server, and the amount of traffic on the network.

Refresh Imported Data

Refresh Non-text Data

1 Click any cell inside the imported data.

	A	B	C	D	E	F	G	H
1								
2	Products							
3	Beverages	Chai	10 boxes x 20 bags	$18.00	39	10	0	
4	Beverages	Chang	24 - 12 oz bottles	$19.00	17	25	0	
5	Beverages	Chartreuse verte	750 cc per bottle	$18.00	69	5	0	
6	Beverages	Côte de Blaye	12 - 75 cl bottles	$263.50	17	15	0	
7	Beverages	Ipoh Coffee	16 - 500 g tins	$46.00	17	25	0	
8	Beverages	Lakkaliköōri	500 ml	$18.00	57	20	0	
9	Beverages	Laughing Lumberjack Lager	24 - 12 oz bottles	$14.00	52	10	0	
10	Beverages	Outback Lager	24 - 355 ml bottles	$15.00	15	30	0	
11	Beverages	Rhönbräu Klosterbier	24 - 0.5 l bottles	$7.75	125	25	0	
12	Beverages	Sasquatch Ale	24 - 12 oz bottles	$14.00	111	15	0	
13	Beverages	Steeleye Stout	24 - 12 oz bottles	$18.00	20	15	0	
14	Condiments	Aniseed Syrup	12 - 550 ml bottles	$10.00	13	25	0	
15	Condiments	Chef Anton's Cajun Seasoning	48 - 6 oz jars	$22.00	53	0	0	

2 Click the Data tab.

3 Click the Refresh All down arrow.

4 Click Refresh.

Note: *You can also refresh the current data by pressing Alt+F5.*

A To refresh all the imported data in the current workbook, you can click Refresh All, or press Ctrl+Alt+F5.

Excel refreshes the imported data.

Refresh Text Data

1. Click any cell inside the imported text data.
2. Click the Data tab.
3. Click the Refresh All down arrow.
4. Click Refresh.

Note: *You can also refresh the current data by pressing Alt+F5.*

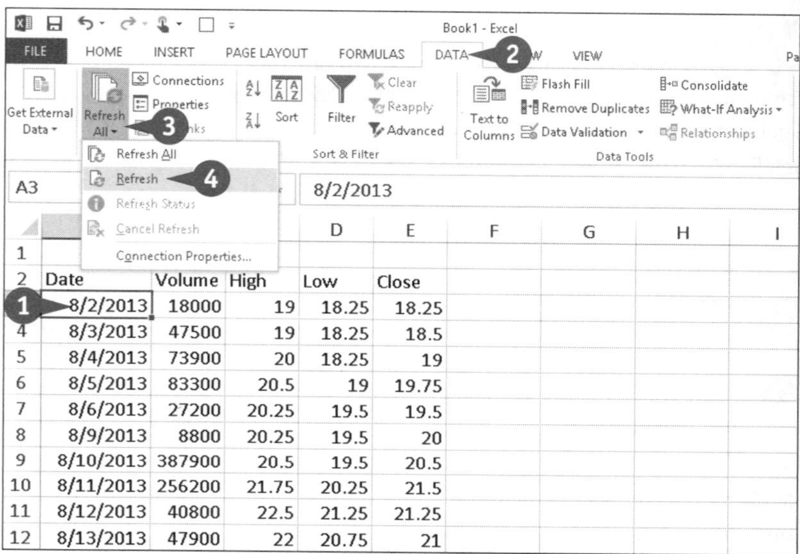

The Import Text File dialog box appears.

5. Open the folder that contains the text file.
6. Click the text file.
7. Click Import.

Excel refreshes the imported text data.

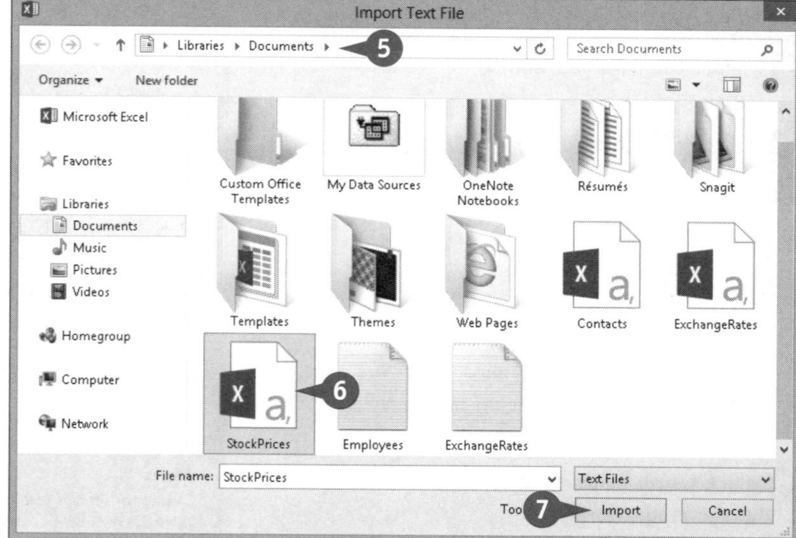

EXTRA

In most cases, you can set up a schedule that automatically refreshes the data at a specified interval. Follow steps 1 to 3 under "Refresh Non-text Data," and then click Connection Properties. Click the Refresh Every check box (☐ changes to ☑) and then use the spin box to specify the refresh interval, in minutes. Note that not every type of imported data supports this feature.

If the refresh is taking a long time, check the refresh status by following steps 1 to 3 under "Refresh Non-text Data" and then clicking Refresh Status to display the External Data Refresh Status dialog box; click Close to continue the refresh. If the refresh is taking too long, follow steps 1 to 3 again, and then click Cancel Refresh to stop it.

Separate Cell Text into Columns

You can make imported data easier to analyze by separating the text in each cell into two or more columns of data. An imported data column may contain multiple items of data. In imported contact data, for example, a column might contain each person's first and last name, separated by a space. This is problematic if you want to sort the contacts by last name, so you need some way of separating the names into their own columns. Excel makes this easy by offering the Text to Columns feature, which examines a column of data and then separates it into two or more columns.

Separate Cell Text into Columns

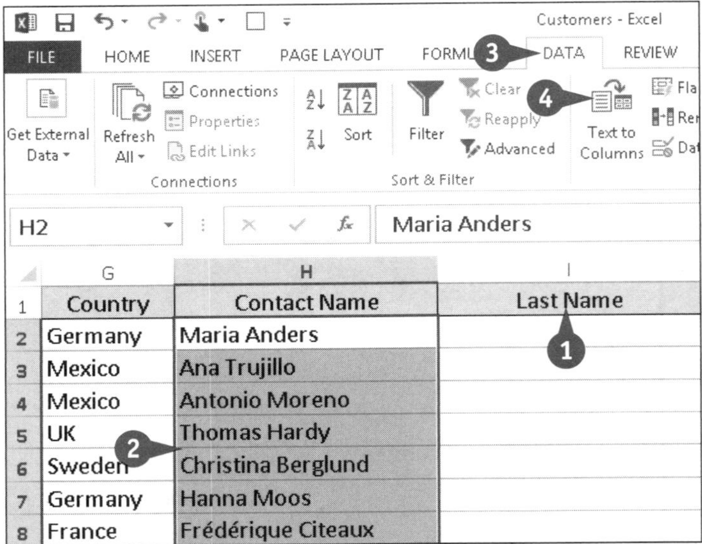

1. Insert a column to the right of the column you want to separate.

Note: *If the data will separate into three or more columns, you can insert as many new columns as you need to hold the separated data.*

2. Select the data you want to separate.
3. Click the Data tab.
4. Click Text to Columns.

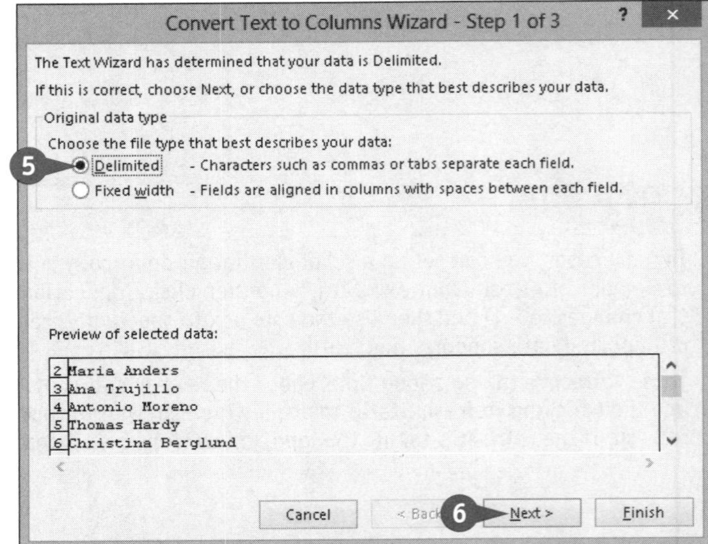

The Convert Text to Columns Wizard – Step 1 of 3 dialog box appears.

5. Click the Delimited option (○ changes to ◉).
6. Click Next.

7 Click the check box beside the delimiter character that your text data uses (☐ changes to ☑).

A If you choose the correct delimiter, the data appears in separate columns.

8 Click Next.

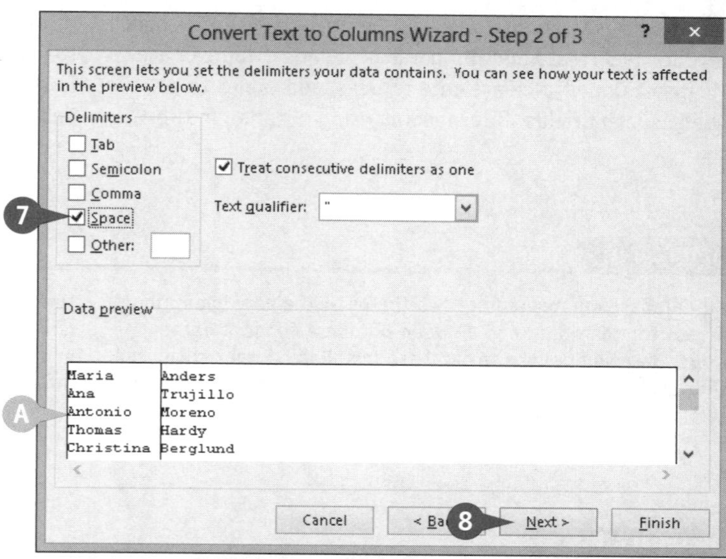

9 Click a column.

10 Click to select the data format you want Excel to apply to the column.

B If you click the Date option, you can use this list to click the date format your data uses.

11 Repeat steps 9 and 10 to set the data format for all the columns.

12 Click Finish.

Excel asks if you want to replace the contents of the destination cells.

13 Click OK (not shown).

Excel separates the data.

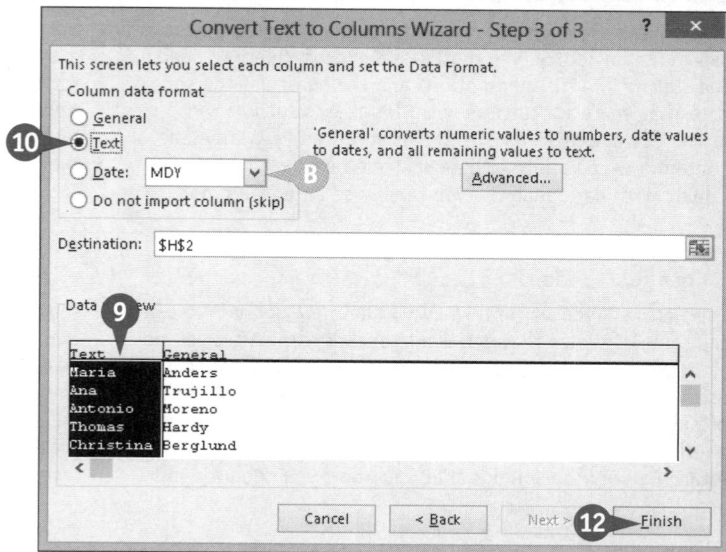

EXTRA

If your column contains fixed-width text, follow steps 1 to 4 to start the Convert Text to Columns Wizard. Click the Fixed Width option (○ changes to ◉), and then click Next. Click and drag a break line to set the width of each column, and then click Next. Follow steps 9 to 13 to complete the wizard.

Excel does not always create just one extra column from the data. For example, in a column of contact names, if any of those names use three words, Excel assumes that you want to create two extra columns for the data. Unfortunately, this may cause Excel to overwrite some of your existing data. Therefore, before separating data into columns, check the data to see how many columns Excel will create.

Understanding Microsoft Query

In Excel, you can use a special program, called Microsoft Query, to create and run database queries. You can use Microsoft Query to create data sources, add tables to a query, specify fields, filter records using criteria, and sort records. You can also save your queries as query files so that you can reuse them later. If you start Microsoft Query from within Excel, you can return the query records to Excel and use them in a table or PivotTable.

Data Source

All database queries require two things at the very beginning: access to a database and an *Open Database Connectivity*, or *ODBC*, data source for the database installed on your computer. ODBC is a database standard that enables a program to connect to and manipulate a data source. An ODBC data source contains three things: a pointer to the file or server where the database resides; a driver that enables Microsoft Query to connect to, manipulate, and return data from the database; and the login information that you require to access the database.

Database Query

If you want to analyze data using a sorted, filtered subset of an external data source, you must use Microsoft Query to specify the sorting and filtering options and the subset of the source data that you want to work with. Databases such as those used in Microsoft Access and SQL Server are often very large and contain a wide variety of data scattered over many different tables. With data analysis, you rarely use an entire database as the source for the report. Instead, you can extract a subset of the database: a table, or perhaps two or three related tables. You may also require the data to be sorted in a certain way and you may need to filter the data so that you only work with certain records. You can accomplish all three operations — extracting a subset, sorting, and filtering — by creating a database query.

Select Tables and Fields

The first task you perform when you define a query is to select the table or tables that you want to work with. After you do that, you select the fields from those tables that you want to use in your worksheet or PivotTable. Because external databases often contain a large amount of data, you can speed up your queries and reduce the amount of memory Excel uses by returning only those fields that you know you need for your analysis.

Filter Records

You may not require all of a table's records in your analysis. For example, if a table contains invoice data for several years, you may only want to work with records from a particular year. Similarly, you may be interested in records for a particular product, country, or employee. In each case, you can configure the database query to *filter* the records so that you only get the records you want.

Sort Records

A database query also enables you to sort the data that you are extracting. This does not matter too much with a PivotTable because Excel sorts the field items in ascending alphabetical order by default. However, the sorting option is important if you import the data into your Excel worksheet.

Query Criteria

You can specify the filtering part of a database query by specifying one or more *criteria*. These are usually logical expressions that, when applied to each record in the query's underlying table, return either a true or a false result. Every record that returns a true result is included in the query, and every record that returns a false result is filtered out of the query. For example, if you only want to work with records where the Country field is USA, then you can set up criteria to handle this, and the query discards all records where the Country field is not equal to USA. The following table lists the operators you can use to build your criteria expressions:

Operator	Value in the Field
Equal (=)	Is equal to a specified value
Does not equal (<>)	Is not equal to a specified value
Is greater than (>)	Is greater than a specified value
Is greater than or equal to (>=)	Is greater than or equal to a specified value
Is less than (<)	Is less than a specified value
Is less than or equal to (<=)	Is less than or equal to a specified value
Is one of	Is included in a group of values
Is not one of	Is not included in a group of values
Is between	Is between (and including) one value and another
Is not between	Is not between one value and another
Begins with	Begins with the specified characters
Does not begin with	Does not begin with the specified characters
Ends with	Ends with the specified characters
Does not end with	Does not end with the specified characters
Contains	Contains the specified characters
Does not contain	Does not contain the specified characters
Like	Matches a specified pattern
Not like	Does not match a specified pattern
Is null	Is empty
Is not null	Is not empty

Microsoft Query

You can use Microsoft Query to create data sources, add tables to the query, specify fields, filter records using criteria, and sort records. You can also save your queries as query files so that you can reuse them later. If you start Microsoft Query from within Excel, you can return the query records to Excel and use them in a worksheet or PivotTable.

Define a Data Source

Before you can do any work in Microsoft Query, you must select the data source that you want to use. If you have a particular database that you want to query, you can define a new data source that points to the appropriate file or server.

Most data sources point to database files. For example, the relational database management program Microsoft Access uses file-based databases. You can also create data sources based on text files and Excel workbooks. However, some data sources point to server-based databases. For example, SQL Server and Oracle run their databases on special servers. As part of the data source definition, you need to include the software driver that Microsoft Query uses to communicate with the database, and any information that you require to access the database.

Define a Data Source

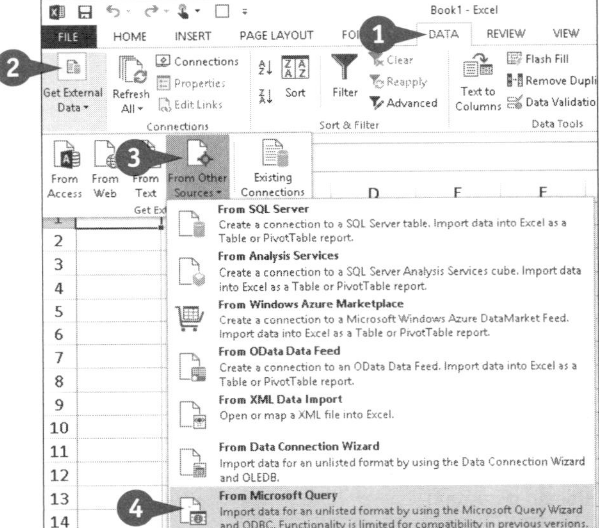

1. Click the Data tab.
2. Click Get External Data.
3. Click From Other Sources.
4. Click From Microsoft Query.

The Choose Data Source dialog box appears.

5. Click New Data Source.
6. Click to deselect the Use the Query Wizard to Create/Edit Queries check box (☑ changes to ☐).
7. Click OK.

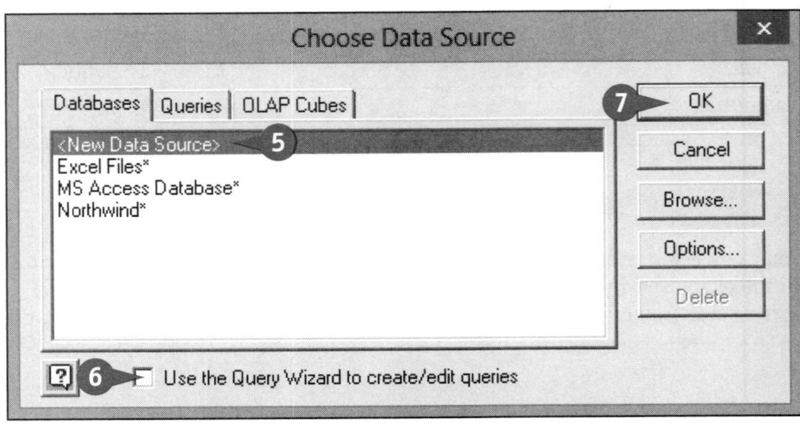

The Create New Data Source dialog box appears.

8. Type a name for your data source.
9. Click the Select a Driver for the Type of Database down arrow and then select the database driver that your data source requires from the drop-down list.
10. Click Connect.

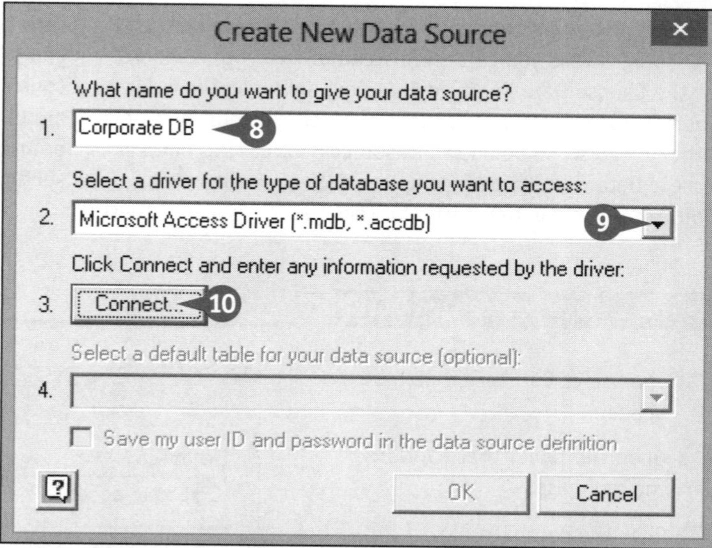

The dialog box for the database driver appears.

Note: *The steps that follow show you how to set up a data source for a Microsoft Access database.*

11. Click Select.

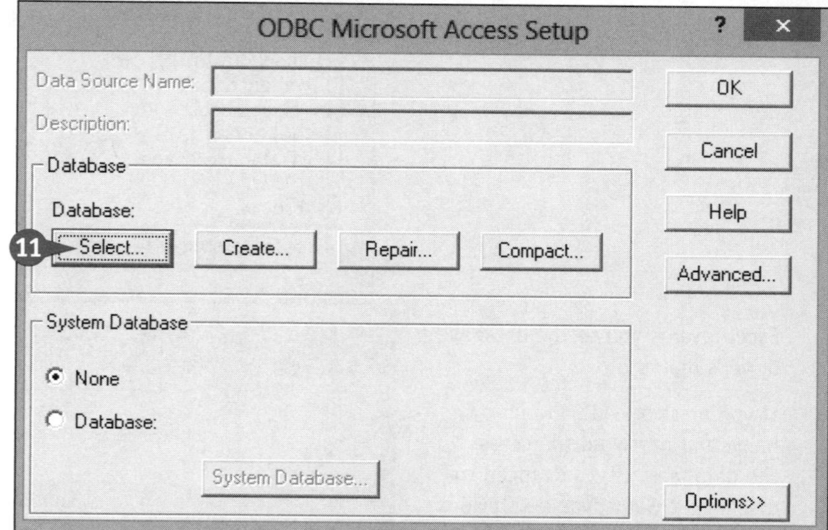

APPLY IT

Many businesses store their data in Microsoft SQL Server databases. This is a powerful server-based system that can handle the largest databases and thousands of users. To define a SQL Server data source, first follow steps 1 to 8. From the database drivers drop-down list, select SQL Server. Click Connect to display the SQL Server Login dialog box. Ask your SQL Server database administrator for the information you require to complete this dialog box. Type the name or remote address of the SQL Server in the Server text box, type your SQL Server login ID and password, and then click OK. Perform steps 16 and 17 later in this section to complete the data source.

continued

Your system probably comes with a few predefined data sources that you can use instead of creating new ones. In the Choose Data Source dialog box, any predefined data sources appear in the Databases tab. For example, Microsoft Office creates two default data sources: Excel Files and MS Access Database. These incomplete data sources do not point to a specific file. Instead, when you click one of these data sources and then click OK, Microsoft Query prompts you for the name and location of the file. These data sources are useful if you often switch the files that you are using. However, if you want a data source that always points to a specific file, you need to follow the steps in this section.

Define a Data Source (continued)

The Select Database dialog box appears.

12 Open the folder that contains the database.

13 Click the database file.

14 Click OK.

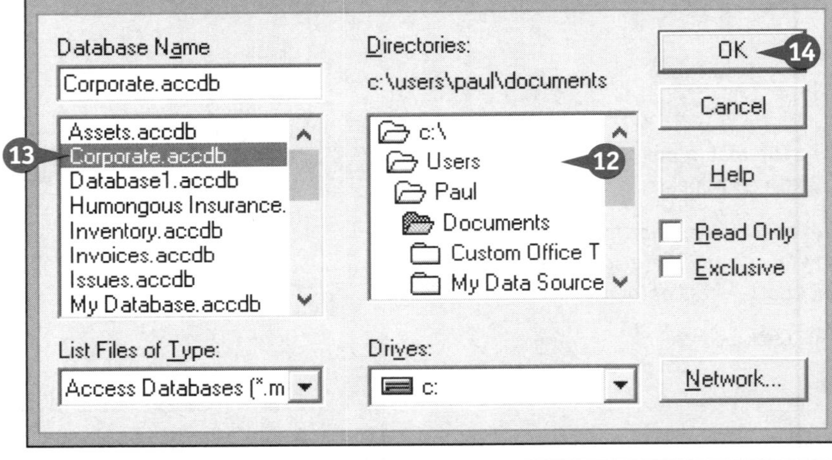

Excel returns you to the database driver's dialog box.

A If you must provide a login name and password to access the database, click Advanced to display the Set Advanced Options dialog box. Type the login name and password and then click OK.

15 Click OK.

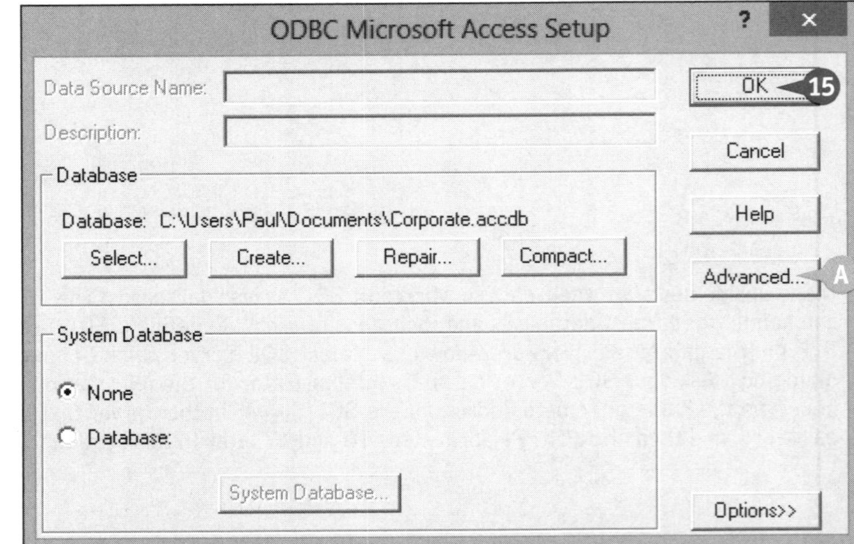

Excel returns you to the Create New Data Source dialog box.

B If you specified a login name and password as part of the data source, you can click the Save My User ID and Password in the Data Source Definition check box (☐ changes to ☑) to save the login data.

16 Click OK.

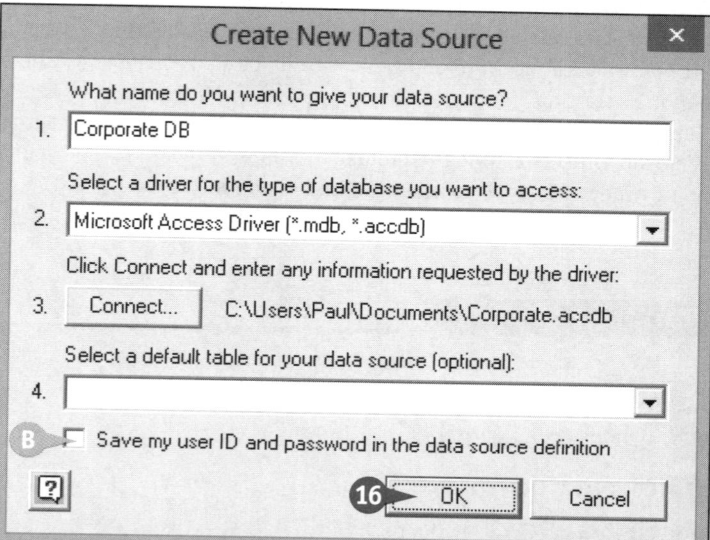

You return to the Choose Data Source dialog box.

17 Click Cancel to bypass the steps for importing the data.

You can now use the data source in Microsoft Query.

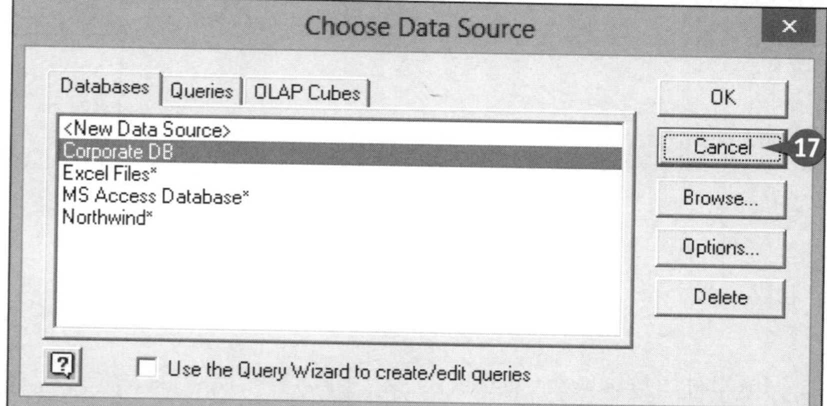

EXTRA

In the Create New Data Source dialog box, you can click the Select a Default Table for Your Data Source down arrow and then click a table from the Access database. When you do this, each time you start a new query based on this data source, Microsoft Query automatically adds the default table to the query, thus saving you several steps. If you have a data source that you no longer use, you should delete it to ensure that only usable data sources appear in the Choose Data Source dialog box. Follow steps 1 to 4 to display the Choose Data Source dialog box. Click the data source and then click the Delete button. When Microsoft Query asks you to confirm the deletion, click Yes.

Start Microsoft Query

To create a query that defines the fields and records that you want to return to and work with in Excel, you must begin by starting the Microsoft Query program. Microsoft Query is part of the Office Tools collection that ships with Microsoft Office. To start the program on its own, you press Windows Logo+R to open the Run dialog box, type %programfiles%\microsoft office 15\root\office15\msqry32.exe, and then click OK. You can also start it from within Excel. That way, the data you configure with the query is automatically returned to Excel so that you can perform your analysis or build your PivotTable report.

Start Microsoft Query

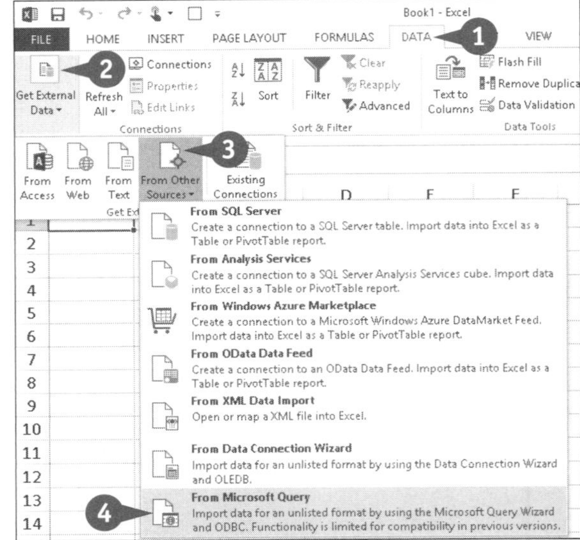

1. Click the Data tab.
2. Click Get External Data.
3. Click From Other Sources.
4. Click From Microsoft Query.

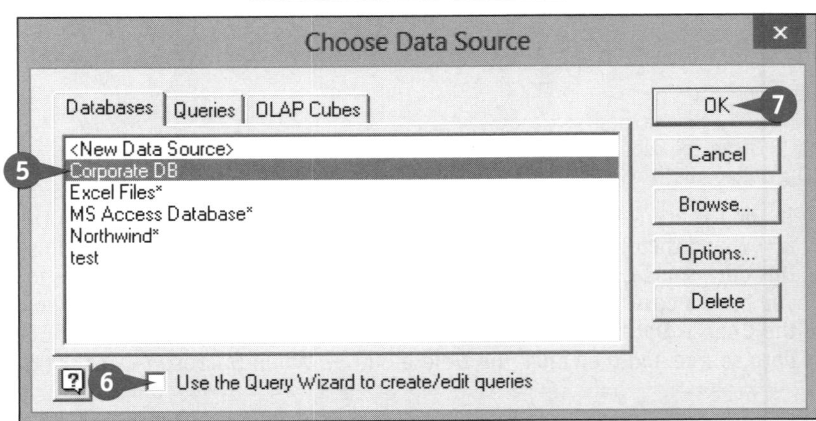

The Choose Data Source dialog box appears.

5. Click the data source you want to work with.
6. Click to deselect the Use the Query Wizard to Create/Edit Queries check box (☑ changes to ☐).
7. Click OK.

The Microsoft Query window and the Add Tables dialog box appear.

Tour the Microsoft Query Window

You can get the most out of Microsoft Query if you understand the layout of the screen and what each part of the Microsoft Query window represents. Although you have not yet created a query using the Microsoft Query program, it is worthwhile to pause now and look at the various elements that make up the Microsoft Query window. Do not worry if what you currently see on your screen does not look like the window shown in this section.

A Microsoft Query Window

This window is where you create and edit, as well as preview, the results. The Microsoft Query window is divided into three panes: the table pane, the criteria pane, and the query results pane.

B Toolbar

The toolbar contains buttons that give you one-click access to many of the most useful features in Microsoft Query.

C Table Pane

This pane displays one list for each table that you add to the query. (For more information, see the section, "Add a Table to a Query.") Each list shows the fields that are part of the table. Click View and then click Tables to toggle this pane on and off.

D Criteria Pane

This pane is where you define the criteria that filter the records you want to return to Excel. (For more information, see the section, "Filter the Records with Query Criteria.") Click View and then click Criteria to toggle this pane on and off.

E Query Results Pane

This pane gives you a preview of the fields and records that your query will return to Excel. As you add fields to the query, change the query criteria, and sort the query (see the section, "Sort Query Records"), Microsoft Query automatically updates the query results pane (also called the *data grid*) to show you what effect your changes will have.

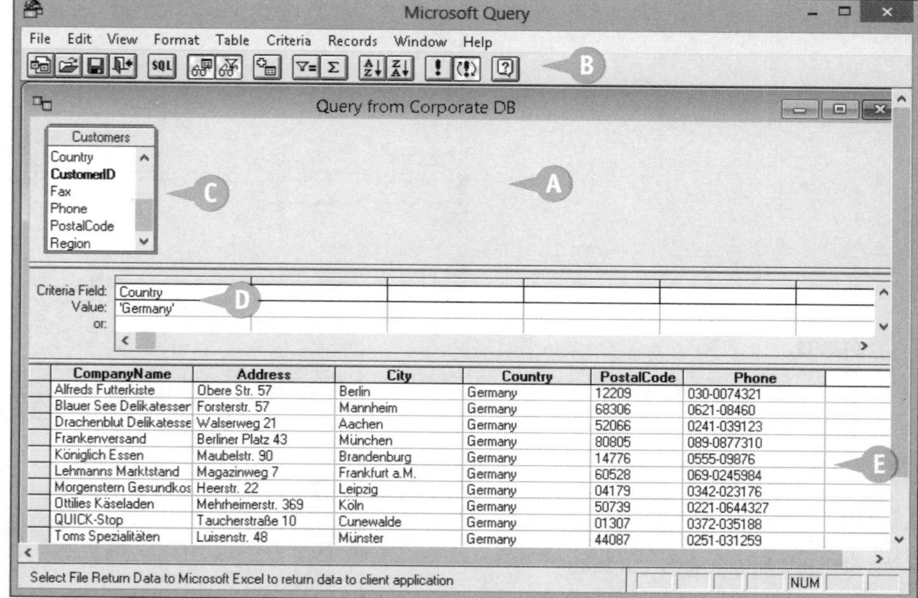

CompanyName	Address	City	Country	PostalCode	Phone
Alfreds Futterkiste	Obere Str. 57	Berlin	Germany	12209	030-0074321
Blauer See Delikatesser	Forsterstr. 57	Mannheim	Germany	68306	0621-08460
Drachenblut Delikatesse	Walserweg 21	Aachen	Germany	52066	0241-039123
Frankenversand	Berliner Platz 43	München	Germany	80805	089-0877310
Königlich Essen	Maubelstr. 90	Brandenburg	Germany	14776	0555-09876
Lehmanns Marktstand	Magazinweg 7	Frankfurt a.M.	Germany	60528	069-0245984
Morgenstern Gesundkos	Heerstr. 22	Leipzig	Germany	04179	0342-023176
Ottilies Käseladen	Mehrheimerstr. 369	Köln	Germany	50739	0221-0644327
QUICK-Stop	Taucherstraße 10	Cunewalde	Germany	01307	0372-035188
Toms Spezialitäten	Luisenstr. 48	Münster	Germany	44087	0251-031259

Add a Table to a Query

With your data source created and Microsoft Query started, the next step you must take is to add a table to the query. In a database, a *table* is a two-dimensional arrangement of rows and columns that contain data. The columns are *fields* that represent distinct categories of data, and the rows are *records* that represent individual sets of field data. In some database management systems, the actual database files are tables. However, in most systems, each database contains a number of tables. Therefore, your first Microsoft Query task in most cases is to select which table you want to work with. Microsoft Query also shows you a list of the queries that are defined in the database, so you can add these objects to your query, if required.

Add a Table to a Query

1. Click Table.
2. Click Add Tables.

Note: *When you start Microsoft Query from Excel, the Add Tables dialog box appears automatically, so you can skip steps 1 and 2.*

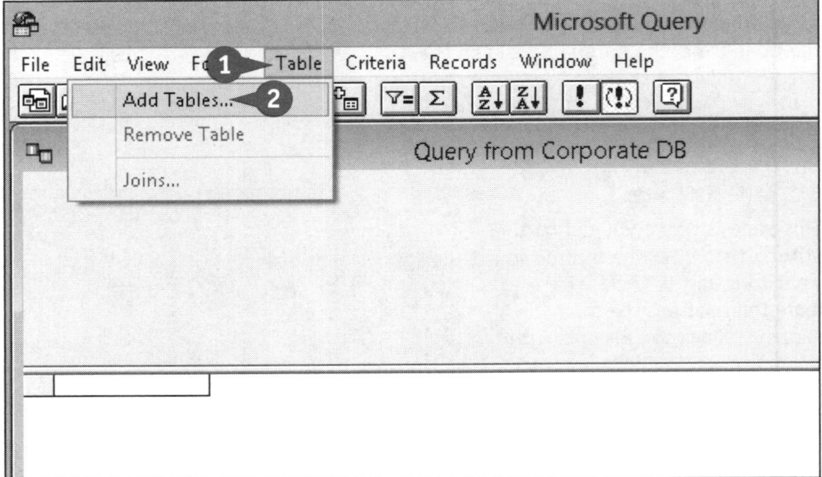

The Add Tables dialog box appears.

A You can also open this dialog box by clicking Add Tables.

3. Click the table you want to add.
4. Click Add.

B Microsoft Query adds the table to the table pane and displays a list of the table's fields.

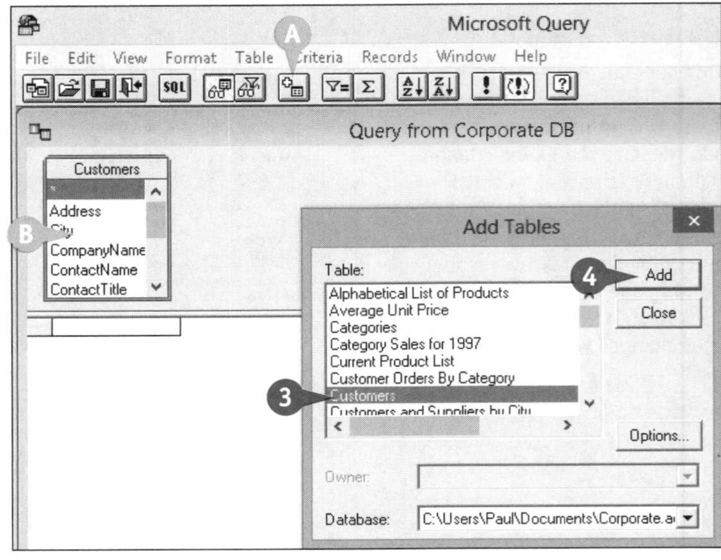

5 Repeat steps 3 and 4 if you want to add multiple, related tables to the query.

C If the tables are related, Microsoft Query displays a join line that connects the common fields.

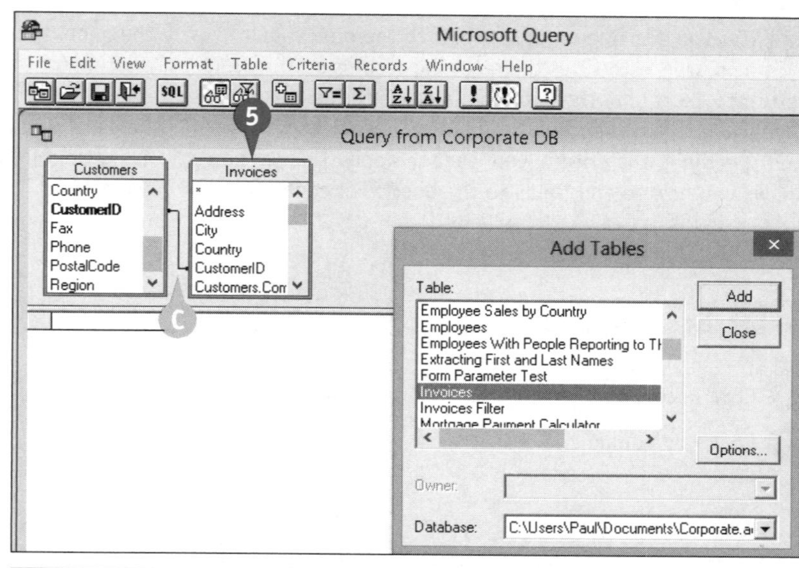

6 Click Close.

You are now ready to add fields to the query, as described in the next section.

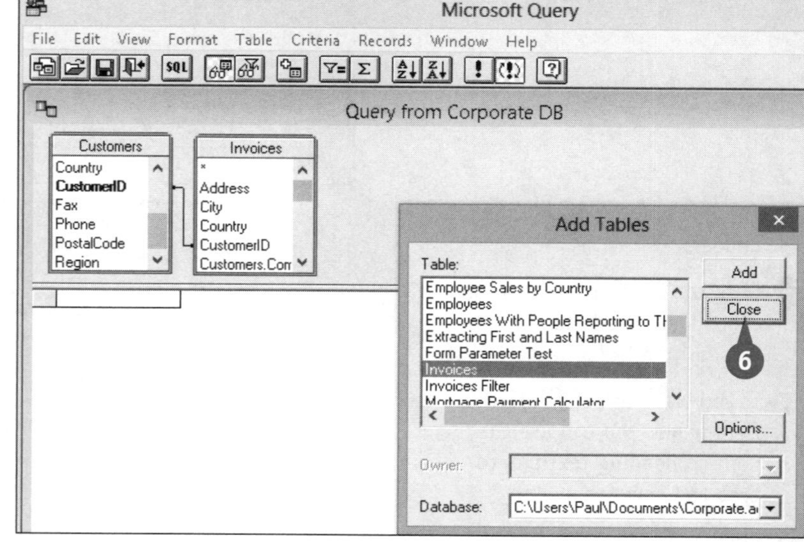

APPLY IT

To join two tables manually, click Table and then click Joins to display the Joins dialog box. Click the Left down arrow and then click the common field from one of your tables. Click the Right down arrow and then click the common field from the other table. Click the Operator down arrow and then click = (equal). Click Add to add the join to the query and then click Close. To remove a table from the query, first click the table in the table pane. Click Table and then click Remove Table. Alternatively, click the table and then press Delete. Microsoft Query deletes the table list. If you added fields from the table to the criteria pane or the query results pane, Microsoft Query removes those fields as well.

Add Fields to a Query

After you add one or more tables to the query, your next step is to filter the resulting records so that you return to Excel only the data you need. Filtering the records involves two tasks: adding the fields you want to work with and specifying the criteria you want to apply. This section shows you how to add fields to the query. For each table, the query window's table pane displays a list that contains an item for each table field. At the top of the list, you also see an asterisk (*) item, which represents *all* the table's fields. If you know that you want to include in your query every field from a table, you can do this easily by adding the asterisk "field" to the query.

Add Fields to a Query

1. Click Records.
2. Click Add Column.

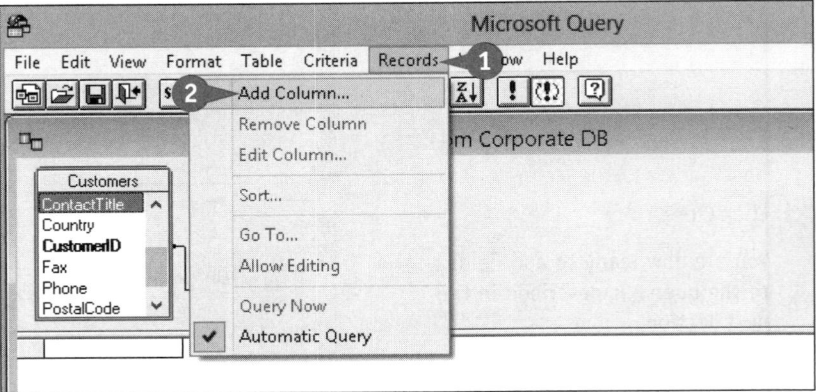

The Add Column dialog box appears.

3. Click the Field down arrow and then select the field you want to add from the drop-down list.

Ⓐ If you want to use a different field name, you can use the Column heading text box to type the new name.

4. Click Add.

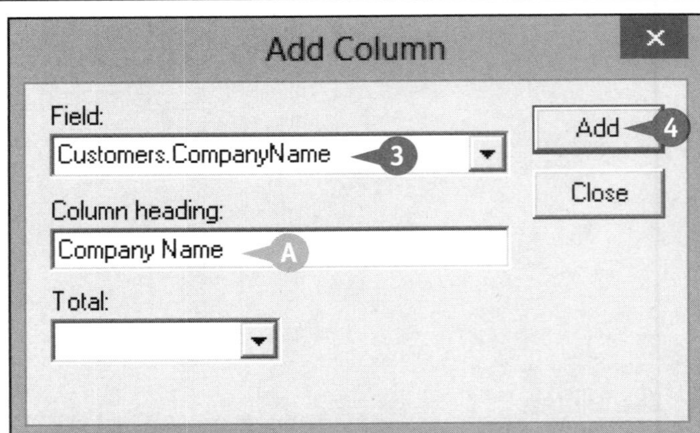

B Microsoft Query adds the field to the query results pane.

C You can also either double-click a field name in a table list, or click and drag a field name in a table list and drop it inside the query results pane.

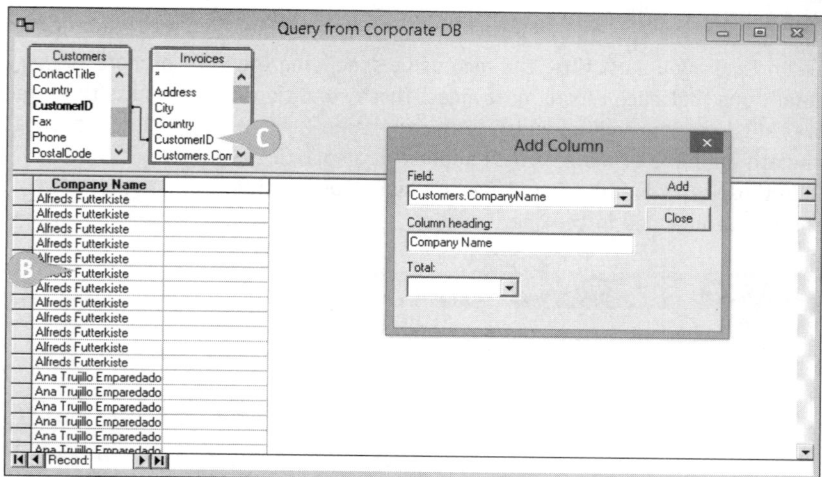

5 Repeat steps 3 and 4 until you have added all the fields that you want to appear in the query.

6 Click Close.

Note: *To change where a field appears in the data grid, first click the field heading to select the entire field. Then click and drag the field heading to the left or right and drop the field into the new position.*

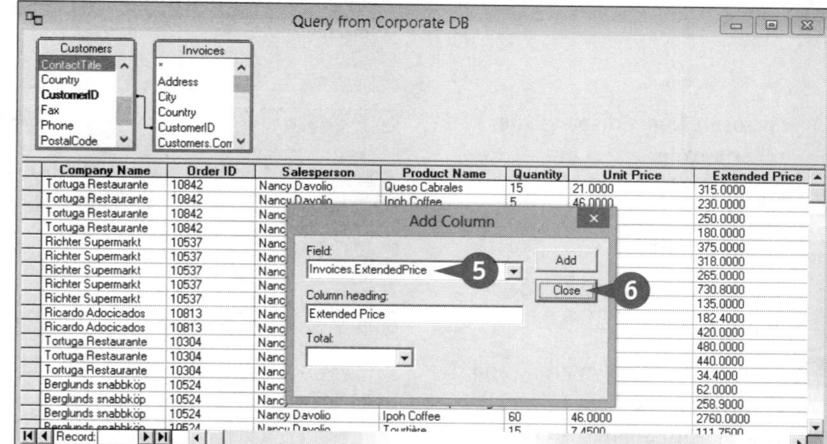

EXTRA

If you want to change to a different field or edit the name displayed in the field heading, double-click the field heading. You can use the Edit Column dialog box to change the field or edit the field heading, and then click OK.

To delete a field from the query, click the field heading or click any cell in the field; note that Microsoft Query does not ask for confirmation when you delete a field, so be sure you click the correct field. Then press Delete.

To display the specific records that you want to return to Excel, you must filter the records by specifying the conditions that each record must meet. These conditions are called *criteria*, each of which is an expression (an operator and one or more values) applied to a specific field. Only those records for which the expression returns a true answer are included in the query results.

You can enter just a single criterion, or you can enter two or more. If you use multiple criteria, you can include in the results those records that match *all* the criteria, or those records that match *any one* of the criteria.

Filter the Records with Query Criteria

1. Click Show/Hide Criteria.

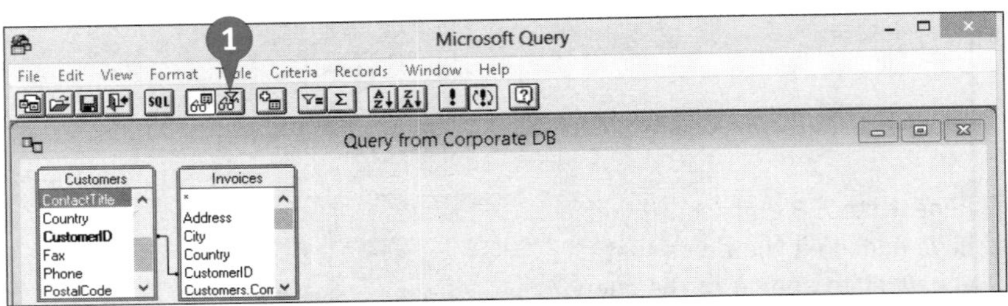

A. Microsoft Query displays the criteria pane.

2. Click Criteria.
3. Click Add Criteria.

   The Add Criteria dialog box appears.

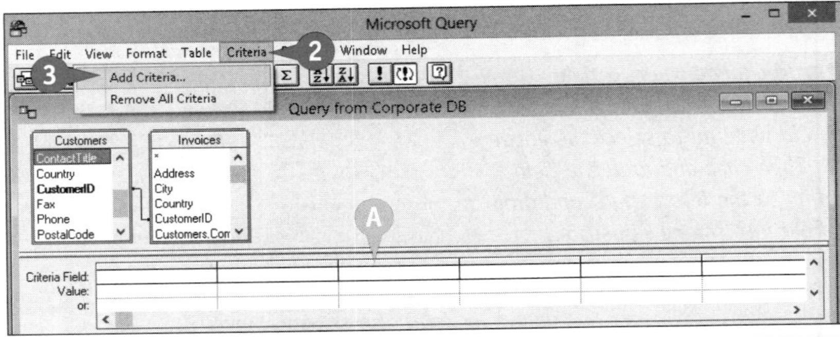

4. Click the Field down arrow and then select the field to which you want to apply the criteria from the drop-down list.
5. Click the Operator down arrow and then select the operator you want to use from the drop-down list.
6. Type the value or values for the criteria.

   B. To use a value from the selected field, you can click Values, click the value you want to use, and then click OK.

7. Click Add.

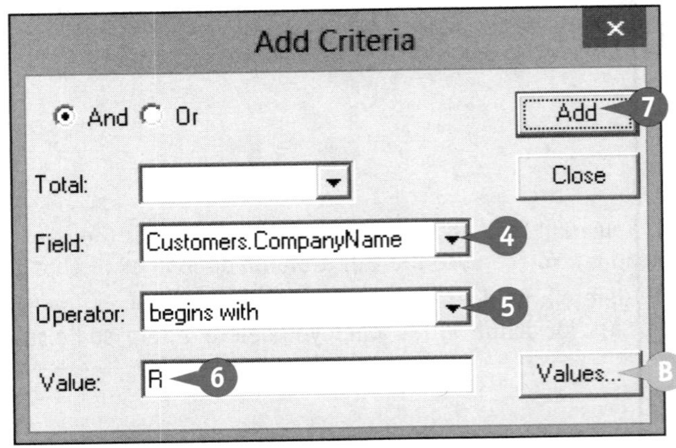

C Microsoft Query adds the criteria to the criteria pane.

D Microsoft Query filters the results to show only those records that satisfy the criteria.

***Note:** If you do not want to specify multiple criteria, skip to step 10.*

8 Click the And option (○ changes to ◉) to add another criterion and to display records that meet all the criteria you specify.

E Alternatively, click the Or option (○ changes to ◉) to display records that meet at least one of the criteria that you specify.

9 Repeat steps 3 to 7 until you have added all the criteria that you want to appear in the query.

10 Click Close.

F Microsoft Query filters the records to show just those records that match your criteria.

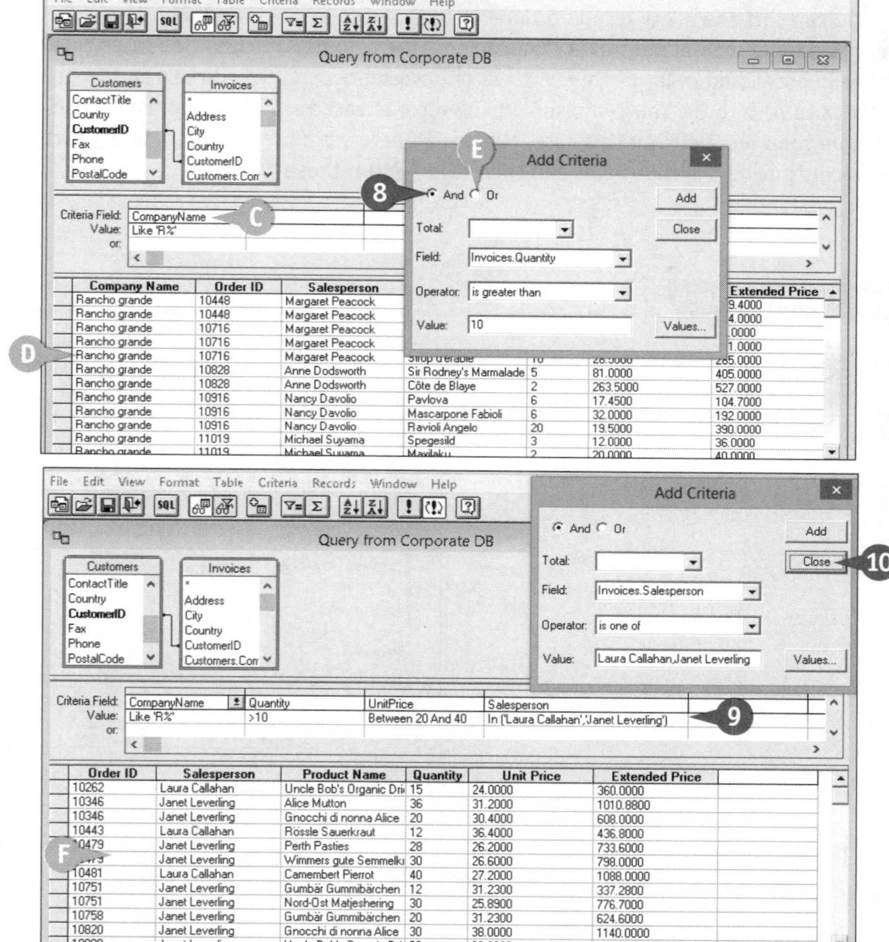

EXTRA

To change the field to which a criteria expression applies, use the criteria pane to click the field name, click the down arrow that appears, and then click the field you want to use. To change the criteria expression, either edit the expression directly in the criteria pane, or double-click the expression to display the Edit Criteria dialog box.

To delete a criterion from the query, click the bar just above the field name to select the entire criterion; note that Microsoft Query does not ask for confirmation when you delete a criterion, so be sure you click the correct one. Then press Delete. If you want to remove all the criteria, click Criteria and then click Remove All Criteria.

Sort Query Records

You can sort the query results on one or more fields to get a good look at your data. You can sort the records either in ascending order (0 to 9, A to Z) or descending order (Z to A, 9 to 0). You can also sort the records based on more than one field. In this case, Microsoft Query sorts the records using the first field, and then sorts within those results on the second field. For example, in the invoice data, suppose you are sorting first on the OrderID field and then on the Quantity field. Microsoft Query first orders the records by OrderID. Then, within each OrderID value, Microsoft Query sorts the Quantity field values.

Sort Query Records

1. Click Records.
2. Click Sort.

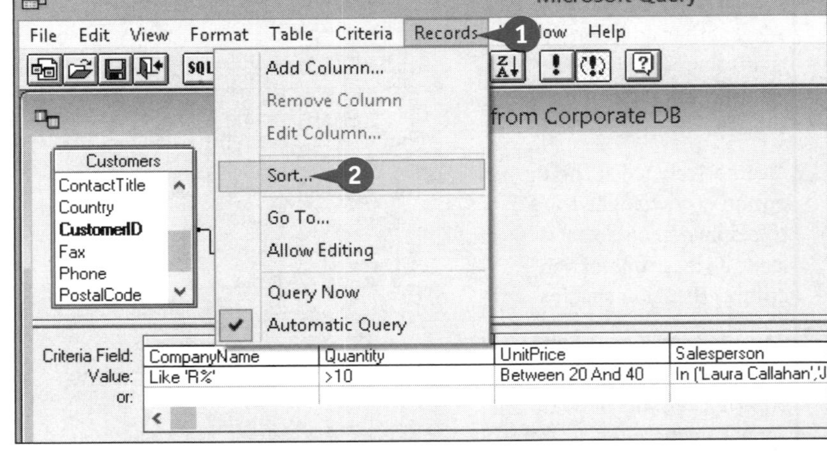

The Sort dialog box appears.

3. Click the Column down arrow and then select the field you want to sort from the drop-down list.
4. Click the Ascending or Descending option to select a sort order (◯ changes to ◉).
5. Click Add.

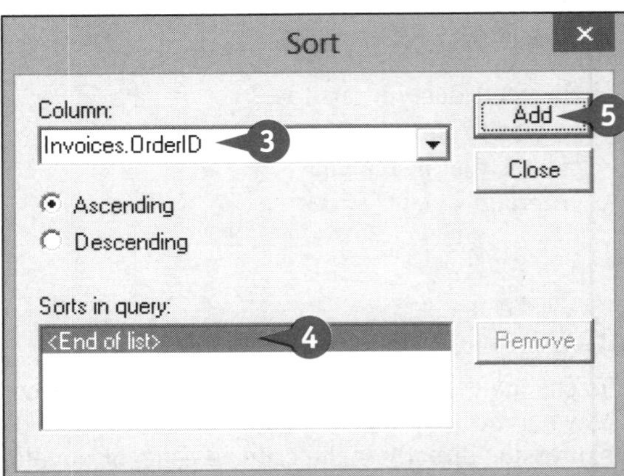

Ⓐ Microsoft Query sorts the records in the query results pane.

Ⓑ Microsoft Query adds the sort to the Sorts in Query list.

6 Repeat steps 3 to 5 until you have added all the sorts that you want to use.

7 Click Close.

Microsoft Query sorts the records.

If you only want to sort the query results on a single field, you can click any cell in that field and then click one of the following icons:

Ⓒ Click Sort Ascending to sort the field in ascending order.

Ⓓ Click Sort Descending to sort the field in descending order.

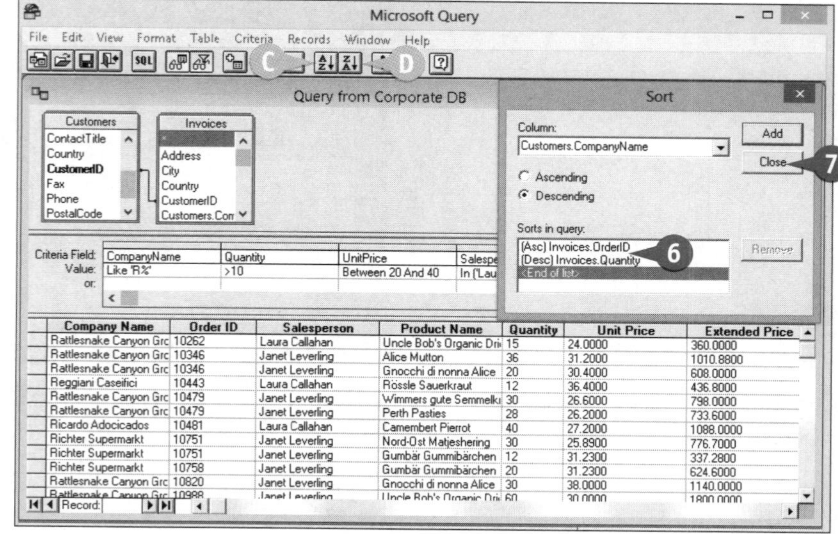

APPLY IT

You can use the toolbar to sort on multiple fields. First, organize the fields in the query results pane so that all the fields you want to use in the sort are side by side, in the order you want to apply the sort. Click and drag the mouse pointer from the heading of the first sort field to the heading of the last sort field. You should now have all the sort fields selected. Finally, click either Sort Ascending or Sort Descending. To remove a sort that you no longer need, click Records and then click Sort to display the Sort dialog box. In the Sorts in Query list, click the sort that you want to delete, and then click the Remove button.

Return the Query Results

After you finish adding fields to the query, filtering the data using criteria, and sorting the data, you are ready to return the results to Excel for use in your worksheet. Microsoft Query is just a helper application, so the data that resides in the query results does not really "exist" anywhere. To manipulate or analyze the query data, you need to return the query results to Excel, and then start a new table or PivotTable based on those results. If you think you will reuse the query later, you should save the query before returning the results.

Return the Query Results

1. Click File.

   A. You can combine steps 1 and 2 by clicking Return Data.

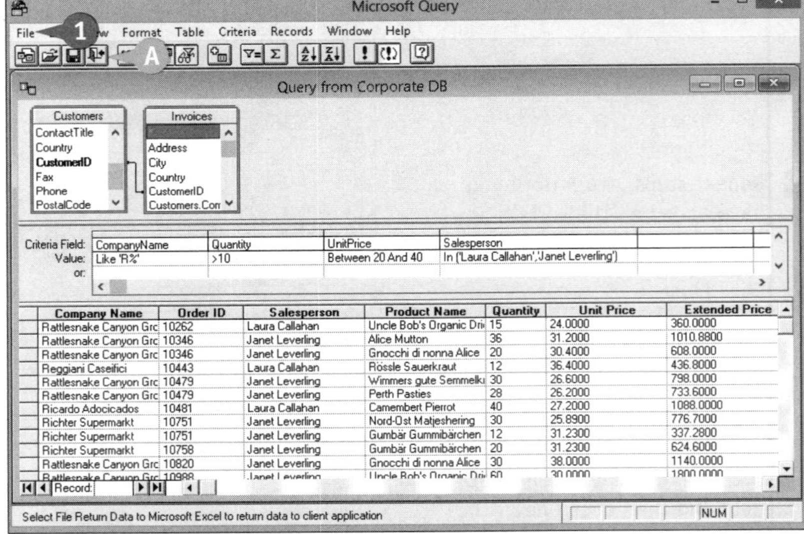

2. Click Return Data to Microsoft Excel.

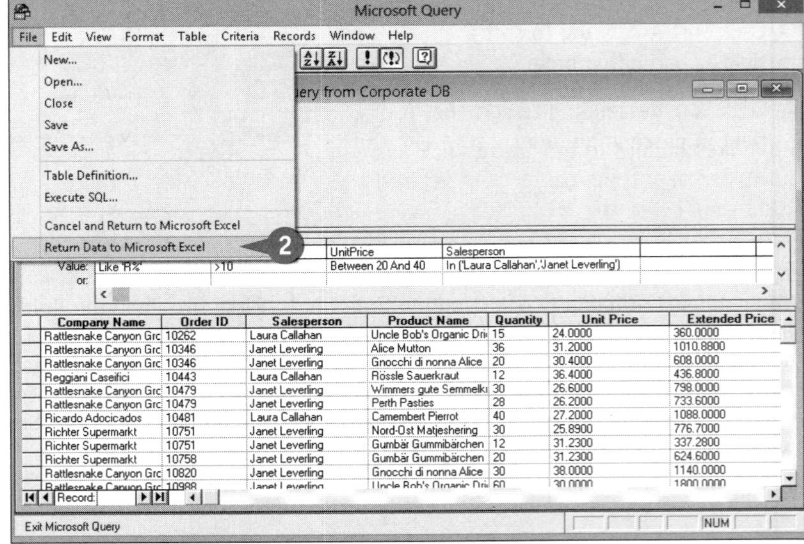

The Import Data dialog box appears.

3 Click the Table option (○ changes to ◉).

B If you want to create a PivotTable instead, click the PivotTable Report option (○ changes to ◉).

4 Click the Existing Worksheet option (○ changes to ◉).

5 Click the cell where you want the imported data to appear.

C If you want the data to appear in a new sheet, click the New Worksheet option instead (○ changes to ◉).

6 Click OK.

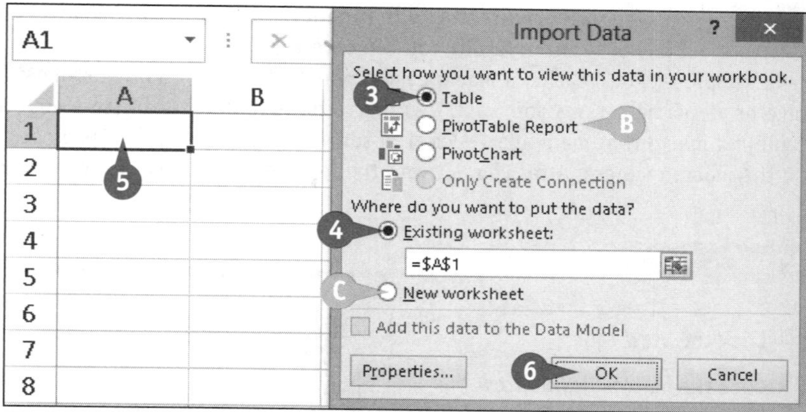

	A	B	C	D	E
1	'Company Name'	'Order ID'	'Salesperson'	'Product Name'	'Quantity'
2	Rattlesnake Canyon Grocery	10262	Laura Callahan	Uncle Bob's Organic Dried Pears	15
3	Rattlesnake Canyon Grocery	10346	Janet Leverling	Alice Mutton	36
4	Rattlesnake Canyon Grocery	10346	Janet Leverling	Gnocchi di nonna Alice	20
5	Reggiani Caseifici	10443	Laura Callahan	Rössle Sauerkraut	12
6	Rattlesnake Canyon Grocery	10479	Janet Leverling	Wimmers gute Semmelknödel	30
7	Rattlesnake Canyon Grocery	10479	Janet Leverling	Perth Pasties	[illegible]
8	Ricardo Adocicados	10481	Laura Callahan	Camembert Pierrot	40
9	Richter Supermarkt	10751	Janet Leverling	Nord-Ost Matjeshering	30
10	Richter Supermarkt	10751	Janet Leverling	Gumbär Gummibärchen	12
11	Richter Supermarkt	10758	Janet Leverling	Gumbär Gummibärchen	20
12	Rattlesnake Canyon Grocery	10820	Janet Leverling	Gnocchi di nonna Alice	30
13	Rattlesnake Canyon Grocery	10988	Janet Leverling	Uncle Bob's Organic Dried Pears	60
14					

Sheet1

D Excel imports the query data into the worksheet.

APPLY IT

To make changes to the query, click any cell in the table (or PivotTable), click the Design tab, click the Refresh All down arrow and then click Connection Properties to open the Connection Properties dialog box. Click the Definition tab and then click Edit Query. This starts Microsoft Query and loads the query results. Make your changes and then return the data to Excel.

To save a query using Microsoft Query, click File and then click Save to display the Save As dialog box. Select a folder to store the query file, type a filename, and then click Save. To use the query file, start Microsoft Query, click File, click Open to display the Open Query dialog box, click the query file, and then click Open.

Record a Macro

A *macro* is a sequence of instructions that perform one or more actions or return a result. You can save time and make the process of creating a macro easier by recording some or all of the actions you want your macro to perform. To build a macro that manipulates Excel in some way, you use the macro recorder. After you activate the recorder, you use Excel to perform the action or actions that you want in the macro, which Excel then translates into the equivalent VBA statements and stores as a macro for later use. You can store your recorded macros in any workbook, but Excel provides a special workbook for this purpose: the Personal Macro Workbook.

Record a Macro

1. Click the View tab.
2. Click the Macros down arrow.
3. Click Record Macro.

A You can also click the Macro Recording icon in the status bar.

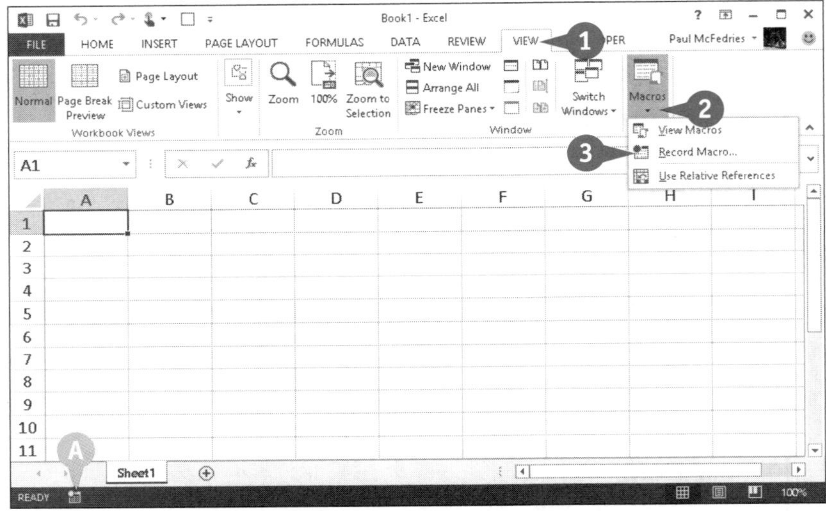

The Record Macro dialog box appears.

4. Type a name for the macro.
5. Click the Store Macro In down arrow and then select the workbook you want to use to store the macro from the drop-down list.

Note: *For most macros, it is best to store the code in the Personal Macro Workbook.*

6. (Optional) Type a description of the macro.
7. Click OK.

Excel starts the macro recorder.

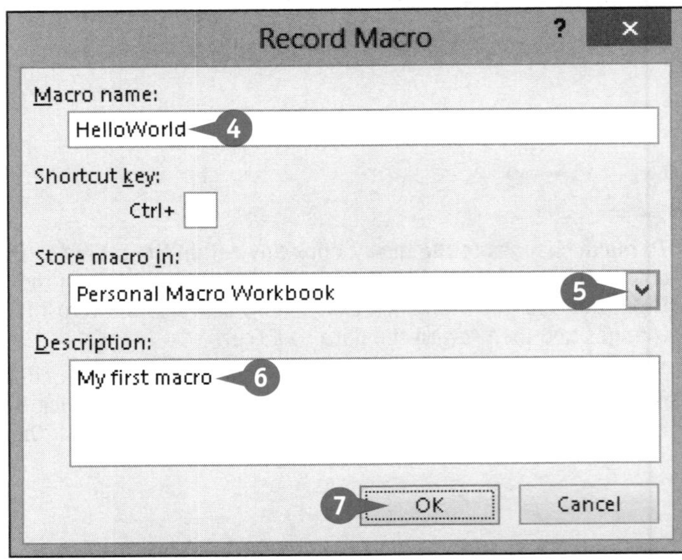

Ⓑ The Recording icon appears in the status bar.

8 Perform the Excel actions you want to record.

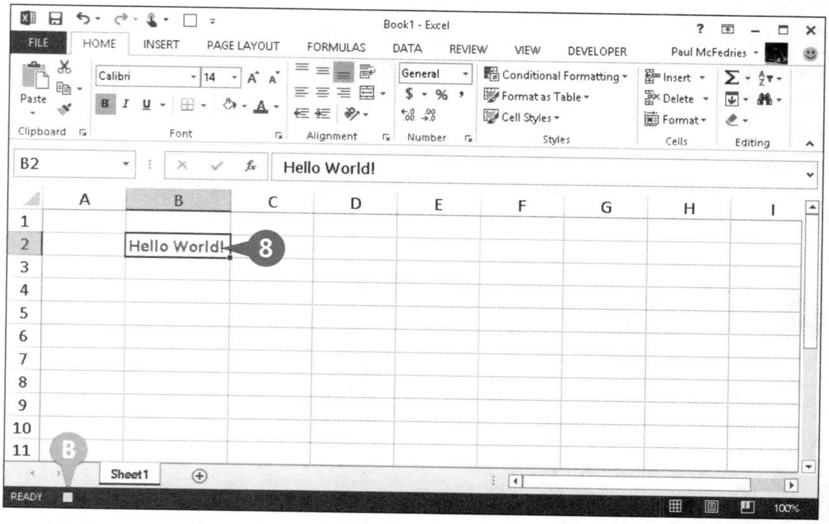

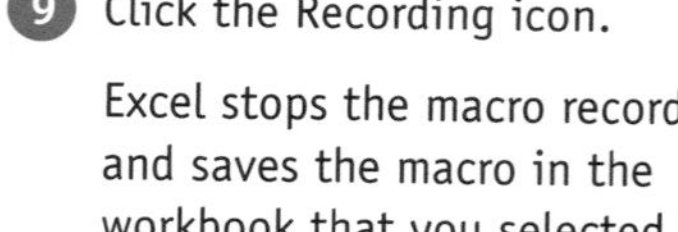

9 Click the Recording icon.

Excel stops the macro recorder and saves the macro in the workbook that you selected in step 5.

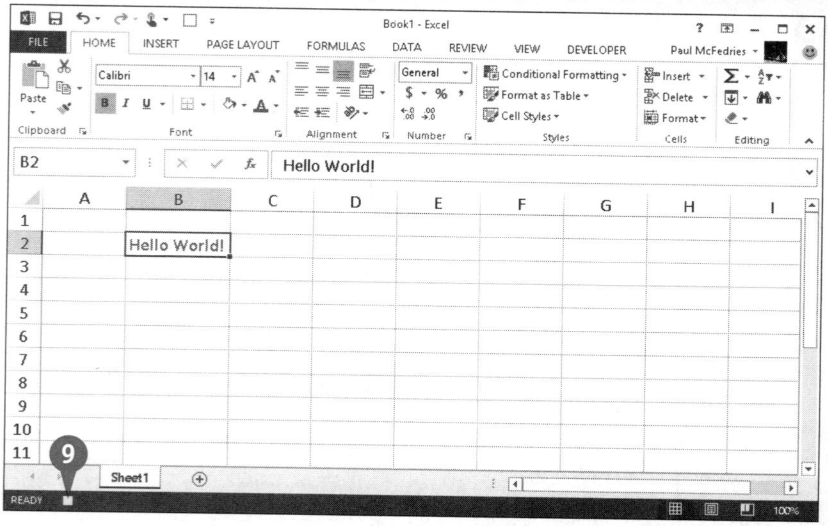

EXTRA

When you specify the macro name in step 4, keep in mind that there are some restrictions you must observe: the name must not be longer than 255 characters; the name must begin with either a letter or an underscore (_); the name cannot contain a space or a period; and the name cannot be the same as an existing Excel function.

You can perform many macro-related actions faster and easier using the Developer tab. To display the Developer tab, right-click the Ribbon, click Customize the Ribbon, click the Developer check box (☐ changes to ☑), and then click OK. To start a macro recording, click the Developer tab and then click Record Macro.

Open the VBA Editor

If you want to add a macro to a workbook, or to create a macro from scratch, you can do this in the VBA Editor, a program that enables you to view, create, edit, and run VBA macros. After you finish recording your actions, Excel translates them into VBA statements and saves the macro in a *module*, a special window in which you can view, edit, and run macros; you access the module using the VBA Editor. If you make mistakes during the recording, or if you want to augment the recorded macro with other VBA statements, then you need to do this in the module. Similarly, you also require access to the module if you want to paste code from other sources or create new macros from scratch.

Open the VBA Editor

1 Click the Developer tab.

Note: *See the section, "Record a Macro," to learn how to display the Developer tab.*

2 Click Visual Basic.

You can also press Alt+F11.

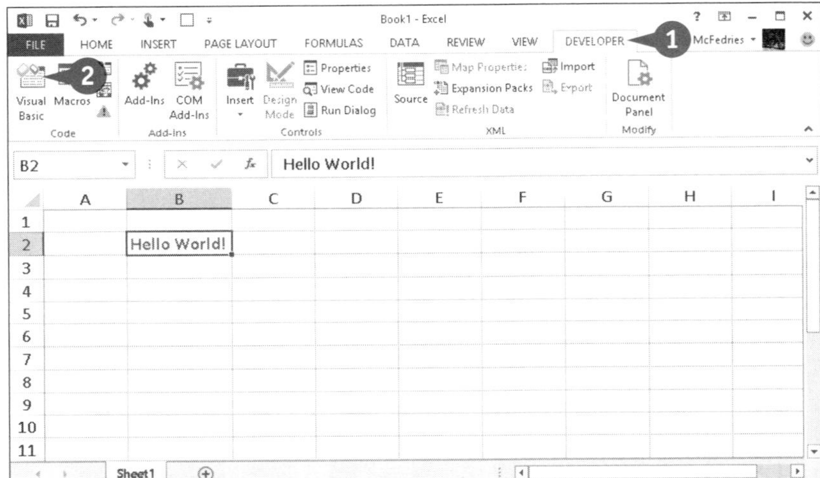

The Microsoft Visual Basic for Applications window appears.

3 Double-click the workbook that contains the recorded macro.

A PERSONAL.xlsb is the Personal Macro Workbook.

If you do not see the Project pane, you can click View and then click Project Explorer, or press Ctrl+R.

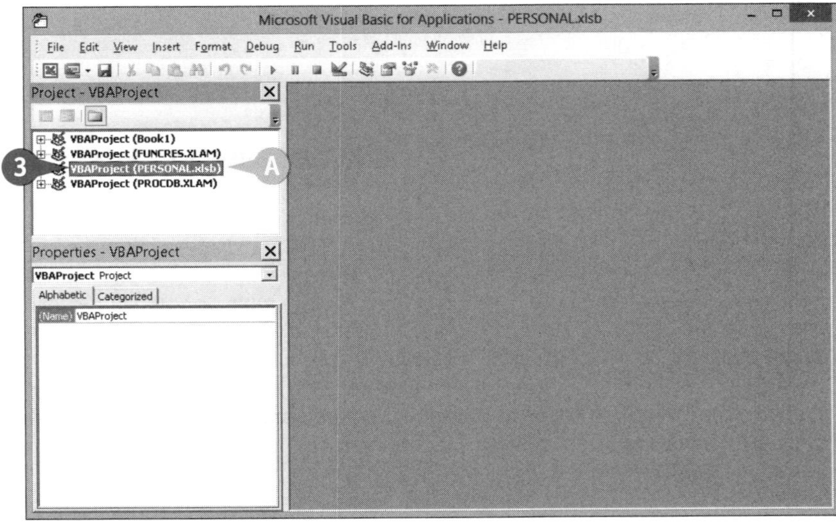

B Excel displays the workbook's modules.

4 Double-click the module you want to open.

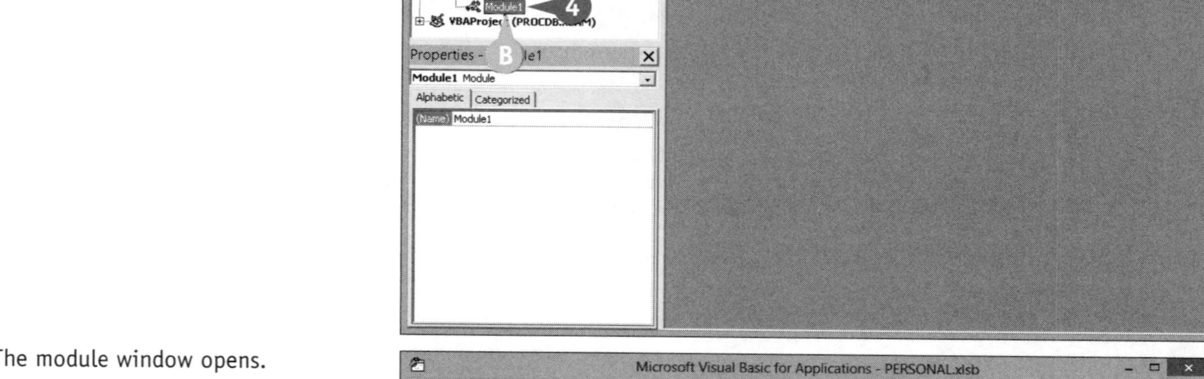

The module window opens.

C The VBA Editor opens the module in a new window.

D If you recorded a macro and are working with the workbook that you used to store that macro, the recorded code appears in the module window.

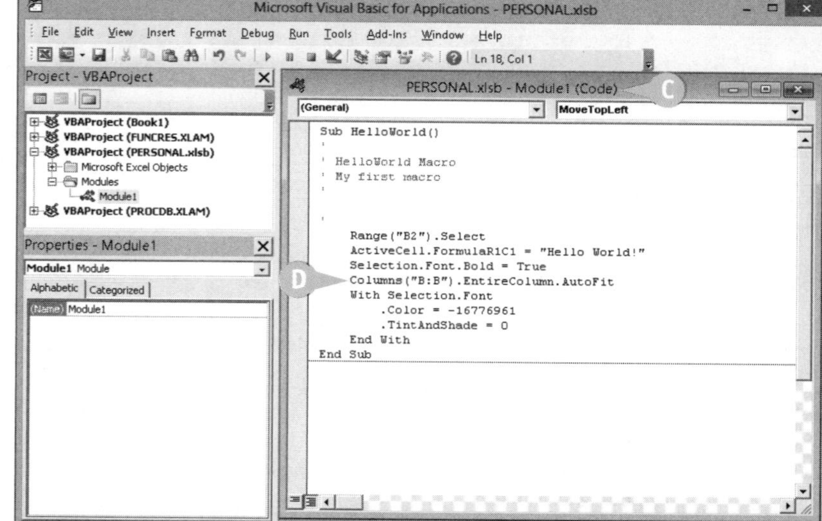

APPLY IT

Excel keeps the Personal Macro Workbook hidden, which is why you do not see it when you are working in Excel. To see the Personal Macro Workbook, you must unhide it. Switch to Excel, click View, click Unhide Window, click Personal, and then click OK.

If the Unhide command is disabled, or if you do not see the Personal Macro Workbook in the Unhide dialog box, then the Personal Macro Workbook may not exist. In most cases, Excel only creates this workbook after you use it to store a recorded macro for the first time. In the Record Macros dialog box, select Personal Macro Workbook from the Store Macro In drop-down list.

Explore the Excel Object Model

To program Excel with VBA, you need to understand the Excel object model. In the programming lexicon, an *object model* is a complete summary of the objects associated with a particular program or feature, the hierarchy used by those objects, and the properties and methods supported by each object. Here an *object* is a distinct, manipulable item such as a worksheet or range.

A *property* is a programmable characteristic of an object, such as a worksheet's name, or whether a range is formatted with bold text. A *method* is an action you can perform on an object, such as creating a new worksheet or clearing the formatting from a range. This section shows you a few properties and methods for the three main Excel objects: the workbook, worksheet, and range.

Workbook Object

You can use VBA to create new workbooks, open, save, and close workbooks, and more. You can reference a specific workbook either by using the `ActiveWorkbook` object, which represents the workbook that currently has the focus, or by using the `Workbooks` collection, which represents all the workbooks currently open in Excel. Here are some examples:

```
Workbooks(1)
Workbooks("Budget.xlsx")
```

Workbook Properties

Property	Description
`Workbooks.Count`	Returns the number of open workbooks.
`Name`	Returns the filename of the workbook.
`Path`	Returns the location of the workbook.
`FileFormat`	Returns the Excel file format of the workbook.
`FullName`	Returns the location and filename of the workbook.
`PivotTables`	Returns the collection of PivotTables in the workbook.
`Saved`	Returns False if the workbook has unsaved changes.
`VBASigned`	Returns True if the workbook has been digitally signed.

Workbook Methods

Method	Description
`Activate`	Switches to a workbook.
`Workbooks.Add`	Creates a new workbook.
`Workbooks.Open`	Opens an existing workbook.
`Protect`	Protects a workbook.
`Save`	Saves a workbook.
`SaveAs`	Saves a workbook to a different file.
`PrintOut`	Prints a workbook.
`Close`	Closes a workbook.
`Unprotect`	Unprotects a workbook.

Worksheet Object

You can use VBA to create new worksheets, copy, move, and delete worksheets, and more. You can reference a specific worksheet either by using the `ActiveSheet` object, which represents the worksheet that currently has the focus, or by using the `Worksheets` collection, which represents all the worksheets currently open in Excel. Here are some examples:

```
Worksheets(1)
Worksheets("Sheet1")
```

Worksheet Properties

Property	Description
`Worksheets.Count`	Returns the number of worksheets in the workbook.
`Name`	Returns the name of the worksheet.
`StandardHeight`	Returns or sets the standard row height.
`StandardWidth`	Returns or sets the standard column width.
`Visible`	Hides or displays a worksheet.

Worksheet Methods

Method	Description
`Worksheets.Add`	Creates a new worksheet.
`Activate`	Switches to a worksheet.
`Calculate`	Calculates a workbook.
`Copy`	Copies a worksheet.
`Move`	Moves a worksheet.
`Delete`	Deletes a worksheet.

Range Object

You can use VBA to select a range, add data to a range, format a range, and more. You can reference a specific cell by using the `ActiveCell` object, which represents the worksheet cell that currently has the focus. You can also use the `WorkSheet` object's `Range` method to specify a range using a reference or a defined name. Here are some examples:

```
Worksheets(1).Range("A1:B10")
ActiveSheet.Range("Expenses")
```

Range Properties

Property	Description
`Address`	Returns the address of the range.
`Count`	Returns the number of cells in the range.
`NumberFormat`	Returns the numeric format of the range.
`Value`	Returns or sets the data or formula for the range.

Range Methods

Method	Description
`Cut`	Cuts a range to the Clipboard.
`Copy`	Copies a range to the Clipboard.
`Clear`	Clears all data and formatting from a range.
`Select`	Select a range.

Add a Macro to a Module

If you have a macro that you want to create or copy, you need to add the VBA code for the macro to a module in the VBA Editor. As you become familiar with manipulating Excel using VBA, you will likely come up with many ways to simplify complex tasks and automate routine and repetitive chores using macros. To implement these macros, you need to type your code into a module in the VBA Editor.

Similarly, you may run across a macro that you want to use for your own work, either as it is or by modifying the code to suit your needs. You can either transcribe this macro into a module on your system, or better yet, copy the macro and then paste it into a module.

Add a Macro to a Module

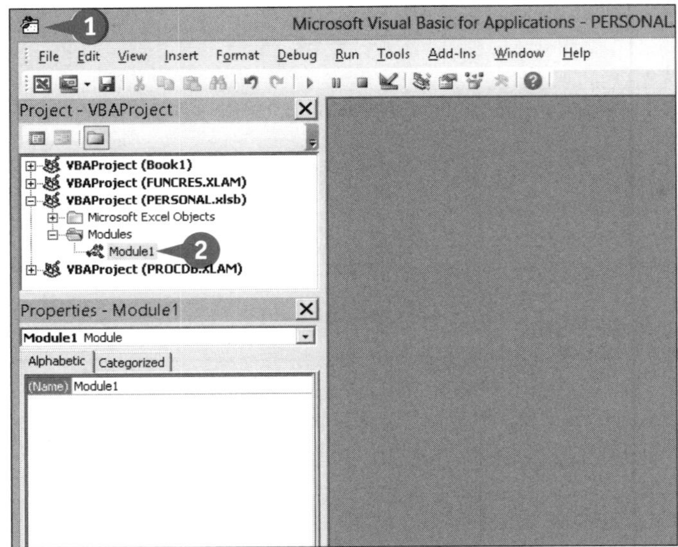

1. Start the VBA Editor.
2. Double-click the module into which you want to add the macro.

   If you prefer to add your code to a new module, you can click Insert and then click Module, instead.

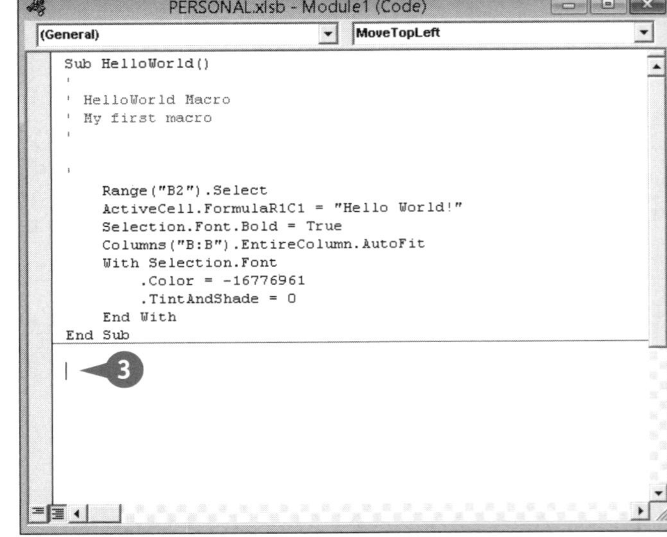

Excel opens the module window.

3. Position the cursor where you want to start the new macro.

Note: *You must add the new macro either before or after an existing macro.*

4. Type **Sub**, a space, the name of the new macro, and then press Enter.

Note: *Make sure the name you use is not the same as any existing macro name in the module.*

PERSONAL.xlsb - Module1 (Code)

(General) | HelloVBAWorld

```
Sub HelloWorld()
'
' HelloWorld Macro
' My first macro
'

'
    Range("B2").Select
    ActiveCell.FormulaR1C1 = "Hello World!"
    Selection.Font.Bold = True
    Columns("B:B").EntireColumn.AutoFit
    With Selection.Font
        .Color = -16776961
        .TintAndShade = 0
    End With
End Sub

Sub HelloVBAWorld
```

A The VBA Editor adds the line `End Sub` to denote the end of the macro.

If you copied the macro code from another source, click Edit and then click Paste, instead.

5. Type the macro statements between the `Sub` and `End Sub` lines.

B As you type a VBA function, object, property, or method, the VBA Editor displays the syntax in a pop-up box.

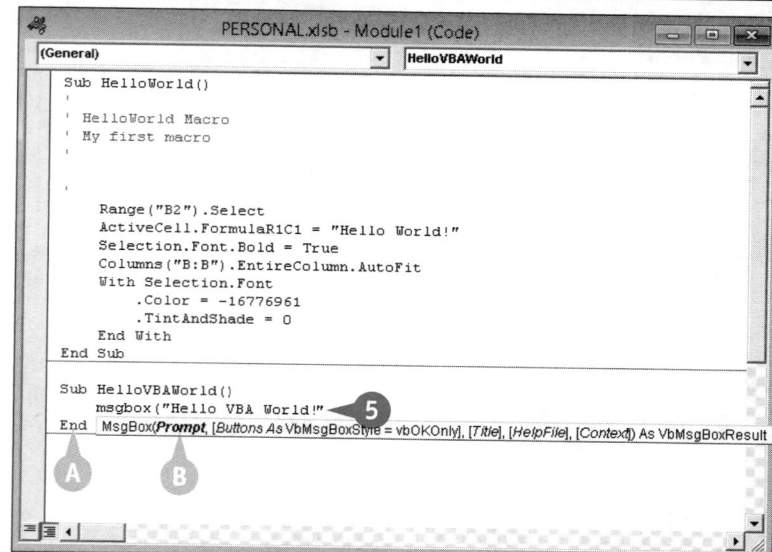

APPLY IT

To create a macro that returns a value, you can create a function macro, which uses the `Function` keyboard instead of `Sub`. Here is the general syntax:

```
Function Name (arg1, arg2...)
    Statements
    Name = result
End Function
```

Name is the name of the function; `arg1` and so on are the function input values; Statements are the VBA statements that calculate the result, which is then assigned to Name.

Run a Macro

You can run a macro from any open workbook. You have the option of running the macro from the VBA Editor or from Excel. Excel maintains a list of the macros that are stored in each open workbook. When you want to run a macro, you can either open the module that contains the macro or display the list of available Excel macros. Either way, to run a macro, you must first open the workbook in which the macro is stored.

It is best to use the VBA Editor if you are testing the macro, because although VBA switches to Excel to execute the code, it returns to the VBA Editor when it is done. Therefore, you can run the code, see whether it works properly, and then adjust the code as necessary.

Run a Macro

Run a Macro from the VBA Editor

1. Open the module that contains the macro.
2. Click any statement within the macro you want to run.

   A. The macro name appears in the list of macros.
3. Click Run.
4. Click Run Sub/UserForm.

   You can also click the toolbar's Run icon (▶) or press F5.

   The VBA Editor runs the macro.

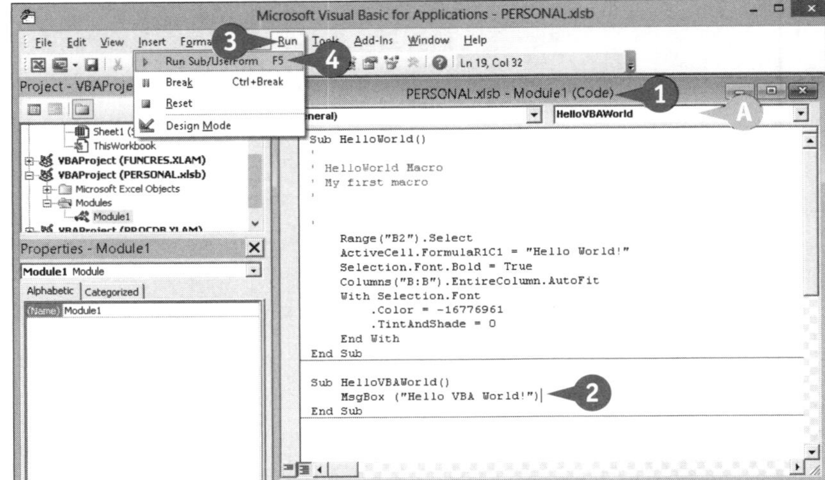

Run a Macro from Excel

1. Open the workbook that contains the macro.

   You can skip step 1 if the macro is stored in the Personal Macro Workbook.
2. Click the View tab.
3. Click Macros.

   If you have the Developer tab displayed, you can also click the Developer tab and then click Macros.

   You can also press Alt+F8.

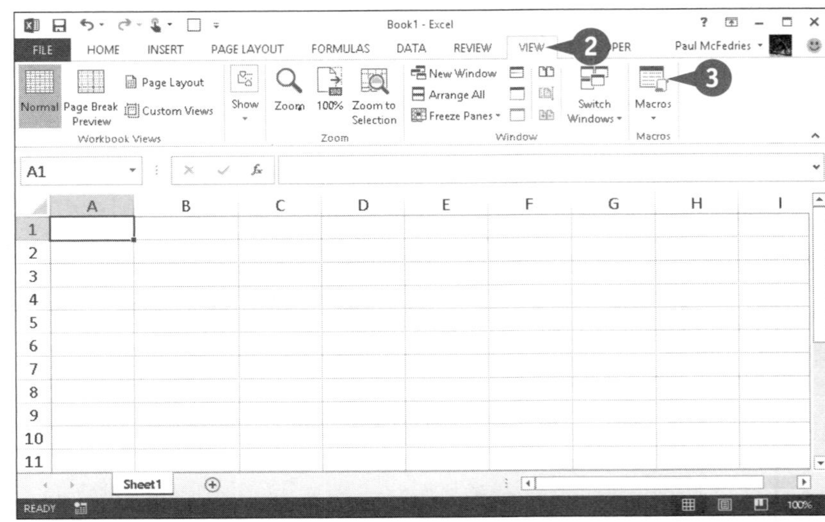

The Macro dialog box appears.

4. Click the Macros In down arrow and then select the workbook that contains the macro you want to run from the drop-down list.

   If you are not sure which workbook contains the macro, select All Open Workbooks, instead.

B. Excel displays a list of macros in the workbook.

5. Click the macro you want to run.
6. Click Run.

   Excel runs the macro.

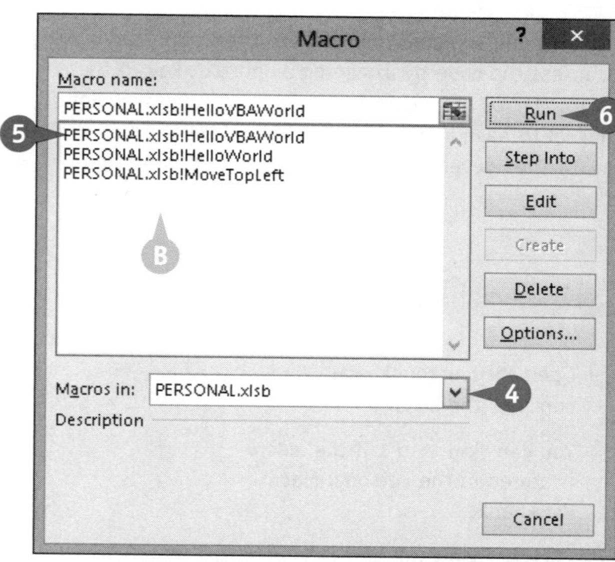

Include a Function Macro in a Formula

1. Type = and whatever formula operators and operands you need before the function.
2. Click Insert Function.

   The Insert Function dialog box appears.

3. Select the User Defined category.
4. Click the function.
5. Click OK.
6. Specify the function's argument, if any, and click OK (not shown).

   Excel inserts the function macro into the formula.

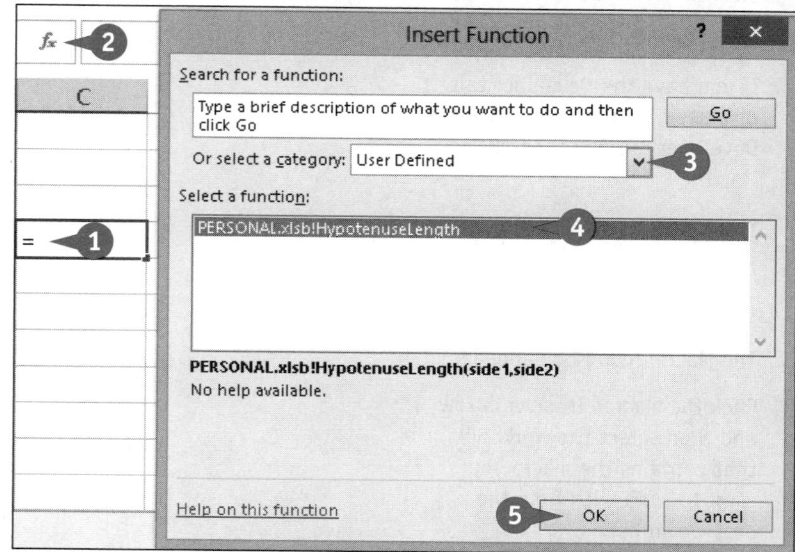

APPLY IT

The default macro security settings in Excel may prevent you from running any macros stored outside the Personal Macro Workbook. If you cannot perform the steps in this section — particularly after you create one or more macros and then close and restart Excel — then you need to either lower the macro security settings in Excel or self-sign your own macros. To jump directly to a macro in the VBA Editor, you can use the Macro dialog box. Follow steps 1 to 3 to open the Macro dialog box and select the macro you want to work with. Click the Edit button. Excel launches the VBA Editor, opens the module that contains the macro, and then displays the macro code.

Assign a Shortcut Key to a Macro

If you have a macro that you use often, you can quickly access the code by assigning a shortcut key to the macro. Macros are meant to be timesavers, so it is not unusual to have a macro that you run several times each day, or even several times in a row. In such situations, those mouse clicks can add up and you may wonder whether the macro is really saving you time. To work around this problem, you can assign a shortcut key to the macro. As long as the macro's workbook is open, you can press the shortcut key within Excel to run the macro.

Assign a Shortcut Key to a Macro

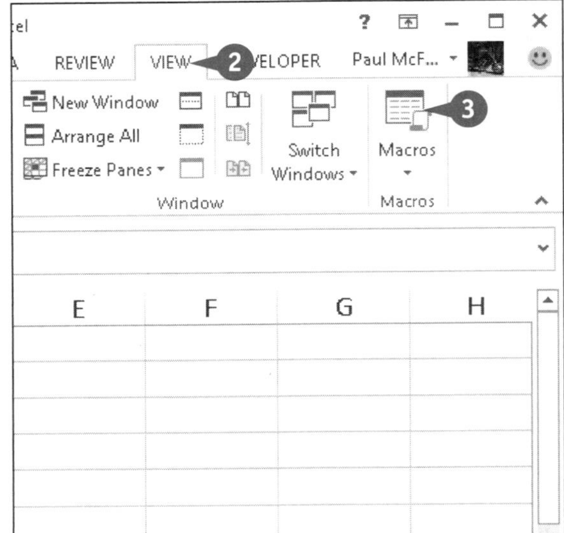

1. Open the workbook that contains the macro.

   You can skip step 1 if the macro is stored in the Personal Macro Workbook.

2. Click the View tab.
3. Click Macros.

   If you have the Developer tab displayed, you can also click the Developer tab and then click Macros.

   You can also press Alt+F8.

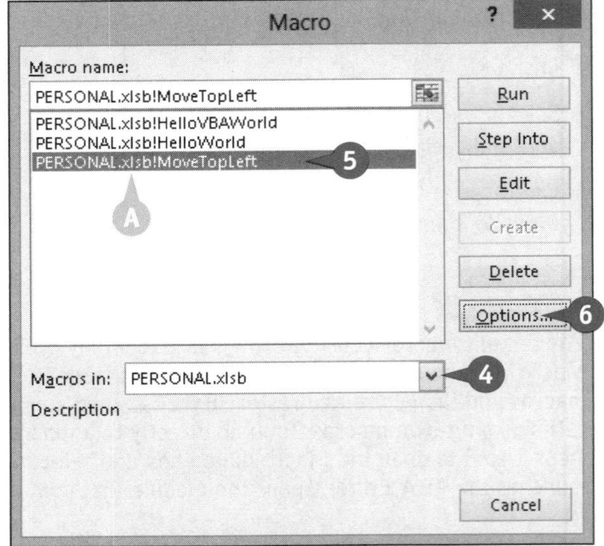

The Macro dialog box appears.

4. Click the Macros In down arrow and then select the workbook that contains the macro you want to work with from the drop-down list.

   If you are not sure which workbook contains the macro, select All Open Workbooks, instead.

- A Excel displays a list of macros in the workbook.

5. Click the macro.
6. Click Options.

The Macro Options dialog box appears.

7 Type the character you want to use as part of the shortcut key.

8 Click OK.

Excel assigns the shortcut key to the macro.

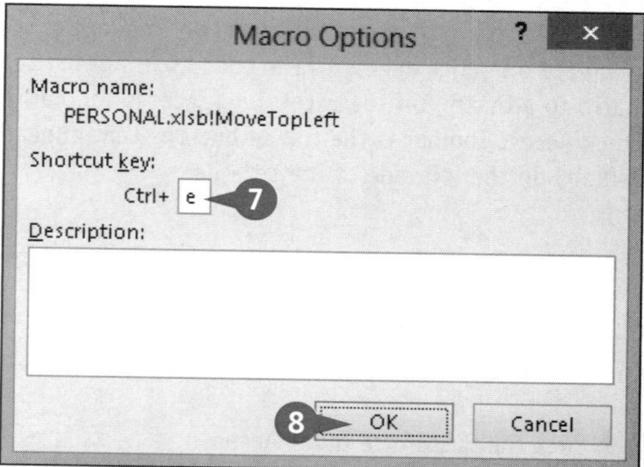

9 Click Cancel.

You can now run the macro by pressing the shortcut key.

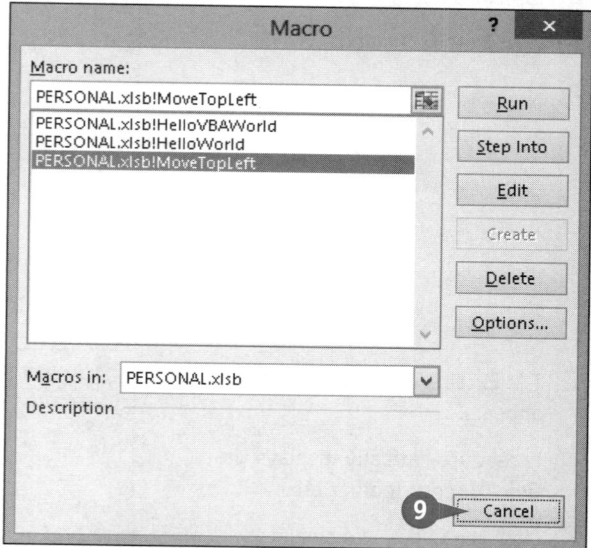

EXTRA

Do not specify a shortcut key that conflicts with the built-in Excel shortcuts, such as Ctrl+B for bold formatting or Ctrl+C for copying text. Otherwise, Excel overrides its own shortcut and runs your macro instead, if the macro workbook is open. Only five letters are not assigned to Excel commands that you can use with your macros: e, j, m, q, and t. You can create extra shortcut keys by using uppercase letters. For example, if you type e into the Ctrl+ text box, you press Ctrl+E to run the macro. However, if you type E into the Ctrl+ text box, you press Ctrl+Shift+E to run the macro. Note that Excel uses four built-in Ctrl+Shift shortcuts: A, F, O, and P.

Assign a Macro to the Quick Access Toolbar

If you have a VBA macro that you use frequently, you can create one-click access to the code by assigning that macro to a button on the Excel Quick Access Toolbar. The Quick Access Toolbar is the row of buttons that appears, by default, on the left side of the title bar.

As long as you leave open the workbook in which the macro is stored, you have one-click access to the macro. Because you must have the macro's workbook open, it is a good idea to only create toolbar buttons for macros in your Personal Macro Workbook, which is always open.

Assign a Macro to the Quick Access Toolbar

1. Click the Customize Quick Access Toolbar button.
2. Click More Commands.

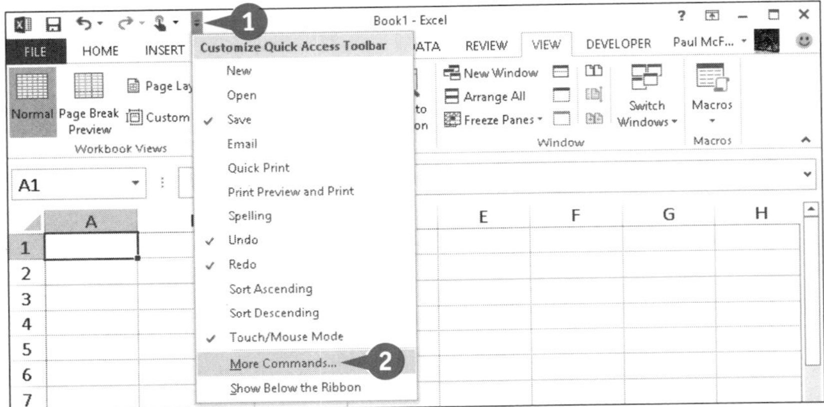

The Excel Options dialog box appears.

A Excel automatically displays the Quick Access Toolbar tab.

3. Click the Choose Commands From down arrow.
4. Click Macros.

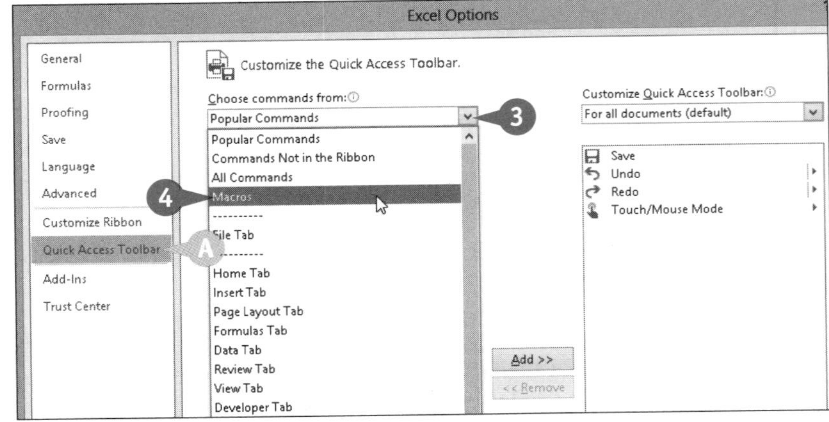

5 Click the macro you want to add.

6 Click Add.

B Excel adds the command.

7 Click OK.

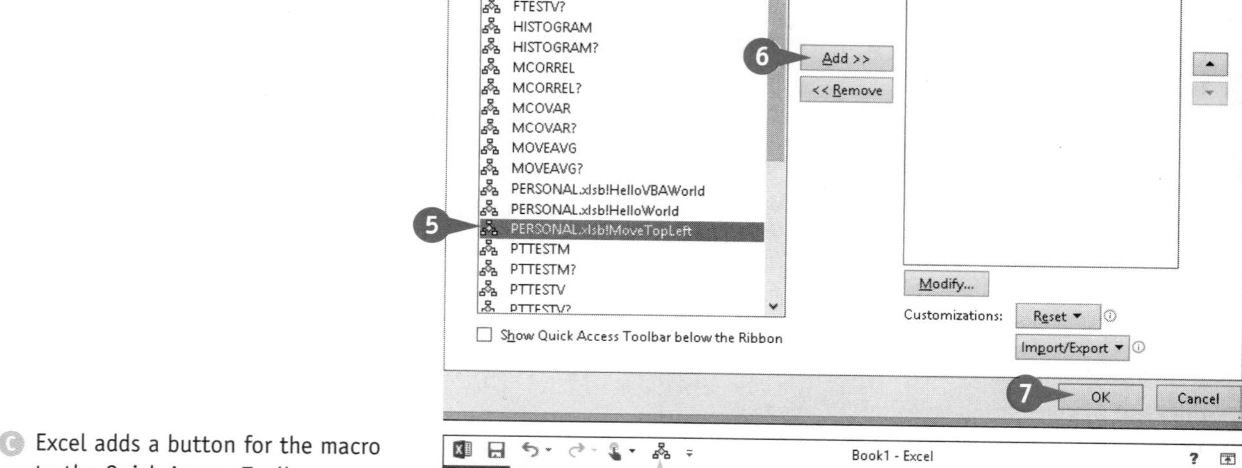

C Excel adds a button for the macro to the Quick Access Toolbar.

EXTRA

To help distinguish one macro button from another, you can customize each button with a suitable icon image. Follow steps 1 and 2 to open the Quick Access Toolbar tab. Click the macro you want to customize and then click the Modify button. In the Modify Button dialog box, click the icon you want to use and then click OK.

You can create more space to add macros by moving the Quick Access Toolbar below the Ribbon. The easiest way to do this is to click the Customize Quick Access Toolbar button and then click Show Below the Ribbon.

Assign a Macro to the Ribbon

You can improve your Excel productivity by customizing the Ribbon with buttons that run the macros you use frequently. It is often useful to organize your macros in some way. For example, you might have a set of macros related to formatting, another set related to file management, and so on. To organize these and other related macros, you can add them to the Excel Ribbon. To add a new command to the Ribbon, you must first create a new tab or a new group within an existing tab, and then add the command to the new tab or group.

Assign a Macro to the Ribbon

Display the Customize Ribbon Tab

1. Right-click any part of the Ribbon.
2. Click Customize the Ribbon.

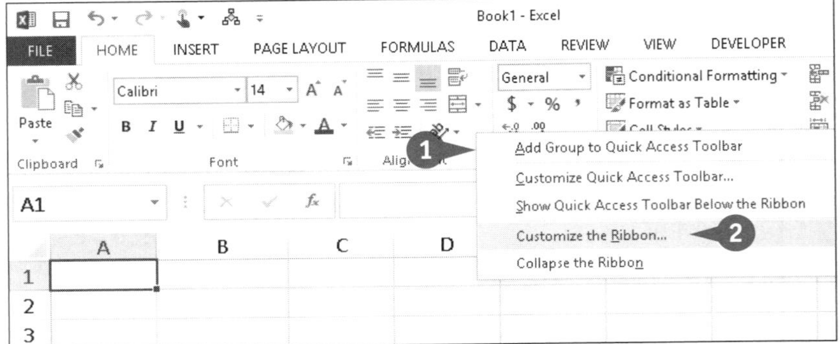

Add a New Tab or Group

The Excel Options dialog box appears.

A. Excel automatically displays the Customize Ribbon tab.

1. Click the tab you want to customize.

B. You can also click New Tab to create a custom tab.

2. Click New Group.

C. Excel adds the group.

3. Click Rename.
4. In the Rename dialog box, type a name for the group.
5. Click OK.

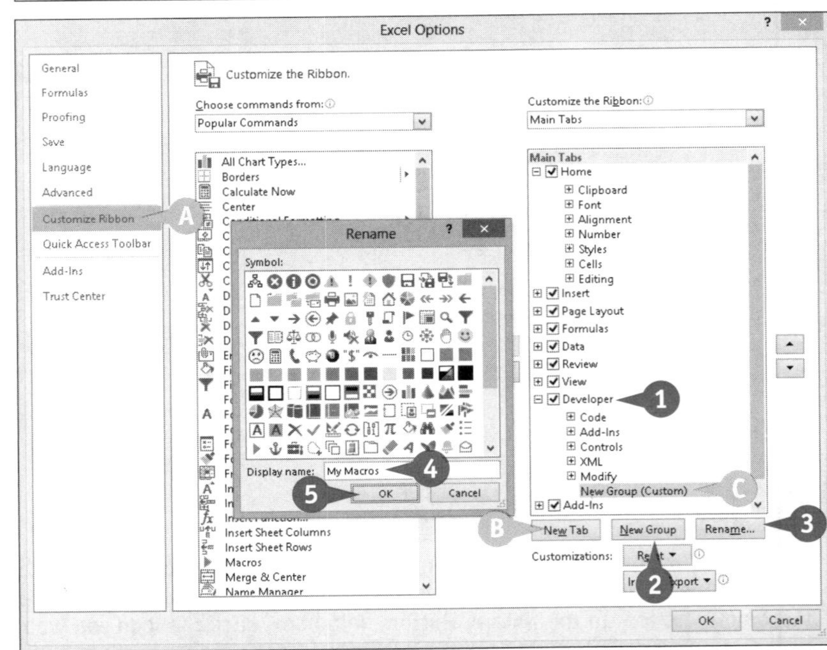

Assign a Macro

1. Click the Choose Commands From down arrow and then click Macros.
2. Click the macro you want to add to the Ribbon.
3. Click Add.
   - D Excel adds the macro to the tab.
4. Click OK.

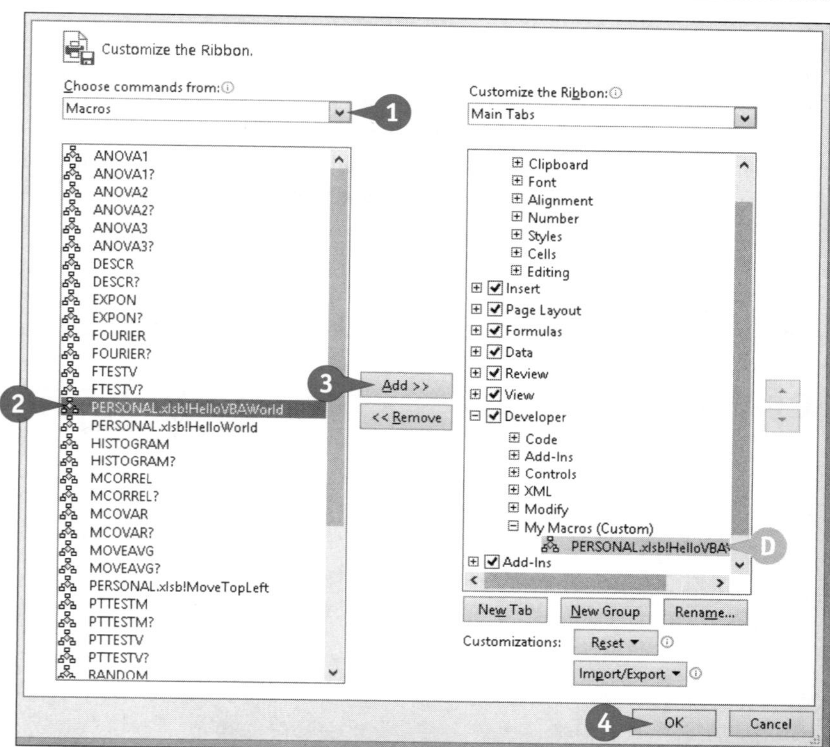

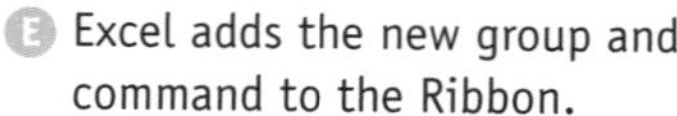
E Excel adds the new group and command to the Ribbon.

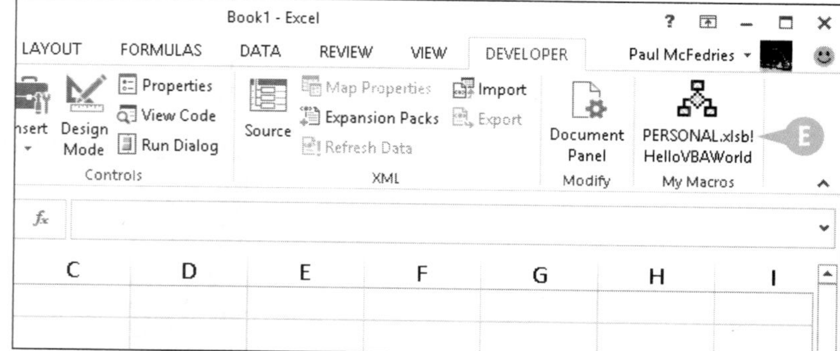

EXTRA

To use a shorter name for a Ribbon macro button, right-click any part of the Ribbon and click Customize the Ribbon to display the Excel Options dialog box with the Customize Ribbon tab displayed. Click the macro button, click the Rename button, type a new name, and then click OK.

To remove macro buttons from the Ribbon, right-click any part of the Ribbon and then click Customize the Ribbon to display the Customize Ribbon tab. To restore a tab, click the tab, click Reset, and then click Reset Only Selected Ribbon Tab. To remove all customizations, click Reset and then click Reset All Customizations.

Set the Macro Security Level

VBA is a powerful language that is all too often used for nefarious ends. Fortunately, you can adjust the macro security setting to one of four options to protect your system. The Disable All Macros without Notification option enables you to disable all macros, without a way to enable them. The Disable All Macros with Notification option notifies you that a document contains macros and disables the macros, but gives you the option of enabling them. The Disable All Macros Except Digitally Signed Macros option enables macros only if they come from a source that has digitally signed the VBA project. The Enable All Macros option runs all macros without prompting.

Set the Macro Security Level

1 Click File.

2 Click Options.

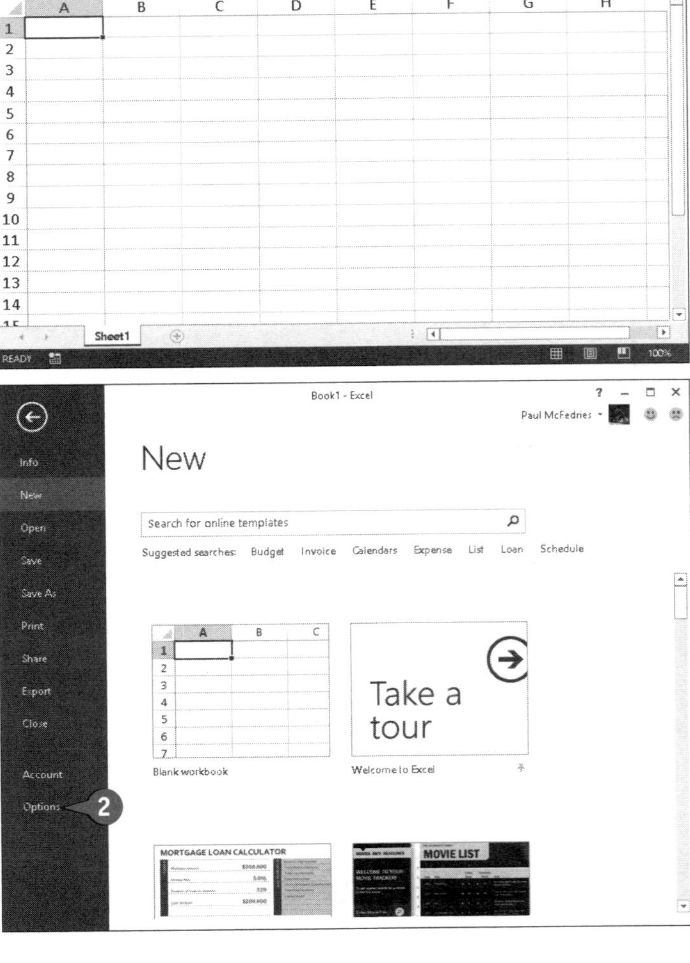

The Excel Options dialog box appears.

3. Click Trust Center.
4. Click Trust Center Settings.

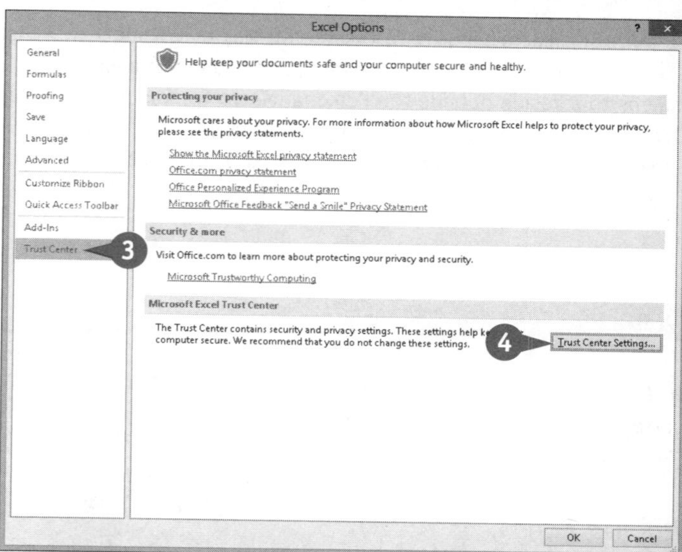

The Trust Center dialog box appears.

5. Click Macro Settings.
6. Click to select the security level you want to use (○ changes to ◉).
7. Click OK.
8. Click OK.

Excel puts the new macro security level into effect.

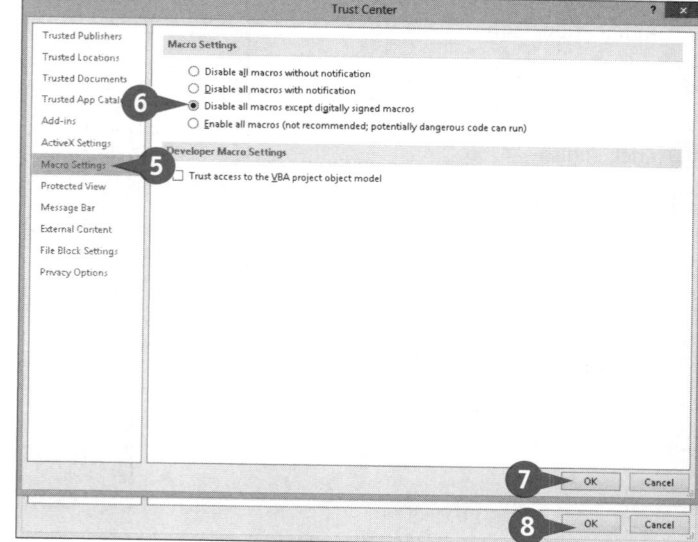

EXTRA

If you are not sure which macro setting to use, consider Disable All Macros Except Digitally Signed Macros. With this setting, Excel only enables macros if the VBA project has been digitally signed using a trusted code-signing certificate. Macros from any other source are automatically disabled. This gives you almost total macro safety. However, you need to self-sign your own macros. If you do not have an antivirus program installed, use the Enable All Macros level if you only run your own macros and you never open documents created by a third party. If you do have an antivirus program, this level is probably safe if you only open third-party documents from people or sources you know.

Digitally Sign Your Excel Macros

If you set macro security to Disable All Macros Without Notification, Excel does not allow you to run your own macros that reside outside the Personal Macro Workbook. Does this mean you must store all your macros in the Personal Macro Workbook? That would make it difficult to distribute your macros to other people. Fortunately, it is possible to "prove" that you are the author of your own macros. You can do that by *self-certifying*, which creates a trust certificate that applies only to your own work and to using that work on your own computer.

Digitally Sign Your Excel Macros

Note: *Before proceeding, create your personal digital certificate by running the SelfCert.exe program, as described in the Apply It section.*

1. Press Alt+F11.

   Excel opens the Visual Basic for Applications Editor.

2. Click the project to which you want to assign the certificate.
3. Click Tools.
4. Click Digital Signature.

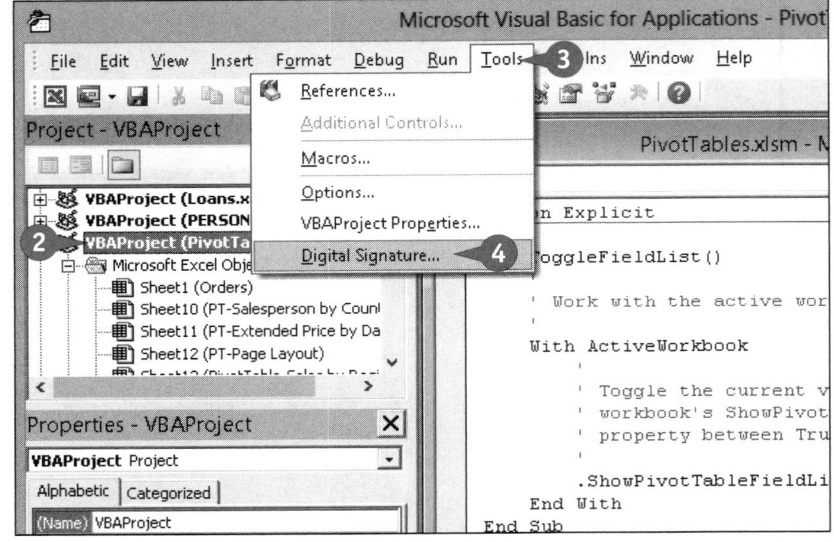

   The Digital Signature dialog box appears.

5. Click Choose.

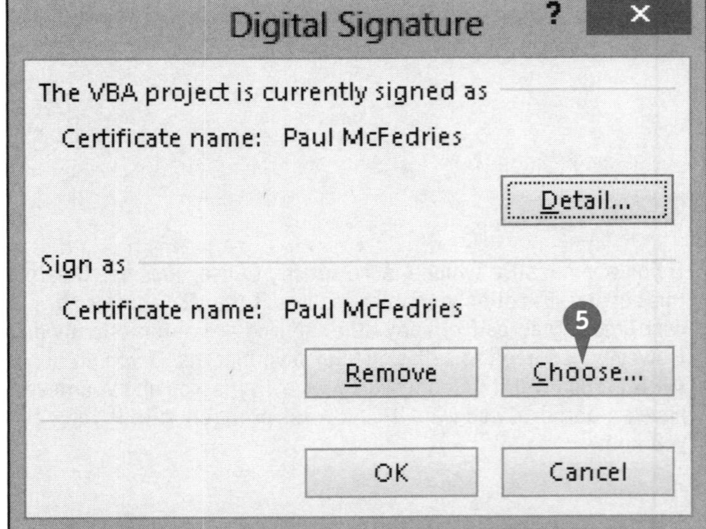

The Windows Security dialog box appears.

Ⓐ Windows displays your digital certificate.

Note: *Remember that you only see this digital certificate after you have run the SelfCert.exe program, as described in the Apply It section of this task.*

6 Click OK.

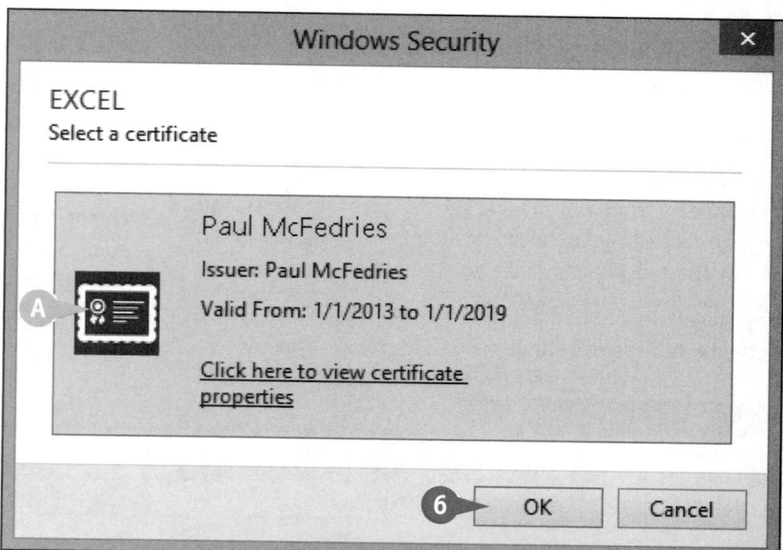

Ⓑ The certificate appears in the Digital Signature dialog box.

7 Click OK.

Excel applies the digital certificate to the project.

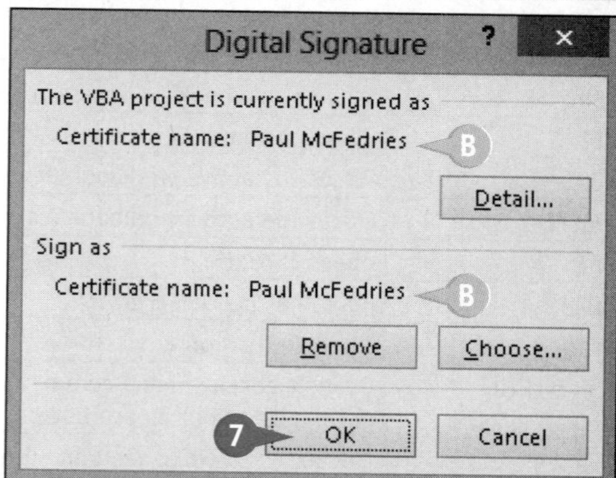

APPLY IT

Before you can digitally sign a VBA project, you must create a digital certificate for signing your macros. Press Windows Logo+R to open the Run dialog box, type the following address in the Open text box and then click OK.

```
%ProgramFiles%\Microsoft Office 15\root\Office15\SelfCert.exe
```

In the Create Digital Certificate dialog box, type your name in the Your Certificate's Name text box, and then click OK. Excel creates a digital certificate in your name and displays a dialog box when it is done. Click OK. You can now use the digital certificate to sign your VBA code, as described in this section.

Using Excel Keyboard Shortcuts

You can execute Excel ribbon commands without taking your hands off the keyboard. This enables you to work quickly, especially if you are an excellent typist. The process is simple. You press the Alt key, and Excel displays KeyTips — letters or numbers that you can press to display more KeyTips or to execute a command. If a menu or dialog box appears after you press a KeyTip, you can use the arrow keys to move to your selection. You then press the Enter key or the spacebar to make your selection.

KeyTips are useful in many ways. For example, you can activate KeyTips to change the color of your type by clicking the keys shown in a KeyTip and then using the arrow keys to select the color you want. To cancel a KeyTips session, you simply press F10.

In Excel 2003, you can execute menu and toolbar commands by pressing the Alt key. Excel 2007, 2010, and 2013 do not use menus and toolbars, but if you have memorized those commands, you can use them. As you execute Excel 2003 commands, Excel displays a message. For example, pressing Alt+E+A+A clears a cell. As you execute the command, Excel displays the message, Office 2003: ALT, E, A, A.

General Program Shortcuts

SHORTCUT	RESULT
Ctrl+N	Creates a new workbook.
Ctrl+O	Opens the Open dialog box.
Ctrl+F12	Opens the Open dialog box (same as Ctrl+O).
Ctrl+S	Saves a workbook. (The Save As dialog box opens if you have not previously saved the workbook.)
Shift+F12	Saves a workbook (same as Ctrl+S).
F12	Opens the Save As dialog box.
Ctrl+W	Closes the active workbook; if it is the only workbook open, it also closes Excel.
Alt+F4	Closes the active workbook (same as Ctrl+W).
F1	Opens Excel Help.
F7	Runs the spell checker.
F10	Turns KeyTips on and off.
Shift+F10	Opens a context menu containing options related to the current worksheet selection. This is the same as clicking the right mouse button.
F9	Calculates all worksheets in all open workbooks.
Ctrl+F9	Minimizes the workbook.
Ctrl+F10	Restores or maximizes the workbook.
Ctrl+P	Opens the Print dialog box.
Ctrl+Shift+F12	Opens the Print dialog box (same as Ctrl+P).
Alt+F8	Opens the Macro dialog box.
Alt+F11	Opens Visual Basic for Applications.

Data Entry Shortcuts

SHORTCUT	RESULT
Enter	Completes the cell entry and moves to the next cell.
Alt+Enter	Starts a new line within the same cell.
Shift+Enter	Completes the cell entry and moves up to the cell above.
Tab	Completes the cell entry and moves to the next cell on the right.
Shift+Tab	Completes the cell entry and moves to the next cell on the left.
Esc	Cancels the cell entry and restores the original cell contents.
Ctrl+D	Fills the active cell with the contents of the cell above it.
Ctrl+R	Fills the active cell with the contents of the cell to the left of it.
Ctrl+F3	Displays the Name Manager dialog box.
Ctrl+K	Displays the Insert Hyperlink dialog box.
F2	Gives you the ability to edit the active cell by placing the insertion point at the end of the cell contents and in the Formula bar.

Editing Shortcuts

SHORTCUT	RESULT
Ctrl+C	Copies the selection to the Office Clipboard.
Ctrl+X	Cuts the selection and places it on the Office Clipboard.
Ctrl+V	Pastes the information from the Office Clipboard.
Backspace	Deletes the entire contents of a cell, or deletes the character on the left of the insertion point if you are editing the cell contents.
Delete	Deletes the entire contents of a cell, or deletes the character on the right of the insertion point if you are editing the cell contents.
Ctrl+Delete	Deletes text from the insertion point to the end of the cell contents.
Ctrl+Z	Undoes an action.
Ctrl+Y	Repeats an action (Redo).
F4	Repeats an action (same as Ctrl+Y).
Ctrl+-	Opens the Delete dialog box.
Ctrl+Shift++	Opens the Insert dialog box.

continued

Formula Shortcuts

SHORTCUT	RESULT
Alt+Shift+Right Arrow	Displays the Group dialog box.
Alt+Shift+Left Arrow	Displays the Ungroup dialog box.
Ctrl+9	Hides the selected rows.
Ctrl+Shift+(	Unhides the hidden rows within the range selection.
Ctrl+0	Hides the selected columns.
Ctrl+Shift+Enter	Enters a formula as an array.
Ctrl+Shift+A	Inserts the argument names in parentheses for the specified function name.
F3	Opens the Paste Name dialog box when you have range names defined.
Shift+F3	Opens the Function Arguments dialog box.
=	Starts a formula.
Alt+=	Inserts the AutoSum formula.
Ctrl+;	Enters the current date.
Ctrl+Shift+:	Enters the current time.
Ctrl++'	Copies the formula in the cell above the active cell.
Ctrl+Shift+"	Copies the value in the cell above the active cell.
Ctrl+`	Alternates between displaying the value of the cell and the cell formula.

Formatting Shortcuts

SHORTCUT	RESULT
Alt+'	Opens the Style dialog box.
Ctrl+1	Opens the Format Cells dialog box.
Ctrl+B	Applies or removes bold formatting.
Ctrl+I	Applies or removes italic formatting.
Ctrl+U	Applies or removes underlining.
Ctrl+5	Applies or removes strikethrough formatting.
Ctrl+Shift+~	Applies the General number format.
Ctrl+Shift+$	Applies the Currency format with two decimal places and negative numbers in parentheses.
Ctrl+Shift+^	Applies the Scientific format with two decimal places.
Ctrl+Shift+#	Applies the Date format with dates formatted as dd-mm-yy.
Ctrl+Shift+@	Applies the Time format with hour, minute, and AM or PM.
Ctrl+Shift+!	Applies the Number format with two decimal places, a thousands separator, and a minus sign for negative numbers.
Ctrl+Shift+%	Applies the Percent format.
Ctrl+Shift+&	Applies outside borders.
Ctrl+Shift+_	Removes outside borders.

continued

Selection Shortcuts

SHORTCUT	RESULT
Shift+Right Arrow	Expands the selection one cell to the right.
Shift+Left Arrow	Expands the selection one cell to the left.
Shift+Up Arrow	Expands the selection up one cell.
Shift+Down Arrow	Expands the selection down one cell.
Ctrl+Shift+*	Selects the current region, or cells containing values, around the active cell.
Ctrl+Shift+Right Arrow	Expands the selection right to the next nonblank cell in the row.
Ctrl+Shift+Left Arrow	Expands the selection left to the next nonblank cell in the row.
Ctrl+Shift+Up Arrow	Expands the selection up to the next nonblank cell in the column.
Ctrl+Shift+Down Arrow	Expands the selection down to the last nonblank cell in the column.
Shift+Home	Expands the selection to the beginning of the row.
Ctrl+Shift+Home	Expands the selection to the beginning of the worksheet.
Ctrl+Shift+End	Expands the selection to the end of the active area of the worksheet.
Ctrl+Spacebar	Selects the entire column.
Shift+Spacebar	Selects the entire row.
Ctrl+A	Selects the entire worksheet.
Shift+Page Down	Expands the selection down one screen.
Shift+Page Up	Expands the selection up one screen.
Ctrl+Shift+Spacebar	Selects all objects if an object is selected.
Ctrl+6	Alternates between hiding objects, displaying objects, and displaying object placeholders.
Shift+F8	Adds another range of cells to the selection.

Worksheet Navigation Shortcuts

SHORTCUT	RESULT
Up Arrow	Moves the active cell up one row.
Down Arrow	Moves the active cell down one row.
Left Arrow	Moves the active cell left one column.
Right Arrow	Moves the active cell right one column.
Home	Moves to the beginning of the current row.
Ctrl+Home	Moves to the beginning of the worksheet (typically cell A1).
Ctrl+End	Moves to the last cell in the worksheet (the cell at the intersection of the last used row and column in the worksheet).
Page Up	Scrolls up one screen.
Page Down	Scrolls down one screen.
Alt+Page Up	Scrolls right one screen.
Alt+Page Down	Scrolls left one screen.
Ctrl+Page Up	Moves to the previous worksheet in the workbook.
Ctrl+Page Down	Moves to the next worksheet in the workbook.
Ctrl+F6	Switches to the next open workbook.
Ctrl+Shift+F6	Switches back to the previously viewed open workbook.
F6	Moves the focus from the status bar to the Ribbon to the worksheet, and if the worksheet is split, from pane to pane.
F5	Opens the Go To dialog box.
Shift+F5	Opens the Find and Replace dialog box.
Shift+F4	Repeats the last Find command.
Tab	Moves between the unlocked cells of a protected worksheet.
Ctrl+.	Moves clockwise to the next corner of the selected range of cells.

Index

D

G

H

I

S

T

U

V

W

X

Y